FIFTEEN AMERICAN AUTHORS
BEFORE 1900

FIFTEEN AMERICAN AUTHORS BEFORE 1900

Bibliographical Essays on Research and Criticism

Revised Edition

EDITED BY
EARL N. HARBERT and
ROBERT A. REES

THE UNIVERSITY OF WISCONSIN PRESS

Published 1984

The University of Wisconsin Press
114 North Murray Street
Madison, Wisconsin 53715

The University of Wisconsin Press, Ltd.
1 Gower Street
London WC1E 6HA, England

First printing

Printed in the United States of America

For LC CIP information see the colophon

ISBN 0-299-09590-8

PS
55
.F53
1984

To HENRY A. POCHMANN
Teacher, Scholar, Friend

Contents

Preface

WHEN *Fifteen American Authors before 1900: Bibliographic Essays on Research and Criticism* first appeared in 1971, we expressed our special indebtedness to two companion titles: *Eight American Authors* (edited by Floyd Stovall) and *Fifteen* (now *Sixteen*) *Modern American Authors* (edited by Jackson Bryer). Both books helped to shape the original conception of what this book should be; and now, both have encouraged us in the work of serious revision, having led the way by appearing in newer, more modern editions. So, despite some changes of our own design in this revised edition, our original debt remains. To it must be added a hundred similar obligations to titles, authors, editors, critics — to all the resources, human and otherwise, that have kept scholarship in American literature alive and prospering throughout the past decade. We are especially grateful for the friendly cooperation of co-workers who patiently answered questions and cheerfully supplied information. By the time this revised edition sees print, our editorial debts will have mounted beyond any practical repayment. We trust that all those concerned in this enterprise will accept our simple "Thank you."

This revised edition omits two chapters found in the original edition: "The Literature of the Old South" and "The Literature of the New South." Since 1971, these subjects have simply grown too large for inclusion here. All other chapters from the first printing of *Fifteen American Authors before 1900* have been retained — and much enlarged with references to recent scholarship and criticism. As it now appears, this volume includes fifteen chapters devoted to fifteen important American writers, arranged alphabetically, from Henry Adams to John Greenleaf Whittier. Each author is considered individually, and each essay has been divided into sections appropriate to that author. All the essays have been revised and updated through a judicious review of scholarship of the last decade.

The essayists themselves — with two exceptions — are the same ones who contributed to the earlier edition.

For the chapters on Howells and Irving, the editors were pleased to obtain the expert services of David J. Nordloh and James W. Tuttleton, respectively, each of whom wrote an original essay for this revised edition. Every contributor to *Fifteen American Authors before 1900* was selected on the basis of both knowledge about and interest in his subject. Once assigned, he was free to choose the materials he would consider; selection (and omission) of essays and books, and, in particular, the use of graduate dissertations and foreign criticism were left to individual judgment. The editors insisted only that each contributor be familiar with all of the material on his subject.

Within each essay, the most complete citation of a book or article is normally found in its first appearance. Later citations appear in abbreviated form, unless the text requires a fuller description for clarity. Short titles for periodicals and standard reference works are included in the Key to Abbreviations, which precedes the essays. Essayists have included information about reprints whenever they judged it useful to the reader.

Together with the Key to Abbreviations, the appropriate discussion in each chapter should supply adequate bibliographical information on the American writers covered here. Yet it may be useful to note a few additional titles that represent the bibliographical foundation for the study of American literature. Jacob Blanck, since 1955, has been issuing his monumental *Bibliography of American Literature* (New Haven, Conn.), cited as *BAL* in the Key to Abbreviations, describing according to modern principles the first editions and other separates of American writers who died before 1931. Among continuing projects, the annual volumes of *American Literary Scholarship* or *ALS* (Durham, N.C., 1965–) have proved to be indispensable because critical evaluation accompanies the bibliographical citations. Listing without evaluation may be found in the *PMLA International Bibliography*, *AL*, and the *Annual Bibliography of English Language and Literature* (issued by the Modern Humanities Research Association). *CHAL* and *LHUS* (especially the bibliographical *Supplements*) remain useful as standard authorities. In recent years, many journals, such as *ALR* and *EAL*, have offered special numbers, essay reviews, and bibliographical listings of scholarship centering on American writers, including some of those considered here. Of course, all these titles (and many others) will be cited in the essays that follow.

At this writing, even more than in 1971, it is clear that current interest in American literature, abroad and at home, remains very high indeed. Almost every essayist found it necessary to complain to one or the other of us (sometimes to both) about the problem of making a judicious selection from the wealth of available material. We were all agreed that only the most significant studies could claim space in these essays. For the priority of economy over completeness in the following essays, we bear the chief responsibility.

Earl N. Harbert   Robert A. Rees
Boston, Massachusetts   Los Angeles, California

November 1983

Acknowledgments

THE preparation of the revised edition of *Fifteen American Authors before 1900: Bibliographic Essays on Research and Criticism* was supported in part by a grant from Northeastern University's Research and Scholarship Development Fund.

Key to Abbreviations

AH   American Heritage
AHR   American Historical Review
AI   American Imago: A Psychoana-
   lytic Journal for Culture, Science,
   and the Arts
AL   American Literature
ALR   American Literary Realism
AM   American Mercury
AmerS   American Studies
AmLS   American Literary Scholar-
   ship: An Annual
AN&Q   American Notes & Queries
AQ   American Quarterly
Archiv   Archiv für das Studium der
   Neueren Sprachen und Litera-
   turen
ArQ   Arizona Quarterly
AS   American Speech
ASch   American Scholar
AtM   Atlantic Monthly, Atlantic
ATQ   American Transcendental Quar-
   terly
AWS   American Writers Series
BAL   Bibliography of American Lit-
   erature
BB   Bulletin of Bibliography
BFHA   Bulletin of the Friends Histori-
   cal Association
BJRL   Bulletin of the John Rylands
   Library
BNYPL   Bulletin of the New York
   Public Library

Bookman   Bookman (U.S.)
BRH   Bulletin of Research in the Hu-
   manities
BSUF   Ball State University Forum
BuR   Bucknell Review
BUSE   Boston University Studies in
   English
Caliban   Caliban (Toulouse)
Carrell   The Carrell: Journal of the
   Friends of the U. of Miami (Fla.)
   Library
CE   College English
CEA   CEA Critic: An Official Journal
   of the College English Association
CEAA   Center for Editions of Ameri-
   can Authors (now CSE)
CentR   The Centennial Review
Century   Century Illustrated Monthly
   Magazine
CH   Church History
CHAL   Cambridge History of Amer-
   ican Literature
CLAJ   College Language Association
   Journal
CLC   Columbia Library Columns
CLQ   Colby Library Quarterly
CLS   Comparative Literature Studies
CMHS   Collections of the Massachu-
   setts Historical Society
Col   Colophon
CP   Concerning Poetry
CR   The Critical Review

CSE   Center for Scholarly Editions (formerly CEAA)

CRevAs   Canadian Review of American Studies

DAB   Dictionary of American Biography

Daedalus   Daedalus (Proceedings of the American Academy of Arts and Sciences)

DAI   Dissertation Abstracts International

DicS   Dickinson Studies

DLB   Dictionary of Literary Biography

DN   Delaware Notes

DR   Dalhousie Review

DVLG   Deutsche Vierteljahrschrift für Literaturwissenschaft und Geistegeschichte

EA   Études Anglaises

EAL   Early American Literature

EALN   Early American Literature Newsletter

ECS   Eighteenth-Century Studies

EDB   Emily Dickinson Bulletin

EIHC   Essex Institute Historical Collections

EJ   English Journal

EL   Essays in Literature

ELH   Journal of English Literary History

ELN   English Language Notes

ES   English Studies

ESQ   Emerson Society Quarterly

Expl   Explicator

FAR   The French-American Review

FI   Forum Italicum

FMod   Filologia Moderna (Madrid)

ForumH   Forum (Houston)

Forum NY   Forum (New York)

FR   French Review

The Friend   The Friend: A Quaker Weekly Journal

GaR   The Georgia Review

GJ   Gutenberg-Jahrbuch

GM   Gentleman's Monthly

GyS   Gypsy Scholar

HLB   Harvard Library Bulletin

HLQ   Huntington Library Quarterly

HM   Harper's Magazine, Harper's New Monthly Magazine, Harper's Monthly Magazine, Harper's

HSE   Hungarian Studies in English (Debrecen)

HTR   Harvard Theological Review

IJHP   Iowa Journal of History and Politics

JA   Jahrbuch für Amerikastudien

JAAC   Journal of Aesthetics and Art Criticism

JAC   Journal of American Culture

JAmS   Journal of American Studies

JEGP   Journal of English and Germanic Philology

JFI   Journal of the Franklin Institute

JHI   Journal of the History of Ideas

JML   Journal of Modern Literature

JNT   Journal of Narrative Technique

JRUL   Journal of the Rutgers University Library

KR   The Kenyon Review

L&P   Literature and Psychology

LHJ   Ladies' Home Journal

LHUS   Literary History of the United States

LW   Literary World

MagA   Magazine of Art

MarkhamR   Markham Review

MF   Midwest Folklore

MFS   Modern Fiction Studies

MissQ   Mississippi Quarterly

MLA   Modern Language Association

MLN   Modern Language Notes

MLQ   Modern Language Quarterly

MLR   Modern Language Review

Monatschefte   Monatschefte für Deutschen Unterricht, Deutsche Sprache und Literatur (Wisconsin)

MP   Modern Philology

MQ   Midwest Quarterly

MR   Massachusetts Review
N&Q   Notes and Queries
NAR   North American Review
NCF   Nineteenth-Century Fiction
NDEJ Notre Dame English Journal
NDQ   North Dakota Quarterly
NEHGR New England Historical
   and Genealogical Register
NEM   New England Magazine
NEQ   New England Quarterly
NR   New Republic
NS   Die Neueren Sprachen
NYFQ New York Folklore Quarterly
NYH   New York History
NYHTBR New York Herald Tribune
   Book Review
NY Review of Books   New York Re-
   view of Books
NYTBR   New York Times Book Re-
   view
Outlook   Outlook (U.S.)
PAAS   Proceedings of the American
   Antiquarian Society
PAPS   Proceedings of the American
   Philosophical Society
PBSA   Papers of the Bibliographical
   Society of America
PHR   Pacific Historical Review
PLL   Papers on Language and Litera-
   ture
PMASAL   Papers of the Michigan
   Academy of Science, Arts, and
   Letters
PMHB   Pennsylvania Magazine of
   History and Biography
PMHS   Proceedings of the Massachu-
   setts Historical Society
PMLA   Publications of the Modern
   Language Association
PNJHS   Proceedings of the New Jersey
   Historical Society
PQ   Philological Quarterly
PrS   Prairie Schooner
QH   Quaker History: Bulletin of the
   Friends' Historical Society

RALS   Resources for American Liter-
   ary Study
RR   Romanic Review
RS   Research Studies
SA   Studi Americani (Rome)
SAB   South Atlantic Review
SAF   Studies in American Fiction
SAH   Studies in American Humor
SAQ   South Atlantic Quarterly
SatR Saturday Review
SB   Studies in Bibliography: Papers of
   the Bibliographic Society of the
   University of Virginia
SCN   Seventeenth-Century News
SCraneN   Stephen Crane Newsletter
SELit   Studies in English Literature
   (Tokyo)
SFQ   Southern Folklore Quarterly
SHR   Southern Humanities Review
SIR   Studies in Romanticism
SLitI   Studies in the Literary Imagi-
   nation
SN   Studia Neophilologica
SNNTS   Studies in the Novel
SoR   Southern Review
SP   Studies in Philology
SR   Sewanee Review
SSASH   Studia Slavica Academiae Sci-
   entiarum Hungaricae
SSF   Studies in Short Fiction
Sym   Symposium: A Quarterly Jour-
   nal in Modern Foreign Literature
TLS   Times Literary Supplement
   (London)
TQ   Texas Quarterly
TSE   Tulane Studies in English
TSL   Tennessee Studies in Literature
TSLL   Texas Studies in Literature and
   Language
TUSAS   Twayne's United States Au-
   thors Series
UKCR   University of Kansas City
   Review
UMPAW   University of Minnesota
   Pamphlets on American Writers

VQR   *Virginia Quarterly Review*   WWR   *Walt Whitman Review*
WAL   *Western American Literature*   YR   *Yale Review*
WHR   *Western Humanities Review*   YULG   *Yale University Library Ga-*
WMQ   *William and Mary Quarterly*   *zette*

FIFTEEN AMERICAN AUTHORS
BEFORE 1900

Henry Adams

EARL N. HARBERT

THE ORIGINAL VERSION of this essay appeared in print more than a decade ago. Clearly these years have been kind to both popular and scholarly interest in Henry Adams. He has been increasingly talked and written about, on radio, in magazines, journals, books, and even on television. In fact, the thirteen-part PBS series "The Adams Chronicles" probably did more to make Henry and the other Adamses household names than did all other sources combined. Such fame, however, can be short-lived, and on balance Henry Adams deserves a better fate. The revised essay which follows represents its author's convictions that Adams appears more important today as a human measure of American experience than he seemed in 1971, and that it is still possible to identify the most usable studies of the man and his work.

BIBLIOGRAPHY

Bibliographical interest in Henry Adams has been considerable; yet there is still no comprehensive primary or secondary bibliography. The need is evident, although a workable substitute can be pieced together from a variety of checklists. Perhaps the easiest to use is Earl N. Harbert's *Henry Adams: A Reference Guide* (Boston, 1978), which combines "Major Writings by Henry Adams," "Writings about Henry Adams, 1879–1975," and a short historical "Introduction." The selective listings are arranged chronologically, and divided between "Books" and "Shorter Writings." Both listings, unfortunately, are highly selective. The recent ap-

From Earl N. Harbert and Robert A. Rees, editors, *Fifteen American Authors before 1900: Bibliographic Essays on Research & Criticism* (Madison: The University of Wisconsin Press; © 1984 by the Board of Regents of the University of Wisconsin System); may be reproduced only by permission of the publisher.

3

pearance of *Literary Writings in America: A Bibliography* in eight volumes (Millbrook, N.Y., 1977) makes a massive collection of cards, gathered by the W.P.A. from 1938–1942, available in print for the first time. Adams's writings, reviews, and commentaries are brought together in Volume One. All entries are unedited and unverified.

A more substantial discussion of primary materials may be found in Jacob Blanck's standard *Bibliography of American Literature* (*BAL*), which includes Henry Adams in Volume One and provides the usual description of editions, reprints, and "References." Of special interest is an illustration: "Syllabus. History II. Political History of Europe from the 10th to the 15th Century." It may surprise the academic reader who does not look upon a course syllabus as imperishable literature. Elsewhere, the most nearly complete chronology of Adams's writings has been printed in the three volumes of Ernest Samuels's biography: *The Young Henry Adams* (1855–1877); *Henry Adams: The Middle Years* (1878–1891); *Henry Adams: The Major Phase* (1892 and after). Samuels's list supersedes the "Bibliography of the Writings of Henry Adams" in James T. Adams, *Henry Adams* (New York, 1933) and improves upon the list of published writings in Elizabeth Stevenson, *Henry Adams: A Biography* (New York, 1956). Important additions to all earlier treatments of Henry Adams's writings from England around the time of the Civil War are proposed in the text and notes of *Both Sides of the Ocean: A Biography of Henry Adams: His First Life: 1838–1862* by Edward Chalfant (Hamden, Conn., 1982). Two additional volumes of his book are promised.

Concentrating largely on secondary material, including literary and historical criticism, Charles Vandersee has reviewed the subject in two excellent essays, both titled "Henry Adams (1838–1918)" (*ALR*, Summer 1969 and Winter 1975). Vandersee divides his material into criticism, bibliography, manuscripts, etc., and his index simplifies its use. Although less appealing because of its age, the selected bibliography in William H. Jordy's *Henry Adams: Scientific Historian* (New Haven, Conn., 1952) has been modernized and, with a new preface, appears in the 1963 (Yale paperback) reprint; the result is a sound discussion of important work pertinent to Jordy's topic. The *LHUS* with *Supplement* also offers a list of studies. George Hochfield, *Henry Adams: An Introduction and Interpretation* (New York, 1962), Robert A. Hume, *Runaway Star: An Appreciation of Henry Adams* (Ithaca, N.Y., 1951), and Max I. Baym, *The French Education of Henry Adams* (New York, 1951, 1969) all contain specialized bibliographies, the last directing attention to Adams's reading and to the contents of his library.

A German essay, "Henry Adams: Ein Forschungsbericht 1918–1958" by Bernhard Fabian (Archiv für Kulturgeschichte, 1959) may be helpful

— the citations are mostly in English — but it is dated and unreliable. Many foreign libraries contain Henry Wasser's *American Literature and Language: A Selected and Annotated Bibliography* (Publication of the Center for European Studies, City Univ. of New York, 1980), with its brief list of books on Adams among others. Ph.D. dissertations that have not been published (to the time of writing) are treated in Vandersee's two surveys (see above) and in greater detail by Barrie Hayne and Katherine Morrison, (*ALR*, Summer, 1975). The high quality of many dissertations becomes apparent here; this listing deserves to be continued. Less helpful are the *Magill Surveys*, or at least, *American Literature: Realism to 1945*, edited by Frank N. Magill (Pasadena, Cal., 1981). The *Dictionary of Literary Biography*, vol. 12, *American Realists and Naturalists* (Detroit, 1982) opens with "Henry Adams" by Earl N. Harbert and contains far more material, bibliographical and otherwise, including many illustrations.

Among specialized items, Howard M. Mumford's "Thayer, Ford, Goodspeed's and Middlebury: A Missing Copy of *The Education of Henry Adams* Found" is noteworthy because it records Adams's own annotations (*PMHS*, Boston, 1971). Norman E. Tutorow, "A Bibliographical Appraisal of Henry Adams' Scientism," (*Social Sciences*, Feb. 1972), on the other hand, tells more about Adams as historian than about the sources. *Articles on Twentieth Century Literature: An Annotated Bibliography, 1954 to 1970* (New York, 1973), compiled by David E. Pownall, brings together a variety of titles first collected in *Twentieth Century Literature*. Other listings of current scholarship can be found in standard bibliographies, such as the yearly *MLA International Bibliography*. Still, to echo an earlier version of this essay, "a modern enumerative bibliography" on Henry Adams "would be a major contribution."

EDITIONS

At this time no authoritative standard edition of the writings of Henry Adams is yet in prospect, although recent developments have encouraged our hopes for one. The appearance of Ernest Samuels's Riverside edition of *The Education of Henry Adams* (Boston, 1973) provided (for the first time) a reliable text for the scholar and teacher, available in paperback and reasonably priced. Samuels's "Introduction" and editorial apparatus explain the complex publication history of this most popular of Adams's titles. The edition is a landmark in editorial scholarship on Adams, rivalled only by the handsome series, *The Letters of Henry Adams*, volumes 1, 2, 3, 1858–1892 (Cambridge, Mass., 1982) edited by J. C. Levenson, Ernest Samuels, Charles Vandersee, and Viola Hopkins Winner. Although the editors have chosen to omit the correspondence that Henry Adams sent to the Boston *Advertiser*, which is fundamental to the argument in the first volume of Chalfant's biography (*Both Sides of the Ocean*), these handsome volumes of *Letters* offer complete and reliable texts, a clear discussion of principles of selection for the entire series, attractive illustrations (especially Adams's watercolors in Volume Three), and useful but unobtrusive notes. Already it is clear that the *Letters* — although not a complete edition — will supersede other printings of Henry Adams's letters. At least three more volumes of letters will follow.

In addition to these important editorial advances, The Library of America has announced *The Works of Henry Adams*, a selection of his most popular titles, printed in authoritative texts and attractively bound, which should begin to appear in 1984. Once in print, the *Works* will remain available, unlike those titles by Adams that only sporadically find a place in publishers' catalogues. In fact, although many excerpts from Adams's writings have appeared in popular anthologies, substantial works like the *Letters of John Hay and Extracts from His Diary* (3 vols., privately printed, Washington, 1908), with its confidential key to names and places, remain unavailable. Still, of the writing in print, in the absence of a standard edition, individual titles must be sought from a confusing array of hardcover and paperback editions, abridgments, and reprints.

The corrupt text of the *Education* remains available in a Sentry paperback, with an introduction by Sir Denis Brogan. *Mont Saint-Michel and Chartres* can be found in many university libraries in the 1912 (private) printing, and the 1913 text has been reprinted in paperback, with introductions by various hands. After its appearance in several abridgments, the complete *History of the United States During the Administrations of Jefferson and Madison* (New York, 1889–1891) has been reprinted (Hillary House, among others), although again, changes in the text from the first private printing (Cambridge, Mass.) are ignored. One particularly brilliant segment of the *History* — the six-chapter opening to Volume One — has been made available in a separate paperback: *The United States in 1800* (Ithaca, N.Y., 1955). Elizabeth Stevenson compiled *A Henry Adams Reader* (Garden City, N.Y., 1958); George Hochfield collected *The Great Secession Winter of 1860–61 and Other Essays* (New York, 1958; reprinted, Cranbury, N.J., 1962); and Edward Saveth added his own analysis of Adams's importance as a historian in *The Education of Henry Adams and Other Selected Writings* (New York, 1963). Both Henry Adams and Charles Francis Adams, Jr., are represented in *Chapters of Erie and Other Essays* (Boston, 1871, 1886), which has been reprinted (New York, 1966) and abridged (Ithaca, N.Y., 1956).

Democracy: An American Novel (anon., New York, 1880) and *Esther:*

A Novel (pseud., Frances Snow Compton, New York, 1884) have also appeared in English editions (and the former in a French translation, Paris, 1883); both have been reprinted in paperback, most conveniently in a combined edition (Garden City, N.Y., 1961) introduced by Ernest Samuels. The Scholars Facsimiles and Reprints edition of *Esther* (New York, 1938; now Gainesville, Fla.) remains a bookman's favorite, even though Robert Spiller's pioneering introduction (see *Criticism*, below) has been reprinted elsewhere. *John Randolph* (Boston, 1882) and the collection of essays on history edited by Henry's brother Brooks Adams as *The Degradation of the Democratic Dogma* (New York, 1919) have also appeared in paperback editions. In a noteworthy introduction to the Harper Torchbook *Degradation*, Charles Hirschfeld discusses Brooks's "insensitivity" to Henry Adams's "work as a first-rate historian and conscious literary artist" and finds that the essays move toward a remarkably modern philosophy of scientific history. *The Life of George Cabot Lodge* (Boston, 1911) is combined with Edmund Wilson's commentary in *The Shock of Recognition* (Garden City, N.Y., 1943; reprinted with corrections, 1955). Much of Henry Adams's other work is now listed in reprint catalogues, including such previously hard to find items as *Memoirs of Marau Taaroa Last Queen of Tahiti* (privately printed, Washington, 1893), *Historical Essays* (New York, 1891), both the *Life* and *Writings of Albert Gallatin* (Philadelphia, 1879), and Adams's edition of *Documents Relating to New England Federalism, 1800–1815* (Boston, 1877). Additional information about reprints is included in Vandersee's two *ALR* essays. For details concerning the poems and other short pieces, consult the appropriate section below.

MANUSCRIPTS AND LETTERS

Henry Adams is believed to have destroyed many of his own manuscripts, including diaries, letters, and the never-published biography of Aaron Burr (1882). In addition, the manuscripts of his most famous books — the *History, Mont-Saint-Michel and Chartres, The Education of Henry Adams* — have not survived. Yet among the rich collections of the Massachusetts Historical Society (Boston, Mass.) are papers and microfilms in number and quality great enough to define the characteristic nature of Adams's personal writing habits. The Society remains the chief resource for serious study of his manuscripts and letters.

To the more than 600 microfilm reels of Adams Papers through 1889, the Massachusetts Historical Society has added (1979) a 36-reel "Microedition of the Henry Adams Papers" with an "Introduction" by Charles Vandersee. This set of microfilms brings together letters and other materials from the three most significant holders: the Massachusetts Historical Society (more than a dozen separate collections), the Houghton Library of Harvard University, and the John Hay Library of Brown University. Vandersee's careful summary of Adams's surviving manuscripts, letters, books, and miscellaneous items makes the "Introduction" invaluable. A less detailed but more generally available version, which contains most of the information has also appeared (*RALS*, Spring 1979) as "Henry Adams: Archives and Microfilm" by Charles Vandersee. For Adams's printed letters, *The Letters of Henry Adams* (1982 f.), issuing from the Belknap Press of Harvard University Press (Cambridge, Mass.) will replace all other collections when it reaches a projected length of six volumes. It will not, however, reprint every letter published elsewhere or print every word in manuscript. To date the three published volumes print 1,277 of the surviving (all or in part) 1,519 letters written between 3 November 1858 and 3 February 1892. Of these, 549 "appear in print for the first time in a complete text" ("Bibliographical Note," 39).

The scholarly value of the Harvard Press *Letters of Henry Adams* cannot be ignored.[1] For many important letters, these volumes present the only printing of a reliable text. Volume One provides clear statements of editorial philosophy and method in the "Bibliographical Note" and "Editorial Note." Together with attractive illustrations, including maps, Henry Adams's watercolors, family genealogies, and many photographs, the texts and apparatus in the first three volumes fit beautifully together, to compliment the various skills of an expert editorial team that includes J. C. Levenson, Ernest Samuels, Charles Vandersee, and Viola Hopkins Winner as principals. The historical and biographical "Introduction" (vol. 1) is a model of brevity and good sense; and the entire project, now moving toward early completion, should serve to justify support for the publications program of The National Endowment for the Humanities.

Other guides to Adams's manuscripts and letters will continue to be used. Perhaps the most helpful is *American Literary Manuscripts* (Austin, Tex., 1960 and revisions) which contains a listing of important library holdings. Robert A. Hume, *Runaway Star: An Appreciation of Henry Adams* (Ithaca, N.Y., 1951), includes in his bibliography a list of "Works Containing Letters of Henry Adams." Some of Adams's apprentice writing has never reached print (undergraduate essays and poetry, for example) but other incidental pieces are emerging: "Henry Adams Reports on a Trades-Union Meeting," edited by Charles I. Glicksberg (*NEQ*, Dec. 1942); "Henry Adams Reports on a German Gymnasium," edited by Har-

---

1. For a dissenting view, see Norman Podhoretz's review of the Harvard edition in *The New Criterion* (June 1983).

old Dean Cater (*AHR*, Oct. 1947); and "Henry Adams Silenced by the Cotton Famine," edited by Joseph A. Boromé (*NEQ*, June 1960). Cater's inclusion in his *Henry Adams and His Friends: A Collection of His Unpublished Letters* (Boston, 1947) of "a hitherto unknown Henry Adams manuscript" brought to light an important essay in letter form, designed to accompany *The Rule of Phase Applied to History* (1909). More recently, Edward Chalfant's discussion of Henry Adams's (usually unsigned) letters to Boston newspapers, found in *Both Sides of the Ocean*, has opened a rich vein of letters-intended-to-be-published to fresh examination. In both the "Notes" and the biographical text, Chalfant discusses the subsurface content of Adams's life and letters during this important one-third of his existence; subsequent volumes should add to Chalfant's insights.

Meanwhile, Henry Adams's marginalia have been summarized by Henry Wasser, *The Scientific Thought of Henry Adams* (Thessaloníki, 1956) and closely examined by Max Baym, "William James and Henry Adams" (*NEQ*, Dec. 1937), and *The French Education of Henry Adams*, and by Paul H. Bixler, "A Note on Henry Adams" (*Col*, part 17, 1934). In addition, a microfilm of pages containing annotations from books in Adams's personal library has been compiled by Ernest Samuels and placed on deposit at the Massachusetts Historical Society; and a listing of undergraduate holdings, "The 1858 Catalogue of Henry Adams' Library," is also available (*Col*, Autumn 1938), thanks to the industry of Max Baym. Among Henry Adams's personal papers, found neatly packaged after his death, was the bulk of the correspondence published as *The Letters of Mrs. Henry Adams 1865–1883*, edited by Ward Thoron (Boston, 1936), which includes a sample page from the Adamses' engagement book.

Of course some probability remains that Adams's letters will continue to be found and printed. Already 4,500 are extant; and usually several can be grouped attractively around a single theme, as in Evelyne de Chazeaux's volume, *Lettres des Mers du Sud* (Paris, 1974), which offers French translations of 28 previously unpublished letters as well as parts of others. Here, Adams wrote mainly from Hawaii, Samoa, Tahiti, and Fiji during 1890–1891, as the "Introduction" (in French) explains; illustrations and a brief bibliographical note are also included. Chazeaux first published a series of these letters in "Lettres de Hénry Adams: Tahiti 1891" (*Revue de Deux Mondes*, Sept. 1968).

Other scholars have reported on rich materials being mined from Adams's correspondence: Ronald M. Meldrum, "The Epistolary Concerns of Henry Adams," *Research Studies: A Quarterly Publication of Washington State University* (Pullman, 1969) traces a "highly subjective account of the same problems and interests" found in the *Education*. Elsewhere "Henry Adams Looks at Contemporary English Poets: A Survey of the Letters of Henry Adams" (*MarkhamR*, May 1970) by Carol M. Kay collects some of Adams's scattered literary criticism. Robert I. Levy concentrates on the letters from the South Seas (like Chazeaux) and on Adams's *Memoirs of Marau Taaroa*; Levy's book, *Tahitians: Mind and Experience in the Society Islands* (Chicago, 1973) places Adams's reportage in a larger modern frame. Cruce Stark looks at family relationships in "The Development of a Historical Stance: The Civil War Correspondence of Henry and Charles Francis Adams," (*CLIO*, June 1975) to find important roots of Henry's "historical career." In a usable Ph.D. dissertation (Brown Univ.), Philip B. Eppard wrote on "The Correspondence of Henry Adams and John Hay, 1881–1892" (*DAI* 40:5913A), helping to trace yet another direction taken by Adams's letters. Just how substantial (and interesting) the discussion of a single letter *to* Henry Adams can be is shown in the detailed discussion provided by Richard A. Hocks, *Henry James and Pragmatist Thought* (Chapel Hill, N.C., 1974), who uses one of James's letters to Adams, written in March, 1914, as a key to James's artistic thought. Hocks's method deserves close attention; it can be applied to Adams and to other writers of great letters.

As we await the appearance of new volumes in the Harvard *Letters of Henry Adams*, other editions must be used with caution. Aside from Cater, the standard published collections are: *A Cycle of Adams Letters, 1861–1865* (2 vols., Boston, 1920), and *Letters of Henry Adams, 1858–1891* (2 vols., Boston, 1930, 1938), both edited by Worthington C. Ford. Deletions and omissions make the texts unreliable by modern standards; yet these volumes did establish the foundation of Henry Adams's considerable reputation as a letter-writer. Mabel La Farge in 1920 edited *Letters to a Niece and Prayer to the Virgin of Chartres* (Boston), the first printing of Adams's long poem. Some of the letters printed here will not be reprinted in the Harvard edition; this is also true of twenty-nine (of thirty-nine) letters from Adams to William Dwight Whitney published by Max Baym in the *Yale University Library Gazette* (Oct. 1967) as "An Historian Prods a Philologist: The Letters of Henry Adams to William Dwight Whitney." One critic's selection from these several collections (except for one letter) appears in the "Great Letters Series" as *The Selected Letters of Henry Adams* (New York, 1951). Newton Arvin's introduction is reprinted, along with his review of Ford's Letters, as "A Warning; not an Example," in *American Pantheon* (New York, 1967). Another influential American estimate of Henry Adams's talent has been set down by Louis Kronenberger in "The Letters and Life of Henry Adams" (*AtM*, Apr. 1967; reprinted in *The Polished Surface*, New York, 1969). Elsewhere, British opinion is offered by Marcus Cunliffe, in *The Literature of the*

United States (3rd ed., Baltimore, Md., 1967), who calls Adams "one of the best letter-writers in the language."

BIOGRAPHY

In general, his biographers have served Henry Adams well. His reputation as a son and brother, thinker and writer, husband and intellectual "uncle," has developed steadily as the details of his life are set down with a high seriousness that carefully avoids hero worship but also denigration. Adams's weaknesses as much as strengths, his characteristic human failings, have by now begun to color the established outlines of his life. Perhaps the best demonstration can be found in the first (of three) volume of Edward Chalfant's on-going biography, *Both Sides of the Atlantic: A Biography of Henry Adams: His First Life, 1838–1862* (Hamden, Conn., 1982), which adds importantly to what we have known about the young Henry Adams at Harvard and abroad. Chalfant, in this volume at least, provides new materials for psychological interpretation, while leaving intact the general outlines of Adams's life to be found in Ernest Samuels's standard three-volume biography: *The Young Henry Adams*, *Henry Adams: The Middle Years*, and *Henry Adams: The Major Phase* (Cambridge, Mass., 1948, 1958, 1964).

In the preface to the first volume, Samuels tells us that he intends to correct misrepresentations of Adams that emerge from the *Education*, and he threads a careful way through a massive accumulation of documents. His biographical formula—"a coherent body of fact with a modicum of interpretation"—allows ample room for discussion while correcting many mistakes, especially those founded upon such unreliable documentation as bowdlerized letters. The volumes grow in size as the subject becomes more complex, but lucidity never disappears. The notes explain such matters as Samuels's use of quotations and provide, in addition, a prodigious collection of supporting detail for the core narrative. Appendix A in *The Major Phase* summarizes "The Travels of Henry Adams." More than its predecessors, this final volume demonstrates the limitations (often self-imposed, especially where psychological theorizing and literary interpretation are concerned) and the more numerous advantages of Samuels's method. Faced with a variety of seductive temptations that might have turned him toward pessimistic philosophy, popularized science, or historical determinism, Samuels manages to bring his man through it all. To date, then, any serious biographical study of Henry Adams must begin with these three volumes.

A sprightly one-volume account, Elizabeth Stevenson's *Henry Adams:*

A *Biography* (New York, 1956; reprinted, 1961) focuses on the enigmatic relationship between Henry Adams the author and the subject of the *Education*, and adds a feminine touch by highlighting the "private world of women" in which Adams lived. Something of the drawing room charmer, rather than the intellectual dynamo, emerges in this portrait of a "Satanic gentleman." Unfortunately, all the correspondence between Adams and his female friends was not available to this biographer; other letters must have added to the picture provided by the subject himself. About Henry Adams's writings, Elizabeth Stevenson is often perceptive, especially in matters of style, but she is also sometimes guilty of oversimplification, reducing the contents of the later works to a series of questions, themes, and outline summaries. Nevertheless, she makes the man worth looking for, even while the literary artist escapes.

Among the figures in Adams's life, two women—his wife, Marian Hooper Adams, and Elizabeth Cameron—have attracted special attention from both biographers and their critics. Samuels's restrained treatment of Marian's tragic suicide refuses to countenance gossip or admit psychological speculation. Otto Friedrich, *Clover* (New York, 1979), begins in effect with what Samuels (and Adams) left him, the omission of any mention of Marian "Clover" Adams from the *Education* and the statue at the Adamses' grave in Rock Creek Cemetery, Washington, D.C., and goes on to fashion a highly speculative account of what their marriage might have been like. A sample of Friedrich's approach appeared in "Clover and Henry Adams—A Most Unusual Love Story" (*Smithsonian*, Apr. 1977). For a more sympathetic treatment of Marian Adams, one that stresses her own achievements as a photographer (with ample illustrations) and her conflicts as a talented American woman, consult *The Education of Mrs. Henry Adams* (Philadelphia, 1981) by Eugenia Kaledin. Her focus is a useful corrective to much commentary on Henry's marriage, which stresses Mrs. Adams's peculiarities. The first full-scale biography of Mrs. Cameron is briefly previewed later in this section.

Marian Adams attracted another perceptive commentator in William Dusinberre, as he proves in "Clover," Chapter Three of *Henry Adams: The Myth of Failure* (Charlottesville, Va., 1980). Dusinberre concentrates on Henry Adams's family (including his grandfather, father, and brothers, as well as Marian), his achievements as a historian, and especially the value of his experience in and with England, to make a larger case for the *History* among Adams's notable works. In his earlier "Henry Adams in England" (*JAmS*, Aug. 1977) the author shows how Adams's English experience and his friendship with Charles Milnes Gaskell found their way into the *History*; Dusinberre's book tells us much about Adams's life and also about his later writings, including *Chartres* and the *Education*.

Some of the same ground is covered by Lee Clark Mitchell in "'But this was History': Henry Adams' 'Education' in London Diplomacy" (*NEQ*, Sept. 1979). Again, the question of Henry Adams's attitude toward writing is a central concern, and Charles Vandersee comes at it from a different direction in "Henry Adams and the *Atlantic:* Pattern for a Career" (*PLL*, Fall 1972). The "three long pieces" that Adams wrote between 1858 and 1861 were never published in the *Atlantic*; yet they are used by Vandersee to demonstrate Adams's "complex ambivalence toward the literary trade," a trait that proved characteristic throughout the long remainder of his life.

As further evidence, we can cite *The Gilded Age Letters of E. L. Godkin*, ed. William M. Armstrong (Albany, 1974), which reviews Adams's relationships with Godkin, the *Nation*, and the *North American Review*. What is said about *Democracy* here can be amplified and expanded by a look at Philip B. Eppard's "Frances Snow Compton Exposed: William Roscoe Thayer on Henry Adams as a Novelist," (*RALS*, Spring 1975). Thayer's piece in the *Boston Evening Transcript* for 10 August 1918 named Adams as the author of *Democracy* and *Esther*. Another contemporary, Oliver Wendell Holmes, used his letters to Albert Einstein as a sketch book; after Adams's death, Holmes remembered him "playing the old Cardinal . . . pointing out that everything was dust and ashes" (*The Holmes-Einstein Letters* [New York, 1964]). Ferris Greenslet recalls a "coolly polite" but equally determined author, who defeated the young bookman's initial attempts to bring the privately printed *Education* to general publication, in "Adams Interlude," a chapter of Greenslet's autobiographical *Under the Bridge* (New York, 1943).

Of course various brief descriptions of Henry Adams's life are included in anthologies of American literature, and many critical studies review at least some of the biographical details. The curious nature of the *Education* guarantees a close association of Adams's life with his writings. Brooks Adams showed the way in 1919, when he wrote "The Heritage of Henry Adams" for *Degradation of the Democratic Dogma*. Pointing to the Adams family as the most relevant frame of reference, Brooks fixes upon the intellectual kinship of "two powerful and original men, the grandfather and the grandson" (John Quincy Adams and Henry Adams). To understand Henry's *Education* (published a year before), the reader (according to Brooks) must know the history of the Adamses through four generations, in order to understand where Henry fitted the family mold and where he did not. More recently, Katherine L. Morrison has provided a more complete context for Brooks's remarks in "A Reexamination of Brooks and Henry on John Quincy Adams" (*NEQ*, June 1981). This essay shows the usefulness of Henry's (and Brooks's) letters as literary and

biographical evidence, as well as the powerful nature of experience in
the Adams family.

Yet the relationship between Brooks and Henry Adams was special,
even for this special family. Some of their correspondence remains unavailable in print, and what we have must be used with caution. Arthur
Beringause draws heavily upon the letters (especially those of the 1890s)
for his *Brooks Adams: A Biography* (New York, 1955). This book adds
substantially to our understanding of their father's influence on Henry
and Brooks, the two sons who worked most closely with him, and of the
intellectual exchanges between the brothers that led to Brooks's *Law of
Civilization and Decay*. Still, many questions remain unanswered, as Marc
Friedlaender makes clear in "Brooks Adams *en Famille*" (*PMHS*, 1968).
A more narrowly defined examination especially useful to students of historiography, is *Henry Adams and Brooks Adams: The Education of Two
American Historians* (Norman, Okla., 1961); after systematically describing four "traditions" in family thinking, Timothy P. Donovan documents
their potency. He is less successful, however, at showing how Henry Adams
gave artistic expression to inherited ideas in his historical writing. A more
informal and personal account of life among the four Adams brothers
can be found in Abigail Adams Homans's *Education by Uncles* (Boston,
1966), which amplifies her essay "My Adams Uncles: Charles, Henry,
Brooks" (*YR*, Mar. 1966). Mrs. Homans remembers Uncle Henry as a
kindly tutor and sage counselor, surrounded by a youthful entourage during the years after the death of his wife.

Looking deeply into family history, in order to review Samuels's *Major
Phase* ("Impressionist of Power," *NY Review of Books*, 14 Jan. 1964), Alfred Kazin finds that Henry (and Brooks) personified, more than heredi-
tary skepticism, a fascination with power as both a practical and an intellectual possession. Kazin enlarges on the same general theme in another
important review essay, "The Fascination of Henry Adams" (*NR*, 1 Aug.
1983), which places Adams among those intellectuals who shared a "sense
of the tragedy of modern history." A generation before Henry, Brooks,
John, and Charles Francis, Jr., were active, the mantle of power was worn
by their father, the subject of Martin Duberman's biography, *Charles Francis Adams, 1807–1886* (Boston, 1960). Henry was his father's favorite, and
this volume shows that the younger man had in his father a model of
intellectual and political achievement that suddenly became an example
of senile incapacity—one powerful enough to frighten any student of
heredity.

Hints of what the family meant to its members pervaded the dramatic
episodes of television's (PBS) "The Adams Chronicles," which included
in thirteen installments some account of four generations. A book ver-

sion, *The Adams Chronicles: Four Generations of Greatness* (Boston, 1975) by Jack Shepherd "was prepared in conjunction with" the television series, largely illustrated, and supplied with an introduction, "A Family in the Public Service," by Daniel J. Boorstin. Francis Russell's book, *Adams: An American Dynasty* (New York, 1976) covers about the same ground. The family homestead is pictured in *House & Garden* (June 1983) with a text by Phyllis Lee Levin ("The Family Treasures of a Great American Dynasty"). In *The Force So Much Closer Home: Henry Adams and The Adams Family* (New York, 1977) Earl N. Harbert provides an intellectual measure of "The Great Inheritance" that was Henry's, although Harbert's purpose is chiefly critical rather than biographical. A reversal of this priority prevails in *Henry Adams and the American Experiment* (Boston, 1980), which David R. Contosta prepared for the Library of American Biography. Contosta earlier wrote "Henry Adams on the Role of Woman" (*New Scholar*, Spring 1974). As an introduction to Henry Adams, however, his book tells more about ideas than about people; what we miss is the rich texture of Adams family life that emerges from Paul C. Nagel's *Descent from Glory: Four Generations of the John Adams Family* (New York, 1983). By laying heavy stress on such themes as "duty" and such habits as diary writing, Nagel is able to keep the continuity of family experience central to his narrative; yet each of the figures from four generations comes alive. By judicial use of his voluminous sources (chiefly the Adams Papers), Nagel keeps everyone in proportion. Woman, man, and child; sister and brother; daughter, son, or grandchild; each Adams has something to tell us about the family and about himself. In particular, Nagel's account is the best yet available of Henry Adams's relationships with his siblings.

Some special qualities of family life were first identified by James Truslow Adams (not a family member) in *The Adams Family* (New York, 1930), subtitled "biography of a family," which was followed by his *Henry Adams* (New York, 1933). Cater's biographical introduction to his 1947 collection of letters added fresh material. A year later, Robert Spiller brought together in his *LHUS* account (reprinted in *The Oblique Light*, New York, 1968) critical and biographical commentary, to form a well-balanced appreciation of Henry Adams and to warn readers against accepting the unauthorized subtitle of the *Education* ("An Autobiography") at face value. Meanwhile family history and genealogy had begun to develop some of its modern popularity, and the Adams family became a favorite study for writers who also held some larger theme in view. Karl Schriftgiesser used "The Admirable Adams'" as a chapter in *Families* (New York, 1940) and Henry Adams as a representative "amateur" lobbyist in *The Lobbyists: The Art and Business of Influencing Lawmakers* (Boston, 1951).

Nathaniel Burt told the family story in the generously illustrated *First Families: The Making of an American Aristocracy* (Boston, 1970). Such acknowledgments of the family's importance are by now too numerous to recount in detail, and much of the recent commentary has expanded on earlier psychological insights. David F. Musto's "Continuity across Generations: The Adams Family Myth," *Kin and Communities: Families in America* (Wash. D.C., 1979) presents the family as an influential pattern of mind; his assessment is both challenging to interpreters and carefully thought out. Another persuasion—different in content, form, and application—is apparent in Joseph F. Byrnes's *The Virgin of Chartres: An Intellectual and Psychological History of the Work of Henry Adams* (Rutherford N.J., 1981).

Again and again, biographical interpreters have foundered on the rock that Henry Adams placed in their path: his imaginative yet inconsistent attempts at self-portraiture in letters and books. Simply and supremely, Adams knew how to hide. Alfred Kazin measures his (and Richard Hofstadter's) fascination with Henry Adams—despite Adams's expressions of anti-Semitism—in the pages of *New York Jew* (New York, 1978), and Joseph Epstein discusses the case of Adams and failure (or "anti-success") in a like idiom: *Ambition: The Secret Passion* (New York, 1980). Yet there are important sources aside from Adams's own writings. Much of his life was spent among the few friends and family members who could be classed as intimates, and their accounts of Henry Adams should be placed alongside his own. Brooks Adams's "The Heritage of Henry Adams" encouraged other critics to consider the Adams family history a kind of key to the writings of Henry and the other Adamses. Worthington Chauncey Ford's "The Adams Family" (*Quarterly Review*, Apr. 1922) reviews six books by family members (including the *Education, Chartres, Chapters of Erie*, and two by Charles Francis Adams, Jr.), finding in them evidence to support a general conclusion: "Exclusion from a public career fostered a family trait which has enriched American history and example —the habit of self-examination." V. L. Parrington preferred his own thesis about the family, which he labeled the "most distinguished in our history" (*Beginnings of Critical Realism in America* [New York, 1930]). "Ancestral bias," according to Parrington, accounted for the "skepticism of the House of Adams" (particularly noticeable in Henry and Brooks) which prevented their understanding of "men and measures."

For better or worse, this view accepts without serious reservation the report of "failure" offered in the *Education*. But more sympathetic evaluations of the Adams clan have also been recorded: Stephen Hess celebrates the industry and energy of the Adamses in *American Political Dynasties: From Adams to Kennedy* (Garden City, N.Y., 1966), although he does not advance his case beyond the limits of popular biography. Cleveland Amory too has found room for the Adamses in his society trilogy, bringing the family story briefly but entertainingly up to date in *Who Killed Society?* (New York, 1960). A rare opportunity to see in print what an undergraduate student thinks of Adams is provided by Margaret A. Good, "Theodore Roosevelt and Henry Adams in the Age of Enterprise," *William and Mary Review* (Spring 1966); while Henry Adams's Washington house (shared with John Hay), rather than the man, is featured in James F. O'Gorman's beautiful catalogue: *Selected Drawings: H. H. Richardson and His Office* (Boston, 1974). An impressive shortened version, handsomely illustrated, appeared in *Harvard Magazine* (Oct. 1974). Both texts are tributes to Richardson and to Adams, who employed him; both owe a debt to Marc Friedlaender, who outlined the relevant human relationships in "Henry Hobson Richardson, Henry Adams, and John Hay" (*Journal of the Society of Architectural Historians* and *PMHS*, 1970).

Among Henry Adams's friendships, several were remarkable. Almost a family member was Aileen Tone, the "secretary-companion and adopted niece," who shared Henry Adams's last years (1913–1918). Her story, gathered from notes, letters, and personal interviews, has been summarized by Louis Auchincloss, "'Never leave me, never leave me'" (*AH*, Feb. 1970; revised as "Aileen Tone and Henry Adams," in Auchincloss, *A Writer's Capital* [Minneapolis, 1974]). It paints a difficult yet fascinating Henry Adams, thirty years Aileen's senior, who punctuated his pathetic expressions of loneliness with moments of fitful charm. Another unusual tribute, this one from a Harvard student who grew into a sometimes stormy friendship with his history teacher, is found in the pages of *Early Memories* (New York, 1913) by Henry Cabot Lodge. Lodge knew all the Adamses, and his comments about the family in the "Memorial Address," included as a preface to *Charles Francis Adams, 1835–1915: An Autobiography* (Boston, 1916), exhibit a New England understanding of the Brahmin mind. The *Education*, of course, sends us back again and again to think about New England, just as it requires us to ponder the characterizations of Henry Adams's friends. Several studies are helpful for the latter undertaking: *The Life and Letters of John Hay* (2 vols., Boston and New York, 1915), by William Roscoe Thayer, portrays the talented gentleman whose political career fascinated Adams. Hay's letters make this old-fashioned biography an especially valuable register of Adams's complex personality upon a sensitive, intelligent man of great good humor. Another symbolic figure in the *Education* is Clarence King, the thoroughly modern scientist. David H. Dickason's "Henry Adams and Clarence King: The Record of a Friendship" (*NEQ*, June 1944) recognizes the importance of learning more about the mysterious geologist; yet the essay depends too much upon a narrow selection of source materials. The Adams-King friendship must be studied in Thurman Wilkins's *Clarence King: A Biography* (New York, 1958) if the details of King's life (such as his secret marriage) and his influence upon Adams are to be grasped. Henry Adams's personal tribute to his recently dead friend, "King," in *Clarence King Memoirs* (New York, 1904), is also indispensable.

Miscellaneous sources touch upon one facet or another of Henry Adams's variegated life. In *Roman Spring: Memoirs* (Boston, 1934), Mrs. Winthrop Chanler devotes a short chapter to the "Friendship of Henry Adams" and discusses the vexing question of his attraction to Roman Catholicism. Indeed, Adams's travels — intellectual, spiritual, physical — have fascinated almost as many observers as has the grip of New England Puritanism on Henry and the Adams family. Louise Fant Fuller, "Henry Adams: Pilgrim to World's Fairs" (*TSL*, 1964), uses evidence from Adams's letters to study his responses "to the three fairs that he attended": the 1893 World's Columbian Exposition; an 1895 visit to Chartres cathedral, "where he met the Virgin"; and the Paris Exposition of 1900. The *Education* and *Chartres*, Mrs. Fuller finds, distort the chronology of sensibility established by the letters and confuse Adams's impressions of the moment. Motoshi Karita reports on "Henry Adams in Japan" (*SELit*, 1962), including books he read and places he visited, and concludes that Adams always remained "unable to penetrate to the inner life of the Japanese." Donald Richie's earlier essay with the same title (*Japan Quarterly*, Oct.–Dec. 1959) reached a similar conclusion. Perhaps the East was just too far from Boston. Louis Auchincloss, "In Search of Innocence" (*AH*, June 1970; reprinted in *Life, Law and Letters: Essays and Sketches* [Boston, 1979]), looks at records of the second journey that Adams made with John La Farge (1890) to Hawaii, Samoa, and Tahiti, and finds that La Farge's watercolors display greater objectivity than Adams's writings. A bonus is the color illustrations of work done by both La Farge and Adams.

Drawing upon an unsurpassed knowledge of the subject, Ernest Samuels has added some afterthoughts to his biography. "Henry Adams' 20th Century Virgin" (*Christian Century*, 5 October 1960) connects Adams's personal theology with nineteenth-century anthropology. Mariolatry offered an explanation for the natural superiority of women, a belief Adams had long held without being able to explain; since Adams's death, Samuels finds, the "Marian development" of Roman Catholic theology has assimilated Henry Adams's views. In another essay, "Henry Adams and the Gossip Mills" (*Essays in American and English Literature Presented to Bruce Robert McElderry, Jr.*, edited by Max F. Schulz [Athens, Ohio, 1967]), Samuels replies to an English critic by explaining the hearsay rule used in the biography: "Whether a rumor deserved a page, a line, a footnote or charitable oblivion would depend on the credible evidence for it and not on its piquancy." Samuels dismisses claims of Henry Adams's paternity of Martha Cameron and labels "inconclusive" the evidence of any liaison between Adams and Martha's mother, Elizabeth Cameron, who, in modern terminology, cannot be labeled his "mistress." The full story of Elizabeth Cameron's eventful life, which did not merely parallel that of Henry Adams, is the subject of *Henry Adams in Love: The Pursuit of Elizabeth Sherman Cameron* (New York, forthcoming) by Arline B. Tehan. This first biography of Mrs. Cameron draws on Sherman family letters.

Finally, it is worth noting that the many poetic and fictional representations of Henry Adams—apart from his appearances on television—have added a certain sparkle to his collective biography. Without attempting to be exhaustive, this survey acknowledges the pervasive force of three: Allen Tate in his novel, *The Fathers* (New York, 1938), pictures Adams as "a young man to be better known later, Henry Adams, a great snob even then, who got on Charles's nerves by pretending friendship with Rooney Lee, the Colonel's son, having been with him at Harvard, and yet ridiculing him for his lack of learning." Conrad Aiken, in Section 8 of *The Kid* (New York, 1947), "The Last Vision," pays a verse tribute to the courageous but ever dark and painful journey of the intellectual Henry Adams, who engaged in a lifelong search for "godhead." And a sensitive characterization, which captures a very different, sunshiny side of Adams during the happy years of his marriage, comes from Henry James, who knew both Marian and Henry Adams well. As Mr. and Mrs. Bonnycastle of Washington, D.C., the Adamses appear in James's "Pandora," where Henry is described by the omniscient narrator: "Her husband was not in politics, though politics were much in him." So fiction may be truer than fact.

CRITICISM

Although the modern reputation of Henry Adams may be traced from 1918, the year of his death and of the publication of *The Education of Henry Adams*, critical interest has developed its individual character and force largely in the years since 1950. As Ernest Samuels worked to put together the puzzle of Adams's life, the way was also being cleared for critical exercises of many different kinds. Now, in 1983, the results of such investigations are before us in profusion. If they seem at times impressively masterful but too often uneven in quality, confused and partial in comprehension, and contradictory in conclusion, no experienced reader of literary criticism will be surprised. Perhaps commentary must be expected to mirror every feature of Henry Adams's personality that found its way into a single letter or sentence or line of poetry. The critical situation, in short, remains lively. It can best be considered in a discussion of individual works, after a brief look at the most important general estimates.

General Estimates

Many readers first meet Henry Adams in one of the anthology introductions which are critical essays in their own right and deserve separate reprinting. Ernest Samuels's discussion in *Major Writers of America*, edited by Perry Miller (New York, 1962), places Adams in a New England literary tradition that prized dissent. Rebellion rather than conformity marked Henry Adams: "the question of fame and success haunted him more, perhaps, than it did any other American writer." Samuels rejects the label "sentimental pessimism" for Adams's philosophy and wisely insists upon crediting fully the ambiguities of a complex mind. Another anthology introduction concentrates on literary artistry: Charles R. Anderson, in *American Literary Masters* (New York, 1965), shows that Adams "uses language like a poet" throughout his work; he experimented as he searched for an adequate mode of self-expression to record the "meaning of history and man's place in it." These two fine introductions have been reprinted, along with a sampling of criticism on Adams, old and new, in *Critical Essays on Henry Adams* (Boston, 1981) ed. by Earl N. Harbert (hereafter, *Critical Essays*). Harbert also has written the "Henry Adams" entry in *Dictionary of Literary Biography: American Realists and Naturalists* (vol. 12). A later *DLB* volume, *Twentieth Century American Historians* is expected to supply another introduction to Adams, written by Michael O'Brien. For readers of French, Charles Cestre's treatment of Adams in *La Littérature Americaine* (Paris, 1945) may be helpful, although it is very brief.

A longer introductory evaluation appears in George Hochfield's *Henry Adams: An Introduction and Interpretation*, in the American Authors and Critics Series. It contains these basic materials: a chronology of Adams's life, brief but incisive discussions of the chief writings, and a selected bibliography. Robert Spiller's "Henry Adams" (*LHUS*) remains richly suggestive many years after its initial appearance. A skillful mixture of biography and criticism yields a commanding overview of the subject; the discussion draws upon the well-known *Chartres* and *Education* to document the thesis: "Throughout his life Adams thought of himself as a man of letters rather than primarily as a historian, scientist or philosopher." Spiller also found a place for Adams in *The Cycle of American Literature* (New York, 1955; reprinted, Mentor, 1957) as "a literary man

who could at least state the issues of the new order both in human and
cosmic terms." An "ability to reconcile reality and myth by the use of
symbols" forms the "secret" of Adams's considerable success. Other observers have carried Spiller's idea further but none holds a higher opinion of Henry Adams: "Adams laid the foundations for modern literature
even more than for modern history by asking questions with which literature alone was competent to deal."

Like Spiller, the scholar-editor-critic J. C. Levenson ranks among the
chief interpreters of Adams's writings. *The Mind and Art of Henry Adams*
(Boston, 1957; reprinted, Stanford, 1968) has become indispensable. *Mind
and Art* is neither an easy book nor a simplified introduction; it best serves
a reader already familiar with Adams by laying down basic lines of inquiry and exploration, and by documenting every assertion. More than
most lengthy critical studies, this book achieves a unity and comprehensiveness which add formal completeness to its argument and make difficult any adequate representation in summary or quotation. Levenson
traces the chronology of Adams's literary development, allowing for the
influences of family, school, reading, and so on. We follow the artist and
the thinker, stopping from time to time to measure his growth. The chief
academic performance of Professor Adams, "Anglo-Saxon Courts of Law"
(1876), for example, displays "his ability not only to test historical facts,
but to organize his knowledge." An emphasis upon literary (rather than
biographical) considerations does not, however, prevent the author's using
explanations to illuminate dark corners: "While earlier Adamses wrote as
public men even in their correspondence, Henry Adams wrote as a private citizen — whether he was a private secretary or a professional scholar
who put his work before so limited an audience that publication served
to conceal." Levenson's treatment of the major works offers a remarkable
range of explications, designed not only to do justice to the peculiar qualities of individual genres and examples but also to show their place and
importance in the larger pattern of Adams's thought and writing. Close
reading and wide reference achieve a happy conjunction in *Mind and
Art*; as a result Levenson's whole achievement becomes something more
than the sum of its parts. No serious reader should miss this book.

Levenson has made other important contributions to critical understanding. "Henry Adams and the Art of Politics" (*SoR*, Winter 1968; reprinted in *Critical Essays*) turns an old biographical question decisively
toward a literary answer: "The idea of politics as an art clarifies at once
Adams's relation to twentieth-century estheticism and to his eighteenth-
century political inheritance." In an earlier piece, "Henry Adams and
the Culture of Science," in *Studies in American Culture: Dominant Ideas
and Images*, edited by Joseph J. Kwiat and Mary C. Turpie (Minneapolis,

1960), Levenson surveys Adams's intellectual approach to science and concludes: "His own way of taking action was to ask, more cogently than any of his countrymen then or since, the leading questions about science — in what spirit to cultivate it, in what ways to use it, how to relate it to other kinds of knowledge." By capturing the tentative and interrogatory qualities of Adams's thought, Levenson provides a necessary check against too literal interpretation of "scientific" history or philosophy.

One possible objection has been raised by Martin Green in *The Problem of Boston* (New York, 1966), which acknowledges a debt to Yvor Winters. Believing "that the history of nineteenth-century Boston is also the history of the American mind," Green finds in Adams's thought a spectrum of "prudish" attitudes, and "deterioration" overall. Because Levenson celebrates "the power of mind," he wrongly suggests, according to Green, that Henry Adams achieved transcendence over "fact" and "experience." This thesis reopens an old argument, which owes something to Van Wyck Brooks, who identified Henry Adams as a representative "New England Mind" in *The Flowering of New England* (New York, 1936, 1957). Another observer, T. K. Whipple, deserves more credit than he usually receives; his *Spokesmen* (New York, 1928) selected Adams as one of ten American writers whose "Poetic Temper" set them against "practical society." A provocative although irritatingly tentative consideration of Adams's cultural significance can be found in Ferner Nuhn, *The Wind Blew from the East: A Study in the Orientation of American Culture* (New York, 1942); his chapter "Henry Adams and the Hand of the Fathers" (reprinted in *Literature in America*, edited by Philip Rahv [New York, 1957]) concentrates upon "the feminine element" in Adams's thought and the importance of polarities in his writing. Another weakness of the cultural approach shows itself in Nuhn's verdict: finally, Henry Adams remains "not quite the artist." Many readers do not agree.

In "Henry Adams: His Passage to Asia" (*Critical Essays*), Margaret J. Brown opens the question of Eastern influences on Adams to a full investigation, which she had earlier initiated in a Ph.D. dissertation, "Henry Adams and the Orient" (Tulane, 1976). In his own gracefully written AWS (no. 93) pamphlet, Louis Auchincloss finds artistry to be a supreme quality in Adams's thought and writing; *Henry Adams* (Minneapolis, 1971) has been reprinted in *Makers of American Thought: An Introduction to Seven American Writers* (Minneapolis, 1974) edited and introduced by Ralph Ross. This volume represents some of the best of the AWS. Among the more extended arguments for Adams as artist, two formula volumes have appeared in two separate series published by Twayne: *Henry Adams* (Boston, 1979) by Ferman Bishop, is the more useful general introduction to Adams and a representative title (no. 293) in Twayne's United States

Authors Series; James G. Murray's *Henry Adams* (New York, 1974), a volume in Twayne's World Leaders Series, is impressionistic throughout and liable to confuse any reader who resists its tripartite division of Henry Adams's thought: "Triangulation," "Transcendentalism," "Existentialism." As one of Murray's reviewers remarked in *AmLS* (1975): "The book cannot be recommended as an introduction to Adams."

A more conventional approach to Adams as literary artist can be found in *The Force So Much Closer Home: Henry Adams and the Adams Family* (New York, 1977) by Earl N. Harbert. As the reviewer for *AmLS* (1977) declared: "What most amazes one . . . is that the book was not written long ago. To view the works of the family-conscious Adams in terms of the family's heritage as it existed in his ancestors' writings is an approach that guarantees interesting results." Harbert's thesis is stated in the "Preface": "'Family' offered him [Henry Adams] a special key to self-understanding, a path for exploring the basic causes of his actions and his thoughts, and a unique resource which he made use of in both his writings and his life." Five chapters apply this concept to all of Adams's most important works except *Chartres*. Elsewhere, Harbert deals respectfully with the literary reputation of Henry Adams in "Henry Adams and the Critics of His Time" (*TSE*, 1978), which usefully supplements the material in *Henry Adams: A Reference Guide* (see *Bibliography* above).

Other important works also demonstrate the vitality of Adams criticism. Vern Wagner's *The Suspension of Henry Adams: A Study of Manner and Matter* (Detroit, 1969) follows his "The Lotus of Henry Adams" (*NEQ*, Mar. 1954); the book focuses upon "technique," especially "juncture" (which welds together "manner" and "matter"), and the "humor" of Adams's sardonic variety. Their overall effect, Wagner feels, is to create an "inconclusive, irresolute, uncertain, doubtful" silence — the philosophical and artistic "suspension" in his title. His thesis forces Wagner to make nonsense of many passages, but he presents the best analysis yet of the "genuine humorist" in Adams. *Symbol and Idea in Henry Adams* (Lincoln, Neb., 1969) by Melvin Lyon combines detailed explications of six major works with a broad discussion of "eight or nine primary aspects" of Adams's thought, to form a remarkably complete treatment of "imaginative symbolism," its development, use, and meaning. More than forty pages of critical notes summarize other interpretations; and the introduction attempts to define with unusual precision the author's terms and method. Unfortunately, some repetitions between text and notes and between critical notes and footnotes bring the organization into question; but its comprehensiveness makes Lyon's book valuable. John J. Conder's *A Formula of His Own: Henry Adams's Literary Experiment* (Chicago, 1970) is limited in size and scope, concentrating upon the literary form and technique of *Chartres* and the *Education*, which together form "a single unit of art." (For a contrasting view, which insists upon the aesthetic unity of the *Education* and which treats the book as an "apotheosis" of the autobiographical form and its author as both "orderer" and "interpreter" of failure, see Chapter Six in David L. Minter's *The Interpreted Design as a Structural Principle in American Prose* [New Haven, Conn., 1969].) Conder allows a place to other writings, but he emphasizes their secondary values, studying them for clues to Adams's developing artistry or as supporting evidence for interpretations of the "masterpieces." Whether such an approach is justified, each reader will have to decide for himself. Conder's method reveals the poetic possibilities in Adams's best prose, and it yields some surprises. Neither *Chartres* nor the *Education*, the author finds (unlike Lyon), "depends upon symbols to achieve a unity of form"; instead, "the various elements of historical and personal experience [are] united by a fictional persona and by recurrent methods of presenting material in a widely varying, often sharply opposed, set of contexts." Conder's closely reasoned explications defy summary treatment. Yet, by anatomizing the "works themselves," he forces us to reconsider older readings, even if our notions of the "internal necessity" within "fictional" forms do not exactly correspond to his. Like Wagner and Lyon, Conder supplies a sustained form of literary (rather than biographical) criticism, and one worth pondering.

Another approach attempts to measure Adams and his writing against the intellectual (or psychological) climate of his time. Although a number of short essays have sought to capture and label the exact philosophical position held by Adams, the larger frame provided by John Carlos Rowe in *Henry Adams and Henry James: The Emergence of a Modern Consciousness* (Ithaca, N.Y., 1967) seems most satisfying. Many readers will probably agree that *Chartres* and the *Education* point toward existentialism, if any such label is required. Of course other possibilities also remain open, as shown in Jay Martin's *Harvest of Change: American Literature, 1865–1914* (Englewood Cliffs, N.J., 1967). Martin nominates "Sages of Society," of whom Adams and Twain best illustrate a consciousness "of the push of history against human ideals." Warner Berthoff, *The Ferment of Realism: American Literature, 1884–1919* (New York, 1965), displays a very different literary persuasion. He classes Henry Adams among those realists who discovered that traditional forms "would not serve." Berthoff shows that Adams's major writings belong to a "Literature of Argument" which we have not recognized and do not fully understand. But we may be getting closer. Harold Kaplan began his own investigation with "The Metapolitics of Henry Adams" (*Social Research,*

Autumn 1979) before proposing a case for Adams as a "Naturalist" in *Power and Order: Henry Adams and the Naturalist Tradition in American Fiction* (Chicago, 1981). This short book is suggestive yet diffuse. It should be read along with the cautionary arguments provided by Ronald E. Martin's *American Literature and the Universe of Force* (Durham, N.C., 1981), especially Chapters One and Four, firmly in mind.

As we have already noted, Henry Adams is often associated with a family political or social position. Perhaps the clearest short example, Lynn Hudson Parsons, "Continuing Crusade: Four Generations of the Adams Family View Alexander Hamilton" (*NEQ*, Mar. 1964), applies the idea of a family prejudice to Henry's chief works. Other observers have preferred to fit the views of the Adamses into a grander intellectual design — the usual designation is "conservative"— where the problem of accurate definition often remains unsolved. In *The Conservative Mind* (London, 1954; reprinted, Avon, 1968) Russell Kirk sketches a line of conservative thought from Edmund Burke to Henry Adams by way of John Adams, but Allen Guttmann, *The Conservative Tradition in America* (New York, 1967), refuses to accept the label "Conservative" for Henry Adams, who is called a "Liberal stripped of illusions." Other students of Adams's thought have insisted upon bypassing politics and finding the critical key in education, considered by several Adamses to be "a central business in life." Clarence K. Sandelin's dissertation (Wisconsin, 1956), "The Educational Philosophy of Henry Adams: A Brahmin Contribution to Critical Realism," brings all the evidence together but pushes the thesis too hard. A more balanced discussion, "Henry Adams: Educator" (*Serif*, June 1967), by John L. Gribben, looks closely at the relationship between the life and writings. Henry Adams's education from books and his uses of an important literary heritage are the subjects of Max Baym's *The French Education of Henry Adams*, to which should be added Baym's "Three Moths and a Candle: A Study of the Impact of Pascal on Walter Pater, Henry Adams and Wallace Stevens," in *Comparative Literature: Proceedings of the Second Congress of the International Comparative Literature Association*, edited by Werner P. Friederich (Chapel Hill, N.C., 1959). The French influences have been studied by others as well, and Samuels surveys the situation with care; new material is added in André Monchoux, "Propos inédits sur la France dans les lettres de Henry Adams" (*Revue de Littérature Comparée*, Apr.–June 1967). William Dusinberre, as stated earlier, focuses on the important English influences in *Henry Adams: The Myth of Failure*. See also (under *Mont-Saint-Michel and Chartres* below) the discussion of *Henry Adams on the Road to Chartres* by Robert Mane.

One of the first full-scale attempts to understand the complexity of

Henry Adams's work, Robert A. Hume's *Runaway Star: An Appreciation of Henry Adams* (1951), remains a useful demonstration (even for
those who do not distinguish three levels in "the sensibility of Henry
Adams") of what had to be done to make Adams a respectable subject
for literary criticism. Yvor Winters, for example, insisted with characteristic vigor (*The Anatomy of Nonsense* [Norfolk, Conn., 1943]) that Adams's
late works (including *Chartres* and the *Education*) represent "the radical
disintegration of mind," probably brought on by an "accumulation of
emotion." Winters's chapter "Henry Adams" (reprinted in *In Defense of
Reason*, New York, 1947) raised its own emotional response, chiefly in
William Jordy's fine book, *Henry Adams: Scientific Historian*, and in Stanley Edgar Hyman's *The Armed Vision* (rev. ed., New York, 1955). From
1931 on, an important general estimate of Adams emerged in the many
essays by R. P. Blackmur, written as preliminary studies for a book that
remained unfinished at his death. Their variety makes them an unsatisfactory basis for determining Blackmur's critical "stance"; fortunately,
the most important pieces have been reprinted in *The Expense of Greatness* (New York, 1940) and *A Primer of Ignorance*, edited by Joseph Frank
(New York, 1967). An additional source of Blackmur's opinions concerning Adams is: *Henry Adams* (New York, 1980), a posthumous volume
edited by Veronica A. Makowsky, with her Introduction and a thoughtful Foreword by Denis Donoghue. Some of the material included here
is indebted to Makowsky's "R. P. Blackmur on Henry Adams" (*Princeton
Univ. Library Chronicle*, Winter 1978); still, all of the tributes to Blackmur's perceptive work on Adams are well deserved. The complex story
of Blackmur's nearly lifelong fascination with Adams may be found in
Russell Fraser's impressionistic biography, *A Mingled Yarn: The Life of
R. P. Blackmur* (New York, 1981), which uses both Blackmur and Adams
to underscore a single moral: "Death is the expense of life and failure
is the expense of greatness."

A recent trend in general studies has encouraged revaluation and greater
self-scrutiny among Adams's critics. Harry M. Campbell's short but provocative "Academic Criticism on Henry Adams: Confusion About Chaos"
(*Midcontinent American Studies Journal*, Spring 1966) claims that Spiller
and Winters (among others) have bent Adams to fit their own designs;
the pessimistic prophet, rightly understood, belongs to a brotherhood of
"atheistic existentialists," with Sartre, Camus, and their followers. Other
critics have found that philosophy, science, history, and biography are
finally secondary to the art of Henry Adams, whose irony, symbolism,
and humor need further explanation. A more methodical charting of
critical response up to the 1950s is contained in a Ph.D. dissertation, "The
Reputation of Henry Adams" (Chicago, 1954), by Moreene Crumley; by

1983, however, the record has grown much longer. Denis Donoghue adds to it a comparison of Adams with other American writers (such as Tate, Trilling, Veblen, and Henry James) which studies "The American Style of Failure" (*SR*, Summer 1974; reprinted, *The Sovereign Ghost: Studies in Imagination* [Berkeley, 1976]). Daniel Aaron views Adams's "discomfort" as "the story of his class" in a different but equally stimulating appraisal, *The Unwritten War: American Writers and the Civil War* (New York, 1973). Elsewhere, the historical and "progressive imagination" of Henry Adams receives attention in two works: *Versions of the Past: Imagination in American Fiction* (New York, 1974) by Harry B. Henderson III; and Daniel Bell's *The Coming of the Post-Industrial Society* (New York, 1973). Another measure of Adams's influence, especially among academics, is provided by Robert L. Church in "Economists as Experts: The Rise of the Academic Profession in the United States," *The University in Society*, vol. 2 (Princeton, 1974), ed. by Laurence Stone. Paul F. Boller, Jr., writes more generally about Henry and Brooks Adams and their contemporaries in *American Thought in Transition: The Impact of Evolutionary Naturalism, 1865–1900* (Chicago, 1969). The summaries found here may be useful in placing non-scientists (or at best amateurs) like the Adamses in relation to their increasingly professional scientific age. More general still is "An Appreciation of Henry Adams," The Skidmore College Faculty Research Lecture for 1974 (Saratoga Springs, 1974) by David Marcell, which tells us something about why Adams continues to read by academics and non-academics alike.

A long chapter, "From Filial Loyalty to Religious Protest," in Jackson Lear's *No Place of Grace: Antimodernism and the Transformation of American Culture, 1880–1920* (New York, 1981) raises many of the questions that have led to the current outpouring of commentary on Adams's cultural importance. The Allen Nevins Prize for 1977, for example was awarded to Mark Schwehn for his Stanford Ph.D. dissertation (1976) in American history, "The Making of Modern Consciousness: The Works and Careers of Henry Adams and William James." Peter W. Williams, "Henry Adams on Religion: An Introduction" (*Ohio Journal of Religious Studies*, Nov. 1974) adds to the interest in Adams as a modern man, as does Charles Vandersee's "The Attractive Genius of Henry Adams" (*The Cresset* [Valparaiso Univ.], Dec. 1982).

Assessing the effects of Henry Adams's writings on such readers, in groups or as individuals, has become as difficult and interesting as the study of influences on Adams. For the former pursuit, Richard H. Pells, *Radical Visions and American Dreams: Culture and Social Thought in the Depression Years* (New York, 1973) offers a provocative point of departure. William Wasserstrom's "Phoenix on Turtle Island: D. H. Lawrence in Adams's America" (*GaR*, Spring 1978) is representative of his several attempts to measure later writers against Adams's standards of thought and expression. A more humorous application of Adamsian "failure" characterizes "SATs are ruining the GNP" (*CHEMTECH*, Sept. 1982) by Nicholas Lemann; and the catalogue of possible uses for various ideas of Henry Adams now seems in practice to be endless. Yet the obvious need for thoughtful reconsideration has been generously served as well. *The Sewanee Review* for Spring 1980, for example, includes four essays or essay-reviews that deal with Henry Adams in general terms: "Learning Through Ignorance: *The Education of Henry Adams*" by James M. Cox; "The View From the Side" by B. L. Reid; "A Grammar of Assent" by Laurence Holland; and "Clover Adams, Henry Adams, and the Conviction of Failure" by Earl N. Harbert. Robert M. Adams covers much of the same ground in "The Sweet Taste of Defeat" (*TLS*, 11 July 1980), as does another veteran observer, Marcus Cunliffe, who also uses the pages of *TLS* (23 Oct. 1981) for another retrospective treatment of Adams. Some of these essays will find a place in the following sections devoted to individual works.

History of the United States of America during the Administrations of Thomas Jefferson and James Madison

"I never yet heard of ten men who had ever read my history," Henry Adams claimed, fifteen years after its publication, and the *Education* allows no room for doubt about the author's disappointment. Status as a classic of American historical writing has since been granted to the *History*, but only after the author's death, when almost everything he had written began to share the almost magical spell cast by the *Education*. The *History*, however, deserves to stand alone. Its volumes contain the best of Adams's political biographies (including the never-published life of Aaron Burr), and every page shows the technique and style of a master historian who had learned his art in a lengthy apprenticeship.

The value of such training is recognized in William Jordy's *Henry Adams: Scientific Historian*. In part because of its excellent bibliography, the book has become a chief resource for all students of Adams's thinking about history. The preface to the 1963 edition surveys recent scholarship and answers questions raised by Howard M. Munford, "Henry Adams and the Tendency of History" (*NEQ*, Mar. 1959), who views Adams's exposition of scientific history as a Delphic joke, full of "elaborate irony" and "grim humor." Jordy assures us that he considered that possibility before dismissing it from his book. He also claims that he did not ignore Adams's value as a seer, despite the accusations of Lewis Mumford in "Apology to Henry Adams" (*VQR*, Spring 1962), nor did he set out to demolish a set of half-baked, pseudoscientific notions. Jordy does try (with large success) to be fair to Adams, science, and history; if his efforts fail to satisfy every specialist, they succeed in combination (as narrower investigations have not done) by fixing the *History* and the historical essays within a workable biographical and literary frame. Adams was not merely a historian, even less was he a scientist. His "awareness of literary values," as Jordy understands them, "with all that such awareness implied for his personality, saved Adams from a blind faith in science." Jordy tells us where and why Adams failed, but also how he succeeded.

The Scientific Thought of Henry Adams by Henry Wasser includes much of the same material about Adams and science, without this useful frame. Wasser's "The Thought of Henry Adams" (*NEQ*, Dec. 1951) makes a case for the primacy of science. Two well-reasoned European accounts discuss the problem with special intelligence: Robert Mane, "Henry Adams et la science" (*EA*, Jan.–Mar. 1963) and Ursula Brumm, "Henry Adams als Historiker: Seine Bedeutung für die amerikanische Literatur- und Geistesgeschichte" (*Archiv*, Oct. 1962). Two essays in *JHI* provide a measure for a change in thinking about Adams's use of science: W. Stull Holt, "The Idea of Scientific History in America" (June 1940), surveys the sources, assumptions, development, and value of "scientific history," placing Adams among his contemporaries and asserting that "no generally accepted verdict can as yet be said to have been rendered." Joseph Mindel's "The Uses of Metaphor: Henry Adams and the Symbols of Science," published twenty-five years later (Jan.–Mar. 1965), applies modern scientific knowledge to correct not only Adams's mistakes but those made by Levenson (*Mind and Art*) and Jordy as well. Mindel studies his subject against a background of the "uses and misuses of metaphors in science"; Adams emerges as a knowledgeable (if amateurish) commentator, who imaginatively fashioned a "metaphorical link between history and science." Mindel's essay reminds nonscientists that Henry Adams (and how many others?) could more easily misinterpret the "philosophy and methodology" of science than the meaning of laws and facts. Howard M. Munford, in "Henry Adams: The Limitations of Science" (*SoR*, Winter 1968; reprinted, *Critical Essays*), acknowledges that "Adams did know what he meant" when he wrote about science. Not "revealing objective truth" but rather making use of the opportunity science offered for "redoing, remaking, reforming the world" was Adams's goal.

Thomas N. Bonner opens his brief introduction, "Henry Adams: A Sketch and an Analysis" (*Historian*, Nov. 1957), with the declaration that Adams "is the one important American historian whose life is more significant than the history he wrote." Here, Bonner echoes Henry Steele Commager, who set his colleagues the task of explaining the why and

how of the *History*, rather than simply accepting the text as "good history
— better had not been written." Commager's chapter, "Henry Adams,"
in *The Marcus W. Jernegan Essays in American Historiography*, edited
by William T. Hutchinson (Chicago, 1937; reprinted, *Critical Essays*),
raises Adams's banner high: "Adams illuminates, better than any of his
contemporaries, the course of American history." Commager goes on to
explain: "All his life Henry Adams made it a rule to ask questions which
he could not answer — questions which were, perhaps, quite unanswer-
able . . . his true function was to provoke speculation, not to satisfy it."
Commager himself achieves something similar.

An issue of *American Heritage* (Aug. 1975) pictures Adams among its
eighteen "Eminent Historians," ranging from Herodotus to Winston
Churchill. Elsewhere, Samuel Eliot Morison discusses "A Letter and A
Few Reminiscences of Henry Adams" that throw some light on the *History* (*NEQ*, Mar. 1954). As yet the broadest background and most useful
context within which to view Henry Adams's achievement is set forth in
"History As Art: An Annotated Checklist of Criticism" (*Style*, Winter
1979); the listing is understandably incomplete but nevertheless full of
promising approaches to historical writing of all periods. James R. Bennett headed the team of compilers, all of whom deserve our thanks and
encouragement. At least one example of how history and Adams's *History* can be used as evidence for generalizing about national attitudes
toward "progress," geographical expansion, government, etc., Walter
Allen's *The Urgent West: An Introduction to the Idea of the United States*
(London, 1969), makes fascinating reading. It can be contrasted with the
darker views of Bert James Loewenberg, *American History in American
Thought* (New York, 1972), where Adams becomes "a study in paradox,"
irony, and pessimism. Concentrating on the later thought of Adams,
David W. Marcell, "Henry Adams's Historical Paradigm: A Reexamination of the Major Phase," in *American Character and Culture in a Changing World: Some Twentieth Century Perspectives* (Westport, Conn., 1979),
finds material enough to justify an analysis based on the now-popular
theory of paradigmatic history. Still, something of the complexity of
Adams's thought seems to have been sacrificed in the process.

For the novice, a usable introduction to the *History* can be found in
*The American Historian: A Social-Intellectual History of the Writings
of the American Past* (New York, 1960); in it Harvey Wish devotes a chapter, "Henry Adams and the Dream of a Science of History," to surveying
where Henry stands among historians, critics, and other Adamses, and
where the *History* fits among his writings. Robert Allen Skotheim, *American Intellectual Histories and Historians* (Princeton, N.J., 1966), discerns
few faults in the *History*; his emphasis upon "intellectual" content serves

to disconnect the introduction and conclusion from the body of political history by judging the parts separately. This approach reverses conventional assessments, which weigh heavily all the materials of politics and diplomacy, even if the result is damaging to Adams's reputation. Ferdinand Schevill (*Six Historians*, Chicago, 1956) calls the political matter "too detailed"; he argues that the portrayal of character (rather than diplomacy or ideas), especially Jefferson's character, an "unquestioned masterpiece of the Adams gallery," is the real strength of a flawed classic. As one might expect, the premier Jefferson biographer, Julian P. Boyd, has also taken time to consider Adams's Jefferson. Boyd finds that the portrait in the *History* "has influenced historians and others from that day to this," even though Adams was "misled" by the subtlety of Jefferson's true character ("Jefferson's Expression of the American Mind," [*VQR*, Autumn 1974]). One result proved to be a notable "irony" in the *History*, about which Stow Persons, in *The Decline of American Gentility* (New York, 1973), and Peter Shaw (see next paragraph below) have much to say. Yet we should not forget that irony may be classed as both a form of literary artistry and a question of the writer's (or historian's) real attitude.

For one of the most serious questions raised about the *History* concerns Adams's objectivity; he has been examined on grounds of filial loyalty, regional bias, political persuasion, racism, and scientific accuracy, among others. Richard Beale Davis rubs an old sore with his suggestion that Adams is unfair to the South (*Intellectual Life in Jefferson's Virginia, 1790–1830* [Chapel Hill, N.C., 1964]), and Peter Shaw adds specific accusations of family favoritism in "Blood Is Thicker Than Irony: Henry Adams' *History*" (*NEQ*, June 1967). More recently, Shaw has amplified his concern with family interests in "The War of 1812 Could Not Take Place: Henry Adams's *History*" (*YR*, Summer 1973). Further possibilities of political bias are explored by Edwin C. Rozwenc's "Henry Adams and the Federalists," in *Teachers of History: Essays in Honor of Laurence Bradford Packard*, edited by H. Stuart Hughes (Ithaca, N.Y., 1954). The chief measure of Adams's political attitudes has always been the intriguing figure of Thomas Jefferson, who is studied by Merrill D. Peterson in *The Jefferson Image in the American Mind* (New York, 1960; reprinted, Galaxy, 1962) and "Henry Adams on Jefferson the President" (*VQR*, Spring 1963). A defense of Adams's efforts to achieve historical objectivity can be found in Earl N. Harbert's "Henry Adams' New England View: A Regional Angle of Vision?" (*TSE*, 1968), which concentrates upon literary technique. Nathalia Wright looks at the problem created by Adams's "Puritan" mind in "Henry Adams's Theory of History: A Puritan Defense" (*NEQ*, June 1945); and Daniel Sisson's *The American Revolution of 1800*

(New York, 1974) tells us that Adams did not interpret events fairly enough, although his *History* nonetheless stands as "archetypal." Another valuable reminder concerning "the temptations both to literary craft and craftiness," provided especially by the historical figure of Andrew Jackson, may be found in Cruce Stark's keen analysis of the *History*, "The Historical Irrelevance of Heroes: Henry Adams's Andrew Jackson" (*AL*, May 1974). Stark fairly credits Adams with "intentions of objectivity"; but another critic, William Ander Smith, finds that the historian seems to have put (wrongly) some famous words into the mouth of Alexander Hamilton. See "Henry Adams, Alexander Hamilton, and the American People as a 'Great Beast'" (*NEQ*, June 1975).

When we apply the rigorous requirements of modern social science, the *History* must be judged unscientific. "The Limits of Social Science: Henry Adams' Quest for Order" (*American Political Science Review*, Dec. 1956) reports the findings of Henry S. Kariel, who admits that Adams anticipated significant developments in social science, even though he could not keep himself from pushing his theories to hasty (and often unwarranted) conclusions. Yet Adams's thinking, unlike his writing, was never "dogmatic" in Kariel's view; Adams "actually accepted no law . . . as complete." He searched for an impossible answer, beyond the reach of both "positivist science and negativist art," one which even today "defies denotation and symbolization." This essay may be difficult reading for a nonscientist, but it uncovers a number of Adams's scientific missteps. A less tenable critique, based on an alleged failure of Adams to respond fully to the system of Karl Marx, is Richard Greenleaf's "History, Marxism, and Henry Adams" (*Science and Society*, Summer 1951); Greenleaf finds that Adams approached no closer to the truths of Marxian analysis than "impure materialism," which left him an apologist for capitalism. Arthur Schlesinger, Jr., in "The Historian As Participant" (*Historical Studies Today* [New York, 1972], ed. Felix Gilbert and Stephen R. Grauhard), credits Adams and his *History* more largely: "Henry Adams was the first among historians to understand" the increasing momentum of modern life—"the acceleration of the rate of social change—an acceleration produced by the cumulative momentum of science and technology." If Adams's version of historical truth still remains of a lower order than that of the scientific law he sought, it nevertheless has impressed many astute readers; and the *History* has been central to their findings.

For other readers, such as Edward Stone, Adams's historical writings serve to classify him among the *Voices of Despair* (Athens, Ohio, 1966). Gerrit H. Roelofs's "Henry Adams: Pessimism and the Intelligent Use of Doom" (*ELH*, Sept. 1950) opened this theme to literary (as well as philosophical) considerations; and recently, the despair motif has figured in

"The Lost America—The Despair of Henry Adams and Mark Twain" (*Modern Age* [Chicago], Summer 1961) by Tony Tanner, and Charles Vandersee's "The Mutual Awareness of Mark Twain and Henry Adams" (*ELN*, June 1968), among many comparative studies. The latter reviews previous scholarship and enters a dissenting conclusion: Adams *did* meet Twain and did become his model for the "unhappiest man" in *What Is Man?* Two essays by Harvey Gross comprise a highly eclectic attempt to show how Adams's conception of history influenced modern literature: "'Gerontion' and the Meaning of History" (*PMLA*, June 1958) and the less convincing "History as Metaphysical Pathos: Modern Literature and the Idea of History" (*Denver Quarterly*, Autumn 1966). Conveniently, Chapter two, "Henry Adams," in Gross's *The Contrived Corridor: History and Fatality in Modern Literature* (Ann Arbor, Mich., 1971) brings together many of his best ideas about Adams, including some observations concerning the influence of Nietzsche (among others).

Many matters of historiography lie beyond the scope of the present essay. Nevertheless, some attempt to locate Henry Adams among American historians has a place here. An examination of the subtle yet powerful "involvement" with life experienced by Adams as a historian can be found in Edward Lurie's "American Scholarship: A Subjective Interpretation of Nineteenth-Century Cultural History," in *Essays on History and Literature*, edited by Robert H. Bremner (Columbus, Ohio, 1966). Lurie sketches the elitist limitations of Adams and his peers, such as John Hay and Clarence King, who approached politics and culture with a serious handicap based upon preconceptions. Adams memorialized in prose both his failure to grasp the real value of Willard Gibbs's science and his ability to master the intellectual and moral "currents" in history and life, which his heritage had better prepared him to comprehend. Other historians, Lurie tells us, have followed Adams's lead, taking only what they please from him — Populist or Jeffersonian history or elitist "assumptions about cultural vapidity"— and in the process they have created an "irony of historiography" by which Adams is made to seem what he was not. Alfred Kazin agrees that it is Adams who "more than any other created our image of history; who in fact shapes our idea of history" ("History and Henry Adams" [*NY Review of Books*, 23 October 1969, 6 November 1969]), and he attributes Adams's attitude to a simple attraction to (perhaps an obsession with) power in every form. In the longest single chapter of *The Force So Much Closer Home: Henry Adams and the Adams Family* (New York, 1977), Earl N. Harbert discusses the artistry and achievement of the *History* in terms different from the "power" defined by Kazin. Harbert's separate consideration of "Sources and Method," "The Adams Ancestors," "Albert Gallatin and John Randolph in the *History*,"

"A Study of Men and Issues," "The Union and the Constitution," and other similar themes may seem to dictate an artificial division of the whole work (as Harbert admits). Overall, however, *Force* makes a strong case for the greatness of the *History*, and not merely for the nine volumes as an extended exercise in Henry Adams's self-education, a mere stop on the way to the *Education*. A recent (1980) Ph.D. dissertation written at the University of Virginia by Ruth Lassow Barolsky, "A Study of Henry Adams' *History of the United States,*" demonstrates in a larger way why the *History* must be given its due.

Adams sought from first to last to bring the didactic potential of history under personal control, and specific literary techniques offer important clues to his success and failure. "Henry Adams' Paraphrase of Sources in the *History of the United States*" (*AQ*, Spring 1965) by Richard C. Vitzhum looks at "some 130 of the 190" published sources for the nine volumes. Vitzhum has extended his comparative study in *The American Compromise: Theme and Method in the Histories of Bancroft, Parkman, and Adams* (Norman, Okla., 1974), a book that places the *History* among American historical classics (unlike Dusinberre's book discussed below). John S. Martin's "Henry Adams on War: The Transformation of History into Metaphor" (*ArQ*, Winter 1968) treats the usefulness of metaphor as both literary and historical expression. Ralph Maud ("Henry Adams: Irony and Impasse," *Essays in Criticism* [Oxford], Oct. 1958) warns that "no amount of investigation into the irony will . . . reveal an answer that counteracts the surface despair." These studies can be used to document in their several ways Ernst Scheyer's thesis in "The Aesthete Henry Adams" (*Criticism,* Fall 1962) that Adams's "theory of history was primarily aesthetically conditioned." More recently, Scheyer has collected from this and four other of his essays a series of topical impressions about Adams's tastes in art objects, history, and artistic friends, and expanded them into *The Circle of Henry Adams: Art and Artists* (Detroit, 1970). Building upon the work of Robert A. Hume, Scheyer brings the training and knowledge of an art historian to the task of studying Adams the aesthetic historian (especially in *Esther, Chartres,* and the *Education*) against the background of the art movements that influenced his epoch. Here, Max I. Baym has also added a few details in "Clio's Quest for Color: Henry Adams's Interest in Titian" (*Journal of Aesthetic Education,* July 1977). The English contributions to both the artistic and historical talents of Adams dominate the valuable book by William Dusinberre, *Henry Adams: The Myth of Failure* (Charlottesville, Va., 1979), who reminds us: "Adams's *History* — as he himself always wished — must be set not against those of Prescott and Parkman but against Macaulay's *History of England, 1685–1702,* and Gibbon's *Decline and Fall.* The process is exclusive, but Adams's

achievement can be defined, in its extent and its limits, in no other way."
His point is well documented.

J. C. Levenson has contributed in large measure to our understanding
of the *History* in both *Mind and Art* and "Henry Adams and the Culture
of Science." His treatment of family and cultural heritage and his informed
interest in literary artistry make these discussions invaluable. More recently, Levenson has summarized his estimate in "Henry Adams," an important chapter in *Pastmasters: Some Essays on American Historians,*
edited by Marcus Cunliffe and Robin W. Winks (New York, 1969; reprinted, *Critical Essays*). Reviewing Adams's whole career as a teacher
and writer of history, Levenson notes an increasing "professionalization."
Adams learned to use larger and larger quantities of historical evidence
to reach progressively grander generalizations about history and life,
which in turn required more sophisticated means for expression: careful
selection of material, suppression of judgments in favor of "facts," skillful
manipulation of a narrative point of view, reliance upon symbols rather
than words. As he achieved mastery, Adams did not abandon political
convictions, Levenson asserts; they remain hidden in the fabric of the
History, to argue a case for "the primacy of foreign policy." Levenson's
chapter strikes a note of serious reconsideration (rather than introduction) which will appeal to those who have read Adams's historical writings with care. It shows that the *History* has attracted readers for a
variety of reasons but that, without exception, the best critics have discovered for themselves the truth of Henry Adams's remark to fellow historian Frederic Bancroft: "I doubt if there is a chapter in my history that
I have written less than four or five times."

Closer to the present, Kenneth S. Lynn takes on a host of contemporaries, viewed as "The Regressive Historians" (*ASch*, Autumn 1978; reprinted, *The Air-Line to Seattle: Studies in Literary and Historical Writing About America* [Chicago, 1983]), before praising "the achievement
of Henry Adams, who may be said to have discovered complexity in American history in the course of writing his nine-volume *History*." William
Appleton Williams, in "Thoughts on Rereading Henry Adams" (*Journal
of Amer. History*, June 1981) also pays his compliment to Adams:

We can learn something important by watching Adams at his work. As he understood and demonstrated, the words *history* and *historian* encompass several significantly different meanings and activities. He explored all those nuances; and
in each he was intensely aware that the historian is struggling to make sense of
past and present experience, and in the process demonstrating the nature and
dynamics of critical and imaginative thought. Any given lecture or written work
is a position report on the voyage of comprehending who we are, what we are
about, and the probable consequences.

Selected as Williams's exemplary historian, Henry Adams fills a high calling indeed. And the *History* stands as a crucial part of the relevant
testimony.

Poetry and Essays

Although the first appearance of "Prayer to the Virgin of Chartres"
has been noted, it will be helpful to list other printings: Robert A.
Hume, *Runaway Star*; *The American Poets 1800–1900*, edited by Edwin H. Cady
(Glenview, Ill., 1966); and Elizabeth Stevenson, *Henry Adams Reader*
(which also contains "Buddha and Brahma"). Three sonnets appear in
Samuels's *Middle Years*, and there is an Adams jingle in Wasser's *Scientific Thought of Henry Adams*. No other poetry has reached print, although more does exist. Mrs. Jane Wilson Hipolito's dissertation, "The
Secret World of Henry Adams" (UCLA, 1968), expands upon what was
known about Adams as poet, and her discussion makes good use of previously unpublished material. Denis Donoghue adds some interesting
speculations in *Connoisseurs of Chaos: Ideas of Order in Modern American Poetry* (New York, 1965)), as well as in other places, such as *The
Sovereign Ghost: Studies in Imagination* (Berkeley, 1976).

Aside from general estimates, which usually treat the poetry as a helpful but clearly secondary evidence of Adams's art, several commentators
have studied the poems closely. Yosal Rogat, "Mr. Justice Holmes: Some
Modern Views" (*University of Chicago Law Review*, Winter 1964), makes
"Buddha and Brahma" the core statement of a philosophical theme that
unites Henry James and Oliver Wendell Holmes, Jr., with Adams. All three
shared an "ambiguous" social position: "Distinguished" by birth, they
nevertheless "had to achieve [further] distinction" by their own efforts
in the separate spheres which satisfied their individual needs for "power"
or "force." Although the essay concentrates upon Holmes, Adams's poem
is used to speak for all three about their peculiar relationship with an
unfriendly world—"both attached and detached." This well-documented
excursion into cultural history corrects a popular misunderstanding that
Adams was an exotic disciple of doom. The same poem receives detailed
explication in Eusebio L. Rodrigues's "Out of Season for Nirvana: Henry
Adams and Buddhism," in *Indian Essays in American Literature: Papers
in Honour of Robert E. Spiller*, edited by Sujit Mukherjee and D. V. K.
Raghavacharyulu (Bombay, 1969). The author finds that Adams "never
did surrender himself completely to Buddhism," although "the way to
the Perfect Life did provide Adams with a sense of direction." Margaret J.
Brown studies more comprehensively just what the East meant to Adams,
in both a Tulane Ph.D. dissertation (1976), "Henry Adams and the Orient," and a summary essay, "Henry Adams: His Passage to Asia" (*Critical*

Essays on Henry Adams). "In enlarging his own understanding of the Orient" through reading and travel," Brown finds, "Henry Adams has become a fully Representative Man, who articulates the aspirations of a people." All of Adams's published verse is reviewed in Stephen Mooney's "The Education of Henry Adams (Poet)" in *TSL* (1961), which shows that Adams demonstrated the "imagination of a poet" even when he wrote prose. Mooney finds the verse to be "occasional" and Adams a "poet of ideas." Only the "Prayer to the Virgin of Chartres" emerges as an unqualified success, "a poetic microcosm" of *Mont-Saint-Michel and Chartres.* Such prose works as "The Great Secession Winter of 1860–61" also reveal important themes that Adams later used in books like the *History.* Robert Sklar shows us how in "Henry Adams and Democratic Society" in *Kyushu Amerika* (Kyushu, Japan [Kyushu American Literature Society], 1972). Not Adams's ideas alone, but the artistic techniques of the young essayist also played their special roles in the grander works of his maturity. In *The Force So Much Closer Home,* Earl N. Harbert concentrates on "Captain John Smith," "Lyell's *Principles of Geology* (10th. ed.) a review," and "Civil Service Reform" to demonstrate how Adams moved away from literary apprenticeship, to master new forms other than the poem and essay.

Any collective consideration of Henry Adams's essays unfortunately blurs important distinctions based upon chronology, type, subject, and value; convenience alone is served. The early nonhistorical essays have attracted less attention than they deserve; apart from introductions to reprint collections, the most helpful discussions are to be found in the appropriate volume of Samuels's biography. The question of social prejudices, especially anti-Semitism, remains unresolved (at least until publication of the Bernard Berenson – Henry Adams correspondence); the basic evidence is brought together in a chapter ("Henry Adams' Norman Ancestors") of Edward N. Saveth's *American Historians and European Immigrants* (New York, 1948), where the essays receive adequate attention. Additional information may be found in "Henry Adams and the Jews" (*Chicago Jewish Forum,* Fall 1966) by Abraham Blinderman, and "Henry Adams and the Invisible Negro" (*SAQ,* Winter 1967), in which Charles Vandersee measures Adams's "skepticism and indifference" toward the attitudes of Boston, finding that Henry was much less "racist" than his outspoken brothers, Brooks and Charles Francis Adams II.

Among the late essays, "The Rule of Phase Applied to History" (1909) and "A Letter to American Teachers of History" (1910) are often treated, along with the final third of the *Education* (and sometimes *Chartres*), as exercises in historiography. A separate discussion of these essays will not be attempted here, except to note that William H. Jordy's *Henry*

Adams: Scientific Historian is the indispensable guide through the intricacies of scientific theory and speculation. As noted above, a comparative study of Adams's philosophical position in his late writings (largely but not exclusively) is available in a special number of the *University of Chicago Law Review* (Winter 1964) devoted to "Mr. Justice Holmes: Some Modern Views." In "The Judge As Spectator," Yosal Rogat suggests important differences between the thinking of Oliver Wendell Holmes, Jr., and that of his contemporary, Henry Adams, over a range of political, legal, and social problems. On this highly selective basis, Adams's importance as a philosophical thinker and writer is clearly demonstrated here; Rogat's essay, however, does assume a large familiarity with Adams's writings.

Biographies and Novels

   Over a thirty-year period Henry Adams exercised his skills as biographer, completing four printed works and the manuscript of a fifth. *The Life of Albert Gallatin* (1879), *John Randolph* (1882), *Memoirs of Marau Taaroa: Last Queen of Tahiti* (1893), and *The Life of George Cabot Lodge* (1911) are different enough to discourage generalizations about their author's attitudes and techniques; taken together they prove at least his remarkable versatility. The never-printed, book-length life of Aaron Burr is generally believed to have been transferred in part from manuscript to the pages of the *History*. Of all these, the *Lodge* has received the least attention, although it has been attractively treated in Edmund Wilson's *The Shock of Recognition*, which reprints the text. Lodge's tragic story represented a deep personal loss to Adams, a much older friend of the young poet; this brief biography registers an authentically emotional response and one that helps us to locate the elusive figure of Henry Adams in his final years. Of use here is an essay by John W. Crowley, who traces the genesis of *Lodge* and Adams's late essays in "The Suicide of the Artist: Henry Adams' Life of George Cabot Lodge" (*NEQ*, June 1973). The more exotic *Tahiti*, too, has suffered unmerited neglect, as Robert E. Spiller testifies in the introduction to his Facsimile reprint edition. The rarity of copies from the 1893 (private) printing is explained by Ira N. Hayward in "From Tahiti to Chartres: The Henry Adams–John La Farge Friendship" (*HLQ*, Aug. 1958), which describes the author's presentation copy to his artist friend. *Tahiti* is one of "the few sources of information on pre-Christian society" in the Pacific, as Robert Langdon reminds us. In "A View on Arii Taimai's Memoirs" (*Journal of Pacific History*, 1969), Langdon describes the circumstances of composition and reassesses *Tahiti*'s importance. The article is followed by a bibliographical note describing "one of the only three known" copies of the 1893 *Tahiti*, one that may have belonged to "Queen Marau herself"; this accounting does not include the Huntington Library copy.

Adams's reputation as a biographer rests upon the volumes devoted to American statesmen and the chief character portrayals in the *History*. The old-fashioned qualities of *Gallatin* are generally acknowledged; perhaps its author's admiration for his subject made for a dull book. The most influential evaluation is that of Gallatin's modern biographer, Raymond Walters, Jr. (*Albert Gallatin* [New York, 1957]), who found that Adams's version "was written with scholarly care" although it showed less "literary skill" than the *History*. Barbara Oberg, current editor of the Papers of Albert Gallatin, believes that Walters "rather lets Adams off the hook" by failing to recognize the selective patterning in Adams's biography (*Newsletter of the Association for Documentary Editing* [May 1982]). Oberg writes not to condemn Adams for his omissions or his (unstated) methods as editor or biographer, but rather to remind us sagely: "To decide to edit someone's papers is to make a subjective statement." That valuable idea is also central to Earl N. Harbert's appreciation of both *Gallatin* and *Randolph* in *The Force So Much Closer Home*. Harbert focuses on family influences and discusses the literary artistry of Adams as biographer and novelist. Most of what Adams learned as he wrote, in Harbert's view at least, would eventually find a place in the method and manner of such works as the *History* and the *Education*.

Few critics have been so understanding about *John Randolph*. William Cabell Bruce devoted much of his preface to *John Randolph of Roanoke* (New York, 1922) to "correcting" with fresh vitriol the portrait that Adams had fashioned: "He has fully availed himself of the opportunity . . . to direct against the memory of Randolph the thrice-refined venom which filtered into his own veins from those of his great-grandfather, grandfather and father. The book is really nothing but a family pamphlet, saturated with the sectional prejudices and antipathies of the year 1882." Henry B. Rule documents some of these accusations in "Henry Adams' Attack on Two Heroes of the Old South" (*AQ*, Summer 1962), focusing upon "Captain John Smith" and *John Randolph*, and concluding that both family pride and the Adamses' antislavery views are as important as the pursuit of historical truth. In the Epilogue to his broadly inclusive *Intellectual Life in the Colonial South, 1585–1763*, 3 vols. (Knoxville, Tenn., 1978) Richard Beale Davis provides a summary corrective, not only to Adams's *John Randolph*, but to his other writings as well: "Thus the southern men Henry Adams refers to as only lawyers — politicians and farmers, among them our Founding Fathers in the Continental Congress and in the signing of the Declaration of Independence and in debates (including *The Federalist*) on the Constitution and the adoption of the

latter document, were far more and other than attorneys and politicians
and planters, though they were all three." John Randolph's personal case
is defined in modern terms of individual temperament and cultural diversity in *The Education of John Randolph* (New York, 1979) by Robert
Dawidoff. The title indicates a debt to Adams, and Lewis P. Simpson
explores some implications to good effect in his thoughtful review-essay,
"The Inwardness of History" (*VQR*, Winter 1981). All together, these commentaries on *Gallatin* and *John Randolph* are suggestive; they indicate
that much more remains to be said about Adams as biographer.

Already Henry Adams's two novels, *Democracy: An American Novel*
(1880) and *Esther: A Novel* (1884), have established his stature as an interesting "novelist of ideas," but they are generally regarded as too "thin"
to rank among the best of the genre. Neither was issued in the name of
Henry Adams: his publisher, Henry Holt, recounts the amusing secrets
of authorship in *Garrulities of an Octogenarian Editor* (Boston, 1923).
A discussion of Adams's politics can be found in Ernest Samuels's *Middle
Years*, and a good introduction to both novels is George Hochfield's *Henry
Adams*. R. P. Blackmur ("The Novels of Henry Adams" [*SR*, Apr. 1943;
reprinted in *A Primer of Ignorance*]) reminds us of a basic problem —
"Adams' two novels . . . unlike those of a professional novelist, do not
show their full significance except in connection with his life" — and concentrates upon the themes of social condemnation, prophecy, and feminine superiority which tie the novels together. A philosophical frame large
enough to fit both is provided by Michael Colacurcio ("*Democracy* and
Esther: Henry Adams' Flirtation with Pragmatism" [*AQ*, Spring 1967]);
while Robert I. Edenbaum prefers to consider the novels as a double answer to one (reductive) question, in "The Novels of Henry Adams: Why
Man Failed" (*TSLL*, Summer 1966). "It is very easy to underestimate
Henry Adams as novelist," D. S. R. Welland cautions ("Henry Adams as
Novelist" [*Renaissance and Modern Studies*, 1959]) at the beginning of his
well-informed discussion, which shows how the circumstances of Adams's
life and the popularity of other writers prevented a fair reception of the
novels in England. Welland reviews Adams's often-noticed debt to Hawthorne and enlarges the study of influences by making a good case for
both George Eliot and the "comedy of manners." Don W. Harrell, "Coun-
terpoint in the Fiction of Henry Adams" (*Journal of the American Studies
Association of Texas*, Mar. 1971) finds a narrative pattern common to both
novels; while Patrick Wolfe concludes that a thorough understanding of
Democracy and *Esther* can tell us much about the reasons behind Adams's
"life-style of pessimism and despair" (*NEQ*, Sept. 1976).

Although we have yet to see the celebration of Henry Adams as a
prophet of women's liberation, R. P. Blackmur and Robert E. Spiller long

ago pointed to the fascinating women in Adams's novels as the symbolic center of his thought. Adams believed, as Spiller explains, "that women still could supply the secret knowledge that men had lost, that they held the key to the ultimate mysteries" (*The Cycle of American Literature*). The quest for the "eternal woman" has been adopted by a covey of critics, who seem not to have advanced explanations very far. In "Henry Adams and the Influence of Women" (*AL*, Jan. 1947) R. F. Miller notes that "neither heroine can be convinced by reason." Edward N. Saveth, in two essays that cover much the same ground ("The Heroines of Henry Adams" [*AQ*, Fall 1956] and "The Middle Years of Henry Adams: Women in His Life and Novels" [*Commentary*, May 1959]), finds that Adams's "prototype" women display a mixture of great strength and equally great destructiveness. Saveth sees Adams's "ideal women" as both "life-affirming" and "life-denying" and Adams himself as a victim of "bad luck" with a series of "cold comfort" heroines in his novels and his life. Leslie A. Fiedler (*Love and Death in the American Novel* [Cleveland, Ohio, 1962]) agrees that the "divine ideal" imposed itself upon Adams's relationships with "actual ladies whom he knew" and declares further that Henry Adams "cannot imagine a truly sexual heroine." This conclusion, as well as other opinions regarding the fictional women in Adams's life, may require some reconsideration, especially in light of new biographical studies of Marian Adams (see *Biography*) and the dramatic treatment of both novels by Romulus Linney, printed in *The Love Suicide at Schofield Barracks [and] Democracy and Esther* (New York, 1973). Unfortunately, this writer has seen no production, and cannot offer any evaluation of the effects on a theater audience.

By itself, *Democracy* holds an important place among "political novels." In a pioneer survey, *The Political Novel: Its Development in England and America* (New York, 1924), Morris Edmund Speare calls Adams's book "the first true political novel written in America." Joseph Blotner's *The Modern Political Novel: 1900–1960* (Austin, Tex., 1966) recognizes *Democracy* as an important "predecessor" of those novels (in his period) which "set national politics in an atmosphere of moral sickness." W. Gordon Milne in *The American Political Novel* (Norman, Okla., 1966) explains more of Adams's "expertise" and decides that *Democracy* appeals because of wit, urbanity, and polish — and fails because "it is a novel *about* things rather than an imaginative recreation of things." Irving Howe also finds fault with Adams's inhibitions in *Democracy*, his refusal to allow "a little more of the original pain and anger" to break through the stylish veneer (*Politics and the Novel* [New York, 1957; reprinted, Fawcett, 1967]). Granville Hicks, in the revised edition of *The Great Tradition* (New York, 1933; rev., 1969) reconsiders his earlier complaint, that Adams wrote "merely to amuse himself," without fully reneging: "I still think Adams was a strong combination of prophet and crybaby." Among more limited discussions, in "The Democracy of Henry Adams" (The "Democracy" of Henry Adams and Other Essays [Bern, 1950]) H. Lüdeke sees "political practice in America" with the sharp eyes of a foreigner. C. Vann Woodward (The Burden of Southern History [Baton Rouge, La., 1960]) locates in Adams's view of the South "ambivalent attitudes" that include admiration for those "antique values" preserved in Virginia. In "The Pursuit of Culture in Adams' Democracy" (AQ, Summer 1967), Charles Vandersee concentrates upon the first chapter of Democracy, to explain how Adams builds a satire which directs its attack not only against American "culture" but against Henry Adams himself. To be read along with Vandersee is Robert Mane's treatment of Mount Vernon in both Democracy and the Education (SA, July–Sept. 1976). Democracy also finds a place (among ten titles) in David C. Stineback's Shifting World: Social Change and Nostalgia in the American Novel (Lewisburg, Pa., 1976).

Walter Allen, in The Urgent West: An Introduction to the Idea of the United States, treats Democracy as a key to the attitudes of an American elite; while Neil Schmitz, "The Difficult Art of American Political Fiction" (WHR, Spring 1971), declares that it is "the only [American] political novel in the nineteenth century that succeeds as a novel." Other critics have compared Adams with one or another contemporary novelist, such as Gore Vidal, Allen Drury, and Ward Just (Business Week, 6 Dec. 1982), but the most comprehensive treatment of Democracy in its political setting is Stephen Miller's "The Washington Novel" (The Public Interest, Summer 1978). Although less narrowly focused, Versions of the Past by Harry B. Henderson III, directs additional attention to Democracy by examining closely just what Adams seems to be saying there about the possibilities of human progress, whether in politics or outside. In many ways, the continuing popularity of Adams's first novel seems assured; the New York Times Book Review (19 Sept. 1982) announces a new reprinting of Democracy with excerpted statements of praise for the novel from one literary scholar and two United States senators.

Esther, of course, has a very different history, in part because of a close association with the tragic figure of Marian Adams and in part because the subject of religious faith discourages the sort of free-and-easy commentary that politics encourages. The historical importance of Esther as a document of disbelief has been established in two essays: Wallace Evan Davies, "Religious Issues in Late Nineteenth-Century American Novels" (BJRL, Mar. 1959), and Elmer F. Suderman, "Skepticism and Doubt in Late Nineteenth Century American Novels" (BSUF, Winter

1967). The latter pays tribute to Adams's use of "science" and "comparative religion" as innovations in theological debate. Millicent Bell, in "Adams' *Esther:* The Morality of Taste" (*NEQ*, June 1962; reprinted, *Critical Essays*), makes the novel into coterie literature, written only for "a private group of friends" who could supply the necessary "annotation from the record of Adams' life." Her sensitive reading rests upon the acceptance of an almost complete "biographical parallel" between Marian Adams and Esther; and the emphasis upon "private" readers conflicts with Henry Adams's declarations about *Esther* as a public experiment, as Ernest Samuels reports. In many ways the most satisfying discussion, Robert E. Spiller's introduction to the 1938 Facsimile edition (reprinted as "The Private Novel of Henry Adams" in *The Oblique Light*) has prevailed for almost fifty years. *Esther*, Spiller suggests, "probes to deeper levels of experience" than does *Democracy*; a "thoroughly good" novel, *Esther* must be read without undue emphasis upon Marian Adams's life but with a sense of history that allows appreciation of the "costume" quality which the novel has acquired "with the passing of time." Henry Wasser insists on a larger role for "scientific evolution" in "Science and Religion in Henry Adams' *Esther*" (*MarkhamR*, May 1970) but no either/or choice is imposed on the reader. At a deeper level of identification with *Esther*'s author, David S. Barber finds that Adams's search for usable ideas doomed the novel to "failure" as a work of art. Overall, Barber's "Henry Adams' *Esther*: The Nature of Individuality and Immortality" (*NEQ*, June 1972) provides a stimulating supplement to the more conventional views of Earl N. Harbert in *The Force So Much Closer Home*. As always, *Esther* remains less popular than *Democracy*, yet food for the thoughtful.

Mont-Saint-Michel and Chartres

From the moment it reached those friends of Adams fortunate enough to be sent a privately printed copy, *Chartres* has evoked from readers as literary as Henry James and as knowledgeable as the historian Ferdinand Schevill a stream of praise. In a letter, James celebrated the charm of *Chartres*; Schevill's *Six Historians* pronounced it "the most penetrating book on the medieval spirit ever produced by an American." Although that "spirit" has sometimes puzzled Roman Catholic theologians and systematic historians, finally *Chartres* rises above all controversy to enjoy nearly unalloyed approval. A special relationship with the *Education* is often suggested, most notably by Samuels, Levenson (*Mind and Art*), Lyon, and Conder; while other critics such as Harbert and Mane seem to prefer that *Chartres* be considered alone, as in many ways a unique achievement among Adams's various masterworks (see *General Estimates*, above). This problem of context for discussion remains unresolved, but the book is clearly too important to be ignored or left to religious enthusiasts only.

One good survey of the problems in *Chartres* (especially its treatment of St. Thomas Aquinas) may be found in Michael Colacurcio's "The Dynamo and the Angelic Doctor: The Bias of Henry Adams' Medievalism" (*AQ*, Winter 1965). In a very personal way Adams believed that "reason inevitably destroys faith"; and his own testimony, as Colacurcio demonstrates, never loses sight of the need for individual human conviction. John P. McIntyre, S. J., in "Henry Adams and the Unity of *Chartres*" (*Twentieth Century Literature*, Jan. 1962), allows for imaginative freedom in Adams's handling of philosophy and history; but Frederick J. Hoffman's chapter, "Nostalgia and Christian Interpretation: Henry Adams and William Faulkner," in *The Imagination's New Beginning: Theology and Modern Literature* (Notre Dame, Ind., 1967), insists that Adams's "rebellious irritation with Puritanism" leads to a theological distortion that raises the Trinity to an "Absolute" and "ignores the Incarnation." History, rather than theology, provides a frame for Alice Chandler's discussion of *Chartres* in *A Dream of Order: The Medieval Ideal in Nineteenth-Century English Literature* (Lincoln, Neb., 1970), which claims "failure" for Adams's medieval vision. His book is considered here as a part of the literary "revival" of interest in medieval life, and *Chartres* is pronounced "the culminating work" of that cultural movement.

Of course comparative study can sometimes help us gauge similarities and differences that otherwise go unnoticed; Kermit Vanderbilt's *Charles Eliot Norton* (Cambridge, Mass., 1959) uses the attitudes of Adams and Norton toward Chartres Cathedral as a proof of the variety in New England thinking. Elsewhere, Roger B. Stein, in *John Ruskin and Aesthetic Thought in America, 1840–1900* (Cambridge, Mass., 1967), allows for a larger measurement of influence on Adams's ideas about both life and art. This subject has long been fruitful. An earlier essay makes the feelings evoked by *Chartres* an important key to Adams's art. R. P. Blackmur, in "The Harmony of True Liberalism: Henry Adams' *Mont-Saint-Michel and Chartres*" (*SR*, Jan.–Mar. 1952; reprinted, *A Primer of Ignorance*), attempts to reconstruct the personal feelings about faith and intellectual equilibrium which underlie Adams's message: "Faith, to work, cannot be exacerbated; and yet, to work, faith seems always either to have persecuted the unfaithful or put them beyond the pale of faith's benefits." Accepting this, Adams knew that "unity was in the convergence of straight lines in the *general* mind and was most likely never unity at all in any single mind — unless in Saint Thomas'." Blackmur examines Adams's figures one by one, describing the role each plays out in a thematic drama and showing how "the emotion of incertitude is put against the emotion of conviction." During the final "phase" of Adams's art, this passion play "reaches into his own experience," Blackmur contends, and a goal of "organic unity" controls both the artist and the man.

Vern Wagner prefers to view *Chartres* as a "major formal" work (along with the *History* and the *Education*) which demonstrates that "decisive conclusion is exactly what Adams teaches us we cannot find" in art or life. Yet vision alone is not sufficient, as Paul L. Kegel points out in "Henry Adams and Mark Twain: Two Views of Medievalism" (*Mark Twain Journal*, Winter 1970); Kegel contrasts in some detail *Prince and the Pauper* and *Connecticut Yankee* with *Chartres*. In their various ways, these approaches to Adams's book make important contributions; but they all seem fragmentary when placed alongside the results of a careful (and richly documented) investigation by Robert Mane, who has set a high standard for every other commentator in *Henry Adams on the Road to Chartres* (Cambridge, Mass., 1971). His title actually describes only the first (and shorter) of the two parts that compose the book. As he traces New England roots and then Adams's development into a cosmopolitan figure, Mane (himself a Frenchman) touches upon the keys in art, literature, philosophy, culture that become essential for understanding his last two chapters: "The Meaning of *Mont-Saint-Michel and Chartres*" and "The 'Unity' of *Mont-Saint-Michel and Chartres*." For Mane, *Chartres* is a "prose poem" and "undoubtedly Adams's greatest work." Mane makes its chosen "allegory" legible and gives us, perhaps for the first time, sufficient evidence on which to judge the book as an "affirmation of Art."

The Education of Henry Adams

Since its publication in 1918, the *Education*[2] has held a place as the central document upon which every broad consideration of Henry Adams is based. An unlikely best seller, the book first invited comparison with other autobiographies of the New England Puritan kind. Later, as Ernest Samuels cleared away the confusion, readers began to concentrate on the nonbiographical possibilities of the *Education*—history, prophecy, pathos, humor, and most of all, literary artistry. Overall, the years have

2. T. S. Eliot's early review of the *Education* deserves special attention. In the *Athenaeum*, 23 May 1919 (reprinted as "A Sceptical Patrician" in *Major Writers of America*, vol. 2), Eliot showed a lack of sympathy with both the matter and the manner of the *Education*, although he recognized its peculiar fascination: "The really impressive interest is in the mind of the author, and in the American mind, or that fragment of it, which he represents." Eliot also sounded a warning which all too few of Adams's readers have taken seriously: "It is doubtful whether the book ought to be called an autobiography, for there is too little of the author in it."

been kind to the *Education*, continually revising the terms of its success to meet the needs of one critic after another, and establishing the book more firmly with each passing decade as a landmark in American literature. Yet the *Education* remains unique and defiant to all attempts at easy categorization; it will not fit the boundaries of any narrow historical or literary tradition, American or foreign.

One avenue of understanding has led us to antecedents. For Adams himself tells of his literary debts to Rousseau, Augustine, Gibbon; and critics have freely suggested additional sources and influences. Among these critics are Samuels, Dusinberre, Mane, Baym in the *French Education*, and Henry A. Pochmann in *German Culture in America* (Madison, Wis., 1957), whose conclusions are enlarged in "The German Education of Henry Adams," written by Foster Park for *Appalachian State Teachers College Faculty Publications* (1962). Other essays concentrate more narrowly upon possible sources: Gene H. Koretz, "Augustine's *Confessions* and *The Education of Henry Adams*" (*Comparative Literature*, Summer 1960), and Richard Ruland, "Tocqueville's *De la Démocratie en Amérique* and *The Education of Henry Adams*" (*Comparative Literature Studies*, Fall 1965). "'But This was History': Henry Adams' 'Education' in London Diplomacy" (*NEQ*, Sept. 1979) by Lee Clark Mitchell also adds something to what we know of the London years from Dusinberre's book and Chalfant's first volume. All three writers point ahead to the *Education* and Jonel C. Sallee, "Henry Adams' Emersonian Education" (*ESQ*, First Quarter 1981) tells another part of the story.

All together, the suggestions point up the many ways in which Adams read and used books; but even more clearly, sources and influences fall far short of explaining the *Education*, which simply cannot be dismissed as derivative. This caution applies to other studies of influence, beginning with Stuart P. Sherman's "Evolution in the Adams Family" (*Nation*, 10 April 1920), and including two Ph.D. dissertations, "The American Adams" (Columbia, 1965) by Peter Shaw and "The Influence of the Family Tradition upon Selected Works of Henry Adams" (Wisconsin, 1966) by Earl N. Harbert. Sherman finds the *Education* to be "only the last or the latest chapter of a continued story" which began in the *Diary* of John Adams and ran its course in the writings of John Quincy and Charles Francis Adams. Shaw uses all available evidence to prove a reversal in literal meaning of failure, the term Adams habitually applied to himself when he meant something else. In "The Success of Henry Adams" (*YR*, Autumn 1969), Shaw interprets the idiom of self-condemnation as an ironic expression of success in the traditional (among the Adamses) arts of politics and diplomacy. His book, *The Character of John Adams* (Chapel Hill, N.C., 1976) gives primary attention to John Adams and the earlier generations of the family, rather than focusing on Henry or the *Education*. Harbert, on the other hand, added to his Wisconsin dissertation a chapter on the *History*, and published the result as *The Force So Much Closer Home: Henry Adams and the Adams Family*. His chapter on the *Education* treats Adams as artist rather than as heir to political greatness; and this approach has been amplified by Harbert in "*The Education of Henry Adams*: The Confessional Mode as Heuristic Experiment" (*Journal of Narrative Technique*, Jan. 1974) and "Henry Adams's *Education* and Autobiographical Tradition" (*TSE*, 1977). Both are reprinted in *Critical Essays*.

John Conder's *A Formula of His Own: Henry Adams's Literary Experiment* reaches out in a different direction, by insisting that *Chartres* and the *Education* must be read together as "a single unit of art"; while Melvin Lyon details the "imaginative symbolism" of the *Education* in *Symbol and Idea in Henry Adams*. Here, Harvey Cox adds to the possibilities in "The Virgin and the Dynamo Revisited: An Essay on the Symbolism of Technology" (*Soundings*, Summer 1970), by treating Adams's symbols as a possible bridge of understanding between religion and modern technology. As we would anticipate from his title, Howard Mumford Jones finds space to discuss the *Education* as an example of a similar "tension" in *The Age of Energy: Varieties of American Experience, 1865–1915* (New York, 1971), and Herbert J. Muller, (*In Pursuit of Relevance* [Bloomington, Ind., 1971]) uses many of the same ideas from the *Education* to point out that even now, "Most of Adams's critique of American democracy remains valid." In *American History in American Thought*, however, Bert James Loewenberg seems less certain about just what "irony" does to the instructional value of the *Education*, a point that Henry B. Rule considers at greater length in "Henry Adams' Satire on Human Intelligence: Its Method and Purpose" (*CentR*, Fall 1971). Useful as a warning here is "*The Education of Henry Adams* by Henry Adams" (*Daedalus*, Winter 1974), in which Judith N. Shklar makes a case for the book as a "matchless contribution to the literature of pure sadness." Martha Banta, to the contrary, labels the *Education* "a repository of comic attacks and counter-attacks — Joe Miller's Joke Book for the aristocratic circuit" (*Failure and Success in America: A Literary Debate* [Princeton, 1978]). Perhaps we might anticipate that one critic's sadness would prove to be another critic's humor.

Other studies have muted the original accusations of philosophical pessimism and "sentimental nihilism" (in the words of Paul Elmer More, *Shelburne Essays* [Boston, 1921]). Better understanding of the author has opened new ways to read the *Education*, making older views seem too simple, as in Richard Hofstadter's *Anti-Intellectualism in American Life*

(New York, 1962). This influential historian of ideas concedes that the *Education* stands as a "towering literary monument" to post–Civil War reform; yet he rates the book "a masterpiece in the artistry of self-pity." Austin Warren comes to a different conclusion, after studying Adams as a regional spokesman, in *The New England Conscience* (Ann Arbor, Mich., 1966); caught between the conflicting demands of acting as both researcher and interpreter, Adams could reach no literary solution that satisfied his "conscience." Unfortunately, Warren's chapter stops short of showing how these polar possibilities work themselves out in the *Education.* Other current views of Adams's problematical book are indebted to Thomas Kuhn and his "paradigm" theory of history; and exemplified by Wayne Lesser, "Criticism, Literary History, and the Paradigm: *The Education of Henry Adams*" (*PMLA*, May 1982), which argues along the "deconstructive" lines established by Carlos Rowe in *Henry Adams and Henry James: The Emergence of a Modern Consciousness.* In a different way, Lesser also bases his case on David Minter's *The Interpreted Design as a Structural Principle in American Prose*, where literary form — rather than "history" or "fact"— is seen as central to Adams's purpose. With a bow to Georg Lukács and his principle of *reification*, Carolyn Porter moves interpretation of the *Education* in yet another direction (while also paying her respects to Minter) in *Seeing and Being: The Plight of the Participant Observer in Emerson, James, Adams, and Faulkner* (Middletown, Conn., 1981). At times, however, Porter's treatment of historical evidence (such as Adams's letters) seems to ignore the considerable artistic skill of writers who shaped their letters as carefully as Adams built his "trap" for readers of the *Education.*

One method for avoiding every impasse in interpretation is to treat the *Education* as a window looking out upon the world. Ralph Gabriel's *The Course of American Democratic Thought* (New York, 1940)) admits Adams to an official position as a witness to history, chosen "to illustrate trends in the thinking of American historians." The *Education* has offered varied testimony: Leo Marx finds that "a sense of the transformation of life by technology dominates *The Education* as it does no other book"; accordingly he uses Adams's metaphorical measurement, the "Two Kingdoms of Force" (the Virgin and the Dynamo), as an index of attitude in *The Machine in the Garden: Technology and the Pastoral Ideal in America* (New York, 1964)). Marx always retains a sensitivity to the literary merits of the *Education*, discussing the combined techniques of the "cool historian and the impassioned poet" which show themselves in Manichean polarities, "technological determinism," and a frenzied appeal for human response. "Doubleness" seems to Marx characteristic of twentieth-century American "pastoralism," but Morton and Lucia White

(*The Intellectual Versus the City: From Thomas Jefferson to Frank Lloyd Wright* [Cambridge, Mass., 1962]) insist that Adams finds fault with the American city "out of concern for civilization" and not "in the name of nature." (Of special value is the Whites' use of Adams's letters to point up once again how much the retrospective *Education* differs from other accounts of the author's feelings, expressed at the time of the experiences themselves.) Alan Trachtenberg's *Brooklyn Bridge: Fact and Symbol* (New York, 1965) treats Adams as a keen observer of politics in the Gilded Age. Borrowing, as Leo Marx does, from the metaphoric possibilities of the two "Kingdoms of Force," Trachtenberg shows that Adams was not alone in seeking a symbolic reconciliation of conflicting cultural forces and that the bridge may have greater symbolic value than the Virgin and the Dynamo. This study also corrects Adams's view of Abram S. Hewitt. One other broad evaluation, a controversial classic of its kind, W. J. Cash's *The Mind of the South* (New York, 1941), registers a southerner's agreement with the portrayal of southern character in the figure of Roony Lee. As noted already (see *Biography*), Allen Tate, in contrast, uses a scene in his novel *The Fathers* to criticize Adams as hypocritical and condescending in portraying Lee. Clearly the evidence in the *Education* opens to many interpretations.

In a volume provocatively titled *Books That Changed Our Minds*, edited by Malcolm Cowley and Bernard Smith (New York, 1939), Louis Kronenberger shows how the "bitterly ironic tone" of the *Education* endeared it to post–World War I readers, while a "validity of predicament" guarantees that it will speak to men and women of all times. Mortimer Adler places the *Education* among the great books of the twentieth century (*Time*, 7 March 1977). F. O. Matthiessen, in *American Renaissance* (New York, 1941), points to an unlikely kinship between Walt Whitman and Henry Adams, built upon their mutual awareness "of the power of sex." Adams's view was simply larger than those of many contemporaries; his appreciations of sex, science, history, politics, art, and education helped to make life interesting, as Robert Spiller shows (*Cycle of American Literature*). And J. C. Levenson ("Henry Adams and the Culture of Science") prefers to measure Adams's intentions and success by his interest in teaching: "assertion of mind" for the author and the reader become the only possible solution to the ultimate problem posed in the *Education*; Adams "shaped his comments to stimulate younger men and make them seek better answers than his own." Jeanne M. Schinto, "The Autobiographies of Mark Twain and Henry Adams: Life Studies in Despair" (*Mark Twain Journal*, Summer 1975), fixes on their common sense of "nostalgia" and "distrust of those who wield power" as central to the age that both didactic writers addressed in their work. For Robert Bingham Downs,

Famous American Books (New York, 1971), the *Education* constitutes an essay in "Explaining the Universe," and the real surprise is that Adams "wrote 500 pages called *Education* and never defined the word." Other readers prefer to direct attention to symbols instead of language, as in "Myths, Machines and Markets: The Columbian Exposition of 1893" (*Journal of Popular Culture*, Winter 1972) by Justus D. Doencke, and "The Goad of Guilt: Henry Adams, Scott and Zelda" (*JML*, Apr. 1977), in which William Wasserstrom treats the Fitzgeralds and Adams together as symbolic representatives of a modernist view that "makes nothing of something."

Looking backward from Adams's lifetime, and forward to the present, many observers have sought to place the *Education* along a continuum of autobiographical art. Certainly since 1973, when Lawrence Buell (in *Literary Transcendentalism*) labeled as "puzzling" the "lack of critical attention" to an "autobiographical tendency in American writing," the responses have been almost overwhelming. Adams and the *Education* are now compared with countless authors and titles; and the American autobiographical tradition (of which everyone claims the *Education* to be a part) fairly seems to have no limits. None of this explanation is meant, however, to deny the usefulness of the best among such studies. Thomas Cooley's *Educated Lives: The Rise of Modern Autobiography in America* (Columbus, Ohio, 1976), for example, places autobiography somewhere between "fiction and history" and discusses Adams, along with Twain, Howells, Henry James, Steffens, Sherwood Anderson, and Gertrude Stein. Anderson is central to John W. Crowley's "The Education of Sherwood Anderson" in *Sherwood Anderson: Centennial Studies* edited by Hilbert H. Campbell and Charles E. Modlin (Troy, N.Y., 1956). In her short book, *The Art of Life: Studies in American Autobiographical Literature* (Austin, Tex., 1977), Mutlu Konuk Blasing adds to this list William Carlos Williams and Frank O'Hara. On Adams and James, Cooley is more convincing; although even here, we may miss the sturdy foundation of historical concern provided by Sacvan Bercovitch, first in "Horologicals to Chronometrics: The Rhetoric of the Jeremiad" (*Literary Monographs*, 1970) and later in his book *The American Jeremiad* (Madison, Wis., 1978). James M. Cox has also contributed here, especially in a series of essays, including "Autobiography and America" (*VQR*, Spring 1971; reprinted, *Aspects of Narrative* [New York, 1971] ed. by J. Hillis Miller); and "Learning Through Ignorance: *The Education of Henry Adams*" (*SR*, Spring 1970). This number of *Sewanee Review* also contains B. L. Reid's "The View From the Side," which traces Adams's thought in the *Education*, as well as review-essays by Laurence B. Holland and Earl N. Harbert about Henry and Clover Adams.

The *Georgia Review* for Summer 1981, prints six essays in a "Focus on Biography & Autobiography" section, none of which is limited to the *Education* but all of which may be said to bear on that book, as does another thoughtful treatment of theory, "Notes for an Anatomy of Modern Autobiography" by Francis R. Hart, in *New Directions in Literary History* (Baltimore, Md., 1974) edited by Ralph Cohen. A rich mixture of literary theory and critical practice is: *Autobiography: Essays Theoretical and Critical* (Princeton, 1980) edited by James Olney, which includes essays from the hands of James M. Cox, Robert F. Sayre, Jean Starobinski, William L. Howarth, among others. Here, the "Bibliography" provides a good start toward comprehending the wealth of material on the subject. Selective as it necessarily is, Olney's listing comprises a good mix of old and new, in which several items bear directly on the *Education*. One, G. Thomas Couser's *American Autobiography: The Prophetic Mode* (Amherst, Mass., 1979), reads Adams's book with particular care, as the author's earlier essay in *Hudson Review* for 1978, "The Shape of Death in American Autobiography," suggested he would. Ross Lincoln Miller's "Henry Adams: Making It Over Again" (*CentR*, Summer 1974) is omitted from Olney's list; while an earlier essay in the same journal, signed "Ross Miller" ("Autobiography as Fact and Fiction: Franklin, Adams, Malcolm X," Summer 1972) is included.

In a collection of essays by many hands, *The American Autobiography: A Collection of Critical Essays* (Englewood Cliffs, N.J., 1981), editor Albert E. Stone also finds room for "A Selective Bibliography of American Autobiography" divided into three sections. Adams and the *Education* appear throughout this volume; but neither receives as much serious attention here as in Stone's own book, *"Autobiographical Occasions and Original Acts: Versions of American Identity from Henry Adams to Nate Shaw* (Philadelphia, 1982). This study features practical (rather than theoretical) criticism, in which the *Education* provides a touchstone for demonstration. Elsewhere, Allen Guttmann's Voice of America talk, printed as *"The Education of Henry Adams"* in *Landmarks in American Writing* (New York, 1969)) acknowledges this status, as does Tony Tanner in *City of Words* (New York, 1972). George Monteiro shows how the *Education* influences later generations of readers and writers in "The Education of Ernest Hemingway" (*JAmS*, Apr. 1974; reprinted, *Critical Essays*), and Gordon Taylor concentrates on Norman Mailer in "Of Adams and Aquarius" (*AL*, Mar. 1974). At present, the favorite target for studies of Adams's influence seems to be Thomas Pynchon, whose *V.*, in particular but not alone, is often compared with the *Education*. A rich discussion of the Adams-Pynchon relationship may be found in *The Grim Phoenix: Reconstructing Thomas Pynchon* (Bloomington, Ind., 1978) by Wil-

liam M. Plater. When he assures us that "Inescapably, Pynchon's novels both parody and affirm the idea of the *Education of Henry Adams,*"
Plater reflects a view that is shared by many readers. Elsewhere, in "One
Continuous Force: Notes on Faulkner's Extra-Literary Reading" (*MissQ,*
Summer 1970) M. F. Gridley traces the influence of the *Education* on
another modern novelist, but without explaining why his reading should
be thought "Extra-Literary" in name or use. Looking abroad, none of
the non-English criticism seems to have caught the flavor of post-modern
implications. Philippe Lejeune is representative in *Je est un autre* (Paris,
1980), which places Adams in a continental tradition of autobiographical writing.

Still, everywhere in the criticism of the *Education* one special difficulty arises — how to grasp and assimilate the full symbolic value of
Adams's narrative. Kenneth Burke acknowledges the problem in *A Grammar of Motives and A Rhetoric of Motives* (combined ed., Cleveland,
Ohio, 1962), although "attenuated self-immolation" may not strike every
reader as the result Adams seeks to achieve: "*The Education of Henry
Adams . . .* exemplifies ritual transformation by a shift from personal
images to impersonal ones," and an "imaging of a fall" dominates the
sections of historical speculation. Burke's insistence upon mythic and
imagistic interpretation (and vocabulary) simply allows no room for biographical discussion. His work has been a rich resource for critics concerned primarily with finding symbolic patterning in all of Adams's work.
Their many-sided conversation has been neatly catalogued in Melvin
Lyon's volume (see *General Estimates,* above); nevertheless a few additional essays deserve attention here: Lynn White, Jr., "Dynamo and Virgin Reconsidered" (*ASch,* Spring 1958), applies to Adams a great familiarity with medieval history and technology, to show that the famous
chapter in the *Education* is not necessarily a discussion of polar oppo-
sites. Various uses of symbols and images have been identified and discussed by Kenneth MacLean, "Window and Cross in Henry Adams' *Education*" (*University of Toronto Quarterly,* July 1959), and James K. Folsom,
"Mutation as Metaphor in *The Education of Henry Adams*" (*ELH,* June
1963). A single issue of *ArQ* (Winter 1968) contained both William J.
Scheick's "Symbolism in *The Education of Henry Adams*" and Charles
Vandersee's study of animal imagery, "The Four Menageries of Henry
Adams." Also helpful is the more general "Poetry and Language," contributed by Norman Holmes Pearson to *A Time of Harvest: American
Literature, 1910–1960,* edited by Robert E. Spiller (New York, 1962)); Pear-
son raises Adams to high station: "The book which, more than any other,
represents the American writer's entrance into the twentieth century is
The Education of Henry Adams." A look at the busy year when Henry

Adams was elected to membership in the American Academy of Arts and Letters can be found in Charles Vandersee's "Henry Adams and 1905: Prolegomena to *The Education*" (*JAmS*, Oct. 1968).

The difficulty of "placing" the *Education* in some respectable literary tradition encourages comparative discussion, as noted above. This has led to a recognition of American autobiography as a genre inclusive enough to contain the Mathers, Franklin, James, Thoreau, and others, as well as Adams. A. D. Van Nostrand, in *Everyman His Own Poet: Romantic Gospels in American Literature* (New York, 1968)), for example, matches the *Education* with the writings of Edgar Allan Poe; another modest contribution, a brief note on narrative tone in *Walden* and the *Education*, is Taylor Stoehr's "Tone and Voice" (*CE*, Nov. 1968). A more satisfactory study of the *Education* as autobiography and a seminal discussion overall is Robert F. Sayre's *The Examined Self: Benjamin Franklin, Henry Adams, Henry James* (Princeton, 1964); Sayre compares and contrasts the autobiographical efforts of James and Adams, showing that both men relied upon Franklin's *Autobiography* as a kind of model. This common debt tells us less about Adams than does the examination of the relationship between the two Henrys: "from time to time they met until the time when, influenced to some degree by each other, they transformed . . . family traditions of personal narrative into their contrasting autobiographies." Adams took a larger role as teacher, a lesser as artist; he converted popular themes — religion, Darwinism, failure — into literary strategies that "connect" to his age. By mistreating himself in his account, Sayre contends, Adams bombarded his readers with a powerful kind of education, an "examination of life." Tony Tanner's "Henry Adams and Henry James" (*Tri-Quarterly*, Winter 1968) enlarges on Sayre's analysis, especially by pointing to the psychological gap between the self-satisfaction James knew from his art and the torment that haunts Adams (in the aftermath of theorizing about life), until "consciousness itself ceases to have any value for him." *Spiritual Autobiography in Early America* (Princeton, 1968), by Daniel B. Shea, Jr., identifies Quaker and Puritan modes of autobiography, both of which show up in a "late" form in the *Education*. Together with the titles mentioned earlier, these studies offer an inclusive sense of how the elusive term "Autobiography" may be applied to Adams's most celebrated book.

Yet a cautionary note should also be sounded. Several important essays warn against misreadings of various kinds and call for further attention to unresolved critical problems. The possible exaggeration of Adams's failure concerns Herbert F. Hahn in "*The Education of Henry Adams* Reconsidered" (*CE*, Mar. 1963); and Max I. Baym, "Henry Adams and the Critics" (*ASch*, Winter 1945–46), sounds a similar alarm. Henry Wasser's brief footnote to the critical history of Adams's best known book, "*The Education of Henry Adams* Fifty Years After" (*Midcontinent American Studies Journal*, Spring 1969), confesses to critical inadequacies in the name of us all: we remain "still troubled by the problem of how to explain his mind."

Of course, the "trouble" caused us by the *Education*, and by the mind that shaped it, accounts for our continuing fascination with Adams. More than anything else, the discussion printed here (and the much longer unprinted bibliography from which these titles are drawn) represents a collective tribute to the compelling force of the interest created by Adams. Charles Vandersee captures much of the power of the man and his work in a brief poem, "Henry Adams, December 1885," printed as a preface to *Critical Essays on Henry Adams*. Eleanor Wilner, in her own poetic statement, "Henry Adams' Wife in Washington, D.C.," in *Maya* (Amherst, Mass., 1979) provides a parallel view of his less well-known wife. And, as if to call attention to another avenue for reaching the pair, who perceptively commissioned more art than either could execute alone, *The New York Times* for the day on which this essay was finally closed out for publication (7 June 1983) carries a brief item about the "thousands" of persons who "find their way" each year to a "secluded grotto" in Washington's Rock Creek Cemetery. There, these pilgrims sit "on the circular bench designed by Stanford White and contemplate the meaning" of a seated figure sculpted by Augustus Saint-Gaudens—the only marker at the grave of Marian and Henry Adams. As the *Times* article, "Adams Memorial Draws Responses" by Marjorie Hunter, carefully notes, Henry Adams long ago explained what he had in mind, both as a patron of White and Saint-Gaudens and as a literary artist in his own right. The *Education* says of Saint-Gaudens's masterpiece, which Adams elsewhere called "the Peace of God": "The interest of the figure was not in its meaning, but in the response of the observer." Like the visitors to his grave, his critics have proved the wisdom of Henry Adams.

William Cullen Bryant

JAMES E. ROCKS

WILLIAM CULLEN BRYANT's importance in the history of nineteenth-century American life and letters is unquestioned; yet, since the first edition of *Fifteen American Authors before 1900* appeared over a decade ago, very little new critical material about this progenitor of American Romantic poetry has come forth. An edition of letters and a long biography (see below) are the only important new contributions to Bryant scholarship. That Bryant was a prolific writer and that his manuscripts are scattered and often difficult to decipher certainly help to explain why authoritative editions and scholarly studies have been slow to appear. Without a good text of the poems critics cannot make a major evaluation of his thought and craft. Individual essays that examine a part of his career or a particular topic are abundant, but assessments of a wider scope, especially in the past decade or two, are lacking. Necessary groundwork has been prepared, based largely on the distinguished writings of the most important Bryant scholar of this century, Tremaine McDowell.

BIBLIOGRAPHY

A rather complete description of Bryant's works is in Jacob Blanck's *Bibliography of American Literature* (New Haven, Conn., 1955), which divides the listings into three sections: primary books and books containing first edition material, collections of previously published poems, and books that contain material reprinted from the books listed in the first section. Blanck admits that there must be errors in his compilation, since

From Earl N. Harbert and Robert A. Rees, editors, *Fifteen American Authors before 1900: Bibliographic Essays on Research & Criticism* (Madison: The University of Wisconsin Press; © 1984 by the Board of Regents of the University of Wisconsin System); may be reproduced only by permission of the publisher.

it is difficult to identify all of Bryant's poems because of the extensive number of reprintings and the revised titles in various anthologies. Many of Bryant's poems have never been accurately dated: Parke Godwin's *A Biography of William Cullen Bryant, with Extracts from His Private Correspondence* (2 vols., New York, 1883; reprinted, 1967) is frequently erroneous. The only substantial bibliography of Bryant published before Blanck, and often in error, was Henry C. Sturges's *Chronologies of the Life and Writings of William Cullen Bryant, with a Bibliography of His Works in Prose and Verse* (New York, 1903; reprinted, 1968), which appeared also as a part of the 1903 Roslyn Edition of Bryant's poetry. Sturges's compilation is divided into lists of the different kinds of writing that Bryant did and is "inaccurate and incomplete," according to Tremaine McDowell, in *William Cullen Bryant*, the American Writers Series volume of representative selections (New York, 1935); in the notes McDowell corrects some of Sturges's errors. Judith Phair's *A Bibliography of William Cullen Bryant and His Critics: 1808–1972* (Troy, N.Y., 1975) is a very helpful compilation, with annotations, of varied materials. In "The Chronology of a Group of Poems by W. C. Bryant" (*MLN*, Mar. 1917), A. H. Herrick points out errors in Godwin's and Sturges's dating of seven poems. Some of the articles discussed under *Biography* and *Criticism*, below, also correct the misdatings of poems, particularly of "Thanatopsis," which was written later than has been commonly thought. A full and accurate chronology of Bryant's poems needs to be done and will be served by the collecting of poems for a new edition. Richard Beale Davis's Goldentree Bibliography, *American Literature through Bryant, 1585–1830* (New York, 1969), updates the annotated listing in McDowell's AWS volume but is now rather dated.

EDITIONS AND TEXTS

Since not all of Bryant's poems or prose writings have been identified or collected, none of the many editions of his works is complete or textually authoritative. The most important editions appeared in the late nineteenth century and have been reprinted. Although Bryant's poetry may not be his most important achievement, it is the poetry that would take priority in any new edition of his works, yet no new edition has appeared in years.

Although many volumes of Bryant's writing were published during his lifetime and shortly thereafter, only a few can be regarded as in any way "standard." *The Poetical Works of William Cullen Bryant* (New York, 1876) is the last edition to have passed through the poet's hands. Parke Godwin's six-volume *Life and Writings of William Cullen Bryant* includes the two-volume *Poetical Works of William Cullen Bryant* (New York, 1883; reprinted, 1967); the two-volume *Prose Writings of William Cullen Bryant* (New York, 1884; reprinted, 1964), which has additional materials not found in earlier editions and some textual revisions and notes by the editor; and the two-volume biography discussed below. The Roslyn Edition, *The Poetical Works of William Cullen Bryant* (New York, 1903; reprinted, 1969), is an inclusive one-volume collection, without Godwin's notes. *Tales of Glauber-Spa* (New York, 1832), in which two of Bryant's prose tales and sketches appeared, has been reprinted in the American Short Story Series of Garrett Press (New York, 1969).

Bryant's early political satire, *The Embargo*, has been reprinted in a facsimile edition, with a short but comprehensive introduction by Thomas O. Mabbott (Gainesville, Fla., 1955). Previously uncollected poems are to be found in Seymour L. Gross's "An Uncollected Bryant Poem" (*N&Q*, Aug. 1957), which reproduces a poem written hastily for the fiftieth anniversary of Washington's inauguration, and in Tremaine McDowell's "An Uncollected Poem by Bryant" (*Americana*, July 1934), which reprints a mediocre gift-book poem entitled "To William." In "The Exhibition in the Palace: A Bibliographical Essay" (*BNYPL*, Sept. 1960), Earle E. Coleman includes the three drafts of a short ode that Bryant wrote for the New York Crystal Palace Exhibition in 1853. (Other uncollected poems can be found in essays discussed under *Criticism*.) Robert B. Silber, in his dissertation (State University of Iowa, 1962), "William Cullen Bryant's 'Lectures on Mythology'" (*DAI*, 23, 4021–22), edits the five unpublished lectures that were presented at the National Academy of Design in New York in 1827.

MANUSCRIPTS AND LETTERS

The only large collection of published letters until the mid-seventies was that in Parke Godwin's biography of Bryant (see *Biography*, below). Godwin, Bryant's son-in-law, extracted from rough drafts of the letters, most of which he did not have access to. Bryant's letters are at long last being collected and tabulated in a modern edition. The first three volumes of a proposed six-volume edition by William Cullen Bryant II and Thomas G. Voss have been published (New York, 1975, 1977, 1981); the first volume covers the years 1809–1836, the second 1836–1849, and the third 1849–1857. Bryant and Voss's editing is scrupulous and detailed; each volume offers full documentation of sources, a chronology of Bryant's life during the years covered by the volume, introductions to each section of letters and extensive notes. What the letters in this handsome edition show us is a man of integrity preoccupied with his duties as editor yet warm and loving to his family and friends; the letters from abroad, written for the *Evening Post*, descriptive of cultural differences and historic change, are particularly valuable. Unfortunately these letters don't reveal as much as we might want of Bryant the poet, concerned with the problems of his art.

These letters come from many manuscript sources in more than 135 institutional and private collections. The largest holders are the college or university libraries of Amherst, Brown, Columbia, Duke, Johns Hopkins, Princeton, Virginia, Williams, and Yale. These historical societies hold manuscript letters: Bureau County at Princeton, Illinois; Chicago; New York; and Pennsylvania. Manuscript letters are to be found in these libraries: Huntington; New York Public; New York State at Albany; Pierpont Morgan; Queensborough, New York, Public; and the Library of Congress.

The listing of manuscript holdings, including letters, in the second edition (1977) of *American Literary Manuscripts,* cannot be considered a complete guide for the scholar because in some instances the reports are inflated or do not reveal new acquisitions. Before the work of Bryant and Voss, Herman Spivey examined the major manuscript collections in "Manuscript Resources for the Study of William Cullen Bryant" (*PBSA,* Third Quarter 1950). Spivey provides brief descriptions of eighteen collections, thirteen of which he considers significant in extent and value; he also gives a partial list of correspondents. Six of the collections — the most important — are housed in the New York Public Library: The Bryant-Godwin Collection, the Bryant Family Papers, the Bryant Miscellaneous Papers, the Berg Collection, the Goddard-Roslyn Collection (including hundreds of manuscript versions of Bryant's poems), and the John Bigelow Collection. Other important holders are the New York Historical Society, the Boston Public Library, the Massachusetts Historical Society, the Houghton Library at Harvard, and the Longfellow House in Cambridge, Massachusetts. Included in these major collections are manuscripts, journals, letters to and from Bryant, and other documents relating to the poet, including a good collection of first editions at Yale. A list of correspondents in the Bryant-Godwin Collection of the New York Public Library is given in Kenneth Cameron's "Bryant's Correspondents: A Checklist" (*ATQ,* Winter 1972). Much of this extensive material has remained essentially untapped by Bryant scholars.

From these various collections some of the letters written to and from Bryant have been printed in a score of articles and notes in the past fifty years. Many of the letters clarify biographical problems or add somewhat to our understanding of Bryant's opinions as a poet and editor. Some of these essays may be less reliable with the publication of the new Bryant-

Voss edition, which has now gathered many of the letters that appeared for the first time in the following essays. The first group of articles under consideration here offers information relevant to a discussion of Bryant's life. Tremaine McDowell's "William Cullen Bryant and Yale" (*NEQ*, Oct. 1930) contains letters to and from his former Williams roommate, John Avery, about his ill-fated determination to enter Yale. The Sedgwick family's influence during his unhappy years as a lawyer in Great Barrington and later is revealed in an exchange of letters between Bryant and Charles, Henry, and Catherine Sedgwick, many published for the first time in C. I. Glicksberg's excellent essay, "Bryant and the Sedgwick Family" (*Americana*, Oct. 1937). Letters written from about 1833 to 1839 to his brother Cyrus and Austin and to his mother concerning family matters are in Helen L. Drew's "Unpublished Letters to William Cullen Bryant" (*NEQ*, June 1937). Of greater importance are the fourteen letters (1831 to 1878), mostly from Cullen to his brother John, which reveal Bryant's plans to leave the *Post*, probably to devote himself to poetry; in "Bryant and Illinois: Further Letters of the Poet's Family" (*NEQ*, Dec. 1943), Keith Huntress and Fred W. Lorch point out that much of Bryant's wealth came from investments in Illinois farmland.

In "William Cullen Bryant Changes His Mind: An Unpublished Letter about Thomas Jefferson" (*NEQ*, Dec. 1949), Herman Spivey shows that Bryant changed from a strong anti-Jeffersonian attitude in his youth to a pro-Jeffersonian stance in his later years. Spivey has also written a significant study of Bryant's attitudes toward Lincoln during the Civil War; this essay, "Bryant Cautions and Counsels Lincoln" (*TSL*, 1961), includes previously unpublished letters — there are thirty-one to Lincoln — with Bryant's comments on slavery, the war, and, particularly, federal appointments. Spivey makes it clear that Lincoln read Bryant's letters, respected his opinions, replied in his own hand to some of them, and heeded his advice on a number of appointments. Some remarks on public affairs, particularly the Civil War, can be found in nineteen letters (1849 to 1866) to a close friend at Roslyn, Long Island; they involve personal matters of perhaps limited significance but reveal the warmth of Bryant's personality (William D. Hoyt, Jr., "Some Unpublished Bryant Correspondence" [*NYH*, Jan. and Apr. 1940]). Bryant's opinions on some major questions of his day are to be found in three letters printed in Paul Crapo's "Bryant on Slavery, Copyright, and Capital Punishment" (*ESQ*, Third Quarter 1967).

Several essays collect for the first time letters to and from Bryant and editorials by Bryant that shed additional light on his relationships with important writers. C. I. Glicksberg reprints editorials and reviews by Bryant and letters by Cooper in "Cooper and Bryant: A Literary Friendship" (*Col*, part 20, 1935); these materials reveal Bryant's admiration for and defense of Cooper during the novelist's "war with the press." Longfellow and Bryant were but casual acquaintances, as Glicksberg shows in "Longfellow and Bryant" (*N&Q*, 3 February 1934). Bryant's arduous trip to St. Augustine, Florida, is described in a letter to William Gilmore Simms, with whom he was friendly, in John C. Guilds, "Bryant in the South: A New Letter to Simms" (*Georgia Historical Quarterly*, June 1953). Paul Hamilton Hayne also admired Bryant, as is shown in several letters Hayne wrote in 1873 requesting that Bryant write a memorial ode to Simms for the *Evening Post* (Edward G. Bernard, "Northern Bryant and Southern Hayne," *Col*, n. s., Spring 1936). Frank Smith's "Schoolcraft, Bryant, and Poetic Fame" (*AL*, May 1933) includes several letters in which Bryant criticizes a poem by William Hetherwold, presumably a protégé of Schoolcraft but who Smith thinks was actually Schoolcraft.

Correspondence that treats of random matters having to do with Bryant's poetic and editorial careers is extensive. Letters (1823 to 1825) to Theophilus Parsons dealing with Bryant's writing for the *Literary Gazette* are in Joseph George Ornato's "Bryant and the *United States Literary Gazette*" (*ESQ*, Third Quarter 1967). Eight letters (1841 to 1874) covering a variety of topics, including Bryant's remarks on the genesis and publication of "Thanatopsis" and his response to South Carolina's secession, can be found in David R. Rebmann's "Unpublished Letters of William Cullen Bryant" (*ESQ*, Third Quarter 1967). Three uncollected travel letters written in 1873 and subsequently published in the *Evening Post* appear in C. I. Glicksberg's "Letters of William Cullen Bryant from Florida" (*Florida Historical Society Quarterly*, Apr. 1936). Another Bryant letter (1848), concerning an obscure play by a woman's rights advocate, appears in Robert H. Woodward's "Bryant and Elizabeth Oakes Smith: An Unpublished Letter" (*Colby Library Quarterly*, Dec. 1959). Jay B. Hubbell's "A New Letter by William Cullen Bryant" (*Georgia Historical Quarterly*, Sept. 1942) reprints Bryant's review of a history of Georgia. Bryant's letter of regret that he cannot attend the Revolutionary War Centennial appears in Arthur Eugene Bestor, Jr.'s, "Concord Summons the Poets" (*NEQ*, Sept. 1933), and his refusal to write a poem on the battle of Oriskany is in Robert H. Woodward's "Bryant and the Oriskany Centennial" (*ESQ*, Second Quarter 1963). Peter B. Morrill's "Unpublished Letter of William Cullen Bryant" (*ESQ*, Second Quarter 1962) deals with personal matters. Some miscellaneous personal letters (1838 to 1877) are in Edward J. Lazzerini's "Bryant as a Writer of Friendly Letters" (*ESQ*, Third Quarter 1967). A brief letter in Benjamin Lease's "William Cullen Bryant: An Unpublished Letter" (*N&Q*, Sept. 1953) reveals Bryant's humorous side. Recent reprinted letters are in Kenneth Cameron's "A Bryant Letter with Poem (1825)" (*ATQ*, Spring 1972) and George Monteiro's "The Patriarchal Mr. Bryant: Some New Letters" (*N&Q*, Oct. 1975). The Bryant-Voss edition of the letters will provide important background essential for future studies of Bryant's life and work; and examination of the manuscripts of Bryant's poetry and prose will be necessary for any future editions of his writings and any new evaluations of his poetic career.

BIOGRAPHY

There is no definitive biography of Bryant; until the last three decades, there were substantial gaps in our knowledge of his life. Many of the more recent essays on Bryant have continued to address biographical questions as well as critical ones; and with the new edition of letters under way, a new, "definitive" biography seems likely. Charles H. Brown's *William Cullen Bryant* (New York, 1971) comes closest to being the only complete and authoritative modern biography we have. Carefully researched, utilizing the manuscripts and the best of recent research, Brown's study places Bryant in his milieu and examines the editor's life and times, his complex personality and his varied writing style; as a literary biography, showing the poet's artistic growth and his importance in the history of American literature, this work falls rather short. A biography that more perfectly balances the two halves of Bryant — the man of affairs and the artist — awaits another scholar.

The "standard" biography of Bryant was by his son-in-law and *Evening Post* associate, Parke Godwin. *A Biography of William Cullen Bryant, with Extracts from His Private Correspondence* (2 vols., New York, 1883; reprinted, 1967) is part of Godwin's six-volume edition of Bryant's writings. Godwin's study, which combines discussion of his subject's life with many lengthy, and often misquoted, letters, is a rather slow-moving if careful work. Chapter One of Godwin's book is Bryant's own autobiography, written in 1874 and 1875, that ends with the year 1811 and is full of chatty reminiscences but sparing of details. Chapters Six and Seven, on the period from 1811 to 1815, incorrectly date some of Bryant's poems and thus are misleading on the development of his mind and art. (The biographical inaccuracies of these early chapters have been largely corrected by more recent scholars.) Although Godwin is understandably vague and incorrect about his father-in-law's early life, he is quite informative about the *Evening Post* years, particularly in his treatment of Bryant's European travels — he slights the American journeys — and the letters Bryant contributed to the paper. In fact, the three volumes of travel sketches, *Letters of a Traveller* (New York, 1850), *Letters of a Traveller,*

Second Series (New York, 1859), and *Letters from the East* (New York, 1869), provide information about Bryant that biographers and scholars have not utilized sufficiently; these letters are being republished in the Bryant-Voss edition. Throughout his rambling biography Godwin portrays honestly Bryant's public side; but Godwin offers little insight into the private man, a regrettable lack, but as he and others, like Charles Brown, indicate, Bryant maintained a distinct separation between his two lives, finding in his family and books an escape from the discomforts of the editor's uneasy chair. Godwin, in a speech on Bryant published in his *Commemorative Addresses* (New York, 1895), sees Bryant's birth and life paralleling that of a young nation; but, unlike the official biography, this speech is highly sentimental. Godwin's major biography forms the basis of the chronology of Bryant's life by Henry C. Sturges which appears in the 1903 Roslyn Edition. Richard Henry Stoddard's short but inaccurate memoir is also included in this edition.

Many of the book-length biographies of Bryant are little more than reminiscences or scissors-and-paste redoings of Godwin's work. In the two concluding chapters of his life of Bryant, Godwin refers to the funeral oration delivered by Henry W. Bellows, *In Memoriam, William Cullen Bryant* (New York, 1878), and to subsequent commemorative addresses by G. W. Curtis, *The Life, Character, and Writings of William Cullen Bryant* (New York, 1879); Samuel Osgood, *Bryant Among His Countrymen* (New York, 1879); and Robert C. Waterston, *Tribute to William Cullen Bryant* (Boston, 1878). These eulogistic statements are minor additions to the record of Bryant's death. Five other book-length studies of Bryant are more ambitious but of varying worth. David J. Hill's *William Cullen Bryant* (New York, 1879) is sketchy, uncritical, and overly appreciative, as is Andrew James Symington's *William Cullen Bryant: a Biographical Sketch* (New York, 1880). John Bigelow, an associate on the *Evening Post*, wrote the American Men of Letters biography, *William Cullen Bryant* (Boston, 1890), dividing his material by topic, rather than using the conventional chronological approach. Bigelow's recollections of Bryant are honest and valuable, although Bryant's early years receive rather sketchy treatment; he discusses the poet (see particularly Chapter Seven) as well as the editor. Bigelow's biography has deservedly been reprinted (New York, 1980) with a short introduction by John Hollander. William Aspenwall Bradley's English Men of Letters biography, *William Cullen Bryant* (New York, 1905), draws on earlier biographies but offers more astute and frequently critical judgments; this judicious book is marred, however, by Bradley's overemphasis on Bryant's Puritanism. Harry H. Peckham's *Gotham Yankee* (New York, 1950) is a derivative and effusive rehashing of earlier biographies that makes little if any attempt to incorporate the new scholarly materials and facts that have been revealed in works published up to the time it was written. Peckham argues for Bryant's importance in American literary history in an overblown style.

Specific periods of Bryant's life, particularly his first thirty years, have been examined carefully by modern scholars, and their essays contribute to the fuller picture of Bryant's family background and of his intellectual and artistic development that is necessary for a comprehensive study of his life. Bryant was deeply influenced by his parents, Peter and Sarah Snell Bryant. Hallock P. Long, in "The Alden Lineage of William Cullen Bryant" (*NEHGR*, Apr. 1948), outlines his several Mayflower ancestors, while Tremaine McDowell, in "The Ancestry of William Cullen Bryant" (*Americana*, Oct. 1928), characterizes the individualism of the Bryant family and the practical, worldly temperament of the Snells. Dr. Peter Bryant wrote some passable verse before Cullen's birth; the possible influence (on, for example, *The Embargo*) of his father's Augustan poetry and political opinions is discussed in Donald M. Murray's "Dr. Peter Bryant: Preceptor in Poetry to William Cullen Bryant" (*NEQ*, Dec. 1960). The extent of Sarah Snell Bryant's influence on her poet son is discussed in a chatty essay by Amanda Mathews, "The Diary of a Poet's Mother" (*Magazine of History with Notes and Queries*, Sept. 1905); some extracts from her diary suggest the strong-willed, stern, pioneer Yankee that George V. Bohman characterizes in "A Poet's Mother: Sarah Snell Bryant in Illinois" (*Journal of the Illinois State Historical Society*, June 1940). This interesting account relates Mrs. Bryant's property-minded move to Illinois in her late sixties to join her sons, Cyrus, John, and Arthur.

The personality and development of the teen-age Cullen has been rather fully chronicled in two highly informative and entertaining essays by Tremaine McDowell, "Cullen Bryant Prepares for College" (*SAQ*, Apr. 1931) and "Cullen Bryant at Williams College" (*NEQ*, Oct. 1928). The former discusses Bryant's study of the classics at the home of his severe and orthodox uncle, the Reverend Thomas Snell, and at a school in Plainfield; the latter, his disappointing year at the recently founded college in Williamstown. Here, as a shy youth who valued close friendships, he confronted new and diverse religious views, developed his ability as a versifier, and was stimulated generally to more independent thinking. In his later life Bryant always regretted that he had not continued his college work, and he mistakenly attributed little indebtedness to his year at Williams. Between 1816 and 1821, when he married Frances Fairchild, he debated the abandonment of poetry for law. But stimulated by the *North American Review*, he determined to continue writing, thereby winning the approval of the Boston literati (particularly for his recitation of the

Harvard Phi Beta Kappa poem, "The Ages"), and published his first volume of poems. These important years are recorded by Tremaine McDowell in "Bryant and *The North American Review*" (*AL*, Mar. 1929). His residence in Great Barrington, Massachusetts, from 1816 to 1825, was a time of intellectual loneliness and dull legal work, until he met Catherine Sedgwick, a member of a distinguished family, who encouraged Bryant's literary life there and later in New York. The years 1825 to 1827 are recorded in two excellent essays, Richard D. Birdsall's "William Cullen Bryant and Catherine Sedgwick—Their Debt to Berkshire" (*NEQ*, Sept. 1955) and C. I. Glicksberg's "Bryant and the *United States Review*" (*NEQ*, Dec. 1934). These essays show how arduous and uncertain were Bryant's early months as an editor away from the New England region that had given him his early reputation.

Bryant's half-century editorship of the *Evening Post* and his residence in the New York area have been extensively chronicled, particularly by his contemporaries. Although Godwin and Bigelow were Bryant's associates on the newspaper, they did not provide as exhaustive an examination of his editorial career as Allan Nevins does in *The Evening Post: A Century of Journalism* (New York, 1922). Nevins's book is important because it compares the *Evening Post*'s editorial opinions with those of other major New York newspapers and provides a rather full view of the city as it was growing during those years; Nevins gives lively accounts of William Leggett, John Bigelow, John R. Thompson, Charles Nordhoff, and Parke Godwin, whose biography of Bryant he occasionally corrects. Nevins delineates the growth of Bryant's political liberalism and emphasizes the varying moods of the editor's personality, offering in Bryant's insistence on a regimen of diet, exercise, and sleep in order to keep his body fit one other reason for his supposed coldness and social aloofness. Bruce E. Petree's dissertation "*The Evening Post* and American Poetry, 1830–1860: A Study of William Cullen Bryant's Influence" (*DAI*, 35, 2236A), discusses Bryant's support of new American poetry, which he printed and reviewed extensively; his newspaper fostered native literature in the early nationalistic years. When not hard at work at his newspaper, Bryant protected his and his family's privacy at his home in Roslyn, Long Island, from the early 1840s on. Joan D. Berbrich, in *Three Voices from Paumanok: The Influence of Long Island on James Fenimore Cooper, William Cullen Bryant and Walt Whitman* (Port Washington, N.Y., 1969), writes in guide-book fashion of Bryant's country retreat and the influence of it on his poems.

Most of the material in Curtiss S. Johnson's study, *Politics and a Belly-Full* (New York, 1962), comes from other books on Bryant, notably those by Godwin, Bigelow, and Nevins, but his study offers a conveniently short and readable survey, with a conclusion that summarizes and assesses Bryant's years as editor rather well. Frank L. Mott, in *American Journalism, a History: 1690–1960* (3rd ed., New York, 1962), briefly assesses Bryant's editorship and praises the man and his paper for distinguished publishing. In "William Cullen Bryant — Puritan Liberal" (*The Romantic Revolution in America*, New York, 1927), Vernon L. Parrington calls Bryant "the father of nineteenth-century American journalism." Understandably, Parrington's essay focuses upon Bryant's editorial career, as does Part Two of Tremaine McDowell's introduction to the AWS volume; both summarize Bryant's political idealism judiciously. In an essay with a misleading title, "William Cullen Bryant and Communism" (*Modern Quarterly* [New York], July 1934), C. I. Glicksberg argues effectively that the editor, although a courageous liberal, was reactionary in his attitudes toward economic conflicts between labor and capital. Eva B. Dykes's "William Cullen Bryant: Apostle of Freedom" (*Negro History Bulletin*, Nov. 1942) praises the editor's liberal views on the black man's condition. Edward K. Spann examines a friendship divided over economics and politics in "Bryant and Verplanck, the Yankee and the Yorker, 1821–1870" (*NYH*, Jan. 1968).

Several other studies also treat Bryant's editorial years, and although they are in part critical, the studies are further examinations of his opinions, his involvement in New York intellectual life, and his editorial practices. William Cullen Bryant II, in his 1954 Columbia dissertation, "Bryant: the Middle Years; a Study in Cultural Fellowship" (*DAI*, 14, 1218), discusses Bryant's influence on American culture from 1825 to 1850; included is a list of works by Bryant that have not heretofore been credited to him. His relations with the South, both as traveler and editor, were always cordial, even though he was strongly antislavery and believed ardently in a determined prosecution of the war. In "Bryant and the South" (*TSE*, 1949), Max L. Griffin discusses in admirable detail Bryant's trips to the South, his friendships with southern writers, and the laudatory notices of his poems in southern reviews. Howard R. Floan, in "The New York *Evening Post* and the Ante-bellum South" (*AQ*, Fall 1956), covers much of Griffin's ground but looks more specifically at the *Post*'s extensive presentation of news about the South up to the 1850s. A 1966 University of Wisconsin dissertation by Thomas G. Voss, "William Cullen Bryant's *New York Evening Post* and the South: 1847–1856" (*DAI*, 28, 698A–99A), examines closely the period from the newspaper's opposition to the Mexican War to its acceptance of the Republican party, and reviews Bryant's principles of government and the southern opposition to some of those views. Bernard Weinstein argues persuasively in "Bryant, Annexation and the Mexican War" (*ESQ*, Spring 1971), that despite his disapproval of Texas entering the union because it would threaten American relations with Mexico, Bryant, once war was declared, supported it. Bryant encouraged a laissez-faire economy and free trade while at the same time affirming social justice. Finally, three articles by C. I. Glicksberg further amplify Bryant's role as editor: "William Cullen Bryant and the American Press" (*Journalism Quarterly*, Dec. 1939) and "William Cullen Bryant: Champion of Simple English" (*Journalism Quarterly*, Sept. 1949) discuss his campaigning for an enlightened American press against the abuses of contemporary newspaper practices and his efforts to write in a simple, uninflated editorial style. Glicksberg's third essay is on the feminist Fanny Wright, whose New York lectures occasioned Bryant to write a satiric ode. The essay is "William Cullen Bryant and Fanny Wright" (*AL*, Jan. 1935). When the Emperor of Brazil visited New York in 1876 and would not keep to a set schedule, Bryant could not present his address; Ottavio M. Casale recounts the amusing episode in "Bryant's Proposed Address to the Emperor of Brazil" (*ESQ*, Spring 1971). Bryant's New York is the subject of Chapter Eleven of Van Wyck Brooks's *The World of Washington Irving* (New York, 1944). In *The Raven and the Whale* (New York, 1956), Perry Miller makes cursory references to Bryant's aloof position as an editor in the midst of the Young America movement. Miller's remarks would suggest that Bryant was less interested generally in the intellectual and artistic life of New York than we know he was. Bryant may have been reticent, but he was not indifferent to the quest for literary nationalism; he wrote friendly literary notices for his newspaper and knew many painters whose artistic ideas influenced his own poetry. In order to see the problem of Bryant and the New York milieu in its clearest perspective, one needs to read other studies, such as those discussed under *Criticism*.

Although Bryant's European travels during these years have been discussed in detail, only one essay has been written about his American journeys and his attitudes toward the country as expressed in the letters for the *Post*. Donald A. Ringe, in "William Cullen Bryant's Account of Michigan in 1846" (*Michigan History*, Sept. 1956), indicates that little use has been made of these documents and describes the last of three trips Bryant made to visit his mother and brothers in Illinois, including a journey of more than a week in northern Michigan which Bryant recorded in lively accounts. Ringe's essay suggests a direction for subsequent inquiry into Bryant's literary methods as an interpreter of the American scene and into his evaluation of it. More recent work examines in greater detail Bryant's investment in Illinois property: David J. Baxter, "William Cullen Bryant: Illinois Landowner" (*Western Illinois Regional Studies*, Spring 1978). (Since it is difficult to separate a man's life from his writings, some information pertaining to Bryant's biography will be found in books and essays that are largely critical and therefore are discussed below.)

Charles Brown's biography is the only full modern treatment of Bryant's life, which has been studied closely in isolated fragments during the past fifty years. However good the pieces, we lack a whole view of the mind, art, and milieu of the poet-editor; significant work for such a study has certainly been done.

CRITICISM

Although there is extensive critical writing on Bryant, major essays of a general evaluative nature are few in number. Despite their excellence in synthesizing his career and the themes and techniques of his poetry, no really long significant critical work, with the possible exception of Albert F. McLean, Jr.'s admirable Twayne United States Authors Series volume, *William Cullen Bryant* (New York, 1964), has been completed. For the student interested in the history of criticism on Bryant, there is a well-edited collection of essays and excerpts by his contemporaries— John Neal, Hugh Swinton Legaré, John Wilson, and Edgar Allan Poe— in Tremaine McDowell's AWS *William Cullen Bryant*. McDowell's important collection, which should be reprinted, is both well selected and handy, and it does offer a variety of critical reactions to Bryant's work; other nineteenth-century articles are listed in his evaluative bibliography. Of more than simply historical interest are the following essays, most of which point out Bryant's limitations in a direct but judicious fashion: Thomas Powell, "William Cullen Bryant," in his *The Living Authors of America* (New York, 1850); E. S. Nadal, "William Cullen Bryant" (*Macmillan's Magazine*, Sept. 1878); E. C. Stedman, "William Cullen Bryant," in his *Poets of America* (Boston, 1885); Henry D. Sedgwick, Jr., "Bryant's Permanent Contribution to Literature" (*AtM*, Apr. 1897); W. R. Thayer, "Bryant," in his *Throne-Makers* (Boston, 1899); Augustus Hopkins Strong, "William Cullen Bryant," in his *American Poets and Their Theology* (Philadelphia, 1916); Fred Lewis Pattee, "The Centenary of Bryant's Poetry," in his *Sidelights on American Literature* (New York, 1922); and Rémy de Gourmont, *Deux Poètes de la Nature: Bryant et Emerson* (Paris, 1925). Harriet Monroe's attacks (*Poetry*, July 1915; *Dial*, 14 October 1915 and 25 November 1915) against Bryant, with blustery defense by John L. Hervey (*Dial*, 15 August 1915, 28 October 1915, and 9 December 1915), represent the disillusionment caused by the apparent materialism of nineteenth-century establishment writers and the reaction of a critic armed to protect the American pantheon.

Those general essays that offer praise tempered by balanced judgment and keen critical insight are not numerous, although they do give the student a good background for his reading of Bryant; the best of these essays were written primarily before the mid-forties, and since then most Bryant scholarship, however good, has treated more specific critical problems. The first of these broad assessments that remains valuable is W. E. Leonard's "Bryant" in *CHAL*. Leonard does overstate his arguments that Wordsworth and other poets were not an influence on Bryant, and that the poet did not really develop over the years because he experienced no moral or intellectual crises; but, despite what some might consider his undervaluing of Bryant's imagination and intellectual abilities, Leonard's survey is fair and perhaps painfully honest. Leonard's discussion is decidedly appreciative, as is Vernon L. Parrington's "William Cullen Bryant — Puritan Liberal," in his *The Romantic Revolution in America*. Parrington's essay provides a good companion piece to Leonard's, for Parrington is interested mainly in Bryant's journalistic reputation, which he finds to be of extraordinary dimensions. Parrington does not outline much of Bryant's intellectual growth, with the exception of his readings in political economy, saying incorrectly that the steps of his development cannot easily be traced, but Parrington does find in Bryant's mature liberalism a rather good example of his own socioeconomic view of American literary history. In "William Cullen Bryant: A Reinterpretation" (*Revue Anglo-Américaine*, Aug. 1934), C. I. Glicksberg offers astute insight into the two halves of Bryant's creative life, the poet and editor; he argues that the older Bryant had little more to say about the subjects he had poetized in his youth and that, although journalism provided him needed experience, he could not treat contemporary material in his poetry because of his view that art must reveal the universal. (Glicksberg here suggests that Bryant wrote less occasional verse than he actually did.) By giving himself to a business career, Bryant, says Glicksberg, compromised his Romantic devotion to art. Glicksberg's thoughtful and laudatory essay comes to the almost inevitable conclusions about Bryant as a poet: had he been more intense and versatile, his writings would have been considerably enriched.

No critical and scholarly examination has done more to instruct modern students of Bryant than has Tremaine McDowell's introduction to the AWS volume; with the exception of some questionable dating of the poems before 1821, this assessment remains the best single work on the poet's whole career — as poet, critic, and editor. The discussion of Bryant's religion is especially strong; the treatment of his politics is overly concise and has been more amply articulated by others, notably Allan Nevins. McDowell's approach to his subject is both topical and chronological, and his footnotes and notes to the works amplify considerably and specifically the arguments in the introduction. McDowell readily acknowledges that Bryant was a poet of minor rank, as he does even more emphatically in his synopsis of Bryant in *LHUS*. For its length this discussion is quite inclusive; it summarizes Bryant's life and his ideas briefly but pointedly. McDowell emphasizes the twin streams of Calvinism and Unitarianism in Bryant's family heritage and his long years of fearing death that, along with readings in his father's library, lay behind the composition of "Thanatopsis." Also, McDowell argues that because Bryant was quite uncomfortable in New York society, he cultivated an austerity that many mistook for his real personality. Bryant, he goes on to say, had a patriarchal demeanor and was a hard-working but not brilliant editor; his small output shows him to be a man of modest genius. In contrast to the AWS introduction, McDowell offers, in his *LHUS* essay, a tougher-minded analysis of his subject.

Another essay of similar scope but of less value is by Arthur Hobson Quinn in *The Literature of the American People* (New York, 1951). Quinn's appreciative essay is long on biography and quotation from the poetry but rather short on synthesis of Bryant's ideas or on the question of his growth as a thinker. Benjamin T. Spencer's article of general evaluation, "Bryant: The Melancholy Progressive" (*ESQ*, Second Quarter 1966), argues that Bryant was a believer in a qualified millennium. Although Bryant thought there was a possibility for a limited utopia, he saw it finally displaced by the vicissitudes of human life. Spencer's short essay makes interesting points that he does not elaborate or document as thoroughly as he might have. Alan B. Donovan's "William Cullen Bryant: 'Father of American Song'" (*NEQ*, Dec. 1968) praises Bryant for assimilating the prevailing intellectual trends of his day: the Puritan perceptual process, the neoclassic appreciation for the order of nature, and the Romantic emphasis on feeling and imagination. From these disparate traditions, says Donovan, Bryant formulated a theory of verse that is "the first native articulation of the art of poetry." Donald A. Ringe's "William Cullen Bryant," in *American Writers: A Collection of Literary Biographies* (New York, 1979), provides the only concise but detailed overview and defense of Bryant's life and his mind and art to appear in many years; an excellent survey, it emphasizes the blend of past tradition and American perception in the varied philosophical themes of his poems.

Albert F. McLean, Jr.'s TUSAS *William Cullen Bryant* is the only lengthy critical study of Bryant and the most complete discussion of his achievement since McDowell's AWS introduction. The book minimizes biographical fact, although the introductory chapter does present an outline of Bryant's life. Here McLean concentrates on the influences on Bryant's mind; and his device of the concentric circles of Bryant's expanding sensibility, although perhaps too neat, provides a workable approach. Mc-Lean argues that Bryant's thought and art did not really mature in any important way, yet his discussion at times belies this point. The strength of his study is his assessment of about thirty important poems, particularly "Thanatopsis." McLean brings much material to bear upon his analysis of the poems and his discussion of Bryant's limited intellectual development; the book is informative, challenging, and polished. In its freshness of approach and in its able and learned synthesis of Bryant's varied career, it should be considered one of the important studies in Bryant criticism.

The topic of Bryant as a theoretical and practical critic has been treated in a variety of essays and longer works of American criticism; several books mentioned earlier—Nevins's, McDowell's AWS introduction, and McLean's—have some relevant discussions of this important aspect of Bryant's career. Bryant was an important early critic in American literature, second only to Poe in the pre-Civil War period, even if many of his ideas were largely derived from his readings in late eighteenth-century estheticians. He bridged the change in literary taste from the Neoclassical to the Romantic periods, and in the four *Lectures on Poetry*, which still need more analysis and evaluation, he wrote the earliest important critical statements in America. A significant influence on his theory was that of Archibald Alison's *Essays on the Nature and Principles of Taste* (Edinburgh, 1790), a work which argued that esthetic pleasure arises through mental associations. According to William P. Hudson, in "Archibald Alison and William Cullen Bryant" (*AL*, Mar. 1940), the young poet read this work before he went to Williams College and was impressed with Alison's ideas about nature as a healing power and poetry as a suggestive rather than imitative art. John P. Pritchard's three studies of American criticism, particularly *Return to the Fountains: Some Classical Sources of American Criticism* (Durham, N.C., 1942), which shows how Horace's and Aristotle's poetics influenced American critics, help explain Bryant's relevance as critic to his age. The most recent work on Bryant's critical theories in the lectures is William J. Free's "William Cullen Bryant on Nationalism, Imitation and Originality in Poetry" (*SP*, July 1969); Bryant rejected the extremes of *imitatio* and originality. References to Bryant are much more cursory in Pritchard's *Criticism in America* (Norman, Okla., 1956); most of them concern the influence of Coleridge on Bryant's theory. In *Literary Wise Men of Gotham: Criticism in New York, 1815-1860* (Baton Rouge, La., 1963), Pritchard refers generally to the power of Bryant's critical voice as an editor. For a contrasting opinion about Bryant's possible importance, one might consult Perry Miller's *The Raven and the Whale* (see *Biography*, above).

Other significant books and essays refer, at times rather sketchily, to Bryant's criticism in the context of broader discussions and offer background for the study of Bryant as critic: William Charvat's *The Origins of American Critical Thought, 1810–1835* (Philadelphia, 1936); Floyd Stovall's *American Idealism* (Norman, Okla., 1943), which argues that Bryant's eighteenth-century roots kept him from becoming fully a Romantic; John Stafford's *The Literary Criticism of "Young America": A Study in the Relationship of Politics and Literature, 1837–1850* (Berkeley, Calif., 1952); M. F. Heiser's "The Decline of Neoclassicism, 1801–1848," in *Transitions in American Literary History*, edited by Harry H. Clark (Durham, N.C., 1953; reprinted, 1967); Harry H. Clark's "Changing Attitudes in Early American Literary Criticism: 1800–1840," in *The Development of American Literary Criticism*, edited by Floyd Stovall (Chapel Hill, N.C., 1955); and Clarence A. Brown's editing of *The Achievement of American Criticism: Representative Selections from Three Hundred Years of American Criticism* (New York, 1954), which reprints Bryant's first and second lectures on poetry and has a very general introductory essay on the background of American criticism but a very helpful bibliography of primary and secondary works. Rebecca Rio Jelliffe's dissertation (Calif.–Berkeley, 1964), "The Poetry of William Cullen Bryant: Theory and Practice" (*DAI*, 25, 4148–49), discusses the influence of English and Scottish associationism on his criticism and poetry. Bryant's critical evaluations of contemporary works have received some notice in books and essays dealing with his *Evening Post* years: C. I. Glicksberg's "New Contributions in Prose by William Cullen Bryant" (*Americana*, Oct. 1936) looks back to his work as a reviewer for the *United States Review and Literary Gazette*. The related matter of the oral delivery of his poems, particularly "The Ages," is discussed in C. I. Glicksberg's "From the 'Pathetic' to the 'Classical': Bryant's Schooling in the Liberties of Oratory" (*AN&Q*, Mar. 1947) and a minor correction is suggested in Louis S. Friedland's "Bryant's Schooling in the Liberties of Oratory" (*AN&Q*, May 1947). Bryant was "the forefather of American prosody," according to Gay Wilson Allen, in *American Prosody* (New York, 1935), an extensive review of Bryant's mechanics which shows that he was, nevertheless, rather conservative in his use of stanzaic devices.

Scholarship on Bryant as critic has certainly not been exhausted, but the picture becomes more complete if we examine the research done on Bryant's interest in art and his relationships with important American artists of the Hudson River School, one of the more fully researched topics in Bryant studies. He wrote extensively on art, particularly on what he saw during his European travels, and found in the landscape paintings of his friends Thomas Cole and Asher Durand a pictorial view of nature which corresponded directly with his own efforts to verbalize responses to nature. Donald A. Ringe has written three excellent essays on Bryant and art; the most general one, "Bryant's Criticism of the Fine Arts" (*College Art Journal*, Fall 1957), considers Bryant's interest in art and those characteristics he most prized—realistic depiction, the presence of light and shadow, the harmony of the unified whole, and moral significance. After arguing that Bryant was limited by his judgment of the choice of subject in an art work, the essay moves to a consideration of Bryant and Cole, a relationship more elaborately examined in Ringe's earlier essay, "Kindred Spirits: Bryant and Cole" (*AQ*, Fall 1954). According to Ringe, the two men considered the external scene an intermediary between man and God and were aware of man's need for profound humility in nature and of the concept of inexorable time that destroys man's creations. The essay concludes with comparisons of several of Bryant's poems and Cole's paintings in respect to theme and technique. In "Painting as Poem in the Hudson River Aesthetic" (*AQ*, Spring 1960), Ringe discusses again the influence on Bryant (also on Cole and Allston) of the Scottish associationists; because beauty is in the mind of the beholder, the artist tries to suggest rather than to imitate. To Bryant, however, poetry is superior to painting because it more directly involves the imagination and because language can be more suggestive than painting; the weakness of the artistic tendency toward allegorization is, to Ringe, the decided emphasis on content over form. Ringe's work on Bryant and art culminates in his important book, *The Pictorial Mode: Space and Time in the Art of Bryant, Irving and Cooper* (Lexington, Ky., 1971), which discusses the themes in Bryant, influenced as they were by Hudson River painters, of the continuity of time and the expanse of nature and the use of precise detail and chiaroscuro.

Ringe's essays and book provide a fuller treatment of the topic than does Charles L. Sanford's "The Concept of the Sublime in the Works of Thomas Cole and William Cullen Bryant" (*AL*, Jan. 1957). Of relatively little value is Evelyn L. Schmitt's "Two American Romantics—Thomas Cole and William Cullen Bryant" (*Art in America*, Spring 1953). The most thorough history of the relationship between Bryant and artists is James T. Callow's study, *Kindred Spirits: Knickerbocker Writers and American Artists, 1807–1855* (Chapel Hill, N.C., 1967). Callow discusses extensively Bryant's acquaintance with many contemporary artists, and he offers abundant documentation to support his impressive scholarship. William Cullen Bryant II's "Poetry and Painting: A Love Affair of Long Ago" (*AQ*, Winter 1970) gives a detailed history of the fine arts and literary associations in New York City. "Bryant and Cole in the Catskills" (*BNYPL*, Spring 1975) is a reprint of a rather recently discovered letter from Cole to Bryant inviting him on a walk in the mountains; Asher Durand's painting "Kindred Spirits" is an idealization of that area of the Catskills. Douglas Noverr offers an interesting symbolic interpretation of the characters and setting of the well-known Durand work.

Bryant's poetry has also been treated extensively, in the general works discussed above and in essays that look more directly at the techniques and themes of his poems and place him in the context of his age. The following group of essays provides some background for a reading and evaluation of Bryant's poems, particularly "Thanatopsis." Along with these essays one must consider, of course, the scholarship on Bryant's theories as a critic and his opinions on art. Although Bryant's poetry is usually considered humorless, C. I. Glicksberg finds some humor in the poet's satiric political poems; "Bryant, the Poet of Humor" (*Americana*, July 1935) also identifies some of Bryant's poems in the *Evening Post*. One essay that argues Bryant's fundamental inability to break with traditional rhetorical poetry and write in a more private and therefore less didactic tone of "pure" poetry is Marvin T. Herrick's "Rhetoric and Poetry in Bryant" (*AL*, May 1935), which seems to suggest that Bryant's poetry would have been better had he written in the style of Poe. Behind Herrick's essay is the usual suggestion of Bryant's deficiencies, which George Arms discusses in his prefatory essay to a selection from Bryant in *The Fields Were Green: A New View of Bryant, Whittier, Holmes, Lowell and Longfellow, with a Selection of Their Poems* (Stanford, Calif., 1953); this essay was a reprint, with some slight changes, of "William Cullen Bryant: A Respectable Station on Parnassus" (*UKCR*, Spring 1949). Arms does not present a particularly new view of Bryant; and he tends to damn by faint praise, particularly since he points out so many inconsistencies in Bryant's thought and action and argues that a lack of complexity, thin diction, and an indecisiveness about theory were among Bryant's faults. Jane Donahue Eberwein's recent edition, *Early American Poetry: Selections from Bradstreet, Taylor, Dwight, Freneau and Bryant* (Madison, Wis., 1978) offers only a simple survey of Bryant's life and some critical commentary but a good selection of his poems.

Roy Harvey Pearce, in his distinguished study *The Continuity of American Poetry* (Princeton, N.J., 1961), refers to Bryant as a representative poet whose works were meant to reinforce and confirm the people's opinions and prejudices, in short, their dreams. For Pearce, Bryant's poems and, particularly, his essays on poetry are cautionary, an opinion with which Bernard Duffey disagrees in his essential article on nineteenth-century American poetry, "Romantic Coherence and Romantic Incoherence in American Poetry" (*Centennial Review* [Michigan State Univ.], Spring 1963 and Fall 1964). Duffey considers that the "coherent" poets, among them Emerson and Bryant, spokesmen for the Protestant spirit, used religion or something akin as a medium of analogy; for the poets of "incoherence" the dogmas of naturalism acted upon their Protestant tenets of deism and evangelicalism. Duffey deals at length with Bryant and offers one of the most effective explanations ever advanced of Bryant's important historical position. Duffey's *Poetry in America: Expression and Its Values in the Times of Bryant, Whitman and Pound* (Durham, N.C., 1978) argues the same thesis. Bryant, he says, celebrated nature "as a means of divine grace; his was chiefly a rhetoric of thanksgiving and praise."

Evans Harrington, in "Sensuousness in the Poetry of William Cullen Bryant" (*University of Mississippi Studies in English*, 1966), discusses Bryant's sensory responses to the world in his poems and concludes that since the sense of sight is most outstanding he uses pictorial imagery extensively. The majority of Bryant's poems are animated by simple perceptions, feelings, and instincts, says Harrington, although it is death that elicits the keenest and most persistent response from Bryant. Sidney Poger's "William Cullen Bryant: Emblem Poet" (*ESQ*, Second Quarter 1966) suggests the possibility of further work on Bryant and the tradition of the emblem. Norman Ferdinand Christensen's 1960 University of Wisconsin dissertation, "The Imagery of William Cullen Bryant" (*DAI*, 21, 195), classifies Bryant's leading images (earth and flowers are used most frequently) and finds that they represent a clearly ordered world view that reflects tension between change and permanence. The traditional sonnet form did not serve well those American poets who were seeking native American expression because it derived from the Old European values and language, according to John Freeman and Gregory Green in an interesting essay, "A Literary Cul-de-Sac: The Sonnet and the Schoolroom Poets" (*ATQ*, Spring 1979); Bryant's "To Cole" is perhaps the best sonnet of the period because it is not tied to the tradition of the form.

Bryant's themes are discussed, of course, in all the writings on him; however, some essays treat his thinking about important nineteenth-century ideas and movements and try to determine his response to changing intellectual fashions. One of the continual topics in Bryant studies, about which there are differing opinions, is the influence of Puritanism on his cast of mind. Most critics are rightly aware of his development away from this tradition, but they often disagree about its residual effects. An overemphasis on Bryant's Puritanism can be found in Norman Foerster's essay, "Bryant," in *Nature in American Literature* (New York, 1923), reprinted — with some elaboration on the differences between Wordsworth and Bryant — from "Nature in Bryant's Poetry" (*SAQ*, Jan.

1918). Foerster was among the first to enumerate the variety of concrete images in Bryant's poetry and to suggest that the sensuousness prominent in his relation to external nature precludes the indictment that he was essentially a cold man. Even though Foerster deemphasizes the occasional echoes of Wordsworthian sentiment in Bryant's poetry, he still subscribes in the main to the traditional view that Bryant was vastly influenced by the English poet and therefore deserves the title the American Wordsworth. Foerster's essay is still valuable.

Bryant's use of the European past has been documented rather thoroughly in numerous works (although influence studies are certainly not exhausted), but, as Donald A. Ringe points out in "Bryant's Use of the American Past" (*PMASAL*, 1956), Bryant also looked back to the short history of his own country not merely to respond to the call for nationalistic poetry but to emphasize the moral that when man places faith in material success and disregards spiritual values he is doomed to fall through the sin of pride. The culture of the mound builders was important to him, as Ringe notes and as Curtis Dahl explains in his well-researched essay, "Mound-Builders, Mormons, and William Cullen Bryant" (*NEQ*, June 1961). Bryant's references to this extinct civilization in "Thanatopsis" and "The Prairies" are supported by highly respected contemporary archaeological works, which Dahl discusses at length. As Ringe indicates, Bryant thought of the displaced American Indians as the victims of American settlement and portrayed them as proud, fierce, and magnificent in the face of death. Bryant's Indians have been only cursorily treated in an early essay by Jason Almus Russell, "The Romantic Indian in Bryant's Poetry" (*Education,* June 1928).

Bryant's interest in science was more extensive than is usually thought, as Frederick William Conner argues in *Cosmic Optimism: A Study of the Interpretation of Evolution by American Poets from Emerson to Robinson* (Gainesville, Fla., 1949). Bryant encouraged the dissemination of scientific knowledge but had no sympathy with Darwinian evolution or the frequent reaction of agnosticism; he did, however, accept the ideas of process, flux, and amelioration—the impermanence of human life and the perpetual renewal of nature in the cycle of seasons were Bryant's themes of change. To what extent new discoveries in geology influenced his belief in the dynamic state of nature within an inflexible rule of order, which derives its purpose and direction from God, is problematical, according to Donald A. Ringe's "William Cullen Bryant and the Science of Geology" (*AL,* Jan. 1955), which builds on Conner's previous work. Ringe believes that these ideas were present in Bryant's earlier works (like "The Ages") and that new geological studies gave him evidence for his own beliefs. His interest in a variety of contemporary scientific questions is briefly examined by C. I. Glicksberg in "William Cullen Bryant and Nineteenth-Century Science" (*NEQ*, Mar. 1950).

Bryant emphasized the emotional origin of art, but although he usually composed in moments of inspiration he revised cautiously and carefully in order to find the right word, usually a simple one, to express precisely his original idea. Bryant's poems were usually improved in this manner, as Tremaine McDowell shows in his important study, "Bryant's Practice in Composition and Revision" (*PMLA*, June 1937). McDowell examines early drafts in manuscript and compares them with the printed versions, particularly of "Thanatopsis." In "The Juvenile Verse of William Cullen Bryant" (*SP*, Jan. 1929), McDowell discusses Bryant's early career from 1803 to about 1811 and illustrates his development through five stages: the religious, the satirical, the pastoral, the political, and the classical. This essay adds to our understanding of Bryant's practice in composition and includes some previously unpublished juvenilia written before "Thanatopsis." Richard E. Peck's "Two Lost Bryant Poems: Evidence of Thomson's Influence" (*AL*, Mar. 1967) studies two uncollected poems, "The Seasons" (1806) and "A Thunderstorm" (1807), which foreshadow themes and natural settings treated by the adult poet.

"Thanatopsis," among the most important early works in American literature, has received rather wide analysis. Bryant has always been considered something of a child prodigy, for it has always been assumed that the poem was composed in 1811, after his one year at Williams; Bryant, moreover, was inclined to date the poem earlier as he grew older. Among the more important arguments advanced is William Cullen Bryant II's contention that the poem was composed in 1815, during the time in which "The Yellow Violet," "Inscription for the Entrance to a Wood," and "To a Waterfowl" were written. Bryant's "The Genesis of 'Thanatopsis'" (*NEQ*, June 1948) treats in detail, including the influences of the Graveyard poets, Byron, Cowper, and Wordsworth, the years 1811 to 1815, when the young poet was growing into maturity and when his religious doubts and fear of death were intensifying. Bryant's argument has the force of logic, clear exposition, and documentation; this essay has done more than any other to clarify the poet's early years. Two earlier essays on "Thanatopsis" have long been considered of historical value and should be noted for their attempts to suggest sources and revisions. Carl Van Doren's "The Growth of 'Thanatopsis'" (*Nation*, 7 October 1915) attributes to the Graveyard school a significant influence; William Cullen Bryant II, however, dates the reading of these works as 1813, rather than 1811. Willis Fletcher Johnson's "Thanatopsis, Old and New" (*NAR*, Nov. 1927) contends that the original introductory four quatrains provide a logical introduction to the poem and are harmonious with it; the article compares the first published version in 1817 with the revised poem in 1821, which included an introduction and conclusion that Johnson considers must have been written at the time of its first draft; both opinions are decidedly dubious.

Albert F. McLean, Jr.'s "Bryant's 'Thanatopsis': A Sermon in Stone" (*AL*, Jan. 1960) sees in the poem a tripartite division like the Puritan plain-style sermons, with a pattern of *doctrine, reasons,* and *uses* — one which Bryant did not necessarily imitate consciously. McLean also discusses the question of voice, which is that of nature, a voice that could be detached and universal. (McLean in addition writes at length about the poem, expanding this essay and discussing sources and revisions, in his Twayne volume.) E. Miller Budick's "'Visible' Images and the 'Still Voice': Transcendental Vision in Bryant's 'Thanatopsis'" (*ESQ*, Second Quarter, 1976) argues that this poem attempts successfully to define man's perception of transcendent truth in natural images. Yvor Winters contrasts in some interesting ways "Thanatopsis" with Stevens's "Sunday Morning" in *The Anatomy of Nonsense* (Norfolk, Conn., 1943); Arthur I. Ladu suggests the influence of Byron on one passage in "A Note on *Childe Harold* and 'Thanatopsis'" (*AL*, Mar. 1939); in "A Passage in 'Thanatopsis,'" Charles Washburn Nichols finds in the poem an echo of the Book of Job (*AL*, May 1939); Thomas O. Mabbott discusses the allusions inherent in "the Barcan wilderness" in "Bryant's 'Thanatopsis'" (*Expl*, Dec. 1952); and Vernon F. Snow presents reasons for Bryant's mentioning the Oregon River in "'Where Rolls the Oregon . . .'" (*WHR*, Summer 1956). The Bible and Thucydides are sources, according to Robert H. Woodward in "'The Wings of Morning' in 'Thanatopsis'" (*ESQ*, First Quarter 1970) and to Gerald J. Smith in "Bryant's 'Thanatopsis': A Possible Source" (*AN&Q*, June 1975).

In the light of his suggested redating of "Thanatopsis," William Cullen Bryant II, in "The Waterfowl in Retrospect" (*NEQ*, June 1957), argues that manuscript evidence places the composition of "To a Waterfowl" between 1812 and 1815, several months before "Thanatopsis" instead of four years after it. Bryant's second most famous poem receives a good explication in Donald Davie's essay, "Bryant: 'To a Waterfowl,'" in *Interpretations: Essays on Twelve English Poems*, edited by John Wain (London, 1955). E. Miller Budick, in "The Disappearing Image in William Cullen Bryant's 'To a Waterfowl'" (*Concerning Poetry*, Fall 1978), offers the interesting reading that ". . . the 'Power' which creates nature's symbolism in the first place compels the poet to go beyond symbols to the unsymbolizable, transcendent idea which is the 'Power' itself." Cecil D. Eby, Jr., corrects one of Parke Godwin's notes in "Bryant's 'The Prairies': Notes on Date and Text" (*PBSA*, Third Quarter 1962). "The Prairies" as a refutation of Buffon and others who believed in the degradation of America is treated well in Ralph N. Miller's "Nationalism in Bryant's 'The Prairies'" (*AL*, May 1949). In "Timothy Flint and Bryant's 'The Prairies'" (*AN&Q*, December 1977), David J. Baxter contends that since Bryant began his important poem one and a half years after his trip to Illinois, his visit with Flint close to the time of the poem's composition was a more direct influence. Edwin R. Booker writes an extensive analysis in "The Garden Myth in 'The Prairies'" (*Western Illinois Regional Studies*, Spring 1978). In "Bryant and James Grahame" (*N&Q*, 14 December 1935), Thomas O. Mabbott finds in Grahame's "The Sabbath" a possible source of "A Forest Hymn." G. Giovannini explains the meaning of "the primal Curse" in "Inscription for the Entrance to a Wood" (*Expl*, Apr. 1946). Bryant's tales receive brief comment in Fred Lewis Pattee's *The Development of the American Short Story* (New York, 1923) and Arthur Hobson Quinn's *American Fiction: An Historical and Critical Survey* (New York, 1936).

Comparative studies of Bryant and other writers are rather extensive. Whitman and Bryant have been contrasted in two essays: C. I. Glicksberg, in "Whitman and Bryant" (*Fantasy*, 1935), shows that the two men, although vastly different in poetic practice, thought kindly of one another's work; Bryant objected to the form of *Leaves of Grass* and must have disapproved of the content as well, says Glicksberg. Donald A. Ringe goes more deeply into their related philosophical world views in "Bryant and Whitman: A Study in Artistic Affinities" (*BUSE*, Summer 1956); Ringe compares their themes as religious nature poets, their imagery, and their prosodic techniques. Bryant, the poet of universal themes, respected Whittier's crusading verse, according to C. I. Glicksberg's "Bryant and Whittier" (*EIHC*, Apr. 1936). Tremaine McDowell's "Edgar Allan Poe and William Cullen Bryant" (*PQ*, Jan. 1937) recounts Poe's curious adulation of Bryant, both as poet and public figure, and Bryant's lack of sympathy for Poe. In "Bryant on Emerson the Lecturer" (*NEQ*, Sept. 1939), C. I. Glicksberg considers Bryant's admiration if not wholehearted enthusiasm for Emerson's philosophy. Melville, who met Bryant in 1847, apparently thought him cold and aloof and patterned the Man with the Weed, one of the disguises of the Confidence Man, after him; Helen P. Trimpi's "Three of Melville's Confidence Men: William Cullen Bryant, Theodore Parker and Horace Greeley" (*TSLL*, Fall 1979) draws a number of interesting parallels but the whole thesis is questionable. Jacob H. Adler's "A Milton-Bryant Parallel" (*NEQ*, Sept. 1951) points out several similarities between the poets. Bryant's interest in French literature and his possible debt to Gautier are discussed generally in Joseph S. Schick's "William Cullen Bryant and Théophile Gautier" (*Modern Language Journal*, Jan. 1933), and the likelihood that Mallarmé knew of Bryant in Poe's reviews is suggested by Henry A. Grubbs in "Mallarmé and Bryant" (*MLN*,

June 1947). Bryant's enthusiasm for German culture is examined in A. H. Herrick's "William Cullen Bryants Beziehungen zur Deutschen Dichtung" (*MLN*, June 1917) and in Henry A. Pochmann's *German Culture in America* (Madison, Wis., 1957). J. Chesley Mathews's "Bryant's Knowledge of Dante" (*Italica*, Dec. 1939) and "Bryant and Dante: A Word More" (*Italica*, Sept. 1958) cover that topic well. Bryant's interest in Spanish and Spanish-American culture was most profound, as Stanley T. Williams discusses at length in *The Spanish Background of American Literature* (vol. 2; New Haven, Conn., 1955). The controversy surrounding the possible meeting of Bryant and José María Heredia and whether Bryant translated his "Ode to Niagara" is treated in numerous essays, the most important of which in English are E. C. Hills, "Did Bryant Translate Heredia's 'Ode to Niagara'?" (*MLN*, Dec. 1919); José de Onís, "The Alleged Acquaintance of William Cullen Bryant and José María Heredia" (*Hispanic Review*, July 1957); Manuel Pedro González, "Two Great Pioneers of Inter-American Cultural Relations" (*Hispania*, May 1959); and in Frederick S. Stimson and Robert J. Bininger, "Studies of Bryant as Hispanophile: Another Translation" (*AL*, May 1959). Essays in Spanish are Manuel Pedro González, "Bryant y Heredia" (*Revista Nacional de Cultura* [Caracas], Nov–Dec. 1962) and Héctor H. Orjuela, "Revaloración de una vieja polémica literaria: William Cullen Bryant y la oda 'Niágara' de José María Heredia" (*Thesaurus: Boletín del Instituto Caro y Cuervo*, May–Aug. 1964).

Bryant's contemporary reputation in Britain, France, and Germany is surveyed or referred to briefly in William B. Cairns's *British Criticisms of American Writings, 1815–1833* (Madison, Wis. 1922); Clarence Gohdes's *American Literature in Nineteenth-Century England* (New York, 1944); Robert W. Duncan's "The London *Literary Gazette* and American Writers" (*Papers on English Language and Literature*, Spring 1965), which corrects Cairns; Harold Elmer Mantz's *French Criticism of American Literature Before 1850* (New York, 1917); Sidney L. McGee's *La littérature américaine dans la "Revue des deux mondes" (1831–1900)* (Montpellier, 1927); and Harvey W. Hewett-Thayer's *American Literature as Viewed in Germany, 1818–1861* (Chapel Hill, N.C., 1958).

The most important scholarly and critical writing on Bryant has appeared in the last fifty years; the best of it has focused on Bryant as a product of his heritage and his age, and has made a valuable contribution to our knowledge of American cultural history in the nineteenth century. The way of future Bryant scholarship seems clear; although the bibliographical problems are complex, a new edition of the letters is being done. Bryant's reputation may never change, but our awareness of his importance and complexity can and will.

James Fenimore Cooper

JAMES FRANKLIN BEARD

RANKING COOPER with Hawthorne, Melville, and James in *The Eccentric Design* (New York, 1959) as "the four greatest novelists America produced in the nineteenth century," Marius Bewley expressed a personal judgment of Cooper shared by an increasing minority of readers. Whether or not Bewley's unconventional estimate of the novelist's importance achieves general critical acceptance, Cooper scholarship and criticism have been moving in the last three decades towards a major revaluation.

BIBLIOGRAPHY

The most generally useful Cooper bibliography is still *A Descriptive Bibliography of the Writings of James Fenimore Cooper* (New York, 1934; reissued, 1968) by Robert E. Spiller and Philip C. Blackburn. Introduced by Spiller's pioneering essay on Cooper's publishing practices, this work provides information on first editions and printings, lists many American and British reprints, and cites some translations into French, German, and other languages. It identifies sets, including some foreign sets, and locates Cooper titles published serially or miscellaneously. Jacob Blanck's *Bibliography of American Literature* supplements Spiller and Blackburn with publication dates drawn from contemporaneous trade journals and with details on states, bindings, and other variants. Copies of numerous American printings are located in Lyle H. Wright's *American Fiction, 1774–1850* (2nd rev. ed., San Marino, Calif., 1969), and other copies are located in *The National Union Catalog of Pre-1956 Imprints*,

From Earl N. Harbert and Robert A. Rees, editors, *Fifteen American Authors before 1900: Bibliographic Essays on Research & Criticism* (Madison: The University of Wisconsin Press; © 1984 by the Board of Regents of the University of Wisconsin System); may be reproduced only by permission of the publisher.

vol. 121. Warner Barnes has prepared a manuscript census and finding list of Cooper imprints in English to 1861, containing almost 900 individual titles and 12 sets, which the American Antiquarian Society in Worcester, Massachusetts, has extended, annotated, and employed as one of the bases for its comprehensive collection of early Cooper editions. The most nearly complete short title list of Cooper's published works, excluding items in the edition proper, is given in Volume Six of *The Letters and Journals of James Fenimore Cooper* (6 vols., Cambridge, Mass., 1 and 2, 1960; 3 and 4, 1964; 5 and 6, 1968), edited by James Franklin Beard.

A new descriptive bibliography of Cooper editions in English, exhaustive in its study of settings, states, issues, and variants of all kinds, is much needed. Incomplete but helpful guides to individual printings and sets of the French translations are contained in appendixes to Margaret M. Gibb's *Le Roman de Bas-de-Cuir: Étude sur Fenimore Cooper et Son Influence en France* (Paris, 1927) and Marcel Clavel's *Fenimore Cooper: Sa Vie et Son Oeuvre: La Jeunesse, 1789–1826* (Aix-en-Provence, 1938). The most extensive list of Cooper editions published in France in French and English during the nineteenth century appears in *Catalogue Général des Livres Imprimés de la Bibliothèque Nationale* (Paris, 1897). Preston A. Barba, finding no other nineteenth-century novelist so widely circulated in Germany in translation, supplies a partial calendar of German translations to 1911 (*Indiana University Studies*, 2, 1914). After the 1820s, German translations of Cooper are reported in the cumulative volumes of Christian Gottlob Ranser's *Vollständiges Bücher-Lexikon* and its successors. John DeLancey Ferguson, declaring Cooper to have been the most frequently translated American writer in Spain, gives a preliminary bibliography of Spanish translations in *American Literature in Spain* (New York, 1916). In his initial investigation of Italian translations, James Woodress discovers 148 editions of Cooper published in Italy between 1828 and 1964, approximately half of which were published after World War II (*Studi Americani*, 1965). Curiously, Valentina A. Libman's *Russian Studies of American Literature* (Chapel Hill, N.C., 1968), translated by R. V. Allen and edited by Clarence Gohdes, refers to few early translations, though Cooper was widely read in Russia in the nineteenth century in French, translated there into Hebrew, and certainly into Russian. Joseph Sabin's *Dictionary of Books Relating to America*, 4 (New York, 1870) lists tantalizing examples of translations of Cooper; but there has never been a comprehensive inventory of translations, though Cooper's books have been translated into Dutch, Danish, Norwegian, Swedish, Polish, Finnish, Hungarian, Greek, Czech, Persian, and other languages. Indeed, the incomplete evidence suggests that no nineteenth-century American writer, not even Whitman, has been so widely translated.

Robert E. Spiller's selective, annotated list of books and articles about Cooper in the AWS *James Fenimore Cooper: Representative Selections* (New York, 1936; reissued 1977) supersedes all earlier compilations. Good selective bibliographies for later scholarship and criticism are supplied in the *Bibliography* of *LHUS* (1948), its *Supplements*, and in studies of Cooper by Marcel Clavel, Dorothy Waples, James Grossman, Donald A. Ringe, Warren S. Walker, Thomas Philbrick, Kay Seymour House, and others. Various specialized bibliographies are more exhaustive: Lewis Leary, *Articles on American Literature 1900–1950* (1954), *1950–1967* (1970), *1968–1975* (1979); James Woodress, *Dissertations in American Literature 1891–1966* (1968); Thomas F. Marshall, *An Analytical Index to American Literature* (1954); the yearly bibliographies in *Annual Bibliography of English Language and Literature*, *AL* and *PMLA*; and, since 1963, *American Literary Scholarship: An Annual.*

Warren S. Walker's *Plots and Characters in the Fiction of James Fenimore Cooper* (Hamden, Conn., 1978) is the standard reference work on its subject, accurate and extremely useful.

EDITIONS

Reprints and reissues of Cooper texts — individual and collected — are innumerable; but until recently no work by Cooper had been edited according to exacting modern critical standards. No collected edition complete for the fiction and nonfiction exists. Recognizing the need for reliable texts and encouraged by the MLA's Center for Editions of American Authors, by Professor Robert E. Spiller and other Cooper scholars, the Fenimore Cooper family generously authorized the present writer in the late 1960s to organize an edition of the *Writings of James Fenimore Cooper* to be sponsored by Clark University and the American Antiquarian Society and published by the State University of New York Press. Since even Cooper scholars did not know how many of his literary manuscripts were extant or where they were or how many contemporaneous editions of his books had been published in English or where they could be located, the preliminary stages of this effort included extensive searching and prolonged efforts to collect books and manuscript facsimiles.

By 1976, when the National Endowment for the Humanities provided timely assistance, an Editorial Board had been formed consisting of the writer, of James P. Elliott, Kay Seymour House, Thomas Philbrick, Donald Ringe, and Warren S. Walker, and an Advisory Committee with Robert E. Spiller as Chairman, C. Waller Barrett, and representatives of the Cooper Family, Clark University, the American Antiquarian Society, and the State University of New York Press. By 1976 also, the Editor-in-Chief and the Textual Editor had prepared in preliminary draft the editorial manual, *The Cooper Edition: Editorial Principles and Procedures* (Worcester: Clark University Press, 1977); and editors had already begun work on the five Leatherstocking Tales, the five European travel books, and the four Revolutionary romances. To date (July, 1982), six volumes have been published (*The Pioneers; The Pathfinder; Gleanings in Europe: Switzerland; Gleanings in Europe: Italy; Gleanings in Europe: England;* and *Wyandotté*).[1] The remaining volumes in these series have been delivered to the publisher or, with the exception of *The Spy*, are almost ready for delivery. *Notions of the Americans*, several sea novels, and *Satanstoe* are assigned or in progress. All these editions, conforming to the requirements of the Center for Editions of American Authors or the Center for Scholarly Editions of the Modern Language Association, are critical, eclectic, unmodernized texts.

Unless and until authoritative editions are available, readers must continue to rely on texts of varying and uncertain quality. Though modern editors have shown that Cooper was far more demanding in his habits of composition, revision, and supervision of printers than critics have hitherto supposed, they have also found that his script was difficult for compositors to decipher, that he did not read proof against his manuscripts, and that his procedures in preparing and transmitting manuscripts and correcting copy were improvised and subject to chance. These circumstances have impaired the accuracy of his texts in unpredicted and unpredictable ways. Two incomplete collections of the fiction published before his death in 1851 are important for his authorial corrections: works revised between 1831 and 1833 for Richard Bentley's "Standard Novels," and eleven of the twelve volumes of the Author's Revised Edition (*The Ways of the Hour* was not revised) issued by George P. Putnam (1849–1851). Yet neither series conforms to Cooper's intentions in all respects. Most texts widely available today derive directly or indirectly from W. A. Townsend's Darley-illustrated edition which descended from the Putnam and other early American editions. Among later sets, the Household Edition, published by Houghton, Mifflin and Company (also by Hurd and Houghton), 1876, 1881–1884, in thirty-two volumes is useful mainly for introductions by Susan Fenimore Cooper to fifteen of the volumes. For several decades the Mohawk Edition, published by G. P. Putnam's Sons, 1895–1896, was the most reliable and accessible edition. Sad to say, the collected edition most readily available today is the old double-columned P. F. Collier set, 1891–1893, reissued some years ago with the usual thirty-

---

1. For reviews, see *Choice*, Jan. 1981; *AL*, May 1981; *NCF*, Sep. 1981; *EAL*, Fall 1981; *WAL*, Feb. 1982; *NYH*, July 1982.

two titles of the fiction compressed into ten volumes, with texts appallingly corrupt.

The Leatherstocking Tales, Cooper's most popular books now as always, are perennially reissued by such paperback publishers as the New American Library, Washington Square Press, Airmont, and Bantam, and in such familiar textbook series as Rinehart, Riverside, and Modern Library. These publications—all modernized reprintings of old, more or less corrupt texts—are far less authoritative than the introductions or afterwords by such respected critics and scholars as Robert E. Spiller, Allan Nevins, John William Ward, Leon Howard, William Charvat, and Norman Holmes Pearson might lead the reader to suspect.

While the Leatherstocking Tales have been in print in one or another edition since their first appearance, Cooper's other fiction has not been so favored. It may therefore be worth noting here as indicative of a renascence of interest in Cooper that all or almost all, even of his lesser known novels, are available today, many reissued by reprint houses in their original formats at extremely high prices. Among the few modern editions whose texts have been prepared with special (if not definitive) care and supplied with substantial introductions should be mentioned *The Crater*, edited by Thomas Philbrick (John Harvard Library, 1962), *The Spy*, edited by James H. Pickering (College and University Press, 1976), and *The Bravo*, edited by Donald A. Ringe (College and University Press, 1963). To facilitate their use as college or university texts, each of the volumes in the State University of New York series is available in paperback as well as cloth covers.

Much of Cooper's nonfiction has also been reissued in the last thirty years. An entirely new entry in the Cooper canon, *Early Critical Essays (1822) by James Fenimore Cooper*, consisting of book reviews written for *The Literary and Scientific Repository, and Critical Review*, was published in facsimile by Scholars' Facsimiles & Reprints in 1956 (reissued 1977) with an introduction and headnotes by J. F. Beard. *Notions of the Americans* (1828), introduced by R. E. Spiller, was reissued in a facsimile of the first American edition by the Ungar Publishing Company in 1963. A *Letter to His Countrymen* (1834) was reprinted in *Jahrbuch für Amerikastudien* (1960). *Gleanings in Europe: France* (1837) and *England* (1837) were reissued (1970) by the Kraus Reprint Company in texts edited by R. E. Spiller in 1928 and 1930; and *The American Democrat* (1838), reprinted with an introduction by H. L. Mencken in 1931, was reissued by Vintage in 1956 (with a supplementary introductory note by R. E. Spiller). The *Democrat* was also reissued by the Liberty Press (1981) and by Pelican (Baltimore, 1969), edited and introduced by George Dekker and Larry Johnston. *The Chronicles of Cooperstown* (1838) is included in histories of Cooperstown, New York, reissused at intervals by publishers of the *Freeman's Journal*. Facsimiles of the French first (in English) of the *History of the Navy of the United States* (1839) and of the American first of *Lives of Distinguished American Naval Officers* (1846) were published in 1969 by the reprint houses of Gregg and Garrett respectively. *New York* (1864), part of the introduction to Cooper's uncompleted *Towns of Manhattan* reprinted as a separate in 1930 by William Farquhar Payson and introduced by Dixon Ryan Fox, is supplemented by J. F. Beard, "The First History of Greater New York: Unknown Portions of Fenimore Cooper's Last Work" (*New-York Historical Society Quarterly*, Apr. 1953). R. E. Spiller's *James Fenimore Cooper: Representative Selections* (1936; reissued 1977) remains a useful anthology of Cooper's nonfictional prose.[2]

Temporarily helpful as they have been and are, these editions cannot be considered satisfactory substitutes for a comprehensive, critical, unmodernized edition of Cooper's fictional and nonfictional writings. That work, necessarily slow and complicated, is proceeding satisfactorily in many localities with the generous cooperation of numerous scholars and institutions under the joint sponsorship of Clark University and the American Antiquarian Society in Worcester, Massachusetts, funded (in part) by the Program for Editions of the National Endowment for the Humanities.

LETTERS AND MANUSCRIPTS

With the generous cooperation of the Fenimore Cooper family, librarians, collectors, scholars, institutions, and foundations, one part of the larger effort, *The Letters and Journals of James Fenimore Cooper*, has been edited by J. F. Beard and published by the Belknap Press of Harvard University Press.[3] This edition provides full, annotated texts of all letters

2. Other miscellaneous writings by Cooper introduced by Spiller but not recently reissued are: an article on slavery in the United States written for the *Revue Encyclopédique* (Apr. 1827) and originally published in French, but first printed from the English manuscript in *AHR* (Apr. 1930); *Letter to Gen. Lafayette . . . and Related Correspondence on the Finance Controversy* (1831–1832), published (New York, 1931) for the Facsimile Text Society; and *The Lake Gun*, an allegorical short story published in *The New York Parthenon* in 1850, issued as a separate (New York, 1932) by William Farquhar Payson. *The Home Book of the Picturesque* (1852), containing Cooper's essay "American and European Scenery Compared," has been published in facsimile with an introduction by Motley F. Deakin (Gainesville, Fla., 1967). J. A. Kouwenhoven (*Col*, Autumn 1938) has located a scene from Cooper's lost play *Upside Down* in W. E. Burton's *The Cyclopaedia of Wit and Humor* (New York, 1858).

3. Reviewed, among others, by Perry Miller (*NYHTBR*, 10 April 1960), Kenneth Lynn (*The Reporter*, 23 June 1960), Oscar Cargill (*SatR*, 16 April 1960), R. E. Spiller (*NYTBR*,

and journals known and available to the editor when the work was in preparation. The texts are arranged in convenient chronological units, and each unit is preceded by a brief introduction. Volume Six contains the index. Texts of additional letters are being collected by the editor as they become available for future publication. *Correspondence of James Fenimore-Cooper* (New Haven, Conn., 1922; reissued, 1971), edited by Cooper's grandson James Fenimore Cooper, contains letters to Cooper not reprinted in *Letters and Journals* and also "Small Family Memoirs," an account of her childhood by Susan Fenimore Cooper, daughter of the novelist. Lafayette's letters to Cooper, so far as they were then available, were edited by Stuart W. Jackson (*YULG*, Apr. 1934). Other important or interesting letters to Cooper, often summarized or quoted in *Letters and Journals*, have been or are being published with collected letters of his correspondents.

As Cooper's literary executor, J. F. Beard has been responsible since 1948 for collecting and assembling facsimiles of letters, documents, and literary manuscripts whose holographs have become widely scattered in the United States and abroad since the novelist's death in 1851. The four largest collections are papers owned by the Fenimore Cooper family; the Cooper Collection of the Beinecke Rare Book and Manuscript Library, Yale University; the Clifton Waller Barrett Library of American Literature, University of Virginia; and the Berg Collection of the New York Public Library. The list most nearly complete for locations of Cooper's letters (some letters have new owners and new locations are known) is provided in *Letters and Journals*, 6. Cooper's literary manuscripts, like his letters, are widely scattered. Some, indeed, were scissored to pieces for nineteenth-century autograph collectors. Many have yet to be located, and the writer is grateful to all who assist in the search.

BIOGRAPHY

The earliest significant biographical treatment of Cooper is William Cullen Bryant's "Discourse on the Life, Genius, and Writings of J. Fenimore Cooper." Brief as it is, this encomium by a friend and literary confidant, delivered at the Public Memorial Meeting at Metropolitan Hall, New York City, on 25 February 1852 and printed with other tributes in

---

15 May 1960), Lewis Leary (*VQR*, Autumn 1960; Summer 1965; Summer 1968), Willard Thorp (*NYH*, Oct. 1960; *NYHTBR*, 24 January 1965), Marcel Clavel (*EA*, Oct. 1963), James H. Pickering (*NCF*, Dec. 1968, *NYH*, Oct. 1970), and Donald A. Ringe (*Papers on Language & Literature*, Fall 1970).

G. P. Putnam's *Memorial of James Fenimore Cooper* (New York, 1852), remained for thirty years the closest approach to formal biography. Believing that living celebrities should eschew biographies of themselves, Cooper supplied the scantiest biographical data for brief essays by Samuel Carter Hall and Rufus Wilmot Griswold (see *Letters and Journals*, 2, 58–60; 4, 340–47, 459–62) and, shortly before his death, enjoined his family emphatically not to authorize a biography.

Recognizing Cooper's prohibition as a form of literary hari-kari, some members of his family wished to disregard it. A few months after his death, his publisher son-in-law Henry F. Phinney proposed to reissue *The American Democrat* with a biographical sketch of the author. Mrs. Cooper objected to the sketch as violating "my Husband's earnest charge, against any authorized biography" and suggested instead the inclusion of Cooper's replies to invitations from literary societies and printers' organizations. In 1854, after their mother's death, Cooper's daughters, acting apparently with the novelist's closest friend, Commodore William Branford Shubrick, made tentative arrangements with Dr. James Wynne for "a memoir of about 500 octavo pages, giving the chief incidents of [Cooper's] life, illustrated by his own journals . . . interspersed with views of his works." This project failed also, seemingly because Paul, the novelist's only son, shared his mother's stricter attitude. Cooper's daughter Susan, an author who understood the deleterious effect of the ban on accurate information, was left to sustain her father's literary reputation as well as she could through fugitive publications. *Pages and Pictures* (1861), her selection of passages and illustrations from his fiction with her brief introduction, was conceived as "a substitute for a Life of him." She later revised and extended these introductions for the Household Edition of Cooper's *Works* (1876–1884), published several autobiographical documents from Cooper's papers in *Putnam's Magazine* (1868–1869), and wrote two articles reminiscent of her childhood for the *Atlantic Monthly* (1887). Her "Small Family Memories," begun in 1883 at the instance of her nephew, Cooper's grandson and namesake, and published in his *Correspondence of James Fenimore-Cooper,* is an informal record of her life to 1828. Susan Fenimore Cooper's accounts of her father and her family remain invaluable biographical sources, though she wrote from memory and must be constantly checked and supplemented.

When Yale's great Chaucer scholar Thomas R. Lounsbury agreed to write the American Men of Letters *Cooper* (New York, 1882; reissued, 1968), the family attitude had not relaxed. Some twenty years later, Lounsbury stated in a letter to DeWitt Miller (owned by the writer and dated New Haven, 9 January 1902):

The writing of the life of Cooper was . . . a sort of *tour de force*. I had little knowledge of him when I set about it, had no special interest in his writings, & had read but few of them. Warner [Charles Dudley Warner, editor of the series] stood over me with a club & said I must take the man's life; & so, like a good or a bad boy, I did.

Lounsbury's assassination of Cooper the man, unlike Mark Twain's assassination of Cooper the artist a bit later, was unintentional. Cut off from most documentary material, Lounsbury rummaged wherever he could for information, in a few files of letters preserved by Cooper's friends, but especially in newspapers and other ephemeral printed sources, many of them hostile to Cooper. His book was impressive for its wit, industry, and style; but no biography written under these circumstances could be satisfactory. Susan Cooper, always an unwilling agent in enforcing her father's restriction, complained to the publisher Houghton Mifflin in a letter quoted by James Grant Wilson in *Bryant, and His Friends* (New York, 1886):

Mr. Lounsbury's book has been a disappointment. While he has done justice to the high moral tone of the novelist, the sketch of his social character is absurdly distorted. He represents Cooper as a cold, gloomy cynic; in fact, he was generally considered a very agreeable companion, full of animated conversation. His social feelings were very strong. He was remarkably fond of children, and very indulgent to young people, entering with zest into their pleasures. Had Mr. Lounsbury known Cooper personally, he would have written a very different book. Some of his comments are absurdly erroneous, as for instance where he says Cooper was a "Puritan of the Puritans"; for never was there a nature more opposed to the narrow prejudices of Puritanism. And what could be more absurd than to say that he had a lingering weakness for poor George the Third!

Years later, reliving his chagrin when Houghton Mifflin showed him Miss Cooper's letter, the exasperated biographer wrote, in the letter to DeWitt Miller previously quoted:

Susan was a nice old lady, but not gifted with much penetration, which however had its compensation in a peculiar capacity to misunderstand. I represented Cooper as being by *nature* a Puritan of the Puritans: dear Susan thought I referred to his *beliefs*, not being aware that Puritans existed in England centuries before Puritanism, or special Puritanic views which we associate with the name. One has, however, to content himself with supplying knowledge: he can not supply comprehension.

In the absence of more satisfactory sources, subsequent Cooper scholars have accepted Lounsbury's scholarly distortions and Susan Cooper's unscholarly reminiscences, many of them shadowy memories from her childhood, as more authoritative than they are. Miss Cooper, despite

Lounsbury, was an intelligent woman; and she understood her father better than his biographer, though she did not write about him as a scholar might. Lounsbury, though he lacked the intimate knowledge to portray Cooper as a complex human being, had sufficient scholarly aplomb to compose a "model biography," which, according to the *LHUS* in 1948, "is not yet superseded."

Actually, the task of correction was begun in the brief, admirably balanced Beacon Biography *James Fenimore Cooper* (Boston, 1900), by W. B. Shubrick Clymer, who inherited holographs of Cooper's letters to Clymer's grandfather, Admiral Shubrick. Quoting generously from these letters to demonstrate Cooper's personal warmth and social and political acuteness, Clymer attributed much of the novelist's acerbity to his "Horatian hatred of the mediocrity which is a foe to excellence." Clymer's contribution was augmented by Mary E. Phillips, whose *James Fenimore Cooper* (New York, 1913) was designed as a "simply told *personal life*," profusely illustrated by pictures "of men, women, places and things" figuring in the story of the man. In her search for fresh biographical materials, Miss Phillips was greatly assisted by Cooper's grandnephew George Pomeroy Keese, who had known the novelist well during the last eighteen years of his life, had collected assiduously, and had published his own reminiscences (*Harper's Weekly*, Supplement, 29 July 1871). Though Clymer and Phillips owed much to Lounsbury (and were perhaps less exacting in details than he), they began at last to demonstrate, despite Lounsbury's forbidding portrait, that the author of the Leatherstocking Tales was an interesting, complicated, and, in many respects, delightful man.

Biographical study of Cooper entered a new phase with the publication of the *Correspondence of James Fenimore-Cooper*, edited by Cooper's grandson. Aware of the need for a fuller understanding of his grandfather, the editor selected from his collection of family papers letters he thought would contribute most to an understanding of Cooper and his times. However, he warned in his introduction, he considered *all* the sources then available to be inadequate for the purpose of satisfactory biography; and he expressed Victorian reservations about publishing details of a private life. His *Correspondence* contained letters to and from Cooper in about equal proportions, with many passages silently expunged. Without purporting to be comprehensive or cohesive, it afforded unsuspected glimpses of a fascinating social and intellectual life marked by extraordinary vigor, variety, and depth of involvement. One reviewer, Henry Seidel Canby, expressed amazement that "a great romancer, producing a shelf of books in his lifetime, of which a number attained the widest international reputation . . . did not take his work seriously except as a means of livelihood and reputation." Instead of cultivating aesthetic, critical, or stylistic refinements, Canby continued in *Definitions* (Second Series, New York, 1924), "the man's intellect turned always towards social criticism or politics."

The young Robert E. Spiller, whose publications were to have a decisive influence on Cooper scholarship and criticism, made the same discovery independently and unexpectedly at about the same time, while preparing a chapter on Cooper for his first book, *The American in England* (New York, 1926). Spiller recalls (*NYH*, Oct. 1954) that while examining Cooper's travel books in what he imagined would be a routine encounter he suddenly found in the novelist's "struggle to discover a meaningful relationship between literary expression and American life . . . the epitome of the birth-struggle of a national culture." This recognition of Cooper's unsuspected stature by Spiller, repeated soon after by Vernon L. Parrington, John F. Ross, and others, invested Cooper with a new and exciting importance as a Representative Man, a writer whose intellectual and emotional tensions tallied with peculiar sensitivity to the tensions of the evolving national culture. To study Cooper was to study American civilization at a crucial point in its development, to probe its contradictions, and to discern its past and future patterns. It is this emblematic, often enigmatic Cooper, responding profoundly and fearlessly to the challenges of his age, who attracted Spiller and his colleagues. The received image of Cooper today is, to a remarkable extent, an elaboration of the image they created.

Recovery of biographical detail was not, however, a primary consideration for scholars interested in Cooper's social and political ideas. John F. Ross referred to his *Social Criticism of Fenimore Cooper* (Berkeley, Calif., 1933) as a "study of American civilization as reflected in Cooper's work," and Parrington and Mencken relied on the biographical sources already available. Even Spiller presented his seminal study *Fenimore Cooper: Critic of His Times* (New York, 1931) as "a record of the evolution of a point of view" and "not biography in the ordinary sense." Nevertheless, Spiller displayed in this book, in his editions of *France* (New York, 1928; reissued, 1970), and *England* (New York, 1930; reissued, 1970), in his introduction to *James Fenimore Cooper: Representative Selections*, and in numerous other introductions and articles, a full appreciation of the uses of biographical and cultural detail; and he extended factual knowledge at every opportunity, especially in his careful retracing of Cooper's European travels. Spiller's major contribution in the 1930s was his bold, imaginative comprehension of the intricate gyrations of Cooper's mind as it grappled with the significant issues of his times. These issues, Spiller saw, could be most effectively defined in a biographical matrix. If this emphasis neglected Cooper the artist, except as Cooper employed his art as a vehicle for his ideas, it seemed a valid and necessary reversal of Lounsbury's portrait of Cooper the irritable malcontent who forsook his art to meddle stubbornly and irresponsibly in social and political preachment. Most important, Spiller's approach opened a new, serious, timely dimension for other scholars.

In the wake of Spiller's early books appeared Henry W. Boynton's *James Fenimore Cooper* (New York, 1931), a biography that professed to be "not a book of criticism, but a study of a man whose genius stands beyond challenge while his personality, singularly complex, baffling, and deserving of study has been almost unregarded." Boynton was in fact less concerned to penetrate baffling complexities than to explore human interest in his subject. Shown mainly in action, his Cooper is the bluff, impulsive, good-humored sailor, tenacious in friendship or hostility, uxorious, combative, vain, and tactless at times, but dedicated with peculiar fervor to his image of the United States, "the *patria*, the mystical entity for which men gladly die." The late Dorothy Waples credited Boynton with restoring Cooper "as a hearty, active, attractive man, inclined to argue, certainly, and loving to shine, but thoroughly kind, gay, and attractive." Boynton's breezy, amost garrulous style and his access, greater than that of earlier biographers, to manuscript sources, enabled him to give vivid surface impressions; but the man Boynton portrayed with so much relish is hardly the "man whose genius stands beyond challenge." The distance between the two, measured in intellect and imagination, is immense.

Two potentially important studies of Cooper's reputation have a semibiographical focus: Ethel R. Outland's *The "Effingham" Libels on Cooper* (Madison, Wis., 1929) and Dorothy Waples's *The Whig Myth of James Fenimore Cooper* (New Haven, Conn., 1938). Drawing mainly on contemporaneous newspapers and magazines, Miss Outland attempted to document Cooper's complicated quarrels with the press, including his libel suits against Andrew Barber, William Leete Stone, Park Benjamin, Thurlow Weed, James Watson Webb, and Horace Greeley. Though she reprinted useful materials, her sources were far less complete and more strongly biased than she realized, and her conclusion that Cooper's suits were influential in shaping New York State's libel laws has been contested by legal authorities. Miss Waples's more ambitious study sought to explain how America's most popular novelist, more through his virtues and circumstances than through his faults, became one of the most unpopular men of his time. Her thesis, that Cooper was an innocent victim of a cabal of Whig editors because he was more than a nominal party Democrat, proposed a drastic oversimplification. Cooper was undoubtedly victimized by the Whig press, but the nature of his involvement was far more complex than Miss Waples suggested. Her book is perhaps more valuable for the evidence she collected than for the restrictive logic of her argument.

Much the weightiest and most methodic biographical study is Marcel Clavel's *Fenimore Cooper: Sa Vie et Son Oeuvre, La Jeunesse, 1789–1826*, accompanied by *Fenimore Cooper and His Critics: American, British and French Criticisms of the Novelist's Early Work* (Aix-en-Provence, 1938). These works, which earned Clavel his *doctorat-ès-lettres* at the Sorbonne and a Montyon prize from the French Academy, deserve much more attention than they have received from American scholars. Their preparation, which Clavel has charmingly described in *À Propos du Centenaire de la Mort de Fenimore Cooper et du Congrès de Cooperstown de Septembre 1951: A French Tribute to James Fenimore Cooper* (Aix-en-Provence, 1956), required fifteen years of research in the United States, England, and France, and a personal devotion matched by few other Cooper scholars. While not definitive, even for the portion of Cooper's life treated, Clavel's work was encyclopedic in aim and scope and remarkably complete considering the sources available to him. His biographical volume contains long, appreciative, academic discussions of six of Cooper's early books, discussions that contravened the popular tendencies in the United States to belittle Cooper and his art. Though World War II interrupted Clavel's plan to complete his work on the same ample scale, he remained an unabashed champion, describing Cooper in 1951 as "still one of my most constant and congenial companions." His contributions to Cooper scholarship have been impressive, all the more because so few American scholars have considered Cooper worthy of such sustained attention.

In the second American Men of Letters *James Fenimore Cooper* (New York, 1949; Stanford, Calif., 1967), James Grossman, a practicing lawyer of much taste, wit, and discernment, retold Cooper's story with interpretive comments on his works. The richness of this book lies mainly in its happy blend of curiosity, enthusiasm, sympathy, restraint, and intuition. Though his research in primary sources was limited, Grossman's psychological insights are rewarding. He recognizes, for example, that Cooper's most emphatic public gestures often contradicted his real feelings. Grossman is not, as an experienced barrister, dismayed by Cooper's legal squabbles. His critical remarks are also perceptive, though his final estimate of Cooper's art is ambivalent. Cooper "was a loose, slovenly writer throughout his entire career," says Grossman of *The Spy*, "but on great occasions, especially in his early work, he kept quiet so well that we can only wonder idly how he learned such restraint, or whether—and this is perhaps the highest form of critical praise—he really knew what he was doing." If so, Grossman never tells. Perhaps it does not matter. His often brilliant seriatim remarks, betraying the strong hold of Cooper's fiction on a highly sophisticated mind, may reveal more than Grossman is willing to admit explicitly. Despite some condescension, his book remains possibly the best one-volume introduction to Cooper the man and his writings.

Grossman pointed to the crux of the modern biographical problem when he commented that "too much is known about [Cooper] to accept the literary personality at face value, too little to create a man independently of it." Largely, one suspects, because of this crucial dearth of biographical information, subsequent book-length studies of Cooper have employed biographical detail mainly as a convenient framework for critical discussion. The disappointing state of our information is not the fault of Cooper's biographers or of the authors of the several valuable biographical articles,[4] but the inevitable result of Cooper's ban on a biography. In the period immediately following his death, his friends were not interviewed, his letters were not collected, and information then readily available was not recorded. The loss is, of course, irreparable, but not total. Though the biographical materials were almost inconceivably scattered, much that was supposed irretrievably lost has, in fact, miraculously survived. The publication of Cooper's *Letters and Journals* was, it is hoped, merely the first phase of the necessarily slow, collaborative effort to increase the biographical store. The next phase, drawing upon a very much larger quantity of documentation, to which the editing of the writings has been contributory, should be the publication of the critical biography which the writer has had in progress for many years.

CRITICISM

In *Fenimore Cooper: The Critical Heritage* (London and Boston, 1973), George Dekker and John P. McWilliams provide, with an excellent introduction, a representative selection of nineteenth-century criticism of Cooper's writings, drawing upon a vast, uneven, only partly inventoried body of contemporaneous reviews and occasional commentary. Studies

4. Among the more useful biographical articles are studies of Cooper's Otsego inheritance by Lyman H. Butterfield (*NYH*, Oct. 1949; Oct. 1954), of his naval career by Louis H. Bolander (*United States Naval Institute Proceedings*, Apr. 1940), and of the Bread and Cheese Club by Nelson F. Adkins (*MLN*, Feb. 1932) and Albert H. Marckwardt (*AL*, Jan. 1935). See also three brief biographical sketches: Robert E. Spiller, *James Fenimore Cooper* (University of Minnesota Pamphlets on American Writers, No. 48, 1965), James Grossman, "The Development of the Novelist," *The Chief Glory of Every People*, ed. Matthew J. Bruccoli (Carbondale and Edwardsville, Ill., 1973); and Lewis Leary, "JFC's Lover's Quarrel with America," *Soundings: Some Early American Writers* (Athens, Ga., 1975).

of Cooper's early reception (see the following section on *Influence*) have dealt with portions of this material, but its full extent defies the energies of any individual scholar. Systematic efforts to locate, collect, and list it are in progress. Warren S. Walker's *Leatherstocking and the Critics* (Chicago, 1965) remains an extremely useful collection of criticism, parody, and burlesque of the Leatherstocking Tales; and Wayne Fields's *James Fenimore Cooper: A Collection of Critical Essays* (Englewood Cliffs, N.J., 1979) is a good, all-too-brief selection from twentieth-century criticism.

Secondary studies of Cooper and his writings (books, articles, and doctoral dissertations) have multiplied rapidly since the late 1960s. Bibliographers record, probably incompletely, some sixty-three doctoral dissertations between 1970 and 1980 in which Cooper figures alone or prominently, approximately 150 articles or chapters in books, and eleven books or monographs, not including general studies in which Cooper has an increasingly important role. In no previous decade has so much energy been focused on Cooper, perhaps not in the century and a quarter since his death. He wrote voluminously (the equivalent of forty-eight volumes in thirty years), and his interests intersect the entire range of American culture in the first half of the nineteenth century. Despite their variety, the published studies accommodate to familiar academic categories.

Source Studies

Since no catalog of Cooper's reading or library is or can be complete, and since personal information sufficiently detailed to confirm real-life sources is largely missing, source studies have usually depended on evidence in published works, a circumstance that has complicated research. Cooper was an omnivorous reader of fiction in his youth and nonfiction in his maturity, collecting and dispersing the equivalent of several private libraries; and he registered sensitively and retentively in his writings impressions of an extremely varied life.

In *James Fenimore Cooper: An Introduction and Interpretation* (New York, 1962) and in numerous articles (see especially *NYH*, Oct. 1954), Warren S. Walker has pioneered in showing how Cooper employed and transmuted in his fiction the most familiar elements of folk culture: traditional character types, legends of the supernatural, Negro lore, folkways, and dialects. He lists (*MF*, no. 3, 1953) several hundred proverbs from the fiction, describes Cooper's more colorful naming practices (*NYFQ*, Summer 1979), and argues persuasively that much of the popular appeal of Cooper's frontiersmen, sailors, Indians, Yankees, squatters, and Negroes rests on the authentic folk flavor of their manners, habits, beliefs, superstitions, and dialectal peculiarities. In "Cooper's Fictional Use of

the Oral Tradition" (*Papers, 1980 Cooper Conference*, Oneonta, N.Y.),
he has summarized and documented much of this scholarship, providing
a fresh study, "Cooper's Yorkers and Yankees in the Jeffersonian Garden,"
in the same collection.

Following Walker's precedent, Florence H. French (*NYFQ*, Mar. and
Sept. 1970) shows how Cooper adapted proverbs to his special dramatic
and ideological purposes in the "Anti-Rent" novels. Robert A. Fink (*NYFQ*,
June 1974) examines Harvey Birch in the tradition of the Yankee peddler,
and Barton L. St. Armand (*AL*, Nov. 1978) places him in the perspective
of the Wandering Jew, as a "domestication of an international Romantic
archetype." John M. Vlach (*NYFQ*, Dec. 1971), reviews the folk antecedents of the Leatherstocking, and James H. Pickering (*NYFQ*, Mar. 1966)
comments on Cooper's skillful use of the festival of Pinkster in *Satanstoe*.
Cooper's mastery of the folklore of the sea has been remarked in commentary on his nautical fiction, especially in Thomas Philbrick's *James
Fenimore Cooper and the Development of American Sea Fiction* (Cambridge, Mass., 1961) and John H. Clagett (*Southern Folklore Quarterly*,
Dec. 1966). W. H. Bonner (*MLN*, Jan. 1946) demonstrates how Cooper
drew variously on the legend of Captain Kidd in *The Red Rover, The
Water-Witch, The Deerslayer*, and *The Sea Lions*.

Even before Lewis Cass remarked (*NAR*, Apr. 1828) that Cooper's
Indians followed "the book of Mr. Heckewelder, instead of the book of
nature," the authenticity of Cooper's portrayal of Indian life had been
questioned; and commentary on this subject still accumulates. Such fastidious Indian historians as Paul A. W. Wallace (*American Philosophical
Society Proceedings*, no. 4, 1952; *NYH*, Oct. 1954) and Arthur C. Parker
(*NYH*, Oct. 1954) complain that Cooper was insufficiently expert as an
ethnologist to distinguish fact from bias in the Indian authorities he employed. More recently, William A. Starna (*Papers, 1979 Cooper Conference*, Oneonta, N.Y.) has shown that from the standpoint of modern anthropology Cooper's knowlededge of Indians was seriously deficient. Surely,
however, such arguments are beside the point. Cooper wrote as a novelist
and he wrote before the science of anthropology existed. All scholars who
have examined his printed sources, Gregory L. Paine (*SP*, Jan. 1926), J. A.
Russell (*Journal of American History*, First Quarter, 1929), John T. Frederick (*PMLA*, Dec. 1956), and James A. Sappenfield and E. N. Feltskog,
eds., *The Last of the Mohicans* (Albany, 1983), agree that he selected his
sources with care (even supplementing them with personal observation)
and followed them carefully. Indeed Edwin L. Stockton, Jr., in his intensive investigation of *The Influence of the Moravians upon the Leather-
Stocking Tales* (*Transactions of the Moravian Historical Society*, 1964)
shows that such celebrated exploits as those involving "moccasin lore,"

"bent Twigs," and "animal-skin masquerades" derive not from Cooper's supercharged fancy but from Heckewelder, who, Stockton also suggests, influenced the presentation of religious and social ideas in the Leatherstocking Tales. In short, while Cooper obtained much of his information on Indian life at second hand, he was as faithful to his sources as his knowledge and the exigencies of his craft allowed. He did not, like many of his critics, confuse the boundaries of historical and imaginative truth.

Much heated, inconclusive, and doubtfully useful speculation has arisen from the search for real-life prototypes of two Cooper characters: Harvey Birch and Natty Bumppo. Tremaine McDowell in "The Identity of Harvey Birch" (*AL*, May 1930) explores thoroughly and dismisses the often-advanced claims of Enoch Crosby (subject of H. L. Barnum's *The Spy Unmasked; or, Memoirs of Enoch Crosby, Alias Harvey Birch*, New York, 1828 (reissued with an introduction by James H. Pickering, Harrison, N.Y., 1975), and other proposed models for the hero of *The Spy*. James S. Diemer (*AL*, May 1954) nominates a new candidate, John Champe. Warren S. Walker's "The Prototype of Harvey Birch" (*NYH*, Oct. 1956) dismisses Champe and suggests that Harvey's exploits were based on the combined adventures of the "Culvers" (Abraham Woodhull and Robert Townsend), secret agents described in Morton Pennypacker's *General Washington's Spies on Long Island and in New York* (Brooklyn, N.Y., 1939). Dispute concerning the prototype of Natty Bumppo involves conflicting claims of Nathaniel and David Shipman, both hunters whom the youthful Cooper may have known. When Nathaniel's protagonists planned a monument at his grave (behind the Baptist Church in Hoosick Falls, New York, not on the prairie), descendants of David (buried at Fly Creek, near Cooperstown) threatened suit. Edith Beaumont summarizes this hundred-year-long, mock-epic contest, fought in the local New York State press, in *The Valley Sampler* (Bennington, Vt., 24 and 31 July 1969). Carl Suesser (*Westermanns Monatschefte*, May 1934) nominates a German prototype, Johann Adam Hartmann.

A more authentic genealogy of the Leatherstocking Tales, as Joel Porte suggests in *The Romance in America* (Middletown, Conn., 1969), would include Homer and Milton; for Cooper's writings are thoroughly indigenous to the western literary tradition. John J. McAleer (*NCF*, Dec. 1962), identifying only a few of Cooper's Biblical analogies as "tentative experiments in symbolism," explains them as efforts to expose "the practices of Calvinism as they had survived in nineteenth-century America." E. P. Vandiver (*Shakespeare Assoc. Bull.*, Apr. 1940; *PMLA*, Dec. 1954) maintains that in 1,089 lines drawn from 36 plays Cooper displays thorough assimilation of Shakespeare, even of the lesser plays, revealing Shakespeare's influence in imaginative suggestions and characterizations as well as in functional use of quotations. W. B. Gates, "Cooper's Indebtedness to Shakespeare" (*PMLA*, Sept. 1952), finds in one-third of Cooper's fiction incidents and plot elements apparently derived from Shakespeare and many significant adaptations of character. The subtlety of these echoes, Gates notes, shows that Shakespeare's influence operated on a subconscious as well as a conscious level. Similarly, as David B. Kesterson demonstrates (*South Central Bulletin*, Winter 1969), Milton's Satan was a formative influence on Magua in *The Last of the Mohicans* and Mahtoree in *The Prairie*. Analogous investigations would disclose heavy indebtedness to other earlier classic authors and also to such contemporaries as Wordsworth and Byron.

Commenting on Sir Walter Scott's assumed originality as a writer of romance, Cooper observed (*Knickerbocker Mag.*, Apr. 1838) that Jane Porter's *The Scottish Chiefs* (1810) was a work of Scott's "own country, class, and peculiar subject, differing from a Waverly [1814] merely in power." Cooper saw his pattern of romance, like Scott's, as a generic synthesis of earlier fictional idioms, including Scott's; and he was vexed, for other reasons as well, by his unflattering cognomen, "the American Scott." The most recent and perceptive treatments of this still-controversial subject are in Donald Davie's *The Heyday of Sir Walter Scott* (London, 1961) and George Dekker's *James Fenimore Cooper: The Novelist* (London, 1967; New York, 1968). Davie and Dekker both argue that one of the best approaches to an understanding of Cooper is through an understanding of Scott. "Sir Walter Scott and Fenimore Cooper," Chapter Three of Nicolaus Mills' *American and English Fiction in the Nineteenth Century* (Bloomington, 1973), contains an excellent application of this approach to a comparison of *Rob Roy* and *The Prairie*. Barrie Hayne, "Ossian, Scott and Cooper's Indians" (*JAmS*, July 1969), mediates the seemingly conflicting demonstration of Georg Fridén in *James Fenimore Cooper and Ossian*, Essays and Studies on American Language and Literature, 8 (Uppsala, 1949), that the rhetoric of Cooper's Indians derives from Byron and Ossian and the contention of John T. Frederick, "Cooper's Eloquent Indians" (*PMLA*, Dec. 1956), that it derives from transcriptions and translations of Indian speech by Heckewelder and other American authorities. Hayne explains the similarities of primitive elegiac speech in Ossian, Scott, Cooper, and American Indian sources by assuming that it expressed a contemporaneous concept of a decorous language for the melancholy contemplation of dying races.

Efforts to adduce close parallels between Cooper's fiction and that of other novelists have not been notably successful. Thus, H. H. Scudder (*SR*, Apr.–June 1928), seeking to show that *Precaution* was written in imitation of Jane Austen's *Pride and Prejudice*, and G. E. Hastings (*AL*,

Mar. 1940), that it was more probably Jane Austen's *Persuasion*, tell us more about Cooper's general indebtedness to the women novelists than they do about the specific inspiration for *Precaution*. The parallels between *The Headsman* and Balzac's *Jésus-Christ en Flandres*, described by Thomas R. Palfrey (*MP*, Feb. 1932), may or may not be accidental. Quite different is the case for Cooper's obvious and extended borrowings from *Gulliver's Travels* in *The Monikins*, fully investigated by Willi Müller in *The Monikins von J. F. Cooper, in ihrem Verhältnis zu Gulliver's Travels von J. Swift* (Rostock, Germany, 1900). As W. B. Gates remarks (*MLN*, June 1952) in considering Cooper's indebtedness to *Robinson Crusoe* in *The Crater*, Cooper deliberately invites comparison of his hero and Defoe's.

Following a regionalist approach, Joan D. Berbrich in *Three Voices from Paumanok* (Port Washington, N.Y., 1969) traces the influence of Long Island — its geography, people, history, folklore, and associations — on the writings of Cooper, Bryant, and Whitman.

Insofar as Cooper derived facts, details, and substantive suggestions for his fiction from printed sources, he usually preferred nonfiction, especially works of history, biography, travel, exploration, and social, economic, and political commentary. Students of these sources agree on the thoroughness of his assimilation. The borrowings present themselves, as James H. Pickering has accurately observed, as a conglomeration of bits and pieces. Since most such studies depend on direct or indirect disclosures by Cooper, who was characteristically coy on the subject, many of his printed sources may still be unidentified.

The more sensitive source studies demonstrate that Cooper used his materials freely as an artist, varying his method from book to book to obtain the total effect desired. Thus, as Thomas Philbrick indicates in "The Sources of Cooper's Knowledge of Fort William Henry" (*AL*, May 1964), Marcel Clavel in *Fenimore Cooper: Sa Vie et Son Oeuvre* and David P. French (*AL*, Mar. 1960) probably erred in ascribing to Cooper's treatment of historical events in *The Last of the Mohicans* the circumstantial care he lavished on them in *Lionel Lincoln* and *Mercedes of Castile*, works which were historical novels in a very special sense. E. S. Muszynska-Wallace's "The Sources of *The Prairie*" (*AL*, May 1949) and James P. Elliott in his forthcoming CSE edition of *The Prairie* (Albany, SUNY) suggest the subtle imaginative process by which details from Cooper's Indian sources were intermingled and fused in the scenes of the fiction. Emilio Goggio (*RR*, July–Sept. 1929) asks implicitly the question as to how, if at all, Cooper's use in good faith of possibly misleading historical sources in *The Bravo* complicates the critic's task.

Other studies that inform and enrich our knowledge of Cooper's sources are articles by James E. Tanner (*AL*, Mar. 1975) on *The Prairie;* by Horace H. Scudder (*PMLA*, Sept. 1947) on *Homeward Bound;* by Donald M. Goodfellow (*AL*, Nov. 1940) on *Mercedes of Castile;* by Richard Van-DerBeets (*AL*, Jan. 1971) and Roberta F. Weldon (*NYFQ*, Summer 1976) on *The Deerslayer;* by R. H. Ballinger (*AL*, Mar. 1948) on *The Two Admirals;* by Dorothy Dondore (*AL*, Mar. 1940) and James H. Pickering (*AL*, Jan. 1967) on *Satanstoe;* by James H. Pickering (*NYH*, Apr. 1968) on *Wyandotté;* by Horace H. Scudder, (*AL*, May 1947) and W. B. Gates (*AL*, May 1951) on *The Crater;* and by W. B. Gates (*PMLA*, Dec. 1950) on *The Sea Lions.*

Influence Studies

No detailed, comprehensive study of Cooper's influence exists, though his writings have had enormous impact, direct and indirect, on the patterns of American and world fiction, an impact including serious literature but extending to subliterary forms — dime novels, pulps, juveniles, and the most jejune formulae of media entertainment. Ironically, this degree of familiarity, which Cooper could never have intended or foreseen and which amounts almost to notoriety, has continued to usurp the attention of readers and impede his acceptance as a serious writer. "Even today," Ray Allen Billington tells us, "German blades salute the final bottle of the evening as '*Der letzte Mohikaner*.'" Disinterested, comprehensive studies establishing clearly the nature and extent of Cooper's influence at home and abroad are much needed. Willard Thorp's excellent brief paper "Cooper Beyond America" (*NYH*, Oct. 1954) gives a foretaste of their potential interest and value.

Curiously, since Cooper was a major shaper of American romance in the 1820s, 1830s, and 1840s, his influence even on his American contemporaries seems not to have been fully investigated, though Alexander Cowie in *The Rise of the American Novel* (New York, 1948) and Ernest E. Leisy in *The American Historical Novel* (Norman, Okla., 1950) point invitingly in this direction. Most such studies are severely limited in scope and purpose. C. Hugh Holman (*AL*, May 1951) differentiates carefully the influence of Scott and Cooper on the romances of William Gilmore Simms, suggesting that Cooper might have been a better model than Scott for Simms' Revolutionary romances; Edward P. Vandiver, Jr. (*MLN*, Apr. 1955) concludes that Simms' Porgy in *The Partisan* was based, in part, on Cooper's Lawton in *The Spy* and his Polwarth in *Lionel Lincoln;* Nathalia Wright (*AQ*, Fall 1952) traces a generic kinship between Cooper's Steadfast Dodge in *Homeward Bound* and Melville's Frank Goodman in *The Confidence Man;* Morton L. Ross (*AL*, Nov. 1965) identifies Captain Truck's "mania of introducing" in *Homeward Bound* with that of

Captain Boomer in *Moby-Dick;* Christine M. Bird (*The Nassau Review*, 3, 5: 1979) finds anticipations of *Redburn* in *Afloat and Ashore;* Kay S. House (*SA* 19–20, 1973–74) compares the executions in Cooper's *The Wing-and-Wing* and Melville's *Billy Budd* in a subtly woven argument to insinuate more than an accidental connection between Cooper's treatment of Horatio Nelson and Melville's treatment of Captain Vere; and E. C. Jacobs suggests (*Poe Studies*, 923, 1976) that Poe borrowed the Latin motto of Montresor's family from *The Last of the Mohicans*. Studies of Cooper's influence on later American writers include: Sacvan Bercovitch's investigation of the "intimate relationship between *The Pioneers* and *Tom Sawyer*" (*Mark Twain Journal*, Summer 1968); Ryōichi Okada's plausible argument (*AN&Q*, Jan. 1976) that the title of Crane's *The Red Badge of Courage* was suggested by the identical phrase in Cooper's *The Last of the Mohicans:* Gordon Mills's notation of similarities in the paradoxical values of the wilderness and civilization in Cooper and Jack London (*NCF*, Mar. 1959), and articles by David R. Mesher (*SSF* 12, 1975) and H. Harbour Winn III (*Notes on Contemporary Literature*, 5.11, 1975) on Malamud's "Last Mohican."

While more an accomplished essay in literary history than a study of influences, Thomas Philbrick's *James Fenimore Cooper and the Development of American Sea Fiction* (Cambridge, Mass., 1961) documents admirably Cooper's formative influence on American nautical fiction. Philbrick shows how Cooper's early sea tales established an "idealized conception of maritime life" for novelists like Joseph C. Hart and short story writers like William Leggett in the 1820s and 1830s and how subsequent efforts by Cooper and his followers to construct a "meaningful alternative to that conception" included experiments by Edgar Allan Poe, Richard H. Dana, Jr., Robert M. Bird, and Charles J. Peterson. The imitations of Cooper's sea tales by E. Z. C. Judson ("Ned Buntline") and others parallel the flood of early imitations of Cooper's frontier fiction. Jeanne-Marie Santraud's *La Mer et Le Roman Américain dans la Première Moitié du Dix-Neuvième Siècle* (Paris: Didier, 1972) focuses mainly on the maritime experience, knowledge, and fiction of Cooper, Dana, Poe, and Melville. Unfortunately, limits of scope do not permit Philbrick or Santraud to place Cooper's nautical romances in the context of those by Frederick Marryat, Eugène Sue, Joseph Conrad, and countless other writers who profited from his example.

More inviting, apparently, as a subject of investigation has been the influence of the Leatherstocking Tales on the development of the mass-entertainment industry. Henry Nash Smith's classic study *Virgin Land: The American West as Symbol and Myth* (Cambridge, Mass., 1950) traces the Leatherstocking type from John Filson's archetypal Daniel Boone leg-

end through its transfiguration in Cooper's imagination and on through
the successive phases of its deterioration and perversion at the hands of
professional dream merchants. Though he finds "the character of Leatherstocking . . . by far the most important symbol of the national experience
of adventure across the continent," Smith denies the Leatherstocking Tales
stature as "a major work of art" and fails to appreciate the ironic night-
mare that knowledge of the so-called "sons of Leatherstocking" would
have occasioned both to their imputed father and his creator. Taking
Cooper more seriously as artist, James K. Folsom in *The American Western Novel* (New Haven, Conn., 1966) generally supplements Smith, observing that "every major theme of the Leatherstocking Tales is picked
up by later writers about the West." Folsom maintains that, in addition
to evident formulae, these novels derive their elegiac tone and their concern with the nature of law and justice, especially their distinction between rights of use and ownership, from Cooper. Unavoidably, many
popular or semipopular articles, like Warren S. Walker's "Buckskin West:
Leatherstocking at High Noon" (*NYFQ*, June 1968), associate Cooper with
the symbols of mass culture. The possible danger of this kind of identification is illustrated in the distinguished social historian Henry Bamford
Parkes's "Metamorphoses of Leatherstocking" (*Modern Writing*, no. 3,
edited by William Phillips and Philip Rahv, New York, 1956), in which
Parkes makes Leatherstocking a convenient "expression of some deep compulsion of the American spirit" to reject law and civilization and to accept the notion that "organized society is somehow antagonistic to individual integrity." No greater misinterpretation of Cooper is possible. An
ingenious and instructive corrective to this approach is provided in "Natty
Bumppo and The Godfather" (*The Colorado Quarterly*, Autumn 1975)
by Wilson Carey McWilliams.

Curiosity about Cooper's British influence seems not to have progressed
beyond George Wherry's reminder (*N&Q*, 16 September 1911) that
Thackeray modeled Col. Newcome's death scene on Leatherstocking's.
Selective summaries of contemporaneous British reviews are provided in
William B. Cairns's *British Criticisms of American Writings, 1815–1833*
(Madison, Wis., 1922) and Marcel Clavel's *Fenimore Cooper and His
Critics: American, British and French Criticisms of the Novelist's Early
Work*. For William S. Ward's more nearly complete listing of British re-
views of the first six novels, see *AL*, March 1977.

Cooper's early influence in France has been much more actively investigated, beginning with George D. Morris's *Fenimore Cooper et Edgar
Poe: D'après la Critique Française du Dix-neuvième Siècle* (Paris, 1912),
which surveys French criticism of Cooper in such periodicals as *Le Globe*
and *La Revue Encyclopédique* and by such critics as Balzac, Sainte-Beuve,

Charles Romey, Louis de Laménie, Philarète Chasles, and George Sand. Georgette Bosset's *Fenimore Cooper et le Roman d'Aventure en France vers 1830* (Paris, 1928) concentrates on the high point of Cooper's popularity in France, between 1826 and 1830, and the period of his greatest influence on French fiction, between 1829 and 1836. Mlle Bosset finds much evidence of Cooper's influence on Balzac's first acknowledged work, *Le Dernier Chouan* (1829) or *Les Chouans*, and traces of intermittent influence on Balzac's fiction until his last, unfinished work *Les Paysans* (1844). She maintains that *The Pilot* (1824) and *The Red Rover* (1827) infected the French imagination with ideas of natural glory and inspired the great vogue of French maritime fiction by Eugène Sue, Edouard Corbière, Auguste Jal, Jules Lecomte, and others, beginning with Sue's *Kernock le Pirate* (1830).

Measuring influence more rigidly, Margaret Gibb in *Le Roman de Bas-de-Cuir: Étude sur Fenimore Cooper et Son Influence en France* (Paris, 1927) minimizes Cooper's effect on Balzac and depreciates the importance of his effect on Alexandre Dumas père, Gabriel Ferry, and Gustave Aimard, since these writers addressed themselves at least partly to adolescents. Other students of Cooper's impact on French literature, E. Preston Dargan ("Balzac and Cooper: *Les Chouans*," *MP*, Aug. 1915), James L. Shepherd III ("Balzac's Debt to Cooper's *Spy* in *Les Chouans*" (*FR*, Dec. 1954), Eric Partridge ("Fenimore Cooper's Influence on the French Romantics," *MLR*, Apr. 1925), Regis Messac ("Fenimore Cooper et Son Influence en France," *PMLA*, Dec. 1928), and Roger Asselineau, "The Impact of American Literature on French Writers," (*CLS*, 1971), take account of the possible indirection and intricacy of imaginative influences, especially on writers themselves strongly imaginative. This possibility is reinforced by Jacques G. A. Bereaud (*CLS*, Sept. 1971), whose examination of the career of A. J. B. Defauconpret, the chief French translator of Cooper and Scott, maintains that "the handling of translation . . . acted as a screen that modified the foreign influence, sometimes profoundly."

As the nineteenth-century American most often translated into German, Cooper rivaled Scott almost as equal in Germany and inspired numerous "German Fenimore Coopers." Ray Allen Billington's *Land of Savagery/Land of Promise: The European Image of the American Frontier in the Nineteenth Century* (New York, 1981) terms Cooper's European reception "Coopermania" and provides a graphic account of this phenomenon, especially in Germany. As early as 1826, *The Spy* apparently affected specific details (C. D. Brenner, *MLN*, Nov. 1915) in Wilhelm Hauff's *Lichtenstein*. A fascinated Goethe began reading Cooper methodically in 1826, borrowed from *The Pioneers* for the setting and characerization of his *Novelle* (1827) according to Spiridion Wukadinović's *Goethes "Novelle": Der Schauplatz, Coopersche Einflüsse* (Halle, 1909), and would doubtless have borrowed further had he completed his *Wilhelm Meisters Meisterjahre* and brought his hero to America. After Goethe, Karl Postl ("Charles Sealsfield"), the Moravian ex-monk and *émigré*, was the best-known German writer to fall early under Cooper's spell. Postl was not uncritical of his model (Karl J. R. Arndt, "The Cooper-Sealsfield Exchange of Criticism," *AL*, Mar. 1943), which he sought to "improve" upon rather than repudiate. By the mid-1850s, four other German *émigrés* with personal experience of America (Friedrich A. Strubberg, Baldwin Möllhausen, Friedrich W. C. Gerstäcker, and Otto Ruppius) were producing voluminously in fiction strongly reminiscent of Cooper. The debts of these writers to Cooper are well documented in various studies, individual and collective, published and unpublished, listed in Lawrence M. Price's *The Reception of United States Literature in Germany* (Chapel Hill, N.C., 1966), a work which usefully digests Cooper's impact on German literature. Harvey Hewett-Thayer's *American Literature as Viewed in Germany, 1818–1861* (Chapel Hill, N.C., 1958) and Morton Nirenberg's *The Reception of American Literature in German Periodicals, 1820–1850* (Heidelberg, 1970) review Cooper's early critical reception in Germany. By the 1860s, even before his influence had yielded to the Mayne Reids and the Karl Mays, Cooper's books were being regularly abridged and edited for juveniles. Anneliese Bodensohn argues eloquently and persuasively in her *Im Zeichen des Manitu: Coopers "Lederstrumpf" als Dichtung und Jugendlektüre* (Frankfurt am Main, 1963) that Cooper should be rescued from this plight. Karlheinz Rossbacher in *Lederstrumpf in Deutschland* (Munich, 1972) performs this task by attempting to reconstruct the literary situation (tastes, reading motivations, structural elements of text, conventions governing response, etc.) controlling the original reception of the novelist in Germany.

Although past and present interest in Cooper in the Soviet Union is not easy to assess, Maria Bobrova's appreciative *James Fenimore Cooper: An Essay on His Life and Creative Work* (Saratov, USSR, 1967) provides fascinating hints of Cooper's impact on the Russian and Soviet mind. Quoting the well-known critic V. Belinsky on Cooper ("Marvelous, mighty, great artist!"), Bobrova suggests that his influence in Russia much exceeded Sir Walter Scott's and that "Our Cooper" remains in the Soviet Union the most appealing of nineteenth-century American writers. Without approving "feudalistic" elements in his thinking, she praises his courage and merciless truth-telling and credits him with showing the role of the people in the creation of American society, with articulating the faults of bourgeois capitalism, and with opposing the racist and genocidal treatment of the Indian. Several Soviet scholars, including V. N. Sheinker of the Murmansk Teacher's Institute and D. M. Urnov of the Gorky Institute, have been actively pursuing Cooper studies; and it is to be hoped that they or other interested Soviet scholars will investigate Cooper's influence on Russian writers of the nineteenth century and publish their results. Professor Sheinker's publications include a study of the first three Leatherstocking Tales, a study of *The Pilot* and other sea tales, and a comparison of the romantic and realistic modes in American literature as illustrated by Cooper and Twain.

While foreign scholars have made distinguished contributions to Cooper scholarship,[5] they have not, except in France and Germany, chosen to investigate his reception and influence in their own countries. Indeed, most such studies — when they have been made at all — have usually been random investigations of Cooper's influence on particular writers. For example, Dorothy S. Vivian shows the Argentine novelist Domingo Faustino Sarmiento drawing on Leatherstocking for his hero of the pampa Facundo Quiroga (*Hispania*, Dec. 1965); Robert L. Johnson suggests that the Australian novelists Henry Lawson and Joseph Furpy owe something to Cooper (*Southern Review* [U. of Adelaide], no. 3, 1965); and Julian Krzyanowski rebuts earlier scholars who said Cooper's fiction did not visibly affect Adam Mickiewicz (*International Journal of Slavic Linguistics and Poetics*, 1961). Since Cooper is probably the first American writer of whom it may be fairly said that he achieved an important position in world literature, it seems not inappropriate to suggest that thorough and systematic surveys, however brief, of his impact abroad in translation, criticism, and influence would be worthy scholarly objectives.

Cooper and His Age

Following the example of Robert E. Spiller, an ever-increasing number of scholars have sought to define the reciprocal relationships between Cooper and his age. Since his thought and attitudes involve a multiplicity of unsorted ideas, assumptions, problems, and values, this effort has been necessarily complex. It has been further complicated, as Spiller notes in "Second Thoughts on Cooper as a Social Critic" (*NYH*, Oct. 1954), by Cooper's incorrigible experimentation with fiction as a medium for ideas and also, as James Grossman in "James Fenimore Cooper: An Uneasy American" (*YR*, Summer 1951), Robert H. Zoellner in "Fenimore

5. See, for example, Teut Riese's *Das Englische Erbe in der Amerikanischen Literatur: Studien zur Entstehungsgeschichte des Amerikanischen Selbstbewusstseins im Zeitalter Washingtons und Jeffersons*, Beiträge zur Englischen Philologie, no. 39 (Freiburg, 1958).

Cooper: Alienated American" (*AQ*, Spring 1961), and Eric J. Sundquist in "Incest and Imitation in Cooper's *Home as Found*" (*NCF* 32, 1977) attest, by the paradoxes and psychic depth of his commitment to his country's destiny. Despite apparent and sometimes real inconsistencies, closer scrutiny suggests that an essential coherence has been obscured by differences of presupposition and emphasis among his critics, as well as by inadequate information.

Cooper's socio-political ideas have elicited especially varied responses. In V. L. Parrington's *The Romantic Revolution in America* (New York, 1927), Cooper is a Platonic Jeffersonian, an anachronistic agrarian, defending a nonexistent republic in which self-restraint and disinterested intelligence can somehow be made to prevail. H. L. Mencken's introduction to *The American Democrat* (New York, 1931), Russell Kirk's *The Conservative Mind* (New York, 1953), and George J. Becker's "James Fenimore Cooper and American Democracy" (*CE*, Mar. 1956) portray Cooper as a superior mind resisting the threat to individuality from the ignorant and irresponsible. Arthur M. Schlesinger, Jr., in *The Age of Jackson* (Boston, 1945) and John C. McCloskey in "Cooper's Political Views in *The Crater*" (*MP*, Nov. 1955) interpret his development as retrogression from a Jeffersonian-Jacksonian stance to a conservatism little short of Whiggery. The ease with which his meanings have been unconsciously warped to fit pre-existing critical categories is illustrated by Schlesinger's unintentional misquotation from *New York* (p. 56): " . . . we do not believe any more in the superior innocence and virtue of a rural population than in that of the largest capitals" as "We do not believe any more in the superior innocence and virtue of a rural population" (*The Age of Jackson*, p. 380). In short, Cooper was not so much a Hamiltonian, Jeffersonian, or Jacksonian as a political independent whose philosophic position, however eclectic, should be considered on its own terms.

The underlying unity of Cooper's thought is recognized in several useful studies which point significantly to earlier, mainly eighteenth-century origins for Cooper's key ideas. Examining *Notions of the Americans* as a commentary on democracy, Morton J. Frisch (*Ethics*, Jan. 1961) finds its Enlightenment assumptions thoroughgoing. Contrasting *Notions* and the Effingham novels as representative of Cooper's thinking in the 1820s and 1830s, Marvin Meyers's *The Jacksonian Persuasion* (Stanford, Calif., 1957) shows Cooper less a proper Jacksonian than an advocate of that Tory phase of Jacksonism which mourned the "Great Descent" from the Doric or First American Republic. Comparing Cooper's economic suppositions in his European trilogy of the 1830s and in his Littlepage trilogy of the 1840s, Marius Bewley, in *The Eccentric Design* (New York, 1959), discovers not a diametrical contrast or reversal but a dialectical continuity which stresses different aspects of the problem of a ruling elite and provides repeated analogies to the writings of John Adams. In his detailed study of Cooper's various expressions of the interplay between the melioristic premise and the premise of "innate corruption," Frank M. Collins, "Cooper and the American Dream" (*PMLA*, Mar. 1966), reveals in still another dimension the pertinence of the eighteenth-century heritage. The conflict, Collins concludes, "did not so much end in an outright victory for either view as subside in a faltering synthesis."

Accepting Cooper's statement in 1834 that his intention was "to illustrate and enforce the peculiar principles of his own country by the agency of polite literature," John P. McWilliams, Jr., in *Political Justice in a Republic: James Fenimore Cooper's America* (Berkeley and Los Angeles, 1972), and in several articles (*AQ*, Fall 1970 and *TSLL*, Winter 1971), has examined the implications of these "principles," mainly legal and political, in representative works of fiction and nonfiction. To make the fiction available for the extrapolation of ideas, McWilliams defines "the Neutral Ground," Cooper's phrase for the setting of *The Spy*, as a *constant* applicable to the settings of each of the novels he discusses, arenas exhibiting "power struggles for possession of the American land." Thanks to McWilliams's native insight and ingenuity, this stratagem is not as reductive as it might appear in such statements as " . . . a Cooper tale is an uneasy melange of derring-do with abstract political and social commentary" (p. 6) or Cooper "was willing to let the literary quality of American literature wait upon its political instruction" (p. 2).

Among studies of Cooper prepared during the Bicentennial, Mike Ewart's "Cooper and the American Revolution: The Non-Fiction" (*JAmS* 11, 1977) is of particular interest. Ewart's method suggests the possibility of extremely exact definition of Cooper's ideological constructions and takes account of the imaginative freedom Cooper required to function as artist. Comparing the "remarkable diversity of justificatory attitudes to revolution in the nonfiction," Ewart elicits "the implicit theory of revolution that comprehends them," demonstrates the consistency with which Cooper maintained it, and indicates the inappropriateness of attempting to read these constructions directly into the fiction. There is a sharp difference, he posits, between "the controlling definitions of the Revolution in each mode. In the nonfiction the Revolution is most commonly a 'war of principle'; in the novels it is a 'civil war.'" In "Cooper and the Revolutionary Mythos" (*EAL*, Spring 1976), James F. Beard reviews the four explicitly Revolutionary novels in the context of themes recalled from early Federalist thought. H. Daniel Peck, in "A Repossession of America: The Revolution in Cooper's Trilogy of Nautical Romances" (*SIR*, Fall 1976) proposes that "Cooper's early nautical trilogy [*The Pilot, The Red Rover,* and *The Water-Witch*] represents an attempt to solve the problems that the Revolution posed for him," especially the introduction to colonial America of "dangerous forces of social disruption." Donald A. Ringe examines the Revolutionary novels of Cooper, Neal, Kennedy, and Simms in "The American Revolution in American Romance" (*AL*, Nov. 1977), pointing out local differences, but finding that these books reveal "the popular view of the American Revolution during the second quarter of the nineteenth century when it filled — as it no longer does — the imaginations of the American people."[6]

Cooper's comments on European society and politics aroused Robert E. Spiller's earliest interest in Cooper; and, in a long series of books, articles, and introductions, beginning with the chapter in *The American in England* and extending to his UMPAW *James Fenimore Cooper* (1965), Spiller early established himself as the leading authority on Cooper's intellectual response to Europe. His most important statements on the subject are in *Fenimore Cooper: Critic of His Times* (New York, 1931), in introductions to *France* and *England* from Cooper's *Gleanings in Europe* series, and articles on Cooper's involvement with Lafayette, especially in the Finance Controversy of 1831–32 (*AL*, Mar. 1931) and the struggle for Polish freedom in 1830–32 (*AL*, Mar. 1935).

In other articles on Cooper's European interests, Russell Kirk ("Cooper and the European Puzzle," *CE*, Jan. 1946) argues that in his three European romances "Cooper was holding up the failings of European systems as a warning to America that her free institutions, too, could perish"; and Anne C. Loveland ("Cooper and the American Mission," *AQ*, Summer 1969) considers the attacks on these books and on Cooper's European political involvements generally as the conservative or Whig response to the effort to export American political principles. Readers interested in Cooper's European observation and experience should also consult the five volumes of the *Gleanings in Europe* series, in publication by the State University of New York Press.

The most comprehensive study of American society in Cooper's fiction is Kay Seymour House's *Cooper's Americans* (Columbus, Ohio, 1965). Regarding the American settings as a kind of Yoknapatawpha County, with its heartland in New York State, Ms. House describes the inhabitants as defined either by the social characteristics of their group or class (women, aborigines, blacks, Dutch, New Englanders, gentry, sailors) or — for characters able to transcend these categories — by their responses to open experience. According to Ms. House, characters of the second type,

6. For studies of the failure of *Lionel Lincoln*, see Donald A. Ringe (*ESQ*, part 1, 1974) and Jeffrey Steinbrink (*EAL*, Winter 1976/1977).

including Leatherstocking and other heroes of romance, "identify the uniquely American opportunity" and explore the limits and possibilities of democratic life, while characters of the first type reveal "America's connections with aboriginal and European cultures." Historically, the first type is important because it established the first persuasive images in American fiction of such groups as Indians, frontiersmen, blacks, and sailors.

With her chapter "Women as Women" in *Cooper's Americans*, House and others began to question Lowell's long-accepted dictum that Cooper's "females" are "sappy as maples and flat as a prairie." Nina Baym ("The Women of Cooper's Leatherstocking Tales," *AQ*, Dec. 1971) and House in two further essays, the last with Genevieve Belfiglio (*Papers, 1978 Cooper Conference*, [Oneonta, N.Y.] and *American Novelists Revisited: Essays in Feminist Criticism*, ed. Fritz Fleischmann [Boston, 1982]) suggest that, even within some nineteenth-century attitudes Cooper could hardly have escaped, his portraits of women have remarkable interest and variety; that they are not, with some possibly intended exceptions, the pitiful, passive, powerless creatures they have often been considered. According to Ms. Baym (and Ms. House), women in Cooper have "a central social significance" and "an important place in his works even when they themselves seem like insignificant beings, or are very crudely drawn." Ms. House and Ms. Baym agree also that Cooper's "females" may be complex, may — like Cora in *The Last of the Mohicans* — be "highly charged," may combine "enough qualities to take on the semblance of a rich life." In fact, Ms. Baym credits Cooper with having invented in Ellen Wade in *The Prairie* "an entirely new, unprecedented kind of social being. She is the first heiress of all the ages." In "Cooper and the 'Cup and Saucer' Law" (*AQ*, Winter 1980), Barbara Ann Bardes and Suzanne Gosset point out that in *The Ways of the Hour* Cooper voiced fears of the possible excesses of the movement towards women's liberation, fears based on his personal observation.

Albert Keiser's *The Indian in American Literature* (New York, 1933) describes Cooper's intentions and accomplishments in presenting Indians in the thirteen tales in which they appear, finding the portraits "remarkably complete and faithful." Agreeing that Cooper tried to use his Indian materials responsibly, Roy Harvey Pearce in *Savagism and Civilization* (Baltimore, Md., 1965; first published in 1953 as *The Savages of America*) and "Civilization and Savagism: the World of the Leatherstocking Tales," in *English Institute Essays, 1949* (New York, 1950), sees Cooper's Indians shaped by "savagism," the concept that whatever the Indian's virtues in the wilderness, his inferiority and doom were irrevocably decided by his obstinate refusal to become civilized. However useful for intellectual history, this idea — which synthesized the conventions of "noble" and "ignoble" savages — is too abstract and reductive to account wholly for Cooper's intentions. Thus, the "doctrine of gifts," a corollary of "savagism," may explain difficulties in race-assimilation; but it also embodies, as Cooper employs it, a plea for ethnic self-respect and for warm human sympathies across ethnic barriers. Some Cooper Indians are — by design — more truly civilized than their white destroyers. James F. Beard's historical introduction to *The Last of the Mohicans* (Albany, N.Y., 1983) links this romance to Cooper's personal interest in Indians and their welfare, an attitude anticipating Helen Hunt Jackson's *A Century of Dishonor* by more than fifty years.

Lucy L. Hazard in *The Frontier in American Literature* (New York, 1927) and indeed all commentators on Cooper's frontiersmen remark that Leatherstocking mediates between savage and civilized worlds, while his other frontiersmen illustrate combinations of qualities drawn from both worlds. In "The Frontiersman in Popular Fiction, 1820–60," *The Frontier Re-examined*, edited by John F. McDermott (Urbana, Ill., 1967), Jules Zanger contrasts the popular images of Daniel Boone and Davy Crockett, showing Natty to be a mixture of the two, progressively dominated by characteristics of Boone, and such Cooper frontiersmen as Hurry Harry and Ishmael Bush to conform more nearly to the Crockett image. Stressing Natty's closeness to the Boone legend, Henry Nash Smith's *Virgin Land* finds Leatherstocking's greatest profundity as symbol in his expression of the tension between social order and individual freedom, a tension endemic to frontier conditions but one that Cooper could not resolve satisfactorily. In "Consciousness and Social Order: The Theme of Transcendence in the Leatherstocking Tales" *WAL*, Fall 1970), Smith returns to the subject and, invoking the insights of Edwin Fussell in *Frontier: American Literature and the American West* (Princeton, N.J., 1965) and Leslie Fiedler in *The Return of the Vanishing American* (New York, 1968), concludes that, despite some ambivalence in Cooper's attitudes, his commitment to the values of a "cultivated white elite" and an "hierarchic social order" quite overshadows the subversive wilderness values of the frontier. On the other hand, Fussell in *Frontier* and House in *Cooper's Americans* regard the frontier and its conflicts as a metaphorical field or microcosm in which Cooper achieved some of his happiest and most complex effects and see no necessarily irreconcilable conflicts between frontier and civilized values, at least as they are embodied in the Leatherstocking.[7]

Though the reviewer for the *North American* commented on the novelty

---

7. S. B. Liljegren's *The Canadian Border in the Novels of J. F. Cooper* (Uppsala, Sweden, 1968) summarizes the tales and portions of tales set on or near the Canadian border.

and verisimilitude of the black servant Caesar in discussing *The Spy* in 1822, the first detailed description of Cooper's gallery of sympathetically drawn blacks is evidently that by Ms. House. Characters like Neb in *Afloat and Ashore* and *Miles Wallingford* are probably far better guides to Cooper's understanding of black experience than statements like his 1827 article on Slavery for the *Revue Encyclopédique* (printed in its English original by Spiller, *AHR*, Apr. 1930), where he was cast by circumstance as apologist for an institution he deplored.

Tracing the evolution of his attitudes towards the South, Max L. Griffin (*SP*, Jan. 1951) shows that Cooper conceived of emancipation as a necessary but slow and complex process requiring education of blacks and compensation of owners. Opposed as he was to slavery on moral grounds, he understood (and feared) the bloody civil war that might be necessary to emancipate the slaves and preferred a gradual, humane manumission within an evolving social and political fabric. This cautionary attitude has sometimes, as in *Race and the American Romantics*, ed. by Vincent Freimarck and Bernard Rosenthal (New York, 1971), been interpreted as racist. Certainly Cooper was no advocate of violence by North or South; but he concluded early that if the issue had to be decided by force, the Union — and freedom — would be the victor.

"Cooper's was the first significant [American] literary mind," writes Edwin H. Cady in *The Gentleman in America* (Syracuse, N.Y., 1949), "stirred by the philosophy of gentility." Cady argues persuasively that Cooper's concept of the gentleman pervades his thought and fiction, informing even his treatment of Leatherstocking and Uncas. Stow Persons' *The Decline of American Gentility* (New York, 1973), an excellent supplement to Cady, glances usefully at Cooper's importance in the history of American gentility.

Yet critics of Cooper's gentry, who usually confine themselves to the Effinghams and Littlepages, have seldom been kind from the time of Thackeray to the present. Granville Hicks in "Landlord Cooper and the Anti-Renters" (*Antioch Review*, Spring 1945) laments that the novelist's anachronistic notions of landed gentry led him to betray his talents and "his generous hopes for his fellow-countrymen" by waging reactionary class warfare in the Littlepage trilogy. Donald A. Ringe, in "Cooper's Littlepage Novels: Change and Stability in American Society" (*AL*, Nov. 1960), points out that the Littlepage family undergoes progressive democratization from novel to novel and so may be regarded as advocates of an ordered change as opposed to the chaotic change threatened by the Newcome family. Telescoping author and fictitious narrator, Jesse Bier (*TSLL*, Winter 1968) complains that *Satanstoe* (and presumably the entire Littlepage series) exudes a noxious class consciousness that Cooper unconsciously parodies; and James W. Tuttleton (*BNYPL*, May 1966) suggests that Cooper indulged a strong private bias in creating his bigoted, greedy New Englanders as offsets to his New York gentry. David M. Ellis's "The Coopers and New York State Landholding Systems" (*NYH*, Oct. 1954) is a useful, comprehensive account of Cooper's involvement in the Anti-Rent War on the side of the landed aristocracy, and A. N. Kaul's chapter on Cooper in *The American Vision: Actual and Ideal Society in Nineteenth-Century Fiction* (New Haven, 1963) balances the Littlepage Trilogy and the Leatherstocking Tales effectively as "Cooper's response to the history and the myth of American civilization."

The reissue of *Home as Found* in 1961 as Capricorn Book with an excellent introduction by Lewis Leary has stimulated lively interest in this much-neglected work. Leary attributes its failure, despite its interest and significance as an early American *roman de société*, to Cooper's inability to order his materials to art. Jack Kligerman ("Style and Form in James Fenimore Cooper's *Homeward Bound* and *Home as Found*," *JNT*, Jan. 1974) locates the failure in Cooper's return to the abstract stylistic milieu of *Precaution* in which the "style categorizes and judges experience instead of portraying it realistically." Joy S. Kesson in "Templeton Revisited: Social Criticism in *The Pioneers* and *Home as Found*" (*SNNTS*, Spring 1977) points to the radical discontinuities between these two books as the key to Cooper's comment on the social dislocation of the 1830s, while Eric Sundquist in "Incest and Imitation in Cooper's *Home as Found*," (*NCF* 32, 1976), reprinted in Sundquist's own book *Home as Found* (Baltimore, 1977) explores continuities, explicating Cooper's work in terms of the author's assumed state of mind, "a repression that cannot be sustained."

As Howard Mumford Jones indicated in his introduction to *James Fenimore Cooper: A Re-Appraisal*, several papers read at the three-day Cooper centennial observance, sponsored by the New York State Historical Association in Cooperstown in September 1951 and published as a special issue of *New York History* (Oct. 1954), considered neglected aspects of Cooper's relationship to his age. James Grossman revealed how Cooper's struggle with the press in his no doubt ill-advised libel suits was motivated by his deep conviction of the importance of a responsible press. William Charvat explored the then relatively unknown terrain of Cooper's relations with his publishers in a paper reprinted in Charvat's *The Profession of Authorship in America, 1800–1870*, edited by Matthew J. Bruccoli (Columbus, Ohio, 1968). Walter Muir Whitehill brought his expertise as professional naval historian to bear on Cooper's *History of the Navy* (1839), the first thorough, systematic history of the United States Navy, and James F. Beard discussed Cooper's close personal and aesthetic associations with his artist contemporaries, emphasizing his affinity to Thomas Cole and painters of the Hudson River Valley School.

Four subsequent week-long summer conferences, sponsored by the State University of New York College at Oneonta and Cooperstown, New York, in 1978, 1979, 1980, and 1982, inspired by Acting President Carey Brush and coordinated by Professor George A. Test, have provided excellent opportunities for students, scholars and general readers to explore in words and physical space whatever aspects of the writer or his country interested them. Papers emanating from these meetings—on such miscellaneous topics as the geography of the Otsego country, its use in Cooper's fiction, his nautical writing, his treatment of history, his travel books, his aesthetics of space, his use of oral tradition, problems of editing Cooper, etc.—have been prepared for typescript publication by Professor Test and are available from the English Department, SUNY, at Oneonta. Among the speakers have been such students of Cooper as Robert E. Spiller, Leslie Fiedler, Donald A. Ringe, Kay S. House, Thomas Philbrick, H. Daniel Peck, Warren Walker, James P. Elliott, Constance Ayers Denne, and James H. Pickering.

Since the Cooper Conference of 1951, Cooper's affinities with the Hudson River School artists have been reexamined and restated several times from different points of view. Regarding Cooper and the painters as *moralistes*, H. M. Jones finds significant analogies both of technique and philosophic outlook (*TSE*, 1952, reprinted in *MagA*, Oct. 1952; *History and the Contemporary*, Madison, Wis., 1964; and *The Frontier in American Fiction*, Jerusalem, 1956). Donald A. Ringe (*AL*, Mar. 1958) shows that Cooper, like Thomas Cole, used patterned landscape series to convey themes beyond the scope of a single landscape, actually borrowing for *The Crater* the motif of the mountain peak in Cole's great cycle *The Course of Empire* (*AL*, Mar. 1958); Ringe also finds (*PMLA*, Sept. 1963) that in various works, but especially in *The Bravo*, Cooper, like the painters, employed chiaroscuro self-consciously as an expressive device. James T. Callow's *Kindred Spirits: Knickerbocker Writers and American Artists, 1807–1855* (Chapel Hill, N.C., 1967) is useful for biographical and cultural documentation.

Harry Hayden Clark's monograph-length "Fenimore Cooper and Science" (*Proceedings of the Wisconsin Academy of Sciences, Arts and Letters*, 1959, 1960) was definitive at the time it was prepared, and it remains an exhaustive, richly informative study—impervious to summary. Clark concluded that Cooper was enthusiastic towards science as a means of advancing utilitarian ends and as an agency fulfilling Providential purposes, but that he rejected the notion that science could eradicate evil or compensate for irrational impulses in man.

Clark, H. M. Jones, (*Belief and Disbelief in American Literature,* Chicago 1967), and Ringe (*Papers of the Michigan Academy of Science, Arts, and Letters,* 1959; *PMLA,* Dec. 1960) have stressed the importance of Cooper's Episcopalianism, especially in the fiction of his later years. Ringe discusses, for example, the epistemological implications of his religious attitudes for such novels as *Jack Tier, The Crater, The Oak Openings, The Sea Lions,* and *The Ways of the Hour.* In *The Darkened Sky: Nineteenth-Century American Novelists and Religion* (Notre Dame, 1969), John T. Frederick provides an admirably balanced account of Cooper's religious attitudes as they appear in his published writings; and Lakshmi Mani, in *The Apocalyptic Vision in Nineteenth-Century American Fiction: A Study of Cooper, Hawthorne, and Melville* (Washington, D.C., 1981), follows perceptively the Apocalyptic and Millenarian oscillations through the action of much of Cooper's fiction.

In *History and Utopia: A Study of the World View of James Fenimore Cooper* (Norwood, Pa., 1978), Allan M. Axelrad argues that Cooper was, first and last, "a thoroughly committed trinitarian," for whom the Enlightenment paradigm of progress is illogical and incorrect. The idea of progress, the cyclical idea of history, "and the view of the world implicit in each, are incompatible and contradictory," according to Mr. Axelrad. In an exceedingly suggestive chapter on Cooper in *Versions of the Past: The Historical Imagination in American Fiction* (New York, 1974) (a book to which Axelrad does not refer), Harry B. Henderson III admits the "unchanging and exclusive nature" of these two structures, but observes that they "seldom appear in their pristine form in a given narrative, because they are always transformed by the social and artistic vision of the author . . . to respond more fully to his sense of reality." In short, Henderson suggests, Cooper employed his historiographical insights in his fiction in the service of his art.

Cooper's ideas and impressions in and of his times continue to inspire articles on miscellaneous subjects by critics and scholars interested in the American past. For example, Thomas Bender (*NYH,* Apr. 1970) studies Cooper and the City, Jay S. Paul (*SNNTS* 5, 1973) and Irving Malin (*Mosaic* 4, 1971) discuss aspects of the American family, and John Gerlich (*Illinois Quarterly* 35, 1973) examines Cooper's elusive quest for the Kingdom of God in an increasingly secular America. Cooper's writings are, it would seem, so encyclopedic in scope that they lend themselves almost inexhaustibly to studies of early nineteenth-century American life. The danger, as Robert E. Spiller pointed out in "Second Thoughts on Cooper as a Social Critic" (*NYH,* Oct. 1954), has been the inevitable risk of distraction from the primary critical problem: "How, in what stages, and to what extent was this content converted to the purposes of art?"

Cooper as Artist

As Walter Sutton remarked in "Cooper as Found — 1949" (*UKCR*, Autumn 1949), at the nadir of Cooper's reputation as artist, the pattern of "sympathetic criticism . . . reveals a curious paradox." His preeminence as a writer of fiction was acknowledged, directly or indirectly, by all important American writers of his time and by most of his British and Continental peers, including Goethe, Balzac, Sand, and Trollope. With gentle disclaimer, he could repeat to his wife a story that Sir Walter Scott, "while at Naples, declared a person you love had more genius than any living writer." Conrad and Lawrence spoke eloquently of him to a later generation. Yet the first century and a quarter of Cooper criticism produced remarkably little in an idiom acceptable to mid-twentieth-century sophisticates to justify high claims for his art. Sutton recommended that readers, emulating Thoreau who flung out his three superfluous stones to avoid dusting them, "take fresh inventory and eliminate from our shelves books which only habit and traditional veneration have led us to regard as American imaginative literature of the first order."

Nineteenth-century criticism of Cooper, including representative and historically important reviews by William H. Gardiner (*NAR*, July 1826), Francis Bowen (*NAR*, Jan. 1828), Francis Parkman (*NAR*, Jan. 1852), Henry T. Tuckerman (*NAR*, Oct. 1859), and George S. Hillard (*AtM*, Jan. 1862), reveals more about his position in American literature than about his art. Even such writers of fiction as Balzac (*Revue Parisienne*, 25 July 1840), Simms (*Magnolia*, Sept. 1841), Poe (*Graham's Magazine*, Nov. 1843), Melville (*Literary World*, 28 April 1849; 16 March 1850), and Sand (*Autour de la Table*, Paris, 1875) tell the modern reader remarkably little about Cooper's artistry. This criticism is, at best, an impressionistic tapestry in which certain recurrent motifs emerge for comment: Cooper's unmistakable nationality in the selection of scenes, events, and characters; his similarity or dissimilarity to Scott; his powers of graphic observation and description; his "facility in inventing incidents and weaving them together in clear spirited narrative"; the probability or improbability of his plots; his uneven success in character delineation; his inequalities of style; and the appropriateness or inappropriateness of his modes of representation.

Properly noting that Cooper paid much attention to his theory of representation. Arvid Shulenberger in *Cooper's Theory of Fiction* (Lawrence, Kans., 1955) maintains that it was transformed over three decades from "a theory of realism arguing for literal truth of representation" to a theory "that the ideal rather than the literal truth should be presented," so that the fiction exhibits "a progress from realism to romance." This conclusion, based on emphases in the prefaces, is misleading. Cooper's early prefaces stressed "realistic" intentions because the fiction was closer to American realities than that to which readers were accustomed; his later prefaces insisted stoutly on his prerogatives as imaginative writer because literal-minded readers treated his fiction as autobiography or history. Actually, what Cooper sought more or less consistently was an effective fusion between the *real* (conceived as fidelity to human nature and to professional, social, and geographical peculiarities) and the *ideal* (conceived as aesthetic qualities deriving from the operation of the imaginative process). The major shift of emphasis in the fiction was, on balance, in the direction of realistic techniques.

Cooper never articulated his theory of romance fully or systematically, however; and when his vogue persisted into the 1880s and beyond, his forms now thoroughly debased by imitators, he became an inevitable target for attack by realists like Howells and Twain and, later, naturalists like Norris and Crane. Some dozen years after Lounsbury's book on Cooper, Twain took Lounsbury's incautious reference to the Leatherstocking Tales as "pure works of art" and other impressionistic nuggets as points of departure for his hilarious, but coldly calculated, "Fenimore Cooper's Literary Offenses" (*NAR*, July 1895). Cooper soon became, as Sydney J. Krause states in "Cooper's Literary Offenses: Mark Twain in Wonderland" (*NEQ*, Sept. 1965), "the realists' whipping boy, the visible symbol of defunct romanticism, and insofar as he falsified the life they would represent truly, he was its most vulnerable and appropriate symbol." The existence of at least two earlier versions of the Twain essay and the curtailment of the weaker parts of the third version (Bernard De Voto, "Fenimore Cooper's Further Literary Offenses," *NEQ*, Sept. 1946) suggest the care with which Twain proceeded. To reply at all was to risk the damaging admission that one took the essay seriously (see D. L. Maulsby, *Dial*, 16 February 1897); not to reply was to risk seeming to concur silently.

The Twain essay merely aggravated the dilemma of critics who attempted for the next half century to keep Cooper's reputation as artist alive. "On the one hand," as Walter Sutton declared, they "freely acknowledged that Cooper was a clumsy writer who never mastered the niceties of his craft, while on the other hand [they] asserted that he was a golden story teller, a true artist who somehow, through the exercise of a tremendous native energy, overcame his limitations and succeeded in creating the American epic." Even such discriminating critics as W. C. Brownell in *American Prose Masters* (New York, 1909), John Erskine in *Leading American Novelists* (New York, 1910), Carl Van Doren in *The American Novel* (New York, 1921), and Henry Seidel Canby in *Classic Americans* (New York, 1931) found it increasingly difficult during the heyday of realism to make a persuasive case for Cooper's artistry. Critics interested in Cooper primarily for his ideas and social criticism were not required to defend him as artist. The result, of which Marcel Clavel complained on his trip to the United States, was a virtual abandonment from the 1920s through the 1940s of even the pretense that Cooper was an artist. One distinguished professor is reported to have read the Twain essay to his classes with the admonition that it contained all his students needed to know of Cooper. Organizing the Cooper Centennial meetings in Cooperstown for 1951, the writer could find no reputable critic willing to speak on Cooper as artist. Sutton's proposal that Cooper's works be "flung out" seemed an honest recognition of accomplished fact.

Nevertheless, Conrad's disgusted comment on the Twain essay in a 1908 letter to Arthur Symons ("That dismal 'bajazzo' with his debased jargon . . . smirches whatever he touches.") is merely one indication that admirers of Cooper's art did not wholly abandon the field to Twain. D. H. Lawrence, in *Studies in Classic American Literature* (New York, 1923), attributes Cooper's peculiar power in the Leatherstocking Tales to his mythic evocation of the American past ("She starts old, old, wrinkled and writhing in an old skin") and future ("a gradual sloughing of the old skin, towards a new youth"). The spontaneity of Lawrence's enthusiasm is best shown in his original essays written for the *English Review* (Feb. and Mar. 1919) and reprinted in *The Symbolic Meaning*, edited by Armin Arnold (London, 1962). Proceeding quite differently — collating texts of *The Spy* — Tremaine McDowell (*SP*, July 1930) reveals in Cooper an unexpected capacity for stylistic revision; and Yvor Winters (*Maule's Curse*, Norfolk, Conn., 1938), discovering variety and elements of distinction in Cooper's style, remarks that Chapter Seven of *The Deerslayer* "is probably as great an achievement of its length as one will find in American fiction outside of Melville." Moving beyond Winters, who sees Cooper as great only in fragments, Marius Bewley in "Revaluations: James Fenimore Cooper" (*Scrutiny*, Winter 1952–53; reprinted in *The Eccentric Design*) maintains in his provocative examination of *The Deerslayer* and other works that Cooper was a higher kind of storyteller than Scott, able to conceive action as a moral pattern "which becomes the form of the completed tale." Preferring to approach Cooper through Scott, Donald Davie writes warmly and at length of Cooper's art in *The Heyday of Sir Walter Scott* (London, 1961; reprinted, 1971). "However much I may differ from Mr. Winters and Mr. Bewley at specific points," he confesses, "I am impenitently of their opinion that Cooper is a very great writer indeed."

While Richard Chase exaggerated in asserting in *The American Novel and Its Tradition* (Garden City, N.Y., 1957) that interesting criticism of

Cooper "had to be in one way or another an elaboration or revision of Lawrence," the mythic approach provided a halfway station to Cooper as artist, where critics could explore his and their own cultural assumptions. Chase *does* elaborate on Lawrence. Henry Nash Smith, correlating Cooper's assumptions about the West with those from other sources, provides in *Virgin Land* an indispensable panoramic context for all nineteenth-century Western heroes. Roy Harvey Pearce, in "The Leatherstocking Tales Re-Examined" (*SAQ*, Oct. 1947), postulating that Cooper intended Leatherstocking as a tragic figure whose way of life has to be extinguished to permit the advance of civilized society, concludes that Cooper failed as an artist because he did not represent that society successfully. R. W. B. Lewis, in *The American Adam* (Chicago, 1955), characterizes Natty Bumppo as the "Adamic hero unambiguously treated — celebrated in his very Adamism," an Adamism evoked largely in spatial terms. According to David W. Noble in *The Eternal Adam and the New World Garden* (New York, 1968), this mythic construction must be qualified by the realization that Natty is not wholly exempted from time, society, and human weakness. Charles A. Brady in "James Fenimore Cooper: Myth-maker and Christian Romancer" (*American Classics Reconsidered*, edited by Harold C. Gardiner [New York, 1958]) points to elements of classical and Christian myth in Cooper, especially in the Leatherstocking Tales; and Leslie Fiedler, in *Love and Death in the American Novel* (New York, 1960) and "James Fenimore Cooper: The Problem of the Good Bad Writer" (*Papers, 1979 Cooper Conference*, Oneonta, N.Y.), finds in Cooper a congeries of mythic characters and relationships and ample confirmation of his theories of heterosexual-homosexual attitudes in American cultural history. Richard Slotkin, in *Regeneration through Violence: The Mythology of the American Frontier, 1600 – 1860* (Middletown, Conn., 1973), draws suggestively on a much larger stock of anthropological archetypes to explicate the "Leatherstocking myth," attributing to Cooper a mythopoeic awareness and power altogether extraordinary in his time. Though these studies suggest, in their variety, the rich mythopoeic texture of Cooper's fiction, they presuppose, as R. W. B. Lewis notes, "an astonishing lack of co-ordination between the classical ingredients of narrative: plot and character and thought and diction."

Meanwhile, critics interested in rehabilitating Cooper's reputation as artist and in seeing his work as an organic whole began tentatively to follow Marius Bewley and Donald Davie in the direction of formal analysis and close thematic scrutiny. Donald A. Ringe, in *James Fenimore Cooper* (New York, 1962), examines carefully Cooper's ideas, settings, and characters to show the novelist, at his best, "a serious artist who could generate an important moral theme from the skillful handling of his materials." Quite properly considering Cooper a *moraliste*, Ringe contributes exceedingly perceptive interpretations of individual books, including some usually neglected, and demonstrates, in addition, the underlying unity in Cooper's developing moral vision. George Dekker's *James Fenimore Cooper* is, as the author says, basically "a critical survey of Cooper's fiction," in which he argues that Cooper, though "not a novelist of the very first rank," has "real strengths . . . great and richly compensating." Approaching Cooper, like Donald Davie, through Scott and in the manner of Georg Lukács, Dekker is concerned with patterns of tension created by large, impersonal social, political, and economic forces within the novelist's world. His method is eclectic and his conclusions, some refreshingly irreverent, are usefully calculated in this transitional period of Cooper criticism to challenge readers to think for themselves. In *The New World of James Fenimore Cooper* (Chicago, 1982), Wayne Franklin attempts in a semi-biographical context "to reinvent the original" in four extended and several brief "readings" of the "border" romances designed to communicate the "imaginative energy" that invests them with "lasting significance." The result is enthusiastic and impressionistic, sometimes insecure in its facts, often open to debate, but interesting and suggestive.

In *The Pictorial Mode: Space and Time in the Art of Bryant, Irving and Cooper* (Lexington, Ky., 1971), Donald A. Ringe developed for the first time in an extended analysis analogies between techniques of three early American writers and certain graphic artists he and others had perceived as containing a "common core of meaning." An understanding of form and meaning in Cooper's fiction, Ringe demonstrated, depends at least in part on the reader's capacity to visualize scenes carefully crafted in the manner of painters of the Hudson River School, especially of Thomas Cole. Blake Nevius in *Cooper's Landscapes: An Essay on the Picturesque Vision* (Berkeley and Los Angeles, 1976) reinforced Ringe's study by examining Cooper's landscapes more explicitly in the context of the British and European aesthetic of the picturesque, especially of such British theorists as Gilpin, Knight, Repton, and Price. Nevius enlarged the focus by suggesting that Cooper's knowledge of the picturesque was deepened by his European experience and by discussing Cooper's interest in and literary use of landscape gardening. In historical introductions to Cooper's European travel books in the new Cooper Edition (R. E. Spiller and J. F. Beard to *Switzerland*, John Conron and Constance A. Denne to *Italy*, and Ernest Redekop and Maurice Geracht to *The Rhine*), editors discussed the implications of picturesque aesthetics for these particular books. Approaching Cooper's fiction with insights afforded by Gaston Bachelard's doctrine of "the primacy of the image," H. Daniel Peck in *A World by Itself: The Pastoral Moment in Cooper's Fiction* (New

Haven, Conn., 1977) achieved a remarkably satisfying and evocative treatment of Cooper's sensory rendition of space and spatial qualities. Spatial
structures equate to psychic structures in Bachelard's phenomenology;
and Peck, like Ringe, Nevius, and others, stressed the preeminently visual
quality of Cooper's imagination.

Interpretations attempting to employ insights derived from psychoanalysis have been much less successful. The most ambitious of such efforts,
Stephen Railton's *Fenimore Cooper: A Study of His Life and Imagination* (Princeton, N.J., 1978), posited (contrary to the experience of editors
who have worked with the manuscripts) that Cooper wrote in a completely "spontaneous," "unconscious" manner and that a critic may therefore "use the texts . . . as the basis for an analysis of the particular emotional demand which, throughout his life, he was forced to try to fulfill."
This "emotional demand," Railton theorizes (disregarding contravening
evidence), was Cooper's "complex and ambivalent" attitude towards his
father. The insistent application of these gratuitous assumptions to the
biographical and literary evidence is a less than constructive exercise. In
a far more sophisticated, much less literal manner, Eric J. Sundquist, in
*Home as Found: Authority and Genealogy in Nineteenth-Century Ameri-
can Literature* (Baltimore and London, 1977), employs a Freudian idiom
to explain the peculiar power — chiefly a power of badness — he finds in
Home as Found. Though the argument is highly ingenious, and perhaps
not intentionally sensationalized, the reader may find the Freudian the-
ogony irrelevant. On the other hand, the chapters on Cooper in Annette
Kolodny's *The Lay of the Land: Metaphor as Experience and History
in American Life and Letters* (Chapel Hill, N.C., 1975) and Joel Porte's
*The Romance in America: Studies in Cooper, Poe, Hawthorne, Melville
and James* (Middletown, Conn., 1969) are particularly sensitive in their
psychological treatment of image and theme in the Leatherstocking Tales.

Recent criticism of Cooper as artist has been most often attracted to
the separate tales of the Leatherstocking series, on the assumption, presumably, that these include his best works of fiction and that they are
semi-autonomous units in a loosely connected sequence whose significant elements of design are invested in the several parts. Recognizing the
presence of Leatherstocking as the obvious and appealing link, Cooper
proposed in his general "Preface" (1850) to determine the sequence by
the hero's ages, though these do not correspond to the sequence of the
writing or to any self-evident thematic imperative. As Terence Martin
has demonstrated in "Beginnings and Endings in the Leatherstocking
Tales" (*NCF*, June 1978), Cooper imposed a minimal unity by introducing retrospective references and allusions, but neither backward- nor
forward-looking glances could have fused the action of five separately

conceived plots into a single tightly constructed cycle. As Allan M. Axelrad states in "The Order of the Leatherstocking Tales" (AL, May 1982),
"most scholars believe that the series is best understood when read in the
chronological order of publication," the proximate sequence preferred by
D. H. Lawrence. Axelrad proposes, however, that the "real order" follows Natty's life cycle because Cooper built his belief "in a cyclical idea
of history" into "individual Leatherstocking novels" and also into "the
central meaning of the series as a whole when read in the chronological
order of Leatherstocking's life." The argument seems strained, not only
because the theory of probability is invoked to suggest that the alphabetical sequence of titles when arranged according to Natty's ages is cryptic
confirmation of Cooper's intention, but also because it is not necessary
to conceive of his concept of history as an "Iron Trap." Until a more persuasive case is advanced, readers will probably do well to follow the more
usual order or invent their own.[8]

Always a favorite among admirers of Cooper, The Pioneers ranks first

8. The following comparatively recent articles or chapters (not mentioned elsewhere
in this essay) contain useful or interesting discussions of the Leatherstocking series:
Haas, Rudolf. "James Fenimore Cooper—Epiker der 'frontier?'" Amerikanische Litera-
    turgeschichte 1. Heidelberg, 1972;
Hirsh, David H. "Cooper: Ideas and Lessons." Reality and Idea in the Early American
    Novel. The Hague and Paris, 1971;
Howard, David. "James Fenimore Cooper's Leatherstocking Tales: 'without a cross,'" In
    Tradition and Tolerance in Nineteenth-Century Fiction, ed. David Howard, John Lucas,
    and John Goode. New York, 1967;
Kelley, William P. "History, Language, and the Leatherstocking Tales." Papers, Cooper
    Conference 1979. Oneonta, N.Y.;
Lanzinger, Klaus. Die Epik im Amerikanischen Roman. Frankfurt/Main, Berlin, Bonn,
    and Munich, 1965;
Lynen, John F. "Irving and Cooper." The Design of the Present: Essays on Time and Form
    in American Literature. New Haven and London, 1969;
Martin, Terence. "The Negative Character in American Fiction." In Toward a New American
    Literary History, ed. L. J. Budd, E. H. Cady, and C. L. Anderson. Durham, N.C., 1980;
Martin, Terence. "Surviving on the Frontier: The Doubled Consciousness of Natty Bumppo."
    SAQ (Autumn, 1976);
Maxwell, D. E. S. "Politics and Pastoral in Cooper." American Fiction: The Intellectual
    Background. New York, 1965;
Nevins, Allan. Introduction to The Leatherstocking Saga. New York, 1954;
Nikoliukin, Aleksandr Nikolaevich. "The Natural Man and the New Society (James Feni-
    more Cooper's Novels)." American Romanticism and Modern Times. Moscow, 1968;
Peck, H. Daniel. "Place into Space." Papers, Cooper Conference 1979. Oneonta, N.Y.;
Poirier, Richard. A World Elsewhere. New York, 1966;
Seelye, John, "Some Green Thoughts on a Green Theme," TriQuarterly (Winter/Spring 1972);
Sühnel, Rudolf. "Coopers Lederstrumpf Saga." In Der Amerikanische Roman im 19. und
    20. Jahrhundert: Interpretationen, ed. Edgar Lohner. Berlin, 1974;
Zoellner, Robert H. "Conceptual Ambivalence in Cooper's Leatherstocking." AL (Jan. 1960).

today among the Leatherstocking Tales and in the Cooper canon in the quantity and quality of critical attention it has attracted and in the variety of critical approaches it has successfully sustained. Inspired perhaps by Thomas Philbrick's extremely thorough and suggestive explication, "Origins and Structure" (*PMLA*, Dec. 1964), study after study has appeared, gradually increasing critical awareness of the substantiality, complexity, and subtlety of Cooper's art. Thus, E. Arthur Robinson (*PMLA*, Dec. 1967), regarding its theme of conservation from an informed historical perspective, shows how Cooper employed actual conflicts of pioneering life to "give artistic unity to the novel and make it an expression of powerful forces at work upon human destiny." In "Cooper's 'Composite Order': *The Pioneers* as Structured Art" (SNNTS 2, 1970) Gerry Brenner attempts a strictly formalistic reading, proposing that the form of the novel predicates a deliberate and successful effort by the author to combine "disparate elements." In a particularly informative article, "'The Ordering of God's Providence': Law and Landscape in *The Pioneers*" (*SAF*, Autumn 1979), Peter Valenti argues that "the language and rhetoric of the picturesque tours underlie the novelistic structure and provide the basic tension in the novel," allowing Cooper to actualize his characters in the process of "responding to a challenging environment." Leland S. Person, Jr., in "Cooper's *The Pioneers* and Leatherstocking's Historical Function" (*ESQ*, First Quarter 1979) represents the novel as a cultural drama in which the Leatherstocking's role is principally "tutorial: not only to exist as avatar of a state of being-in-nature, but also to inculcate a conservative vision of the future in those who will assume responsibility for the land"; and Geoffrey Rans, in "'But the Penalty of Adam': Cooper's Sense of the Subversive" (*Canadian Review of American Studies*, Spring 1972), finds in the character Hiram Doolittle an ironic prefiguring of the fate that is to overtake the village of Templeton in *Home as Found*.[9]

The Last of the Mohicans, second and perhaps most famous of the

9. The following articles, introductions, and chapters, too numerous and varied to weave into continuous discussion, should be mentioned here:

Barton, Robert. "Natty's Trial, or the Triumph of Hiram Doolittle." *Cimarron Review* (July 1976);

Beard, James Franklin. Historical Introduction to *The Pioneers*. Albany, N.Y., 1980;

Cohen, Lester H. "What's in a Name?: The Presence of the Victim in *The Pioneers*." *Massachusetts Review* (Autumn 1975);

House, Kay Seymour. "James Fenimore Cooper: *The Pioneers*." *The American Novel from James Fenimore Cooper to William Faulkner*, ed. Wallace Stegner. New York and London, 1965;

Howard, Leon. Introduction to *The Pioneers*. New York: Rinehart, 1959.

Leatherstocking Tales, is also the most enigmatic, certainly the least con-
ducive to critical agreement. For James Grossman (*James Fenimore
Cooper*, p. 44), it is a "'pure' adventure story," "deliberately superficial,"
having "no serious concern with the outside world which it uses as a deco-
ration and an aid to the action." Other sophisticated readers, as different
as D. H. Lawrence, Leslie Fiedler, and George Sand, have found the book
a deeply moving experience. Thomas Philbrick, in his prize-winning essay "*The Last of the Mohicans* and the Sounds of Discord" (*AL*, Mar.
1971), entertains the possibility that its materials may not be "ordered
in an ideological scheme which, once identified, will unlock the meaning of the book," and suggests perhaps prematurely, that the "disintegration of order in confusion and obscurity is repeated in virtually every unit
of action, large and small, in the novel."

Other students have circumscribed this "ideological elusiveness" in
quasi-allegorical hypotheses. Michael D. Butler, in "Narrative Structure
and Historical Process" (*AL*, May 1976), proposes, for example, that the
action traces "a historical process in which a physical, masculine, red
culture embodied in the futureless bachelorhood of Uncas, Magua, and
Chingachgook gives way to a more spiritual, more feminine, white culture represented by the promising union of Alice and Duncan." Robert
Milder in "*The Last of the Mohicans* and the New World Fall" (*AL*, Nov.
1980) thinks the action reenacts "the fall from paradise, with paradise
understood as a post-lapsarian Arcadia, not an Eden" and then inquires
"whether paradise lost can become paradise regained," paradise being
"the limitless possibilities of America" and the fall a "loss of imaginative
vision." In an argument much less strained (*AL*, Nov. 1965), Donald Darnell reasons that since Cooper employed Uncas (not Hawkeye) as the hero
and relied consistently on the "Ubi sunt" formula, it is not unreasonable

---

Kehler, Joel R. "Architectural Dialecticism in Cooper's *The Pioneers.*" *TSLL* (Spring 1976);

McWilliams, John P., Jr. "The Pioneers" in "Innocent Criminal or Criminal Innocence:
   The Trial in American Fiction." *Law and American Literature: A Collection of Essays.*
   Commission on Undergraduate Education in Law and the Humanities. The American
   Bar Association. Chicago, 1980;

Mills, Nicolaus C. "Prison and Society in Nineteenth-Century American Fiction." *WHR*
   (Autumn 1970);

Otten, Kurt, "Cooper: *The Pioneers.*" *Der Amerikanische Roman: Von den Anfängen bis
   zur Gegenwart*, ed. Hans-Joachim Lang. Düsseldorf, 1972;

Paul, Jay S. "The Education of Elizabeth Temple." *SNNTS* (Summer 1977);

Ringe, Donald A. "Cooper's Mode of Expression." *Papers, Cooper Conference 1978.* Oneonta, N.Y.;

Ross, Morton L. "Cooper's *The Pioneers* and the Ethnographic Impulse." *American Studies*
   (Fall 1975);

Spiller, Robert E. Afterword to *The Pioneers.* New York: New American Library, 1964.

to assume that the book does concern the fate of the Indian. In the historical introduction to *Mohicans* in the Cooper Edition (Albany, N.Y., 1983), the present writer suggests that this reference be enlarged to include all mankind and that the ordering principle is not an "ideological scheme," but the symbol that inspired the book and determined the shape of the action.[10]

Except for *The Pioneers*, recent critics of the Leatherstocking Tales have been most often attracted to *The Prairie*, some to the aesthetic and philosophic values of the setting—the central symbol—and some to the historical, political, social, and psychological implications of the action. Among the former, Donald A. Ringe (*NCF*, Mar. 1961) locates the moral or philosophic import of the tale mainly in the "immensity of the natural landscape in contrast to the smallness of man." Jesse Bier (*TSLL*, Spring 1962) finds in the implicit interrelations of man and nature a "philosophic substructure" insistent that "the human condition is perennially lapsarian," expressing "a type of ardent Christian realism" in which man "is the perennial corrupter of God's world and . . . the agent and inheritor of the inevitable and successive falls of the Gardens of Eden." Merrill Lewis (*WAL*, Fall 1970) examines the pervasive desert metaphor to suggest that all the characters are questers whose relationships with landscape disclose their essential condition; and William L. Vance (*PMLA*, Mar. 1974) shows how the abundant interrelationships between man and beast (practical, scientific, and philosophic) are employed to reveal theme and define "man's own ambiguous identity as an animal with a difference." William Bysshe Stein (*Bucknell Review*, Spring 1971) explicates the book from the vantage point of its central character, finding the Trapper a "Wise Old Man," a "mystagogue," "an archetypal psychopompos," with a "dowry of wisdom [that] never changes. . . . though articulated in different terms from one period to another and from one culture to another." Interpreting the book as "elegiac comedy," Edwin Haviland Miller (*Mosaic* 9, 1977) notes that Natty was originally conceived as a comic character and that the

10. The following introductions and articles, not mentioned elsewhere in this essay, are recommended:

Charvat, William. Introduction to *The Last of the Mohicans*. Boston: Houghton Mifflin, 1958;

Haberly, David T. "Women and Indians: *The Last of the Mohicans* and the Captivity Tradition." *AQ*, (Fall 1976);

Martin, Terence. "From the Ruins of History: *The Last of the Mohicans*." *Novel* (Spring 1969);

Martin, Terence. "Leatherstocking and the Frontier: Cooper's *The Last of the Mohicans*." *The Frontier in American History and Literature*. Frankfort am Main, Berlin, and Bonn: Verlag Moritz Diesterweg, 1961;

Weidman, Bette S. "White Men's Red Man: A Penitential Reading of Four American Novels." *MLS* (Fall 1974).

rich incongruities of his speech, manners, and behavior in *The Prairie* are part of Cooper's strategy for making him, despite his elevation, human, lovable, and dramatically acceptable.

As William Wasserstrom has indicated in an influential essay, "The Origins of Culture: Cooper and Freud" (*The Psychoanalytic Study of Society* 1, 1960), *The Prairie* has had a special interest for social scientists because its action seems to anticipate Freud's theory of the tribal horde (in *Moses and Monotheism*), the mythic process by which primeval societies evolve as civilized cultures. Moving outside the Freudian context, Mary E. Rucker (*WAL*, Nov. 1977) explicates the action in terms of conflicting concepts of natural, tribal, and civil law. Though his contribution is perhaps more historical than critical, Orm Øverland's *The Making and Meaning of an American Classic: James Fenimore Cooper's "The Prairie"* (Oslo and New York, 1973) is a conscientious compendium of information (biographical, bibliographical, textual, and historical) useful and generally reliable in its facts. Much of the textual material will be superseded in James P. Elliott's forthcoming CSE edition of the book.[11]

In his most important essay on Cooper (*Scrutiny*, Winter 1952–53), reprinted in *The Eccentric Design*, Marius Bewley expatiated warmly on the artistry of *The Deerslayer*, proposing this romance as "the greatest masterpiece of American literature before *The Scarlet Letter*, and . . . as serious in its meaning." Recent critics have been silent or noncommittal in response to Bewley's challenge, though he has not been alone in his high opinion of the later Leatherstocking Tales. Cooper himself thought *The Pathfinder* (1840) and *The Deerslayer* (1841) not inferior and perhaps superior to the first three. Yet, curiously, the later tales have not attracted a body of recent criticism comparable to that on *The Pioneers* or *The Prairie*. Though the biographical studies with a critical orientation and the critical studies mentioned earlier (by Donald Davie, David Howard, Annette Kolodny, John F. Lynen, H. Daniel Peck, Joel Porte, and Yvor Winters) make perceptive comments on *The Deerslayer*, their remarks on *The Pathfinder* have usually been muted or qualified. Only two semi-critical articles on *The Pathfinder*, "Leatherstocking in Love" (*British Association for American Studies Bulletin*, June 1965) by

11. The following works also contain useful discussions of *The Prairie*:
Chase, Richard. *The American Novel and Its Tradition*. New York, 1957;
Goetzmann, William H. "James Fenimore Cooper: *The Prairie*." *Landmarks of American Writing*, ed. Hennig Cohen. New York and London, 1969;
Nelson, Carl. "Cooper's Verbal Faction: The Hierarchy of Rhetoric, Voice, and Silence in *The Prairie*." *West Virginia University Philological Papers* 24 (1977);
Smith, Henry Nash. Introduction to *The Prairie*. New York: Rinehart, 1950;
Ward, John William. Afterword to *The Prairie*. New York: New American Library, 1964.

George Dekker, and "Similes and Metaphors in Cooper's *The Pathfinder*," by Lura Nancy and Duilio T. Pedrini (*NYFQ*, June 1967), appear to have been published in the last thirty years. Few more are recorded for *The Deerslayer*.

Disclaiming any wish to be thought a professional re-evaluator, Beniamino Placido ("James Fenimore Cooper e *The Deerslayer*," SA 13, 1967) suggests that Americans have seriously underestimated Cooper and that American literature comes not from *Huckleberry Finn*, as Hemingway maintained, but from *The Deerslayer*, much as Russian literature may be said to come from Gogol's *The Overcoat*. Professor Placido finds embodied in the action of this book significant characteristics and paradoxes of the American response to experience: a capacity for accumulated violence, for example, together with a need for an aggressive enemy presence to release its force; a peculiar tendency in the community to relegate its unpleasant assignments to self-sacrificing strangers, outsiders, who reestablish order and then withdraw unrewarded; and a requirement that manifestations of violence be restrained within a pattern of civility or code. Adopting a less generalized approach, Donald Darnell (*Studies in the Novel*, Winter 1979) argues that *The Deerslayer* is, in part, a domestic tragedy of manners in which Judith is a victim of class distinction, caught in the "tension between Cooper's antipathy to social aspiration and his recognition of his heroine's legitimate claims to position in the social world." Frieda K. Bradsher (*Renascence* 31, 1978) finds Cooper's treatment of Judith positively unjust, a violation of the Episcopalian teaching he seemingly professed, a teaching which should, according to Ms. Bradsher, have caused him to make Deerslayer more receptive to Judith's repentance. Natty, therefore, "not only fails to treat [Judith] fairly but actually abandons her to a life of sin." On an entirely different tack, Alan F. Sandy, Jr., argues (*ESQ*, Summer 1970) that the discernable levels of voice or diction in *The Deerslayer* are functional, that they enable Cooper "to hem in the truth" by fragmenting and insinuating it from several points of view.[12]

Recent studies of Cooper's art in the eighty-five percent of his fiction not included in the Leatherstocking Tales are still relatively few and tentative. They are beginning to appear, however; and they suggest a higher artistic accomplishment than earlier Cooper critics were willing to accord. Thomas Philbrick maintains, for example, in "Language and Mean-

12. The following discussions of *The Deerslayer*, not mentioned elsewhere in this essay, may be of interest:
Beard, James F. Introduction to *The Deerslayer*. New York: Harper's Modern Classics, 1960;
Bowden, Edwin T. *The Dungeon of the Heart: Human Isolation and the American Novel*. New York, 1961;

ing in *The Water-Witch*" (*ESQ*, Summer 1970) that this romance, which Yvor Winters described as stylistically "probably Cooper's ablest piece of work . . . one of the most brilliant . . . masterpieces of American prose," does, despite Winters' reference to its "comic-opera plot," employ its verbal pyrotechnics to make a serious thematic statement. In "Cooper's Artistry in *The Headsman*" (*NCF*, June 1974), Constance Ayers Denne finds in this work, generally neglected as sociopolitical, independent claims to critical consideration, claims that redeem and explain the otherwise unsatisfactory ending. In "History and Progress: Some Implications of Form in Cooper's Littlepage Novels" (*NCF*, June 1971), Edgar A. Dryden discovers in this trilogy, usually discussed in the local context of the Anti-Rent War in New York State, Cooper's most elaborate and satisfying statement of the relationship between past and present, an almost Faulknerian sense of the present as an indefinite extension of the past, in which "the key to self-knowledge and self-determination" is a constant awareness and assessment of its hidden influence. Paul Stein, in "Cooper's Later Fiction: The Theme of 'Becoming'" (*SAQ*, Winter 1971) contends that the later fiction adopts "a characteristically different mode of narration" that "invests [it] with a dynamic quality missing from the earlier work." Instead of depicting his characters "in the grip of circumstances brought about by previous decisions or by the force of social pressures beyond their control," Stein says, Cooper shows them after 1838 "in the process of making choices, of struggling forward to their proper goals, of being active agents" in their own affairs. Whether or not one agrees, such responses indicate that Cooper's fiction is at last being read and evaluated freshly without the unspoken obeisance to critical fashion.[13]

The massive quantity of Cooper's fictional production (no American writer of comparable stature has been more prolific), the severe limitations of our present knowledge in matters of biographical and bibliographical detail, the marked disparities in present critical attitudes, and the radical nature of the revaluation seemingly in progress suggest that

---

Davis, David Brion. "The Deerslayer, A Democratic Knight of the Wilderness." In *Twelve Original Essays on Great American Novels*, ed. Charles Shapiro. Detroit, 1958;

Mizener, Arthur. "The Deerslayer." In *Twelve Great American Novels*. New York, 1969;

Nevins, Allan. Afterword to *The Deerslayer*. New York: New American Library, 1963;

Paine, Gregory L. Introduction to *The Deerslayer*. New York: Harcourt, Brace & Co., 1927.

13. On Cooper's European trilogy, see also:

Fabris, Alberta. "La Trilogia Europa di J. F. Cooper." *SA* 15 (1969);

Riese, Teut Andreas. "Fenimore Cooper als Gestalter Deutscher Geschichte, Betrachtungen zu seinem Roman *Die Heidenmauer*." Ruperto-Carola 41 (Heidelberg, 1967);

Williams, J. Gary. "Cooper and European Catholicism: A Reading of *The Heidenmauer*." *ESQ* (Third Quarter, 1976).

Cooper studies are likely to continue for the immediate future in a state of flux. Though it would be rash to predict the outcome or to attempt to hasten it by premature synthesis, Robert Penn Warren has summarized admirably the attitude of most thoughtful students and readers of Cooper today:

> The relevance of Cooper is greater now than ever. If Cooper's notion of a class of "gentlemen" sounds quaint to modern ears, we may still realize that the problems of the tyranny of the majority and of maintaining standards of excellence are yet painfully with us. Even more painfully with us is the problem of man's relation to nature and to other men in the great modern state.
>
> One index of the relevance of Cooper is indicated in his resemblance to Faulkner. Cooper, like Faulkner, came from a personal world that seemed retarded and stood outside his "modernity." Both saw a "doom" in history, in Cooper's case involving the crime against the Indian, in Faulkner's that against the Negro. For both, the violation of the fellow man is associated with a violation of nature, and both hold a vision of a world of "communal brotherhood" in nature. . . . If neither believes in a gospel of progress, both see life as redeemed by human kindness, valor, and fidelity.[14]

14. *Atlantic Brief Lives, A Biographical Companion to the Arts*, ed. Louis Kronenberger (Boston and Toronto: Little, Brown, 1971), p. 182.

Stephen Crane

DONALD PIZER

I HAVE ATTEMPTED to include all major work on Stephen Crane. A special problem in citing articles about Crane is that many have been reprinted, often more than once, in texts designed for student use. Rather than attempt to note every instance of this kind of republication, I have noted the existence of collections of critical writings about Crane at appropriate points in my discussion. I have, however, listed other forms of republication.

MANUSCRIPTS

The two principal Crane manuscript collections are at Columbia University and the University of Virginia. The Columbia collection, some thirteen hundred items, consists mainly of material preserved by Cora Crane and acquired by the library in 1952. Its greatest strengths are in manuscripts of Crane's poems, stories, and sketches, and in scrapbooks of his published journalism. The provenance of the Columbia Crane Collection is amusingly detailed by Lillian Gilkes in her "The Stephen Crane Collection Before Its Acquisition by Columbia: A Memoir" (*CLC*, Nov. 1973). A description of the collection and a partial list can be found in Joan H. Baum, *Stephen Crane (1871–1900): An Exhibition of His Writings Held in the Columbia University Libraries . . .* (New York, 1956). The University of Virginia manuscript holdings represent the collecting efforts of Clifton Waller Barrett. The Barrett Collection boasts, above all, the manuscript of *The Red Badge of Courage* (the only surviving com-

From Earl N. Harbert and Robert A. Rees, editors, *Fifteen American Authors before 1900: Bibliographic Essays on Research & Criticism* (Madison: The University of Wisconsin Press; © 1984 by the Board of Regents of the University of Wisconsin System); may be reproduced only by permission of the publisher.

plete holograph of a Crane novel) and contains as well a sizable body of miscellaneous material. Some of its most significant items are noted by Miss Baum in her 1956 catalogue (the exhibition was a joint one of the Columbia and Barrett collections). David A. Randall provides a history of the *Red Badge* manuscript in his *Dukedom Large Enough* (New York, 1969), while the manuscript itself has been published in facsimile in *Stephen Crane: The Red Badge of Courage: A Facsimile Edition of the Manuscript*, 2 vols. (Washington, D.C., vol. 1, 1973; vol. 2, 1972). Volume Two contains facsimiles of both the final manuscript and the earlier draft; Volume One contains an extended textual introduction by Fredson Bowers, much of which also appears in Volume Two of the Virginia Edition of *The Works of Stephen Crane* (10 vols., Charlottesville, 1969–76) (hereafter cited as the Virginia Edition).

Additional Crane collections of some importance are those in the Syracuse University and Dartmouth College libraries and in the private possession of Charles Feinberg and Melvin H. Schoberlin. The Arents Collection at Syracuse is described in an appendix to *Stephen Crane: Love Letters to Nellie Crouse*, edited by Edwin H. Cady and Lester G. Wells (Syracuse, N.Y., 1954); the Dartmouth collection is listed in Herbert F. West, *A Stephen Crane Collection* (Hanover, N.H., 1948). The Virginia Edition includes all hitherto unpublished Crane material from these and other collections, principally in Volume Ten, *Poems and Literary Remains*.

BIBLIOGRAPHY

Early Crane primary bibliographies were superseded by Ames W. Williams and Vincent Starrett, *Stephen Crane: A Bibliography* (Glendale, Calif., 1948). The Williams and Starrett bibliography played a major role in the Crane "revival" of the early 1950s, but in the more than three decades since its appearance many scholars have noted errors and gaps, particularly regarding Crane's journalism. Unfortunately, Joseph Katz's promised descriptive bibliography has not appeared, which means that the most authoritative analytical account of Crane's books lies scattered throughout the textual sections of the Virginia Edition. The Virginia Edition also includes much new information on Crane's periodical publication, but a more useful complication for most scholars is the section entitled "Writings of Stephen Crane Arranged Alphabetically by Individual Titles" in R.W. Stallman's *Stephen Crane: A Critical Bibliography* (Ames, Iowa, 1972). For each item Stallman provides a history of printings from the earliest to the latest.

Of considerable importance to the prospective descriptive bibliographer are two accounts of Matthew J. Bruccoli's distinguished Crane collection: *Stephen Crane: 1871–1971, An Exhibition from the Collection of Matthew J. Bruccoli* (Department of English, University of South Carolina, Bibliographical Series, no. 6, 1971), and *The Stephen Crane Collection from the Library of Prof. Matthew J. Bruccoli* (Auction Catalogue, Swann Galleries, New York, 1974).

There have been surprisingly few attribution controversies in Crane scholarship despite his extensive anonymous journalism. Nevertheless, two cruxes are "Veterans' Ranks Thinner by a Year" and "Stephen Crane's Pen Picture of the Powers' Fleet Off Crete." Although Thomas A. Gullason attributed the first item to Crane (*NCF*, Sept. 1957), Daniel G. Hoffman has convincingly dismissed the attribution (*NCF*, June 1959). The second was the center of a running controversy between R. W. Stallman and Lillian Gilkes over whether or not Crane could have been in Crete at the time the article was written and filed. (See, in particular, Gilkes's *Cora Crane: A Biography of Mrs. Stephen Crane*, Bloomington, Ind., 1960; Stallman and Gilkes in *SSF*, Fall 1964; Stallman's *Stephen Crane: A Biography*, New York, 1968; Gilkes in *AL*, May 1969; and Stallman in *AL*, May 1972.)

Another attribution controversy concerns the authorship of various portions of the London newsletter published under Crane's name in the *New York Press* between August and November 1897. There seems little doubt that the newsletter was produced collaboratively by Crane and Cora Crane. However, Lillian Gilkes argued in "The London Newsletters of Stephen and Cora Crane: A Collaboration" (*SAF*, Autumn 1976) that Fredson Bowers, in Volumes Eight and Nine of the Virginia Edition, attributes too little of this material to Cora and too much to Crane. Both scholars use the same manuscript evidence, but Miss Gilkes's more intimate knowledge of Cora's interests and prose style suggests that she may be correct in contesting Bowers's attribution of specific portions of the newsletter to Crane.

Finally, two recent attribution efforts fail to convince: Lillian Gilkes's attempt, in "A New Stephen Crane Item" (*SAF*, Autumn 1977), to identify a newspaper story about the millionaire Barney Barnato as by Crane; and Lyle D. Linder's attempt, in "'The Ideal and the Real' and 'Brer Washington's Consolation': Two Little Known Stories by Stephen Crane?" (*ALR*, Spring 1978), to place Crane as the author of two unpublished black dialect stories in the Cora Crane Collection.

The secondary bibliography section of Williams and Starrett has been superseded by later, fuller lists. One of the best of these is by Stanley Wertheim in Theodore L. Gross and Stanley Wertheim, *Hawthorne, Melville, Stephen Crane: A Critical Bibliography* (New York, 1971). Wertheim's judicious and balanced 100-page annotated list of Crane research is distinguished by the incidental light cast on Crane himself within Wertheim's mini-essays on major Crane scholarship. On the whole, though less complete, Wertheim's survey is far more reliable (as I will shortly note) than Stallman's massive critical bibliography. Wertheim also provides an invaluable descriptive survey of doctoral dissertations on Crane in "Guide to Dissertations on American Literary Figures, 1870–1910: Part One – Stephen Crane" (*ALR*, Summer 1975).

The major work in Crane secondary bibliography is of course Stallman's *Stephen Crane: A Critical Bibliography*. Shock and dismay characterized much of the initial response to the work. (Two caustic reviews are by Joseph Katz in *Proof* [1973] and James E. Kibler in *Costerus* [1974].) The first several sections of the book reprint slightly revised material long available in the standard Crane bibliographies; the longest section consists of a year by year annotated commentary of Crane criticism which is complete through 1969 and selective through 1972. Rarely has a bibliographer more blatantly seized the opportunity afforded by an annotated list to pay old debts and prolong old quarrels. Crankiness and crotchetiness in a major critic can sometimes be both entertaining and informative, but in this instance Stallman's neglect of descriptive analysis and his massive exercise in self-puffery, in loaded selectivity of comment, and in studied neglect are an embarrassment. The wonder is that this 642-page effort in repetitiousness and contentiousness was published. A further example of Stallman's apologia can be found in "That Crane, That Albatross Around My Neck: A Self-Interview" (*JML*, Feb. 1979).

Two extremely useful essay reviews of Crane research are Joseph Katz, "Afterword: Resources for the Study of Stephen Crane," in *Stephen Crane in Transition: Centenary Essays*, edited by Joseph Katz (DeKalb, Ill., 1972) (hereafter cited as *Crane Centenary Essays*), and Marston LaFrance, "Stephen Crane Scholarship Today and Tomorrow" (*ALR*, Spring 1974). Katz begins with an excellent account of the Crane collections at Columbia and Virginia and then discusses at length the state of Crane research in bibliography, editing, and biography. LaFrance concentrates on identifying the critical approaches to Crane which have emerged since the beginning of the Crane revival in the early 1950s. His own commitment to Crane as an ironic humanist colors much of his commentary, particularly in his bias against naturalist and religious symbolist readings of Crane, but nevertheless there is much good sense in his review. Both Katz and LaFrance offer useful suggestions on current needs in Crane studies. A more limited but nevertheless trenchant review of tendencies in Crane criticism is offered by Edwin Cady in his new first chapter, "The Elusive Stephen Crane," in the revised edition of his *Stephen Crane* (Boston, 1980).

EDITIONS, TEXTS, AND REPRINTS

Wilson Follett's edition of *The Work of Stephen Crane* (12 vols., New York, 1925–27; 6 vols., New York, 1963) made available a large body of Crane's work which had long been out of print. The collection was very much a creature of its time in its somewhat precious bookmaking, in its array of generally uninformed and irrelevant introductions by contemporary literary and journalistic lights, and in its haphazard and undescribed editorial methods. It was superseded, of course, by the Virginia Edition, edited by Fredson Bowers. In the course of the appearance of the 10 volumes of the Virginia Edition, a number of reviewers noted flaws both in the textual theory and practice of the edition — most notably in the decisions to produce a single eclectic version of the 1893 and 1896 texts of *Maggie* and to regularize the dialect of *The Red Badge of Courage*. The most authoritative review of the text of the edition on its completion is by David J. Nordloh (himself a CEAA editor) in "On Crane Now Edited: The University of Virginia Edition of *The Works of Stephen Crane*" (*SNNTS*, Spring 1978). Nordloh concludes that "The texts of the Virginia Edition are not reliable. They are theoretically and practically a chaos." He bases this evaluation on a number of major inadequacies in the edition, among which are inaccurate reporting of texts, obscure editorial commentary, and imposition of the editor's standards on Crane in an effort to present "an ideal Stephen Crane, better than real life."

Nevertheless, the Virginia edition is a landmark in Crane scholarship and does make several valuable contributions to the study of Crane and his work. Most of all, it is a great advantage to have an edition which is truly complete, or almost so, unlike the 1925–27 Follett edition. Only Crane's letters are omitted; otherwise every known miscellaneous bit of journalism, every scrap of writing whether previously published or unpublished, is included. In addition, the task of editing Crane's minor work has generated some important new information about and critical commentary on Crane in the introductions to the various volumes of the edition, since minds of a caliber not usually engaged with this level of a writer's work have perforce had to struggle with its implications for Crane's life and art. And finally one cannot help applauding the remarkable energy and will which produced so massive a body of research in so comparatively brief a period.

The edition, however, has a number of serious flaws even for the general user who is not deeply concerned with textual matters. Let me start with weaknesses of editorial planning and then proceed to those of editorial commission. First, the overall organization of the edition appears haphazard. In some instances, such as Crane's Whilomville stories, similarity of subject matter is preserved by placing all the similar material in one volume; in other instances, such as Crane's Bowery or western stories, the material is dispersed over several volumes. In one notable instance, Volume Five, the contents of Crane's miscellaneous 1898 collection, *The Open Boat and Other Tales of Adventure,* is preserved, but in all other instances the contents of such collections are dispersed, by genre and subject matter, over several volumes in the edition.

Another problematical and troublesome editorial procedure is the omission of all historical annotation of Crane's work. It seems absurd not to supply, for example, the geographical and historical annotation which would make understandable specific references in Crane's Greco-Turkish and Cuban war reporting and not to annotate equally obscure allusions and references elsewhere in his work. If the purpose of an edition is to achieve an approximation of what the author intended, the editor should make available not only the text of that intention but also the now lost or obscure historical context of what the author wrote. This omission, I should note, was not imposed upon the Virginia Edition by the CEAA, since other CEAA editions do include annotation.

One wonders if the extraordinary disproportion in the size of the various volumes of the edition arises from the failure initially to realize the extent of Crane's writing in certain areas or from the discovery of the need for an unexpectedly full editorial commentary in some instances once the edition was under way. In any case, the size of the volumes ranges from 282 pages for Volume One to 1224 for Volume Eight. Volume Eight, *Tales, Sketches, and Reports,* it probably the most unwieldly book produced within the entire CEAA project. It requires steady hand pressure to maintain one's place in the book, since otherwise the weight on one side or the other will cause the book to close. Somewhat related to this disproportion in overall length is the disproportion in the length of the introductions. Edwin Cady is responsible for one introduction, James Colvert for four, and J. C. Levenson for five. Colvert's and Cady's introductions average 20 pages, Levenson's 72. This disproportion does not derive from the significance of the works being introduced; Colvert's introduction to the Bowery Tales (*Maggie* and *George's Mother*) is 28 pages, Levenson's to *The O'Ruddy* is 62. It derives rather from the differing conception of the role and nature of the introduction held by these scholars. This varying conception is of course of considerable importance to the user of the edition, since the "accident" of assignment of a particular scholar to a particular volume thus determines the kind of information he will receive in the introduction to that volume. From Colvert he will receive principally biographical and historical information bearing on the genesis of the works in question; from Levenson he will receive this and a great deal of Levenson's critical interpretation of the works as well. The point of this observation is neither to quarrel with the presence of Levenson's criticism nor to call for uniformity for its own sake. It is rather to note that in the Virginia Edition the amount of critical discussion of Crane's work has little relationship to either the intrinsic interest of the work under consideration or the extent of critical discussion of the work elsewhere.

Much of the criticism that appears in the edition — whether in the "historical" introductions or in the textual introductions — is of great interest. Nevertheless, the mode of critical inquiry in the Virginia Edition significantly weakens its usefulness. First, there is the "mixed" content of Bowers's critical commentary — mixed in that it appears in his textual introductions and textual notes in fragmentary form and intertwined with technical textual analysis. Bowers's textual introductions in the ten volumes of the edition contain roughly 900 pages of closely argued bibliographical and textual commentary. Embedded in this vast amount of material are such important critical discussions as Bowers's toward "a distant home" reading of *Maggie,* discussions which are of importance to the Crane critic but which are rendered obscure and unavailable by their location and context.

Moreover, all the criticism which appears in the edition, whether in the historical or textual introductions, shares the even more significant weakness of occuring in a critical vacuum. The reader has little sense that a major and much explicated Crane work had ever before been the subject of a critical intelligence other than that of the critic at hand. If criticism is to be a function of an edition of this kind, it should be put into the historical perspective which is the underlying principle of all editing. Just as the reader is told, in introductions and tables, the process by which the editor determined upon an eclectic text which constitutes the author's final intentions, so he should be made aware of the critical traditions in the reading of a specific work upon which the writer of the introduction is building. Otherwise, the story is incomplete and editions of the magnitude and "definitiveness" of the Virginia edition should strive toward completeness. Also, there is an unpleasant savor of critical pride in the isolation of much of the critical commentary in the introductions. Levenson, for example, devotes many pages in his introduction to the *Red Badge* to demonstrating his belief that there are important similarities between the novel and Tolstoy's *Sebastopol.* But he does not even mention, let alone discuss, in his lengthy essay the landmark discovery by Harold Hungerford of Crane's detailed dependence upon the Battle of Chancellorsville in the *Red Badge.*

A number of earlier editions of Crane's work are still of interest, despite the appearance of the Virginia Edition, because of their specialized purposes. Among the most important of these are *The Sullivan County Sketches of Stephen Crane*, edited by Melvin Schoberlin (Syracuse, N.Y., 1949) and *Stephen Crane: Sullivan County Tales and Sketches*, edited by R. W. Stallman (Ames, Iowa, 1968); *The War Dispatches of Stephen Crane* (New York, 1964) and *The New York City Sketches of Stephen Crane* (New York, 1966), both edited by R. W. Stallman and E. R. Hagemann; *The Complete Short Stories and Sketches of Stephen Crane* (New York, 1963) and *The Complete Novels of Stephen Crane* (New York, 1967), both edited by Thomas A. Gullason; and *Stephen Crane in the West and Mexico*, edited by Joseph Katz (Kent, Ohio, 1970) and *The Western Writings of Stephen Crane*, edited by Frank Bergon (New York, 1979).

It would be well to mention at this point four general collections which have played a major role in Crane studies. William M. Gibson's *Stephen Crane: "The Red Badge of Courage" and Selected Prose and Poetry* (New York, 1950; rev. 1956 and 1968) and R.W. Stallman's *Stephen Crane: An Omnibus* (New York, 1952) helped to establish both the canon of Crane's major work and important areas of critical interest. Joseph Katz's *The Portable Stephen Crane* (New York, 1969) and Maurice Bassan's *Stephen Crane: A Collection of Critical Essays* (Englewood Cliffs, N.J., 1967) continued the unending attempt to isolate the best in Crane's writing and in writing about him.

In addition to complete or special collections of Crane, there have been major editions of specific works and of his poems and letters. I will discuss these in the order of their composition, beginning with *Maggie*. The novel has received much editorial attention in recent years, most of it stemming from the discovery that the 1893 *Maggie* is a significant work in its own right. In "Stephen Crane's Revision of *Maggie*" (*AL*, Jan. 1955), R. W. Stallman discussed in some detail the differences between the 1893 and 1896 versions and stressed that future editions should include the paragraph from Chapter Seventeen which was omitted from the 1896 edition. Joseph Katz, in "The *Maggie* Nobody Knows" (*MFS*, Summer 1966), also emphasized the distinctiveness of the 1893 edition, though his contention that the curtailing of profanity in the 1896 version weakens the religious theme in the novel is unconvincing. In response to this interest in the 1893 *Maggie*, Joseph Katz and Donald Pizer prepared facsimile editions of the 1893 text (Gainesville, Fla., 1966, and San Francisco, 1968), and Maurice Bassan prepared a particularly useful edition — *Stephen Crane's "Maggie": Text and Context* (Belmont, Calif., 1966) — in which he republished the 1893 text and introduced the substantive 1896 variants in footnotes. This shift of interest to the 1893 text of *Mag-*

gie (Katz also chose it for his *Portable Stephen Crane*) was momentarily halted by Fredson Bowers's decision to attempt to produce an eclectic text of the novel for the Virginia Edition. But the widespread attack on the results of this effort — see in particular Hershel Parker and Brian Higgins, "Maggie's 'Last Night': Authorial Design and Editorial Patching" (*SNNTS*, Spring 1978) — suggests that the 1893 text (emended of its typographical errors) will continue to supplant the 1896 version as the basic reading text of the novel. It is, for example, the text which Thomas A. Gullason has recently chosen, after careful consideration, for his Norton Critical Edition of *Maggie* (New York, 1979).

The text of *The Red Badge of Courage* has proven to be a major crux in modern bibliographical studies. Until 1951, when John T. Winterich included unpublished material from *The Red Badge* manuscript in his London Folio Society edition of the novel, the 1895 Appleton text had sole authority. (Joseph Katz has prepared facsimiles both of the December 9, 1894, *New York Press* syndicated version of *The Red Badge* [Gainesville, Fla., 1967] and the 1895 Appleton text [Columbus, Ohio, 1969].) A fuller description and use of the manuscript, including an important distinction between an early short version (SV) and a later long version (LV), were provided by R. W. Stallman in his 1952 *Omnibus* volume. Winterich and Stallman noted that not only did the long version bear the mark of significant revision by Crane, but also that a number of passages left uncanceled in the LV manuscript were not published in the Appleton text. Both Winterich and Stallman (and Gibson in 1956) printed this omitted material in brackets as part of their integral text. In more recent years, however, most editors have concluded that Crane himself was responsible for the excision of this material and that the inclusion of it within the text is unjustified. Editors of *The Red Badge* have therefore either placed the omitted material in footnotes or appendices (Richard Lettis et al. in 1960; Sculley Bradley et al. in 1962; Thomas A. Gullason in 1967; and Donald Pizer in 1976) or have omitted it entirely (Daniel G. Hoffman in 1957; Richard Chase in 1960; Frederick C. Crews in 1964; and Joseph Katz in his 1969 *Portable Stephen Crane*).

The most important discussions of the text of *The Red Badge* are by Stallman in his Signet edition (New York, 1960); by William L. Howarth in "*The Red Badge of Courage* Manuscript: New Evidence for a Critical Edition" (*SB*, 1965); by Fredson Bowers in Volume One of the facsimile edition of the manuscript and in the Virginia Edition; by Henry Binder in "*The Red Badge of Courage* Nobody Knows" (*SNNTS*, Spring 1978); and by Donald Pizer in "'*The Red Badge of Courage* Nobody Knows': A Brief Rejoinder" (*SNNTS*, Spring 1979). Stallman's Signet volume can best be described as a tentative critical edition. Relying on the Appleton version as copy-text, he supplies uncanceled LV passages in brackets within the text and canceled LV passages and "critically interesting [SV] variants" in footnotes. Howarth's article is the first full discussion of the physical state of *The Red Badge* manuscript and of the relationship of its condition to problems bearing on the preparation of a critical edition. Howarth is particularly valuable in establishing the order and extent of Crane's revisions (he notes seven distinct writing states), in discovering several corruptions in the Appleton text, and in correcting Stallman's account of the manuscript. Bowers builds on these and other studies to produce the first bibliographically sophisticated text of *The Red Badge*. His attempt is marred, however, by his effort to "improve" on Crane—to regularize the dialect which Bowers believes Crane intended to regularize but in fact did not. Binder in his essay, and in the text of *The Red Badge* which he prepared for the new *Norton Anthology of American Literature*, edited by Ronald Gottesman et al. (New York, 1979), opens up a new area of contention in textual studies of the novel. Most scholars have believed that Crane was well advised to cut the manuscript of *The Red Badge*, since they held that the omitted passages are heavy-handed ironic accounts of Henry's motives which are out of key with Crane's final conception of the novel and Henry. (See, for example, Olov W. Fryckstedt, "Henry Fleming's Tupenny Fury: Cosmic Pessimism in Stephen Crane's *The Red Badge of Courage*" [*SN*, 1961] and Edwin Cady's *Stephen Crane*.) Binder, however, contends that Crane was forced by his Appleton editor Ripley Hitchcock to revise the manuscript and that the uncut version is the novel we should be reading. Pizer rejects this notion on the grounds that Binder has supplied insufficient external evidence of Hitchcock's intervention and that the revised version is by far the more significant work of fiction. He notes in passing that after thirty years of the availability of and interest in the manuscript version of *The Red Badge*, only Binder and his mentor Hershel Parker have recognized its legitimacy and virtues. An additional contribution to this controversy is by another of Parker's students, Steven Mailloux, who in his "*The Red Badge of Courage* and Interpretive Conventions: Critical Response to a Maimed Text" (*SNNTS*, Spring 1978) argues that the critical disagreement over the meaning of the novel can be attributed to its maimed text.

Crane's poems were collected by Wilson Follett in his 1925–27 edition and in *The Collected Poems of Stephen Crane* (New York, 1930). Neither volume is of bibliographical interest. The two modern critical editions are by Joseph Katz, *The Poems of Stephen Crane* (New York, 1966) and by Fredson Bowers in the Virginia Edition.

The first major collections of Crane's letters were by Stallman in his *Omnibus* and by Edwin H. Cady and Lester G. Wells in *Stephen Crane:*

Love Letters to Nellie Crouse. Stallman and Lillian Gilkes then published their invaluable *Stephen Crane: Letters* (New York, 1960), which remains the standard edition. Like much of Stallman's editorial work, the collection is occasionally faulty in its transcriptions and facts. But in this instance Stallman's tendency toward excessive editorial commentary has resulted in a volume which has an old-fashioned life-in-letters usefulness. Indeed, in some ways the edition is a more satisfactory introduction to Crane's life than Stallman's full-scale biography. However, a new edition of Crane's letters is needed, since a sizable number of new letters has appeared since 1960 and since Stallman and Gilkes's annotation requires updating and correction.

One of the most active areas of Crane editing in recent years has been the preparation of collections of critical material on Crane. Two important general collections are *Stephen Crane in Transition: Centenary Essays*, edited by Joseph Katz, and *Stephen Crane's Career: Perspectives and Evaluations* (New York, 1972), edited by Thomas A. Gullason. The first contains nine original essays on Crane (I will discuss these individually in their appropriate places); the second is a massive, eclectic, and well-prepared selection of previously published Crane criticism and in particular of Crane criticism since 1950. Three more specialized collections of secondary material are Stanley Wertheim's *Studies in "Maggie" and "George's Mother"* (Columbus, Ohio, 1970); Thomas A Gullason's edition of *Maggie* in the Norton Critical Editions series (New York, 1979); and Donald Pizer's second edition of Bradley, Beatty, and Long's edition of *The Red Badge* in the same series (New York, 1976).

The *Stephen Crane Newsletter* (Fall 1966–Fall 1970), edited by Joseph Katz, was a principal vehicle for the publication of bibliographical, textual, and biographical notes on Crane. It was occasionally not unlike other author-newsletters in its failure to distinguish between the trivial and the significant. (One group of letters from Crane's boarding school headmaster to Mrs. Crane is for the most part a collection of bills, including some for laundry.) But many of the enterprises of the *Newsletter* served important functions — its census of 1893 *Maggies*, for example, or such continuing features as its quarterly checklist, its reviews, and its work-in-progress reports. It has been missed.

BIOGRAPHY

There are at present five major biographical studies of Crane: Thomas Beer, *Stephen Crane: A Study in American Letters* (New York, 1923); John Berryman, *Stephen Crane* (New York, 1950); Edwin H. Cady, *Stephen Crane* (New York, 1962; 2nd rev. ed., Boston, 1980); R. W. Stallman, *Stephen Crane: A Biography* (New York, 1968); and Jean Cazema-jou, *Stephen Crane (1871–1900) Écrivain-Journaliste* (Paris, 1969). In addition, a sixth important biographical study of Crane lies "buried" in the ten volumes of the Virginia Edition. The almost 500 pages of intro-duction as well as the 900 pages of textual commentary contain a wealth of biographical detail. Much of this detail, of course, is concerned with the facts of composition and publication of Crane's work and therefore does not pertain to major moments of his life when he was not writing. But other moments, such as his war reporting or his English years, are here presented with a fullness and accuracy (as well as in fragmentary fashion and repetitiously) not elsewhere available.

Beer's work has so often been called brilliantly impressionistic but faulty that I would like to approach it from another direction after noting the crux which it represents in Crane studies. Beer relied on many letters and interview notes which are no longer extant. (His most severe critics would argue that much of this material was never extant.) In the years since the publication of his biography, students of Crane's life have frequently found demonstrable errors in this presently unavailable but supposedly documentary base of biographical detail. Yet because Beer still remains our only source of knowledge about many phases of Crane's life, scholars must continue to rely upon him despite his proven untrustworthiness.

Beer's declared intent was to destroy the myth of Crane as a demonic artist, but his biography, though it achieved this end, created several new myths about Crane. First, his book is less a biography of Crane than a study of Crane and his time. Crane emerges from Beer's pages not as a fully realized personality but as "A Study in American Letters," that is, as an artist misunderstood and crushed by the philistine culture of the 1890s. This myth of Crane survived well into the 1950s when E. H. Cady and others revealed that Crane shared many of the popular assumptions and beliefs of his time. A second myth introduced by Beer was that of the role of fear in Crane's psychical makeup — an approach which imme-diately suggested the need for a Freudian reading of Crane's life and work. Beer's oft-noted impressionistic style is therefore less significant as a characteristic of the twenties than is his interpretation of Crane in terms of two widely held views of the American artist current during that decade — that our best artists are victimized by American life and that their work expresses above all the drama of their suppressed inner life.

Like Beer, Berryman is usually a delight to read. Beer's strength lies in his ability to gather seemingly disparate concrete details into a single ironic or (less often) pathetic effect. Berryman also has an ironic touch, but his sense of narrative pace is far superior to Beer's, since Beer, in-deed, was not interested in narrative coherence. Moreover, Berryman, unlike Beer, was aware of his responsibilities as a literary biographer. So we are rewarded with graceful accounts of the sources, composition, publishing history, and reputation of Crane's major works. Some of this detailed information has proven to be faulty or incomplete, but the basic outline of Crane's life and work emerges firmly and, on the whole, authoritatively from Berryman's book.

Berryman's long final chapter, "The Color of This Soul," has had some notoriety in American literary criticism as an extreme example of Freudian biography. His thesis, that Crane's Oedipus complex was responsible for his lifelong interest in older, disreputable women, is open to question, since the early death of Crane's father would seem to preclude a heavy reliance upon an Oedipal interpretation of Crane. Moreover, Berryman's collage technique — that is, his gathering together of similar images and symbols from the entire corpus of Crane's work in order to "paste up" a Freudian reading of Crane — is ingenious at best. Horses, the color red, and Negroes do appear in Crane's work, but so do many other symbols. Although it is sometimes dangerous to call upon common sense as a guide when discussing a complex literary figure, A. J. Liebling's criticism of Berryman nevertheless rings true. As Liebling noted in "The Dollars Damned Him" (*New Yorker*, 5 August 1961), a highly intelligent, very young man is apt to get involved with women older than himself, and a man who liked horses is apt to include them in his work.

Although Berryman's final chapter has often been singled out for adverse criticism, many readers are apparently unaware that Berryman's Freudian thesis shaped his interpretation of works discussed at some length earlier in the book, for example, "The Monster" and "The Blue Hotel." In short, Berryman is very much an advance over Beer as a usable scholarly biography but his is still too much a "poetic" biography in a pejorative sense. That is, his imaginative response to his subject colors and controls the work more than most readers would prefer.

Although Edwin H. Cady's study is a critical biography, with more criticism than biography, his section on Crane's life is nevertheless a valuable contribution to Crane biography. Reacting no doubt to the single-thesis approach of Beer and Berryman in biography and Stallman in criticism, Cady refuses to categorize Crane or his work but rather views him as "an uncrystallized experimenter, a youthful pluralist." In two brief but cogent chapters, he defines the tone of the principal moments in Crane's life, confronts the major cruxes in Crane biography, and places Crane firmly in the context of his family, his time, and his friends. In short, Cady's fifty-odd pages constitute an excellent introduction to Crane's life.

In the years following Berryman's *Stephen Crane*, a great deal of Crane biographical material became available. The Columbia and Barrett collections, the Stallman and Gilkes edition of the letters, and the Gilkes biography of Cora Crane, to name but a few such aids, all seemed to open the way for a definitive biography, with R. W. Stallman, the doyen of Crane scholars, the obvious biographer. Unfortunately, the best that can be said of Stallman's massive work is that it will do until a better book is written. It has all of Stallman's weaknesses and few of his strengths. It is discursive, repetitive, poorly organized, padded, overpolemical, and thesis-ridden. Almost every work by Crane, from the most familiar to the most obscure, is subjected to a pedestrian summary of its contents and to a cursory critical discussion, the latter often a rehash of standard Stallman opinions available in superior form elsewhere. And after almost twenty years of berating Beer and Berryman for their errors, Stallman still feels obliged to note every point at which he corrects them.

Saddest of all, Stallman is simply not a good biographer. Important moments in Crane's life, such as the *Commodore* disaster or his Cuban war experiences, are narrated poorly, and Stallman often slips into the cardinal sin of the literary biographer, the too easy translation of biographical fact into literary event. For example, we are told of a college tug-of-war in which Crane participated and are then informed, "That Lafayette College tug-of-war became the flag that is wrenched from the enemy in *The Red Badge.*"

There are flashes of Stallman at his best in character vignettes (Crane and Conrad) or in an occasional provocative remark, but all in all the biography is poorly written and, despite its over 100 pages of documentation, poorly researched. (Many reviewers noted its inaccuracies.) In truth, it is a tired book: it should have been compressed, reorganized, rewritten, and checked fully for accuracy. Stallman had the knowledge and the intellect to produce a major Crane biography, and he was poorly served by those editors and readers who permitted what is essentially a draft to appear in print.

Cazemajou's lengthy study offers in its first part a 225-page survey of Crane's life. Drawing upon all extant scholarship and seeking to resolve the principal problems in the interpretation of Crane's life, Cazemajou on the whole provides a more balanced biography than does Stallman in his *Stephen Crane.* Though he presents no radical rereading of Crane's life, Cazemajou does make important contributions in at least three areas: the religious context of Crane's boyhood, Crane's early New York years, and the role of Cora's personality and life style in Crane's decline after 1896.

I will now discuss biographical studies which bear significantly on particular phases of Crane's career. In general, I omit reminiscences of Crane by friends and relatives. Most such accounts have long been available and their pertinent information has been absorbed into later biographical studies.

Thomas Gullason has explored Crane's family background as it relates to Crane's character and work. His *Stephen Crane's Career: Perspectives and Evaluations* contains a collection of previously unpublished documents bearing on Crane's family, while his "The Fiction of the Reverend Jonathan Townley Crane, D.D." (*AL*, May 1971) republishes four Sunday school stories by Crane's father. Some of the most important articles on Crane's school years are Thomas A. Gullason, "The Cranes at Pennington Seminary" (*AL*, Jan. 1968) for Crane's first prep-school; Lyndon U. Pratt, "The Formal Education of Stephen Crane" (*AL*, Jan. 1939), David E. E. Sloane, "Stephen Crane at Lafayette" (*RALS*, Spring 1972), and Claude Jones, "Stephen Crane at Syracuse" (*AL*, Mar. 1935) for Claverack, Lafayette, and Syracuse. Crane's boyhood and young manhood at Asbury Park are well surveyed by Victor A. Elconin, "Stephen Crane at Asbury Park" (*AL*, Nov. 1948), with particular emphasis on the summer of 1892.

Crane's early years in New York are still obscure, despite the continuing effort by Crane scholars to answer such basic questions as what he was reading and writing, who his friends were, and where he was living. The most important sources of information about this period are Corwin K. Linson's *My Stephen Crane*, edited by Edwin H. Cady (Syracuse, N.Y., 1958), and the various recollections of Hamlin Garland. Neither writer is completely dependable, though Garland's invaluable accounts have been more or less untangled and interpreted by a number of scholars. Donald Pizer, in "The Garland-Crane Relationship" (*HLQ*, Nov. 1960),[1] corrects Garland's confused and contradictory chronology by reference to his contemporary journals and letters, while Olov W. Fryckstedt, "Crane's *Black Riders*: A Discussion of Dates" (*SN*, 1962); Robert Mane, "Une recontre littéraire: Hamlin Garland et Stephen Crane" (*EA*, Jan.–Mar. 1964); and Stanley Wertheim, "The Saga of March 23rd: Garland, Gilder, and Crane" (*Stephen Crane Newsletter*, Winter 1968) refine and correct Pizer's restructuring of Garland's account of the relationship. Also of much interest is a reminiscence of Crane by Nelson Greene, one of the "Indians" Crane shared a room with during 1894–95, in Stanley Wertheim, "Stephen Crane Remembered" (*SAF*, Spring 1976).

Two other early literary associations which have been explored are those

---

1. Reprinted in Pizer's *Realism and Naturalism in Nineteenth-Century American Literature* (Carbondale, Ill., 1966). Other Pizer articles cited below which are reprinted in this collection are: "Late Nineteenth-Century American Naturalism: An Essay in Definition," "Romantic Individualism in Garland, Norris, and Crane," and "Stephen Crane's *Maggie* and American Naturalism."

of Crane and William Dean Howells and Crane and Elbert Hubbard. The best discussion of Howells and Crane is in Edwin H. Cady's *The Realist at War* (Syracuse, N.Y., 1958), though Clara and Rudolf Kirk also present a useful summary in their edition of Howells's *Criticism and Fiction, and Other Essays* (New York, 1959). Crane and Hubbard are the subject of David H. Dickason's "Stephen Crane and the *Philistine*" (*AL*, Nov. 1943) and Joseph Katz's "How Elbert Hubbard Met Stephen Crane" (*Stephen Crane Newsletter*, Spring 1968).

Most studies of Crane's early New York years have understandably concentrated on such verifiable matters as his friendships. Few scholars have attempted, as does Joseph J. Kwiat in "The Newspaper Experience: Crane, Norris, and Dreiser" (*NCF*, Sept. 1953), to discuss the impact of Crane's free-lance reporting experiences on his work and thought. (Kwiat's "Stephen Crane and Frank Norris: The Magazine and the 'Revolt' in American Literature in the 1890s" [*WHR*, Autumn 1976] and his "Stephen Crane, Literary-Reporter: Commonplace Experience and Artistic Transcendence" [*JML*, 1980] add little to his earlier essay.) But as Ellen Moers demonstrated in her *Two Dreisers* (New York, 1969), the New York newspaper and magazine world of the 1890s was alive with ideas and enthusiasms and with personal intrigue and gossip. Crane was very much part of this life, and we will not fully understand this phase of his experience until we know more about his relationship to the journalistic subculture of the 1890s.

We know much more, of course, about Crane's post-1894 years, after *The Red Badge* brought him fame and notoriety. Saving his English experiences for later discussion, the most important events of this period were his trip west, his filibustering experiences in Florida, his relationship with Cora, his Tenderloin misadventure with Dora Clark, and his reporting of the Greco-Turkish and Cuban wars.

Joseph Katz's introduction to his *Stephen Crane in the West and Mexico* contains a lengthy account of Crane's western trip of late 1895. Bernice Slote, in two important essays, covers somewhat the same ground but with detailed attention to Crane's visit to Nebraska and his encounter there with Willa Cather: "Stephen Crane in Nebraska," in "Stephen Crane: A Portfolio" (*PrS*, Summer 1969) and "Stephen Crane and Willa Cather" (*Serif*, Dec. 1969). The first essay clarifies the itinerary and weather conditions of Crane's visit, the second corrects a number of important details in Cather's widely used "When I Knew Stephen Crane."

Crane's filibustering experiences are fully documented. William Randel has filled in the Jacksonville background in "Stephen Crane's Jacksonville" (*SAQ*, Spring 1963) and "From Slate to Emerald Green: New Light on Crane's Jacksonville Visit" (*NCF*, Mar. 1965), supplemented by Joseph Katz, "Stephen Crane, 'Samuel Carlton,' and a Recovered Letter" (*NCF*, Sept. 1968). Crane's shipwreck adventure has occasioned a controversy over the accuracy of his later account, both in his news story and in "The Open Boat." The problematic issues are: was there treachery aboard the *Commodore*, how many men were in the boat, did the captain shirk his duty, and were the seas rough? Berryman in 1950 and Cyrus Day in "Stephen Crane and the Ten-foot Dinghy" (*BUSE*, Winter 1957) doubt the factual accuracy of Crane's accounts of these matters. Crane has been defended by William Randel, "The Cook in 'The Open Boat'"(*AL*, Nov. 1962); William T. Going, "William Higgins and Crane's 'The Open Boat': A Note About Fact and Fiction" (*PLL*, Winter 1965); and R. W. Stallman, "Journalist Crane in That Dinghy" (*BNYPL*, Apr. 1968). The controversy has served the useful purpose of reminding us that, as in most disasters, the *Commodore* shipwreck produced varying impressions on its participants and observers. Crane's brilliance, most critics would now agree, lay in his shaping of his own impressions into a work of art, whether the waves were high or low on January 2, 1897.

Crane's Jacksonville period also marked the beginning of his relationship with Cora. (He had apparently just escaped from a difficult entanglement with Amy Leslie; see Joseph Katz, "Some Light on the Stephen Crane-Amy Leslie Affair" [*Mad River Review*, Winter 1964–65] and John D. Conway, "The Stephen Crane-Amy Leslie Affair: A Reconsideration" [*JML*, Feb. 1979].) This all-important relationship, first hinted at by Beer and discussed at greater length in later biographies, is in part the subject of Lillian Gilkes in *Cora Crane: A Biography of Mrs. Stephen Crane*. Crane, however, is a somewhat shadowy figure in this study, for Miss Gilkes's interest is centered firmly on Cora. In the author's view, Cora was not the overblown, matronly figure recalled by Conrad, Ford, and James but a heroic late nineteenth-century New Woman riding full-tilt against Victorian conventions. Miss Gilkes's work is based on extensive research in Florida and England and among the Columbia Crane papers, but her biographical method is nevertheless suspect because of her close identification with her subject. (For example, she is confident enough of her material to create dialogue.) The principal value of her biography is not in increasing our understanding of Crane's inner life. Rather, her work is a fascinating account of late nineteenth-century Anglo-American social practice (as distinct from morality) and of the amazingly disordered circumstances of Crane's final years.

Crane's 1896 New York experiences and his adventures as a war correspondent are well surveyed in Stallman and Hagemann's two editions noted above. These may be supplemented by Olov W. Fryckstedt's "Stephen Crane in the Tenderloin" (*SN*, 1962), which is still the best account of the Dora Clark affair, and by Scott C. Osborn's "The 'Rivalry-Chivalry' of Richard Harding Davis and Stephen Crane" (*AL*, Mar. 1956). Two useful reminiscences of Crane's still obscure period in Havana after the conclusion of the Spanish-American War have come to light, the first by Otto Carmichael, "Stephen Crane in Havana: A Newly Discovered Biographical Sketch," in "Stephen Crane: A Portfolio," and the second by Walter Parker, "Re Stephen Crane," in Stanley Wertheim's "Stephen Crane Remembered."

Our knowledge of Crane's English years is based in part on excellent reminiscences and pen portraits by such friends as Conrad, Wells, James, and Ford. Their accounts and the friendships themselves are the subject of Eric Solomon's slight *Stephen Crane in England: A Portrait of the Artist* (Columbus, Ohio, 1964) and Stanley Weintraub's breezy but accurate and substantial *The London Yankees: Portraits of American Writers and Artists in England, 1894–1914* (New York, 1979). The tangled history of Crane's personal relationships, writing, and finances during his English years also receives much attention, as noted earlier, in the introductions to the Virginia Edition. Lillian Gilkes's "Stephen Crane and the Harold Frederics" (*Serif*, Dec. 1969) is a lengthy account not only of this relationship but of the social world of Cora and Crane during their final English phase. Miss Gilkes's essay contains her usual oblique defense of Cora and much unsupported conjecture. But it is also an important attempt to understand the social milieu of the Cranes at Oxted and Brede. Miss Gilkes and Thomas F. O'Donnell contribute as well two notes on the Crane-Frederic relationship which correct Stallman's account in his biography: "Hall Caine, R. W. Stallman and 'The Kate Lyon Fund'" (*Frederic Herald*, Jan. 1969) by O'Donnell; and "Frederic, Crane, and the Stallman Biography" (*Frederic Herald*, Apr. 1969) by Gilkes.

The Brede period itself receives full attention in Gordon Milne's brief monograph *Stephen Crane at Brede: An Anglo-American Literary Circle of the 1890s* (Washington, D.C., 1980) and in a number of essays. No doubt the definitive study of the Christmas play escapade is Jesse S. Crisler's "'Christmas Must Be Gay': Stephen Crane's *The Ghost* — A Play by Divers Hands" (*Proof*, 1973). Crisler devotes over 50 pages to correcting Stallman's version and to providing a detailed history of the occasion; included is a facsimile of the surviving manuscript of the play. Several other useful documentary accounts of the Cranes at Brede have appeared. Sir Shane Leslie recalls the Cranes in a brief memoir, "Stephen Crane in Sussex," in Matthew Bruccoli's *Stephen Crane: 1871–1971, An Exhibition . . .* , while Mark Barr also reminisces about Crane in "The Haunted House of Brede," in Stanley Wertheim's "Stephen Crane Remembered." And in a major research article, "The Library of Stephen and Cora Crane" (*Proof*, 1971), James E. Kibler, Jr., presents an annotated list, based largely on Cora's catalogues, of the Crane library at Brede. Since we have so little hard evidence about Crane's reading, Kibler's article serves an extremely useful purpose.

A number of scholars have held that Crane overproduced and catered to popular taste while in England in order to maintain the style of life represented by Brede Place. An acceptance of this possibility is implicit in Stallman and Gilkes's full accounts of the Cranes in England and it is also the explicit thesis of A. J. Lieblings's "The Dollars Damned Him" and James B. Stronks's "Stephen Crane's English Years: The Legend Corrected" (*PBSA*, July–Sept. 1963). Daniel G. Hoffman's revelation, in "Stephen Crane's Last Novel" (*BNYPL*, June 1960), that Crane was planning to write a Revolutionary War novel in order to capitalize upon the vogue for such fiction also supports this view of his last years. And, finally, E. R. Hagemann's "The Death of Stephen Crane" (*PNJHS*, July 1959) is an exhaustive account, based largely on documents in the National Archives, of Crane's illness, death, and burial, while Stanley Wertheim's "H. G. Wells to Cora Crane: Some Letters and Corrections" (*RALS*, Fall 1979) adds to our knowledge of Crane's final days.

CRITICISM

General Estimates and Interpretations

Some of the early estimates of Crane remain among the best general introductions to his work. George Wyndham's "A Remarkable Book" (*New Review*, Jan. 1896); Edward Garnett's "Mr. Stephen Crane: An Appreciation" (*Academy*, 17 December 1898; reprinted, with additions, in Garnett's *Friday Nights*, New York, 1922); and H. G.Wells's "Stephen Crane: From an English Standpoint" (*NAR*, Aug. 1900; reprinted in *The Shock of Recognition*, edited by Edmund Wilson, New York, 1943) helped to establish such permanent areas of critical interest as Crane's irony and psychological realism, the canon of his best work, and the relationship of his technique and form to painting. Vincent Starrett's "Stephen Crane: An Estimate" (*SR*, July 1920; reprinted in Starrett's *Buried Caesars*, Chicago, 1923) played an important role in the "rediscovery" of Crane and continues to have intrinsic value. Alfred Kazin's pages on Crane in *On Native Grounds* (New York, 1942) and Grant C. Knight's section in *The Critical Period in American Literature* (Chapel Hill, N.C., 1951) have not weathered as well as the essays by Garnett and Wells. The best more recent general estimates, most of which combine biographical and critical interpretation, are by Warner Berthoff, *The Ferment of Realism* (New

York, 1965); Larzer Ziff, *The American 1890s* (New York, 1966); Jay Martin, *Harvests of Change* (Englewood Cliffs, N.J., 1967); and Jean Cazemajou, *Stephen Crane* (UMPAW, 1969).

I will now discuss, more or less in chronological order, the major critical approaches to Crane's work. My classification is, of course, in part arbitrary, but some classification is necessary if the basic tendencies in Crane criticism are to be made discernible.

In Crane's own day it was common to call him an impressionist and to associate his techniques with those of the studio. Garnett and Wells stressed this aspect of Crane, as did Ford Madox Ford in his later and influential article "Techniques" (*SoR*, July 1935). Impressionism, however, has often served merely as a vague description of Crane's color sense and of his highly distinctive narrative technique and prose style. More recent critics who are absorbed in the possibility of discussing Crane as an impressionist have refined their use of the term in several ways. One group has sought to define his impressionism by locating its source in Crane's contemporary world. Joseph J. Kwiat, in "Stephen Crane and Painting" (*AQ*, Winter 1952), builds valiantly on a base of scanty evidence to claim that Crane's association with various minor illustrators during 1891–93 led to his acceptance of impressionistic ideas and techniques. On the whole, it has been less difficult to find literary sources for Crane's impressionistic aesthetic. James B. Colvert, in "The Origins of Stephen Crane's Literary Creed" (*University of Texas Studies in English*, 1955), persuasively contends that Crane's voiced literary ideals ("I understand that a man is born into the world with his own pair of eyes," etc.) parallel those of the artist Dick Heldar in Kipling's *The Light That Failed*. Donald Pizer, in "Romantic Individualism in Garland, Norris, and Crane" (*AQ*, Winter 1958), and Stanley Wertheim, in "Crane and Garland: The Education of an Impressionist" (*NDQ*, Winter 1967), stress the impact of Garland's impressionistic beliefs on Crane during the vital 1892–93 period. Even Crane's color sense has been associated with a literary source, by Robert L. Hough, in "Crane and Goethe: A Forgotten Relationship" (*NCF*, Sept. 1962).

The difficult task of attempting to pinpoint what is meant by Crane's stylistic impressionism was first undertaken at any length by R. W. Stallman in his 1952 *Omnibus* volume. Stallman's belief that Crane's style is "prose pointillism" suffers from the inevitable fuzziness that results from the translation of brush and canvas terminology into literary practice and effect. Much more useful are the important articles by Sergio Perosa, "Stephen Crane fra naturalismo e impressionismo" (*Annali di Ca'Foscari* [Venezia], 1964; translated and reprinted in *Stephen Crane: A Collection of Critical Essays*, edited by Maurice Bassan); by Orm Øverland, "The

Impressionism of Stephen Crane," in *Americana Norvegica*, edited by
Sigmund Skard and Henry H. Wasser (Philadelphia, 1966); and by Rodney O. Rogers, "Stephen Crane and Impressionism" (*NCF*, Dec. 1969).
Perosa and Øverland closely examine Crane's point-of-view technique,
his episodic structure, his imagery and symbolism, and his syntax and
diction. Rogers means by impressionism in Crane not the usual emphasis
on his color imagery and fragmentary narrative method but rather Crane's
belief that reality is shifting, fleeting, and evanescent and therefore that
experience is ultimately solipsistic. (His point anticipates Frank Bergon's
major study.) On the other hand, Bert Bender, in "Hanging Stephen Crane
in the Impressionist Museum" (*JAAC*, Fall 1976), dismisses the traditional
view that Crane's fictional style owes much to his conscious or unconscious absorption of impressionist ideals and methods from painting.
Bender believes that painting and fiction are incomparable and that
Crane's aesthetic principles, in any case, differ significantly from those
of the impressionist painters. His essay is a healthy corrective to the almost universal acceptance of a relationship between Crane and impressionism. Bender fails to realize, however, that the attempt to describe
Crane as an impressionist may be a useful way of identifying certain characteristics of his mind and style whether or not these in fact have their
sources and analogues in painting.

The long-standing interest in Crane as an impressionist is brought to
a climax by James Nagel's excellent *Stephen Crane and Literary Impressionism* (University Park, Pa., 1980). The major advance represented by
Nagel's book is in the fullness, clarity, and precision of his examination
of this difficult area of Crane studies. Nagel does not so much cast new
light on Crane's impressionism (except perhaps in the relationship between Crane's irony and his impressionistic techniques) as sum up with
admirable good sense where we stand. He is perhaps weakest in his excessive preoccupation with naturalism as the "villain" in Crane criticism,
but this is a minor aberration in an important watershed study of Crane's
literary sensibility.

A significant variation in the interpretation of Crane as an impressionist was first introduced by Charles C. Walcutt in *American Literary Naturalism, A Divided Stream* (Minneapolis, Minn., 1956) and pursued at
greater length by David R. Weimer in *The City as Metaphor* (New York,
1966). Walcutt's remark that Crane is probably closer to expressionism
than impressionism is fully and brilliantly explored by Weimer, who concludes that Crane's fragmentation and stylization of experience are less
related to the eye of the impressionist painter than to the intellect of the
expressionist playwright.

Although Crane's fellow writers have tended to consider him principally as an impressionist, academic criticism, with its ideological bent, has more frequently approached him as a naturalist. Much of this criticism straitjacketed Crane in an abstract definition of naturalism ("pessimistic determinism" or the like) and served little purpose except to pigeonhole him neatly. Two influential studies of this kind are Oscar Cargill's *Intellectual America* (New York, 1941) and Malcolm Cowley's "'Not Men': A Natural History of American Naturalism" (*KR*, Summer 1947; reprinted in *Critiques and Essays on Modern Fiction, 1920–51*, edited by John W. Aldridge [New York, 1952]). This simplistic view of Crane persists even in such otherwise sophisticated works as Desmond Maxwell's *American Fiction: The Intellectual Background* (New York, 1963) and Edward Stone's *Voices of Despair* (Athens, Ohio, 1966). Occasionally it appears in somewhat disguised form, as in Gordon O. Taylor's *The Passages of Thought: Psychological Representation in the American Novel, 1870–1900* (New York, 1969), but is essentially the same old naturalistic wolf.

The three most important studies of Crane as naturalist are Lars Åhnebrink, *The Beginnings of Naturalism in American Fiction* (Uppsala, Sweden, 1950); Charles C. Walcutt, *American Literary Naturalism*; and Donald Pizer, "Nineteenth-Century American Naturalism: An Essay in Definition" (*BuR*, Fall 1965). Åhnebrink seeks to place Crane fully in the European naturalistic tradition, particularly that of Zola. His critical method consists largely of the examination of parallel passages and themes in the work of Crane and such writers as Zola, Tolstoy, Turgenev, and Ibsen. His parallels, however, reveal primarily that descriptions of a slum tenement, for example, will often include odors, noise, and violence. They do not cast light on the distinctive qualities of mind that produced works as different as *Maggie* and *L'Assommoir*. Nevertheless, Åhnebrink's voluminous documentation convincingly establishes the pervasiveness of such subjects as alcoholism and slum conditions in the late nineteenth-century social and literary consciousness of both Europe and America. Walcutt's study of Crane as a naturalist appears to work at cross-purposes with his general thesis that American naturalism is a divided stream — that is, that the nineteenth-century currents of intuitional idealism and mechanistic determinism reach an uneasy and inconsistent union in the naturalistic novel. To Walcutt, Crane is the one major example in American naturalism of a complete and coherent determinist. Walcutt successfully discusses *Maggie* as a deterministic novel, but in his analyses of Crane's later work, including *The Red Badge*, he overemphasizes deterministic threads in a complex pattern of themes. Paradoxically, Walcutt's greatest impact on Crane criticism has probably been less his discussion of Crane than his general thesis in *American Literary Naturalism*. For since 1956 many critics have accepted his belief that American naturalism — including the work of Crane — must be approached as a complex literary phenomenon rather than as merely a weak-minded illustration of a particular philosophical doctrine. Pizer's article follows in the path blazed by Walcutt with two major differences. What Walcutt views as thematically and artistically inept (particularly the mixing of philosophical attitudes), Pizer views as a source of depth and power. And Pizer places Crane in a definition of naturalism which derives from the practice rather than the theory of late nineteenth-century American fiction and which therefore refuses to consider deviations from Zolaesque or other concepts of naturalism as aesthetically or thematically significant.

Two more recent approaches to Crane's naturalism are by Thomas A. Gullason, "Stephen Crane: In Nature's Bosom," in *American Literary Naturalism: A Reassessment,* edited by Yoshinobu Hakutani and Lewis Fried (Heidelberg, 1975) and by Donald Pizer, "Nineteenth-Century American Naturalism: An Approach Through Form" (*ForumH*, Winter 1976). Gullason attempts to identify the various threads of naturalism apparent in all of Crane's work and career; he concludes that Crane has naturalistic qualities but is an untypical naturalist in theme and style. Pizer seeks to isolate in *The Red Badge* the symbolic structure characteristic of much late nineteenth-century American naturalistic fiction.

I have already noted the Freudian aspects of the biographies by Beer and Berryman. Maxwell Geismar, in *Rebels and Ancestors* (Boston, 1953); Daniel G. Hoffman, in *The Poetry of Stephen Crane* (New York, 1957); and Stanley Wertheim, in "Stephen Crane and the Wrath of Jehova" (*Literary Review*, Summer 1964), also view Crane as a classic Oedipal case. Geismar in particular vigorously searches out Oedipal symbols in most of Crane's work. Hoffman, however, adopts this angle of approach as one of several critical methods, and Wertheim explores less blatantly than most Freudian critics the theme of guilt in Crane. Inevitably, *George's Mother* has attracted the greatest attention from Freudian-minded critics. Often a Freudian reading of this novel is awkwardly applied to other major works by Crane, as in Norman Lavers's "Order in *The Red Badge of Courage*" (*University Review*, Summer 1966). Jungian readings of Crane tend to concentrate on *The Red Badge* and Crane's concept of the hero. John E. Hart's "*The Red Badge of Courage* as Myth and Symbol" (*UKCR*, Summer 1953) remains the best of such studies. Donald B. Gibson's *The Fiction of Stephen Crane* (Carbondale, Ill., 1968) is ostensibly a study of Crane in relation to Erich Neumann's Jungian *The Origins and History of Consciousness*. In fact, it is reading of Crane in which the author mechanically applies a free will-determinism formula to the interpretation of work after work.

Crane's social themes are often mentioned in discussions of his New York slum writing, but there is little full-scale discussion of him as a critic of his society. (He appears only briefly, for example, in W. F. Taylor's standard *The Economic Novel in America*.) Two exceptions, both of which discover a strong sense of the reality of the class struggle in his work, are Russell B. Nye's "Stephen Crane as Social Critic" (*Modern Quarterly*, Summer 1940) and M. Solomon's "Stephen Crane: A Critical Study" (*Masses & Mainstream*, Jan. and Mar. 1956). Neither study is entirely persuasive, primarily because of the difficulty in separating Crane's social attitudes from other, more prominent aspects of his thought—his views of God and nature, for example. Moreover, it is obvious that his social ideas cannot be adequately described by summarizing the plots of his fiction, as Robert W. Schneider does in *Five Novelists of the Progressive Era* (New York, 1965), or by a cursory treatment of a complex subject, as in Donald Vanouse's "Women in the Writings of Stephen Crane" (*SHR*, Spring 1978). An essay of a far different order of merit is Robert Shulman's "Community, Perception, and the Development of Stephen Crane: From *The Red Badge* to 'The Open Boat'" (*AL*, Nov. 1978). Concentrating on Crane's visual and journey imagery, Shulman cogently traces the movement in Crane's fiction (and presumably in Crane himself) from an "outcast" to a "community" social ethic, culminating in an excellent reading of "The Open Boat."

Studies of Crane as religious symbolist tend to concentrate on *The Red Badge* and on his poetry. Since examination of religious themes in his poetry usually occurs within full-scale discussions of his poetic art, I will reserve commenting on these themes until later. More pertinent at this point is the controversial reading of *The Red Badge* by R. W. Stallman, a reading which implies that Christian symbolism is at the heart of all of Crane's work. Stallman's interpretation of *The Red Badge* as a story of Christian redemption first appeared in his 1951 Modern Library edition of the novel. Since then he has repeated it many times (with occasional variations in emphasis), most notably in his "Stephen Crane: A Revaluation," in *Critiques and Essays on Modern Fiction, 1920–51*, edited by John W. Aldridge, in his 1952 *Omnibus* volume, in his essays on Crane in *The Houses That James Built* (East Lansing, Mich., 1961), and in his Crane biography. Few readers of Crane would deny that Christian symbols and themes pervade his work, but most would probably echo Isaac Rosenfeld's early comment in "Stephen Crane as Symbolist" (*KR*, Spring 1953) that Stallman "is working his poor horse to death." I shall take up Stallman's reading of *The Red Badge* at greater length later, but it is appropriate at this time to note such major negative responses to his methods and thesis as Philip Rahv, "Fiction and the Criticism of Fiction" (*KR*,

Spring 1956); Norman Friedman, "Criticism and the Novel" (AR, Fall 1958); and, in particular, Stanley B. Greenfield, "The Unmistakable Stephen Crane" (PMLA, Dec. 1958). The general import of these responses is that Stallman has woven a disparate group of images into a theme which is extraneous to or contradicted by the themes present in the plot and characterization of the novel.

Concern with Crane's religious themes continues, ranging from the obsessional ingeniousness of Daniel Knapp's "Son of Thunder: Stephen Crane and the Fourth Evangelist" (NCF, Dec. 1969) to the reasoned moderation of George Monteiro's "Stephen Crane and the Antinomies of Christian Charity" (CentR, Winter 1972). Knapp, who believes that Crane's major work is largely an allegorization of the Gospel according to John, devotes his essay to a demonstration of the buried Christ allegory in Maggie, George's Mother, and "The Blue Hotel." The result is a massive collection of forced readings which derive inevitably from the clarity and fixity of the determining pattern in the critic's mind. Monteiro, on the other hand, while acknowledging Crane's conscious repudiation of much Christian belief, convincingly demonstrates his acceptance in such works as Maggie and "The Monster" of the Christian ideal of charity or caritas. Yet another "religious" reading of Crane is "Stephen Crane's Calvinism" (CRevAS, Spring 1971), by Leverett J. Smith, Jr., in which Smith awkwardly and tenuously places Crane's theme of the transforming power of the imagination in a Calvinist context. In all, perhaps the most substantial reading of Crane as essentially a religious writer occurs in Jean Cazemajou's lengthy 1969 Docteur ès Lettres study of Crane, Stephen Crane . . . Écrivain-Journaliste. Thus, for example, Cazemajou interprets Maggie as an allegory of redemption, George's Mother as a banal allegory of the Fall, and The Red Badge as largely shaped by the imagery and theme of Pilgrim's Progress. But both Cazemajou's method of offering several readings and then selecting the Christian for emphasis and his full documentation of the major criticism bearing on a work suggest the judicious rather than the doctrinaire critic.

Another important critical tendency has been to attempt to define Crane's moral position without recourse to the absolutes of pessimistic determinism or Christian redemption. In a series of closely reasoned articles which usually draw upon Crane's best work, a number of critics have discussed Crane's cosmic vision as a complex entity the defies easy classification. The first such writer was John W. Shroeder, in "Stephen Crane Embattled" (UKCR, Winter 1950); followed by Greenfield; by James B. Colvert, in "Style and Meaning in Stephen Crane's 'The Open Boat'" (University of Texas Studies in English, 1958) and "Structure and Theme in Stephen Crane's Fiction" (MFS, Autumn 1959); by George W.

Johnson, in "Stephen Crane's Metaphor of Decorum" (*PMLA*, June 1963); by Max Westbrook, in "Stephen Crane: The Pattern of Affirmation" (*NCF*, Dec. 1959), "Stephen Crane and the Personal Universal" (*MFS*, Winter 1962–63), and "Stephen Crane's Social Ethic" (*AQ*, Winter 1962); by J. C. Levenson, in his introductions to the Virginia Edition; and by Forest Caroll Edwards, in "Decorum: Its Genesis and Function in Stephen Crane" (*TQ*, Summer 1975). Most of these critics accept Greenfield's view that Crane's work exhibits a "balance between the deterministic and volitional views of life." Each, however, asserts this position somewhat differently. Colvert, for example, stresses Crane's ironic relationship to his characters, Johnson their roleplaying, and Westbrook their ethical limitations yet ultimate responsibility. Levenson (like Cady earlier) emphasizes pluralistic reading of Crane, and Edwards discusses Crane's search for a workable principle of decorum to mediate between the pulls of rebellion and acceptance. With the exception of Shroeder's early, tentative article, all are major efforts.

Our greater knowledge of Crane's life and times and the growth of American Studies as a discipline have encouraged critical studies which stress the American roots of his subjects and themes. A pioneer "Americanist" study of Crane was Marcus Cunliffe's "Stephen Crane and the American Background of *Maggie*" (*AQ*, Spring 1955). Cunliffe ably demonstrates that the sources of Crane's story are less attributable to Zola than to American social reform tracts of the 1880s and 1890s. In other attempts to dispel the notion that Crane was a "sport" on the American scene, Donald Pizer, in "Romantic Individualism in Garland, Norris, and Crane," notes the similarity between Crane's aesthetic beliefs and an Emersonian faith in the artist's private vision, and Daniel G. Hoffman, in *The Poetry of Stephen Crane*, locates the specific source of Crane's symbolic technique in an Emersonian aesthetic. Edwin H. Cady has opened up two rich areas of interest of Crane in an American context: Crane and the American enthusiasm for sports, in "Stephen Crane and the Strenuous Life" (*ELH*, Dec. 1961), and Crane and the code of the Christian gentleman, in *Stephen Crane*. Crane's career as an American journalist has also been perceptively characterized by Cady in his introduction to Volume Eight, *Tales, Sketches, and Reports*, of the Virginia Edition and by Bernard Weinstein (more superficially) in his "Stephen Crane: Journalist" (*Crane Centenary Essays*). Another wide-ranging but thin effort is Donald Vanouse's citing of popular images in Crane's work in his "Popular Culture in the Writings of Stephen Crane" (*Journal of Popular Culture*, Fall 1976). And Crane has belatedly and unconvincingly been discussed by David W. Noble in connection with the Edenic myth in *The Eternal Adam and the New World Garden* (New York, 1968).

Perhaps the most important study of Crane in relation to his American setting is Eric Solomon's *Stephen Crane: From Parody to Realism* (Cambridge, Mass., 1966). Solomon believes that many of Crane's themes have their origin in his conscious parody of late nineteenth-century popular literary formulas and subjects—slum reform and temperance writing, romantic war fiction, the dime western, and children's stories. His book is both the best study of the literary origins of Crane's fiction and one of the few full-length studies of Crane which discusses the various major divisions in his work with a coherent and acceptable analytical device, that of Crane as parodist. Nevertheless, this device is also the source of some of the book's weaknesses. Least significant of these is Solomon's neglect of his thesis when he is confronted by an essentially nonparodic work, such as "The Open Boat." More vital are his bypassing of a theoretical discussion of parody as a literary mode and his fuzzy and limited concept of "realism." For Solomon, realism seems to be merely the opposite of what Crane is parodying in particular works, and he concludes that most of Crane's major fiction moves from a parody half to a realistic half. In short, Solomon is often formulistic and he is weak on theory. But no student of Crane can neglect his discussion of the relationship between Crane's writing and the literature of his time.

Crane also has come within the compass of the critical movement which finds most major writers to be existentialists. Two articles which adopt this view toward his work are William B. Stein's "Stephen Crane's *Homo Absurdus*" (*BuR*, May 1959) and Florence Leaver's "Isolation in the Work of Stephen Crane" (*SAQ*, Autumn 1962). Both critics find that Crane's work exhibits the existential themes of the absurdity of ethical values and the isolation of man in an amoral, Godless universe. Although these are by no means novel conclusions, both writers state their case persuasively.

Recent major Crane criticism has been characterized by increased attention to his prose style and fictional technique as means of reaching both his fundamental character as a writer and his themes in individual works. Earlier significant studies of this kind, as those by James Colvert and Max Westbrook, have been supplemented and advanced by the work of Jean Cazemajou, Marston LaFrance, Frank Bergon, James Nagel (whose study of Crane's impressionism I have already discussed), and others.

Of the five books on Crane in the last decade, Milne Holton's *Cylinder of Vision: The Fiction and Journalistic Writing of Stephen Crane* (Baton Rouge, 1972) is the least satisfying. Holton's central point—that Crane is concerned with the related problems of seeing and knowing—is flatly and tediously applied to the entire Crane canon (except the poetry) with almost always predictable results. The two major values of Holton's study derive principally from its genesis as a revised dissertation: he has something to say about even the most minor and usually slighted Crane work, and he cites almost all pertinent Crane criticism in his 55 pages of notes and bibliography. Jean Cazemajou's *Stephen Crane . . . Écrivain-Journaliste* also contains unusually extensive accounts of Crane's minor fiction and journalism but is a far more polished and important study than Holton's. And Cazemajou's final chapter, in which he attempts to demonstrate Crane's stylization of experience through metaphor, symbolism, and allegory, is one of the most ambitious such efforts in recent criticism.

Marston LaFrance's *A Reading of Stephen Crane* (Oxford, 1971) is a major study of Crane's technique as a novelist. LaFrance's thesis — and the term "thesis" suggests the strength and pervasiveness of his central position — is that Crane was a moral ironist; that is, that he was always an ironist but that his irony was directed principally against those who refuse to accept responsibility for their actions and beliefs. LaFrance has a fine ear for the nuances of Crane's various ironic tones and devices and we are unlikely to get for some time as full and well written a reading of the ironic permutations and modulations in Crane's work. But in the end LaFrance's study has some of the flavor of a moral tract, of a work in which the critic does not so much shed light on the subject under discussion as seek to persuade us of the rightness of a particular way of life. One feels this moralism particularly in LaFrance's interpretation of Crane's New York fiction, where he has to struggle against the evidence to find threads of the theme of moral responsibility, and in his frequent strident repetition of his thesis. (LaFrance restates his basic position in his lively and intelligent essay "Stephen Crane in Our Time," in *The Chief Glory of Every People*, edited by Matthew J. Bruccoli [Carbondale, Ill., 1973].)

Frank Bergon, in his *Stephen Crane's Artistry* (New York, 1975), also chooses to concentrate on Crane's form and technique but does so with a conscious rejection of LaFrance's view of Crane as a moralist. To Bergon Crane is not seeking to judge man but rather to render the complexity and ambiguity of immediate experience as it is encountered by a distinctive temperament. In one of the most satisfying efforts in all Crane criticism to work closely with the idiosyncrasies of Crane's prose and fictional styles, Bergon convincingly demonstrates the nature and implications of Crane's preoccupation with the individual perception of the immediate in his major fiction. In one sense Bergon's book is a series of "enormous repudiations" in that he finds beside the point the usual approaches to Crane as naturalist, parodist, religious symbolist, etc. But in another sense he himself works within the recent tendency in Crane criticism which seeks to identify Crane's attitude toward life in his techniques.

An interest in Crane's style also characterizes a number of major essays in the *Crane Centenary Essays* collection. In "Stephen Crane: Style as Invention," James B. Colvert summarizes the position which he has been evolving over the past decades. Crane, he believes, is not a realist in the sense that he attempts to describe what he sees; rather, he constantly stylizes his depiction of experience to conform to his inner vision of life as largely a confrontation between weak and deluded man ("the little man") and the world at large, a world dominated by an indifferent nature ("the mountain"). Crane's work is a variation on this theme from its "clever school" shape in the Sullivan County Sketches to its final mythic statement in his major work of 1897–98. Jean Cazemajou works along similar lines in his provocative short essay "*The Red Badge of Courage*: The 'Religion of Peace' and the War Archetype" in which he seeks to identify Jungian archetypes in Crane's consciousness to which adhere permanent clusters of imagery and diction. And Max Westbrook, in his "Whilomville: The Coherence of Radical Language," studies the complex relationship between Crane's language and the degree of distance between author and character suggested by his language.

Also of considerable interest as a speculative essay on Crane's style is Dietmar Haack's "Stephen Crane und die 'kühne' Metapher" (*Jahrbuch für Amerikastudien*, 1969). Haack suggestively argues that Crane's "bold" imagery, and particularly his color imagery, is not only a personal characteristic but is also a permanent vestige of Crane's early allegiance to the "clever school" of writers. Far less successful attempts to approach Crane through his form and technique are Joseph X. Brennan, "Stephen Crane and the Limits of Irony" (*Criticism*, Spring 1969); C. B. Ives, "Symmetrical Design in Four of Stephen Crane's Stories" (*BSUF*, Winter 1969); and Arno Karlen, "The Craft of Stephen Crane" (*GaR*, Fall 1974). Brennan offers a rather jaundiced view of Crane's faults and limitations as an ironist, a view undermined by Brennan's apparent misunderstanding of the technique of indirect discourse. Ives's belief that Crane's short stories rely on the device of the "turning point" seems more useful for some stories than others and in any case adds little to our understanding of Crane's technique. And Karlen's essay must surely be one of the most superficial and uninformed discussions of Crane ever published in a major literary quarterly.

Maggie and Other Early Work

Most critical discussions of Crane's early journalism have appeared in editions of the Sullivan County sketches (Schoberlin and Stallman) and in general studies of his work and career. Inevitably, almost all of this criticism is devoted to isolating those characteristics of Crane's early newspaper work which anticipate later themes and techniques. An excellent demonstration of the possibilities of this approach is Marston LaFrance's "The Ironic Parallel in Stephen Crane's 1892 Newspaper Correspondence" (*SSF*, Fall 1968). LaFrance reveals that a basic Crane technique — the ironic juxtaposition of two seemingly diverse yet essentially similar moral climates — appears in his early accounts of Asbury Park and Ocean Grove. Although limited in scope, LaFrance's discussion is probably more useful than the many analyses which attempt to locate complex philosophical positions in such slight and "clever" works as the Sullivan County sketches.

Crane's New York sketches and tales have attracted the special attention of Maurice Bassan: "Misery and Society: Some New Perspectives in Stephen Crane's Fiction (*SN*, 1963); "The Design of Stephen Crane's Bowery 'Experiment'" (*SSF*, Winter 1964); and "Stephen Crane and 'The Eternal Mystery of Social Condition'" (*NCF*, Mar. 1965). Bassan's first article usefully places Crane's Bowery sketches in the context of the depression of 1893–94, but his final study is a somewhat strident attempt to demonstrate the literary worth of "An Experiment in Luxury." Several of Crane's New York stories receive brief but useful explications in Stanley Wertheim's "Stephen Crane's 'A Detail'" (*MarkhamR*, Fall 1975), George Monteiro's "Society and Nature in Stephen Crane's 'The Men in the Storm'" (*PrS*, Spring 1971), James Nagel's "Structure and Theme in Crane's 'An Experiment in Misery'" (*SSF*, Spring 1973), and Thomas Bonner, Jr.'s "Crane's 'An Experiment in Misery'" (*Expl*, Apr. 1976). One significant trend noted in these essays as well as in the more extensive studies of Crane's fiction already discussed is that "An Experiment in Misery" is gaining stature as a major story equal in interest to "The Bride Comes to Yellow Sky," "The Blue Hotel," etc.

Among general examinations of Crane's New York fiction, Yoshie Itabashi's "New York Sketches — Crane's Creed and Art" (*SELit*, Mar. 1972) diffusely and unsuccessfully seeks to locate Crane's creed of personal honesty in the themes and form of his New York stories and sketches. A much more significant effort — indeed, one of the major recent essays on Crane — is Alan Trachtenberg's "Experiments in Another Country: Stephen Crane's City Sketches" (*SoR*, Spring 1974). Working closely with "The Men in the Storm" and "An Experiment in Misery," Trachtenberg seeks not so much to explicate the stories as to associate Crane's various fictional strategies and narrative voices with an emerging late nineteenth-century urban sensibility. His essay is rich and suggestive and deserves careful study by anyone interested in Crane as a writer of the 1890s.

Maggie is of course the early work by Crane which has received the greatest critical attention. The fullest and most useful introductions to the novel are by James Colvert, in the Virginia Edition, and by Donald

Pizer, in his facsimile edition of the 1893 Maggie. Both Colvert and Pizer stress the native sources of the novel, as do Marcus Cunliffe in "Stephen Crane and the American Background of *Maggie*" and Thomas A. Gullason in "The Sources of Stephen Crane's *Maggie*" (*PQ*, Oct. 1959). The search for native roots, however, has occasionally resulted in straining analogous to earlier attempts to discover French sources for Crane's work. Two examples are Sholom J. Kahn, "Stephen Crane and Whitman: A Possible Source for *Maggie*" (*WWR*, Dec. 1961) and Donald B. Kuspit, "Charles Dana Gibson's Girl" (*Jahrbuch für Amerikastudien*, 1962).

As with *the Red Badge*, critical opinion is divided in its belief as to what constitutes the main thrust of *Maggie*. Most early critics, and more recently David Fitelson in "Stephen Crane's *Maggie* and Darwinism" (*AQ*, Summer 1964), envision the novel as portraying above all an uncompromising Darwinistic determinism. Another group of readers, while accepting the conditioning force of environment as a principal theme, notes the presence of other major themes as well, particularly those which suggest the continuing significance of character even in a slum world. Howells viewed *Maggie* in this light as early as 1896, in his introduction to the Heinemann edition (reprinted in *Prefaces to Contemporaries [1882–1920]*, edited by George W. Arms et al. [Gainesville, Fla., 1957]), when he noted that the novel resembled a Greek tragedy in its account of a soul "struggling vainly with inexorable fate." Thomas A. Gullason in "Thematic Patterns in Stephen Crane's Early Novels" (*NCF*, June 1961) and Max Westbrook in "Stephen Crane's Social Ethic," however, have stressed that the characters of *Maggie* are either unfilfilled dreamers or do indeed have responsibility for their fates. Perhaps the most pervasive approach to the novel in recent decades holds that Crane's satire is directed against middle class and romantic attitudes rather than against the slum dwellers who unwittingly ape these attitudes. Some critics reach this position by an analysis of Crane's ironic techniques: W. B. Stein, "New Testament Inversions in Crane's *Maggie*" (*MLN*, Apr. 1958); Joseph X. Brennan, "Ironic and Symbolic Structure in Crane's *Maggie*" (*NCF*, Mar. 1962); and Janet Overmyer, "The Structure of Crane's *Maggie*" (*UKCR*, Autumn 1962). Others have concentrated on such particulars as Crane's portrayal of the theater or of Maggie's mother to reach a similar conclusion: R. W. Stallman, "Stephen Crane's Primrose Path" (*New Republic*, 19 September 1955) and "Crane's *Maggie*: A Reassessment" (*MFS*, Autumn 1959); Donald Pizer, "Stephen Crane's *Maggie* and American Naturalism" (*Criticism*, Spring 1965); and William T. Lenehan, "The Failure of Naturalistic Techniques in Stephen Crane's *Maggie*," in *Stephen Crane's "Maggie": Text and Context*, edited by Maurice Bassan.

A good deal of the recent criticism of *Maggie* either covers old ground or adds little to our understanding of the novel. So, for example, Stanley R. Harrison's "Stephen Crane and Death: A Moment Between Two Romanticisms" (*MarkhamR*, May 1971), is an extraordinarily overblown and finally silly reading of *Maggie* and *George's Mother* in relation to the closing of the frontier, while Philip H. Ford's "Illusion and Reality in Crane's *Maggie*" (*ArQ*, Winter 1969) and Katherine G. Simoneaux's "Color Imagery in Crane's *Maggie*" (*CLAJ*, Sept. 1974) are conventional and obvious noncontributions to these well worn topics. Two major recent contributions to the criticism of *Maggie*, however, occur in David M. Fine's "Abraham Cahan, Stephen Crane, and the Romantic Tenement Tale of the Nineties" (*AmerS*, Spring 1973) and in Fredson Bowers's textual commentary in Volume One, *Bowery Tales*, of the Virginia Edition. Fine builds on the work of Marcus Cunliffe and Eric Solomon in seeking to determine the specific base of popular slum fiction against which Crane was reacting; his findings sharpen our awareness of the conventions of plot and characterization which Crane parodies. Bowers's defense of his omission from Chapter Seventeen of the paragraph describing the "huge fat man" leads him into an extended discussion of the religious connotations of Maggie's death. Seldom outside of Biblical explication has one seemingly innocuous phrase—Crane's description of Maggie early in the chapter as "intent upon reaching a distant home"—been subject to such extended and convoluted attention. Ultimately, Bowers's reading—and thus his argument for omission of the paragraph—appears weak in the light of both the casual impact of the phrase in context and the characterization of Maggie elsewhere in the novel.

The aspect of *Maggie* which has received the least satisfactory criticism is its form. R. W. Stallman (in his *Omnibus*) has described *Maggie* as a novel of alternating moods, but a description of this kind is applicable to most fiction. Malcolm Bradbury, in an offhand but suggestive article, "Sociology and Literary Studies. II. Romance and Reality in *Maggie*" (*JAmS*, July 1969), claims that Crane's ironic juxtaposition of deluded characters and a Darwinistic universe results in a breakdown of the traditional linear plot. Although Bradbury does not describe what has replaced plot as structural principle in *Maggie*, three recent essays do reach toward a cohesive reading of the form and technique of the novel. Picking up on Walcutt's remark that the city in *Maggie* is a "landscape of hysteria," both Robert J. Begiebing, in "Stephen Crane's *Maggie*: The Death of the Self" (*AI*, Spring 1977) and Thomas A. Gullason, in "The Prophetic City in Stephen Crane's 1893 *Maggie*" (*MFS*, Spring 1978), find Crane's device of expressionistic distortion a unifying element in the novel. And Biancamaria Pisapia, in "Stephen Crane: La 'Lunga Logica' di *Maggie*" (*SA*, 1977–78), applies a number of structuralist critical principles in an effort to come to grips with the form of the novel.

George's Mother has received surprisingly little adequate attention.

Joseph X. Brennan, in "The Imagery and Art of *George's Mother*" (*CLAJ*, Dec. 1960), analyzes the imagery of the novel and unconvincingly concludes that George's mother is one of the few "really sympathetic" figures in all of Crane's fiction and that the work is better than *Maggie*. Bernard Weinstein echoes this evaluation, on the basis of Crane's greater knowledge of the Bowery after completing *Maggie*, in his "*George's Mother* and the Bowery of Experience" (*MarkhamR*, Spring 1980). Katherine G. Simoneaux's "Color Imagery in Crane's *George's Mother*" (*CLAJ*, June 1971) throws no more light on the novel than her equally thin study of the imagery of *Maggie*. Marston LaFrance's "*George's Mother* and the Other Half of *Maggie*" (*Crane Centenary Essays*) adds little to his point in *A Reading of Stephen Crane* that Crane holds his slum characters — in this instance George Kelcey and Jimmie Johnson — morally responsible for their failure of will. And though James B. Colvert, in his introduction to the Virginia *Bowery Tales*, deals successfully with the complicated problem of the dating of the composition of the novel (see also Maurice Bassan, "An Early Draft of *George's Mother*" [*AL*, Jan. 1965]) he appears to be forcing his contention that Crane wrote the work as a "realistic" novel in the manner of Howells and Garland because of their criticism of *Maggie*. Colvert and many other critics have noted that *George's Mother*, because of its mother-son center and its temperance and religious themes, is the most personal of Crane's novels. This characteristic and the comparatively low-keyed techniques of the novel have perhaps deterred critics from full consideration of what is undoubtedly a major work.

The Red Badge of Courage

The best general introductions to *The Red Badge of Courage* are those by Richard Chase and Frederick C. Crews in their editions of the novel (Boston, 1960, and Indianapolis, Ind., 1964) and by Edwin H. Cady in his *Stephen Crane*. Two useful collections of criticism are *Stephen Crane's "The Red Badge of Courage": Text and Criticism*, edited by Richard Lettis et al. (New York, 1960) and *The Red Badge of Courage*, edited by Sculley Bradley et al., 2nd revised edition (New York, 1976).

At one stage in the history of Crane scholarship, *The Red Badge* was an active field for source hunters. Crane's reading of Zola and Tolstoy, his acquaintance with Civil War veterans, his knowledge of various Civil War novels and historical works — all were pursued with vigor and often with the intent of establishing a major source. Today, the tendency in general accounts of *The Red Badge* is to deemphasize the importance of sources and to acknowledge the existence of several different threads of influence without stressing one or the other. Nevertheless, some kinds of source study have undoubtedly been more fruitful than others, with the search for literary antecedents perhaps among the less productive because the least demonstrable.

Lars Åhnebrink's *The Beginnings of Naturalism in American Fiction* includes lengthy studies of Crane's possible debts to Zola's *La Débâcle* and to Tolstoy's war fiction. E.C.Brody, in "Tolstoy and Crane's *The Red Badge of Courage*" *(SSASH,* 1978), adds almost nothing to Åhnebrink, but J. C. Levenson, as noted earlier, provides in his introduction to Volume Two of the Virginia Edition a convincing expansion of Åhnebrinks's belief that Tolstoy's *Sebastopol* was a major source. Crane's Homeric parallels have been discussed by Warren D. Anderson, in "Homer and Stephen Crane" *(NCF,* June 1964), and Robert Dusenbery, in "The Homeric Mood in *The Red Badge of Courage"* *(Pacific Coast Philology,* Apr. 1968). And Olga Vickery notes a similarity between the imagery of Dante's Inferno and *The Red Badge* in "The Inferno of the Moderns," *The Shaken Realist,* edited by Melvin J. Friedman and John B. Vickery (Baton Rouge, 1970).

A group of Civil War novels are offered as sources by H. T. Webster, "Wilbur F. Hinman's *Corporal Si Klegg* and Stephen Crane's *The Red Badge of Courage"* *(AL,* Nov. 1939); Thomas F. O'Donnell, "De Forest, Van Petten, and Stephen Crane" *(AL,* Jan. 1956) *(Miss Ravenel's Conversion);* and Eric Solomon, "Another Analogue for *The Red Badge of Courage"* *(NCF,* June 1958) (Joseph Kirkland's *The Captain of Company K).* Alexander R. Tamke, somewhat less convincingly than Solomon, attempts to demonstrate that *The Captain of Company K* is not merely an analogue of *The Red Badge* but a major source —"The Principal Source of Stephen Crane's *Red Badge of Courage," Essays in Honor of Esmond Linworth Marilla,* edited by Thomas A. Kirby and William J. Olive (Baton Rouge, 1970). Several critics have cited essays which contain ideas about war that appear to resemble Crane's. Eric Solomon, in "Yet Another Source for *The Red Badge of Courage"* *(ELN,* Mar. 1965), suggests Horace Porter's "The Philosophy of Courage," and Neal J. Osborn, in "William Ellery Channing and *The Red Badge of Courage"* *(BNYPL,* Mar. 1965), offers Channing's sermon on "War."

The search for the sources of the *Red Badge* often occasions a good deal of thin and unproductive criticism. Some examples are Donald S. Thomas's attempt to link the question which Henry asks the corpse to the religious writings of one of Crane's uncle's, in "Crane's *The Red Badge of Courage"* *(Expl,* May 1969); Frank Sadler's discovery of a "delightful ambiguity" in the obsolete meaning of "fleme" in "Crane's *Fleming:* Appellation for Coward or Hero?" *(AL,* Nov. 1976); and the forced comparison attempted by Toby Fulwiler in "The Death of the Handsome

Sailor: A Study of *Billy Budd* and *The Red Badge of Courage*" *(ArQ,* Summer 1970).

A much more profitable vein of source hunting is that which concerns Crane's use of Civil War material. Lyndon U. Pratt, in "A Possible Source of *The Red Badge of Courage*" *(AL,* Mar. 1939), and Thomas F. O'Donnell, in "John B. Van Petten: Stephen Crane's History Teacher" *(AL,* May 1955), note Crane's association with the Union veteran General Van Petten, his history teacher at Claverack. The most important study of this kind is Harold R. Hungerford's "'That Was at Chancellorsville': The Factual Framework of *The Red Badge of Courage*" *(AL,* Jan. 1963). Hungerford demonstrates beyond doubt that Henry's "Various Battles" are those of Chancellorsville and that Crane's source was principally *Battles and Leaders of the Civil War.* Frederick C. Crews, in his edition of *The Red Badge of Courage,* supplements Hungerford's article by supplying several maps of the battle and by textual annotation which notes references and allusions to the Chancellorsville campaign. Three additional persuasive efforts which suggest that Crane was not drawing upon a single source but was rather writing within a tradition of depiction of the Civil War recruit are Daniel Aaron, *The Unwritten War: American Writers and the Civil War* (New York, 1973), Stanley Wertheim, "*The Red Badge of Courage* and Personal Narratives of the Civil War" *(ALR,* Winter 1973), and John Wilmerding, *Winslow Homer* (New York, 1972). All contribute to our sense that there were enough unromanticized portrayals of the trials of the recruit in Civil War personal narratives, art, and photography to supply a foundation for Crane's own rejection of the conventions of popular Civil War romance.

R. W. Stallman's well-known discussion of the wafer image at the close of Chapter Nine has stimulated interest in the source of the image. Scott C. Osborn, in "Stephen Crane's Imagery: 'Pasted Like a Wafer'" *(AL,* Nov. 1951), locates the image in Kipling's *The Light That Failed* and believes that both Kipling and Crane intended a sealing wax rather than a communion allusion. Stallman came to the rescue of his reading in "The Scholar's Net: Literary Sources" *(CE,* Oct. 1955) but was answered in turn by Edward Stone, in "The Many Suns of *The Red Badge of Courage*" *(AL,* Nov. 1957), and by Eric W. Carlson, in "Crane's *The Red Badge of Courage*" *(Expl,* Mar. 1958). In "Stephen Crane's 'Fierce Red Wafer'" *(ELN,* Dec. 1963), Cecil D. Eby, Jr., indirectly defends Stallman when he claims that the presence of "fierce" in the manuscript does not invalidate a religious allusion. Jean G. Marlowe, however, finds an entirely different source of the metaphor in "Crane's Wafer Image: Reference to an Artillery Primer?" *(AL,* Jan. 1972). In addition, Crane's red badge metaphor has called forth two unconvincing efforts to locate literary sources

— Ryōichi Okada, "Another Source of Crane's Metaphor, 'The Red Badge of Courage'" (*AN&Q*, Jan. 1976) (Cooper's *The Last of the Mohicans*), and Bryant Mangum, "Crane's Red Badge and Zola's" (*ALR*, Summer 1976) (Zola's *La Débâcle*). Another controversy over sources centers on the "hot ploughshares" image which closes the novel. Edward Stone argues in his "Crane and Zola" (*ELN*, Sept. 1963) that Crane derived the image from Zola's *L'Assommoir*. But Marston LaFrance claims, in "Crane, Zola, and the Hot Ploughshares" (*ELN*, June 1970), that the image in fact derives from a medieval legend known to Crane, while A. Bryant Mangum, perhaps most convincingly of all, attributes it, in "The Latter Days of Henry Fleming" (*AN&Q*, May 1975), to Crane's confused and confusing misuse of a Biblical image.

Criticism of *The Red Badge* has been so varied in focus and method that it is difficult to shape a discussion of its major tendencies. It is also often redundant, with the critic unknowingly restating with some slight variation what has been said before by others. Among examples of criticism of this kind are: Tony Tanner, "Stephen Crane's Long Dream of War" (*London Magazine*, Dec. 1968); Carol B. Hafer, "The Red Badge of Absurdity: Irony in *The Red Badge of Courage*" (*CLAJ*, June 1971); Michael J. Hoffman, "*The Red Badge of Courage*: Between Realism and Naturalism," in *The Subversive Vision: American Romanticism in Literature* (Port Washington, N.Y., 1972); Rita K. Gollin, "'Little Souls Who Thirst for Fight' in *The Red Badge of Courage*" (*ArQ*, Summer 1974); and Paul Breslin, "Courage and Convention: *The Red Badge of Courage*" (*YR*, Winter 1977). Of a different order of worthlessness is Jan R. Van Meter's "Sex and War in *The Red Badge of Courage*: Cultural Themes and Literary Criticism" (*Genre*, Mar. 1974), in which the author discovers an extensive layer of buried sexual imagery in the novel (rifles, flags, and the like) and concludes that the *Red Badge* is therefore about sexual initiation and maturity. No doubt it is to some degree, but few readers would accept the degree argued by Van Meter.

Despite the varied character of studies of *The Red Badge*, one problem in particular which has occupied almost all critics is that of Crane's relationship to Henry Fleming at the close of the novel. Does Crane wish us to accept at face value Henry's estimation of himself as a "man"; or is Crane once again ironically depicting Henry's capacity for self-delusion; or is his characterization of Henry consciously or unconsciously ambivalent? To emphasize this particular crux in the interpretation of *The Red Badge* is to oversimplify some critical discussions and to reorient the principal direction of others, but it is perhaps the only way to bring some order in brief compass to a large body of work.

The position that Crane is ruthlessly ironic toward Henry throughout the novel and that the book is therefore a study of man's ability to delude himself under any circumstances is best represented by Charles C. Walcutt in his *American Literary Naturalism, A Divided Stream*. With the principal exception of Jay Martin, in *Harvests of Change*, and, recently, Henry Binder, in "*The Red Badge of Courage* Nobody Knows," most critics have not accepted such an extreme view of Crane's attitude toward Fleming. They argue that evidence both within the novel and in such works as "The Open Boat" reveals Crane's belief that men can become "interpreters" of their experience. A position directly opposed to that of Walcutt can be closely identified with two schools of criticism — the religious and the mythic. If Henry undergoes a sacramental experience in the novel (either in connection with Jim Conklin or in relation to battle in general) or if he is initiated into manhood in any one of several mythic patterns, his final self-evaluation is lent authority, since it is the product of his maturation. The religious interpretation of *The Red Badge* — in particular the interpretation of Jim Conklin's death as a redemption experience — is of course closely associated with the work of R. W. Stallman, from the introduction to his Modern Library edition in 1951 to his 1968 biography. (It would be an interesting exercise, by the way, to trace the permutations in the tone of Stallman's discussions of the redemption theme in *The Red Badge*, from the certainty of the early 1950s to the willingness to hedge in 1968. But major critics, like major writers, should not be held to a foolish consistency, and the religious center of the novel has always been the principal focus of Stallman's interpretation.) The fullest endorsement of Stallman's redemption reading is by Daniel G. Hoffman in his introduction to *The Red Badge of Courage and Other Stories* (New York, 1957). The most elaborate and successful interpretation of the novel as an initiation myth is by John E. Hart, in "*The Red Badge of Courage* as Myth and Symbol." A rather weak echo of Hart's thesis can be found in David L. Evans, "Henry's Hell: The Night Journey in *The Red Badge of Courage*" (*Proceedings of the Utah Academy of Science, Arts, and Letters*, 1967).

In other "affirmative" readings of *The Red Badge*, however, there is less of a sense that a particular critical method, such as symbolic imagery or myth criticism, has produced a predictable interpretation. A sizable number of critics have had the "felt response" that Crane wished to affirm some aspect of experience in his depiction of Henry and they have struggled manfully in order to define the nature of this theme. So James B. Colvert, Eric Solomon, and John Fraser — in "Structure and Theme in Stephen Crane's Fiction"; "The Structure of *The Red Badge of Courage*" (*MFS*, Autumn 1959); and "Crime and Forgiveness: *The Red Badge* in Time of War" (*Criticism*, Summer 1967) — contend that Fleming matures during the novel in his understanding of social and moral reality and that this maturity takes the fictional configuration of his movement from isolation to group acceptance, loyalty, and duty. This is also the position of Marston LaFrance's lengthy and penetrating analysis of Crane's ironic themes in the novel in his *A Reading of Stephen Crane*, and of Ben Satterfield's "From Romance to Reality: The Accomplishment of Private Fleming" (*CLAJ*, June 1981). Other critics, though they also stress some growth on Henry's part, see his development in less positive terms. James T. Cox, in "The Imagery of *The Red Badge of Courage*" (*MFS*, Autumn 1959), and Robert Shulman, in "*The Red Badge of Courage* and Social Values: Crane's Myth of His America" (*CRevAS*, Spring 1981), argue persuasively that Henry "progresses" from a romantic or unformed vision of the world to an awareness that man lives in a hostile and godless universe. A third group of critics often adopts Freudian ideas to maintain that Henry's maturity stems from his ability to exorcise the specter of fear in its various guises. Perhaps the best of such readings is Daniel Weiss's "*The Red Badge of Courage*" (*Psychoanalytic Review*, Summer and Fall 1965), though the articles by Bernard Weisberger, "*The Red Badge of Courage*," in *Twelve Original Essays on Great American Novels*, edited by Charles Shapiro (Detroit, Mich., 1958), and Kermit Vanderbilt and Daniel Weiss, "From Rifleman to Flagbearer: Henry Fleming's Separate Peace in *The Red Badge of Courage*" (*MFS*, Winter 1965–66), should be noted. Somewhat analogous in method and findings is William Wasserstrom's overwrought "Hydraulics and Heroics: William James and Stephen Crane" (*Prospects*, 1979), in which Wasserstrom holds that Crane (as is revealed by Henry's regeneration during the second day's activities) shared James's vitalist notion of human behavior.

The critical approach which stresses that purposeful ambivalence is the key to the close of the novel stems largely from Stanley B. Greenfield's influential article "The Unmistakable Stephen Crane." Greenfield argues that Crane portrays life as an experience in which the individual can both learn and remain deluded. Henry, for example, has gained from his experiences but he is nevertheless deluded in his understanding of what he has gained. Thus, Crane's tone is the mixed one of sympathetic identification and of irony. Ralph Ellison states this view of the novel succinctly in *Shadow and Act* (New York, 1964), when he writes that "although Henry has been initiated into the battle of life, he has by no means finished with illusion — but that, too, is part of the human condition." Further support of Greenfield's thesis can be found in Frederick C. Crews's introduction to *The Red Badge;* Donald Pizer, "Nineteenth-Century American Naturalism: An Essay in Definition"; Larzer Ziff, *The American 1890s;* John J. McDermott, "Symbolism and Psychological Realism in *The Red Badge of Courage*" (*NCF*, Dec. 1968); and Thomas L. Kent, "Epistemological Uncertainty in *The Red Badge of Courage*" (*MFS*, Winter 1981/82).

This position is summed up and advanced by Frank Bergon's account, in his *Stephen Crane's Artistry*, of Crane's rendering through style and form of the complex impact of experience on Henry, and by J. C. Levenson's full and convincing discussion, in his introduction to *The Red Badge* in the Virginia Edition, of what Crane's revisions and excisions can tell us about the themes and form of the novel. Levenson's and Bergon's conclusion, that Crane is more concerned with rendering the unresolvable complexities of the inner life than in depicting a drama of moral redemption, has been evolving in Crane criticism for some time; given Levenson's evidence in the genesis of the text and his and Bergon's critical insight, this view of the novel takes on even greater weight.

To some critics, however, the ambivalences (or ambiguities) at the close of the novel constitute major weaknesses either in Henry or in Crane's artistry. William B. Dillingham, "Insensibility in *The Red Badge of Courage*" (*CE*, Dec. 1963), and John W. Rathbun, in "Structure and Meaning in *The Red Badge of Courage*" (*BSUF*, Winter 1969), believe that Henry's movement from introspective self-analysis to instinctive participation in group action is necessary and triumphant but that it also represents the loss of a distinctively human form of sensitivity. And Clark Griffith, in "Stephen Crane and the Ironic Last Word" (*PQ*, Jan. 1968), holds that Crane's belief that life is an insoluble puzzle led him to undermine, with a final ironic touch, our acceptance of any meaning which his characters think they have gained from experience. Griffith's position is not far from the view that the insoluble ambiguities at the close of *The Red Badge* stem from Crane's conscious or unconscious confusion. John Berryman writes more frankly than most readers who hold this view when he comments, in "Stephen Crane, *The Red Badge of Courage*," in *The American Novel*, edited by Wallace Stegner (New York, 1965), "I do not know what Crane intended. Perhaps he intended to have his cake and eat it too — irony at the end, but heroism too." Mordecai Marcus, in "The Unity of *The Red Badge of Courage*," in *Stephen Crane's "The Red Badge of Courage": Text and Criticism*, edited by Richard Lettis et al., and James B. Colvert, in "Stephen Crane's Magic Mountain," in *Stephen Crane: A Collection of Critical Essays*, edited by Maurice Bassan, also adopt this position. Marcus asserts that Crane could not make up his mind whether Henry had matured or was deluded, while Colvert, in a probing and provocative essay, finds that Crane's joining of sentimental solipsism and ironic deflation in his own self-evaluation is the underlying source of the novel's flawed conclusion.

In addition to the recent attempt to demonstrate that Crane's effort in *The Red Badge* is to dramatize the unresolved complexities of consciousness rather than the certainties of moral growth, there have been a number of valuable studies of the novel which seek to place it in significant historical and literary contexts: Wayne Charles Miller, *An Armed America: Its Face in Fiction: A History of the American Military Novel* (New York, 1970); Harry B. Henderson, *Versions of the Past: The Historical Imagination in American Fiction* (New York, 1974); Robert M. Rechnitz, "Depersonalization and the Dream in *The Red Badge of Courage*" (*SNNTS*, Spring 1974); and Robert Shulman, "*The Red Badge of Courage* and Social Values: Crane's Myth of His America." Concentrating on the novel's social and psychological realism, Miller ably documents its role in the development of American war fiction. Henderson's section on Crane, "*The Red Badge of Courage*: The Search for Historical Identity," is a brilliant attempt to reconcile Crane's historical and naturalistic imaginations — or, put another way, to trace the ironic tension arising from Henry's attempt to define himself in "public recorded history" by means of asserting his private instinctive self. Rechnitz's essay draws heavily on several earlier currents of *Red Badge* criticism — in particular Walcutt's emphasis on the ironic close of the novel and Dillingham's on Henry's loss of sensitivity and individuality — in order to suggest that Henry's vision of peace and escape at the conclusion places him in the American tradition of "lighting out for the territory" when threats to personal freedom and the pressure of responsibility become too great. Shulman believes that the imagery of inchoate violence in the novel accurately mirrors American life of the 1880s and 1890s. A somewhat similar close reading of the interplay of social and psychological reality in the novel (though in this instance not in a historical context) is Leland Krauth's "Heroes and Heroics: Stephen Crane's Moral Imperative" (*South Dakota Review*, Summer 1973). Krauth usefully unravels Crane's complex attitude toward heroism as a key to understanding the ambiguity of the close of the novel.

Studies of the form of *The Red Badge* tend to concentrate on its imagery and symbolism, with Stallman's religious reading often serving as a starting point. Stallman's interpretation of the imagery and symbolism of *The Red Badge* (as well as his reply to critics of this approach) can best be found in *The Houses That James Built*. Edwin H. Cady states the position of those critics who reject Stallman's thesis when he writes in his *Stephen Crane*: "The decisive difficulties with the Christian-symbolist reading of *The Red Badge*, it seems, are that there appears to be no way to make a coherent account of the symbols as referential to Christian doctrine and then to match that with what happens in the novel." A number of critics other than Stallman have pursued various threads of imagery in the novel with less ambitious aims but often with more productive results. Among these are Claudia C. Wogan, "Crane's Use of Color in *The Red Badge of Courage*" (*MFS*, Summer 1960) (a simple listing); Mordecai and Erin Marcus, "Animal Imagery in *The Red Badge of Courage*" (*MLN*, Feb. 1959); James W. Tuttleton, "The Imagery of *The Red Badge of Courage*" (*MFS*, Winter 1962–63) (pagan religious imagery); William J. Free, "Smoke Imagery in *The Red Badge of Courage*" (*CLAJ*, Dec. 1963); John J. McDermott, "Symbolism and Psychological Realism in *The Red Badge of Courage*" (wound symbolism); and Reid Maynard, "Red as a Leitmotif in *The Red Badge of Courage*" (*ArQ*, Summer, 1974). Other than Stallman, the major reading of *The Red Badge* as a work in which theme and form arise out of a complex interaction of image patterns is James T. Cox's "The Imagery of *The Red Badge of Courage*." Cox's brilliant commentary on various imagistic threads (particularly those involving the sun) is a high point in the application of New Criticism techniques to *The Red Badge*. That is, his argument is persuasive but it is occasionally difficult to recall that he is writing about *The Red Badge*.

A secondary area of formalistic analysis has been the overall structure of the novel. R. W. Stallman has often called the form of *The Red Badge* "a repetitive alternation of contradictory moods." Thomas M. Lorch, in "The Cyclical Structure of *The Red Badge of Courage*" (*CLAJ*, Mar. 1967), also stresses repetitive change, though that of action and of Henry's thought rather than of mood. On the other hand, Eric Solomon, in "The Structure of *The Red Badge of Courage*," and John W. Rathbun, in "Structure and Meaning in *The Red Badge of Courage*," suggest that the key to the novel's form is its developmental structure. Clinton S. Burhans, in "Twin Lights on Henry Fleming: Structural Parallels in *The Red Badge of Courage*" (*ArQ*, Summer 1974) expands at length on the frequently noted division of the novel into ironically juxtaposed parallel halves. Mordecai Marcus, in "The Unity of *The Red Badge of Courage*," *Stephen Crane's "The Red Badge of Courage": Text and Criticism*, edited by Robert Lettis et al., finds that Crane's virtuoso irony constitutes the formal unity of the work. And Donald Pizer, in "A Primer of Fictional Aesthetics" (*CE*, Mar. 1968), uses *The Red Badge* to illustrate the ways in which formalistic analysis can be brought to bear on a complex work of fiction.

Major recent interest in the form of *The Red Badge* has centered on its point-of-view technique and its diction. Early studies of Crane's point-of-view technique were by Edwin Cady (in his *Stephen Crane*) and Robert C. Albrecht, in "Content and Style in *The Red Badge of Courage*" (*CE*, Mar. 1966). A more ambitious effort is Clinton S. Burhans's "Judging Henry Judging: Point of View in *The Red Badge of Courage*" (*BSUF*,

Spring 1974). Burhans adds little to Walcutt's thesis that Crane is almost always ironic in his attitude toward Henry but he does supply a careful and full account of Crane's constant undermining of Henry's judgments in the novel.

In his "Crane's Henry Fleming: Speech and Vision" (*ForumH*, Winter 1961), Robert L. Hough comments briefly on Crane's shift in levels of diction in *The Red Badge*. Breaking considerably more new ground are three studies of the language of the novel—Jean Cazemajou, "*The Red Badge of Courage*: The 'Religion of Peace' and the War Archetype" (*Crane Centenary Essays*), which I have already discussed under general estimates of Crane; W. M. Frohock, "*The Red Badge* and the Limits of Parody" (*SoR*, Winter 1970); and Neil Schmitz, "Stephen Crane and the Colloquial Self" (*MQ*, Summer 1972). Both Frohock and Schmitz confront the vexing problem of Crane's use of the stereotyped diction of sentimental fiction, particularly that of bucolic idylity, when representing Henry's thoughts. Frohock argues convincingly that Crane intends no parody when attributing this language to Henry at the close of the novel, while Schmitz sees more conscious irony and defends the validity of the device. Both essays are provocative attempts to come to grips with an important aspect of Crane's diction. The equally troublesome matter of Crane's seemingly inconsistent use of dialect in the novel is dealt with at great length by Fredson Bowers in his introduction to the facsimile of the novel and his textual introduction to Volume Two of the Virginia Edition. Bowers convincingly concludes that much of the inconsistency derives from Crane's only partly completed attempt to revise the dialect after Hamlin Garland read the manuscript.

Major Short Fiction: "The Open Boat," The Monster,"
"The Bride Comes to Yellow Sky," and "The Blue Hotel"

I should begin by noting that Jean Cazemajou's *Stephen Crane . . . Écrivain-Journaliste* contains unusually full and clearheaded (though by no means entirely original) readings of each of Crane's major stories, and that J. C. Levenson's 118-page introduction to Volume Five of the Virginia Edition, *Tales of Adventure*, contains full accounts of the biographical context of each of the stories except "The Monster" as well as capsule critical readings of each story.

There is substantial agreement among Crane critics that "The Open Boat" is his best short work (many would say his best work of any length) and that the story's central theme concerns nature's indifference to man, with a significant corollary theme that man is capable of a sympathetic union with his comrades in adversity, if not with nature. Critical attention has focused, therefore, on various ways of stating this theme and on Crane's mastery of technique. Richard P. Adams, for example, in "Naturalistic Fiction: 'The Open Boat'" (*TSE*, 1954), notes that Crane's covert nostalgia for a natural world of warmth and relatedness is responsible for the emotional and thematic power of the story. Peter Buitenhuis, on the other hand, in "The Essentials of Life: 'The Open Boat' as Existentialist Fiction" (*MFS*, Autumn 1959), looks forward rather than backward for a controlling focus and finds that Camus's idea of the absurd can best describe the central vision of experience expressed by "The Open Boat." And Mordecai Marcus, in "The Three-Fold View of Nature in 'The Open Boat'" (*PQ*, Apr. 1962), notes that nature in the story is portrayed sequentially as malevolently hostile, as thoughtlessly hostile, and, finally, as indifferent.

Much of the recent criticism of "The Open Boat" is of little value. Max L. Autrey, in "The Word Out of the Sea: A View of Crane's 'The Open Boat'" (*ArQ*, Summer 1974), supplies a conventional naturalistic reading; Eddy Dow, in "Cigars, Matches, and Men in 'The Open Boat'" (*Re: Arts and Letters*, 1975), forces a connection between the cigar passage and the theme and form of the story; Joseph X. Brennan, in "Stephen Crane and the Limits of Irony," misjudges the nature of the ironic mode in the story; Kenneth T. Reed, in "'The Open Boat' and Dante's *Inferno*: Some Undiscovered Analogues" (*Stephen Crane Newsletter*, Summer 1970), unconvincingly discovers parallel mythic journeys in the two works; and William K. Spofford, "Stephen Crane's 'The Open Boat': Fact or Fiction?" (*ALR*, Autumn 1979) makes the simplistic point that the themes present in Crane's fictional representation of the event are anticipated in earlier works.

Three essays which also add little that is new to the reading of the story but which nevertheless usefully and sharply recapitulate traditional approaches are Donna Gerstenberger, "'The Open Boat': Additional Perspective" (*MFS*, Winter 1971–72); James Nagel, "The Narrative Method of 'The Open Boat'" (*Revue des Langues Vivantes*, 1973); and Bert Bender, "The Nature and Significance of 'Experience' in 'The Open Boat'" (*JNT*, Spring 1979). All three writers concern themselves with the epistemological center of the story — that is, with how the correspondent attempts to know reality, with Bender reaching the suggestive conclusion that the correspondent's insight resembles one of William James's varieties of religious experience.

On the whole, the best work on "The Open Boat" has dealt with Crane's craftsmanship. Caroline Gordon, in "Stephen Crane" (*Accent*, Spring 1949; reprinted in Caroline Gordon and Allen Tate, *The House of Fiction*, New York, 1950), and James B. Colvert, in "Style and Meaning in

Stephen Crane's 'The Open Boat,'" concentrate on Crane's point-of-view technique, while Peter Buitenhuis, in "The Essentials of Life: 'The Open Boat,'" and John T. Frederick, in "The Fifth Man in 'The Open Boat'" (*CEA*, May 1968), are particularly apt in analyzing Crane's language and imagery. Two of the best overall studies of the story are by Daniel G. Hoffman, in *The Poetry of Stephen Crane*, and Andrew N. Lytle, in "'The Open Boat': A Pagan Tale," in *The Hero with the Private Parts* (Baton Rouge, La., 1966). Hoffman revealingly demonstrates the close relationship between "The Open Boat" and Crane's best poetry, and Lytle discusses with sensitivity and clarity Crane's expert handling of point of view, plot, characterization, and imagery. Two more recent stimulating essays on the formal structure of the story are by E. R. Hagemann, "'Sadder than the End': Another Look at 'The Open Boat'" (*Crane Centenary Essays*) and George Monteiro, "The Logic Beneath 'The Open Boat'" (*GaR*, Fall 1972). After a profitless logic-chopping opening discussion of the subtitle of the story, Hagemann offers an important summary (supplementing Stallman's) of the sinking of the *Commodore* and a carefully thought out reading of the balanced structure of the story. Monteiro, who in a number of essays since 1969 has sought to reinterpret Crane as a religious writer, identifies the "logic" beneath the story as an emblematic though loose and informal Christian allegory in which the sea is the world, the life boat is the church, etc.

"The Monster" has grown in critical reputation during the last several decades. The satiric portrayal of village morality in the story has been recognized from the beginning and has often been well described — see, for example, Wilson Follett's introduction to Volume Three of *The Work of Stephen Crane* — but much early criticism which goes beyond this commonplace was often merely biographical or idiosyncratic. Thus, Sy Kahn, in "Stephen Crane and the Giant Voice in the Night: An Explication of *The Monster*," in *Essays in Modern American Literature*, edited by Richard E. Langford (DeLand, Fla., 1963), suggests somewhat irrelevantly that Crane's experiences with Cora led him to condemn middle class morality on its home grounds, the small town. And James Hafley, in *"The Monster* and the Art of Stephen Crane" (*Accent*, Summer 1959), is blatantly ingenious in his exploration of the imagery of the story. However, Thomas A. Gullason, in "The Symbolic Unity of 'The Monster'" (*MLN*, Dec. 1960), convincingly charts the ironic reversals which are central to the story's satiric thrust. And J. C. Levenson, in a discussion which has wide-ranging implications for Crane's mind and art (in Levenson's introduction to Volume Seven of the Virginia Edition), notes the two major interlocking themes of the story — Crane's portrayal of the "psychological

landscape" of American life by means of the macabre, and his ironic juxtaposition of the pulls of ethical belief on the one hand and the practical
requirements of "civilization" on the other.

Criticism of "The Monster" during the last decade has considerably
advanced our understanding of the story. Max Westbrook's earlier noted
"Whilomville: The Coherence of Radical Language" (*Crane Centenary
Essays*) contributes to our realization of the connection between Crane's
point-of-view technique and role playing in the story. From another direction, John R. Cooley, in "'The Monster'— Stephen Crane's 'Invisible Man'"
(*MarkhamR*, Fall 1975), offers one of the most useful readings so far of
the role and significance of the blackness of Henry Johnson. And in one
of the best recent essays on a Crane story, Charles W. Mayer, in "Social
Forms vs. Human Brotherhood in Crane's *The Monster*" (*BSUF*, Summer 1973), perceptively places the central social themes of the story in
the context of both Crane's career and the fundamental interests of the
nineteenth-century American novelist. Much less successful is the study
by Charles E. Modlin and John R. Byers, Jr., "Stephen Crane's 'The Monster' as Christian Allegory" (*MarkhamR*, May 1973), which resembles the
essay by Daniel Knapp noted earlier in that its authors seek to find exact
parallels between the story and the Gospel According to John.

The most useful extended discussion of "The Bride Comes to Yellow
Sky" is in Eric Solomon's *Stephen Crane: From Parody to Realism.* Solomon establishes without doubt the relationship between Crane's parodic
use of the dime novel and his satire of the cultural assumptions of both
eastern and western readers. Many critics have more or less echoed this
view of the story, with perhaps A. M. Tibbetts's "Stephen Crane's 'The
Bride Comes to Yellow Sky'" (*EJ*, Apr. 1965) the best study aside from
Solomon's. The principal crux in the story is the extent to which it is an
allegory of the Death of the West — the West either as myth or as reality.
Although Robert Barnes, in "Crane's 'The Bride Comes to Yellow Sky'"
(*Expl*, Apr. 1958), and Jay Martin, in *Harvests of Change*, attempt to
demonstrate the existence of this theme, the story's predominantly comic
spirit (as well described by Tibbetts) appears to resist a neat allegorical
formulation. Much recent criticism of the story also appears to be pushing
for themes far beyond the limits of the work. In "Scrathy the Demon in
'The Bride Comes to Yellow Sky'" (*TSL*, 1971), Sanford E. Marovitz discovers a hidden layer of demonic imagery "so subtly applied that readers
for more than half a century have not been able to grasp fully its ingenious function." In "Murder by the Minute: Old and New in 'The Bride
Comes to Yellow Sky'" (*NCF*, Sept. 1971), Ben M. Vorpahl tortuously pur-
sues the relationship in the story between the imagery of space and time
to reach the conventional conclusion that the work is about the end of

an era. And in "Androgyny in Stephen Crane's 'The Bride Comes to Yellow Sky'" (*RS*, Dec. 1977), Shannon Burns and James A. Levernier divide the various figures in the story into "masculine" and "feminine" principles. "The Blue Hotel" is a compelling work, which is more than can be said of most of its criticism. The story seems to attract commentary which can most charitably be described as forced. (Joseph Katz has collected much of the earlier significant writing on the story in *Stephen Crane: "The Blue Hotel,"* Columbus, Ohio, 1969.) With some exceptions the early criticism of the work is still the best. Walter Sutton, in "Pity and Fear in 'The Blue Hotel'" (*AQ*, Spring 1952), identified man's alien position in nature as a central motif, while Stallman (in his *Omnibus*) stated the case for considering the final section of the story superfluous. The best of these early studies, and still the most useful article on the story, is Joseph N. Satterwhite's "Stephen Crane's 'The Blue Hotel': The Failure of Understanding" (*MFS*, Winter 1956–57). Satterwhite comes to grips with the two principal areas of interest in the story — its theme of complicity and its parable form — and he also takes a stand in a debate found in most criticism of the work when he finds that its ending is an appropriate gloss on its theme.

Much of the criticism of "The Blue Hotel" continues to be preoccupied with the themes of misunderstanding and alienation and with the relevance and success of the close of the story. Ray B. West, Jr., in "Stephen Crane: Author in Transition" (*AL*, May 1962); Eric Solomon, in *Stephen Crane: From Parody to Realism*; and Sister Mary Anthony Weinig, in "Heroic Convention in 'The Blue Hotel'" (*Stephen Crane Newsletter*, Spring 1968), refine our appreciation of Crane's ironic themes and techniques, though their readings do not vary significantly from those of Sutton and Satterwhite. William B. Dillingham, however, in "'The Blue Hotel' and the Gentle Reader" (*SSF*, Spring 1964), does add a new note in his comment that Crane's refusal to permit the reader to respond sympathetically to the Swede includes us all in the ironic thrust of the conclusion, since we, too, have failed to understand. H. Alan Wycherley, in "Crane's 'The Blue Hotel': How Many Collaborators?" (*AN&Q*, Feb. 1966), identifies the bartender as yet another contributor to the Swede's death. And Jürgen Wolter, in "Drinking, Gambling, Fighting, Paying: Structure and Determinism in 'The Blue Hotel'" (*ALR*, Autumn 1979) decribes a repetitive pattern of events which he believes contributes to a deterministic theme in the story.

But a great deal of the criticism of "The Blue Hotel" falls into the cateories familiar to anyone who has "read through" the modern criticism of a "difficult" work. Robert F. Gleckner, in "Stephen Crane and the Wonder of Man's Conceit" (*MFS*, Autumn 1959); Hugh N. Maclean, in

"The Two Worlds of 'The Blue Hotel'" (*MFS*, Autumn 1959); and Richard VanDerBeets, in "Character as Structure: Ironic Parallel and Transformation in 'The Blue Hotel'" (*SSF*, Spring 1968), trace elaborate threads of symbolic action in the story in order to announce themes readily available elsewhere in the work. James T. Cox and Edward Stone—in "Stephen Crane as Symbolic Naturalist: An Analysis of 'The Blue Hotel'" (*MFS*, Summer 1957) and in "Stephen Crane," *A Certain Morbidness* (Carbondale, Ill., 1969)—concentrate on symbolism arising out of imagery. Stone's discussion of Crane's color symbolism is often helpful, but Cox's article is a classic of its kind. Centering on the stove as a key symbol, he examines the "symbolic substructure" of the story and concludes that the theme of "The Blue Hotel" is precisely the opposite of the Easterner's final words. Indeed, two other critics have reached a similar unconvincing conclusion. Marvin Klotz, in "Stephen Crane: Tragedian or Comedian: 'The Blue Hotel'" (*UKCR*, Spring 1961), reads the story as a deliberate burlesque of literary naturalism in which most apparent themes are ironic reversals of their true meaning, and Bruce L. Grenberg, in "Metaphysic of Despair: Stephen Crane's 'The Blue Hotel'" (*MFS*, Summer 1968), believes that the existential themes pervading the story cause the Easterner's final words to be Crane's "bitterest irony." More recently, Chester L. Wolford, in "The Eagle and the Crow: High Tragedy and Epic in 'The Blue Hotel'" (*PrS*, Fall 1977) and Ronald E. McFarland, in "The Hospitality Code and 'The Blue Hotel'" (*SSF*, Fall 1981), laboriously and muddily seek to discover analogues from Homer and Greek tragedy in the story.

Many other recent critical readings of "The Blue Hotel" continue to be ingenious and forced. Two extraordinary examples are Jon M. Kinnamon's "Henry James, the Bartender in Stephen Crane's 'The Blue Hotel'" (*ArQ*, Summer 1974) and Sue L. Kimball's "Circles and Squares: The Designs of Stephen Crane's 'The Blue Hotel'" (*SSF*, Fall 1980). Less absurd but equally minor are Richard A. Davison, "Crane's 'Blue Hotel' Revisited: The Illusion of Fate" (*MFS*, Winter 1969–70); Tim A. Pilgrim, "Repetition as a Nihilistic Device in Stephen Crane's 'The Blue Hotel'" (*SSF*, Spring 1974); J. F. Peirce, "Stephen Crane's Use of Figurative Language in 'The Blue Hotel'" (*SCB*, Winter 1974); and James Ellis, "The Game of High-Five in 'The Blue Hotel'" (*AL*, Nov. 1977). Somewhat more useful is Robert Narveson's "Conceit in 'The Blue Hotel'" in "Stephen Crane: A Portfolio" (*PrS*, Summer 1969), which contributes to the debate over possible irony in the conclusion of the story an interpretation of the egotistical limitations present in the Easterner's final remarks. All in all, as I remarked some years ago, Crane studies would profit from a ten-year moratorium on "Blue Hotel" explications. One way to achieve this end would be to require that each would-be explicator read every article published on the story.

Other Fiction

I will discuss criticism of Crane's minor fiction within the following categories: western stories, war stories, Whilomville tales, and the three last novels—*The Third Violet*, *Active Service*, and *The O'Ruddy*. But first I should again note that the book-length studies of Crane by Milne Holton, Marston LaFrance, and Jean Cazemajou contain unusually full accounts of Crane's minor fiction.

A number of major studies of Crane's western stories have appeared since Eric Solomon's pioneering and still important chapter on "The Gunfighters" in his *Stephen Crane: From Parody to Realism*. The most important of these are Joseph Katz's introduction to his *Stephen Crane in the West and Mexico;* Raymund A. Paredes' "Stephen Crane and the Mexican" (*WAL*, Spring 1971); Robert G. Deamer's "Stephen Crane and the Western Myth" (*WAL*, Summer 1972) and "Remarks on the Western Stance of Stephen Crane" (*WAL*, Summer 1980); Frank Bergon's introduction to his *The Western Writings of Stephen Crane;* and Jaime Robertson's "Stephen Crane, Eastern Outsider in the West and Mexico" (*WAL*, Fall 1978). Paredes' stress on Crane's reflection of derogatory stereotypes of the Mexican in his western stories neglects the ironic and parodic context in which many of these occur. Katz and Deamer share a belief in the importance of Crane's western trip (and therefore his writing dealing with the trip) because of its role in completing his mature view of life. Katz is more convincing than Deamer, since Deamer posits an almost absolute bifurcation in Crane's ideas—all determinism before the trip, all free will after, with the western stories moving strongly toward the celebration of free will. Bergon and Robertson (in two of the best essays on Crane's western writing) stress the literary quality rather than personal significance of Crane's western fiction. They find that the stories are essentially exercises in the ironic testing of the myth of the west rather than complete acceptance or rejection of the myth. Superficial and obvious, on the other hand, is James L. Dean's "The Wests of Howells and Crane" (*ALR*, Summer 1977).

Three brief but well-done close readings of minor western stories are George Monteiro's "Stephen Crane's 'Yellow Sky' Sequel" (*ArQ*, Summer 1974), in which Monteiro finds that "Moonlight on the Snow" contains many of the same themes and devices as "The Bride Comes to Yellow Sky"; Charles W. Mayer's "Two Kids in the House of Chance: Crane's 'The Five White Mice'" (*RS*, March 1976), which places the themes of this problematical story in the context of Crane's basic ideas; and Glen M.

Johnson's "Stephen Crane's 'One Dash—Horses': A Model of 'Realistic'
Irony" (*MFS*, Winter 1977–78), in which Johnson discovers a finely
wrought balance between satire and expressionism in the story.

Several scholars have worked on the sources of Crane's war fiction.
James W. Gargano, in "Crane's 'A Mystery of Heroism': A Possible Source"
(*MLN*, Jan. 1959), strains for a Biblical parallel, while Thomas A. Gullason, in "Stephen Crane's Private War on Yellow Journalism" (*HLQ*, May
1959), notes a minor influence on Crane's war fiction, his distaste for
the "new journalism" of Pulitzer and Hearst. Two discoveries of specific
sources are by Hans Arnold, who in "Stephen Crane's 'Wyoming Valley
Tales': Their Source and Their Place in the Author's War Fiction" (*Jahrbuch für Amerikastudien*, 1959) cites Crane's reliance on his grandfather's
Wyoming (1858), and by C. B. Ives, who in "'The Little Regiment' of
Stephen Crane at the Battle of Fredericksburg" (*MQ*, Spring 1967) identifies both the battle and the regiment. Arnold, however, is less successful
in arguing that Crane's Wyoming Valley stories are really early rather
than late works.

Other critics have attempted to distinguish among various phases in
Crane's depiction of battle and soldiers and to relate these phases to significant moments in the development of his literary imagination. E. R.
Hagemann, in "Stephen Crane's 'Real' War in His Short Stories" (*AQ*,
Winter 1956), and Thomas A. Gullason, in "The Significance of *Wounds
in the Rain*" (*MFS*, Autumn 1959), believe that Crane's first-hand experience of battle resulted in war fiction superior to his earlier, entirely imaginative depiction of war. Gullason also seeks to make the point that the
quality of *Wounds in the Rain* undermines the widely held belief that
Crane's writing declined during his last years. Eric Solomon, in "Stephen
Crane's War Stories" (*TSLL*, Spring 1961), adds a third phase to Crane's
war fiction, that of the four Spitzbergen tales written in 1899. In these
stories Crane's two earlier themes of the soldier's isolation or fear and
of his professional pride give way to the theme of the mingled glory and
horror of battle. Solomon has probably defined too neat a pattern for
Crane's war fiction, but his article is nevertheless one of the best attempts
to deal coherently with this aspect of Crane's work.

Finally, a number of critics have worked closely with particular war
stories. Two unsatisfactory readings are Paul Witherington's "Stephen
Crane's 'A Mystery of Heroism': Some Redefinitions" (*EJ*, Feb. 1969), and
Neal J. Osborn's "The Riddle in 'The Clan': A Key to Crane's Major Fiction?" (*BNYPL*, Apr. 1965). Witherington imposes a myth and ritual
interpretation upon "A Mystery of Heroism" and Osborn struggles to
demonstrate that all of Crane's principal themes and techniques can be
found in "The Clan of No-Name." A much more successful article is Wil-

liam B. Dillingham's "Crane's One-Act Farce: 'The Upturned Face'" (*RS*, Dec. 1967), in which Dillingham studies the amalgam of the comic and the grotesque which is the particular effect of this story and of much of Crane's best work.

The most interesting recent development in the criticism of Crane's war fiction is the emergence of "Death and the Child" and, to a lesser extent, "War Memories" as significant Crane stories equal in worth to Crane's other major short fiction. Milne Holton provides a lengthy reading of "Death and the Child" and concludes that the story is Crane's most mature study of the problem of apprehension, and Rodney Rogers uses the story, in his "'Stephen Crane and Impressionism," to demonstrate the power and suggestiveness of Crane's fully developed impressionistic technique. In a related effort Charles W. Mayer's "Stephen Crane and the Realistic Tradition: 'Three Miraculous Soldiers'" (*ArQ*, Summer 1974), demonstrates the link between Crane's deflation of war and his impressionistic technique.

Crane's Whilomville stories have attracted attention both because of their intrinsic interest and because of their critical usefulness as a unified body of work late in his career. J. C. Levenson, in his introduction to Volume Seven of *The Works of Stephen Crane*, has painstakingly detailed the publishing history of the stories. Levenson, as well as most other commentators on the stories, believes that they do not represent a major effort by Crane. Critics, however, have stated this position in varying ways and degrees, from Stallman's contention (in his *Omnibus*) that they are "lightweight stuff" to Solomon's belief (in his *Stephen Crane: From Parody to Realism*) that they are of uneven quality. Those who praise the stories usually base their evaluation on Crane's successful blending of nostalgia for and satire of village life and mores. This is more or less the position of Ima H. Herron, in *The Small Town in American Literature* (Durham, N.C., 1939); Grant C. Knight, in *The Critical Period in American Literature;* and Jean Cazemajou in "Stephen Crane et la petite ville américaine" (*Caliban*, Mar. 1967). John C. Martin, in "Childhood in Stephen Crane's *Maggie*, 'The Monster,' and Whilomville Stories" (*Midwestern University Quarterly*, 1967), takes this view a step further and argues that the theme of the relationship of the individual to society is as well dramatized in these stories as in Crane's major work. J. C.Levenson's stress on the importance of the outsider in this relationship, an approach to the stories as principally social fiction, is also reflected in George Monteiro's well-taken "With Proper Words (or Without Them) the Soldier Dies: Stephen Crane's 'Making an Orator'" (*Cithara*, May 1970). Monteiro, in "Whilomville as Judah: Crane's 'A Little Pilgrimage'" (*Renascence*, Summer 1967), also examines the satiric theme of one of the better stories in the series. Ellen A. Brown's "Stephen Crane's *Whilomville Stories:* A Backward Glance" (*MarkhamR*, May 1973) is a thin reading of the stories as realistic accounts of childhood, but her (and Patricia Hernlund's) "The Source for the Title of Stephen Crane's *Whilomville Stories*" (*AL*, Mar. 1978) successfully locates the origin of "Whilomville" in Crane's family history.

Most Crane critics would not be too much disturbed if *The Third Violet, Active Service,* and *The O'Ruddy* disappeared from the face of the earth, and this sentiment is reflected in the extent of the criticism of the three novels. Nevertheless, useful general accounts of the three works occur in Thomas A. Gullason's "The Jamesian Motif in Stephen Crane's Last Novels" (*Personalist,* Winter 1961); Lillian Gilkes's "*The Third Violet, Active Service,* and *The O'Ruddy:* Stephen Crane's Potboilers" (*Crane Centenary Essays*); and J. C. Levenson's introductions to Volumes Three and Four of the Virginia Edition. Gullason unsuccessfully seeks to demonstrate that the presence of the Jamesian theme of sensitivity to class in these novels lends them significance, while Miss Gilkes, though she finds Crane's "potboilers" weakened by his inability to portray feminine characters, also believes that the novels represent Crane's increasing mastery of the novel form. The importance of Levenson's discussions of Crane's late novels is that these works seldom attract a critic of his discrimination. He thus provides an important base for future discussions of the novels in his conventional but generally well-taken emphasis on *The Third Violet* as a Howellsian comedy of manners, on *Active Service* as an autobiographical novel, and on *The O'Ruddy* as a picaresque romance.

The Third Violet is usually mined for its autobiographical themes and implications, a good early example of which is Wilson Follett's introduction to Volume Three of *The Work of Stephen Crane.* In particular, Crane's inability to portray feminine characters (as well described by Edwin Cady in his *Stephen Crane*) has served as grist for various kinds of mills. William L. Andrews has written the best overall account of the novel in "Art and Success: Another Look at Stephen Crane's *The Third Violet*" (*Wascana Review,* Spring 1978). Andrews convincingly relates the work to Crane's permanent interest in the integrity and nature of the artist's personal vision.

Active Service has had few admirers (and probably few readers). All Carl Van Doren could muster in its favor in his introduction to Volume Four of *The Work of Stephen Crane* was some faint praise for its "incidental detail." Like *The Third Violet,* it will no doubt continue to interest biographers more than critics, as in Lillian Gilkes's discussion of the layer of reference to Cora throughout the novel in her "Stephen Crane and the Biographical Fallacy: The Cora Influence" (*MFS,* Winter 1970–71).

Discussion of *The O'Ruddy* has been concentrated on the tangled history of its authorship and publication. An exception is Lillian Gilkes's study of the suggestive parallels between the novel and Harold Frederic's *The Return of the O'Mahoney* in her "Stephen Crane and the Harold Frederics." The question of precisely how much of *The O'Ruddy* Crane wrote has been resolved with the appearance of Bernard O'Donnell's definitive *An Analysis of Prose Style to Determine Authorship: The O'Ruddy* . . . (The Hague, 1970) and with the discovery of Robert Barr's annotated proof sheets of his portion of the novel. (The proof sheets are described in Volume Four of the Virginia Edition.) And Lillian Gilkes and Joan H. Baum, in "Stephen Crane's Last Novel: *The O'Ruddy*" (*CLC*, Feb. 1957), and Jean Cazemajou, in "*The O'Ruddy*, Robert Barr et *The Idler*" (*Caliban*, Jan. 1968), discuss the serialization of the novel.

Poetry

Joseph Katz has incorporated earlier textual and bibliographical studies of Crane's poetry into his introduction and notes to *The Poems of Stephen Crane*, while Fredson Bowers supplies an extremely full biographical and bibliographical commentary in his textual introduction to Volume Ten, *Poems and Literary Remains*, of the Virginia Edition. Still of independent interest, however, are Thomas F. O'Donnell's "A Note on the Reception of Crane's *The Black Riders*" (*AL*, May 1952) and Jean Cazemajou's "A propos de quelques parodies de l'oeuvre de Stephen Crane" (*Caliban*, 1965) for their bearing on the influence of Crane's poetry on his reputation in the 1890s. In one of those not uncommon coincidences of literary scholarship, two concordances of the poetry appeared within a year of each other—Herman Baron's *A Concordance to the Poems of Stephen Crane* (Boston, 1974) and Andrew T. Crosland's *A Concordance to the Complete Poetry of Stephen Crane* (Detroit, 1975). The first is keyed to Joseph Katz's edition of the poems, the second to Volume Ten of the Virginia Edition.

The problem of sources and influence has been as troublesome for critics of Crane's poetry as it has been for critics of his fiction. The Bible (for its parable form) and Emily Dickinson were frequently mentioned in early criticism. Daniel G. Hoffman, in *The Poetry of Stephen Crane*, added Ambrose Bierce and Olive Schreiner, with particular emphasis on Miss Schreiner's *Dreams*, an emphasis affirmed by Carlin T. Kindilien, in "Stephen Crane and the 'Savage Philosophy' of Olive Schreiner" (*BUSE*, Summer 1957). Hoffman also discounted Emily Dickinson's influence, finding the two poets dissimilar in theme and form. James M. Cox, in "*The Pilgrim's Progress* as Source for Stephen Crane's *The Black Riders*" (*AL*, Jan. 1957), convincingly demonstrates the importance of Bunyan's parable form and techniques. Cox's essay is also an illuminating discussion of major tendencies in Crane's poetry as a whole. A number of critics, however, appear to be mining rather thin veins of possible influence: E. A. Gillis, "A Glance at Stephen Crane's Poetry" (*PrS,*Spring 1954) (Aubrey Beardsley); Thomas A. Gullason, "Tennyson's Influence on Stephen Crane" (*N&Q,* Apr. 1958); and Richard E. Peck, "Stephen Crane and Baudelaire: A Direct Link" (*AL,* May 1965).

The best general introductions to Crane's poetry are Henry Lüdeke's "Stephen Crane's Poetry," in *The "Democracy" of Henry Adams and Other Essays* (Bern, 1950); Daniel G. Hoffman's *The Poetry of Stephen Crane;* Joseph Katz's introduction to *The Poems of Stephen Crane;* and James B. Colvert's introduction to Volume Ten of the Virginia Edition. (Chapter-length discussions of Crane's poetry also occur in the books by LaFrance and Cazemajou.) Lüdeke, in an article which anticipates much later criticism, discusses with good sense such matters as Crane's irony and his religious themes and the relationship between his poetry and Emily Dickinson's. Katz is best for a solid introduction to the biographical setting of the poems. He is less successful in his attempt to demonstrate that *The Black Riders* volume has a coherent structure. Hoffman's study is of course one of the "basic books" (Cady's term) on Crane. Hoffman's forceful revelation that Crane wrote two kinds of religious poems — those involving a God of vengeance and those involving a God of love — is perhaps the best known aspect of his book, since his discussion made obsolete a great deal of earlier criticism which had pigeonholed Crane as an 1890s atheistic iconoclast. (See, for example, Carlin T. Kindilien's *American Poetry in the Eighteen Nineties* [Providence, R.I., 1956].) But Hoffman is perhaps most stimulating in his analysis of Crane's movement from allegorical to symbolic poetry, and in his attempt to define and explore Crane as a symbolic writer in prose as well as in poetry. Moreover, though it is possible to quarrel with some of Hoffman's general ideas about Crane's life and work, his reading of individual poems is of a very high order. Colvert's brief introduction also suggestively and usefully relates Crane's poetic symbolism to symbolic patterns in the remainder of his work.

Criticism of Crane's poetry both before and after Hoffman is overshadowed by his work. Harriet Monroe's "Stephen Crane" (*Poetry,* June 1919), in which she dismisses Crane as a sententious and often sophomoric moralist, still represents a sizable body of critical opinion, though the careful study of Crane's best poetry has tended to qualify that view. Several critics have attempted to find a single "key" to Crane's poetry, particularly to *The Black Riders.* (*War Is Kind* is usually admitted to be a hodge-podge.) Max Westbrook, in "Stephen Crane's Poetry: Perspective and Arrogance" (*BuR*, Dec. 1963), finds the key in Crane's adoption of seemingly opposite yet essentially complementary poetic "voices" to express a central creed of compassion. Much less persuasively, Yoshie Itabashi, in "The Modern Pilgrimage of *The Black Riders:* An Interpretation" (*Tsuda Review* [Tokyo], Nov. 1967), believes that the order of the poems in the volume is that of a spiritual journey culminating in an acceptance of a compassionate God. A larger group of critics has concentrated on Crane's poetic form. Harland S. Nelson, in "Stephen Crane's Achievement as a Poet" (*TSLL*, Winter 1963), unsuccessfully seeks to prove that Crane's parables are as powerful as his symbolic poems. Robert C. Basye's "Color Imagery in Stephen Crane's Poetry" (*ALR*, Spring 1980) is competent though routine. Christof Wegelin, in "Crane's 'A Man Said to the Universe'" (*Expl*, Sept. 1961), and Mordecai Marcus, in "Structure and Irony in Stephen Crane's 'War Is Kind'" (*CLAJ*, Mar. 1966), work closely and well with the form of two of Crane's most reprinted poems. Perhaps it was Wegelin's comments on the device of the confrontation in "A Man Said to the Universe" which stimulated Ruth Miller to write what is probably the best and most important discussion of Crane's poetry since Hoffman's book. In her "Regions of Snow: The Poetic Style of Stephen Crane" (*BNYPL*, May 1968), she examines the various shapes that Crane gave to his basic structural device of the encounter. Her conclusion, that Crane's wisdom is adolescent but that his poetic constructs delight us, has often been felt but has never been so well stated.

Two brief and thin recent general essays on Crane's poetry are Walter Sutton, "The Modernity of Stephen Crane's Poetry: A Centennial Tribute" (*Courier*, Oct. 1971) and J. Lasley Dameron, "Symbolism in the Poetry of Poe and Stephen Crane" (*Emerson Society Quarterly*, Fall 1970). Notes on individual poems are Jean R. Halladay, "A Misdated Crane Poem" (*AN&Q*, Feb. 1974) ("One Came from the Skies" is earlier than Stallman's dating); George Monteiro, "Crane's 'A Man Adrift on a Slim Spar'" (*Expl*, Oct. 1973) (a clarification of an image); and Clarence O. Johnson, "Crane's 'I Was in the Darkness'" (*Expl*, Sept. 1975) (a Biblical source).

Influence and Reputation

Discussions of Crane's influence have centered on Conrad, Hemingway, and Dreiser. Most of the early criticism of Crane's influence on Conrad—R. B. Sewall, "Crane's *The Red Badge of Courage*" (*Expl*, May 1945) (on *The Red Badge* and *Lord Jim*); Guy Owen, Jr., "Crane's 'The Open Boat' and Conrad's 'Youth'" (*MLN*, Feb. 1958); Peter Baasner, "Stephen Crane and Joseph Conrad," in *Kleiner Beiträge zur Amerikanischen Literaturgeschichte*, edited by Hans Galinsky and H. J. Lang (Heidelberg, 1961); Bruce Johnson, "Joseph Conrad and Crane's *The Red Badge* of Courage" (PMASAL, 1963) (on The Red Badge and The Nigger of the "Narcissus"); and Austin M. Fox, "Stephen Crane and Joseph Conrad" (Serif, Dec. 1969) — has been thin in substance and has often adopted Conrad's later, patronizing tone toward Crane. Far more substantial and suggestive are the major essays (largely on the relationship of The Nigger of the "Narcissus" to The Red Badge of Courage) by Elsa Nettles, "Conrad and Stephen Crane" (Conradia, Autumn 1978) and Peter L. Hays, "Joseph Conrad and Stephen Crane" (EA, Jan.–Mar. 1978).

The best general discussions of the personal and literary parallels between Crane and Hemingway are those by Philip Young, in Ernest Hemingway (New York, 1952), and Daniel G. Hoffman, in The Poetry of Stephen Crane. Both critics note the importance of a personal code in the value systems of the two writers as well as similarities in subject matter and theme in various works. Other scholars have dealt in greater detail with the prose style of the two authors and with particular influences. W. Gordon Milne, in "Stephen Crane: Pioneer in Technique" (NS, July 1959), comments on the tendency toward compression and simplicity in the prose style of both writers, characteristics which have also been noted by Harold C. Martin, "The Development of Style in Nineteenth-Century American Fiction," in Style in Prose Fiction, edited by Harold C. Martin (New York, 1959), and Richard Bridgman, in The Colloquial Style in America (New York, 1966). I confess that I am unconvinced by attempts to find links between two such distinctive prose styles. Philip Young's remark that "The Blue Hotel" probably influenced "The Killers" is well documented by J. A. Ward, in "'The Blue Hotel' and 'The Killers'" (CEA, Sept. 1959). But William B. Bache is less persuasive in his "The Red Badge of Courage and 'The Short Happy Life of Francis Macomber'" (WHR, Winter 1961). A somewhat different direction in Crane-Hemingway studies is taken by Earle Labor, in "Crane and Hemingway: Anatomy of Trauma" (Renascence, Summer 1959). Labor compares Frederic Henry and Henry Fleming and makes the useful point that Crane and Hemingway had divergent views about the meaning of war despite similarities in their depiction of the subject. But W. M. White, in "The Crane-Hemingway Code: A Reevaluation" (BSUF, Spring 1969) weakens his thesis that there is a major difference between the two writers' codes by a superficial concept of Crane's central ethic.

Theodore Dreiser has joined Conrad and Hemingway as the writers on whom Crane is held to have been a major influence. Ellen Moers's discussion, in her Two Dreisers (New York, 1969), of the impact of Crane's sketch "The Men in the Storm" on a similar scene in Sister Carrie is supplemented by Joseph Katz's "Theodore Dreiser and Stephen Crane: Studies in a Literary Relationship" (Crane Centenary Essays). Katz's lengthy essay surveys as well Dreiser's later estimates of Crane. Two much thinner contributions to the same subject are Robert McIlvaine's "A Literary Source for Hurstwood's Last Scene" (*RS*, Mar. 1972), which duplicates Moers's earlier discovery, and D. B. Graham's "Dreiser's Maggie" (*ALR*, Spring 1974), which strains at a connection between Crane's *Maggie* and a brief passage in *Sister Carrie*. A convincing demonstration of Crane's influence on Eugene O'Neill is Robert McIlvaine's "Crane's *Maggie*: A Source for *The Hairy Ape*" (*The Eugene O'Neill Newsletter*, 1979).

The study of Crane's contemporary reputation is best begun with Richard M. Weatherford's *Stephen Crane: The Critical Heritage* (London, 1973). Weatherford not only reprints all significant reviews of Crane's work during his lifetime but supplies in his introduction an excellent interpretive survey of the principal characteristics of the response to Crane in the 1890s. Among recent book-length studies of Crane, Jean Cazemajou's is particularly noteworthy for the fullness of discussion of the critical reception of Crane's work. Together, the works of Weatherford and Cazemajou constitute as full an account of Crane's contemporary reputation as most general critics of Crane require. Crane's reputation in the 1920s, when he was often interpreted as a rebel against American puritanism, can best be studied in the criticism of the period, particularly in Beer's biography and in such estimates as Matthew Josephson's "The Voyage of Stephen Crane," in *Portrait of the Artist as American* (New York, 1930). Two overall accounts of Crane's reputation are John W. Stevenson's superficial "The Literary Reputation of Stephen Crane" (*SAQ*, Apr. 1952) and Maurice Bassan's brief but incisive account in the introduction to his *Stephen Crane: A Collection of Critical Essays*.

More specialized articles and notes on Crane's critical reputation are: Thomas F. O'Donnell, "A Note on the Reception of Crane's *The Black Riders*"; R. W. Stallman, "Crane's *Maggie* in Review," in *The Houses That James Built* (the 1896 *Maggie*); Eric Solomon, "Stephen Crane, English Critics, and American Reviewers" (*N&Q*, Feb. 1965) (*The Red Badge*); Joseph Katz, "The 'Preceptor' and Another Poet: Thomas Wentworth Higginson and Stephen Crane" (*Serif*, Mar. 1968); and Marc Ferrara and Gordon Dossett, "A Sheaf of Contemporary American Reviews of Stephen Crane" (*SNNTS*, Spring 1978). Among studies which trace the reaction of specific journals to Crane are: Thomas A. Gullason's "Stephen Crane and the *Arena*: Three 'Lost' Reviews" (*PBSA*, July–Sept. 1971) and George Monteiro's "*The Illustrated American* and Stephen Crane's Contemporary Reputation" (*Serif*, Dec. 1969). The *Stephen Crane Newsletter*, before its demise, carried a number of surveys of references to Crane and his work in contemporary journals: "The Reception of *Wounds in the Rain*" (Winter 1969); Richard M. Weatherford, "Stephen Crane in

The Lotus and *Chips*" (Spring 1970); George Monteiro, "Stephen Crane and *Public Opinion*" (Fall 1970); and E. R. Hagemann, "Stephen Crane and *The Argonaut*" (Fall 1970). And in a major study, Friedel H. Bastein, in *Die Rezeption Stephen Cranes in Deutschland* (Frankfort, 1977), presents an account of Crane's literary reputation (translations, critical discussions, scholarly interest) in Germany, including the DDR, from the beginning to the present.

Emily Dickinson

JAMES WOODRESS

Since 1924 the reputation of Emily Dickinson has been growing steadily, and since Thomas H. Johnson's complete edition of her poetry in 1955 interest has increased spectacularly. The end does not yet seem to be in sight. In 1967 three books and six dissertations were devoted to her work, and in 1968 five books, five more dissertations, and two editions appeared, and a quarterly bulletin was launched. In 1969 another book joined the procession, and the annual MLA bibliography listed nearly three dozen Dickinson items representing scholarly activity in five countries outside the United States: Canada, France, Japan, Roumania, and India. That the interest has reached a high and apparently stable level seems apparent from the yearly MLA listings: thirty items in 1966, twenty-two in 1967, thirty-one in 1968, and thirty-four in 1969. As this book goes to press in 1971, a new and bigger bibliography and a book-length gathering of poetic tributes have come out so far this year. *Books in Print* (1968) listed no less than twenty-six available works about Emily Dickinson. Both quantitatively and qualitatively the attention Emily Dickinson has received in the past decade and a half makes her America's number one woman poet, and she now seems firmly placed in the firmament of the handful of major nineteenth-century figures who long have dominated our literary history. A sizeable problem that the student or teacher of American literature today has in confronting Emily Dickinson is in keeping up with the scholarly and critical explosion. All the essential manuscripts and scholarly tools are now available for studying her poems,

From Earl N. Harbert and Robert A. Rees, editors, *Fifteen American Authors before 1900: Bibliographic Essays on Research & Criticism* (Madison: The University of Wisconsin Press; © 1984 by the Board of Regents of the University of Wisconsin System); may be reproduced only by permission of the publisher.

and of the making of books and articles about Emily Dickinson there seems to be no end.

The growing interest in Emily Dickinson finally has culminated in adequate bibliographical materials. The most important bibliography is Willis J. Buckingham's *Emily Dickinson: An Annotated Bibliography [of] Writings, Scholarship, Criticism, and Ana, 1850–1968* (Bloomington, Ind., 1970). This volume, containing about 2,600 items, is exhaustive in its coverage and a mine of accurate information. It lists all the materials one expects in such a work: earlier bibliographies, a guide to manuscript collections, publication data for both poems and letters, books and articles about Emily Dickinson. It also includes doctoral dissertations, M.A. and B.A. theses (the last two items of doubtful utility), creative tributes, recordings, broadcasts, films, data on commemorations and exhibitions, lists of unpublished papers delivered at scholarly meetings, and miscellanea. Nearly half of the listings (1,214) are in section six ("Parts of Books and Signed Articles"), although hundreds of these items are reviews rather than works of scholarship or criticism. The section on translations and foreign estimates and criticism (326 items) is especially thorough and goes far beyond any other compilation. Yet it must be said that in this *omnium gatherum* there is a lot of trivia. While it is clearly useful to include a large number of reviews of the early editions of the poems, it is hard to see who will have need for a listing of 64 reviews of Genevieve Taggard's *Life and Mind of Emily Dickinson*, and it seems hardly worth listing unpublished concordances based on the pre-Johnson text now that there is in print a good computer-made-post-Johnson concordance.

Although Buckingham's bibliography casts its net more widely, it does not supersede Sheila Clendenning's *Emily Dickinson, A Bibliography: 1850–1966* (Kent, Ohio, 1968), which includes 951 well-organized, annotated, indexed, and cross-referenced items, both primary and secondary sources. Ms. Clendenning's compilation includes some 1967 items so that it is almost as up to date as Buckingham's listings, which do not go beyond 1968. She ignores peripheral items such as poetic tributes and fictional portrayals and lists 12 pages of poetry explications, 585 articles about Emily Dickinson, and 45 books. There is, in addition to the usual information on editions and the publication of individual poems and letters, an annotated list of dissertations and an admirable introductory essay summing up the growth of Emily Dickinson's literary reputation. Furthermore, Mrs. Clendenning's bibliography is a beautifully printed letterpress book, bound attractively in what Emily Dickinson probably would have described as cochineal.

There are other recent bibliographies of less utility: Klaus Lubbers, *Emily Dickinson: The Critical Revolution* (Ann Arbor, Mich., 1968), contains about one thousand unannotated items arranged as a supplemental list of sources rather than as a bibliography. About half of his listings are reviews which appeared between 1890 and 1962. Another less complete list of reviews between 1890 and 1896 may be found in Millicent Todd Bingham's *Ancestors' Brocades: The Literary Debut of Emily Dickinson* (New York, 1945; reprinted, Dover, 1967). A general list of 436 items, now superseded by the Clendenning and Buckingham bibliographies, is found in Susan Freis's "Emily Dickinson: A Checklist of Criticism, 1930–1966" (*PBSA*, Fourth Quarter 1967). Jacob Blanck, in *BAL*, Volume Two, besides describing the primary works in more detail than anyone else, also includes poems set to music, anthologies, and fiction. An extensive list of creative tributes to Emily Dickinson appears in the *Emily Dickinson Bulletin* (Jan. 1969).

Two pioneering bibliographies, now hard to come by, are of historic interest: Alfred Leete Hampson's *Emily Dickinson: A Bibliography* (Northampton, Mass., 1930), and *Emily Dickinson, December 10, 1830–May 15, 1886: A Bibliography* (Amherst, Mass., 1930). The latter, which was compiled by the Jones Library staff, contains a foreword by George Whicher. These are subsumed into the more recent compilations but were the initial efforts to collect bibliographical information, along with the catalogue of a Yale University Library exhibition, also issued in 1930, the centennial year of Emily Dickinson's birth.

A final bibliographical item, although of peripheral importance, should be mentioned, because it appeared too late to be included in either the Buckingham or Clendenning bibliographies: Robert Fraser's *The Margaret Jane Pershing Collection of Emily Dickinson* (Princeton, N.J., 1969). It is a twenty-three-page pamphlet, with an introduction by Richard M. Ludwig, which describes a collection recently presented to the Princeton Library.

For current bibliography one should consult the annual volumes of *American Literary Scholarship* (Durham, N.C.), edited by James Woodress from 1965 to 1969 and by J. Albert Robbins from 1970 on, and the annual listings in *PMLA*. The former reviews briefly and evaluates the annual Dickinson scholarship.

At the beginning of 1968 Emily Dickinson joined the select group of authors to whom an entire journal has been devoted. The *Emily Dickinson Bulletin*, edited by Frederick L. Morey, 4508 38th Street, Brentwood,

Md. 20722, appears quarterly in duplicated format and serves as news-letter, clearinghouse for notes and queries, serial bibliography, and re-pository of short articles.

One service that computer technology can perform for humanistic scholarship is the preparation of concordances. Emily Dickinson is the first American to benefit from the efforts of the Cornell Concordance Center with S. P. Rosenbaum's *A Concordance to the Poems of Emily Dickinson* (Ithaca, N.Y., 1964), an impressive 899-page volume that in-dexes over one hundred thousand of Emily Dickinson's words. It gives not only the word in context but also includes the first line of the poem in which the work occurs and is keyed to the number of the poem in Johnson's text. The appendix includes word-frequency lists (*heaven* ap-pears 143 times, *death* 141, *bride* 14, *husband* 1). Cornell has preserved the tape for the print-out so that future scholars can ask for specific data not included in the concordance. This concordance already is getting heavy use in specialized studies of style, diction, and imagery.

EDITIONS

Emily Dickinson has the most fascinating publication history of any American author. The place to begin this absorbing story is with Mrs. Bingham's *Ancestors' Brocades*, which tells how the poems originally came to be edited by her mother, Mabel Loomis Todd, and Thomas Wentworth Higginson (*Poems by Emily Dickinson and Poems . . . Second Series*, Boston, 1890, 1891). The story also has been told more succinctly and objectively, and with some corrections, by a contemporary scholar, R. W. Franklin, in *The Editing of Emily Dickinson: A Reconsideration* (Madi-son, Wis., 1967). Lavinia Dickinson found the poems among her sister's effects after her death and engaged Mrs. Todd, wife of an Amherst Col-lege astronomy professor, and Col. Higginson of Boston to edit them. They labored to present twentieth-century poems to a nineteenth-century au-dience. "The editors were wise enough to think the poems good, and prac-tical enough to realize that many of their contemporaries would find the poetry offensive in style, if not in content" (Clendenning, p. xii). The two editors tried to make the meter scan and the lines rhyme. By nineteenth-century standards they did not regularize enough; by present criteria, of course, they took unwarranted and indefensible liberties. Mrs. Bing-ham tells this story well, but she is an apologist for her mother's work, and she makes Lavinia too much a villain. When the first two volumes came out, both editors and, most of all, the publisher were surprised at the favorable reception and excellent sales, and Mrs. Todd alone then edited two volumes of letters to satisfy the curiosity about Emily Dickinson that the poems had aroused. Later in 1896 Mrs. Todd alone brought out *Poems . . . Third Series.* By this time 450 poems, less than half the number that Mrs. Todd had transcribed from the MSS turned over to her by Lavinia Dickinson, had been published.

A celebrated feud between the Dickinsons and the Todds broke out after the publication of *Poems . . . Third Series.* It occurred over a piece of land Austin, Emily's brother, intended to give Mrs. Todd for her editorial services. Sister Lavinia, however, filed suit to recover the property after Austin's death, testifying that she had been tricked into signing the deed of conveyance, and she won her case. The Todds appealed to the Massachusetts Supreme Court and lost. Thereupon Mrs. Todd, who was the only person besides Higginson able to edit the poems, put all the materials she had in a camphorwood chest, stored it away, and never spoke to Lavinia Dickinson again. The town of Amherst took sides, and the split was irrevocable. Thus ended the Todd-Higginson dynasty. For students who wish to see these early printings, a facsimile edition has been brought out by George Monteiro, *Poems 1890–1896)* (Gainesville, Fla., 1967), in which all three of the original volumes are reprinted.

The Middle Kingdom belonged to Martha Dickinson Bianchi, daughter of Emily's brother Austin and Susan Gilbert Dickinson. Emily Dickinson's poetry dropped out of sight from 1897 until Mrs. Bianchi published *The Single Hound* (Boston, 1914), which contained another 147 poems (only one of them had been previously published) chosen from among the 276 poems that Emily had sent her sister-in-law, who lived next door. During the succeeding years Mrs. Bianchi continued her editing with the aid of Alfred Leete Hampson and brought out *The Complete Poems* (Boston, 1924), which was far from complete but added five new poems; *Further Poems . . . Withheld from Publication by Lavinia Dickinson* (Boston, 1929), all of which were among those that Mrs. Todd had received from Lavinia, transcribed, and returned; *Poems* (Boston, 1930); and *Unpublished Poems* (Boston, 1935). *Further Poems* added 175 to the canon and *Unpublished Poems* presented another 131. All these, plus six more from *Poems* (1930) and *Life and Letters* (Boston, 1924), made a total of 908 poems published over a period of forty-five years. But this was by no means the total left by the poet.

Before this tangled publishing history moves into its next phase, however, the editorial work of Conrad Aiken should be mentioned. In the same year that Mrs. Bianchi brought out the so-called *Complete Poems*, he became the first outside editor and issued his own *Selected Poems* (London, 1924) chosen from the Todd-Higginson texts. He later began to attack Mrs. Bianchi's editorial work in a running skirmish that went on as late as 1945. Her editions, Aiken charged, except for *The Single Hound*, were full of distortions, misrepresentations, and stupidities, and when he reviewed *Further Poems* in 1929 he demanded a new, corrected edition. His attacks were perhaps too vigorous, but they were typical of the response of the academic and literary community to Mrs. Bianchi's editions.

During the thirties Mrs. Bingham opened the camphorwood chest and resumed the work her mother had abandoned after the lawsuit. Mrs. Todd had died in 1932, and there was no further reason for withholding unpublished poems. The third period in the publication history is the Bingham Dynasty, and it lasted from 1945 until 1955. During this decade, besides publishing *Ancestors' Brocades* (she waited until Mrs. Bianchi died before airing the feud), Mrs. Bingham edited one important collection of poems and two volumes of letters. *Bolts of Melody* (New York, 1945), which also has Mrs. Todd's name on the title page, was the work in progress at the time of the lawsuit. For the first time in all the Emily Dickinson publishing history a carefully edited text appeared, for Mrs. Bingham, trained as a scientist and interested in literature, had a modern notion of an editor's responsibilities. *Bolts of Melody* contained 668 new poems, bringing the total then published to 1,576. But even as late as 1945 no outside scholar ever had seen the manuscripts of these poems.

In the fifties, however, the manuscripts became available, and the Fourth Dynasty or the Age of Johnson began. Johnson issued his three-volume edition of all the poems Emily Dickinson is known to have written — 1,775, together with the variants — as *The Poems of Emily Dickinson* (Cambridge, Mass., 1955). The Johnson edition was a historic event in Dickinson scholarship and for the first time united the papers that had been divided by the Todd-Bingham and Dickinson-Bianchi feud. In addition to listing manuscript variants, the Johnson edition also records previous publication data and the emendations of earlier editors. For the first time Emily Dickinson's idiosyncratic punctuation — mostly dashes — is retained, and the edition attempts to date the poems by studying their location in the packets as left by Emily Dickinson and by a close study of handwriting changes over the years. The front matter and appendices contain a great deal of information about the creation and editing of the poems, the recipients of the poems, and the manuscripts. The Johnson text has been reprinted as *The Complete Poems of Emily Dickinson* (Boston, 1960), in one volume, without critical apparatus (and with some silent textual changes). *Final Harvest* (Boston, 1962) prints a selection of 575 poems from the Johnson text, both in hard-cover and in paper. Later printings added another poem (J-398) at the end of the collection. Another selection based on the Johnson variorum edition is James Reeves, *Selected Poems of Emily Dickinson* (New York, 1959). Reeves has standardized spelling and punctuation in an intelligent way and equipped his edition with an extensive biographical and critical introduction.

While the Johnson edition was a great landmark, careful scrutiny of the manuscripts since 1955 has revealed a few errors and faulty readings. Franklin's *The Editing of Emily Dickinson* finds that about 10 percent of the Johnson edition could be improved: "Mrs. Todd's transcripts, her typewriters, her diaries and journals, as well as the manuscripts themselves have fresh contributions to make to our understanding of Emily Dickinson's poetry and how we should edit it" (p. xvii). David Higgins, in "Twenty-five Poems by Emily Dickinson: Unpublished Variant Versions" (*AL*, Mar. 1966), supplements Johnson with variants taken from the Todd-Bingham Dickinson Papers at Amherst College and one poem at the Library of Congress.

MANUSCRIPTS AND LETTERS

Almost all the extant Emily Dickinson manuscripts are now available in two large institutional collections: the Houghton Library of Harvard University and the Amherst College Library. In 1950 the Harvard Library was given all the papers formerly owned by Martha Dickinson Bianchi and A. L. Hampson. This is a big collection, which includes not only the manuscripts of the poems but also letters by Emily Dickinson and a great many family papers. The library also has books from the Dickinson library and furniture and pictures from the home in Amherst. Many of the holograph poems were stitched into a series of forty packets, the identity of which has been preserved, and about two-thirds are fair copies. The Amherst College collection dates from 1956–57 when Mrs. Bingham gave the college the papers she had inherited from her mother. This too is a large holding, occupying twenty-seven feet of space and containing Mrs. Todd's transcripts, holograph poems, correspondence, ancillary manuscripts, and other papers. This collection has been made available on microfilm by the Folger Shakespeare Library (Washington, D.C., 1957), and Mrs. Bingham has written a *Guide to the Use of the Microfilm . . .* (Amherst, Mass., 1957). Anyone planning to study the manuscripts, which are filled with immense complexities, should first read Franklin's book. It describes the Harvard and Amherst Collections in great detail, suggests some reordering of the packets from Johnson's arrangement, corrects some of Johnson's slips in editing the mass of material which went into the variorum edition, and analyzes exhaustively the early editorial vicissitudes of the manuscripts. Franklin concludes with a thoughtful discussion of the future problems of editing a reader's edition of the poems.

Thomas H. Johnson's edition of the poems was followed by a companion three-volume edition of *The Letters of Emily Dickinson* (Cambridge, Mass., 1958). Aided by an associate editor, Theodora Ward, he managed to round up about 1,150 letters and prose fragments for this collection. The letters are accurately transcribed and arranged chronologically, although dating was difficult and often could only be approximated. Two-thirds of the letters were published from holographs; the rest derive from transcripts or earlier printed versions. The holograph letters are widely scattered in the hands of libraries and individuals, but the Johnson-Ward edition includes in its critical apparatus the location of the manuscript and the data, where appropriate, concerning previous publication. Certainly additional letters will turn up in the future, but since 1958 no significant additions to the letters have been published. Richard Sewall, in "The Lyman Letters: New Light on Emily Dickinson and Her Family" (*Massachusetts Review* [Univ. of Mass.], Autumn 1965, published also as a monograph by the University of Massachusetts Press), has found some excerpts from Emily Dickinson's letters in letters written by Joseph B. Lyman to his future wife (see *Biography*, below).

All of the early letter collections have been subsumed into the Johnson-Ward edition, but it is worth while to point out Mrs. Todd's role as editor of the letters as well as editor of the poetry. She published the first collection (Boston, 1894), and if it had not been for her industry in gathering letters within a decade after Emily Dickinson's death, many would not have survived. Even so, there were other important letters that Mrs. Todd was not able to trace, such as the letters to Benjamin Franklin Newton or to George Gould. Also many of the letters which she collected and returned after transcribing have now disappeared. Mrs. Todd reissued her two-volume collection the year before she died (New York, 1931) with previously suppressed passages restored and six new letters to Charles Clark, which threw new light on the relationship with Charles Wadsworth. Neither of the two letter collections issued by Mrs. Bianchi in 1924 and 1932 is reliable or of any use today. On the other hand, Theodora Ward's edition of *Emily Dickinson's Letters to Dr. and Mrs. Josiah Gilbert Holland* (Cambridge, Mass., 1951) is a carefully edited collection of letters to the editor's grandparents, and Mrs. Bingham's *Emily Dickinson: A Revelation* (New York, 1954) prints accurately the important letters to Judge Lord (see *Biography*, below). The last important letter collection, *Emily Dickinson's Home: Letters of Edward Dickinson and His Family* (New York, 1955), also Mrs. Bingham's work, is not incorporated in the Johnson-Ward edition, except for the three "master" letters written by Emily.

BIOGRAPHY

Emily Dickinson's biography is just as snarled as the publication history of the poems. As early as 1890 her love poems caused a writer in the *Springfield Republican* to wonder what had inspired such passionate outbursts. Mrs. Todd, however, tried to forestall the search for a lover by writing in her introduction to *Poems . . . Second Series* that Emily Dickinson had "lived in seclusion from no 'love-disappointment'" and that her life was the normal blossoming of a nature "introspective to a high degree." Lavinia Dickinson before her death in 1899 apparently dragged a red herring across the trail, but when Mrs. Bianchi's introduction to *The Single Hound* (1914) and later her *Life and Letters* (1924) appeared, there were tantalizing hints about the man in her aunt's life. As biography, Mrs. Bianchi's work was myth-making, misleading, and downright erroneous. Public interest in Emily Dickinson grew in the twenties and produced, among other things, a search to find the missing man. The centennial of her birth brought two books which now have only historic interest: Josephine Pollitt, *Emily Dickinson: The Human Background of Her Poetry* (New York, 1930), and Genevieve Taggard, *The Life and Mind of Emily Dickinson* (New York, 1930). The former nominated Major Hunt, Helen Hunt Jackson's first husband, as the lover, and the latter accorded the honor to George Gould, an Amherst College student whom Emily knew fairly well. Neither candidate deserved the nomination. Both books are enthusiastic and tend to make a cult of Emily Dickinson; Miss Taggard's book attempts to trace intellectual growth and to discuss the poetry, but she lacks aesthetic distance.

The first reliable (and still valuable) biography was George Whicher's *This Was A Poet: A Critical Biography of Emily Dickinson* (New York, 1938; Philadelphia, 1952; Ann Arbor, Mich., 1957). At least, until recently, most students of Emily Dickinson have accepted Whicher's reconstruction of his subject's life. He identified Benjamin Franklin Newton, the young student who had read law in Squire Dickinson's office, and the Reverend Charles Wadsworth, a Presbyterian minister of Philadelphia, as central figures in her life. Newton had encouraged her to write, had introduced her to Emerson's poetry, had gone on to Worcester to continue his studies, and had died early. Wadsworth had been a sort of spiritual father to her and the object of her love, but he never had been aware of his effect upon her. These two men had a strong impact on her development as a poet, and with that, says Whicher, "posterity is legitimately concerned." Whicher also was the first scholar to warn biographers that the *I* in Emily Dickinson's poetry, as she wrote Higginson, "does not mean—me—but a supposed person." Finally, Whicher's book placed Emily Dickinson firmly in the context of her background: "The quintessence of the New England spirit was embodied in Emily Dickinson. She cannot be rightly understood except in terms of her heritage" (Whicher, p. viii).

Since Whicher's biography appeared, other men have shown up in Emily Dickinson's life. The most sensational disclosure came in Mrs. Bingham's *Emily Dickinson: A Revelation* (New York, 1954), which brought to light the relationship with Otis Lord of Salem, judge of the Massachusetts Supreme Court and formerly Edward Dickinson's best friend. In this volume Mrs. Bingham published a biographical essay and a packet of love letters written to Judge Lord during the late seventies and early eighties. The letters show a deep attachment, reciprocated by the much older judge, not an attachment sublimated in poetry, like that which occurred about 1860–1861.

Another man in Emily Dickinson's life was Samuel Bowles, editor of the *Springfield Republican*, long known as a good friend of both Austin and Emily Dickinson. Winfield Townley Scott, "Errand from My Heart" (*Horizon*, July 1961), argues persuasively that Bowles, not Wadsworth, was the man who inspired the love poems. The same argument is developed more fully by David Higgins in *Portrait of Emily Dickinson: The Poet and Her Prose* (New Brunswick, N. J., 1967). This also is the view of Ruth Miller in *The Poetry of Emily Dickinson* (Middletown, Conn., 1968).

Still another candidate for Emily Dickinson's lover was produced by Rebecca Patterson, *The Riddle of Emily Dickinson* (Boston, 1951), in Kate Scott Anthon, a friend and occasional correspondent. This book reads a lesbian relationship that no other Dickinson scholar finds credible. Jay Leyda writes: "Unfortunately the real importance of ED's relation to Catharine Scott has been obscured by a work [*The Riddle*] that constructs a fictitious set of sexual circumstances" (*The Years and Hours of Emily Dickinson*, p. lxix). Kate Scott was an important friend who reacted with excitement when Emily Dickinson showed her some poems at a critical point in Emily's artistic development.

The interest in Emily Dickinson, which had reached a high level by the twenties, produced a number of personal reminiscences, such as Clara B. Green's "A Reminiscence of Emily Dickinson" (*Bookman*, Nov. 1924), Gertrude M. Graves's "A Cousin's Memories of Emily Dickinson" (Boston *Sunday Globe*, 12 January 1930), and MacGregor Jenkins's *Emily Dickinson: Friend and Neighbor* (Boston, 1930). Mrs. Bianchi also contributed a volume, *Emily Dickinson Face to Face: Unpublished Letters with Notes and Reminiscences* (Boston, 1932). Mrs. Bianchi was about twenty when her aunt died, and her reminiscences of life among the Dickinsons are useful if read cautiously. To these memoirs should be added the large collection of family letters in Mrs. Bingham's *Emily Dickinson's Home*, which add significant detail for understanding the context of Emily Dickinson's life, the town of Amherst, family relationships, and daily routine. In addition, the more recently discovered Lyman letters (see *Manuscripts and Letters*, above) give some valuable glimpses of the Dickinson family. Joseph Lyman was a distant Dickinson relative, a schoolmate of Austin's, one of Lavinia's beaus, and a good friend of Emily's. He had warm memories of the days he spent visiting in the Dickinson home. These letters also reveal that Emily's "terror—since September" probably was caused by eye trouble, not unrequited love.

The decade of the forties produced no biographies, unless one includes Henry W. Wells's *Introduction to Emily Dickinson* (Chicago, 1947), which is more criticism than biography. In the fifties, however, there were Richard Chase's volume in the American Men of Letters Series, *Emily Dickinson* (New York, 1951), and Thomas H. Johnson's companion volume to his edition of the poems, *Emily Dickinson: An Interpretive Biography* (Cambridge, Mass., 1955). Both are important critical biographies that deal intelligently with the relationship between Emily Dickinson's poetry and her background, friendships, and cultural context, but neither Chase nor Johnson adds biographical data to Whicher's account.

One of the most important sources of biographical material came out early in the sixties: Jay Leyda's *The Years and Hours of Emily Dickinson* (2 vols., New Haven, Conn., 1960). This is the raw material of biography — 928 pages of entries from the letters and diaries of many people, from newspapers and other printed sources — all arranged chronologically. It begins with the announcement in 1828 of Edward Dickinson's intention to marry Emily Norcross and ends with a letter describing Emily Dickinson's funeral in 1886. The front matter includes a detailed biographical dictionary of "The People Around Emily Dickinson" and an extensive appendix locating sources.

Since Leyda's book came out, no new biographical discoveries have been made, although both Higgins and Miller have reinterpreted the old evidence to argue that Bowles was the object of Emily Dickinson's love and the man she addressed as "master." Higgins's *Portrait* is a competent book based on a close reading of all the letters, and while his evidence is no more conclusive than Whicher's, it is perhaps more plausible. Both Johnson and Chase and more recently Gelpi and Sherwood (see *Criticism*, below) accepted Whicher's identification of Wadsworth, but Mrs. Bingham, who was in a position to know as much as anyone, never advanced a candidate (*Emily Dickinson's Home*). When she first published the three impassioned "master" letters to their unknown recipient, she remained noncommittal. Both Theodora Ward (see below) and Jay Leyda think that neither Wadsworth nor Bowles was the addressee. Actually there were several other male friends in Emily Dickinson's life who have not been mentioned in this discussion, but she probably was stating a fact when she wrote Higginson that "my life has been too simple and stern to embarrass any." There is, of course, no doubt of Wadsworth's importance to her, for she referred to him specifically as "my dearest earthly friend."

Besides Newton, Wadsworth, and Bowles, the role played by Thomas Wentworth Higginson was of great significance. The facts about this relationship have never been obscure, for Higginson wrote the introduction to *Poems* (1890) and two articles about Emily Dickinson (*Christian Union*, 25 September 1890, and *AtM*, Oct. 1891). The latter article printed letters and recounted the friendship, which began when Higginson published "A Letter to a Young Contributor" in the *Atlantic* (Apr. 1862) and she wrote asking him to be her preceptor. He soon dropped the role of literary advisor but remained her friend and correspondent. This friendship is well treated by Whicher, Johnson, and others and fills a good portion of Anna Mary Wells's *Dear Preceptor: The Life and Times of Thomas Wentworth Higginson* (Boston, 1963). Miss Wells's view of Higginson is more favorable than the average estimate.

Most of the books on Emily Dickinson since 1960 have dealt primarily with her poetry, placing it in context, to be sure, but chiefly concerned with thematic development, ideas, imagery, poetic form, and explications. Theodora Ward, however, in *The Capsule of the Mind: Chapters in the Life of Emily Dickinson* (Cambridge, Mass., 1961), is an exception, as are Higgins's *Portrait* and Miller's *The Poetry of Emily Dickinson*. Mrs. Ward traces the inner story through the self-revelation found in the poems, but being aware of the serious danger of drawing false inferences, she proceeds carefully. As Johnson's assistant, she spent a great deal of time studying and ordering the manuscripts, and she writes with authority. She is especially good in her chapters devoted to Mr. and Mrs. Holland, Samuel Bowles, and Col. Higginson. Ms. Miller's book in its early chapters is largely concerned with biography, the Dickinson-Todd relationship, the correspondence with Higginson (which she thinks Johnson misunderstood), and the Bowles friendship. Jack L. Capps, in *Emily Dickinson's Reading: 1836–1886* (Cambridge, Mass., 1966), expands the biographical information previously available on his special topic — but for the purpose of illuminating the art. This is a valuable study. John B. Pickard, in *Emily Dickinson: An Introduction and Interpretation* (New York, 1967), has written a good short study for college students, and he combines both biography and criticism. An even briefer but reliable introduction, prepared for British readers, is Douglas Duncan's *Emily Dickinson* in Oliver and Boyd's Writers and Critics Series (Edinburgh, 1965).

CRITICISM

Eighty years have passed since Roberts Brothers of Boston published *Poems by Emily Dickinson* in 1890. This period divides itself evenly into two eras: the period of judicial criticism and the period of academic criticism. For the first forty years Emily Dickinson's poetry was judged by writers and literary journalists who struggled to evaluate her work and to fit her into categories. The majority of reviewers liked her poems but were hard put to explain why she was good or to defend her violations of nineteenth-century poetic norms. Whether the puzzled reviewers created an audience or interested readers sold her poems by word-of-mouth praise is a moot point. At any rate, the poetry created a considerable stir in the nineties and went through repeated printings. Then there was a second wave of interest after 1914 when Mrs. Bianchi began editing her aunt's poems. Following the centennial year of her birth, 1930, the writing about Emily Dickinson began to be dominated by the academic critics. No longer was it necessary to evaluate her poetry. By that time it belonged to literature and could be treated with the same serious analysis that one applied to Milton or Keats.

There are three useful books that enable one to study the first seventy years of Dickinson criticism, both the judicial and the academic criticism: Lubbers, *Emily Dickinson: The Critical Revolution;* Caesar R. Blake and Carlton F. Wells, eds., *The Recognition of Emily Dickinson* (Ann Arbor, Mich., 1964); and Richard B. Sewall, ed., *Emily Dickinson: A Collection of Critical Essays* (Englewood Cliffs, N.J., 1963). The first traces with great thoroughness the growth of the poet's reputation from the time she first wrote Higginson in 1862 ("Are you too deeply occupied to say if my verse is alive?") until the end of 1962, a century later. It not only charts the vicissitudes of Emily Dickinson's posthumous fame, but it also succeeds in mapping the changing tastes and interests of a hundred years of literary history. The other two books are collections of essays that provide abundant documentation (without much overlap) for Emily Dickinson's developing reputation. Among the forty-five selections in the Blake-Wells volume and the seventeen in Sewall's collection, only four are duplicated. The former volume concentrates on Emily Dickinson's reception before 1930 and the latter, which is one of Prentice-Hall's Twentieth Century Views Series, prints only one essay written before 1932.

The Growth of a Reputation: 1890–1930

Higginson's essay in *The Christian Union* and his introduction to *Poems* (1890) were designed to prepare the way for the poetry. He wrote Mrs. Todd when the volume came from the printer: "I am *astounded* . . . How could we have doubted them." In his preface, however, he had to defend the irregular meter, lack of rhymes, ellipsis, and compression: "In many ways these verses will seem to the reader like poetry torn up by the roots, with rain and dew and earth still clinging to them, giving a freshness and a fragrance not otherwise to be conveyed." He also argued that she had a "rigorous literary standard" of her own and a "tenacious fastidiousness" in her choice of words. He concluded that "when a thought takes one's breath away, a lesson in grammar is an impertinence." Even with Higginson as coeditor, however, Thomas Niles of Roberts Brothers was reluctant to publish the poems and asked the writer-critic Arlo Bates to give an opinion. Bates's report stated: "There is hardly one of these poems which does not bear marks of unusual and remarkable talent; there is hardly one of them which is not marked by an extraordinary crudity of workmanship." He insisted on cutting the proposed selection in half, and the first volume came out with only 116 poems. These "yes, but" reactions to Emily Dickinson's poems were rather typical of the large number of reviews that the volume received.

Only William Dean Howells (*HM*, Jan. 1891) was unequivocal in his praise and unruffled by the apparent lack of form. Where Higginson's preface tried to fit Emily Dickinson into a tradition by comparing her with Blake, Howells noted that it was an Emerson who had read Blake who had influenced her. He also thought there was a bit of Heine in her poetry, but he did not suppose she ever had read the German poet. Although most of the poems were short, Howells thought each "a compassed whole, a sharply finished point" and he believed Emily Dickinson had "spared no pains in the perfect expression of her ideals." Even the poems that seemed to have been left rough or rude gave the impression that "the artist meant just this harsh exterior to remain."

Andrew Lang, the most formidable of the British reviewers, found nothing to admire in the poems. He launched an anonymous diatribe in angry rebuttal to Howells and found fault with the lack of rhyme, the faulty grammar, and general incomprehensibility of the metaphors. He summed up with "balderdash" and wondered if Howells really was serious in praising "this farrago of illiterate and uneducated sentiment" (*London Daily News*, 2 January 1891). Later Thomas Bailey Aldrich, who had succeeded Howells as editor of the *Atlantic*, gazed into a cloudy crystal ball when he predicted that "oblivion lingers in the immediate neighborhood" of Emily Dickinson's verse (*AtM*, Jan. 1892). He was reviewing *Poems, Second Series*, and apparently felt a need to help stamp out "Miss Dickinson's *disjecta membra*" which Howells and Higginson thought so highly of. He was not nasty, like Lang, but he could not take seriously a poet who eschewed rhyme and meter, and in answer to Higginson's preface wrote that "an eccentric, dreamy, half-educated recluse in an out-of-the-way New England village (or anywhere else) cannot with impunity set at defiance the laws of gravitation and grammar."

By the time Mrs. Todd alone edited *Poems, Third Series* (1896) Emily Dickinson's verse no longer was a novelty. The reviewers had her pegged generally as poet *manqué* and fewer notices appeared than before. Higginson, who reviewed the volume in the *Nation* (8 October 1896), still was fond of the poetry "in spite of all its flagrant literary faults." But there were several essays in 1896 which summed up all of Emily Dickinson's poems then published and looked ahead toward the twentieth-century estimate of her place in American literature: Bliss Carmen, "A Note on Emily Dickinson" (Boston, *Transcript*, 21 November 1896); Harry Lyman Koopman, "Emily Dickinson" (*Brown Magazine*, Dec. 1896); and Rupert Hughes, "The Idea of Emily Dickinson" (*Godey's*, Nov. 1896). Both Carmen and Koopman believed that her originality and her flouting of the genteel conventions insured her permanence, and Hughes concluded that along with Poe and Whitman she was one of the three American contributors to world lyric poetry.

The period from 1897 to 1914 was a time of great silence in Emily Dickinson criticism. Lubbers's sources list only seven articles about her in this period; and in twenty-five literary histories published between 1895 and 1913, she is mentioned in only eight. But after 1914 only Bliss Perry's *The American Spirit in Literature* (New Haven, Conn., 1918) fails to discuss Emily Dickinson. Her poems, however, appeared in eighteen anthologies between 1896 and 1914, including twenty poems in Edmund Clarence Stedman's *An American Anthology* (Boston, 1900). Stedman's use of twenty poems is misleading, because Emily Dickinson appears in his collection along with 613 other poets. Yet time was on her side, and the statement she had made in one of her letters was in the process of being demonstrated: "If fame belonged to me, I could not escape her."

When *The Single Hound* appeared in 1914, a new era in American poetry had begun. Harriet Monroe's new magazine, *Poetry*, had been in existence for two years, and Frost, Eliot, Pound, Millay, Amy Lowell, and others were already publishing. Lubbers has found only twelve reviews of this volume, but he believes that only a few review copies were sent out. Only 888 copies were issued in two small printings, and the book quickly became a collector's item. Before it went out of print Emily Dickinson was hailed as a precursor of the imagist movement that was then dominating American poetry. Elizabeth Sergeant reviewed the book for the *New Republic* (14 August 1915) under the caption "An Early Imagist" and noted that for "starkness of vision, 'quintessentialness' of expression, boldness and solidity of thought, and freedom of form" Emily Dickinson could "give the imagists 'pointers.'" Amy Lowell, the demiurge of imagism, began talking about her in lectures on the new poetry and wrote her into *A Critical Fable* (Boston, 1922). Robert Hillyer, Louis Untermeyer, and Conrad Aiken, three more young poet-critics, added their voices to the swelling chorus. Emily Dickinson's form, which had bothered even her strongest supporters in the nineties, no longer was an obstacle, and she began to be linked with Whitman as one of the liberators of American verse. She still troubled academic critics, such as the pioneer professor of American literature, Fred Lewis Pattee, who never admitted her to the pantheon, and Norman Foerster, who wrote cautiously of her in the important *Cambridge History of American Literature* (1921). Foerster felt that her "place in American letters will be inconspicuous but secure."

The most important critical essay on Emily Dickinson to appear before the centennial year was the preface that Conrad Aiken wrote to introduce his selection of the poems (1924). Both Blake-Wells and Sewall reprint it. Aiken analyzed the poetry perceptively, introduced the topics that have occupied the critics ever since, and concluded flatly that she is "among the finest poets in the language." He saw in her the "most perfect flower of New England Transcendentalism." In her mode of life she "carried the doctrine of self-sufficient individualism farther than Thoreau," and in her poetry "she carried it . . . farther than Emerson." Aiken discounted the Puritan strain in her background, a point that later writers have addressed themselves to, but he did single out the large number of poems on death as one of the remarkable things about the verse and he thought the "most characteristic and most profound" aspect of her work was "the remarkable range of metaphysical speculation and ironic introspection." Even Aiken's view of Emily Dickinson's "singular perversity, her lapses and tyrannies" is quite contemporary, and he accepts her erratic but brilliant verse "as an inevitable part of the strange and original genius she was."

One more example from the criticism written before 1930 will have to suffice for this brief survey, but it is a significant essay that looks ahead, like Aiken's, towards present-day views and shows that British opinion was moving in the same direction as the American. Susan Miles discussed with great lucidity "The Irregularities of Emily Dickinson" (*London Mercury*, Dec. 1925) in answer to an earlier essay by Harold Monro (*Criterion*,

Jan. 1925) dismissing Emily Dickinson as overrated. Miss Miles argued that the "irregularities have a definite artistic significance." If a poet wishes to give expression to a world in which he believes "not a worm is cloven in vain" he does well to construct neat stanzas where *sin* rhymes with *in*, *fall* rhymes with *all*, *night* with *light*, and *ill* with *will*. And if the poet sees a world where "all discord is harmony not understood, all partial ill is universal good," he will express his view in heroic couplets of undeviating regularity. "Emily Dickinson viewed a world made up of pieces which often did not dovetail . . . and a little madness in her rhymes was part of her expression of it." The essay goes on to illustrate this point and concludes that Emily Dickinson was one of the "comparatively few poets — Thomas Hardy is another — who have achieved an aesthetic impression of a cleft and unmatching world."

Emily Dickinson and the Academicians: 1930–1955

Dividing the academic criticism of the past forty years at the year 1955 is somewhat arbitrary; but after the appearance of the Johnson variorium edition the quantity of Emily Dickinson scholarship increased sharply, and for the first time critics were able to examine the entire canon and to see it arranged, at least roughly, in chronological order. The academic critics who wrote between 1930 and 1955 worked under difficulties, although their objective in general was to define the nature of the poetry and to subject it to close analysis. The first important essay of the new era was Allan Tate's often-reprinted "New England Culture and Emily Dickinson" (*Sym*, Apr. 1932) which begins with the assumption that "Emily Dickinson is a great poet."

Tate is not at all interested in the biographical problem, "which will never give up the key to anyone's verse." Even if the seclusion had resulted from disappointment in love, "there would remain the discrepancy between what the seclusion produced and the seclusion looked at as a cause." The effect of the seclusion is the poetry, but the cause is really "the whole complex of anterior fact, which was the social and religious structure of New England." Actually, he says, "her life was one of the richest and deepest ever lived on this continent." What does interest Tate is the tension in Emily Dickinson's verse that resulted from the breaking up of the Puritan idea under the impact of Emersonian Transcendentalism. Like Shakespeare at the end of the medieval system and Donne in the seventeenth century, she lived in a time of change, in what Tate calls the perfect literary situation. "Miss Dickinson is the only Anglo-American poet of her century whose work exhibits the perfect literary situation — in which is possible the fusion of sensibility and thought." Her poetry is primarily a "poetry of ideas" and his purpose is to fit her into a tradition;

for "poetry does not dispense with tradition; it probes the deficiencies of a tradition."

Whicher's *This Was A Poet* (1938) also placed Emily Dickinson firmly within her tradition, and aside from its interest as biography, it is in addition a significant work of criticism. Whicher felt obliged to counteract the enthusiastic tendency, after *The Single Hound* appeared, to see Emily Dickinson as a twentieth-century contemporary. His biographical chapters, which recreate vividly the Amherst background and the Mt. Holyoke experience, effectively contribute to this effort. Both Whicher and the poet, as Emily Dickinson put it, "see — New Englandly." Though she lived during the Gilded Age she was not a part of it. Her mental climate was much the same as Emerson's, and what she actually represents is the "last surprising bloom — the November witch-hazel blossom — of New England's flowering time" (Whicher, p. 153). Three of the strongest currents of New England culture came together in her poetry: "the Puritan tradition in which she was nurtured; the Yankee or, more broadly, American humor that was just coming out of the ground; and the spiritual unrest, typified by Emerson, which everywhere was melting the frost of custom" (ibid.)

Richard Sewall notes in the introduction to his collection of essays that one of the characteristics of academic criticism before 1955 was the "tone of grudgingness and apology on the one hand and fulsomeness and cloying unction on the other." Yvor Winters, always a prickly critic, illustrates the former tone in "Emily Dickinson and the Limits of Judgment," one of the chapters in *Maule's Curse* (Norfolk, Conn., 1938). He wrote that "no poet of comparable reputation has been guilty of so much unpardonable writing." It annoyed him that she often was praised for her worst traits, such as the silly playfulness that made "I like to see it lap the Miles" an "abominable" poem; and even her best poems, unlike those of Jonson, Herbert, or Hardy "can never be isolated certainly and defensibly from her defects." He found this state of affairs "profoundly disturbing" because she was "a poetic genius of the highest order." Winters in this essay went on to analyze a number of poems, good and bad, to accuse Emily Dickinson of an occasional "deliberate excursion into obscurity," and to quarrel with Tate because he praised a fine poem ("Because I could not stop for Death") for the wrong reasons. But when Winters called "The last Night that She lived" great poetry, despite a "badly mixed figure and at least two major grammatical blunders," his critical position was in substance not much different from Higginson's in 1890, although he conducted his analysis on a much more sophisticated level.

R. P. Blackmur's essay, "Emily Dickinson: Notes on Prejudice and Fact" (*SoR*, Autumn 1937), was even more sophisticated and grudging than

Winters's.[1] He first had to clear away the undergrowth of prejudice before he could reach the poetry to analyze it. The prejudices were several: Aiken's view that Emily Dickinson was the best woman poet in English; Mrs. Bianchi's contention that her aunt was a complete rebel and that her "slips and roughnesses" were examples of a "revolutionary master-craftsman"; Ludwig Lewisohn's "magnifying her intellectual and mystical force" in his *Expression in America* (New York, 1932); and Tate's prejudice about the poet in relation to his time "as a fatal event in cultural history." The bulk of Blackmur's essay is a detailed analysis of Emily Dickinson's language, for as he argues: "The [possible] greatness of Emily Dickinson . . . is going to be found in the words she used and in the way she put them together." What he concedes to his subject is that she had an aptitude for language and that this sometimes produced great poetry. He concludes, however, that "the failure and success of Emily Dickinson's poetry were uniformly accidental largely because of the private and eccentric nature of her relation to the business of poetry." Blackmur's view might be classed by another critic as an additional prejudice to add to the original list; but this essay is a prime example of the "new criticism" of the thirties and forties, as John Crowe Ransom pointed out in *The New Criticism* (Norfolk, Conn., 1941).

The forties produced two books on Emily Dickinson that fall into Sewall's category of "fulsomeness and cloying unction." In the first, Sister Mary Power read the poetry and discovered that though Emily Dickinson was born a latter-day New England Puritan, she actually was a Roman Catholic in spirit: *In the Name of the Bee: The Significance of Emily Dickinson* (New York, 1943). This book, which was written with the cooperation of Mrs. Bianchi, was attacked by Whicher (*NEQ*, Mar. 1944) as propaganda filled with errors of fact and interpretation. A more important book was H. W. Wells's *Introduction to Emily Dickinson*, which contains many perceptive comments and insights but makes Emily Dickinson far bigger than life size. Wells's enthusiasm is infectious, and he is a cultivated scholar, but one is put off, for example, by such sentences as the one which begins his ten-page chapter entitled "Language of Poetry": "Emily Dickinson is one of the foremost masters of poetic English since Shakespeare, and in the severe economy of her speech comparable to Dante." For Wells, "the significance of Emily Dickinson lies in the fact that her kinship is closer to all great poets than it is to any of her contemporary New Englanders." She stands with the chief poets, seers, mystics, and visionaries, and his aim is "to deliver Emily from the claws of per-

---

1. For a later, more favorable view, see Blackmur's essay "Emily Dickinson's Notation" (*KR*, Spring 1956).

sonal interpretation and to place her personality upon a more distinguished height, not of Amherst Hill, but of Parnassus." Both Wells and Sister Power see Emily Dickinson as a mystic, and this term occurs frequently in the earlier critical writing. Fortunately, Sister Mary Humiliata in "Emily Dickinson—Mystic Poet?" (*CE*, Dec. 1950) corrects the loose use of this term by showing that Emily Dickinson does not really belong in the company of mystics as traditionally defined.

Richard Chase's *Emily Dickinson* (1951) brought a fine critical intelligence to the reading of the poetry. The careful discriminations lacking in Wells are found here in the comparisons of Whitman, Emerson, and others with Emily Dickinson, and Chase is quite severe in limiting to about fifty the poems which "have the substance and the fineness of manner which urge us to accord them equality with much else that is excellent in the literature of lyric poetry." Chase's book also has a clear focus in seeing Emily Dickinson's poetry as possessing "one major theme, one symbolic act, one incandescent center of meaning. Expressed in the most general terms, this theme is the achievement of status through crucial experiences." He goes on to explain that experience was both narrow and profound and typically took the form of a "sudden illumination, an appalling pause in the motion of things, a seizure of an unspeakable power, an ecstatic influx." The core of this book consists of three illuminating chapters on "The Economy of Poetry," "A Poetry of Ideas," and "The Idea of Poetry." Chase agrees with Tate on the importance of Emily Dickinson's historical position, but he also believes that the "used and shopworn furniture of the bygone cultural traditions" were something of a liability and resulted in "a curious personal, poetic convention which can only be called 'rococo.'"

Emily Dickinson's aptitude for language, which Blackmur discussed in 1937, became the subject for Donald E. Thackrey's *Emily Dickinson's Approach to Poetry* (Lincoln, Neb., 1954), the last critical study before the Johnson variorum edition. Writers from Higginson on have been aware of Emily Dickinson's great preoccupation with words; in fact, she wrote Higginson that, after her first tutor died, for several years her lexicon was her only companion. Thackrey's monograph is the first to deal with this subject extensively and competently. For him, her fascination with words explains in part her method of composition. She approached poetry inductively through the "combining of words to arrive at whatever conclusion the word pattern seemed to suggest, rather than using words as subordinate instruments in expressing a total conception." Words to her had a startling vitality, some terrifying mysterious power, and her poetry is full of specific statements about language. Her intense concern with language as a means of communication no doubt accounts for the economy and frugality of her verse. At the same time it made her aware that words really could not communicate at all. This second aspect of her experience . . . led her to a worshipful attitude toward silence," and one might have expected ultimately a withdrawal from attempts to communicate and a devotion "to a mystical experiencing of truth." But she was not a mystical type and went on writing her letter to the world.

Emily Dickinson and the Academicians: 1955–1969

Space in this essay precludes the discussion of the large number of critical articles and explications which appeared in the decade after 1955 at the rate of from ten to twenty per year and since then at a still higher rate. Many of these are significant discussions and are worth attention. It has also been impossible to deal with the forty dissertations written on Emily Dickinson, except for the eight which so far have appeared as books. Summaries of most of the unpublished dissertations may be found in *DA*. It is interesting to note, however, that the first dissertation was written at the University of Vienna in 1940, and none was produced in the United States until 1951. But since the Johnson variorum edition appeared, it has been floodtime for Dickinson dissertations.

After five years of work on the manuscripts and letters, Johnson brought out his complete edition of the poems in 1955 and in the same year issued *Emily Dickinson: An Interpretive Biography* (Boston, 1955). As criticism the biography lacks the brilliant *aperçus* of Chase's work, but it is the first book to be based on a close examination of the manuscripts arranged in approximate chronological order. Johnson was able to study the process of technical mastery as no one before had been able to do, and his discussion of "The Poet and the Muse" is a valuable contribution. He studies her prosody as it derived from Watts's *Christian Psalmody* and *The Psalms, Hymns, and Spiritual Songs*, copies of which were owned by Edward Dickinson. Her first lesson in metrics no doubt came from Watts, and Johnson's discussion of her use of common meter, long meter, and short meter is illuminating. At first she followed the hymn meters closely, but gradually she "perceived how to gain new effects by exploring the possibilities within traditional metric patterns." Her experiments continued until her "prosodic expertness was fully realized in 1862." A further study of this subject is Martha W. England, "Emily Dickinson and Isaac Watts: Puritan Hymnodists" (*BNYPL*, Feb. 1965), which examines the Watts relationship in great detail and with a considerable knowledge of hymnology.

As has been noted, the appearance of the Johnson edition of the poetry was hailed as a momentous literary event, and the three-volume work was widely reviewed. Two interesting review-essays were written by John

Crowe Ransom and Austin Warren. Ransom's pleasantly discursive "Emily
Dickinson: A Poet Restored" (*Perspectives USA;* Spring 1956) surveys the
work with a poet's eye and suggests that about one out of seventeen of
the 1,775 poems is "destined to become a common public property." Warren's review "Emily Dickinson" (*SR,* Autumn 1957), expands this number to about three hundred, but Warren is surprised to discover that there
is no "consistency of method" between the early and late poems. He had
expected the "poems to grow more Dickinsonian" and not occasionally,
as they do, turn back to styles not definitely hers. "Unlike Mozart and
Beethoven and Hopkins and James, she had no 'late manner' so integrally
held that she could not, in conscience, deviate therefrom."

The first comprehensive reading of all the poems based on the Johnson
text appeared in Charles Anderson's *Emily Dickinson's Poetry: Stairway
of Surprise* (New York, 1960). This is an important book that is interested
solely in the poetry as art and winnows from the entire canon 103 poems
for explication under several thematic groupings: "The Paradise of Art,"
"The Outer World," "The Inner World," and "The Other Paradise." As
Anderson explains in his preface, "with a poet like Emily Dickinson who
published nothing and apparently destroyed nothing, the literary remains
may include the miscellaneous sweepings of the poet's workshop, ranging all the way from splendid finished creations down to absent-minded
scribblings." The 103 poems, which he analyzes extensively and perceptively, represent to him the real gold of the total remains. He departs from
Johnson's practice of using as basic text the earliest fair copy, and when
there are variant extant texts, which often is the case, he establishes his
own reading. Many of the poems Anderson includes have long been admired and often explicated, such as "Safe in their Alabaster Chambers"
and "There's a certain Slant of light," but others, like "There is a Zone
whose even Years" and "I went to Heaven," are much less familiar. Still
others like "There came a Day at Summer's full" are surprisingly not
among Anderson's selections.

About the time Anderson's book came out, three poets, Archibald Mac-
Leish, Louise Bogan, and Richard Wilbur, appeared together at an Emily
Dickinson celebration at Amherst College. Their papers were published
in an interesting little book, *Emily Dickinson: Three Views* (Amherst,
Mass., 1960). MacLeish ("The Private World") believes that it is the quality
of the voice in which Emily Dickinson speaks that makes her unique and
important. It is "the tone rather than the words that one remembers
afterwards"— a wholly "spontaneous tone" without any "literary assumption of posture or pose." And the voice "speaks to *you,*" not to herself
as a voice to be overheard, and it speaks with "that New England restraint which is really a self-respect which also respects others." Louise

Bogan ("A Mystical Poet") revives the term mystic for Emily Dickinson but uses it as a metaphor: "We find that the progress of the mystic toward illumination, and the poet toward the full depth and richness of his insight — are much alike." She sees Emily Dickinson as belonging with the great English Romantic poets who "shared the belief that the imagination was nothing less than God as he operates in the human soul." And she elaborates the comparison with Blake that Howells and Higginson had made in 1890. Richard Wilbur's view ("Sumptuous Destitution") is of Emily Dickinson as a poet with a "sense of privation"— the "laureate and attorney of the empty-handed." She questioned God about the economy of His creation and "used her own suffering as experiential evidence about the nature of the deity." She also employed another "emotional strategy" in her "repeated assertion of the paradox that privation is more plentiful than plenty; that to renounce is to possess the more."

A book that belongs on the same shelf with Anderson's is Clark Griffith's *The Long Shadow: Emily Dickinson's Tragic Poetry* (Princeton, N.J., 1964). Griffith sets out to rescue his subject from the favorite public image of her as "an American Mrs. Browning, with a shade less preciousness and minus of course the husband, or of a feminine Walt Whitman, with the 'yawp' tuned down somewhat, and minus of course the whiskers." Anderson anticipated Griffith somewhat in rejecting the "excessively facile" poem "I never saw a Moor" and explicating instead "I know that He exists," but Griffith's book is a provocative study of more than fifty poems that define Emily Dickinson as a tragic poet. This is where her real importance lies, he believes. Her outlook was, "in the sense with which existentialism now defines these terms, an outlook suffused with *Angst*, dread, and terror." Thus Emily Dickinson belongs among her contemporaries with Melville rather than Whitman. "She shared with Melville essentially the same view of man's predicament, seeing him as a finite creature, craving order and infinity, but set down in a 'multiverse' that thwarts his cravings and remains deaf to his appeals." She tried to devise means of escaping but in her most meaningful poems the tragic vision prevails. In this book Emily Dickinson emerges as a modern tragic poet with a "sense of the discrepancy between man's potential glory and the actual horror that contains him." She is more than a tragic poet, of course, and Griffith's book needs to be supplemented by a reading of other studies such as Hyatt Waggoner's (see below).

Another writer who sees Emily Dickinson as a modern existentialist is Thomas W. Ford in *Heaven Beguiles the Tired: Death in the Poetry of Emily Dickinson* (University, Ala., 1966). It is useful to have someone isolate and organize the death poems (though he misses a few), for certainly death was one of her flood subjects; but not many Dickinson scholars will agree with Ford's thesis that "Emily Dickinson's intense interest in death was the most important single factor in shaping the contours of her poetry." Her business was circumference, as she said, and that included death among other things. Ford is simply wrong when he argues that "it can safely be assumed that the [Civil] war heightened her awareness of death still further, and that this heightened awareness was largely responsible for increased literary activities." The limitations of this book, however, lie chiefly with the failure to relate the death poems to the entire corpus of the poetry, as Griffith's book does with its chapter on "The Aesthetics of Dying." Finally, Ford's explications are far less satisfactory than those of either Anderson or Griffith.

A much more satisfactory study that deals with one facet of the poet's work is David T. Porter's *The Art of Emily Dickinson's Early Poetry* (Cambridge, Mass., 1966). Here Emily Dickinson's apprenticeship is investigated with admirable balance and thoroughness. Like Anderson, Porter is concerned only with the poetry and not at all with biography. His purpose is to plot the "boundary of the developmental period in her career" and to discover "the early stylistic habits that equipped her for the enormous flood of poetry in the year 1862." This he does ably in examining the 301 poems Johnson dated before 1862, plus the additional ones she sent Higginson during that year. In the last chapter Porter lists twenty-six early poems that he regards as superior performances. By 1862 Emily Dickinson had mastered her art and on several occasions had reached "that high level of lyric expression at which extraordinary emotional impulses are matched and dominated by even more extraordinary discipline."

Among the thirteen scholarly books on Emily Dickinson that appeared in the past five years (1965–69) are two competing studies of the poet's mind and art: Albert J. Gelpi, *Emily Dickinson: The Mind of the Poet* (Cambridge, Mass., 1965), and William R. Sherwood, *Circumference and Circumstance: Stages in the Mind and Art of Emily Dickinson* (New York, 1968). Gelpi seeks to go beyond biography and textual analysis to comprehend Emily Dickinson "fully and richly as a poet" and in addition "to suggest how central and radial a figure she is in the sweep of the American imagination." This is a very competent and comprehensive study that begins with the poet's preoccupation in an early letter to Susan Gilbert with the Emersonian problem of identity *versus* otherness, the *me* and the *not-me*. It is controlled by the metaphor of circumference throughout and returns full circle at the end to Emily Dickinson's mind as exemplifying "the paradox of the double consciousness spiraling back on itself." The complexity of her mind is not the "complexity of harmony but that of dissonance. Her peculiar burden was to be a Romantic poet with a Calvinist's sense of things: to know transitory ecstasy in a world tragically fallen and doomed." As an American poet, she occupies a pivotal position. She does not belong to the "prophetic or Dionysian strain of American poetry which derived palely from Emerson and descended lustily through Whitman to Carl Sandburg and Jeffers, and more recently to Jack Kerouac and Brother Antoninus." Rather she fits into the "Appollonian tradition which proceeds from Edward Taylor through her to Eliot, Stevens, Frost, and Marianne Moore, and thence to Robert Lowell and Elizabeth Bishop."

Sherwood's book, like Gelpi's, is a post-Johnsonian reading of all the poetry in its present ordering. Where Gelpi is mainly interested in the poet's mind as revealed in her poetry, Sherwood assumes "that poetry is a form of autobiography." He argues the Wadsworth identification again and believes that Higginson played an important part in formulating her aesthetic theory. The weight of scholarly opinion is against him on the latter subject, but nonetheless his book has a good many interesting explications. Unfortunately he does not take into account the books by Griffith, Gelpi, and Higgins, all of which deal differently with matters he treats and which appeared between the completion of his dissertation in 1964 and its publication in 1968. Emily Dickinson scholars in the sixties had to scramble to keep up to date.

Sherwood's study posits four distinct periods in Emily Dickinson's life: a period of questioning of God and immortality; a period of resentment and defiance in which she created her own god in Charles Wadsworth; a period of despair; and a period in which all her wrongs were righted by an orthodox religious conversion. The third and fourth periods occurred during the momentous year 1862 when she was composing more than a poem per day. To arrive at the conclusion that the despair and redemption both occurred in 1862, Sherwood has to reorder the 1862 poems in the Johnson edition into a coherent and logical pattern. Rearranging the poems within a given year is defensible, for Johnson's ordering is fairly arbitrary; but one cannot ever be sure that all the poems assigned to 1862 (largely on the basis of handwriting analysis) were written in that year. Sherwood's thesis, however, is provocative and possible, but what is more controversial about this book is its insistence on the importance of Puritanism in Emily Dickinson's life and the relegation of transcendentalism to an insignificant role. He writes: "Puritanism, far from being the stock from which she manufactured intellectual supports, was live, firm and deeply rooted." In another instance he states: "Emily Dickinson's transcendentalism (or the watered-down version of it that lies behind her early poems about the intimations of nature) was a passing fancy."

A corrective to Sherwood's insistence on Puritanism's importance is a splendid chapter in Hyatt Waggoner's *American Poets: From the Puritans to the Present* (Boston, 1968). Waggoner, like Gelpi, gives Emerson a central role and places Emily Dickinson in a pivotal position in the mainstream of American poetry from Taylor to Frost: "There are very few important American poets either before or after her whose work is not suggested somewhere in hers." Waggoner also corrects Whicher's view that Emily Dickinson owed little specifically to Emerson, though she partook much of transcendentalism. If Whicher had had the Johnson editions of poems and letters, he would have seen the large Emersonian influence, but Waggoner goes on to show that Emily Dickinson eventually rejected both her father's Calvinism and Emerson's transcendentalism for the conviction that "faith was simply a 'first necessity' of our being, resting on nothing but need." Thus she redefined faith as a commitment in the manner of the later existentialists.

After eighty years of Emily Dickinson commentary one hardly expects to come across a study that breaks new ground, but such is Brita Lindberg-Seyersted's *The Voice of the Poet: Aspects of Style in the Poetry of Emily Dickinson* (Cambridge, Mass., 1968). This is a careful, lucid, abundantly documented reading of the poetry by a literary scholar with a working knowledge of modern linguistic theory.[2] It is an important addition to Emily Dickinson scholarship and answers questions previously only guessed at — often wrongly — by impressionistic critics. Mrs. Lindberg-Seyersted approaches Emily Dickinson by isolating three concepts which are realized in her language and language habits: colloquialness, slantness, and privateness.[3] These are the aspects of her style that make her different from other poets, and this study investigates them on the levels of diction, metrics, and syntactic structures.

The study begins with a chapter on "The Voice and the Poet," which establishes the clear relationship between Emily Dickinson's speech and letters on the one hand and her poetry on the other: In the bulk of her poetry there is clearly a single voice speaking directly to a second person (two-fifths of all the poems are I-poems). "This contributes greatly to the prevailing impression conveyed to a reader of the character of 'spokenness' of her poetic message." Next Mrs. Lindberg-Seyersted analyzes the diction, the use of colloquial words, unique usages, shifts from one form

2. A number of articles have treated specific topics dealt with in this book, but this is the first comprehensive literary-linguistic study. See Clendenning, Nos. 516, 578, 621, 626, 689, 785, 799, 912; also Buckingham, Nos. 6.315, 6.498, 6.599, 6.716, 6.893a, 6.924, 6.1191, 8.100.

3. "Slantness" is defined as a poetic technique of indirection, a term coined from the line, "Tell the truth but tell it slant"— Johnson, No. 1129. "Privateness" refers to the idiosyncratic aspects of Dickinson's style.

class to another, the use of paradox and contrast, archaisms and neologisms, the mixtures of Latin roots and Anglo-Saxon words, the interplay of monosyllables and polysyllables. This is all done quite thoroughly and with ample documentation. Then the book moves on to matters of prosody and metrics, speech rhythm, and rhyme. It deals not only with traditional prosody but also with phonology and studies the interplay of linguistic and metrical rhythm. The last chapter moves on to the larger syntactic elements, which in their idiosyncratic usage contribute, just as diction and metrics do, to Emily Dickinson's colloquialness, slantness, and privateness. The book ends with an interesting explication of "Further in Summer than the Birds," using the author's literary-linguistic method.

One final note: *The Voice of the Poet* deals extensively with a problem that has vexed Emily Dickinson scholars since the manuscripts became available, the matter of punctuation and capitalization. Both Mrs. Lindberg-Seyersted and R. W. Franklin (*The Editing of Emily Dickinson*) refute Edith Perry Stamm's widely circulated article "Emily Dickinson: Poetry and Punctuation" (*SatR*, 30 March 1963) which argues that the dashes are elocution markings indicating how the poems are to be read. Franklin reproduces Emily Dickinson's recipe for coconut cake, which has the same eccentricities of punctuation and capitalization as the poems.

Arguments over how to read and interpret Emily Dickinson are likely to go on forever. Ruth Miller's *The Poetry of Emily Dickinson* (Middletown, Conn., 1965) is a case in point, for it begins by dismissing all previous Emily Dickinson scholars as either wrong or wrongheaded and claims that the meaning of the poems can be understood only if they are subjected to "a new kind of scrutiny." But her method is not really different from that of other explicators, and the readings are often less satisfactory than those of Anderson, Griffith, and others. Ms. Miller's chief contribution, however, lies in Chapter Ten ("The Fascicles") in which she subjects the packets to intensive examination and argues that there is structure and meaning in the original arrangement of the poems. "Each is a narrative structure designed to recreate the experience of the woman" or "if the emphasis is on the poet, each fascicle records the poet's effort to understand the truth." She believes that the idea for the arrangements came from Francis Quarles's *Emblems, Divine and Moral*, which was in the Dickinson family library. The book also includes nearly two hundred pages of very useful appendices, especially the first, which tabulates the poems by fascicle in their probable original ordering (based on the work of Johnson, Leyda, and Franklin), and the third ("Emily Dickinson's Reading"), which lists the Emily Dickinson Association Books at Harvard and quotes suggestive excerpts from some of them. This listing is a valuable addition to the appendices in Capp's *Emily Dickinson's Reading.*

Two final items of minor importance will conclude the domestic portion of this survey: Dolores Dyer Lucas, *Emily Dickinson and Riddle* (DeKalb, Ill., 1969), and Marguerite Harris, compiler, *Emily Dickinson: Letters from the World* (n.p., 1970). The former is a slight study that examines Emily Dickinson's poetry in the literary and folk tradition of the riddle, arguing that the poet "consciously exploited the technique of riddle, in much of her work" (p. 14) in order to allow herself "to have her say without reprisal" (p. 133). The latter collects forty-five poems on Emily Dickinson by contemporary poets, including Gregory Corso, Richard Eberhart, William Stafford, and Yvor Winters, to mention some of the more prominent.

Emily Dickinson and the World

As one might expect, Emily Dickinson's emergence as a poet of international stature in the non-English-speaking world has come lately. The Buckingham bibliography lists twenty-six separate books or pamphlet translations into ten languages, including Japanese, Polish, Czech, and Hebrew, all but one published since World War II. Samplings of the poems, however, came out in periodicals much earlier, and the bibliography lists eighteen more translations of this sort. The earliest translations appeared in a German magazine published in Chicago in 1898, but this was a unique instance; and the first translations into German published in Germany are to be found in Ewald Flügel's essay, "Die nordamerikanische Literatur" in *Geschichte der englishen Literatur* (Leipzig and Vienna, 1907). The two poems that Flügel translated may well have been the first appearances of Emily Dickinson in translation outside of the United States. One cannot be sure because the investigation of translations and foreign reception has barely begun, and neither the Buckingham nor Clendenning listing is complete. Hans Galinsky's *Wegbereiter modernen amerikanischer Lyrik: Interpretations und Rezeptionsstudien zu Emily Dickinson und William Carlos Williams* (Heidelberg, 1968) devotes a section to "Emily Dickinson in Deutschland" (pp. 47–61) and for German listings is probably complete. Also Hensley C. Woodbridge has compiled a bibliography of eleven Spanish and Portuguese translations and eighteen critical articles (*Emily Dickinson Bulletin*, Oct. 1968), which have been incorporated into Buckingham's bibliography and somewhat augmented. Three Italian bibliographies list translations, books, articles, introductions, and reviews (many brief): Marialusia Bignami, "La letteratura americana in Italia" (*Studi Americani*, 1964); Centro di Studi Americani, *Repertorio bibliografico della letteratura americana in*

Italia (3 vols., Rome, 1966–69); and Paola Guidetti (see below). In any real sense Emily Dickinson began to be known abroad in the thirties when her poems first were translated into Czech, French, Italian, Hungarian, and again into German.

The appearance in 1968 of two important books by foreign scholars marks a sort of flowering of Emily Dickinson's world reputation. Klaus Lubbers (*The Critical Revolution*) is a member of the faculty at the University of Mainz, and Mrs. Lindberg-Seyersted (*The Voice of the Poet*), who is Swedish, teaches at the University of Oslo. Her book also has been published in Sweden. Interest in Emily Dickinson in both Germany and Sweden has not been extensive until recent years, but Mrs. Lindberg-Seyersted's study was preceded by two Swedish book-length translations in 1949 and 1950, the latter with an extensive introduction. Interest in Emily Dickinson in Germany, as Galinsky's study shows, has lagged, because Germans traditionally have been more interested in American fiction and drama, but there now are at least two post-Johnson selections of the poems available in translation, and Galinsky's study is a pioneering effort.

By all odds the greatest enthusiasm for Emily Dickinson outside of the United States has been shown in Italy. Not only have there been twenty-three translations of her poems into Italian, but five of them appeared in the thirties. The first book-length study of Emily Dickinson to be written in a language other than English also was in Italian, Emilio and Giuditta Cecchi, *Emily Dickinson* (Brescia, 1939). The mongraph, which began as Giuditta's thesis for the *laurea*, was reworked with the aid of her father, who, with Cesare Pavese and Elio Vittorini, was one of the pioneer introducers of American literature to Italy. Since that beginning the Italians have produced two more critical studies, Francesco Strocchetti's *Emily Dickinson* (Naples, 1957) and a more recent book by one of the most active Italian Americanists, Biancamaria Tedeschini-Lalli's *Emily Dickinson: prospettive critiche* (Florence, 1963).[4] The latter is a good introduction for Italians to the poet's cultural background, the relations of her life to her art, her poetic sensibility, and the major themes. Italian interest has even produced a detailed study of Emily Dickinson's reputation in Italy: Paola Guidetti, "La fortuna di Emily Dickinson in Italia" (*Studi Americani*, 1963). Of the two hundred-plus foreign critical pieces listed in the Buckingham bibliography, seventy-seven of them are in Italian. This compares with forty-three German items, twenty-five French, and twenty-eight from all of Spain and Latin America.

---

4. An essay in Italian was published in New York in 1950: Guiseppe Tusiani, *La poesia amorosa di Emily Dickinson.*

Interest in Emily Dickinson in Asia is beginning to develop, but it is a still more recent growth than in Europe and Latin America. The Japanese discovered her in 1952 and since then have produced twenty-six articles and seven translations. A *Study and Selected Poems* appeared in Tokyo in 1961, edited and translated by Toshikazu Niikura, to introduce her to non-English-speaking Japanese. The introduction of American studies to India has brought Emily Dickinson to the attention of students in that subcontinent. Two interesting chapters were devoted to her in a recent volume published in English by the U.S. Educational Foundation in India: C. D. Narasimhaiah, ed., *Indian Response to American Literature* (New Delhi, 1967). In this volume "The Poetry of Emily Dickinson" by C. Vimala Rao finds Emily Dickinson accessible to Indian readers because of the universality of her subjects: nature, love, death, immortality. In her attitude toward time he finds a special appeal for Indians, because "she appears to dwell in timelessness." Salamatullah Khan, writing on "Emily Dickinson and Death," sees parallels between her treatment of death as a suitor ("Death is the supple Suitor" and "Because I could not stop for Death") and the devotional songs of Kabir, one of the saint-poets of India.

DICKINSON SCHOLARSHIP SINCE 1970

Since I wrote the above essay in early 1970, the reputation of Emily Dickinson has continued to grow, and the scholarship on her appearing regularly in journals from every part of the globe increases almost exponentially. Even without the great surge of interest in Dickinson caused by the growth of feminism and academic programs in women's studies in the past decade, there is no doubt today that she has emerged as our greatest woman poet and a co-equal of Poe, Emerson, and Whitman in the Pantheon of 19th Century American poets.

These generalizations are easily documented statistically. When Lewis Leary brought out the first of his checklists, *Articles on American Literature, 1900–1950* (Durham, 1954), he listed only 125 articles on Dickinson, a bare average of two and one-half per year over the first half of this century. His second compilation, *Articles . . . 1950–1967* (1970), contained 217 articles, an average of 12 per year for the years it covered. The third and most recent volume, *Articles . . . 1968–1975* (1979), lists 327 items, an average of 41 items per year for the eight years it spans. The thin trickle of yesteryear has become a hemorrhage.

Dissertations also show the same trends. The first dissertation on Dickinson was written in Vienna in 1940, but down through 1955 only three more appeared. During the next six years there were eight additional ones, and between 1961 and 1966 there were 18. From 1967 through 1972 the rate increased to 27, and in the most recent period, 1973–1980, there were no less than 38. Thus there have been 87 dissertations all told, 47 of them written since the first edition of this book came out. This astonishing activity among graduate students assures us of an undiminished flow of articles and books in the future. General complaints today among academicians that publishing sources are drying up for scholarly writing seem not to hold true for Dickinson scholars.

Bibliography

To keep up with Dickinson scholarship, one needs first of all to consult the annual *MLA International Bibliography* and the annual bibliography that appears in *Dickinson Studies* (new name since 1979 of the *Emily Dickinson Bulletin*). For evaluation of the yearly output of books and articles, there is the annual, *American Literary Scholarship*, which devotes half of one chapter to Dickinson studies. This has been written by Bernice Slote (1971–74), Willis Buckingham (1975–79), and Jerome Loving (1980–81). These sources may be by-passed, if one is interested in explications of individual poems published prior to 1977, for Joseph Duchac's *The Poems of Emily Dickinson: An Annotated Guide to Commentary Published in English, 1890–1977* (Boston, 1979) provides an immensely useful 621 pages of listings, over six thousand items arranged conveniently. This is an indispensable resource. A similar compilation for the growing number of Dickinson studies in Japan appeared at the same time in Takao Furukawa's *Interpretation Index to Emily Dickinson's Poems in Japan* (Tokyo, 1979). This volume analyzes over 500 books and articles published in Japan between 1927 and 1979.

Other bibliographical contributions of lesser scope appeared during the past decade. Willis Buckingham twice has supplied addenda to his book-length bibliography (see p. 186) with 227 items (*EDB*, Dec. 1974) and still more in "Second Addendum" (*EDB*, June 1978). Every student of Dickinson needs to check *EDB* and its successor *DicS* for miscellaneous bibliographical items that appear there from time to time.

Two significant bibliographic essays are now available, the first by Willis Buckingham, "The Bibliographical Study of Emily Dickinson" (*RALS*, Spring 1974), the second by Roland Hagenbückle, "New Developments in Dickinson Criticism" (*Anglia*, no. 3/4, 1978). Buckingham, the leading authority on Dickinson bibliography, surveys the history of descriptive bibliographies of Dickinson's work, checklists of criticism, scholarship, and ana, specialized tools such as guides to MSS, bibliographies of her reading, and concordances. Buckingham concludes that we need a good descriptive bibliography of the poet's work, a census of collections in major libraries, and a handbook to Dickinson studies that will "winnow and appraise the mass of accumulating materials." The Hagenbückle essay offers a review of major critical studies published during the last two decades, a period which pretty well covers the years since the Johnson variorum edition opened the flood-gates for Dickinson scholarship that now threatens to drown us.

One final item of a bibliographical nature that should not be overlooked is the index to *EDB/DicS*. There are two indexes: one covering the years 1968–1974, compiled by Buckingham, the other covering from 1975–1980, compiled by Buckingham and Martin A. Orzeck. In the fourteen years of its existence this journal has published a large amount of Dickinson material, not all of it important, but much that is useful.

Editions

The one significant new edition of Dickinson in the past ten years will be discussed under MSS below. There have been no significant new printed editions of her work since Johnson brought out the variorum edition in three volumes in 1955 and then followed it up with *The Complete Poems* in 1960 and *Final Harvest* in 1962. The quality of Johnson's work is attested to by the fact it has not had to be done over in 27 years. Someday, however, there may be a new edition more nearly definitive than Johnson's. R. W. Franklin, who has been studying the Dickinson MSS and the editing of them for about 20 years, has found a good many misreadings, misdatings, and omissions in the Johnson edition.

Manuscripts and Letters

A new edition of Dickinson's poems probably would follow the ordering of the work to be found in Franklin's two-volume edition of *The Manuscript Books of Emily Dickinson* (Cambridge, Mass., 1981). In this important and long-awaited edition Franklin has arranged the poems in the order in which they originally existed in the fascicles left by the poet on her death in 1886. The vicissitudes undergone by the poems through the work of successive editors resulted in the loss of the original order. Johnson tried to reorganize the MSS but did not fully succeed. Franklin has probably done it as well as it ever can be done, and the result now is a facsimile edition that affords all Dickinson scholars who can't afford to visit Amherst and Harvard a chance to see the MSS pretty much the way Lavinia Dickinson found them.

A facsimile edition of Dickinson's MSS is particularly important, for these MSS have always resisted stubbornly the translation from longhand into print. Dickinson's idiosyncratic punctuation, capitalization, stanza and line divisions and lists of alternate readings make it highly desirable for scholars to have copies of the MSS in front of them. This edition relinquishes the Todd sequence and restores the original forty bound fascicles, arranged chronologically and renumbered. The unbound sheets that Dickinson left but did not sew together are reproduced here and called "Sets" and numbered one through fifteen. There can be no definitive arrangement of these MSS, as the poet did not make any. Franklin, however, was able to use stationery, stains, and pin impressions to give the MSS a rough ordering. The editorial work in this edition is meticulously performed, and the notes are useful, clear, and unobtrusive.

Since the two main collections of Dickinson MSS (the Todd and Dickinson archives) came to rest in institutional collections at Amherst and Harvard, few new manuscripts of poems have surfaced. Two previous published but unlocated MSS, however, have been found at Middlebury College (*PBSA*, Mar. 1975), and three other MSS that were in Millicent Todd Bingham's possession but not discovered in time for Johnson to use were added to the Amherst Collection in 1968 (*AL*, Mar. 1978). These latter are variants, not new poems. Finally, a new version of "Further in Summer than the Birds" is reprinted in *PBSA* (Dec. 1978). All of these accretions to the Dickinson canon are the work of the indefatigable R. W. Franklin.

By now the dust seems to have settled over the controversial subject of Dickinson's punctuation, but early in the seventies Edith Wylder published *The Last Face: Emily Dickinson's Manuscripts* (Albuquerque, N.M., 1971) as a refinement to her earlier much-criticized article (she was then Edith Stamm) in 1963 (see p. 211). Wylder's response to her critics argues that Dickinson's punctuation marks are rhetorical signs rather than guides to oral reading, as she earlier believed, and are associated with Dickinson's "attempt to create in written form the precision of meaning inherent in the tone of the human voice." This theory and all the various comments about Dickinson's eccentric punctuation (especially those by Johnson and Charles Anderson) are carefully surveyed by Brita Lindberg-Seyersted in a monograph, *Emily Dickinson's Punctuation* (Oslo, 1976). Although nothing is ever final, this discussion ought to lay the matter to rest, for Lindberg-Seyersted shows convincingly that "Emily Dickinson's punctuation is part of her poetry, that it is a feature of her style, and of her personality as a poet." Future editors will have to cope with it, baffling and ambiguous though it is.

Just as MSS of poems seldom turn up these days, so do holograph letters rarely appear. A previously unpublished letter to Dickinson's niece, Martha Dickinson, appears on the cover of *PrS* (Winter 1977/78), and three letters from Lavinia Dickinson to Mrs. J. G. Holland and Julia Spear are reproduced in *RALS* (Autumn 1976). Some redating of letters to the

Bowles family has been done by Myra Himelhoch and Rebecca Patterson in *EDB* (Mar. 1972).

Biography

The decade of the seventies was an important one for Dickinson biography. It began with John Cody's important though vigorously attacked psychoanalytical biography and was followed three years later by Richard Sewall's massive, two-volume life. And at other points in the ten-year period there were lesser though significant contributions to the available biographical data, such as Jean Mudge's study of the Emily-Sue relationship.

Cody's book, *After Great Pain: The Inner Life of Emily Dickinson* (Cambridge, Mass., 1971) is the work of a psychiatrist, not a literary critic, but Cody has studied the poetry of his subject with careful attention. Cody believes that Dickinson's personality suffered a traumatic disturbance through her mother's neglect and denial of love, and he argues that as a result she underwent a nervous breakdown during her twenties. Cody believes that a psychoanalytic biography is possible for an artist who is able to reflect on the inner workings of her consciousness, as Dickinson was, and he finds in her work "a vast array of psychological symptoms, each sharply observed and exactly characterized." Her poems both afforded her emotional relief and possessed an analytic and documentary function. There are a lot of penetrating insights in this study and many persuasive readings of individual poems. The analysis of Dickinson's relationships with her brother Austin and her sister-in-law Sue are especially good.

Cody's book received some spirited rebuttal. Simon Grolnick in *L&P* (no. 2, 1973) found the book depersonalized, tangential, and reductionistic. He disagreed with the psychological approach, saw various omissions of fact and context. In another anti-Cody review article (*EIHC*, Apr. 1975) James Hijiya argued that Dickinson's maladjustment derived not from her mother's failure but from her culture's inability to provide an avenue for her to be both poet and woman. Her life was a contradiction: outward submissiveness and inward assertiveness, all of which added up to a great deal of neurosis.

Sewall's biography, the result of years of meticulous scholarship, probably will stand for a good while as the definitive account of Dickinson's life. Sewall has worked his way into the inner and outer worlds of his subject with a great deal of success, although, as he says at the outset, "Almost nothing to do with Emily Dickinson is simple and clear-cut." Volume One deals with forebears and family with individual chapters on Dickinson's grandfather, parents, brother, and sister. It also treats the

"War between the Houses" in great detail and reveals for the first time the long liaison between Mabel Loomis Todd and Austin Dickinson. The result of this volume is a rich assemblage of background data that illuminate the tangled emotional relationships among the various members of the Dickinson circle. Volume Two focuses on Dickinson's life in a chronological order and deals with early friendships, Charles Wadsworth, Samuel Bowles, Thomas Wentworth Higginson, and others like the Hollands, Helen Hunt Jackson, and Judge Lord as they come along. Sewall does not try to solve the old question of identifying the object of Dickinson's love interest, but he leans towards Bowles. One closes Volume Two of this biography with the satisfaction of having read a fascinating and judiciously managed account of a complex personality thrown in sharp relief against her time and place. For a dissenting view of this biography, see Barton St. Armand's attack, "Emily Dickinson at Yale" (*Michigan Quarterly Review*, Winter 1977).

Although there are likely to be few new biographical facts to add to Sewall's life, the mass of assembled data is certain to be scrutinized from various perspectives. One of the new perspectives of the past few years has been that of feminism. Arguing that the most important fact about Dickinson is that she was a female poet in a male-dominated society are Adrienne Rich in "Vesuvius at Home: The Power of Emily Dickinson" (*Parnassus*, Fall-Winter 1976), Suzanne Juhasz in *Naked and Fiery Forms: Modern American Poetry by Women, A New Tradition* (New York, 1976), and Barbara Welter in *Dimity Convictions: The American Woman in the Nineteenth Century* (Athens, Ohio, 1976). Ellen Moers, on the other hand, in *Literary Women* (Garden City, N.Y., 1976) argues that the major influence on Dickinson's life was the women's literature of her day. This is an intelligent handling of material similar to that which John E. Walsh treated naively in his biographical study, *The Hidden Life of Emily Dickinson* (New York, 1971). Walsh believed that Dickinson made extensive use, almost to the point of plagiarism, of Elizabeth Barrett Browning's *Aurora Leigh*, a position that few Dickinson scholars would accept, though it is generally acknowledged that *Aurora Leigh* was a favorite book.

Walsh also argued that the object of the "master" letters was Judge Lord, the same jurist that Dickinson did in fact love later in her life. The case for this conclusion is considerably more convincing than the case for the Browning influence. But a study that readers should be warned away from is Dorothy Waugh's *Emily Dickinson: A Surmise* (New York, 1976). This work reminds one of the Dickinson books of the Thirties when authors busily were advancing candidates for Dickinson's lover. Waugh produces yet another candidate, Richard Salter Storrs, a distant relative and friend of one of the poet's second cousins. There is no hard evidence for this surmise, and it may be dismissed.

Another biographical study of a different sort, but one that should be mentioned because it has received wide attention and no doubt has influenced the public view of Dickinson, is William Luce's play, *The Belle of Amherst*, a one-woman drama that starred Julie Harris both on stage and television. Luce's introduction to the printed version says that he set out to show Dickinson's "humanity and reasonableness." He sees her as a pretty normal human being who also happened to be a poet. Howard Meyer, however, in "A Second Look at *The Belle of Amherst*" (*MQ*, 1980) believes that the play dealt more in myth than in facts. He shows how Dickinson and Higginson are both misrepresented and maligned.

Interest in the important Emily-Sue relationship is a perennial attraction to biographers and critics. It was the subject of a detailed study by Lillian Faderman in "Emily Dickinson's Letters to Sue Gilbert" (*MR*, Summer 1977), which argues, as Cody did earlier, that Dickinson loved Susan Gilbert deeply and could not accept her marriage to Austin. Jean McClure Mudge also tackles this subject, but she believes that the break between Dickinson and her sister-in-law has been over-emphasized and that while there was strain, the affection was constant and enduring (*PrS*, Spring 1978). Mudge's article is convincingly based on a thorough study of notes, poems, and correspondence, published and unpublished.

That Dickinson had eye problems is well established information, and Richard Sewall is the one who discovered that Dickinson's "terror since September" probably referred to eye trouble. Sewall and Martin Wand in "'Eyes Be Blind, Heart Be Still': A New Perspective on Emily Dickinson's Eye problem" (*NEQ*, Sept. 1979) suggest plausibly that Emily, Lavinia, and their mother all suffered from exotropia, a condition in which one eye turns out. This article, based on the expertise of an ophthalmologist, unfortunately got a lot of play in the press, as though the secret of Dickinson's seclusion finally were solved.

Criticism

The past eleven years have been a productive period for Dickinson criticism. During this time books have appeared at the rate of more than one per year, and the articles have been innumerable. This essay will have to confine itself to the book-length works in order to keep within a reasonable length. The decade of the Seventies was preceded by Denis Donoghue's University of Minnesota Pamphlet on Dickinson which appeared too late for the first edition of this book, and ended with David Porter's second full-length study of the poet. Along the way there appeared two monographs, two collections of essays, three long sections of books, and nine complete works. In addition, there were many books that contained chapters on Dickinson, some of them very useful, such as William M. Gibson's new essay on Dickinson for the fourth revision of the *Literary History of the United States* (1974). The trend in the last decade's Dickinson scholarship has been to drop discussions of the poetry in relation to biography and external considerations and to consider the poetry as an autonomous body of work. But there also have been significant studies of Dickinson's literary relations.

Donoghue's pamphlet, *Emily Dickinson* (Minneapolis, 1969), is an excellent forty-seven-page introduction to Dickinson by one of our good contemporary critics. It is compact, well written, lucid, accurate, and a good place for any beginner to start his study of the poet. Donoghue sketches briefly the biographical, intellectual, and social background, outlines major themes and preoccupations, and manages to discuss a good many poems, literary influences, and matters of style and form. His preference is for the poems "in which Emily Dickinson's sensibility encounters the great moral universals: love, pain, loss, doubt, death. What happens to the universals, what happens to the sensibility: the poems are among the greatest in the language."

The decade of the Seventies began with a Finnish study (in English) of Dickinson that has received little attention in the United States. It is Sirkka Heiskanen-Makela's *In Quest of Truth: Observations on the Development of Emily Dickinson's Poetic Dialectic* (Jyväskylä, Finland, 1970), a sophisticated work that takes a developmental approach in focusing on Dickinson's changing approach to reality as it is reflected in the evolving tactics of her style. As a number of critics have done earlier, Heiskanen-Makela sees Dickinson as coming out of the Puritan tradition. The quest for truth is manifested both in her prayer-like poetry that uses the hymn meter and in her logical, argumentative style that moves in syllogistic manner from premise to conclusion. In contrast to Emerson, who found unity between mind and nature, Dickinson's mind worked more like Jonathan Edwards' in locating all truth in the mind. This book also explores Dickinson's analogical method, discusses her use of myth and role-playing, and includes a chapter on "The Physics and Metaphysics of Metaphor."

Richard H. Rupp edited a collection of Dickinson essays, *Critics on Emily Dickinson* (Coral Gables, Fla., 1972), which contains 29 snippets of criticism plus poems by Hart Crane and Adrienne Rich and is divided into sections devoted to "Life and Death," "Partial Views," "Explications," and "Evaluations." There are bits from many familiar essays and standard works beginning with Thomas Bailey Aldrich's wrong-headed review in the *Atlantic* in 1892 in which he expressed the view that Dickinson, had she studied grammar and metrics, might have become a second-rate poet. John Crowe Ransom, Archibald MacLeish, Richard Wilbur, and Louise Bogan are represented, as are well-known Dickinson scholars like Albert Gelpi, David Porter, Thomas H. Johnson, and Charles Anderson. But the selections are maddeningly short.

John Emerson Todd's brief study, *Emily Dickinson's Use of the Persona* (The Hague, 1973), deals with a subject of perennial interest to Dickinson scholars. Beginning with Dickinson's familiar statement to Higginson that "when I state myself as the Representative of the Verse — it does not mean — me — but a supposed person," Todd groups the personae into four categories: the little girl, the lover-wife-queen, the experiencer of death and eternity, and "personae involving psychology and the divided personality." In the last category Todd examines such poems as "the Soul Selects Her Own Society" and "The Soul Unto Itself." There are no surprises in this 88-page monograph, but it is a sensible book and concludes appropriately that Dickinson's "ability to use this variety of Personae so imaginatively is one of the measures of her stature as a poet."

A book of considerably more weight and density is Inder Nath Kher's *The Landscape of Absence: Emily Dickinson's Poetry* (New Haven, 1974). This book is not easy going, but it contains many perceptive insights on specific poems and organizes the general themes in the poetry. It is a good example of the recent trend towards close-reading without biographical reference. Kher deals with the structure, imagery, and symbolism of the poetry, emphasizes the existential nature of the work. He is interested in how the poetry builds "interchangeable and interpenetrating symbolic structures on such perennial themes as life, love, despair, ecstasy, death, immortality, and self." In an organic sense Kher sees the poetry as one long poem of "multidimensional reality, each dimension presenting a certain deep and penetrating mood." Dickinson's poetry, he believes, is both apprehensible and elusive; it is the "landscape of absence." This is a comprehensive, significant study of the poetry that focuses on the work as belonging not to a narrow American literary tradition but to the poetic tradition of world literature. Kher regards the critic's job as the task of enhancing "our appreciation of the mystery at the heart of the poetic perception." One can only applaud this approach.

The year 1975 saw the appearance of three significant works of Dickinson scholarship: Albert Gelpi's eighty-page chapter on Dickinson in *The Tenth Muse: The Psyche of the American Poet* (Cambridge, Mass.), Jean McClure Mudge's phenomenological study, *Emily Dickinson and the Image of Home* (Amherst, Mass.), and Robert Weisbuch's *Emily Dickinson's Poetry* (Chicago).

Gelpi, who began his academic career with a dissertation that eventuated in *Emily Dickinson: The Mind of the Poet* (see pp. 208–9), has now placed Dickinson in the context of major American poets beginning with Edward Taylor. *The Tenth Muse* treats, besides Taylor, Emerson, and Poe, Whitman and concludes with a mature, illuminating, and original chapter on Dickinson. Gelpi's discussion of Dickinson is psychological criticism at its best. He has combined the psychological insights of Freud, Jung, neo-Freudians and others, believing that any single approach is reductive rather than clarifying, to explore the landscape of the poet's psyche. He has dropped the "mind" of his earlier book because it suggests "conscious, cerebral activity engaged with the world or reflecting on it" for the word "psyche," which is "more inclusive [and] . . . recognizes that conscious manifestations cannot be separated from the mysterious promptings and impulses of the unconscious." Gelpi reads the poems as the record of events taking place in a psychic time-space. Dickinson sought self-definition through acts of consciousness. The lover, for example, that critics and biographers have sought to identify is in fact none of the previously suggested candidates but no one at all. "The poems describe a subjective drama, and both figures in the drama are first and last psychological factors." Gelpi sees the poems in general as "battles" of consciousness in which the poet on occasion manages to attain power and self-integration. The study keeps its attention focused clearly on the poetry.

Jean Mudge's book begins with the assumption that "even for a highly imaginative mind, such as Emily Dickinson's, earliest encounters with the concrete world during childhood and adolescence are of primary and lasting importance." She proceeds then to examine Dickinson and her houses, the first objects in her world, "in order to explore an early, fundamental part of her sensitivity to space." This sensitivity subsequently controls the poet's attitudes "toward all of life and to a life beyond." Dickinson's image of house and home is perhaps the most penetrating and comprehensive figure she employs, and as such it is worthwhile organizing a study, though it has a limited scope, from this perspective. As curator of the Dickinson house in Amherst, Mudge knows the physical environment of her subject well and the early chapters on "The House on Pleasant Street" and "The Dickinson Homestead" are especially interesting and integrate the background and the poetry very successfully. Figures of enclosure in Dickinson's poetry produced both positive and negative feelings: fears of isolation and homelessness, hopes of security and happiness. A noteworthy and useful aspect of this book is the large number of illustrations of the Dickinson houses and furnishings.

Whereas both Gelpi and Mudge were concerned with psychology in their studies, Robert Weisbuch is concerned with examining Dickinson's poetry as a continuing effort to reconcile a Transcendentalist desire for ever-expanding consciousness with a more skeptical notion of experiential limitations. He sees this clash between desire and possibility as shaping Dickinson's style and the broad context of her ideas. Like Kher, Weisbuch regards the lyrics as one long poem "to the same extent that Whitman's lyrics constitute a *Leaves of Grass,*" and he isolates their various characteristics with the "hope of finally achieving an integration." Weisbuch argues that Dickinson does not use particulars to refer to real experiences but rather employs analogies and typologies. As in many of the more recent Dickinson books, he focuses on the poetry and eschews biographical criticism. He also concentrates on the dialectical nature of Dickinson's ideas, but it must be said that the book is rather hard going and not as lucidly written as one would like.

It seems surprising that the Twayne United States Authors Series, which now has been going for many years, did not produce a volume on Dickinson until 1976. But Paul Ferlazzo's *Emily Dickinson* (Boston) is number 280 in this sequence. Within the procrustean format of the Twayne series Ferlazzo does a good job of organizing and summarizing the relevant data and themes. He has threaded his way through the large amount of Dickinson scholarship and presented it in succinct and lucid fashion. Like Donoghue's pamphlet, this is an introductory work to which one can safely send undergraduates. It contains, as usual, a selected, annotated bibliography and a chronology of the poet's life.

There was a hiatus of three years before the next round of important Dickinson scholarship appeared. In 1979 Margaret H. Freeman edited a posthumous collection of Rebecca Patterson's essays on Dickinson written over a period of thirty years, *Emily Dickinson's Imagery* (Amherst, Mass.); Karl Keller brought out his study of Dickinson's American literary relations in *The Only Kangaroo Among the Beauty: Emily Dickinson and America* (Baltimore); Sandra M. Gilbert and Susan Gubar devoted a long chapter to Dickinson in their distinguished volume of feminist criticism, *The Madwoman in the Attic: The Woman Writer and the Nineteenth-Century Literary Imagination* (New Haven); and Sharon Cameron's *Lyric Time: Dickinson and the Limits of Genre* (Baltimore) applied the sharp intelligence of a literary theorist to Dickinson's poetry.

Patterson, whose *The Riddle of Emily Dickinson* (see p. 194) stirred up a hornet's nest a generation ago with its suggestion of a lesbian relationship in Dickinson's life, also wrote a good many non-controversial essays over the years. Seven of them appear in this collection. Patterson is concerned with patterns of imagery—Dickinson's use of geography, precious stones, color, points of the compass—all familiar topics to readers of the poetry, but these are clearly written pieces and often include

statistical information comparing Dickinson to other poets. Patterson does
not deal in influences but in relationships; however, she tends to be over-
specific in seeing the meanings of a poet whose objective was to "tell all
the truth but tell it slant." Patterson also sees more sexual meanings in
the poems than most critics would.

Keller's book, *The Only Kangaroo*, is a broad-based study of Dickinson's inheritance of an American literary tradition going back to her
Puritan forebears. Many Dickinson scholars have dealt with Dickinson's
connection with Puritanism, but Keller goes beyond previous efforts and
devotes complete chapters to Dickinson and Bradstreet, Dickinson and
Taylor, and Dickinson and Edwards. Like Bradstreet, she stood up in the
expectation of Puritan womanhood. Like Taylor, she made a place for
herself in the closed Puritan universe, and like Edwards she got "her thrills
out of a dark Puritan sensationalism." These chapters are followed by
a contrasting of two Puritan descendants, Harriet Beecher Stowe and Dickinson, in a very original and arresting chapter, and then Keller moves
on to consider Dickinson's relations with Hawthorne, Emerson, and her
own literary circle (Susan Gilbert, Helen Hunt Jackson, Bowles, and Higginson). There also is a discussion of Whitman, how much Dickinson
might have known of him and a comparison/contrast of these two different but seminal nineteenth-century American poets. Finally Keller concludes with a chapter on the legacy of Dickinson to poets of our century.
All in all, this is a provocative, interesting book. It is well worth reading
and does a good job of siting Dickinson in her American frame of
reference.

The Madwoman in the Attic views Dickinson in the context of a number of nineteenth-century woman writers. Gilbert and Gubar conceived
their study while teaching a course together on woman writers in which
they began to see "a distinctive female literary tradition." In this tradition there were "images of enclosure and escape, fantasies in which mad-
dened doubles functioned as asocial surrogates for docile selves." There
were also "metaphors of physical discomfort manifested by frozen landscapes and fiery interiors." Dickinson fitted into the pattern. The chapter on her poetry (written by Gilbert) tries to assess Dickinson's accomplishment in terms of this tradition. "Emily Dickinson herself became
a madwoman . . . both ironically a madwoman (a deliberate impersona-
tion of a madwoman) and truly a madwoman (a helpless agoraphobic,
trapped in a room in her father's house.)"

Dickinson's life then became a kind of novel or narrative poem in which
she maneuvered about and enacted and eventually resolved both her anxieties about her art and her anger at her female subordination. "Her terse,
explosive poems are therefore, in a sense, the speech of a fictional char-

acter." It is from this perspective that Gilbert reads the poems. The readings are continuously interesting and excellent feminist criticism, but sometimes the explications seem forced to fit the thesis. Women reviewers in general found *The Madwoman in the Attic* exciting and illuminating, but Willis Buckingham in *ALS* (1979) thought there was "something wishful, however, in the way some of the poems are read to reenforce each other and proper self-restraint is not always exercised in plotting the poems."

It takes a high level of literary sophistication to read Cameron's *Lyric Time*, and only students who are both well versed in Dickinson and literary theory will profit from this book. This is a book about time in a particular body of poetry and the author's interest is "unabashedly" theoretical. She suggests that the temporal problems in Dickinson's poems "are frequently exaggerations of those generic features shared by all lyrics, and that it is precisely the distance some of these poems go toward the far end of coherence, precisely the outlandishness of their extremity, which allows us to see, literally magnified, the fine workings of more conventional lyrics." The poems discussed in chapter one shy away from "a dialectical understanding of experience," while the poems of the next chapter "compare narrative conceptions of temporality with lyric conceptions of it." Then Cameron discusses poems that "recoil from temporality," goes on to deal with specific features of Dickinson's poetry, and ends up with a theory of lyric poetry: "Dickinson's poems attempt to stall time to a stasis. . . . The deathless world of no time is a world we lose merely waking up. Dickinson's poems articulate the loss and, like all lyrics, they attempt to reverse it." If all this sounds recondite, it is.

A companion study in feminist criticism to *The Madwoman in the Attic* is Margaret Homans's *Women Writers and Poetic Identity: Dorothy Wordsworth, Emily Brontë, and Emily Dickinson* (Princeton, 1980). Homans sees Dickinson as the only one of the three poets to overcome the inhibitions of being a female writer in a male-dominated society. She did it, Homans argues, by identifying with Eve, who learned from Satan not to trust the language of God or Adam. This study manages to show Dickinson's sense of linguistic dislocation, as Homans applies Emerson's notion that language has been corrupted through the ages to the problem of language for the female poet. Using insights from psychoanalysis, Homans suggests that while Emerson's language was that of the ego, Dickinson penetrated deeper to the language of the id. If her poems are more elusive and pessimistic than Emerson's, it is because she is reaching beyond Emerson's nature to an unnameable nature. Whereas Emerson is concerned with the power of the eye to see, Dickinson is absorbed by what she cannot see. Both were language-makers.

Homans's book was followed by another able study also concerned with gender and feminist poetics, Joanne Feit Diehl's *Dickinson and the Romantic Imagination* (Princeton, 1981). This work attempts a re-evaluation of Dickinson's poetry based on an understanding of her relationship to the major Romantic tradition. The major Romantics that Diehl examines against Dickinson's work are Wordsworth, Keats, Shelley, and Emerson; she omits Byron and Coleridge for valid reasons that she explains. What Diehl is interested in is both what Dickinson shares with the major romantics, and how she departs from the Romantic tradition. The most important divergence, she believes, results from gender. Dickinson subverted the tradition in order to achieve her astonishing original poetry.

The original premise of the book is that Dickinson did not develop in isolation or merely under the lingering influences of Puritanism and nineteenth-century New England Transcendentalism. She had to be influenced by the great Romantics, just as Tennyson and Browning were. "We cannot come to terms with what is most powerful in Dickinson unless we look to her forebears." Diehl then reads Dickinson in juxtaposition with the Romantics, but this is not a sources-and-influence study that hunts for parallel passages and echoes. It is more subtle than that, for Dickinson "characteristically employs obscuring strategies." Because she was a woman she conceived herself "as necessarily apart from this male line of poets." Thus the method adopted is to look for themes, strategies, and uses of language that unify her poems. "By informing such a general vision with close textual analyses, the reader can identify more clearly the dominant structures, the prevailing gestures, which shape Dickinson's problematic relation to her Romantic origins." This is an interesting, well-written, and significant study that casts a wider net than previous critics have done in searching for Dickinson's sources. It is particularly good in its treatment of Dickinson's American predecessor Emerson, who stood between her and the English Romantics. She reshaped his version of Romanticism by rejecting "an Emersonian nature which educated man" and adopted the view that the world is a "deceptive text that cannot be read right, and so must remain a deeply equivocal mystery."

David Porter's *Dickinson: The Modern Idiom* (Cambridge, Mass., 1981) is one of the best books on Dickinson to appear in many years. It ranks with George Whicher's pioneering work, *This Was a Poet*, Charles Anderson's *Emily Dickinson's Poetry*, Richard Sewall's biography, and perhaps a few other works that no student of Dickinson can ignore. Porter's interest in Dickinson began with *The Art of Emily Dickinson's Early Poetry* (see p. 208), and after a decade and a half of thinking about and teaching Dickinson he has distilled his reflections into another study. Whereas too many books on Dickinson begin with theses to be proved, this book seems to come to the material with a fresh, unbiased eye, as though Porter had cast aside all his preconceptions about Dickinson and taken a new look. He has gone back to the documentary evidence, the letters and the poems — not the printed versions that give her a formality she never had, but the manuscripts. The Dickinson who emerges is a startling figure, a character of extraordinary "otherness," a poet whose "My Life had stood — a Loaded Gun" provides a "stunning emblem for her life and work."

Although there is no sense of coherence in the totality of Dickinson's work, the crucial experience for her was the sense of living after things happened, a preoccupation with afterknowledge. But she wrote with such concentration "that barely a handful of poems exists without some measure of inpenetrability." Porter's chapters on "The Puzzling Idiom" and "How Dickinson Wrote" are excellent analyses of her compactness and omitted syntax, written with reference to manuscripts and work sheets. Further, Porter deals with "Disabling Freedom," in which he finds that Dickinson lacked a poetic design and in fact had "no large structure for her poetic energies." She had a "finless mind," one which embraced no social program, no politics, no history, nothing but her existential self. To illustrate this, Porter quotes a paradigmatic letter to her cousin John Graves written in 1856 when she sat in the April sunshine, surrounded by chickens, describing what she saw. And she suffered from the curse of spontaneity.

"Without a line of vision, lacking an axis of conception, there was no Archimedean stance by which to pry the world. The world, thus her work attests, was always a surprise." This explains the lack of movement in her work towards the truth that one finds in other poets, and her work remained fragmentary throughout her life. Finally, Porter sees Dickinson as "an early member of the modern movement of poetry." In her freedom she founded a language. The poems carry an agitated and troubled ignorance. "They are, to use Dickinson's word, haunted." Her poetry inaugurates in American literature two main characteristics: "The menacing ascendance of consciousness and the disappearance of an artistic goal."

A fascinating and original article of monograph length is George Monteiro and Barton Levi St. Armand's "The Experienced Emblem: A Study of the Poetry of Emily Dickinson" in Jack Salzman, ed., *Prospects: The Annual of American Cultural Studies* (1981). This study breaks new ground in its investigations, throws considerable light on some obscure poems, and suggests new readings (perhaps even corrected readings) of other much-explicated poems. Monteiro and St. Armand begin with the fact that emblematic books such as Peter Parley's *Book of Fables* (1834) and William Holmes and John W. Barber's *Religious Emblems* (1846) and *Religious Allegories* (1848) were well known to Dickinson and the premise that she must have alluded frequently to the emblems in these works in her poetry. The article is profusely illustrated from these emblem books, and the illustrations with their accompanying text, when compared with Dickinson's poems, yield new meanings. The authors write: "We contend that the lost language of a significant cluster of Dickinson's poems is primarily a pictorial one, having reference to a popular emblem tradition. . . ." Thus what seems arcane to twentieth-century readers of Dickinson's poems would have been clear, had her poems been published in her lifetime, to nineteenth-century readers nurtured in the same social and cultural milieu of New England. This is excellent scholarship and highly recommended.

Dickinson and the World

As domestic interest in Dickinson continues to grow, so does the attention she gets abroad. Although French scholars do not seem much attracted, Japanese, German, and Italian critics regularly study her work, and the first extended biographical and critical study in Polish appeared in 1980: Aleksander Rogalski's "Emily Dickinson" in *Annetta i Emilia*, pp. 137–258. Two recent books on Dickinson appeared in Japan: Masao Nakauchi's *Emily Dickinson: Tsuyo no Hotosha [Emily Dickinson: The Debauchee of Dew]* (Tokyo, 1981) and Takao Furukawa's *Emily Dickinson no Giho [The Art of Emily Dickinson]* (Tokyo, 1980). There also was a study that combined Dickinson and Whitman: *Whitman and Dickinson: Bunka Shocho o Megutte [Whitman and Dickinson: Cultural Symbols in Their Writings]* by Takiaki Yamakawa *et al.* One German scholar, Franz Link, combined Dickinson and Hilda Doolittle in *Zwei amerikanischen Dichterinnen: Emily Dickinson und Hilda Doolittle* (Berlin, 1979), while another, Gudrun Grabner wrote *Emily Dickinson: Das transzendentale Ich* (Heidelberg, 1981). Finally, the Italians produced Barbara Linati's translation of 96 poems with an introduction in *Emily Dickinson: Poesie* (Rome, 1976).

Jonathan Edwards

EVERETT EMERSON

JONATHAN EDWARDS has become the beneficiary of much solid scholarship in the last dozen years, the result being that many attractive but erroneous assumptions have been discarded. The new Edwards that has emerged was both an inheritor of the New England intellectual tradition and a member of an international community of philosophers and theologians, not an isolated genius transformed by the discovery of John Locke. It was Perry Miller who did most to attract students of literature to Edwards; it was Miller who insisted that Edwards was a literary artist; it was Miller who declared that "theology was Edwards's medium, as blank verse was Milton's." But Miller's *Jonathan Edwards* has been carefully examined, and Norman Fiering, speaking as the best informed of the Edwards experts, has recently declared that Miller's study "can only be judged an unaccountable lapse in the scholarship of one of the greatest of American historians." Miller's book is still readable and exciting, though it obviously must be read with caution. Originally published in New York in 1949, it is best in the reprint containing a learned introductory essay by Donald Weber (Amherst, Mass., 1981).

The scholarship on Edwards is the work of intellectual, church, and social historians, theologians, and philosophers, with some assistance from literary specialists. Few of the most important books on Edwards are addressed to those interested in literature. Among those in this category that can be commended are two that are informed, relatively modest, and not abstruse, those by William J. Scheick and Terrence Erdt.

From Earl N. Harbert and Robert A. Rees, editors, *Fifteen American Authors before 1900: Bibliographic Essays on Research & Criticism* (Madison: The University of Wisconsin Press; © 1984 by the Board of Regents of the University of Wisconsin System); may be reproduced only by permission of the publisher.

BIBLIOGRAPHY

Thomas H. Johnson prepared a careful bibliography of Edwards's works, *The Writings of Jonathan Edwards* (Princeton, N.J., 1940). Its usefulness is somewhat limited by Johnson's decision not to indicate what sermons appear in collections nor to describe the relative value of the various collected editions. Much the best bibliography of scholarship and criticism is M. X. Lesser's *Jonathan Edwards: A Reference Guide* (Boston, 1981), which covers the years through 1978. Its abstracts are judicious. Also valuable are the substantial "Bibliographical Note" in Norman Fiering's study of Edwards's moral thought (discussed below) and the documentation in Patricia J. Tracy's *Jonathan Edwards, Pastor* (also discussed below). In addition to the listing of dissertations in Lesser's *Guide*, one may usefully consult the bibliography of doctoral dissertations on Edwards compiled by Richard S. Sliwoski (*EAL*, Winter 1979/80).

EDITIONS

After a very slow and faltering start, the Yale edition of *The Works of Jonathan Edwards* is now publishing valuable volumes with some regularity. Each contains an extended essay as introduction. So far we have *The Freedom of the Will*, edited by Paul Ramsey (New Haven, Conn., 1957); *Religious Affections*, ed. John E. Smith (1959 — Smith is the General Editor of the project); *Original Sin*, edited by Clyde A. Holbrook (1970); *The Great Awakening*, edited by C. C. Goen (1972); *Apocalyptic Writings*, edited by Stephen J. Stein (1977); and *Scientific and Philosophical Writings*, edited by Wallace E. Anderson (1980). These volumes are reviewed by Philip Gura (*NEQ*, September 1980). In the not distant future the following may be expected: *The Life of David Brainerd*, edited by Norman Pettit; *The Miscellaneous Observations*, edited by Thomas A. Schafer (a much-anticipated volume, Professor Schafer having expertly transcribed the "Miscellanies"); *Early Sermons*, Volumes 1 and 2, edited by Wilson H. Kimnach, Volume 3, edited by Nathan O. Hatch; *History of Redemption*, edited by John F. Wilson; *The Nature of True Virtue* (and other ethical writings), edited by Paul Ramsey. Other volumes being prepared are *Types of the Messiah* and *Images and Shadows of Divine Things*, edited by Wallace Anderson, Mason I. Lowance, Jr., and David Watters; *Letters*, edited by George Claghorn (probably in two volumes); and a collection of writings on the church, edited by David Hall and John F. Jamieson. An important account of this edition and the difficulties faced by editors appears in Thomas A. Schafer's "Manuscript Problems in the Yale Edition of Jonathan Edwards" (*EAL*, Winter 1968/69).

Edwards's earlier editors found his style often incorrect and inelegant and so proceeded to improve and trim it as they saw fit. The least of the offenders, Edward Williams and Edward Parsons, published the *Works* at Leeds in eight volumes (1806–11) supplemented by two additional volumes published at Edinburgh (1847). This ten-volume edition, formerly very scarce, was reprinted by Burt Franklin (New York, 1968). Nearly as satisfactory is the edition of Samuel Austin published in eight volumes (Worcester, Mass., 1808). Each edition contains some materials omitted in the others, but for completeness the most valuable is the four-volume reprint of the Worcester edition "With Valuable Additions and a Copious Index" (New York, 1843). Another edition is that of Edward Hickman (London, 1833). The ten-volume edition prepared by Sereno Edwards Dwight (New York, 1829–30) is the least valuable textually, but it contains works not otherwise available, such as the important "The Mind,"not to be found among Edwards's manuscripts. All of these editions have been reprinted. For other comments on this complicated matter, see Johnson's *Writings of Edwards*, the index to which is of special value in comparing the contents of the various editions.

Many of Edwards's writings do not appear in any collected edition. A full volume of sermons, edited by Tryon Edwards as *Charity and its Fruits* (New York, 1852), was apparently prepared for publication by Edwards from sermons delivered in 1738. Many selections from the *Miscellanies* have appeared at various times, such as the thirty-six page *Observations Concerning the Scripture Oeconomy of the Trinity and Covenant of Redemption*, edited by Egbert C. Smyth (New York, 1880); "Jonathan Edwards on the Sense of the Heart," edited by Perry Miller (*HTR*, Apr. 1948), the important item No. 782, on Edwards's rhetorical theory; and, notably, *The Philosophy of Jonathan Edwards From His Private Notebooks*, edited by Harvey G. Townsend (Eugene, Oreg., 1955). Five other slim gatherings, in addition to those in the *Works*, are listed by Douglas Elwood in *The Philosophical Theology of Jonathan Edwards* (New York, 1960). Three other important publications are *An Unpublished Essay of Edwards on the Trinity*, edited by George P. Fisher (New York, 1903), with a text of sixty-six pages; *Selections from the Unpublished Writings of Jonathan Edwards of America*, edited by Alexander B. Grosart, including a "Treatise on Grace" (Edinburgh, 1865); and, more important than the above, *Images or Shadows of Divine Things*, edited by Perry Miller (New Haven, Conn., 1948). Paul Helm edited the *Treatise on Grace and Other Posthumously Published Writings* (London, 1971); the introduction is valuable. Among the most useful editions of Edwards is Leon Howard's "*The Mind" of Jonathan Edwards* (Berkeley and Los Angeles, 1963).

Important but briefer pieces of Edwards's writings include: seven letters in *Representative Selections*, edited by Clarence Faust and Thomas Johnson (New York, 1935; revised 1962); eight letters and sermon notes in *Princeton University Library Chronicle* (Winter 1954); letters, a diary, and other personal papers, in Sereno Dwight's *Life of President Edwards* (New York, 1830); two letters and two sermons, in *Puritan Sage: Collected Writings of Jonathan Edwards*, edited by Vergilius Ferm (New York, 1953); parts of three sermons that reveal Edwards's attitude toward the Great Awakening, in *NEQ* (Mar. 1948); a sermon, in *Selected Sermons of Jonathan Edwards*, edited by H. N. Gardiner (New York, 1904); six letters in *NEQ* (Apr. 1928); various letters in Winslow's *Jonathan Edwards*; and two single letters, one in *NEQ* (June 1956) and one in *Biblia Sacra* (Aug. 1844).

The best text of the important "Personal Narrative" is in Samuel Hopkins's *The Life and Character of the Late Reverend Mr. Jonathan Edwards* (Boston, 1765), reprinted in David Levin's *Jonathan Edwards: A Profile* (New York, 1969). Edwards's will appears in *Biblia Sacra* (July 1876). Convenient volumes of selections are the aforementioned excellent one by Faust and Johnson and the very full but less useful one by Vergilius Ferm. A paperback edition of *The Nature of True Virtue* (Ann Arbor, Mich., 1960) makes the whole of the brief work available.

MANUSCRIPTS

Students of Edwards will probably continue to find it necessary to consult the manuscripts, since the Yale edition will not be complete. Thomas A. Schafer observes that "of the more than 250 sermons spanning the first decade of Edwards's ministry, only nine have been printed" (*EAL*, Winter 1968–69). Also unpublished are his Latin master's thesis and many letters (more than 200 located so far). The largest collections of manuscripts are at Yale and at Andover-Newton Theological Seminary. The latter is chiefly family letters and documents; the former includes Edwards's "Micellanies," now largely prepared for publication by Thomas A. Schafer, and nearly 120 manuscript sermons. All of these are housed in the Beinecke Rare Book and Manuscript Library. Some items are at Princeton; minor items are scattered. In addition to Professor Schafer's essay, there are discussions of the manuscripts in *CHAL;* Winslow's biography; *PMHS* (1901 – 2 essays by Upham and Dexter); and *Littell's Living Age* (21 January 1853).

BIOGRAPHY

The first of the Edwards biographies is still one of the best. Samuel Hopkins knew Edwards well, and what he said about him has been of great use to other biographers. *His Life and Character of the Late Reverend Mr. Jonathan Edwards*, a short life, has been frequently reprinted, most recently by David Levin in *Jonathan Edwards: A Profile*. It ought to be more widely read. Among its virtues are its inclusion of the best text of Edwards's "Personal Narrative" and extracts from his diary.

Sereno Dwight thought so highly of Hopkins's work that in preparing his own biography of Edwards he remarked, "The life by Dr. Hopkins, which is the testimony of an *eye-witness*, has been incorporated." Dwight's *Life of President Edwards* is a preface to his edition of Edwards's works. Its nearly eight hundred pages include a great many important documents: letters, anecdotes, the text of "The Mind" (the only extant version), and "Notes on Natural Science." Edwards's dismissal from Northampton is fully documented; nearly one hundred pages are devoted to it. The book is a compilation, not a work of art, but it is of immense value. Largely derived from Dwight is Samuel Miller's "Life of Jonathan Edwards" in the *Library of American Biography*, edited by Jared Sparks (New York, 1839).

Primarily studies rather than biographies, the books by Allen, McGiffert, Miller, Aldridge, and Davidson are discussed below. (Aldridge provides an excellent brief biography.)

Henry B. Parkes's *Jonathan Edwards: The Fiery Puritan* (New York, 1930) gets off on the wrong foot with the title. A popular biography by a learned author, it is marred by sensationalism, condescension, and overstatement. Edwards, says Parkes, was "the father of American Puritanism." Parkes is particularly inaccurate on the early American Puritans and provides a very thin treatment of Edwards's works.

The best narrative biography is clearly Ola E. Winslow's carefully documented *Jonathan Edwards*. As Winslow confesses, it was not possible, "in addition to his life story, to do more than indicate the chronology and general import of his ideas, particularly with respect to his changing fortunes." If Perry Miller has increased our understanding of Edwards's rivals and enemies, Patricia Tracy has given us a better knowledge of Edwards's Northampton, and Edwards's part in the Great Awakening is now clearer. Little has been added to our knowledge to alter the shape of his life, although J. P. Carse (see *Criticism*, below) has indeed given it a tragic dimension. Winslow's book is continually interesting and skillfully researched. If the book does not deal adequately with Edwards's ideas, neither does it distort them.

In an earlier version of this essay, I remarked that Edwards's Northampton years deserved fuller treatment than they had been given. That gap has now been effectively filled, though Patricia J. Tracy's study is not exactly biographical. Entitled *Jonathan Edwards, Pastor,* the book is perhaps better described by its subtitle: *Religion and Society in Eighteenth Century Northampton* (New York, 1980). Tracy's interests are those of a social historian, and her book is valuable, intelligent, and thorough. She argues, persuasively, that "Ultimately, Jonathan Edwards's career should be viewed in the broad context of the evolving nature of the church in colonial New England." One of the special virtues of the book is the treatment of Edwards's relationship to his predecessor. She believes that, unfortunately for Edwards, he "was much more like Stoddard than the Northampton of 1750 was like the Northampton of 1700," and she contends that Edwards attempted to abandon Stoddardeanism as a result of the failure of the Great Awakening to have results in his congregation satisfactory to Edwards. It is useful to compare Tracy's treatment of the Stoddard-Edwards relationship with two recent investigations, one by David Laurence in "Jonathan Edwards, Solomon Stoddard, and the Preparationist Model of Conversion" (*HTR*, July–Oct. 1979) and another by John F. Jamieson in "Jonathan Edwards's Change of Position on Stoddardeanism" (*HTR*, Jan. 1981).

CRITICISM

It is difficult to be fair to such older books as Arthur McGiffert's *Jonathan Edwards* (New York, 1932). Although McGiffert's biography with analysis of Edwards's thought is sympathetic, intelligent, and informed, it has been superseded by Winslow, Tracy, and other books of the last twenty years. Not so easy to dismiss is the pioneering work of Alexander V. G. Allen, whose *Jonathan Edwards* (Boston, 1889) remains worth reading. Like McGiffert's combination biography and critical study, Allen's book takes Edwards seriously, and though far from sympathetic, what Allen has to say is frequently penetrating. It is probably fair to call Allen's the best study before Miller's.

Perry Miller's *Jonathan Edwards* (New York, 1949) is the most influential book on Edwards. An intellectual biography by an intellectual who found Edwards constantly stimulating, Miller's *Edwards* is appealing to students of literature partly because of its use of a literary frame of reference: for Miller, Edwards was "an artist in ideas." Scattered through the book are references to Hawthorne, Pope, Melville, and Milton, and most readers will admire Miller's effective shaping of materials, even his use of novelistic methods. Miller sees Edwards both as a thinker who understood the implications of Newton and Locke and was able thereby to anticipate modern philosophical problems and approaches and also as a man whose life was made difficult by petty feuds. In fact, Miller's treatment of the Williamses, the Hawleys, and Edwards's many personal relationships is so lively that at times one forgets that much is based on conjecture, or, to put it more kindly, is interpretive.

It is easy to find fault with Miller's view of Edwards. He dramatically overstated Edwards's rejection of covenent theology. (See Bogue's book, cited below, and Cherry's "The Puritan Notion of the Covenant in Jonathan Edwards' Doctrine of Faith," *CH*, Sept. 1965.) Miller inaccurately described Edwards's adaptation of the Lockean philosophy. (See Fiering's splendid study.) Perhaps most unfortunate is Miller's neglect of Edwards's teachings on grace and his repeated implication and suggestion that Edwards was a philosophic naturalist.

Most of the recent books on Edwards have corrected Miller. Davidson offers the narrative of a Puritan mind and Carse a humanistic study in tragedy; Miller's Edwards is a man who may be a bit too much like his creator but a thoroughly fascinating creature nonetheless. An important review of Miller's book appeared in *CH* (Dec. 1951) and a cruel but lively dissection in *NEQ* (Mar. 1952). See also the very severe comments by Peter Gay in *A Loss of Mastery: Puritan Historians in Colonial America* (Berkeley and Los Angeles, 1966); Gay calls Miller's thesis absurd. A more favorable review is R. W. B. Lewis's in *Hudson Review* (Spring 1950).

Miller's other contributions include essays collected in *Errand into the Wilderness* (Cambridge, Mass., 1956). In a suggestive but vague study "From Edwards to Emerson" Miller notes that the mystic and pantheistic impulses felt by Edwards were in some way connected with the development of Transcendentalism. According to "The Rhetoric of Sensation," Edwards taught (as an extension of Locke's sensationalism) that for an idea to be comprehended it must affect the heart as well as the head: "an idea is a unit of experience, and experience is as much love and dread as it is logic." Grace is a new simple idea, one to be learned only from experience. *Nature's Nation* (Cambridge, Mass., 1967) contains Miller's "Sinners in the Hands of a Benevolent God," which contrasts the Enfield sermon with *True Virtue*.

There are many studies of Edwards's place in New England religious history. Conrad Wright's excellent *The Beginnings of Unitarianism in America* (Boston, 1955), a dissertation under Miller, provides a context for the study of Edwards's thought, or at least aspects of it. Wright's discussion of the Great Awakening, the Edwards-Chauncey debate, and especially Edwards and the Arminians on the will are of fundamental importance. Edwards's treatise on the will is shown to be an unfair attack on the Arminian position, since he ascribed to the Arminians a view of the will not really theirs. (But see Paul Ramsey, *contra* Wright, in his edition of *Freedom of the Will*.) The ironic results of Edwards's attack are amusingly described, and Wright's book is very readable. Only the first four chapters are directly concerned with Edwards.

Another good study of Edwards's thought is more comprehensive but less conveniently organized: Joseph Haroutunian's *Piety Versus Moralism: The Passing of the New England Theology* (New York, 1932). Haroutunian demonstrates a real comprehension of Edwards's religious position, described as "inspired by a piety which sought to glorify God and His sovereignty over man." The study describes the collapse of Edwardeanism more accurately than Frank Hugh Foster's *Genetic History of the New England Theology* (Chicago, 1907), which is, nonetheless, still a useful book. Relevant for an aspect of Edwards's theology is H. Shelton Smith's *Changing Conceptions of Original Sin* (New York, 1955). A solid, briefer study is Clarence H. Faust's "The Decline of Puritanism" in *Transitions in American Literary History*, edited by H. H. Clark (Durham, N.C., 1953). A more controversial book, Alan Heimert's long *Religion and the American Mind From the Great Awakening to the Revolution* (Cambridge, Mass., 1966), also provides an elaborate context for Edwards's thought. Heimert's thesis that "Calvinism and Edwards provided pre-Revolutionary America with a radical, even democratic, social and political ideology" has not been widely accepted. See, for example, E. S. Morgan's review in *WMQ* (July 1967). Much of the analysis of the religious history of the period has been challenged by G. J. Goodwin in "The Myth of 'Arminian-Calvinism' in Eighteenth-Century New England" (*NEQ*, June 1968).

Other studies of Edwards's place in American religious thought of value include Thomas A. Schafer's "The Role of Jonathan Edwards in American Religious History" (*Encounter*, Summer 1969); the chapter on Edwards in Sydney E. Ahlstrom's National Book Award winner, *A Religious History of the American People* (New Haven, Conn., 1972); and William A. Clebsch's *American Religious Thought: A History* (Chicago, 1973), which gives Edwards equal space with Emerson and William James.

Over the years much of the Edwards scholarship has naturally been addressed to students of philosophy and religion. Perhaps none of the valuable studies of this kind is as likely to put readers off as is John H. Gerstner's *Steps to Salvation: The Evangelistic Message of Jonathan Edwards* (Philadelphia, 1960), for it is pious, evangelical in intention, and weakly documented. But it is based on a careful reading of Edwards's many unpublished sermons, and since no other full report on them is in print, it is not to be ignored. The book provides a description of Edwards's teaching on a variety of topics. Gerstner continued his work in a series of four articles (appearing throughout the four numbers of *Biblia Sacra* in 1976) entitled "An Outline of the Apologetics of Jonathan Edwards." The series takes up the argument from being, the unity of God, and the proof of God's special revelation, the Bible. Gerstner and Jonathan N. Gerstner have more recently published "Edwardsean Preparation for Salvation" (*Westminister Theological Review*, Fall 1979), which shows that Edwards's teaching on preparation was not so different from that of Thomas Hooker or Thomas Shepard, and argues that "preparation" is not contrary to strict Calvinism.

Douglas Elwood's *Philosophical Theology of Jonathan Edwards* seeks to provide a general description of Edwards's thought from a sympathetic point of view. Though Elwood argues for Edwards's importance as a forward-looking thinker, the book lacks both seriousness and conviction. With the aid of many quotations, Elwood relates Edwards to some of the great philosophers and suggests that his reliance on his experience, Augustine-like, in reaching his philosophical and theological positions is what makes Edwards distinctive. For Elwood, Edwards was a panentheist: he believed in the unity of all things in God. Robert C. Whittemore has replied to Elwood's thesis in "Jonathan Edwards and the Theology of the Sixth Way" (*CH*, Mar. 1966). He argues that Edwards is better described as a Christian Neoplatonist. (Whittemore also argues, persuasively, against Miller. He calls Edwards a medievalist in the crucial matter of his ontology: Edwards stressed "Being to the exclusion of Becoming.")

Alfred Owen Aldridge's *Jonathan Edwards* (New York, 1964) has many virtues and a few weaknesses. About two-fifths of the book consists of an excellent biography of Edwards, the best thing of its kind. Valuable also is Aldridge's familiarity with the eighteenth-century context of Edwards's thought, not surprising since Aldridge is a biographer of Franklin and Paine. But too often Aldridge looks at Edwards from a Franklinian point of view, and he is far from sympathetic with Edwards and his values. At times he shows a lack of insight into Calvinist thought, as when he cannot understand how a predestinarian can be an evangelist. Some aspects of Edwards's thought, such as his treatise on justification by faith, are slighted. Aldridge is excellent, however, on *The Nature of True Virtue*.

The Theology of Jonathan Edwards: A Reappraisal by Conrad Cherry (New York, 1966), though misnamed, is a very able work of scholarship. Cherry analyzes the concept of faith in Edwards's thought, and while he considers it central to an understanding of Edwards, the study is not quite the general study that both its title and its publication in paperback form suggest. An important chapter shows that Perry Miller had misstated the relationship of Calvin, the seventeenth-century Puritans, and Edwards on covenant theology: "Not only did Edwards retain Puritan covenant categories; inscrutability or distant mystery is not of the essence of God's saving operations in Calvin's system." This study is addressed to readers with a grounding in theology, but because Cherry is very well acquainted with Edwards and his commentators and his fresh insights, the book is an essential one.

Edward H. Davidson's *Jonathan Edwards: The Narrative of a Puritan Mind* (Boston, 1966) is more highly valued by some readers than by this one. The book seeks to provide an overview of Edwards but focuses on a few aspects of his thought. For Davidson, Edwards was a Puritan, but the effort to relate Edwards to Puritanism is neither very knowledgeable nor very satisfying, and the book is marred by inaccuracies and slips: "Each Sunday," Davidson writes, Edward Taylor "penned his Preparatory Meditation in verse on the same text he had used in his sermon." There are other indications that Davidson did not know enough to write a thoroughly sound book on Edwards. The task is not an easy one; it requires much reading in both Edwards's work (Davidson unfortunately used the Dwight text) and Edwards scholarship. For another opinion of the book, see A. O. Aldridge's review in *Seventeenth-Century News* (Summer 1969).

James Carse's *Jonathan Edwards & the Visibility of God* (New York, 1967), is a book with a thesis about Edwards the man. Carse begins with observations on the relationship of Edwards's thought to Locke's; he argues that for Edwards things are what they appear to be because "appearances are all there are," and "beyond what is visible there is nothing at all." Carse then considers the implications of this view in Edwards's major writings. He concludes that when seen in this light the dominant idea in *Freedom of the Will* is that "God can have no part in determining what man actually does in the world unless he becomes man's reason for doing it." After examination of Edwards's other major writings, Carse characterizes Edwards as a preacher of "a radical this-worldliness" who failed to live a life in keeping with this world view: "there was nothing in his visible mien that served as a commanding model for the 'consent of being to being.'" One comes away from Carse's book both with a new understanding of Edwards and a recognition that to support his thesis Carse has had to disregard large facets of Edwards's thought. As Norman Grabo has pointed out in a review that is generally admiring (*EAL*, Spring, 1969), Carse ignores the role of grace in Edwards's theology (much as Perry Miller did, one might add). But the book remains an exciting and thoroughly readable work.

One of the most important studies of Edwards is Roland Delattre's *Beauty and Sensibility in the Thought of Jonathan Edwards* (New Haven,

Conn., 1968). Delattre argues that the aesthetic aspect of Edwards's thought "provides a larger purchase upon the essential and distinctive features of his thought than does any other aspect, such as the idealistic, sensationalist, Platonist, scholastic, Calvinist, or mystic," and that Edwards's peculiar contribution is his elevation of beauty to a prominent place in theology. Except for a few helpful diagrams, Delattre makes few concessions to his readers. It is a pity that a study likely to be of great interest to students of American literature should be so dense. Though the book does not lend itself to summarizing, the last two pages do set forth much of what Delattre concludes. They at least should be read by every student of Edwards, some of whom will as a result be encouraged to tackle the body of the book, or, if not, either his piece in *Sound* (Spring 1967) or the one in *American Philosophy from Edwards to Quine*, edited by R. W. Shahan and K. R. Merrill (Norman, Okla., 1977).

Too pedantic and narrow in its focus to be of much importance is Dorus P. Rudisill's *The Doctrine of the Atonement in Edwards and His Successors* (New York, 1971). A book that has an attractive title, Clyde A. Holbrook's *The Ethics of Jonathan Edwards: Morality and Aesthetics* (Ann Arbor, Mich., 1973), was appropriately described by Norman Fiering as uninformed and anachronistic (*WMQ*, Jan. 1975). Harold P. Simonson's *Jonathan Edwards: Theologian of the Heart* (Grand Rapids, Mich., 1974) is not one of the important studies of Edwards. All of the theses of the book are challenged in a review by W. S. Morris (*CH*, Sept. 1975). A useful corrective to Perry Miller that goes beyond Cherry's considerations, Carl W. Bogue's *Jonathan Edwards and the Covenant of Grace* (Cherry Hills, N.J., 1975), is not widely available. Arguing that Edwards's theology remained within the framework of covenant theology without compromising his Calvinism, Bogue shows how Edwards reconciled divine sovereignty and human responsibility.

The most recent study of Edwards is without question the best informed, if not the most comprehensive. Norman Fiering has produced two companion volumes: *Moral Philosophy at Seventeenth-Century Harvard: A Discipline in Transition* and *Jonathan Edwards's Moral Thought and Its British Context* (both Chapel Hill, N.C., 1981). The serious student should read the two in order, but even selective reading is valuable. Fiering handles with great learning and understanding the vexed question of Locke's influence on Edwards; he judges that it is best to see Edwards as a thinker in a complex philosophic milieu that included Locke. More important than Locke as a single figure influence on Edwards was Malebranche, according to Fiering. There is a useful discussion of "Sinners in the Hands of an Angry God" in Chapter Five of the Edwards volume, which concludes with an admiring analysis of *True Virtue*. Though

Edwards as a human being is not vividly present, Fiering's work has many virtues: clarity, modesty, sophistication, and a deep sense of personal involvement. One hopes that he will continue his work on Edwards, for here he has quite deliberately limited himself. Another recent book on Edwards, the first in Italian, is not addressed to English readers, though happily Marcella de Nichilo is familiar with Edwards's writing and much of the scholarship. Her work is entitled *Realtà e immagine: L'estethica nei sermoni di Jonathan Edwards* (L'Aquila, Italy, 1980).

The Great Awakening and the career of Jonathan Edwards are closely identified. The standard modern study is Edwin S. Gaustad's readable *The Great Awakening in New England* (New York, 1957), but Joseph Tracy's classic *The Great Awakening* (Boston, 1841) still has much to offer. An unusually valuable collection of materials, including selections from Edwards, is *The Great Awakening: Documents Illustrating the Crisis and Its Consequences*, edited by Alan Heimert and Perry Miller (Indianapolis, Ind., and New York, 1967). It has a good introduction and a bibliography. Perry Miller's writings on the Great Awakening include an unconvincing essay on "Jonathan Edwards and the Great Awakening" in his *Errand into the Wilderness*. In it Miller relates the Awakening to the practice of "owning the covenant" and argues that the meaning of the Awakening was that ability rather than social status was to determine who was to lead. Another brief study, an excellent one, also focuses on the results of the Awakening: Robert J. Taylor's *Western Massachusetts in the Revolution* (Providence, R.I., 1954).

Collections of materials for the study of the Great Awakening are available in some abundance. Besides the Heimert-Miller volume, there are J. M. Bumstead, ed., *The Great Awakening* (Waltham, Mass., 1970); Richard L. Bushman, ed., *The Great Awakening* (New York, 1970); Darrett B. Rutman, ed., *The Great Awakening* (New York, 1970); Stephen Nissenbaum, ed., *The Great Awakening at Yale College* (Belmont, Calif., 1972); and J. M. Bumstead and John E. Van de Wetering, eds., *What Must I Do to be Saved?: The Great Awakening in Colonial America* (Hinsdale, Ill., 1976). A few other studies, not to be neglected, include Cedric B. Cowing's *The Great Awakening and the American Revolution* (Chicago, 1971), Cushing Strout's *The New Heavens and New Earth: Political Religion in America* (New York, 1974), and William G. McLaughlin's *Revivals, Awakenings and Reform* (Chicago, 1978), which covers American history from 1607 to 1977.

Readers of Perry Miller's study of Edwards have an obligation to read Peter Gay's chapter on Edwards's *History of the Work of Redemption*, a work that Miller found especially original. Gay, a historian, found the work reactionary and fundamentalist. The second half of Gay's readable essay in *A Loss of Mastery* is an analysis of Edwards as a tragic hero, with the tragedy based on "the complete incompatibility of Edward's system of ideas with the new world of enlightened philosophy." Gay's book has had mixed reviews, despite its charm.

Many valuable general studies of Edwards have been published. One of the most celebrated is Leslie Stephen's readable essay in his *Hours in a Library*, Second Series (London, 1876). Stephen presents a sparkling denunciation of Edwards as "a kind of Spinoza-Mather" who combined "the logical keeness of the great metaphysician with the puerile superstition of the New England divine." A more sympathetic study, and one of continuing value, is that of Williston Walker in his *Ten New England Leaders* (Boston, 1901). George P. Fisher knew Edwards's writings well; his *History of Christian Doctrine* (New York, 1896) provides one of the best brief accounts of Edwards's theology.

Another thoughtful older essay is one by I. Woodbridge Riley in his *American Philosophy: The Early Schools* (New York, 1907); it argues that Edwards's chief weakness was his lack of real learning. In this essay Riley also explores the relationship of Edwards's mysticism to his idealism. Much the same view of Edwards is set forth in Riley's *American Thought from Puritanism to Pragmatism* (New York, 1915). A somewhat longer study, that of Clarence Faust in *Jonathan Edwards: Representative Selections*, edited by Faust and Thomas H. Johnson, is among the best of the general essays, though thirty-five years old. Here Edwards's thought is considered in the context both of his career and of eighteenth-century philosophy.

Edwards naturally finds a place in recent histories of American thought. Paul Conklin devoted a chapter to Edwards in his *Puritans and Pragmatists: Eight Eminent American Thinkers* (New York, 1968). Morton White discusses the character of Edwards's philosophical thought in his *Science and Sentiment in America: Philosophical Thought from Jonathan Edwards to John Dewey* (New York, 1972). Not to be missed is the substantial study in Elizabeth Flower and Murray G. Murphey's *History of American Philosophy* (New York, 1977). Also much admired is Norman Fiering's essay, "Will and Intellect in the New England Mind" (*WMQ*, Oct. 1972).

Several other general essays must be mentioned. Joseph Haroutunian's "Jonathan Edwards: A Study in Godliness" (*Journal of Religion*, July 1931) is an excellent survey of Edwards's ideas. Edward Davidson's "From Locke to Edwards" (*JHI*, July 1963) is far more useful than Davidson's book. It focuses on "Sinners in the Hands of an Angry God" as a central document for an understanding of Edwards; here Edwards "demonstrated that the world's meaning is never known except as it is experienced." Davidson sees Edwards as concerned with "the mystery of the imperilled soul forced to know first itself and then some minute and cloudy portion of the outside world." Thomas A. Schafer wrote a good brief essay for the fifteenth edition of the *Encyclopedia Britannica*. Perhaps the most valuable brief treatment of Edwards for the student of literature is Michael Colacurcios's "The Example of Edwards: Idealist Imagination and the Metaphysics of Sovereignty" (in *Puritan Influences in American Literature*, ed. Emory Elliott [Urbana, Ill., 1979]). Colacurcio argues that the most useful way to look at Edwards is to see how he treats the relationship between philosophical argument and the "data" of Christian Revelation. More comprehensive is the well-informed pamphlet by Edward M. Griffin, *Jonathan Edwards* (Minneapolis, 1971). Griffin's more recent study of Edwards's antagonist Charles Chauncey may be mentioned at this point; *Old Brick: Charles Chauncey of Boston, 1705–1787* (Minneapolis, 1980) sheds much light on Edwards.

Among literary studies of Edwards, the fundamental ones are by Thomas H. Johnson. "Jonathan Edwards's Background of Reading" (*Publications of the Colonial Society of Massachusetts, 1930–33*) provides a necessary beginning for a study of Edwards's literary milieu and influences on his writing; and "Edwards as a Man of Letters," in Faust and Johnson's volume of Edwards selections, has not been superseded. It is, however, quite brief. Another study establishes a point that may not need establishing. Paul R. Baumgartner's "Jonathan Edwards: The Theory Behind His Use of Figurative Language" (*PMLA*, Sept. 1963) argues that the "Puritan mind," especially Edwards's, was "perfectly at home with figurative language," and that there is no tension between Puritan theory and practice. One wonders if it is useful to identify Edwards with the early Puritans on such matters.

Other literary studies include Sang Hyun Lee's "Jonathan Edwards' Theory of the Imagination" (*Michigan Academician*, Fall 1972); Daniel B. Shea's thoughtful essay in *Major Writers of Early American Literature*, ed. Everett Emerson (Madison, Wis., 1972); John Griffith's "Jonathan Edwards as a Literary Artist" (*Criticism*, Spring 1973); Harold P. Simonson's "Jonathan Edwards and the Imagination" (*Andover Newton Quarterly*, Nov. 1975), which argues that Edwards was not a literary artist; the brief but valuable study by Terrence Erdt, *Jonathan Edwards: Art and the Sense of the Heart* (Amherst, Mass., 1980), which is a pleasure to read; and the more comprehensive if not always informative study by William J. Scheick, *The Writings of Jonathan Edwards: Theme, Motif, and Style* (College Station, Tex., 1975). Scheick is a student of literature who is comfortable in theology.

A few specialized studies make contributions to understanding. E. C.

Smyth's "Some Early Writings of Jonathan Edwards, 1714–1726" (*PAAS*, 1895, 1896) considers the manuscripts on the Soul and on Natural Science and discusses their literary merits and the development of Edwards's style. Smyth considers "modesty" an important trait of the early pieces. Edwin H. Cady's "The Artistry of Jonathan Edwards" (*NEQ*, Mar. 1949) should be read along with Davidson's essay, noted above. In an analysis of "Sinners in the Hands of an Angry God" Cady shows how Edwards communicates his "excruciatingly vivid vision" to his hearers. Robert Lee Stuart identifies the "element of comfort" in the sermon in "Jonathan Edwards at Enfield" (*AL*, March 1976), and Alexander Medlicott, Jr., reports Reverend Stephen Williams's response to it in "In the Wake of Mr. Edwards's 'Most Awakening' Sermon at Enfield" (*EAL*, Winter 1980/81).

Wilson Kimnach has produced a series of informative studies that stem from his 1971 University of Pennsylvania dissertation; all concern Edwards as a preacher and provide a context for an understanding of the famous sermons such as "Sinners." In "The Brazen Serpent: Jonathan Edwards's Conception of the Sermon" (in Charles Angoff, ed., *Jonathan Edwards: His Life and Influence* [Rutherford, N.J., 1975]), Kimnach traces the development of Edwards as a preacher. In "Jonathan Edwards' Sermon Mill" (*Early American Literature*, Fall 1975) he shows how Edwards revised his sermons for different audiences and occasions. In "Jonathan Edwards' Early Sermons: New York, 1722–1723" (*Journal of Presbyterian History*, Fall 1977), Kimnach looks at Edwards's earliest sermons. Willis J. Buckingham draws attention to Edwards's rhythms and pacings in "Stylistic Artistry in the Sermons of Jonathan Edwards" (*PLL*, Spring 1969).

Daniel B. Shea's "The Art and Instruction of Jonathan Edwards's *Personal Narrative*" (*AL*, Mar. 1965) is one of several good studies of this work. Shea shows how Edwards skillfully combined spiritual autobiography and instruction. A more historical approach is provided by David C. Pierce in "Jonathan Edwards and the 'New Sense' of Glory" (*NEQ*, Mar. 1968). Pierce suggests that the mysticism of the work belongs to its time, that "the 'new sense' of glory was a specific response to the rapprochement between God and nature which had been effected by the new philosophy."

Another helpful analysis of the *Narrative* is in David L. Minter's *The Interpreted Design as a Structural Principle in American Prose* (New Haven, Conn., 1969). As the title of his book suggests, Minter sees Edwards as finding a definite pattern in his religious life. R. C. De Prospo in "The 'New Simple Idea' of Edwards' Personal Narrative" (*EAL*, Fall 1979) argues that Edwards's account is consistent with his interpretation of Locke. Paul David Johnson in "Jonathan Edwards's 'Sweet Conjuction'" (*EAL*, Winter 1981/82) gives the work a Bachelardian reading. Unduly neglected because of its place of publication, Norman S. Grabo's "Jonathan Edwards' *Personal Narrative:* Dynamic Statis" (*Literatur in Wissenschaft und Unterricht,* 1969) compares the *Narrative* with two other conversion narratives that Edwards wrote. Two studies that might usefully be read together are David L. Weddle's "The Image of the Self in Jonathan Edwards: A Study of Autobiography and Theology" (*Journal of the American Academy of Religion,* Mar. 1975) and Wayne Lesser's "Jonathan Edwards: Textuality and the Language of Man" (in *Critical Essays on Jonathan Edwards,* ed. William J. Scheick [Boston, 1980]). Both consider, from different perspectives, the selves to be found in the *Narrative.* Finally, there are a few good pages on the work in G. Thomas Couser's *American Autobiography: The Prophetic Mode* (Amherst, Mass., 1979).

Some other works of Edwards have been examined individually. William J. Scheick looks at "Family, Conversion, and the Self in Jonathan Edwards' *A Faithful Narrative of the Surprising Work of God*" (*TSL,* 1974); he finds that Edwards exalted the family as a source of order and the proper environment for conversion. Stephen J. Stein looks at No. 348 of Edwards's "Notes on Scripture" to find a creative poet in "Jonathan Edwards and the Rainbow: Biblical Exegesis and Poetic Imagination" (*NEQ,* Sept. 1974). John F. Wilson has published two studies of the *History of Redemption,* the work that Peter Gay had damned as an anachronism. (Wilson is editing the *History* for the Yale edition.) "Jonathan Edwards as Historian" (*CH,* Mar. 1977) identifies Edwards as belonging to the tradition of ecclesiastical historians who emphasize the process of redemption. In "Jonathan Edwards's Notebook for *A History of Redemption*" (in *Reformation, Conformity and Dissent,* ed. R. Buick Knox [London, 1977]), Wilson relates the *History* to Edwards's concerns in the years 1755–57.

Perry Miller introduced the topic of Edwards's use of typology to students of the Massachusetts thinker in his edition of *Images and Shadows.* His work has now been much corrected, notably by Mason I. Lowance, Jr., first in "Images and Shadows of Divine Things: The Typology of Jonathan Edwards" (*EAL,* Spring 1980, reprinted in *Typology and Early American Literature,* ed. Sacvan Bercovitch [Amherst, Mass., 1972]), and more recently in his *The Language of Canaan* (Cambridge, Mass., 1980), in which he looks at Edwards's typological thought in its historical context. Another essay on the subject from Lowance is in *Literary Uses of Typology,* ed. Earl Miner (Princeton, N.J., 1977), which also includes Karl Keller's essay on how Edwards's allegorizing resembles the practice of nineteenth-century American writers, such as Emerson. Another study of how Edwards anticipated Emerson and his contemporaries is in John F. Lynen's *The Design of the Present* (New Haven, Conn., 1969). Many studies deal with special aspects of Edwards's thought. William S. Morris's "The Genius of Jonathan Edwards," in *Reinterpretations in American Church History*, edited by J. C. Brauer (Chicago, 1968), argues that the logic of Burgersdicius had great influence on Edwards. Though the essay is full of philosophical and theological jargon, it makes important points. Morris calls Edwards's philosophy "spiritual realism": "God as a divine Being is alone real." Edwards is an existentialist of sorts, since for him experience is what matters, especially experience of the divine. The essay praises Edwards highly. Edwards's debt to Newton's *Opticks* in his use of metaphors of light is explored in Ron Loewinsohn's "Jonathan Edwards' Opticks: Images and Metaphors in Some of His Works" (*EAL*, Spring 1973). Emily Stipes Watts identifies the influence of Thomas More's *Enchiridion Ethicum* on Edwards's ethical definitions in "The Neoplatonic Basis of Jonathan Edwards' 'True Virtue'" (*EAL*, Fall 1975). David S. Wilson shows that Edwards's famous observations on flying spiders were not so remarkable in "The Flying Spider" (*JHI*, July–Sept. 1971).

Among students of Edwards's theology, Thomas A. Schafer is unusually able. He has examined "Jonathan Edwards and Justification by Faith" (*CH*, Dec. 1951), and "Jonathan Edwards's Conception of the Church" (*CH*, Mar. 1955). In the former he demonstrates that Edwards's treatment of justification by faith was a preliminary means of dealing with Arminianism and of defending piety against the new moralism. Later, in the treatises on the will, original sin, and true virtue, Edwards used a different approach, one that shaped American theological history. In the latter study Schafer shows that though the Great Awakening weakened the concept of the Church, Edwards's teachings strengthened it. On a related topic, Gerhard T. Alexis discusses "Jonathan Edwards and the Theocratic Ideal" (*CH*, Sept. 1966). Alexis establishes the important point that Edwards did not consider the elect, the saints, to be God's instruments, nor was he an advocate of the theocratic ideal. He took a narrower view of religion's role in society than did the early New England Puritans.

Richard L. Bushman undertook an attractive analysis of Edwards. In "Jonathan Edwards and Puritan Consciousness" (*Journal for the Scientific Study of Religion*, Fall 1966) he analyzes Edwards's understanding of the conversion process as a resolution of man's conflict with God. In another study, "Jonathan Edwards as Great Man: Identity, Conversion, and Leadership in the Great Awakening" (*Sound*, Spring 1969), Bushman examines Edwards's quest for identity and its relationship to his sources in the Great Awakening. This thoughtful interpretation is based on the techniques developed by Erik Erikson. It is far more profound than the older essay by Joseph H. Crooker, "Jonathan Edwards: A Psychological Study" (*NEM*, Apr. 1890), which, however, should not be ignored, nor should the discussion of Edwards in the stimulating and controversial study by Philip Greven in *The Protestant Temperament: Patterns of Child-Rearing, Religious Experience, and the Self in Early America* (New York, 1977).

Several studies of Edwards's philosophy can be recommended. Frederick J. E. Woodbridge's "The Philosophy of Jonathan Edwards" was published in *Exercises Commemorating the Two-Hundredth Anniversary of the Birth of Jonathan Edwards* (Andover, Mass., 1904). Woodbridge notes that Edwards's influence in New England was great until about 1890, his influence not being permanent because he did not connect adequately his philosophy and his theology. It was a duality that Edwards may have become aware of toward the end of his life. The essay is of continuing importance. Harvey G. Townsend, who edited *The Philosophy of Jonathan Edwards*, prepared a sympathetic, critical interpretation of his *Philosophical Ideas in the United States* (New York, 1934). Townsend analyzes Edwards's epistemology, ethics, and esthetics. In a more specialized study, Townsend makes clear the role of "The Will and the Understanding in the Philosophy of Jonathan Edwards" (*CH*, Dec. 1947). He summarizes: "Edwards saw quite clearly that there is a difference between propositions formulated by the understanding and strictly subject to logical processes for verification and inference on the one hand; and those willed choices which express our likes and dislikes on the other. From the latter issue all the forms of action which give men their moral and religious characters." In "Jonathan Edwards as Philosophical Theologian" (*Review of Metaphysics*, Dec. 1976), John Smith describes Edwards's position as theological empiricism.

Two discussions focus on Edwards's early idealism. Wallace E. Anderson, in "Immaterialism in Jonathan Edwards's Early Philosophical Notes" (*JHI*, June 1964), observes that though Edwards's conclusions are like Berkeley's, his arguments are quite different. George Rupp's "The Idealism of Jonathan Edwards" (*HTR*, Apr. 1969) attempts to qualify the classification of Edwards as an idealist because for him resistance or solidity exists outside the mind. Those interested in this topic should consult Norman Fiering's volumes, commended earlier.

The sources of Edwards's idealism have been much discussed. Its relation to Cambridge Platonism, treated by Clarence Gohdes in "Aspects of Idealism in Early New England" (*Philosophical Review*, Nov. 1930), has been exhaustively considered by Emily S. Watts in her dissertation "Jonathan Edwards and the Cambridge Platonists" (Illinois, 1963).

Edwards's sensationalism is the subject of David Lyttle's "The Sixth Sense of Jonathan Edwards" (*Church Quarterly Review*, Jan. 1966) and of C. A. Smith's "Jonathan Edwards and 'The Way of Ideas'" (*HTR*, Apr. 1966). Lyttle shows that for Edwards the experience of grace is qualitatively different from other experiences, is like a sensory experience but is not in fact empirical, though it leads to a principle of perception. Smith argues that Edwards considered man to possess "the active power of aesthetic sensitivity and that it was through this channel that man gained access to the materials of the knowledge of God." Among recent discussions, two may be commended, in addition to Fiering's. Paul Helm in "Locke and Jonathan Edwards: A Reconsideration" (*Journal of the History of Philosophy*, Jan. 1969) urges that one should discriminate sharply between Locke's empiricism and Edwards's position. Also emphasizing the distinction is David Laurence's "Jonathan Edwards, John Locke, and the Canon of Experience" (*EAL*, Fall 1980). This exemplary discussion cuts through to decisively central issues. See also the afore-mentioned book-length study by Terrence Erdt.

Edwards and science is the subject of several essays. Clarence H. Faust's "Jonathan Edwards as a Scientist" (*AL*, Jan. 1930) is a fundamental study. Faust argues that: (1) Edwards was never deeply interested in science; he was always more concerned with theology and philosophy, and (2) Edwards planned the composition of theological works while at Yale as early as his sixteenth year. Theodore Hornberger in "The Effect of the New Science Upon the Thought of Jonathan Edwards" (*AL*, May 1937) suggests that Edwards's confidence in the study of nature, a confidence derived from the new science, led him to make use of it in seeking to bring men back to religion. Henry J. Laskowsky argues that Edwards was ahead of his times or at least up-to-date in "Jonathan Edwards: A Philosopher of Science" (*Connecticut Review*, Oct. 1970). In "Edwards' Epistemology and the New Science" (*EAL*, Winter 1973), Jean-Pierre Martin argues that Edwards's scientific thought was "embarrassingly conservative."

Among many articles on Edwards's apocalyptic thought, two should be consulted. The editor of Edwards's apocalyptic writings, Stephen J. Stein, contributed "Providence and the Apocalypse in the Early Writings of Jonathan Edwards" (*EAL*, Winter 1978/79); there he argues that in his pre-1724 writings Edwards gives more attention to providence than to millennialism. In "Interpretation et Utilisation de l'Apocalypse" (*Annales du Centre de Recherches sur l'Amerique Anglophone*, 1981) Jean Beranger argues that for Edwards the book of Revelation was central to his reading of history. Two books in which Edwards's apocalyptic thought is examined in the context of American history are Ernest Lee Tuveson's *Redeemer Nation: The Idea of America's Millenial Role* (Chicago, 1968) and more recently Nathan O. Hatch's *The Sacred Cause of Liberty: Republican Thought and the Millenium in Revolutionary New England* (New Haven, Conn., 1977).

Among the more useful articles surveying the state of Edwards studies, none recent, are William S. Morris, "The Reappraisal of Edwards" (*NEQ*, Dec. 1957), W. J. Burggraff's "Jonathan Edwards: A Bibliographical Essay" (*Reformed Review*, Mar. 1965) and Thomas Werge's "Jonathan Edwards and the Puritan Mind in America" (*Reformed Review*, Spring 1970).

Edwards's influence and connections with later writers have been a major concern of historians. In "Individualism and the Puritan Imagination" (*AQ*, Summer 1970) Ellwood Johnson sees Edwards as participating in American cultural continuity insofar as he was an advocate of individualism. In "From Edwards to Emerson to Thoreau: A Revaluation," (*ATQ*, Spring 1973) Mason Lowance sees a line of continuity but makes useful distinctions: what is revealed to the saints, according to Edwards, is similar to what is available to the "transcendentally redeemed" in the thought of Emerson and Thoreau. Another scholar, William H. Parker, goes so far as to call Edwards a transcendentalist. See his "Jonathan Edwards: Founder of the Counter-Tradition of Transcendental Thought in America" (*Georgia Review*, Winter 1973). John E. Smith looks at Edwards's contributions to pragmatism in "Jonathan Edwards: Piety and Practice in the American Character" (*Journal of Religion*, Apr. 1974). There is a lively chapter on Edwards and Emily Dickinson in Karl Keller's *The Only Kangaroo among the Beauty* (Baltimore, Md. 1979). Daniel B. Shea's "Jonathan Edwards: The First Hundred Years" (*JAmSt*, Aug. 1980) is the most comprehensive study of the impact of Edwards on American history.

Edwards studies are in a healthy state, since the scholarly overkill that so burdens the life of the serious student of American literature is not a major problem for those interested in Edwards; however, uninformed studies, based on out-dated scholarship at best, continue to be published. The use of M. X. Lesser's reference guide, with its excellent index, should make the scholar's work far easier than it has been. Norman Fiering's studies or, for the less ambitious, the pages in the Flower-Murphey *History of American Philosophy* are the best introductions to Edwards at present.

Benjamin Franklin

BRUCE GRANGER

FACED WITH the voluminous record of Franklin's careers as journalist, philomath, civic projector, scientist, and statesman, it is necessary to narrow the focus. This essay will center not on scientific and state papers but on the more obviously literary writings. While Benjamin Franklin dabbled in verse early and late, it is of course as a prose writer that he made his mark in the world of American letters. His literary prose encompasses a wide range of nonfiction genres popular in the eighteenth century, notably the periodical essay, almanac, letter to the press, personal and familiar letter, bagatelle, and autobiography.

BIBLIOGRAPHY

The only formal Franklin bibliography was published almost a century ago: Paul Leicester Ford's *Franklin Bibliography. A List of Books Written by, or Relating to Benjamin Franklin* (Brooklyn, N.Y., 1889). It lists among Franklin's own writings 600 books and pamphlets, 18 periodicals and serials in which his writings appeared, 15 state papers and treatises in the formation of which he aided, 70 works containing letters by him, and 18 writings wrongly or doubtfully ascribed to him; also 211 works relating to, written to, or dedicated to him. Ford was a conscientious bibliographer in his day, but scholarly investigation since 1889 has brought about a drastic revision and expansion of the Franklin canon and has resulted in an ever-growing library of biographical and critical studies. Two selective bibliographies that help bring Ford up to

From Earl N. Harbert and Robert A. Rees, editors, *Fifteen American Authors before 1900: Bibliographic Essays on Research & Criticism* (Madison: The University of Wisconsin Press; © 1984 by the Board of Regents of the University of Wisconsin System); may be reproduced only by permission of the publisher.

date are *Benjamin Franklin: Representative Selections*, edited by F. L. Mott and C. E. Jorgenson (Chicago and New York, 1936), and the *LHUS* and Supplements (1959, 1972). The need for a new and comprehensive bibliography is evident.

C. William Miller's *Benjamin Franklin's Philadelphia Printing, 1728– 1766: A Descriptive Bibliography* (Philadelphia, 1974) is a definitive but specialized bibliography which "undertakes to include all known publications, signed and unsigned, issuing from the Philadelphia printing office of Benjamin Franklin from the spring of 1728, when he first became master of his own shop . . . to January 20, 1766, when the Franklin and Hall partnership was formally dissolved." The first part "is made up of detailed descriptions of the 856 known printed pieces . . . assigned to the Franklin printing house"; the second lists 545 pieces of job printing; and the third removes "86 items attributed inaccurately to the Franklin and Franklin and Hall printing house by other bibliographers." All available title-pages are photographically reproduced. The introduction surveys Franklin's printing career down to 1766, type fonts and foundries, Franklin's role in the establishment of a paper mill industry in the Middle Colonies, and the Franklin printing house's association with American bookbinders.

EDITIONS

Collected Works

Four important collections of Franklin's works appeared during his lifetime, all with his knowledge, several with his active help: *Experiments and Observations on Electricity* (London, 1751); *Oeuvres de M. Franklin . . . Traduites de l'anglois sur la 4 éd. Par M. Barbeu Dubourg . . .* (2 vols., Paris, 1773); *Political, Miscellaneous, and Philosophical Pieces . . .*, edited by Benjamin Vaughan (London, 1779); and *Philosophical and Miscellaneous Papers, Lately written by B. Franklin, L.L.D.*, edited by Edward Bancroft (London, 1787). Francis S. Philbrick, "Notes on Early Editions and Editors of Franklin" (*PAPS*, Oct. 1953), discusses these four collections, as well as the first two important posthumous editions, William Duane's *Works of Dr. Benjamin Franklin* (6 vols., Philadelphia, 1808–18) and William Temple Franklin's *Memoirs of the Life and Writings of Benjamin Franklin* (3 vols., London, 1817–18). There were three major editions, prior to the Yale edition now in progress: Jared Sparks's *Works of Benjamin Franklin* (10 vols., Boston, 1836–40), John Bigelow's *Complete Works of Benjamin Franklin* (10 vols., New York, 1887–88), and Albert Henry Smyth's *Writings of Benjamin Franklin* (10 vols., New York, 1905–7).

When the projected forty volumes of *The Papers of Benjamin Franklin*, edited by Leonard W. Labaree and William B. Willcox (New Haven, Conn., 1959–), are completed, they will contain approximately 30,000 pieces by and to Franklin; twenty-two volumes have appeared to date, covering the period down to 27 October 1776. (For the years after this date Smyth's edition remains the most nearly definitive, though it is not always trustworthy as to either attribution or text.) Unlike earlier editions which "all had to be selective," this Yale edition is "intended to be comprehensive." In the words of the editors, it "will present the full text of every document of Franklin's career, signed or unsigned, that we can locate and establish to our satisfaction to have been written by Franklin or by Franklin with others. . . . The ultimate test to be applied in determining whether to print any document or part of a Franklin document is whether the contents are in any sense the product of his mind." It will also include letters and other communications addressed to Franklin and "third-party" letters, producing as has never before been possible a full and fair view of his very extensive correspondence. But even the Yale edition will not be complete since many of Franklin's papers were lost or destroyed, especially during the Revolution.

In trying to establish the canon of Franklin's writings the Yale editors have erred, wisely I feel, on the side of too great conservatism. J. A. Leo Lemay does not agree. Reviewing the first ten volumes, he finds the editors "too conservative in their attributions" and wishes that "a much larger number of essays and hoaxes [had] been included (or at least discussed) in the *Papers*" (*ECS*, Winter 1967/8). Several writings not included in the Yale volumes already published have since been attributed to Franklin: A. O. Aldridge, "Benjamin Franklin and the *Pennsylvania Gazette*" (*PAPS*, Feb. 1962), attributes to him two essays that appeared in the *Pennsylvania Gazette*, a letter of a husband-hunting maid, Belinda (26 June 1732), and a discourse by "Chatterbox" on the subject of characters with the termination "box" in their names (11 January 1733), and "An Essay on Paper-Currency" in the February 1741 issue of the *General Magazine*; Aldridge, "A Religious Hoax by Benjamin Franklin" (*AL*, May 1964), argues that Franklin almost certainly wrote two pieces that appeared in the 8 August 1734 issue of the *Pennsylvania Gazette*, "companion pieces designed to ridicule a lugubrious 'Meditation on the Vanity and Brevity of Human Life, wrote in Imitation of the Psalms,' which had appeared in the preceding issue"; and Lemay, "Franklin's Suppressed 'Busy-Body'" (*AL*, Nov. 1965), demonstrates that of two editions of the 27 March 1729 issue of the *American Weekly Mercury* the first, which was suppressed before distribution, "contains a hitherto unnoticed addition to Franklin's 'Busy-Body No. 8' which marks Franklin's first entry into Pennsylvania politics." On the other hand, certain deletions from the Yale edition have been proposed, notably the eleven letters calling for total repeal of the Townshend duties of 1767 which appeared in the London *Public Advertiser* between 4 January and 2 March 1770 over the pseudonym, "The Colonist's Advocate." Although previously long attributed to James Burgh, a schoolmaster and fellow member with Franklin of the club of Honest Whigs, Verner Crane, convinced that Franklin was the author, printed them in his edition of *Benjamin Franklin's Letters to the Press;* the Yale editors, "basing their ascription on Crane's work," reprinted them in Volume 17 of the *Papers*. I find convincing Carla Hay's argument that "the entire series is the handiwork not of Franklin but of James Burgh" ("Benjamin Franklin, James Burgh, and the Authorship of 'The Colonist's Advocate' Letters,'" *WMQ*, Jan. 1975). In a response which immediately follows this article William Willcox will go no farther than to concede "that Franklin had a hand, though perhaps a lesser one than we supposed, in 'The Colonist's Advocate.'" In spite of such additions or possible additions to and deletions from the canon, *The Papers of Benjamin Franklin*, a project prepared under the auspices of the American Philosophical Society and Yale University and supervised by Leonard Labaree until his retirement in 1969 and since that time by William Willcox, is an editorial landmark in American literary scholarship.

Editions and Texts by Genre

In *Benjamin Franklin's Letters to the Press, 1758–1775*, edited by Verner W. Crane (Chapel Hill, N.C., 1950), a majority of the 141 documents examined are attributed to Franklin for the first time; 91 letters to the English and American press are reprinted in full for the first time. *Benjamin Franklin's Autobiographical Writings*, edited by Carl Van Doren (New York, 1945), prints, or prints in full, for the first time forty-nine Franklin pieces, chiefly letters; fifty-one of the pieces in this edition do not appear in Smyth. There have been definitive editions of three personal correspondences: *Letters and Papers of Benjamin Franklin and Richard Jackson, 1753–1785*, edited by Carl Van Doren (Philadelphia, 1947); *Benjamin Franklin and Catharine Ray Greene: Their Correspondence, 1755–1790*, edited by William G. Roelker (Philadelphia, 1949); and *The Letters of Benjamin Franklin and Jane Mecom*, edited by Carl Van Doren (Princeton, N.J., 1950). Also Whitfield J. Bell, Jr., "'All Clear Sunshine': New Letters of Franklin and Mary Stevenson Hewson" (*PAPS*, Dec. 1956), quotes extensively from the unpublished Franklin-Stevenson correspondence. Important among editions and samplings of Franklin's familiar correspondences with French friends are *Benjamin Franklin's Letters to Madame Helvétius and Madame La Freté*, compiled by Luther S. Livingston (Cambridge, Mass., 1924); *Les amitiés américaines de madame d'Houdetot*, edited by Gilbert Chinard (Paris, 1924); and — for Franklin-Brillon letters — A. H. Smyth, "Franklin's Social Life in France" (*Putnam's Monthly Magazine*, Oct.–Dec. 1906; Jan. 1907), and W. C. Ford, "One of Franklin's Friendships" (*HM*, Sept. 1906). Dorothy Medlin, "Benjamin Franklin and the French Language: A Letter to Madame Brillon" (*FAR*, Fall 1977), presents an accurate transcript and commentary on Franklin's letter of 12 May 1779 comforting Mme Brillon in her distress over her husband's infatuation with the governess Mlle Jupin. In view of Franklin's many corrections in it (and others he failed to make), the author expresses the hope that "as the complete collection of French documents is prepared for publication in the Yale edition of the Franklin Papers, this letter may be useful as a linguistic *point de repère*, showing Franklin's proficiency in French in the spring of 1779 and giving insight into his method of composition." *Franklin's Wit and Folly: The Bagatelles*, edited by Richard E. Amacher (New Brunswick, N.J., 1953), is the most important edition of Franklin bagatelles, though it does not include any of those he wrote in Philadelphia and England and reprints two pieces, "Information to Those Who Would Remove to America" and "Remarks Concerning the Savages of North America," that are not bagatelles properly speaking. Chinard, "Random Notes on Two 'Bagatelles'" (*PAPS*, Dec. 1959), has transcribed the French text of two bagatelles from manuscript, "The Elysian Fields" and "The Ephemera."

The *Autobiography* is unfinished in two respects: Franklin brought his story only to 1758 and he did not live to revise even this long fragment to his final satisfaction. Indeed, he seems clearly to have conceived of this fragment as lying at the center of a longer autobiographical work. Part One of the *Autobiography* was written in July and August 1771, Part Two in 1784, Part Three in 1788–89, and Part Four in 1789–90. *The Autobiography of Benjamin Franklin: A Genetic Text*, edited by J. A. Leo Lemay and P. M. Zall (Knoxville, Tenn., 1981), approved by the Center for Editions of American Authors, is a definitive scholarly edition. "Our genetic text of Franklin's autobiography," write the editors, "prints in its entirety Franklin's holograph manuscript, showing all the cancellations, revisions, and additions." It "is intended for the scholar who wants to know what Franklin originally wrote, what he canceled, what he revised, and what he added." This is the first edition to be based on "an original transcript of the holograph manuscript" (located at the Huntington Library), and "only the original manuscript contains the last revisions of the author." Although Lemay and Zall point out that *The Autobiography of Benjamin Franklin*, edited by Leonard W. Labaree et al. (New Haven, Conn., 1964), used "only a photocopy — not the original manuscript," a spotcheck of two dozen paragraphs at widely spaced intervals suggests that while the Lemay-Zall text frequently differs substantively from the Labaree text, these differences are not important and do not affect the meaning or style of the *Autobiography* significantly. Scholars will of course need to consult the Lemay-Zall edition, but for the general reader the Labaree clear text remains the most readable and satisfactory edition; the explanatory and biographical notes are full and informative. Persuasively Lemay and Zall call into serious question the scholarly usefulness of *Benjamin Franklin's Memoirs: Parallel Text Edition*, edited by Max Farrand (Berkeley and Los Angeles, 1949), arguing that all four texts printed in that edition are faulty: (1) in the case of the original manuscript "Max Farrand corrected a copy of Mott and Jorgenson for the first part of the autobiography and a reprint of Bigelow for the remainder"; (2) William Temple Franklin's 1818 London edition of Parts One–Three, the only text other than the holograph manuscript that has been thought authoritative, because of Temple's carelessness "has no claim to authority"; (3) the Buisson translation of Part One, *Mémoires de la vie privée de Benjamin Franklin* (Paris, 1791), is evidently based on an unrevised copy of Part One, not on one of the two no longer extant fair copies as has generally been thought; and (4) the Le Veillard version of Parts One–Four in French, which survives in manuscript at the Library of Congress, "usually prints the revisions without regard to the original translation Le Veillard was revising."

The Autobiography of Benjamin Franklin: A Restoration of a "Fair Copy," edited by Max Farrand (San Marino, Calif., 1949), is an untrustworthy hybrid; Farrand, who died in 1945, was responsible only for Part One, and the edition was completed at the Huntington Library under the supervision of Godfrey Davis. Verner Crane, "Max Farrand and Benjamin Franklin's Memoirs" (*MP*, Nov. 1949), demonstrates that where MS and WTF texts differ, Farrand often exercised aesthetic judgment in choosing the version which seemed best supported by Buisson's and Le Veillard's translations and further, that since it is only in Part One that the Buisson text is available to tip the balance between the readings of MS and WTF, Davis and his staff had to be even more subjective than Farrand in completing this restoration.

MANUSCRIPTS AND LETTERS

Eight libraries own more than 500 manuscripts by, to, or about Franklin: the American Philosophical Society, the Library of Congress, the National Archives, the Historical Society of Pennsylvania, the University of Pennsylvania, Yale University, the Massachusetts Historical Society, and the French Foreign Office. The American Philosophical Society holds by far the largest number of Franklin manuscripts, the nucleus of the collection being Mr. Charles Pemberton Fox's presentation in 1840 of 13,800 pieces in nine languages; I. Minis Hays, *Calendar of the Papers of Benjamin Franklin in the Library of the American Philosophical Society* (5 vols., Philadelphia, 1908), describes these seventy-six manuscript volumes. Of manuscripts and letters acquired by the Society since the publication of Hays's *Calendar*, the most important was the purchase in 1936 of a large collection of papers from the Bache family, descendants of Franklin's daughter Sarah. *Guide to the Archives and Manuscript Collections of the American Philosophical Society*, compiled by Whitfield J. Bell, Jr., and Murphy D. Smith (Philadelphia, 1966), lists significant groups of Franklin manuscripts, mostly letters, acquired since 1936. See W. E. Lingelbach, "Benjamin Franklin's Papers and the American Philosophical Society" (*PAPS*, Dec. 1955), which "treats the relations of the American Philosophical Society with Franklin's writings over a period of more than a century and a half [and] surveys the Society's relationship to" *The Papers of Benjamin Franklin*.

Second in importance is the manuscript collection at the Library of Congress, consisting principally of the 2,938 pieces in the Henry Stevens Collection; see W. C. Ford, *List of the Benjamin Franklin Papers in the Library of Congress* (Washington, D.C., 1905). Acquisitions since 1905 are described in C. W. Garrison's *List of Manuscript Collections in the Library of Congress to July, 1931* (Washington, D.C., 1932) and D. M. Mugridge's "Scientific Manuscripts of Benjamin Franklin" (*Lib. of Cong. Jour. of Current Acquisitions*, Aug. 1947). The Franklin papers were reorganized in 1972 and are now available on microfilm; see *Benjamin Franklin: A Register and Index of His Papers in the Library of Congress* (Washington, D.C., 1973). The 840 pieces held by the University of Pennsylvania are listed in an appendix to Volume Five of Hays's *Calendar*. According to the *Guide to the Manuscript Collections of the Historical Society of Pennsylvania* (Philadelphia, 1949), the "Benjamin Franklin Papers, 1747–1794" consist of about a thousand items, among them two volumes of letters and papers (1750–83) and three volumes of miscellaneous papers from his French ministry (1776–85). The Mason-Franklin Collection at Yale University includes manuscript books and correspondence with Joseph Galloway and the Shipley family; see G.S. Eddy, "A Ramble Through the Mason-Franklin Collection" (*YULG*, Apr. 1936), and D. W. Bridgwater, "Notable Additions to the Franklin Collection" (*YULG*, Oct. 1945).

J. Albert Robbins with the assistance of eight regional chairmen and sixty-three regional associates canvassed 600 American libraries (excluding private collections) to produce the second edition of *American Literary Manuscripts* (Athens, Ga., 1977), an item-count finding list arranged by author. This volume reveals that, in addition to the libraries named above, the most extensive Franklin holdings are at the Clements Library, Columbia University, the Houghton Library, and Princeton University. It contains the most nearly definitive find-list of Franklin manuscripts in American repositories presently available.

BIOGRAPHY

General Studies

In "Three Earliest Published Lives of Benjamin Franklin, 1790–93: The *Autobiography* and Its Continuations" (*EAL*, Spring 1974) Betty Kushen examines the three earliest book-length lives of Franklin published outside the United States: *Memoirs of the Late Dr. Benjamin Franklin* (London, 1790) by James Jones Wilmer — and probably, as P. M. Zall argues persuasively if circumstantially elsewhere (*EAL*, Fall 1975), co-authored by the malevolent Andrew Allen; Buisson's *Mémoires* (Paris, 1791); and the anonymous *Private Life of the Late Benjamin Franklin* (London, 1793). It is Kushen's conviction that these early biographies set the pattern of characterization, both laudatory and derogatory, followed in all lives until the twentieth century (that by Weems being a notable exception) when Carl Van Doren attempted definitively "to restore and vindicate Franklin's image." In "The American Image of Benjamin Franklin" (*AQ*, Summer 1957) Richard D. Miles, reviewing 150 years of Franklin biography, writes, "For three-quarters of a century following his death, Franklin appeared to most Americans as a man who, by his charm and practical sagacity, had emerged from an unpromising station to world eminence." After the Civil War, according to Miles, three forces shaped the American image of Franklin: the business ethos, xenophobia, and the works of "scholars, thinkers and creative writers" beginning with Parton. "The major task of recent serious scholarship," Miles concludes, thinking of Van Doren and Crane, "has been to reveal a more human Washington and a nobler, more heroic Franklin. The former may be the more difficult task, but the latter has more definitely been performed with success."

An early popular biography, one which emphasizes the economic and moral rather than the political significance of Franklin, is Mason L. Weem's *Life of Benjamin Franklin; with Many Choice Anecdotes and Admirable Sayings of This Great Man, Never Before Published by Any of His Biographers* (Baltimore, 1815). "Parson" Weems elaborates, often fancifully, on the evidence of the *Autobiography*; thus, Abiah advises Josiah one night as they lie sleepless in bed that for fear he should go to sea instead, little Ben be allowed to go to school (chapter 5), and Ben speaks joyously of the youthful verses he has just composed (chapter 7). The first half of the book treats Franklin's life chronologically to 1730 (that is, to the end of Part One of the *Autobiography*). Thereafter Weems abandons strict chronology and falls back on the biographical strategy suggested in his subtitle; while some of the material is apocryphal, most of it is excerpted or given in its entirety from Franklin's own writings: sayings from *Poor Richard* (chapter 33) and anecdotes like "The Whistle" and Cotton Mather's admonition to "stoop! stoop!" (chapter 34). Some attention is given to Franklin's electrical experiments, but his political activities are scarcely mentioned and his years in France not at all. In "The Legend Maker" (*AH*, Feb. 1962) David Van Tassel speculates, "Perhaps the worldly side of Franklin was too much even for the Parson." The first important biography is James Parton's *Life and Times of Benjamin Franklin* (2 vols., New York, 1864). As the title makes clear, Parton is frequently concerned with the times of Franklin, but always in a way that is relevant; for example, there is a chapter on Old Philadelphia in the 1740s and one on electricity before Franklin. In the Revolutionary period the emphasis is heavily political and diplomatic. This is not a critical biography, though Parton unconsciously reflects the squeamishness of the age ("*Poor Richard*, at this day, would be reckoned an indecent production"). Relatively objective and by mid-nineteenth-century standards carefully researched, Parton's biography stands at the opposite end of the spectrum from Weems's.

Carl Becker's 1931 *DAB* life of Franklin — reprinted separately as *Benjamin Franklin: A Biographical Sketch by Carl L. Becker* (Ithaca, N.Y., 1946) — is precise and clear throughout its short length, striking a judicious balance between the public and the private man. Indicative of Becker's ability to catch the quintessence of his subject is the observation that Franklin "accepted the world as given with imperturbable serenity; without repining identified himself with it; and brought to the understanding and the mastery of it rare common sense, genuine disinterestedness, a fertile and imaginative curiosity, and a cool, flexible intelligence fortified by exact knowledge and chastened and humanized by practical activities." Even as he presented itemized corrections, Carl Van Doren wrote that Becker's sketch "enjoys and deserves a wide reputation as the best biography in the entire collection [DAB] and as the best short account of its subject in existence. Only a little over 10,000 words in length, it says more that is essential to Franklin than biographies ten times as long, and it leaves out literally nothing that is important to the understanding of that vast and versatile genius" (*WMQ*, Apr. 1947).

After almost half a century Carl Van Doren's own *Benjamin Franklin*

(New York, 1938) remains the most nearly definitive biography of its sub-ject. It is sensitive at all times to literary nuance; thus, the proverb bor-rowings in *Poor Richard* are examined and the statement, "letter-writing with him was a form of art," is confirmed throughout by Van Doren's discussion of (especially) private correspondence. Like Parton, but more skillfully and less obtrusively, Van Doren presents the times behind the life. In 1940 at the "Meet Dr. Franklin" conference, his "Concluding Paper" (*JFI*, Nov. 1942) announced: "I hope in 1945 to issue a revised edition of my book, half again as long as the first." Though his interest in Frank-lin continued until his death in 1950, Van Doren was not able to com-plete the revision. Many readers will agree with Clinton Rossiter that we need a fuller biography even than Van Doren's, "something with the sweep and detail of the Freeman *Washington*" (*Seedtime of the Repub-lic*, New York, 1953).

Verner Crane has written two slender but significant biographies. The first of these, *Benjamin Franklin, Englishman and American* (Baltimore, 1936), consists of three lectures entitled "The Education of Benjamin Franklin," "Franklin as a Social Philosopher," and "Franklin and the Brit-ish Empire." Franklin's life, writes Crane, has "a singular correspondence with many of the main elements of American experience in his century. . . . [He] touched in his career and in his various interests almost all of the dominant currents of American life and aspiration in his time. . . . To explore Franklin's world is largely to discover the America of the eigh-teenth century. It is to discover, also, of course, a larger world of Euro-pean philosophy and science from which, however, America was never absolutely cut off." Crane's *Benjamin Franklin and a Rising People* (Boston, 1954) displays a comprehensive grasp of the facts of Franklin's public life, achieving a balance between history and biography. Occa-sionally in the first half of the book Crane engages in just enough critical analysis to make it clear that he, too, is sensitive to literary values, as in his consideration of the *Dogood* papers, *Poor Richard*, and the early letters to the English press. Although this avowedly public biography in-creasingly emphasizes Franklin's political and diplomatic career, the finest chapter is that on Franklin as natural philosopher.

In *Benjamin Franklin: Philosopher and Man* (Philadelphia and New York, 1965) Alfred Owen Aldridge proposes "to reveal Franklin as a man first; as a universal genius second." More than Parton and Crane, more even than Van Doren, he focuses on what Plutarch called "actions of small note." The reader puts down this painstakingly researched and well-informed book with a fuller knowledge of Franklin's private life but with-out any clear sense of the "complete personality" for which Aldridge was striving; which is to say, the full-length portrait of Franklin is somewhat blurred. *The Private Franklin: The Man and His Family* (New York, 1975) by Claude-Anne Lopez and Eugenia W. Herbert is the most significant biography since Van Doren's. In contrast to biographers like Parton and Crane, who concentrate on Franklin's public life, he is here pictured in the midst of his several families: the large Boston family into which he was born, his own Philadelphia family, and the families into which he settled when away from home, notably that of his London landlady Margaret Stevenson and her daughter Polly (Hewson). Constructed almost exclusively from private journals and personal correspondence, the book presents a man who is intensely human, at once more callous and more magnanimous than the Franklin known to history. The most puzzling relationship, say the authors, is that with William Temple Franklin, the grandchild Franklin loved most blindly; Temple seemed to everybody but the grandfather a fop and a cicerone, not much more. Having disinherited his son William, Franklin sought to make this grandson his literary heir and executor by bequeathing him his library and manuscripts, never dreaming that Temple would sell the library and dawdle for almost thirty years before publishing "only a few thousand among the most interesting documents of the enormous collection of manuscripts." Here is a book whose two dozen short chapters deserve to be read with care and savored.

Special Studies

While Arthur Bernon Tourtellot's *Benjamin Franklin: The Shaping of Genius: The Boston Years* (Garden City, N.Y., 1977) adds little biographical information to what Franklin himself tells us about his Boston years (1706–23), through careful research this book adds substantially to our knowledge of the father Josiah Franklin, both in England and in America, and fleshes out the Boston world of Franklin's boyhood and young manhood. Of special interest to students of literature is the lengthy examination of the *New-England Courant* and the *Dogood* papers. Tourtellot concludes that "it was the Boston of the Mathers that had particularly molded the values and resistances of the young Franklin, as he sought to absorb all learning that he could reconcile with reason, increasingly doubted what he found uncongenial with it, and deepened his suspicions of the certainty of absolutes and the prudence of extremes." I find convincing John H. McLaughlin's argument in "His Brother's Keeper: Franklin's Sibling Rivalry" (*SAB*, Nov. 1973) that Franklin's early drive for wealth arose from his rivalry with his brother James, a rivalry that came to an end once he outdistanced James in their mutual profession, journalism. Granted that Franklin's "career as a writer was psychologically related to his earlier childhood goal of attaining a first rate education," I question McLaughlin's attributing Franklin's early drive for education to disappointment at not going to college; it would seem rather that the young Franklin sensed that, in the words of James Parton, "the Harvard of that day would have choked or expelled him."

Franklin's visits to Paris in 1767 and 1769 and his nine-year sojourn there (1776–85) have interested biographers far more than any other period of his life. Morris Bishop calls France Franklin's "spiritual home. [There] he found intellectual companionship and social satisfactions more appropriate and welcome to his character than anything he had known in America" ("Franklin in France," *Daedalus*, May 1957). Two members of his neighbor Mme Helvétius's household, Abbé André Morellet and Pierre-Jean-Georges Cabanis, left valuable recollections of Franklin, *Mémoires inédits de l'abbé Morellet* (Paris, 1822), vol. 1, chapters 9 and 15, and *Oeuvres complètes de Cabanis* (Paris, 1825), vol. 5, 219–74 — recollections which not only portray the patriarchal ambassador at Passy but also add to our knowledge of Franklin's boyhood in Boston. A nineteenth-century Frenchman, Antoine Guillois, pictures the salon world into which Franklin stepped so effortlessly during the years of his French ministry: *Le salon de Madame Helvétius* (Paris, 1894).

In *Franklin in France* (2 vols., Boston, 1887–88) E. E. Hale and E. E. Hale, Jr., undertake "to examine anew the whole mission of Franklin to France," making use of the manuscripts at the American Philosophical Society and the Library of Congress and "printing all the more important letters of Franklin not published heretofore, and also the most important unpublished letters of his correspondents, which would throw light on the history or on his life in France." This biography, conscientious and thorough for its day, has been largely superseded. Willis Steell's *Benjamin Franklin of Paris . . . 1776–1785* (New York, 1928), although somewhat fictionalized and therefore not always trustworthy, gives a vivid account of Franklin's relations with French women of his close acquaintance. Far superior to either of these studies is Claude-Anne Lopez's superbly illustrated *Mon Cher Papa: Franklin and the Ladies of Paris* (New Haven, Conn., 1966). Mrs. Lopez, the Yale editor who will supervise publication of the material relating to Franklin and France, focuses on the pleasure he "and the French men and women of his day found in each other's company." She paints a rich and refined picture of Franklin moving among his French friends, notably Mmes Brillon and Helvétius and Comtesse d'Houdetot. Taking exception to those who have called his written French "semi-wild" (Jusserand) and "fantaisiste" (Chinard), she maintains that "in almost every letter his unedited French had the redeeming flash of one perfect, graceful sentence."

Among shorter studies of Franklin and France two deserve special mention. J. J. Jusserand, in *Essays Offered to Herbert Putnam*, edited by W. W.

Bishop and A. Keogh (New Haven, Conn., 1929), has written a well-informed, succinct account of the years 1776 to 1785, emphasizing Franklin's diplomatic activities more than his private life. At the outset Jusserand observes, "The trend of thought in France, especially since the middle of the century, had been in favor of the very ideas dear to Franklin: simpler lives, nearer to nature, the restriction of privileges, the pursuit of happiness made accessible to all, toleration, freedom of thought." In "Franklin en France" (*FR*, Feb. 1956) Gilbert Chinard surveys "l'éducation française de Benjamin Franklin" from the time he began the study of French in 1733 until the eulogies on him in 1790–91.

Since Franklin throughout a seventy-year career conceived of himself first and always as a printer, it is not surprising that this vocation has attracted considerable attention. Lawrence C. Wroth's "Benjamin Franklin: The Printer at Work" (*JFI*, Aug. 1942) is the best-informed short essay on the subject. C. William Miller gives an account of "the means Franklin used to elbow his way to preeminence as a printer-publisher" beginning in 1728. "There was no printer in America who could rival him as a writer, few who insisted on cleaner presswork, and none in the Middle Colonies who could match the quality of his first text fonts." In less than a decade he became *the* printer in Philadelphia. "Franklin found many ways to make money as a printer, but one point seems clear: his way to wealth lay not in the publishing of memorable books" ("Benjamin Franklin's Way to Wealth," *PBSA*, Fourth Quarter 1969). Richard Cary, in "Benjamin Franklin, Printer-Plenipotentiary" (*Colby Library Quarterly*, Sept. 1965), traces Franklin's "professional progress as printer and publisher." "Fascinated by both the mechanical and graphic possibilities of printing," writes Cary, "Franklin early attained the skills of a master craftsman, adopted improvements to the press, experimented with inks, papermaking, engraving and stereotyping." Luther S. Livingston's *Franklin and His Press at Passy* (New York, 1941) examines in detail Franklin's experiments of this sort while in France. Julius Rodenberg shows how Franklin's printing activities interacted with his politics. Of the Passy years he writes, "Der Journalismus hatte ihn zur Politik geführt, jetzt verhalf ihm die Politik zu den feinsten und schönsten Blüten im Treibhaus seines Journalismus" (*GJ*, 1956). In "The Printer as a Man of Letters: Franklin and the Symbolism of the Third Realm" Lewis P. Simpson observes that the development of printing made clear as never before in Western civilization that in addition to the realms of Church and State there existed a Third Realm, the Republic of Letters. "Franklin's fundamental response to the Age of Printing was his discovery that it opened to the person of talent and ambition a self-education in letters and learning" which he displayed from the time of the *Dogood* papers onward. "Unifying the roles of printer and man of letters like no other figure in the eighteenth century, Franklin expressed the harmony and power — the hegemony — the Third Realm had achieved three centuries after the invention of printing" (*The Oldest Revolutionary: Essays on Benjamin Franklin*, edited by J. A. Leo Lemay [Philadelphia, 1976]).

Four other biographical studies should be mentioned at this point, the first two by J. Bennett Nolan. In *General Benjamin Franklin: The Military Career of a Philosopher* (Philadelphia, 1936) Nolan reconstructs Franklin's seven-week military career in eastern Pennsylvania (18 December 1755 to 5 February 1756), during which time he organized the Moravian settlements and built Fort Allen (or Gnadenhütten). Nolan's book is more trustworthy than the account Franklin gives in the *Autobiography*. *Benjamin Franklin in Scotland and Ireland, 1759 and 1771* (Philadelphia, 1938) is an absorbing day-by-day account of Franklin's visits to Scotland (1759, 1771) and Ireland (1771), "the houses wherein he dwelt, the streets through which he walked, the people with whom he mingled." *Ben Franklin Laughing: Anecdotes from Original Sources by and about Benjamin Franklin* (Berkeley, 1980), explains the editor P. M. Zall, is a collection of anecdotes, not meant to be exhaustive, which "derives from original sources — diaries, memoirs, newspapers, periodicals, scholarly biographies, and popular literature." The first part "includes sixty-six anecdotes from Franklin's correspondence and published writings," excluding such artful works as *Poor Richard*, satires, and bagatelles which are easily found elsewhere. The second part consists of "248 anecdotes from writings by others." The anecdotes are arranged by year in each of the two parts, and there is a concise note about the source of each anecdote. Finally there is C. C. Sellers's definitive *Benjamin Franklin in Portraiture* (New Haven, Conn., 1962). "My purpose in this study," he writes, "has been to define the appearance and character of Benjamin Franklin as revealed in portraiture. A secondary aim has been to show something of the historical role of the portraits themselves in spreading his fame and sustaining the philosophy, the policies, and the nation he represented. My interest has been both in the man and in the symbol." There are forty-four pages of black-and-white likenesses of Franklin, members of his family and friends, and the artists who executed them, preceded by "a general survey in nine chapters telling the story of the life portraits from young manhood to old age" and "a descriptive catalogue of them."

CRITICISM

General Estimates

In 1889 Paul Leicester Ford, in his *Franklin Bibliography*, stated that Franklin "never was a literary man in the true and common meaning of the term," a critical judgment that has been sounded again and again through the years. Paul Elmer More wrote, "There is a certain embarrassment in dealing with Franklin as a man of letters, for the simple reason that he was never, in the strict sense of the word, concerned with letters at all" (*Shelburne Essays*, Fourth Series, New York, 1906). And William C. Bruce added, "Franklin was not a conscious man of letters at all, and is not to be judged by such academic standards" (*Benjamin Franklin, Self-Revealed*, New York, 1917). Henry S. Canby, in *Classic Americans* (New York, 1931), represents the case more fairly: "as a writer from the beginning to the end [Franklin] was first of all a journalist. . . . Regarded as a man of letters — and in his capacity of prime journalist for the colonies, he must be so regarded — Franklin is, indeed, an excellent example of a phenomenon peculiarly American. In his social ideas he was ahead of his time, in his literary expression behind it." Critics who do not regard Franklin as a man of letters take too narrow a view of the prosaic and practical nature of his mind. Sainte-Beuve, for example, not comprehending the rhetorical strategy behind Franklin's famous letter of 26 January 1784 to his daughter, wrote, "He brings everything down to arithmetic and strict reality, assigning no part to human imagination" (*Portraits of the Eighteenth Century*, translated by K. P. Wormeley, New York, 1905). In *The Art of Living* (New York, 1960) F. L. Lucas cautions that "one should not exaggerate Franklin's lack of the imaginative. The kind of imagination that shows itself in whimsical humour, in graceful wit, in vivid apologue and illustration, was his to a high degree."

The underlying assumption of the present essay is that Franklin is an important American man of letters. Five important critical studies, none of which is comprehensive, proceed on this assumption. The earliest by many years is the historian John Bach McMaster's *Benjamin Franklin as a Man of Letters* (Boston, 1887; rpt. of 1893 ed., New York, 1980). Even allowing for faulty knowledge about the Franklin canon in 1887, McMaster's discussion of the writings is disturbingly uneven. The American newspaper essays and pamphlets, Prefaces to *Poor Richard*, English bagatelles, and *Autobiography* (chiefly a review of the history of its composition and publication) are stressed more than the letters to the press, personal letters, and French bagatelles. McMaster's conclusion, though, is sound: "[Franklin] could do so many things that to do one thing long was impossible. A pamphlet that could be written in the heat of the moment; a little essay or a bagatelle that could be finished at one sitting, and trimmed and polished at a couple more, was about all he had the patience and the industry to accomplish. He finished nothing. . . . Except the Bagatelles, which he wrote in his old age for the amusement of his friends, he produced little which did not serve an immediate and practical purpose, and which was not expressed in the plainest and clearest English."

Theodore Hornberger's *Benjamin Franklin* (UMPAW, Minneapolis, 1962) achieves comprehensiveness and depth in brief compass, treating in some detail *The Nature and Necessity of a Paper-Currency*, *Poor Richard*, *Experiments and Observations on Electricity*, *Plain Truth*, three letters to the press ("Edict," "Rules," "Sale"), and the *Autobiography*. The personal and familiar letters and the bagatelles, however, are scarcely mentioned. Hornberger's essay supports his observation that Franklin "was not as uncomplicated a man as he thought he was, nor was his literary style as simple as he believed it to be."

Richard E. Amacher's *Benjamin Franklin* (TUSAS, New York, 1962) is a very uneven book. The central chapters are loosely generic, in the sense that they deal with the *Autobiography*, *Poor Richard*, political journalism, essays, letters, scientific papers, and religious and philosophical tracts. The analysis of the *Autobiography* is largely derivative; and the argument that the work possesses organic unity is not convincing—after all, it is unfinished. Since editing *Franklin's Wit and Folly* Amacher has revised his conception of the term bagatelle to include works other than those printed on the press at Passy, and he is secure in his discussion of them. He says of Franklin's personal correspondence, "Had he written nothing else, this alone would give him claim to a high literary reputation," but the discussion that follows is disappointingly thin. The chapter on political journalism, by far the longest in the book, is steadily rewarding. Here one encounters original observations ("Certainly his twenty-five years of carefully disciplined writing and rewriting in connection with *Poor Richard* did much to weed all irrelevancies from his style") and an examination of such letters to the press as "Rules" and "On the Slave Trade." In extenuation but not in defense of the heavy reliance on secondary sources throughout this book, it should be said that Amacher seems to have wished to familiarize the uninitiated reader with Franklin scholarship.

In *Benjamin Franklin: An American Man of Letters* (Ithaca, N.Y., 1964; rpt. Norman, Okla., 1976) Bruce Granger contends that critics like P. L. Ford who do not regard Franklin as a literary man are "guilty of applying the wrong yardstick, of measuring Franklin the writer against a definition of literature that does not accord with what we now know about colonial culture." This critical study seeks to demonstrate how Franklin, guided by a neoclassic concern for propriety, purity, perspicuity, elegance, and cadence, achieved distinctiveness and vitality through a wide range of nonfiction prose genres: periodical essay, almanac, letter to the press (or editorial), personal letter, familiar letter, bagatelle, and autobiography. The personal letter, "addressed to a single individual with no thought to publication," is to be distinguished from the familiar letter, "wherein the author poses, self-consciously revealing a side of himself, and in effect reaches beyond his audience of one to a larger public." Scientific and official papers except as they are treated incidentally have been excluded from this study.

In "Benjamin Franklin" (*Major Writers of Early American Literature*, edited by Everett Emerson [Madison, Wis., 1972]) J. A. Leo Lemay examines the *Dogood* papers, *Poor Richard's Almanack* ("The Way to Wealth" in detail), personal (as distinct from familiar) letters, letters to the press ("An Edict by the King of Prussia" in detail), bagatelles ("The Ephemera" in detail), and the *Autobiography*, filtering in much new information. In my opinion the most valuable section of this steadily perceptive and quite comprehensive essay is the wide-ranging discussion of Franklin's personal letters which concludes, "No other letter-writer had so many tones and moods; practically no other letter-writer had such a voluminous international correspondence, with such a wide variety of individuals of such disparate interests and personalities; and no other letter-writer of the times took part in so many historic events in America and Europe."

Special Studies by Genre

Until the appearance of Martin Christadler's *Der amerikanische Essay: 1720–1820* (Heidelberg, 1968) there had been only one extensive study of the periodical essay in America, and that an unpublished dissertation by Ernest Claude Coleman, "The Influence of the Addisonian Essay in America Before 1810" (Illinois, 1936). Christadler discusses the *Dogood* and *Busy-Body* papers out of a wide familiarity with the Anglo-American essay and essay serial; especially illuminating is his analysis of the persona and the angle of vision Franklin adopts in the *Dogood* serial. *The New-England Courant. A Selection of Certain Issues Containing Writings of Benjamin Franklin or Published by Him During His Brother's Imprisonment*, edited by Perry Miller (Boston, 1956), reproduces in facsimile some fifty issues of the *Courant* between No. 1 (7 August 1722) and No. 113 (23 September 1723), thereby providing a context in which to view and evaluate the *Dogood* papers. George F. Horner, a longtime student of humor in colonial America, argues convincingly, in "Franklin's Dogood Papers Re-examined" (*SP*, July 1940), that in spite of resemblances in method, purpose, and matter, the *Dogood* papers are not merely imitative of the *Spectator*; "they show peculiar and immediate pertinence to the Boston of 1722 and exhibit significant departures from the *Spectator* convention, in style, point of view, and character-mask of the putative author." Moreover, there is "manifest a lowering of style to the level of literacy of the poorer class." Horner says finally of these earliest extant writings of Franklin: "The style, the point of view, and the character-mask developing in them are to be his henceforth. These, it is now seen, are largely the product of practical necessity and shrewd opportunism rather than slavish imitation." In "Franklin's Apprenticeship and the Spectator" (*NEQ*, Sept. 1979) Albert Furtwangler maintains that during his apprenticeship as a writer for the *Courant*, especially as author of the *Dogood* papers, Franklin witnessed "a struggle between the Puritan will of Cotton Mather and a modern form of wit inspired by Joseph Addison," writers who were counterpoised in his learning. Bruce Granger examines the *Busy-Body* papers in detail. Franklin, whose heart it would seem "was not in this enterprise, as it had so clearly been in the *Dogood* papers," wrote only the first four essays and parts of the fifth and eighth, letting Joseph Breitnall, who "was responsible for the liveliest as well as the dullest essays," carry on the series alone to a total of thirty-two. Franklin's *Busy-Body* essays "imitate the manner and matter of Addison more nearly than anything he ever wrote; it was perhaps his awareness of this fact that led him to abandon his part in the undertaking as quickly as he did" (*American Essay Serials from Franklin to Irving* [Knoxville, Tenn., 1978]).

In "The Character of Poor Richard: Its Source and Alteration" (*PMLA*, Sept. 1940) John F. Ross maintains that "it has not been recognized (1) how extensively Franklin was indebted to Jonathan Swift in his hoaxing of Titan Leeds, the rival almanac-maker; (2) that the source for the characters Richard and Bridget Saunders was almost certainly Swift's Bickerstaff papers [specifically the Partridges]; and (3) that there are *two* Poor Richards — the original comic philomath of 1733 and the final American archetype, the fountain-head of shrewd prudential wisdom." My only quarrel with this steadily perceptive article is Ross's contention that "Franklin forced Richard to play a rôle"; it seems rather that insofar as the conception of Richard underwent a change between 1733 and 1758, it happened unconsciously. Cameron C. Nickels, "Franklin's Poor Richard's Almanacs: 'The Humblest of his Labors,'" in *The Oldest Revolutionary*, demonstrates that "Franklin clearly separated himself from the character he created," a distinction most obvious in the almanacs written in the 1730s, by focusing on not only the delineation of Poor Richard and his wife Bridget in the prefaces, proverbs, and poetry, but also on his astrological prognostications. "Artfully conceived and rendered," writes Nickels, "Poor Richard is a complex, round character that changes over twenty-six years from a rather indolent but affable stargazer to a pompously didactic almanac maker who likes to see himself as an eminent author." Harold A. Larrabee, "Poor Richard in an Age of Plenty," in a statement that is essential to a sensitive reading of *Poor Richard's Almanack*, especially the 1758 Preface (known familiarly as "The Way to Wealth"), says of Franklin: "His moral teaching — like that of John Dewey, now so much under attack — was a dynamic doctrine of 'open ends' rather

than of fixed moral absolutes forcing all individuals into a single mold"
(*HM*, Jan. 1956). In "The Rhetorical Strategy of Franklin's 'Way to
Wealth'" (*ECS*, Summer 1973) Edward J. Gallagher argues that from a
rhetorical standpoint the framing introduction and conclusion, especially
the conclusion, are "the most important part of the essay"; when Poor
Richard reacts to Father Abraham's harangue by denying himself material
for a new coat he had gone to the auction to buy and concludes, "*Reader,
if thou wilt do the same, thy Profit will be as great as mine,*" "the reader
responds humorously to the climactic ironies."

Robert Howard Newcomb's dissertation, "The Sources of Benjamin
Franklin's Sayings of Poor Richard" (Maryland, 1957), treats its subject
definitively, superseding the work of earlier scholars like Stuart A. Gal-
lacher (*JEGP*, Apr. 1949); parts of Newcomb's dissertation have been published. Newcomb demonstrates that Franklin borrowed heavily from
Halifax (*PMLA*, June 1955), Montaigne (*MLN*, Nov. 1957), Richardson
(*JEGP*, Jan. 1958), two English miscellanies, *Wits Recreation* and *A Collection of Epigrams* (*PQ*, Apr. 1961), and proverb collections by Thomas
Fuller, George Herbert, and James Howell. Charles W. Meister, writing
earlier than Newcomb (*AL*, May 1952) and not so fully aware of the
sources, calls Franklin a proverb stylist. He demonstrates that in his proverb borrowings Franklin employed balance (often with alliteration), metaphor or other figures of speech (notably personification), and anticlimax;
"his art was to let his sure ear select the best form of a competing lot,
polish that form through pruning, adding, or supplying a lively metaphor, and then find a strategic use for the particular proverb's message."
Frances M. Barbour's *Concordance to the Sayings in Franklin's 'Poor
Richard'* (Detroit, 1974) covers the *Almanack* during the years of Franklin's direct association with it (1733–58); it is arranged alphabetically
"under key words to the sayings," these words being cross-referenced.

Verner Crane's introduction to *Benjamin Franklin's Letters to the Press*
is reading essential to an understanding of this popular eighteenth-century
genre and Franklin's handling of it. Essential also is Crane's examination
of the dominion view of empire Franklin held from 1766 to 1774. In "Dr.
Franklin's Plan for America" (*Michigan Alumnus Quarterly Review*, Summer 1958) Crane writes, "From experience, from observation of American society, from his reading of the history of English colonization, sooner
than others [Franklin] arrived at the equalitarian principle of empire
which [American patriots] all embraced on the eve of the final crisis."
There have been relatively few studies of individual letters to the press.
Paul Baender, in "The Basis of Franklin's Duplicative Satires" (*AL*, Nov.
1960), explores a duplicative pattern in three of them ("Felons," "Edict,"
"Slave Trade") and concludes: "In these three satires Franklin retraced

the process of perception. From actual events—the transportation of felons, a tyrannical colonial policy, and pro-slavery speeches—he proceeded to analogues, as one naturally did to make experience intelligible. At the same time he put himself as well as his readers through a test of character. For his perceptions had to contain more than private values to be virtuous; they had to imply the goodness of fostering the general welfare and the viciousness of egoism. Not that Franklin needed to reassure himself; on the contrary, in returning to fundamental perceptions he was calling upon all his strength and defying his opponents to match it. They may have refused the challenge, but he was not mistaken in putting it to them." In "Benjamin Franklin" Mary E. Rucker focuses on two famous letters to the English and two to the French press ("Rules," "Edict," "Sale," "Supplement"). Of particular interest is her suggestion that the final paragraph of the "Edict" weakens the force of the irony that has been sustained up to this point: "Not content to let his satire operate dramatically, Franklin there portrays the erstwhile naive correspondent as appalled by Frederick's stating that his regulations are based upon those by which England has governed Ireland and America. To be appalled is obviously to be aware of the gross injustices, and the correspondent directly and passionately judges British ministerial policy" (*American Literature, 1764–1789: The Revolutionary Years*, edited by Everett Emerson [Madison, Wis., 1977]). George Simson illustrates how "An Edict by the King of Prussia" follows closely the form of British parliamentary statutes and thus discloses Franklin's rhetorical strategy in this famous letter to the English press (*AL*, May 1960). In *Political Satire in the American Revolution* (Ithaca, N.Y., 1960) Bruce Granger suggests that like Swift in *A Tale of a Tub*, in "The Sale of the Hessians" Franklin "devises a situational mask the better to objectify and give bite to the satire." And Walter Blair, "Franklin's Massacre of the Hessians," in *Towards a New American Literary History: Essays in Honor of Arlin Turner*, edited by Louis J. Budd, Edwin H. Cady, and Carl L. Anderson (Durham, N.C., 1980), says that Franklin, deliberately distorting what is known about the Battle of Trenton, multiplied the Hessian casualties and minimized the number not harmed and thereby "enlarged the villainy of the count who was responsible and who not only profited from disasters but gloated over them"; moreover, he sees to it that the count's "mathematics are cockeyed" in that the treaty signed in Hesse-Cassel on 15 January 1776 and applicable to the men stationed at Trenton contained no blood-money clause.

Franklin's bagatelles, taken as a generic entity, have not received sufficient critical attention. Richard Amacher, in the introduction to *Franklin's Wit and Folly* and in his discussion of "Dialogue between Franklin and the Gout," "The Whistle," and "Letter to the Royal Academy," provides incisive, if at times too ingenious, commentary on the French bagatelles. Mrs. Lopez's analysis in *Mon Cher Papa* of "The Elysian Fields" is brilliant. Dorothy Medlin, in "Benjamin Franklin's Bagatelles for Madame Helvétius: Some Biographical and Stylistic Considerations" (*EAL*, Spring 1980), argues in a scholarly and convincing fashion that the two bagatelles, "The Elysian Fields" and "The Flies," and "other epistles from Franklin to Madame Helvétius can be read as sprightly, personable jeux d'esprit written with affectionate camaraderie" for her. Maintaining that "the less inhibited form of the bagatelle" offers us the possibility "of getting closer to a genuine revelation of Franklin's personality" than such works as *Poor Richard* and the *Autobiography*, Harriet Rose advances the questionable Freudian argument that in "To the Royal Society" Franklin "identifies the pleasure resulting from the freedom from anal inhibitions with erotic satisfaction, and the more acceptable forms of self-indulgence such as eating, drinking, and using perfume" ("Towards the Pleasure Principle: Character Revelation in Franklin's *To the Royal Academy*," *Paunch*, Feb. 1972). A. O. Aldridge describes Franklin's essay on daylight saving (usually known as "An Economical Project") in the *Journal de Paris*, 26 April 1784, as "a gentle parody [of] articles of practical usefulness and household hints" such as the *Journal* published. "The mild satire of this combined literary parody and moral parable resembles Swift's writings in a mellow mood. It is the type of irony Swift might have written in place of *A Modest Proposal* if he had spent five years in the company of Mmes Helvétius and Brillon" (*AL*, Mar. 1956). There have been a few source studies. Aldridge has demonstrated that "The Ephemera" is based on an essay in the *Pennsylvania Gazette*, 21 October 1731, wherein the antediluvian Pulgah warns his daughter Shual of the brevity of life; not, as is usually cited, the essay in the *Pennsylvania Gazette*, 11 December 1735, on the venerable insect vainglorious of his great age (*NEQ*, Sept. 1954). And A. S. Pitt suggests that Franklin may have derived the theory of the great chain of being, restated in the final paragraph of "An Arabian Tale," from one or more of the following acknowledged sources: Locke's *Essay Concerning Human Understanding* (3, vi, 12), *Spectator* no. 519, Pope, Thomson, Young, Buffon's *Histoire Naturelle*, or Milton's *Paradise Lost*, 5, 153–204 (*PMLA*, Mar. 1942).

Max Hall, having traced in *Benjamin Franklin and Polly Baker* (Chapel Hill, N.C., 1960) the publication history of "The Speech of Miss Polly Baker," concludes that the earliest known text of this bagatelle is that printed in the London *General Advertiser*, 15 April 1747, and that the first known American printing was in the *Boston Weekly Post-Boy*, 20 July 1747. Some years later Hall told the personal story of his research for this book on "the Franklin hoax that reached the largest audience of all" ("An Amateur Detective on the Trail of B. Franklin, Hoaxer," *PMHS*, 1972). J. A. Leo Lemay, in *Men of Letters in Colonial Maryland* (Knoxville, Tenn., 1972), says that Jonas Green printed what he called "a correct Copy" of Polly Baker's Speech in the *Maryland Gazette* of 11 August 1747, one having "a different textual authority (which was, according to Green, better)" than that in the *General Advertiser*. Later Lemay, conceding "that the external evidence concerning the authenticity of Green's version of the Speech of Polly Baker, while strong, is not conclusive," argues persuasively that Franklin wrote the *Maryland Gazette* text and that it "is stylistically superior to and more dramatic than the *General Advertiser* text" in at least twenty of the thirty-three instances in which the two texts differ substantively; unique to this American text is a passage "on the murder of bastard infants," which echoes Swift's *Modest Proposal* ("The Text, Rhetorical Strategies, and Themes of 'The Speech of Miss Polly Baker'" in *The Oldest Revolutionary*).

Far more than any other of Franklin's writings the *Autobiography* has increasingly engaged the attention of scholars. James M. Cox observes that before the emergence of the term "autobiography" early in the nineteenth century, "there were two categories of people's lives written by themselves: the confession and the memoir [Franklin's name for his *Autobiography*]. The confession was an account of a man's private life, centering on his emotions, feelings, secrets, frustrations — essentially his private world. The memoir was more on the order of chronicle, relating the individual's role upon the stage of history. The confession bared the inner thoughts; the memoir recounted the career." Franklin "sees his act of writing as the next best thing to living his life over again and he thus sees his memoir not as a record but as a second edition in which the sins of his life (which would have enormous emotional weight in the confessional form) become the mere errata of the first edition which he can point to and playfully wish to remove" ("Autobiography and America," *VQR*, Spring 1971). Robert Bell, focusing on the models of the confession provided by Augustine and Bunyan, seems not to recognize that Franklin was writing in the very different tradition of the memoir which he unwittingly characterizes when he says that Franklin fails "to convey much sense of inner life and development beneath a multitude of disparate roles and guises, and an apparent disregard for a coherent organizing principle beyond what happened next. The story is episodic, resembling a picaresque novel. . . . Events are not linked by any transcendent Augustinian unity, nor because Franklin has forged any metaphoric connections, but because they occurred, one after another" ("Metamorphoses of Spiritual Autobiography," *ELH*, Spring 1977).

There is sharp disagreement about how organic a work the *Autobiography* is. In "Form and Substance in Franklin's Autobiography" Aldridge writes: "In form Franklin's work is a virtual disaster. . . . His expository method strongly resembles that of the picaresque novel — a rambling series of events joined together by a single protagonist, but with no unity of theme or purpose except for the announced motif of chronicling the author's rise from poverty to affluence. . . . The greatest and most enduring literary value of Franklin's memoirs is psychological rather than artistic — the delight and satisfaction in fulfilling and recording a life of superior achievement" (*Essays on American Literature in Honor of Jay B. Hubbell*, edited by Clarence Gohdes [Durham, N.C., 1967]). Hugh J. Dawson goes so far as to say that Franklin gives thematic unity to Parts One and Two by means of the letters from Abel James and Benjamin Vaughan inserted between these parts, which serve "as a pivot on which he could turn back to join personal history and conduct book in the morally instructive lesson of a young man's rise in the world" ("Franklin's 'Memoirs' in 1784: The Design of the *Autobiography*," *EAL*, Winter 1977/ 78). Elsewhere Dawson indicates that what helps determine the thematic unity of Parts One and Two is the complex and troubling father-presences. He concludes, "Although Franklin's relations with his father were often conflicted, he knew Josiah's personality and example to have been enabling rather than destructive" ("Fathers and Sons: Franklin's 'Memoirs' as Myth and Metaphor," *EAL*, Winter 1979/80). Charles L. Sanford, going too far, calls the *Autobiography* "a great moral fable pursuing on a secular level the theme of John Bunyan's *Pilgrim's Progress*. . . . a work of imagination which, by incorporating the 'race' consciousness of a people, achieves the level of folk myth" ("An American *Pilgrim's Progress*," *AQ*, Winter 1954) — a reading which seems to assume that the *Autobiography* is a finished work, not the long fragment we know it to be. Daniel Shea's view, in *Spiritual Autobiography in Early America* (Princeton, N.J., 1968), is more convincing than Sanford's: "Neither a spiritual autobiography in the tradition of the Puritans and Quakers nor an American achievement in its formal characteristics, Franklin's *Autobiography* yet achieves a distinctly American mixture of naive perfectionism and skeptical empiricism, assuring its reader through autobiographical example that the world has yielded repeatedly to the onslaught of method, while reserving irony as a defense against hoping too much."

Point of view in the *Autobiography*, which is inseparable from form, has interested many scholars. "Surely it must strike any reader of the *Autobiography* as curious," writes John Ward in "Who Was Benjamin Franklin?" (*ASch*, Autumn 1963), "that a character who speaks so openly should at the same time seem so difficult to define." In the *Autobiography*, says

Farrand, Franklin "was not in the least morbidly introspective; if any-thing, he was whimsically amused" ("Self-Portraiture: The Autobiogra-phy," *JFI*, Jan. 1942). David Levin observes that "most of us overlook the crucial distinction, especially in the first half of Franklin's autobiogra-phy, between the *writer* of the book and the chief *character* he portrays. . . . Though the honest autobiographer refuses to invent fictitious inci-dents, he *actually creates himself as a character*" (*YR*, Winter 1964). Robert F. Sayre amplifies this observation, arguing that though the *Auto-biography* as a whole is formless, Franklin's several poses give form to each of the first three parts (Part Four being too short to consider): "The first section of the *Autobiography* is the story of Franklin's building of his roles — sampling sundry occupations, hoaxes, disguises, and literary masks — and of fitting himself out in the 'plain dress' of his first and most lasting public character, flexible and adaptable as it was always to be for him, 'Benjamin Franklin of Philadelphia, Printer.' . . . the two later parts have one important thing in common: both are accounts of proj-ects. . . . the 'Project of arriving at moral Perfection' is his French one of the *naïf* 'Philosophical Quaker.' . . . The disarming quality of the at-tempt to reach moral perfection was the logic of it. . . . Franklin's iden-tity in the third part of the *Autobiography* as patriot and civic projector gives it the form of a series of lessons in 'doing good.' . . . Of all parts of the *Autobiography*, this one is most like a memoir and of most value to the descendants of early American democracy" (*The Examined Self: Benjamin Franklin, Henry Adams, Henry James* [Princeton, N.J., 1964]). Building largely on Sayre's analysis, Morton L. Ross believes that the struc-ture of the *Autobiography* depends upon a calculated opposition between self-advertisement in the first two parts and self-effacement in the last two: "It is this movement from self-advertisement to self-effacement which works to balance the halves of Franklin's ethical program" ("Form and Moral Balance in Franklin's *Autobiography*," *Ariel: A Review of Inter-national English Literature*, July 1976).

Focusing on the rhetorical nature of the book, more especially the use of the persona, John Griffith observes: "The speaker whose voice relates the events of the *Autobiography* plays a kind of dramatic part in the book. He is the end product of the events he describes, the completed, arrived Dr. Franklin, and as such is one of the work's two main characters; the other is the young, unformed Franklin, the essentially mute figure ac-tively engaged in the hectic experiences about which this mature, speak-ing Franklin takes time to reason and speculate." Unlike the memoirs of such younger contemporaries as Colonel John Trumbull, John Adams, Benjamin Rush, and Jonathan Boucher, "the relationship between young and old Franklin . . . is pictured as a discontinuous series of comparisons and contrasts between the speaker and the young man he once was" ("The Rhetoric of Franklin's 'Autobiography,'" *Criticism*, Winter 1971). In "Benjamin Franklin and the Choice of a Single Point of View" John F. Lynen sees the *Autobiography* as controlled by an omniscient authorial consciousness and, drawing essentially the same distinction as Griffith, says of the relationship between author and actor, "the fundamental contrast, so far as the book's form is concerned, is not between the various past selves but between the man who looks back on the past and the man who lived it" (*The American Puritan Imagination: Essays in Revaluation*, edited by Sacvan Bercovitch [Cambridge, England, 1974]). Viewing the persona in the *Autobiography* somewhat differently than Griffith and Lynen, Roger J. Porter contends that like all autobiographers Franklin creates an order in his book that was absent in the life. His project of arriving at moral perfection "may stand for an entire conception of self in the *Autobiography*, in the sense that, fearful of venturing too far into the realm of introspection, he here "wishes to give us the impression that a rational life can be constructed at will." "Everywhere the matter-of-fact tone belies any inner struggle he must have confronted in his choice of behavior," making the book "the performance of a skilled and splendid con-man." Franklin "knows that the self as a concept is something that can be created as much in the writing as in the long process of living" ("Unspeakable Practices, Writable Acts: Franklin's *Autobiography*," *The Hudson Review*, Summer 1979).

In perhaps the best of the few stylistic studies Hans Galinsky, having examined closely the first four paragraphs of the *Autobiography*, points to Franklin's partiality for participial and substantive (rather than verbal) constructions and, more broadly, to three classical qualities that characterize his prose: "fast symmetrische Gliederung weiter Satzräume, Gleichgewicht in der Form des syntaktischen Gleichlaufs, Bevorzugung des Statischen vor dem Dynamischen" (*NS*, May 1957). P. M. Zall, "A Portrait of the Autobiographer as an Old Artificer," in *The Oldest Revolutionary*, demonstrates how an examination of the stylistic and substantive revisions, in particular the interpolations, in the holograph manuscript tells "us much about the way in which Franklin shaped the plot, characters, and theme of Part One."

There have been so many thematic studies of the *Autobiography* that only some of the most noteworthy will be considered. D. H. Lawrence's well-known chapter on Franklin in his *Studies in Classic American Literature* (New York, 1923) centers its attack on the art of virtue, set forth in Part Two of the *Autobiography*. "Why the soul of man is a vast forest, and all Benjamin intended was a neat back garden," he exclaims. "Think of Benjamin fencing it off! . . . He made himself a list of virtues, which he trotted inside like a grey nag in a paddock." Lawrence concludes: "And now I, at least, know why I can't stand Benjamin. He tries to take away my wholeness and my dark forest, my freedom. For how can any man be free, without an illimitable background? . . . Either we are materialistic instruments, like Benjamin or we move in the gesture of creation, from our deepest self, usually unconscious." With critics like Lawrence, he who is not with me must perforce be against me. Jesse Bier calls the *Autobiography* "the most significant book in American literature," in the sense that "it signals almost all of the chief thematic interests of the subsequent course of American letters. . . . the interest of the individual and of society, the claims of democracy and of aristocracy, the relation of Appearance and Reality, and the values of Romantic Idealism and Pragmatic Realism" (*WHR*, Winter 1958). According to Franz H. Link the *Autobiography*, "ein klassisches Dokument der Aufklärung in ihrer amerikanischen Prägung," illustrates that industry, frugality, and doing good are the means to felicity, affluence, and reputation (*DVLG*, 1961). In the view of Ralph L. Ketcham, the *Autobiography*, more than any other work, answered Crèvecoeur's famous question, "What then is the American, this new man?" and "thus helped to further define the revolutionary elements in the national character. . . . It has been as well a persistent reminder, whenever American society tends to stratify and stagnate and vulgarize, of what is being lost or betrayed" ("Benjamin Franklin: *Autobiography*," in *Landmarks of American Writing*, edited by Hennig Cohen [New York, 1969]). It is Lemay's belief that what makes the *Autobiography* so popular and a classic of American literature is "its definitive formulation of the American Dream," five aspects of which he considers in detail: the rise from rags to riches, the movement from impotence to importance, belief in individualism, belief in free will, and a philosophy of hope ("Benjamin Franklin, Universal Genius," in *The Renaissance Man in the Eighteenth Century* [Los Angeles, 1978]).

Julian Smith argues, in "Coming of Age in America: Young Ben Franklin and Robin Molineux" (*AQ*, Fall 1965), that in writing "My Kinsman, Major Molineux" Hawthorne was probably influenced by the *Autobiography*, "especially by the twenty or so pages dealing with the period between Franklin's arrival in Philadelphia at the age of seventeen and his ill-advised voyage to England thirteen months later." Young Franklin and Robin, who "are in some way confronted with the problem of finding a place in the world, . . . desire to be exalted over their peers, and in this desire, contrary to the democratic ideals of the new country, they seek to link their fates and careers to royal officials; both are humiliated by the sudden revelation that their hopes in these officials were ill-founded; and both out of their humiliation, learn the lesson of self-reliance." Agreeing that "Hawthorne has employed several echoes of Franklin's *Autobiography*," A. B. England points out that the similarities which Smith notes "are accompanied by suggestive differences" from the time Franklin and Robin decide "to travel to their new environments," with the result that Hawthorne creates a different kind of story from Franklin's (*JAmS*, Aug. 1972).

Other Special Studies

Stuart P. Sherman's characterization in *CHAL* of Franklin's style remains one of the most comprehensive and acute ever made: "It is the flexible style of a writer who has learned the craft of expression by studying and imitating the virtues of many masters: . . . His mature manner, however, is imitative of nothing but the thoroughly disciplined movement of a versatile mind which has never known a moment of languor or a moment of uncontrollable excitement. . . . the writing of his later years is marked not merely by clearness and force but also by the sovereign ease of a man who has long understood the interrelations of his ideas and has ceased to make revolutionary discoveries in any portion of his own nature. . . . He is seldom too hurried, even in a private letter, to gratify the ear by the turning and cadence of sentence and phrase; and one feels that the harmony of his periods is the right and predestined vesture of his essential blandness and suavity of temper. His stylistic drapery, however, is never so smoothed and adjusted as to obscure the sinewy vigour of his thought. His manner is steadily in the service of his matter." In contrast to Sherman's assessment stands that of Charles Angoff: "To call Franklin 'one of the greatest masters of English expression' [Faÿ] is the veriest nonsense. Almost any one of the Eighteenth Century New England theologians wrote better. Franklin, to be sure, was easier to understand, but there was far less in him worth understanding. His influence on the national letters, in the long run, was probably nil" (*A Literary History of the American People*, 2 vols. [New York, 1931]).

In *Franklin's Vocabulary* (Garden City, N.Y., 1928) Lois M. MacLaurin discovers that of approximately 4,060 words Franklin used in the period 1722 to 1751 only 19 are pure Americanisms. From this, she concludes: "(1) That Franklin consciously avoided any use of 'colloquialisms' or 'Americanisms,' and that his later works show an increasing tendency in this direction. (2) That the spoken language in America must have been very closely related to the written language in England, since otherwise Franklin's vocabulary would surely have contained a larger percentage of variations, which, owing to their familiarity, would have escaped his notice when writing. Even his private letters contain practically no new words."

In *America's Coming of Age* (New York, 1915) Van Wyck Brooks claims to have discovered the basic tension in American literature, a discovery some find profoundly true and others too facile: "Not until the eighteenth century did the rift appear and with it the essential distinction between 'Highbrow' and 'Lowbrow.' It appeared in the two philosophers, Jonathan Edwards and Benjamin Franklin, who share the eighteenth century between them. . . . Were ever two views of life more incompatible than these? What indeed could Poor Richard have in common with an Angry God?" Out of this antithesis, according to Brooks, there emerged a middlebrow synthesis: ". . . it would be hard to say whether Emerson more keenly relished saintliness or shrewdness. . . . He perfectly combined the temperaments of Jonathan Edwards and Benjamin Franklin; — the upper and lower levels of the American mind are fused in him and each becomes the sanction of the other."

A. O. Aldridge's *Benjamin Franklin and Nature's God* (Durham, N.C., 1967) is the most important study to date of Franklin's religious credo, which except for *A Dissertation on Liberty and Necessity* (1725) Aldridge finds steadily deistic, akin to "the benevolent philosophy of Shaftesbury and the English latitudinarian divines." The later chapters on Franklin's ecclesiastical associations, however, seem peripheral to the book's stated purpose, which is to concentrate on "the metaphysical and theological problems which he formulated and discussed as such in his own writings." It is Melvin H. Buxbaum's thesis, in *Franklin and the Zealous Presbyterians* (University Park, Pa. and London, 1975), that for nearly half a century, from the time of the *Dogood* papers (1722) until his *Narrative of the Late Massacres* (1764), "Franklin's animosity toward Presbyterians [and Congregationalists], and theirs toward him, continued," and that when in the Revolutionary period a reconciliation took place it was so complete that there is nothing in the *Autobiography* or his other late writings to suggest that such an animosity had ever existed. To be sure, pushing such a thesis involves blinking at a good many historical facts, but Robert Arner goes too far when he concludes that "Buxbaum has tailored all the evidence to make his own special kind of coat, a coat so strangely cut that only he could be comfortable wearing it" (*AmLS, 1975*).

James A. Sappenfield's *A Sweet Instruction: Franklin's Journalism as a Literary Apprenticeship* (Carbondale and Edwardsville, Ill., 1973) is a frequently insightful survey of Franklin's writings in Boston and Philadelphia. I have a quarrel, though, with its thesis: that Franklin served a thirty-five-year apprenticeship as journalist (1722–57) against the time when he became an autobiographer. Granted that the ironic masks and other rhetorical devices he mastered while a young journalist are effectively employed in the *Autobiography*, are not the more than one hundred letters he addressed to the English press between 1758 and 1775 the true culmination of this literary apprenticeship? This uneven book, whose weakest chapter is on the *Dogood* papers and its strongest on *Poor Richard*, scores many more hits than misses. Stanley Brodwin, surveying Franklin's seventy-year literary career, contends that he "created a comic body of work that sprang from a constant dialectic between 'challenge' and 'response' or 'freedom' and 'constraint' in a revolutionary social context, as well as from the necessity to resolve the conflict between the claims of 'virtue' and the force of 'passion' or instinct within himself." Franklin discovered in *Poor Richard*, for example, "a perfect vehicle that, through satire and humor, would help him to find—however tentatively—that inner unity and, at the same time, would enable him to rise in and shape the outer world" ("Strategies of Humor: The Case of Benjamin Franklin," *Prospects: An Annual Journal of American Cultural Studies*, 1979).

Reputation and Influence

Franklin's international reputation and influence originated in the correspondence, official, scientific, and social, he carried on with men of two continents over a period of sixty-five years; these documents are now scattered in repositories extending from Honolulu on the west to Leningrad and Moscow on the east. As with many another American writer, acceptance at home came later and more slowly than it did abroad. At the time of his death many Americans agreed with the Federalist critic Joseph Dennie that Franklin was "the founder of that Grubstreet sect, who have professedly attempted to degrade literature to the level of vulgar capacities, and debase the polished and current language of books, by the vile alloy of provincial idioms, and colloquial barbarism, the shame of grammar, and akin to any language, rather than English" (*The Port Folio*, 14 February 1801). More persistent than Dennie in his attempts to blacken the name of Franklin at home was John Adams. In view of Adams's indignation over Mercy Otis Warren's *History of the Rise, Progress, and Termination of the American Revolution* (1805), speculates William B. Evans, "one often wonders if Adams' ire was not stirred as much by Mrs. Warren's warmly favorable presentation of Franklin as by her somewhat cool, aloof treatment of her old friend, John Adams." Adams's antagonism toward Franklin, according to Evans, did not arise until 1780, when Adams sailed for Europe to negotiate treaties of peace and commerce with Britain; "regardless of how or why Adams arrived at his opinions of Franklin, he held them sincerely, and acted upon them doggedly" ("John Adams' Opinion of Benjamin Franklin," *PMHB*, Apr. 1968).

Franklin early secured his reputation abroad, nowhere earlier than in France. French contemporaries heralded him "not only as a man of letters, but also as a scientist, as a practical moralist and master of economic theory, and as a diplomat respected by the entire court," according to A. O. Aldridge, *Franklin and His French Contemporaries* (New York, 1957). "He was a double symbol," writes Morris Bishop. "He made visible and concrete the effective blending of two philosophies: Rousseau's return to Nature and Voltaire's skeptical, anticlerical rationalism" (*Daedalus*, May 1957). Small wonder, then, that after his death he was widely eulogized in France. Gilbert Chinard, who has edited some of these eulogies, *L'Apothéose de Benjamin Franklin* (Paris, 1955), concludes that the apotheosis of Franklin in France "présente un phénomène qui s'est rarement manifesté et jamais, croyons-nous, avec une égale intensité," and that it "marque un moment d'espoir et d'enthousiasme dans l'histoire de la Révolution française." At the end of a long appreciative essay on Franklin's achievements by word and deed Charles Cestre says, ". . . le couronnement de sa vie de bienfaisant labeur fut l'alliance avec notre pays, qui sauva l'Amérique de la défaite et hâta l'avènement de la Révolution française" ("Franklin, homme représentatif," *Revue Anglo-Américaine*, Aug. 1928).

Franklin's fifteen-year sojourn in Great Britain (1757–62, 1764–75) and the friendships he formed there with men of varied interests made him, in the words of Leonard Labaree, "this country's first great diplomatic representative" ("Benjamin Franklin's British Friendships," *PAPS*, Oct. 1964). "The Germans," writes Alfred Vagts, "knew Franklin first as the man who had experimented with electricity. . . . Together with Washington's, his name stood for revolution. . . . To the nineteenth century German, he became the guide to winning wealth, health, happiness, friends and influence" ("Benjamin Franklin — Influence and Symbol," *American-German Review*, Dec. 1956–Jan. 1957). It is Antonio Pace's considered view in *Benjamin Franklin in Italy* (Philadelphia, 1958) that "the influence exerted by Italy upon Franklin pales into relative insignificance by comparison with the impact of Franklin upon Italy." In the judgment of José Bataller, Franklin was the only American writer in the colonial period to make an impact in Spain where the *Autobiography* was translated as early as 1798" ("El primer libro norteamericano en España," *FMod*, 1961). Katalin Halácsy, maintaining that Franklin is still well known and honored in Hungary because "he took a leading part in events of world-wide importance like the American Revolution" and because of his versatility, surveys his reputation as physicist, public figure, reformer, capitalist and citizen, historical figure, and private person from 1756 to 1975 ("The Image of Benjamin Franklin in Hungary," *HSE*, 1976). "Franklin was the first great American personality to enjoy great popularity in Romanian literature and culture in the first half of the nineteenth century," writes Adrian Marino. His "name, his biography, and translations of his works can be found in all the Enlightenment publications of the age"; *Poor Richard* "was especially widespread and influential" ("Benjamin Franklin in Romanian Literature," *CLS*, June 1976).

In spite of the range and quality of Franklin scholarship, especially in recent years, four major tasks need to be undertaken: a formal bibliography, a find-list of manuscripts, a definitive biography, and a comprehensive critical study. All four may have to await completion of *The Papers of Benjamin Franklin* some years hence.

Oliver Wendell Holmes

BARRY MENIKOFF

BIBLIOGRAPHY

OLIVER WENDELL HOLMES has never lacked for good bibliographies. At the present time there are three major ones: George B. Ives, *A Bibliography of Oliver Wendell Holmes* (Boston, 1907); Thomas F. Currier and Eleanor M. Tilton, *A Bibliography of Oliver Wendell Holmes* (New York, 1953); and Jacob Blanck, *BAL*. In addition to the primary bibliographical material in all three volumes, the Ives and Currier bibliographies contain extensive sections on biography and criticism. These are virtually exhaustive in their listings of reviews and essays on Holmes, and are essential checklists of criticism.

A number of small and selective bibliographies remain useful. Among these are: Harry Hayden Clark, *Major American Poets* (New York, 1936); Walter F. Taylor, *A History of American Letters* (New York, 1936); S. I. Hayakawa and Howard Mumford Jones, *Oliver Wendell Holmes: Representative Selections* (New York, 1939); Lewis Leary, *Articles on American Literature, 1900–1950* (Durham, N.C., 1954); and the *LHUS* with its *Supplement* (1959).

A convenient listing of Holmes's writings on medical and scientific subjects can be found in the *Boston Medical and Surgical Journal* (11 October 1894). For additions to the Currier bibliography, see Eleanor Tilton, *PBSA* (First Quarter 1957).

EDITIONS

Although the sheer size of the Currier bibliography might suggest something of the popularity of Holmes's writings during his lifetime, the num-

From Earl N. Harbert and Robert A. Rees, editors, *Fifteen American Authors before 1900: Bibliographic Essays on Research & Criticism* (Madison: The University of Wisconsin Press; © 1984 by the Board of Regents of the University of Wisconsin System); may be reproduced only by permission of the publisher.

ber of editions available for present-day readers is rather limited. The standard edition remains the thirteen-volume set brought out by Houghton, Mifflin and Company, *The Complete Writings of Oliver Wendell Holmes* (Boston, 1891). This edition — reprinted by Scholarly Press in 1972 — has been supplemented by Albert Mordell's *The Autocrat's Miscellanies* (New York, 1959), a collection of Holmes's literary reviews and essays which were not included in the standard library edition. An excellent single-volume edition of the poetry is the original Cambridge Edition (Boston, 1895), revised with a new introduction by Eleanor Tilton, *The Poetical Works of Oliver Wendell Holmes* (Boston, 1975). Selections of the poetry can be found in all good modern anthologies of American literature. An inexpensive paperback edition of *The Autocrat of the Breakfast-Table* (1858; New York, 1968) is available, as is a paperback of *Ralph Waldo Emerson* (1884; New York, 1980), with an introduction by Joel Porte. Unfortunately there are no accessible editions for classroom use of *The Professor at the Breakfast-Table, The Poet at the Breakfast-Table,* and *Elsie Venner.*

MANUSCRIPTS AND LETTERS

Oliver Wendell Holmes was a prodigious letter writer. Apart from close friends like John Lothrop Motley (see *The Correspondence of John Lothrop Motley,* edited by George William Curtis, New York, 1889) and James Russell Lowell (see John T. Morse, Jr., *Life and Letters of Oliver Wendell Holmes,* Boston, 1896), Holmes's correspondents were various and numerous, causing him to complain, "I am overburdened with a correspondence which I find almost unmanageable." As long as Holmes was capable of signing his own name, however, he was meticulous in answering his "reading constituency" which he estimated at "three generations" of his own contemporaries. Many of these letters are probably irrecoverable; some are undoubtedly buried in basements and stored in attics. An occasional one, cleansed of its dust, reveals some interesting details. Roland Kent, for example, discovered a letter Holmes had written in 1875 to Kent's father in Wilmington, Delaware. In it Holmes classifies nearly a dozen of his most famous poems according to their mood and intention (*AL*, Nov. 1948). Nevertheless, a substantial body of Holmes's correspondence remains available and accounted for. All of his major biographers — Morse, Howe, Tilton, and Small — have quoted liberally from his correspondence. An appendix to the Currier bibliography provides a convenient list of all of the letters which were published in journals and books. What stands as our most pressing need, then, is a good modern edition of this correspondence.

The majority of Holmes's letters are on deposit in the Houghton Library at Harvard University. A substantial collection, donated by Justice Oliver Wendell Holmes, is in the Library of Congress; smaller collections are in the Henry E. Huntington Library (the Fields Collection) and the New York Public Library (the Berg Collection).

Eleanor Tilton describes the Holmes Collection in the Houghton Library at Harvard University as follows: "The most important items are medical lecture notes taken when Holmes was a student in Boston and Paris, medical casebooks, a bound volume of manuscripts (of which about a third are unpublished), a bound volume of letters (chiefly those written to his parents from Paris), notebooks for his major books after *The Autocrat* and *The Professor*, indexes to periodicals, and four miscellaneous notebooks." Other major repositories for manuscript materials are: the Library of Congress, the Francis A. Countway Library of Medicine in Boston, the Harvard Archives, and the Henry E. Huntington Library. Furthermore, the Oliver Wendell Holmes Library at Phillips Academy, Andover, contains the *Oliver Wendell Holmes Memorabilia Scrapbook*, a collection of notices and reviews of Holmes's books and lectures.

BIOGRAPHY

Doctor Oliver Wendell Holmes, fortunately for his biographers, lived eighty-three of his eighty-five years in Cambridge and Boston with very little to vex him. His private life was singularly without conflict, and he sustained only two antipathies in his public life, Calvinism and homeopathy. If these facts were not enough to dampen any interest biographers might have had in Holmes as a subject, then his writing itself expressed the character of the man more effectively, it seemed, than any mere biography possibly could. It was, after all, Holmes himself who added the subtitle to *The Autocrat of the Breakfast-Table*, "Every Man His Own Boswell." There were, of course, a succession of books that purported to describe the life of Holmes. These were written mainly in the years between 1880 and 1910, and they are largely encomiastic songs that possess neither wit nor point.

The first important biography was published two years after Holmes's death by his nephew, John T. Morse, Jr., *Life and Letters of Oliver Wendell Holmes*. Morse's main purpose is to provide a chronology of Holmes's career; he encloses the letters within the narrative in order to convey a sense of the personal style and tone of the author. The biography suffers, however, from an apologetic tone — Morse does not want to suggest that his subject is all *that* important — and from a fundamental lack of information. Quite simply, there were not enough letters or manuscripts available for Morse to work with. In addition, Morse himself possessed little imagination, and he tended to impose on Holmes some of his own beliefs and convictions. Thus the idea of Holmes's anti-Calvinism is given emphasis, even underlined, by Morse's own apparent hatred for the "promiscuous" doctrine. Morse summarized his impressions in "Oliver Wendell Holmes," *The Encyclopaedia Britannica* (New York, 1910): "By heredity the Doctor was a theologian; no other topic enchained him more than did the stern and merciless dogmas of his Calvinist forefathers. His humanity revolted against them, his reason condemned them, and he set himself to their destruction as his task in literature." Nevertheless, *Life and Letters* remained for nearly fifty years the standard biography of Oliver Wendell Holmes. Earl Harbert, who introduced the Chelsea House reprint (New York, 1980), declared that the book remains valuable for its "highly personal impressions about Holmes and his place in New England society." For a good critique of Morse's biography, see John White Chadwick's review in *The Nation* (11 June 1896).

The next biography of importance was written by M. A. de Wolfe Howe, *Holmes of the Breakfast-Table* (London, 1939). Although Howe depended upon Morse's earlier work, he also made use of manuscripts and letters which had been previously unavailable, particularly materials in the Harvard College Library and the Boston Medical Library. Howe's book has a simplicity of design (only five chapters), an elegance of expression, and a critical perceptiveness that reveal Holmes in his work as well as in his life. Howe recalled for his audience what Morse had barely noticed — that Holmes had been a physician, a professor of anatomy, and an active Lyceum lecturer. *Holmes of the Breakfast-Table* vividly recreates that figure. A briefer version of Howe's excellent sketch of Holmes appears in the *Dictionary of American Biography* (New York, 1932).

It was not until 1947, however, the one hundreth anniversary of Holmes's acceptance of the Parkman Professorship of Anatomy and Physiology at Harvard Medical School, that a "definitive" biography appeared: Eleanor M. Tilton's *Amiable Autocrat: A Biography of Dr. Oliver Wendell Holmes* (New York, 1947). Mentor Williams (*NEQ*, June 1948) describes well just what the book does: "It examines Holmes against the proper socio-cultural background of his century, something the earlier biographers could not do. It evaluates Holmes's literary work from fresh viewpoints and with acute insight. It points up the Autocrat's contribution to the intellectual climate of the period." Miss Tilton's study provided readers for the first time with a detailed account of Holmes's career in Paris as a medical student: "Crowding into his two years what many of his friends acquired more leisurely in three, Holmes had summoned the necessary concentration for his heavy schedule. Never again in his life would he show such whole-hearted devotion to a single pursuit as he was showing now in his study of medicine. When Holmes wrote his family that not one among his fellow students had 'sought knowledge so ardently and courted pleasure so little,' he was taking a high tone, but he was not exaggerating." The significance of Miss Tilton's full exploration of Holmes's student days and his career as a physician and professor in America is evaluated by Miriam R. Small (*AL*, Mar. 1949): "It is time that we should see Holmes as we do here, judged as a part of his own age and its tendencies, pictured colorfully and justly as doctor, medical teacher, and anatomist as well as poet, lecturer, social wit, and Autocrat." Miss Small has herself written a critical biography, *Oliver Wendell Holmes* (New York, 1962), in which she too emphasizes Holmes's importance as a physician and "medical scholar."

In 1979 Edwin Hoyt published *The Improper Bostonian: Dr. Oliver Wendell Holmes* (New York, 1979). Despite the breezy tone and careless writing, the book does add a footnote to the major biographies. Hoyt draws attention to features of Holmes's personality that were previously slighted—his "gentle racism," which Hoyt believed was at the root of Holmes's antagonism to the abolitionists, and his egotism, which impelled him to become a public figure and thereby separated him from his family. Hoyt speculates that Holmes's wife dissuaded him from publishing in order to protect the family from literary "exploitation" rather than to defend Holmes from the attacks of religious fundamentalists. But the critical weakness of *The Improper Bostonian* is its failure to account for Holmes as a significant figure in his own time, either as a writer or a professor of medicine. In effect Hoyt reduces the man to a single worn word—"dilettante."

Among the personal reminiscences of Holmes as a teacher, the most disarming are two accounts by his former students, David W. Cheever, "Oliver Wendell Holmes, The Anatomist" (*Harvard Graduates' Magazine*, Dec. 1894) and Thomas Dwight, "Reminiscences of Dr. Holmes as Professor of Anatomy" (*Scribner's Magazine*, Jan. 1895). Cheever's comment is typical: "As a lecturer he was accurate, punctual, precise, unvarying in patience over detail, and though not an original anatomist in the sense of a discoverer, yet a most exact descriptive lecturer; while the wealth of illustration, comparison, and simile he used was unequaled. Hence his charm; you received information, and you were amused at the same time. He was always simple and rudimentary in his instruction." For confirmation of this view, see "Oliver Wendell Holmes" in the *Boston Medical and Surgical Journal* (11 October 1894) and Charles W. Eliot, "Dr. O. W. Holmes as a Teacher of Anatomy," *Boston Medical and Surgical Journal* (28 September 1911).

An excellent portrait of Holmes as a young, practicing physician appears in Reginald Fitz's "My Dr. Oliver Wendell Holmes," *The Bulletin*

of the New York Academy of Medicine (Aug. 1943). "[By 1938] Dr. Holmes
was beginning to make himself felt as a doctor: not the ordinary kind
of practitioner by whom small fevers were gratefully received but as a
modern internist who was prepared to see only a few cases, to follow
to the autopsy table those that were fatal, who wished to study disease
rather than to treat it, and to advance medical knowledge, as Louis had
said, by eliciting truth through the establishment of facts which were well
and carefully observed." An intimate account of Holmes's role in the development of the Harvard Medical School may be found in Charles W.
Eliot, "Oliver Wendell Holmes," *Harvard Graduates' Magazine* (June
1923); see also Reginald Fitz, "President Eliot and Dr. Holmes Leap Forward" (*HLB*, Spring 1947).[1]

CRITICISM

It would be a convenience for this essay and my own desire for harmony to be able to say that the criticism of Oliver Wendell Holmes reflects the development of American literary criticism in general and the
changing fashions in literary taste in particular. But this is not the case.
In fact the criteria for judging Holmes's work have remained remarkably
constant, and the criticism itself has rarely altered in its general observations. Since the publication of *The Autocrat of the Breakfast-Table* in 1858,
Holmes has been extolled for his virtues and criticized for his limitations.
Today, of course, his virtues seem somehow less visible while his limitations appear all the more obvious. But during his own day he was held
in extremely high regard. The most brilliant conversationalist of a not
undistinguished circle, for a quarter of a century he dominated New
England letters.

General Estimates

Although the criticism on Holmes began as early as 1836, when he published his first volume of poems, and continued throughout his lifetime,

---

1. A convenient medical biography by Charles R. Bardeen can be found in *Dictionary
of American Medical Biography*, edited by H. A. Kelly and W. L. Burrage (New York,
1928). Among the best literary reminiscences of Holmes are those by William Dean How-
ells, *Literary Friends and Acquaintance* (New York, 1900); Annie Fields, *Authors and Friends*
(Boston, 1896); and M. A. de Wolfe Howe, "Dr. Holmes, the Friend and Neighbor," *YR*
(Apr. 1918). Other accounts of Holmes include: J. L. Hughes, *The Canadian Magazine*
(Dec. 1893); Samuel May, *Harvard Graduates' Magazine* (Dec. 1894); H. D. Sedgwick,
Century (Aug. 1895); G. W. Smalley, *Studies of Men* (New York, 1895); E. S. Phelps Ward,
Chapters from a Life (Boston, 1896); J. T. Trowbridge, *My Own Story* (Boston, 1903); and
Sir William Osler, *An Alabama Student* (London, 1908).

the critical evaluations did not appear in abundance until the last twenty years before the turn of the century. A substantial number of these were published in the 1890s, following Holmes's death and the publication in 1896 of Morse's *Life and Letters*. But it by no means took that long for perceptive critics to summarize the importance of Holmes's work. Early in his career, an extensive article, "Dr. Oliver Wendell Holmes and *Elsie Venner*," appeared in the *National Review* (Oct. 1861). The English have always been receptive to Holmes's writing, and he has received his most sympathetic appreciations, as well as his sharpest criticisms, from English reviewers. The *National* reviewer, who must have had one eye on the Civil War, used the occasion of *Elsie Venner* to examine the state of American literature, and the position of Dr. Oliver Wendell Holmes in that literature. First the reviewer commented on the popularity of *The Autocrat of the Breakfast-Table* and of *The Professor at the Breakfast-Table* in England: "Dr. Holmes is indisputably and above all an entertaining writer. He thinks, and he can express his thought articulately. He flashes upon you an ingenious suggestion, or a whimsical paradox, clothed in fantastic guise, and without giving you time to pause upon the truth it contains, or to reflect even whether what seems so plausible is true, presents you with another and another in endless sequence. The general effect is somewhat kaleidoscopic." Although Holmes's books appear indebted to Montaigne, Rabelais, and Sterne, they are, like Holmes himself, essentially American. And it is the American aspect which finally limits them: they are, like the culture itself, unoriginal, imitative, and intellectually "thin." Yet, despite this central criticism, the *National* reviewer details for us certain of Holmes's literary characteristics which he finds attractive: his wit and humor; his shrewd observations of life; his ingenious criticism on art, literature and philosophy; his large and humane sympathies; and especially his aversion toward any tyranny which would suppress free thought. (For an opposing view – Holmes is "unAmerican in style" and subject matter – as well as a thoughtful appreciation, see *Dublin University Magazine*, Sept. 1874.)

Two essays of the 1870s comment upon the humor and satire in Holmes's work. E. P. Whipple (*HM*, Mar. 1876) refers to Holmes's "fleering mockeries of folly and pretension, as in his almost Juvenalian invectives against baseness and fraud." George Stewart in *Evenings in the Library* (Toronto, 1878) emphasizes the "genial" Holmes, an emphasis which might almost be said to damn Holmes in our own day as much as it served to make him admired in his. Stewart then compares Holmes with Oliver Goldsmith: while they both appeal to "the heart and common sympathy of mankind," Holmes lacks Goldsmith's vulgarity. Thus, what the *National Review* critic saw as a weakness in 1861–the "expurgated" or diluted tone of Holmes's essays — Stewart sees as a virtue. He places Holmes in the tradition of the nineteenth-century essayists like Lamb, Hazlitt, and Hunt. The breakfast-table volumes are judged "great books" for their raillery, teasing, fun, and graceful imagery. Holmes's wit does not injure, Stewart concludes, and his writing reflects his humanity and charity.

Two major evaluations, one American and the other English, appeared in the middle eighties: E. C. Stedman's appreciative study for the *Century Magazine* (Feb. 1885) and Edward Delille's sharp critique in the *Fortnightly Review* (Aug. 1886). For Stedman, Holmes's genius reveals itself in the originality of his prose and in the excellence of his society verse. Establishing a principle that was to be repeated in later criticism, Stedman observed that the humor of the poetry and the satire of the breakfast-table books had the effect of relaxing "the grimness of a Puritan constituency." In support of this observation he emphasizes Holmes's "elastic buoyant nature," his zest for life which reveals itself in all the writing, and especially in the Autocrat volumes. Stedman next makes an observation which would be echoed in all future criticism: Holmes by instinct and habit is a man rooted in the eighteenth century, a man whose proper study is mankind. Although Stedman emphasizes Holmes's own brand of contemporary conservatism, that of Cambridge and Boston, he nevertheless admires him as a progressive and speculative thinker. In addition, Stedman is the first important literary critic to insist that Holmes's primary profession was not literature, but medicine.

Edward Delille's criticism stresses the limitations that Holmes's genial temper imposes on his writing. Although his thought is not original, Delille admits, Holmes nevertheless possesses all the talent necessary for great literature. He simply lacks passion, at least the passion of a writer like Thomas Carlyle. Delille's bias seems to be a social one: he would prefer to see Holmes perform for America the kind of satiric service that he admires in the anonymous author of *Democracy*. But Holmes's very sympathy and humane feeling — his "geniality" again — prevent him from accomplishing this. Delille does find in Holmes one trait to admire without qualification — a sympathy for childhood, a sympathy which is expressed more honestly than in Dickens. Delille also rates the novels highly. He believes that "Dr. Holmes could have been . . . *the* American novelist of the century." Delille argues that Holmes had a power for depicting character that was his most genuine literary gift, a gift that is revealed to advantage in the breakfast-table books which "constitute his greatest contribution to literature." Delille's final sentence, however, expresses an important reservation that was to be repeated in later criticism: "But [Holmes's] possession of all these gifts rather enhances than diminishes the regret that they should be, to a certain extent, impaired by the spirit of a *dilettante*."

During the 1890s a substantial number of general evaluations were published. The English criticisms were among the most acute and reflective. *Blackwood's Edinburgh Magazine* (Aug. 1892) commented first on the American aspect of Holmes's work, on the "frankness" and "aggressive independence of attitude" with which Holmes revealed both his personality and his thought in his prose. The *Blackwood's* critic, however, expressed a minority opinion when he declared that Holmes's genius was shown to advantage first in the novels, and particularly in *Elsie Venner*. He compared the book to Hawthorne's *Transformation* (a comparison which had already become common) and admired it for its "fantastic and sensational" qualities as well as for its delightful portrait of a rural New England community. Elsewhere, James A. Noble in *Impressions and Memories* (London, 1895) felt that Holmes's "deeper thought" was revealed in the novels.

Another perceptive article (*Quarterly Review*, Jan. 1895) focused on the importance of the past, on ancestry and education in Holmes's work. The anonymous critic observed that Holmes's concern with the past was not limited to the novels — where the theme of heredity regularly appears — but also filled his prose and verse with "delightful reminiscences" of childhood. Echoing Stedman, the writer remarked that Holmes was a product of the "leisured Augustan age," a detail which was confirmed by his use of classical English measures. His conservatism revealed itself as well in his social and political convictions. But this reviewer saw another, equally important, aspect of Holmes's personality: he was the inquiring man of science, a figure engaged in the extraordinarily various activities of daily life. This side of Holmes reveals itself in the breakfast-table books, those volumes of "practical philosophy" which were best suited to the Doctor's conversational gifts. If Holmes was not a man of literary genius, concludes the reviewer, he nevertheless played an essential role in his day: "No writer did more in his generation to soften the harshness of the Puritan temper, or to disperse with the cheerful warmth of innocent enjoyment the chilling gloom of its austere rule in New England. For this, even more than for his purely literary influences, he deserved, and gained, the affection of his fellow-countrymen." For confirmation of this conclusion by two American critics, see G. W. Curtis, *Literary and Social Essays* (New York, 1894) and John White Chadwick (*ForumNY*, Nov. 1894).

Leslie Stephen's sympathetic appreciation for the *National Review* (July 1896), which was reprinted in *Studies of a Biographer* (New York, 1898), supported the general English view that Holmes was a representative of America. Unlike some of his countrymen, however, Stephen does not believe that the stamp of Boston marks Holmes as a provincial: "The New England of his day, whatever its limitations, was seething with important movements as interesting, in slightly different applications, on this side of the Atlantic as well as on the other; and the fact that Holmes looked at them from a New England point of view does not show that he did not appreciate their wider significance." Stephen did not add anything to what had already been said about Holmes; the most interesting feature of his essay, apart from its informal style, is Stephen's suggestion that Holmes had perhaps never grown to manhood. "Holmes' boyishness means the actual possession of such qualities as are attributed to boys—rashly sometimes—by loving mothers; the perfect simplicity, the confiding trustfulness of a nature which has not been soured into cynicism; and the confident assumption that their own happiness implies the general goodness of all their fellow-creatures."

Two American critics, Henry Cabot Lodge (*NAR*, Dec. 1894) and *The Nation*'s reviewer (11 October 1894), emphasized Holmes's versatility. Lodge saw Holmes as a man possessed of a creative imagination as well as a scientific habit of mind. The two traits complemented each other. "Imagination did not make his medicine or anatomy untrustworthy, nor did his scientific tendencies make either his verse or his prose cold or dry. His wit and humor, it is true, gleamed through his lectures and left behind them to a generation of students a harvest of stories and traditions. The scientific cast of thought, on the other hand, as it often supplied an image or a metaphor, may possibly have had something to do also with the unfailing correctness of the poet's verse." For Lodge, Holmes's literary talent exhibits itself to perfection in occasional verse and in *The Autocrat of the Breakfast-Table*. Continuing what had become almost a mannerism in Holmes criticism, Lodge compared the *Autocrat*, with its "exact combination of wit and humor, of pathos and wisdom, of sense and sentiment," to the best work of all the great essayists from Montaigne through Charles Lamb. *The Nation* shared Lodge's opinion regarding the richness of the *Autocrat* and the "vitality" of the breakfast-table books as a group, but it stressed even more than Lodge had the belief that Holmes's "versatility" was his most exciting, and enduring, characteristic. "He must be regarded as poet, professor, and autocrat at once, if one would have a rounded conception of him, and understand what sort of personal power in him it was that extended a local reputation over a continent." But Holmes's versatility was not universally regarded as a virtue; for an adverse judgment, see the review in *The Bookman* (Sept. 1892). Finally, *The Nation*, anticipating what would become a leitmotif in Holmes criticism, assigned him a place in history: "He belongs to old Boston now—an historical period of the city that cannot be recalled without his name."

A substantial number of essays about Holmes were published at the turn of the century. But the tone of these "appreciations" differed from the earlier criticisms. Few of the critics writing in these years had known Holmes himself, and none had experienced at first hand the forceful personality of the 1860s and 1870s, the author of "Currents and Counter-Currents in Medical Science," *Elsie Venner*, "Mechanism in Thought and Morals," and *The Poet at the Breakfast-Table*. These essays maintain a certain detached attitude towards Holmes's work. They are generous in their praise, but it is a praise they seem never quite certain of. They comment almost as much on Holmes himself as they do upon his writing. The sanity and common sense which he brought to literature, his practical philosophy, his identification with the city of Boston — all are acknowledged with a sort of wistful regard for the character and person of Oliver Wendell Holmes. The writers all are conscious of an obligation to place Holmes in his proper niche in American literature. They are careful to examine his weaknesses and to explore the limitations of his talent, lest they be accused of making too strong a case for his importance.

In 1900 Barrett Wendell published his classic chapter on Holmes in *A Literary History of America*. "Among Boston lives the only other of eminence which was so uninterruptedly local is that of Cotton Mather. The intolerant Calvinistic minister typifies seventeenth-century Boston; the Unitarian physician typifies the Boston of the century just past."[2] Wendell's stress, however, was not on Holmes as a social phenomenon but on Holmes as a vigorous eighteenth-century rationalist, New England's one "uncompromising" enemy of Calvinism. "Among our men of letters this rationalist was the most sturdy, the most militant, the most pitiless enemy of a superstition whose tyranny over his childhood had left lifelong scars." Others who have recognized Holmes's antagonism toward Calvinism are Leon Vincent, *American Literary Masters* (Boston, 1906); G. K. Chesterton, "Introduction" to *The Autocrat of the Breakfast-Table* (London, 1904); and James Ormerod, *Library* (Jan. 1908). Wendell saw in Holmes a figure like Voltaire, devoted to the truth and to battling all those "delusions" which impeded the progress of men toward a better future. It is scarcely surprising that Wendell discovered in "The Deacon's Masterpiece" an allegorical satire on the inevitable destruction of Calvinism. More recently, J. S. Mattson has argued persuasively against this classic judgment on Holmes's comic *tour de force* (*NEQ*, Mar. 1968).

By 1910 the criticism of Oliver Wendell Holmes clearly had become institutionalized. His writings were the subject of an extensive, and perceptive, study in the *Edinburgh Review* (Apr. 1910); his breakfast-table

---

2. For further discussion of Holmes as a Bostonian, see Horace Scudder, *AtM* (Dec. 1894); George Woodberry, *HM* (Feb. 1903); Richard Burton, *The Reader Magazine* (Apr. 1905); and W. G. Ballantine, *NAR* (Aug. 1909).

books were commented upon favorably by Samuel Crothers in a slim volume entitled *The Autocrat and His Fellow-Boarders* (Boston, 1909); and his prescription for life — to live to the utmost of one's powers — received a strong second, made by the reviewer for *TLS* (26 August 1909). If Holmes no longer enjoyed the popular audience that his works had commanded during his lifetime, he nevertheless appeared regularly in literary histories. William Trent and John Erskine in *Great American Writers* (New York, 1912) saluted his liberal spirit; John Macy in *The Spirit of American Literature* (New York, 1913) admired both his rationalism and his "unbroken perfection of style"; and Brander Matthews, in the most concise and judicious statement of these years (*CHAL*), praised Holmes's cleverness — a sort of Yankee ingenuity — and the civilizing influence he exerted on his time. Matthews feels that Holmes's most enduring quality is his talk: "Holmes is not only a man of science and a man of the world, he is also a humorist and a wit, — a wit who has no antipathy even to the humble but useful pun, — a humorist abounding in whimsy. And as a result of this fourfold equipment his talk is excellent merely as talk. It has the flavour of the spoken word; it is absolutely unacademic and totally devoid of pedantry. Therefore it is not only delightful but stimulating; it continually makes the reader think for himself and turn back upon himself. Despite its acuteness, its liveliness, its briskness, its vivacity, it never lacks seriousness without ever becoming ponderous."

Matthews's judgment received confirmation from an unexpected source. Henry James, reviewing the early years of the *Atlantic Monthly* in an essay on James and Annie Fields (*AtM*, July 1915), described how that celebrated magazine "was for years practically the sole organ of that admirable writer and wit, that master of almost every form of observational, of meditational, and of humorous ingenuity, the author of *The Autocrat of the Breakfast-Table* and of *Elsie Venner*." James recalled that Holmes and the Fieldses both lived on the same street. "I find myself couple together the two Charles Street houses, though even with most weight of consideration for that where *The Autocrat, The Professor, Elsie Venner,* and the long and bright succession of the unsurpassed Boston *pièces de circonstance* in verse, to say nothing of all the eagerest and easiest and funniest, all the most winged and kept-up, most illustrational and suggestional, table-talk that ever was, sprang smiling to life."

The reputation of Oliver Wendell Holmes declined dramatically in the 1920s. But, as I have already indicated, Holmes had never been overrated for his intrinsic literary merit. He was always seen to have limitations, and very real ones, which could never be dismissed or discounted from any honest evaluation of his work. The reaction to Holmes that one might expect in the twenties, however, surfaced only in the form of a single short essay; it was appropriately placed where it seemed designed to serve an attractive and sophisticated audience. C. Harley Grattan's article (*AM*, Jan. 1925) might almost be said to characterize our present popular conception of the debunking Jazz Age. "To have written one book of importance and a handful of occasional poems cannot make a man a figure of major significance. The impossibility appears the greater when it is recalled that the one book epitomizes the humor of a single region." Grattan chides Holmes for taking too seriously his Saturday Club friendships. He declares that the novels have no interest for modern readers. He attacks with apparent relish the reticence with which Holmes regarded sex. Grattan's criticism appears motivated mainly by a hostility towards New England regionalism and Boston gentility, and Oliver Wendell Holmes was a fitting scapegoat. "Pleasantness and fastidious conventionalism thus make up all there is of Holmes. His religious radicalism no longer scares anyone, and it didn't scare many of any intelligence in his own day. In him is summed up the humor of literary Boston — in 'The Autocrat' and a handful of poems. His life and works are materials for a footnote to the history of an epoch. The charm of his personality made his contemporaries overrate him, and the adulators of New England continued the error."

A far more judicious account of Holmes as he appeared to a critic in the twenties can be found in Vernon Parrington's *Main Currents in American Thought* (New York, 1927). Parrington, of course, finds Holmes's social conservatism uncongenial to his own egalitarian temper. He also conveys a clear Western disdain toward Holmes's belief that Boston was the freest place in America. Nevertheless he regards Holmes with a certain affection: "A radical in the field of theology where personal concern brought him to serious grappling with the problem, a tolerant rationalist in the realm of the intellect, he remained a cheerfully contented conservative in other fields. He was unconsciously insulated against the currents of social and political thought flowing all about him." For Parrington, following in the tradition of Barrett Wendell, Holmes's single most striking, indeed radical, characteristic is his militant anti-Calvinism. The only poems he admires, for example, are "The Deacon's Masterpiece," "Parson Turell's Legacy," and "The Moral Bully." Although the tone of the essay conveys a certain aloofness, it expresses at least a moderate admiration for the honesty and integrity of the "authentic Brahmin."

If the tone of writers like Harley Grattan, Vernon Parrington, and Ludwig Lewisohn (*Expression in America*, New York, 1932) tended to make us peer down on the diminutive figure of Oliver Wendell Holmes from an Olympian height, in order to see more clearly his minor place in American literature, then this tone marked only a difference in emphasis, or degree, from the earlier criticism. Most critics had agreed in evaluating Holmes's position: he was a minor figure who played a role in New England's literary history, a figure whose artistic importance, however, was rigidly limited. Even those writers who had celebrated Holmes, as E. C. Stedman and Barrett Wendell did, were conscious of the personality of the man rather than the importance of his work. But in the middle of the 1930s a radical change in the criticism of Oliver Wendell Holmes occurred. Van Wyck Brooks, Harry Hayden Clark, and S. I. Hayakawa and Howard Mumford Jones all contributed to the change in Holmes criticism.

Van Wyck Brooks's main purpose in his writing ("Dr. Holmes: Forerunner of the Moderns," *SatR*, 27 June 1936, and "Dr. Holmes's Boston," *HM*, July 1940) was to explore the nature of New England life, to find the source for modern American literature, and to uncover the impulse that kept American writing sane and whole. The figure of Oliver Wendell Holmes, "the most intelligent man in New England," seemed ready-made for Brooks's task. From the outset he dismissed as absurd what had become a minor cliché in the criticism of Holmes during the 1920s, that the Doctor had intended his description of the Brahmin caste in *Elsie Venner* to reflect a "bloated Boston aristocracy." Brooks instead revived a single idea that had informed the best of the earlier criticism — Holmes as a conversationalist. In Brooks's mind, however, conversation was not merely a social gift, a talent to be cultivated for the pleasures of the Saturday Club, but a "mission," a means to expose all those "secrets" and fears which lay hidden and "twisted" within. "Fruits of the old religion of Calvinism, fruits of isolation and provincial conditions, fruits of unconscious living. Out with them, and talk them over!" Language, "expression," was New England's greatest need. "Emotions that can shape themselves in language open the gate for themselves into the great community of human affections." Holmes unfolded his wisdom for his readers — in a way offering them prescriptions for their health, both mental and physical.

Brooks turned next to "Crime and Automatism," to "Mechanism in Thought and Morals," to *Elsie Venner* and *The Guardian Angel*. In all these he saw a fundamentally modern theme: human responsibility as it related to an aberrant or disordered mind. Of course critics had always recognized the theme of limited responsibility in Holmes's work. But Brooks concentrated on that theme and drew attention to its pyschological accuracy as well as to its social significance. The rattlesnake's bite in *Elsie Venner* became a metaphor for any untoward or accidental circumstance that might determine an individual's destiny. In the end the thought of Dr. Oliver Wendell Holmes, "forerunner of the moderns," led to Darwinism, Marxism, and Freudianism.

Harry Hayden Clark supported Brooks's view. His essay "Dr. Holmes: A Reinterpretation" (*NEQ*, Mar. 1939) examined in detail Holmes's literary and aesthetic ideas, his social and political ideas, and his religious and philosophical ideas. Clark discovered that Holmes was "Federalistic" and "traditional" in social, political, and literary matters; while, in his religious and philosophical thought, he was scientific, "progressive," and rational. What distinguishes the essay, however, is Clark's attempt to place Holmes in a modern setting and to find in Holmes's determinism the source for his most radical idea: a belief that pity is often the only attitude society can take toward the criminal. But Clark, like Brooks before him, placed an inordinate stress on what he regarded as the absolute determinism of Holmes. He saw in Holmes's thought the ideas that culminated in the fiction of Theodore Dreiser and the practice of Clarence Darrow.

It was left to S. I. Hayakawa, a student of Clark's, and Howard Mumford Jones to provide a more restrictive, and definitive statement: "His determinism is a hopeful one because he does not make the mistake of regarding causation in the moral world as the same kind of thing as mechanical causation. Like the modern determinists, he sees the *self* as an active principle, so that the human will, while conditioned, is something more than the sum total of its conditioning agencies." The introduction which Hayakawa and Jones contributed to *Representative Selections* (New York, 1939; New York, 1978) must be regarded as the single most comprehensive view of Holmes until that time. He was examined first in relation to his city, to the "Boston of solid mercantile culture" which he had come to represent. Holmes was faulted for his failure to understand Catholic Boston, the Boston of the Irish and the Italians, "the Boston that was undergoing profoundly significant social changes under his very eyes." He was also chided — in no uncertain terms — for his ignorance of American economic imperialism, for his inability to perceive, as Emerson and Thoreau had, the nature of American industrial development. Undoubtedly these criticisms owed a good deal of their force, as well as their impetus, to the economic depression of the 1930s. When Jones reconsidered Holmes some twenty years later, for example, in *History and the Contemporary* (Madison, Wis., 1964), his objections seem to have lost some of their sharpness.

What appeared unique and salutary about the earlier study, however, was the primary role it assigned to Holmes as a physician. Hayakawa revived the earlier judgment of writers like Stedman and Lodge and claimed that literature was never more than a "sideline" for Holmes. But he went beyond that: he studied the medical essays and declared that Holmes's "medical papers sometimes make much better reading than his literary prose," a thoroughly defensible observation. He even suggested that it was Holmes's medical knowledge that prevented his social philosophy from being thoroughly commonplace, indeed, that saved him from literary "oblivion." Mentor Williams confirmed this judgment in his review of *Representative Selections* (*NEQ*, Dec. 1941). Williams, like Hayakawa, had recently written a dissertation on Holmes and his emphasis had been similar: Holmes as a scientific thinker was more interesting than Holmes as a literary artist. Williams also commented forcefully on Holmes as a "realist" and a "hardheaded" liberal who possessed a thorough understanding of his age. He was a "pioneer of scientific humanism" as well as an "educator of the public." For Williams, the modern spirit in Holmes could be found in "Currents and Counter-Currents in Medical Science," in "Mechanism in Thought and Morals," and in "Jonathan Edwards."[3]

Following a hiatus of more than thirty years, Holmes was reconsidered in a number of essays published in the 1970s. Although these assessments revived many earlier judgments as to the merit of Holmes's work, there were significant differences from the previous criticism. For one thing, the writers in the 1970s were more comfortable discussing Holmes's writing in relation to the man himself. This was not altogether original since Holmes had always provided the key for an autobiographical or biographical approach to his life's work. What was new, however, was the willingness on the part of critics like Gail Thain Parker, Eleanor Tilton, Barry Menikoff, and Thomas Wortham to evaluate Holmes's achievement as a function of his biography, rather than to separate the life from the work. Whether the methods reflected a renewed interest in life-writing or merely the decay of the New Criticism would be difficult to say. Holmes had never been a writer who could flourish in the twentieth century largely because his best work was *sui generis* and resistant to the rigid analytic schemes of modern criticism. What proved interesting to these critics, therefore, was the challenge of evaluating a writer whose performance had no analogue in American literature.

Gail Thain Parker ("Sex, Sentiment, and Oliver Wendell Holmes," *Women's Studies*, 1972) offered the most original reading of Holmes to appear in print. Adopting a feminist perspective, Parker was mainly concerned with the "concept of spheres," the segregated roles which were assigned to women and men as a consequence of nineteenth-century cultural patterns. Holmes served as a convenient example because he was

---

3. For useful statements on Holmes's belief in the idea of progress and his faith in science see Neal F. Doubleday, "Dr. Holmes and the Faith in the Future" (*CE*, Feb. 1943); R. W. B. Lewis, *The American Adam* (Chicago, 1955); and Don M. Wolfe, *The Image of Man in America* (Dallas, 1957). For a strong negative evaluation of Holmes's achievement see Alexander C. Kern, "Dr. Oliver Wendell Holmes Today" (*UKCR*, Spring 1948).

a major "public" figure who shared with his male contemporaries a conviction that there were "fundamental differences" between the sexes. He
"embraced the idea of woman's spiritual superiority" and thus contributed to the mid-century movement towards the sanctification of love and
sentiment. What Holmes revealed in his fiction, although unintention-
ally, was the recognition that "adolescence was . . . a greater crisis for
the male," and "pubescent boys had to domesticate their sexual passions."
In effect Parker saw sentimentalism — which eulogized women as tearful
and spiritual creatures — as a means of controlling and suppressing male
sexual drives. *The Guardian Angel*, in her view, dramatized the "evil"
of the phallic principle. In her shrewdest insight with respect to Holmes
himself, Parker connected "sexual energy" with "mental energy" and
"phallicism" with "professionalism," arguing that "Holmes could never
be sure he knew where competence ended and aggression began." His
ambivalence about his own career — artist versus physician, feminine versus masculine — was the sign of his generation's failure to develop any
model of an integrated personality that would accommodate differing
roles for male and female, that would allow for both the profession of
medicine and the pursuit of art.

In a more traditional vein, Eleanor Tilton summarized a lifetime's study
of the Autocrat in a lengthy introduction to *The Poetical Works of Oliver
Wendell Holmes* (Boston, 1975). Tilton's focus always had been biographical, and she was acutely conscious of Holmes's use of masks in order to
explore "the puzzle of his own personality." Holmes's preoccupation with
his identity — poet, professor, autocrat — inhibited or precluded the development of any "single-minded" pursuit that might have led to unquestioned achievement in one particular area. Nonetheless, for Tilton there
was merit in the "diversity" of his pursuits: "It cannot be said that Holmes
was no poet; it has to be said that he was so many other things as well."

Thomas Wortham stressed Holmes's "impassioned" attack on Calvinism in an extensive essay published in *American Writers: A Collection
of Literary Biographies*, edited by Leonard Ungar (New York, 1979).
Wortham revived a theme that had been developed earlier by Barrett
Wendell and Vernon Parrington, but he described it in personal rather
than doctrinal terms. He saw Holmes's antipathy to Calvinism as a form
of concealed "rage" against his father, a rage that expressed itself in
Holmes's lifelong condemnation of the writings of Jonathan Edwards.
When Wortham reviewed Holmes's canon he asserted that the Autocrat
had not distinguished himself in any single area of writing. Although he
judged *The Poet* the "best" of the breakfast-table series (a judgment that
reflected as well the opinions of Tilton and Menikoff) he argued that the
major objective of Holmes's writing was to educate and persuade his read-

ers that they "need not fear science or knowledge." Yet despite Holmes's limitations as a prose stylist, a poet, a thinker and a humorist, he remains "one of the truly civilized figures in our literature." For Wortham, then, as for Tilton, Holmes's achievement was validated in terms of its totality, which appeared far greater than the sum of its individual parts.

Barry Menikoff, in the *Dictionary of Literary Biography*, vol. 1 (Detroit, 1978), supported the view that was implicit in Tilton's and Wortham's assessments—namely that Holmes's achievement was distinguished by its commitment to liberating men and women from bondage to false idols. Thus Holmes's attacks on Calvinism and homeopathy "were motivated by his belief that they impeded the pursuit of truth and retarded mankind's progress toward a lovelier and healthier world." In a survey of the writings, particularly the work produced in the 1860s and early 1870s, Menikoff concluded that the breakfast-table series, Holmes's "trilogy," constituted his major literary achievement. For a contrary view of Holmes during this period ("a miniaturist in literature") see Lewis Leary, "Oliver Wendell Holmes," in *The Comic Imagination in America*, edited by Louis Rubin, Jr. (New Brunswick, N.J., 1973).

Poetry

Although the popularity of Holmes's poetry has diminished with the passage of time and the change in poetic taste, the criticism and evaluation of his verse has remained remarkably consistent. E. C. Stedman's *Century Magazine* study, reprinted in *Poets of America* (Boston, 1885), established the favorable feeling towards Holmes's work that prevailed in the 1880s, and it provided a sane and balanced judgment of his poetic achievement. Stedman sees Holmes's work as a "survival" of the eighteenth century, a poetry which retains the "courtesy and wit" of the Georgian age, as well as its heroic and octosyllabic measures. He finds, however, blended with the Georgian manner, a "vivacity" that contributes a uniquely modern flavor to the verse. Stedman remarks that poetry for Holmes was a diversion rather than a "high endeavor." This attitude enabled him to capture the lightness and ebullience in verse that characterized his occasional poetry, a form that he mastered. Stedman was also the first to suggest that Holmes served as the unofficial poet laureate of Harvard, the heir to the tradition of Phi Beta Kappa recitationists. (See also Thomas F. Currier, "Holmes as Harvard Poet-Laureate," *PMHS*, 1945.)

S. I. Hayakawa in "The Boston Poet-Laureate: Oliver Wendell Holmes" (*SELit*, Oct. 1936) distinguishes between two forms of occasional poetry: "Private occasional poetry is essentially the same as poetry proper in its origination: a poet sees a situation, or is present at an event, and this gives rise to certain reflections or emotions which he feels constitute subject-matter for a poem." But this does not typify Holmes's work. Rather his métier is "public occasional verse," a poetry which "does not express private emotions, but emotions shared with a number of other people. The poet, under these circumstances, is the instrument of a group; he must so far as possible merge his feelings into those of the group. Consequently we properly think of this class of occasional verses as those which are written for public occasions, anniversaries, weddings, funerals, victories, and other events of public importance." In this form, of course, Oliver Wendell Holmes has no rival. Hayakawa in another essay, "Holmes's Lowell Institute Lectures" (*AL*, Nov. 1936), gathered together the newspaper accounts of Holmes's 1853 lectures on English poets.

One of the best descriptions of the poetry appears in Brander Matthews's chapter on Holmes for the *CHAL*. There Matthews argues that Holmes's poetry owes its special character to an intellectual rather than an imaginative impulse; consequently it lacks both intensity of feeling as well as breadth of vision. "It has a French felicity of fancy, a French dexterity of craftsmanship, French point and polish, and also a French inadequacy of emotion." (For additional comment on the French influence, see Rica Brenner, *Twelve American Poets Before 1900*, New York, 1933, and Gay Wilson Allen, *American Prosody*, New York, 1935.) But Holmes's serious poetry was never the serious work of his life. It is in his "familiar" verse, Matthews declares, that Holmes's distinctive gift reveals itself. For in this kind of "easy" poetry—"the lyric commingled of humour and pathos, brief and brilliant and buoyant, seemingly unaffected and unpremeditated"— Holmes has in effect found a poetic equivalent for the essay in its charm and colloquial manner.

The two most sophisticated essays on Holmes's poetic theory and practice are by William Knickerbocker and Karl Wentersdorf. In "His Own Boswell: A Note on the Poetry of Oliver Wendell Holmes" (*SR*, Oct.–Dec. 1933), Knickerbocker begins with an examination of Holmes's poetic theory and declares that poetry is not the triumph of a finished piece of work but rather the experience which the artist himself enjoys in the process of creation, "the psychological richness of an inner state of high emotional ecstasy in the presence of Beauty." But Holmes recognized that he could not expect to achieve, let alone sustain, this kind of poetic joy. Therefore he turned inward and interested himself with recording what he discovered— both for himself and his age. "The single conception which unifies the diversity of themes in Holmes is his frank confession that he is 'his own Boswell.' He was bravely aware of himself, of his ancestral past, and made his chief effort to be the versifying commentator of the emotional experiences of a nineteenth century Yankee Brahmin. It was no slight achievement for one of that quality to overcome the regional taboo against self-revelation." For Knickerbocker, as for Matthews before him, Holmes's intimate revelations in verse (akin to his "congenial table-talk" in prose) confer upon his poetry a special strength, perhaps even durability, that in its own way is a minor literary triumph.

Wentersdorf, on the other hand, restricts himself in "The Underground Workshop of Oliver Wendell Holmes" (AL, Mar. 1963) to a consideration of Holmes's view of the creative process. Drawing largely on "Mechanism in Thought and Morals" and its "mechanistic" psychology, he argues that Holmes conceived of the creative process as a more advanced, or deeper, form of unconscious mental activity. The production of "genuine" poetry was therefore never "anything but a purely mechanical process, divinely inspired, but antecedent to the actual writing and not influenced by conscious effort." Wentersdorf diminishes the role traditionally assigned to Holmes as an expositor of neoclassical ideas — discipline and rational effort — and focuses instead on the contemporary accent in his aesthetic, on his belief that "automatism" affects poetic creation at least as much as it controls human behavior. Holmes fashioned an aesthetic, the result of an artist's "insight" and a scientist's "specialized knowledge," that "contributed materially to the understanding of the psychological processes involved in literary creativity. . . ." For an alternative view of Holmes's poetics (and a cogent reading of his most ambitious poem, "Wind-Clouds and Star-Drifts") see P. T. Dircks, "The Poet and the Astronomer: Neoclassic Aspects of Holmes' Satiric Technique" (Research Studies, Dec. 1969).

General studies of Holmes's poetry that remain valuable are: Augustus Strong, American Poets and Their Theology (Philadelphia, 1916); Alfred Kreymborg, Our Singing Strength (New York, 1929); and George Arms, The Fields Were Green (Stanford, Calif., 1953). Helpful studies of "The Chambered Nautilus" are: Bayard Christy (AL, May 1937), Nelson Adkins, (AL, Jan. 1938), and Cecil Eby (ESQ, Second Quarter 1962). Other studies demonstrate the influence of Dante, Horace, and Motley: J. Chesley Mathews (Italica, Sept. 1957); J. P. Pritchard, Return to the Fountains (Durham, N.C., 1942); The Classical Weekly (16 May 1932); and Eleanor Tilton (AL, Jan. 1965).

Novels

Although much of the best criticism of Holmes's fiction appears in general estimates of his work, a small number of special studies are nonetheless important for their independent observations. Two contemporary English reviews of Elsie Venner, for example, are among the most perceptive: the earlier cited National Review (Oct. 1861) and J. M. Ludlow's

"*Elsie Venner* and *Silas Marner:* A Few Words on Two Noteworthy Novels," in *Macmillan's Magazine* (Aug. 1861). The *National* reviewer comments first on the theme of limited responsibility: "Character [for Holmes] is destiny; but organisation is character, and organisation is an affair of race and parentage and external influences, moulding the individual as clay is moulded. This is the 'destiny,' the 'romance' of which is told in *Elsie Venner.*" Although the reviewer finds the doctrine uncomfortably deterministic, he objects even more to its dramatic presentation. The novel is a kind of "fantastic extravagance," a fiction whose moral lacks the clearness of an "avowed parable" and one whose main character, Elsie, lacks any reality. She is a case for the "morbid pathologist" rather than the novelist.

J. M. Ludlow agrees. He describes the manner in which Elsie assumes the characteristics of a serpent—her powers of fascination, of repulsion, her absence of human affection, and her "instinctive savagery." But what strikes Ludlow beyond all these observations is the peculiar fact that the novel could not have been written by anyone but an American. (Both writers refer to Hawthorne's *Transformation,* which had recently been published; the comparison was to become persistent in all future discussions of Holmes's fiction.) Ludlow speculates on the meaning of this fact, on why America's best writers possess such "morbid" visions: "Perhaps more than all does it come from this,—that America herself has been now for many years but a stage-effect, of which the secession crisis has shown at last the hollowness; that the lie of slavery, which has stultified from the first her Declaration of Rights, has poisoned all her art as well as all her social life. So long as the 'right to wallop one's own niggers' is considered consistent with the constitution of a free country, so long may there well be something diseased in the national mind, which inclines it to the morbid rather than to the wholesome, and which makes its highest fictions studies in human pathology, not broad representations of human life."

For less prescient and more typical contemporary reviews, see James Russell Lowell (*AtM,* Apr. 1861); Andrew Peabody (*NAR,* Apr. 1861); and *Dublin University Magazine* (Apr. 1862). For a scathing account of the fiction, see *The Nation* (14 November 1867): "His characters are figures labelled and set up to be fired at, or are names about which a love story is told, or they embody some physiologico-psychological theory; but they are never to be called characters in any true sense of the word."

Among the most sophisticated modern essays on Holmes's fiction are two by Edouard Roditi and Charles Boewe. Roditi, in "Oliver Wendell Holmes as Novelist" (*ArQ,* Winter 1945), begins by dismissing the notion that Holmes's novels are "psychiatric," an idea popularized by Dr. Clarence P. Oberndorf in *The Psychiatric Novels of Oliver Wendell Holmes* (New York, 1943) and "Psychic Determinism in Holmes and Freud" (*Mental Hygiene*, Apr. 1944) and pursued also by Rose Alexander in "Oliver Wendell Holmes — Psychiatrist" (*Medical Records* Oct. 1939). Roditi argues instead that the purpose of the novels is far more philosophical or theological. The medical "paraphernalia" is nothing more than a rhetorical device which attempts "to achieve a persuasive verisimilitude in tales that otherwise might seem wildly romantic or drily philosophical." The psychology of the novels is no more original than that of any other nineteenth-century novelist who reveals the habits and manners of neurotic characters. And for Roditi all of Holmes's main figures — Elsie Venner, Myrtle Hazard, Maurice Kirkwood — are frustrated and lonely individuals who from infancy have been deprived of a mother's love. What is original and striking about Roditi's essay is his suggestion that Holmes is indebted to Richard Burton and *The Anatomy of Melancholy* for his belief that emotional disturbances can be traced to the deprivation of affection during childhood.

Charles Boewe, "Reflex Action in the Novels of Oliver Wendell Holmes" (*AL*, Nov. 1954), believes that the novels can all be regarded as attacks on Calvinism. Each one is "a study of a different kind of limitation of the will, and all aim to persuade the reader that rational people cannot hold others accountable for acts over which they have no control." The determinism in the novels is dependent upon a theory of "mechanical reflex action" which Holmes derived in part from the English physician Marshall Hall.

During the 1970s *Elsie Venner* was scrutinized and revaluated in modern critical terms. Although the book had always been regarded as a fascinating if eccentric *tour de force*, Stanton Garner and Lewis Fried departed from tradition by analyzing its form and content, a procedure that implied a degree of craftsmanship which previous critics were either unwilling or unable to acknowledge. In "*Elsie Venner*: Holmes's Deadly 'Book of Life'" (*HLQ*, May 1974), Garner focused on the novel as an early expression of fictional realism, a mode that differed sharply from the symbolic romances of Melville and Hawthorne. Indeed, he suggested that Holmes's method redirected American fiction away from the manner of his great contemporaries and toward a darker realism which, ironically, Holmes himself neither liked nor desired.

Turning to the message of *Elsie Venner*, Garner found the same themes that others in this decade were discovering for the first time. Like Judith Fryer in *The Faces of Eve* (New York, 1976), he declared that Holmes recognized "the sexual implications" of his novel, that Elsie as serpent represented the "threat of woman stripped" of the veneer of civilization or gentility. As for the men, Bernard Langdon was an "emasculated member" of Holmes's own Brahmin caste, and served to call into question not only the legitimacy of that caste but the virility of an entire male generation. (For an antithetical view—the Brahmins exhibit the highest class virtues, including the privileged luxury of "moral freedom"—see John Martin, "The Novels of Oliver Wendell Holmes: A Re-Interpretation," in *Literature and Ideas in America*, ed. Robert Falk [Athens, Ohio, 1975]).

Lewis Fried, in *"Elsie Venner:* Holmes and the Naturalistic Tradition" (*Zeitschrift für Anglistik und Amerikanistik*, 1979), also stressed Holmes's realism and called *Elsie Venner* America's "earliest naturalistic novel." He drew attention to the influence of "French critical thought" on Holmes (recalling the crucial years spent in Paris studying medicine) and he noted the physician's predilection for biological and social explanations of personality. Fried argued that Holmes attempted to adjudicate if not resolve the discrepancy between science and religion. "Man can ask rational questions of Nature without denying his religious temper: for the empirical world revealed a redemptive order." Where Garner saw the novel divided between Holmes's official optimism (expressed in his spokesmen's monologues) and the "savageness" of the dénouement, Fried viewed the final avalanche that buried the snake-infested mountain ledge as a symbolic "crumbling of dogmatic beliefs." Holmes's declaration in *Elsie Venner*, Fried concluded, was an existential one: "solutions . . . are historically provisional, and it is by such doubt that we must endure."

Medical Writings

The criticism of Holmes's medical essays, written mainly by physicians, is not nearly as extensive as the criticism of his poetry and his fiction. Yet it is instructive for the literary critic, and for the support it offers modern writers like S. I. Hayakawa, Mentor Williams, and Eleanor Tilton in their views of Holmes's social and literary significance. As a medical writer, Holmes aligned himself with the champions of progress and opposed the forces of reaction. According to Edgar M. Bick, in "A Note on the Medical Works of Oliver Wendell Holmes," Holmes lived through medical revolutions, through "the introduction of pathology, histology, bacteriology, applied electricity, organic chemistry and modern surgery," and "stood as the whip which drove back the objectors and allowed the modern scientific concept of medicine to gain entrance" (*Annals of Medical History*, Sept. 1932). For Holmes's special role in "naming" anesthesia, see A. H. Miller, *Boston Medical and Surgical Journal* (29 December 1927). Holmes's antagonism to homeopathy was as well known among his contemporaries as was his antipathy toward Calvinism. In this too he was at the forefront of medical thought. For the principles he used in exposing homeopathy and other "kindred delusions" were derived from Pierre-Charles-Alexander Louis, the French physician who exerted such a powerful influence on all American medical students of Holmes's generation, as Henry R. Viets recalls in "Oliver Wendell Holmes, Physician" (*ASch*, Winter 1934). Holmes's essay on "Currents and Counter-Currents in Medical Science" was considered by contemporaries and later writers to be one of the finest statements ever written on the philosophy of medicine. Edward O. Otis tells us, in "The Medical Achievements of Dr. Holmes," "No medical writer of his day recognized more clearly than did he, or so persistently opposed, the evils of an inordinate use of drugs, or so insistently advocated the study of the causes of disease and the supreme importance of depending upon nature and nature's remedies for their cure" (*Boston Medical and Surgical Journal*, 30 December 1909).

But Holmes's greatest service as a medical writer, according to Otis, was that of interpreter and critic: "He was a profound student of the past and a clear-visioned prophet of the future. . . . He had an original creative mind, which had not been stifled or attenuated by too much so-called culture or education. He possessed the power of systematizing and generalizing medical knowledge in an orderly form, and, more than all, he possessed that rare ability, genius we may almost call it, of expression or style which captivates and holds fast the reader by its keenness, wealth of illustration, striking analogies, epigrammatic forms of expression and airiness of touch." His essay on the contagiousness of puerperal fever testifies more than anything else to this fact. (For confirmation of the view of Holmes as scholar, see Enoch Hale, *NAR*, July 1838, and Tracy J. Putnam, *Archives of Neurology and Psychiatry*, May 1941.) For studies of Holmes's classic essay on puerperal fever, see C. J. Cullingworth, *The British Medical Journal* (Nov. 1905); F. C. Irving, *New England Journal of Medicine* (July 1943); Henry R. Viets, *Bulletin of the Medical Library Association* (Oct. 1943); C. E. Heaton, *American Journal of Obstetrics and Gynecology* (Oct. 1943); and B. P. Watson, *Bulletin of the New York Academy of Medicine* (Aug. 1943).

From the very beginning of his career the style of Holmes's medical papers was commented upon favorably. Perhaps the best account is Neille Shoemaker's "The Contemporaneous Medical Reputation of Oliver Wendell Holmes" (*NEQ*, Dec. 1953). But what characterizes Holmes's work, even more than the brilliance of its style, and what earned Holmes the respect and love of his colleagues, is that same basic humanity which reveals itself in his literary writings. According to Andrew Peabody (*NAR*, July 1861), "What impresses us most of all in these discourses is the author's profound sense of the humane mission of the medical faculty, and his own unforced and unfeigned sympathy with the sufferings which it is his office to relieve. Some physicians treat the themes within the cognizance of their art as wholly impersonal, and as if muscles, nerves, and organs existed only for their manipulations, and for the cause of science. Dr. Holmes never forgets that he is discussing the members, liabilities, and morbid affections of a suffering body, and that his science exists for its uses, and should be cultivated for humanity's sake."[4]

4. A few reviews and essays on individual works are worth consulting. On "Mechanism in Thought and Morals": James Eliot Cabot, *The Nation* (2 March 1871); and William Dean Howells, *AtM* (May 1871). On *The Autocrat of the Breakfast-Table:* J. T. Winterich, *Publishers' Weekly* (17 January 1931); William Stetson Merrill, *Catholic World* (Feb. 1932); and J. DeLancey Ferguson, *Col* (Feb. 1936).

William Dean Howells

DAVID J. NORDLOH

STUDENTS OF HOWELLS were inclined, even into the early 1960s, to refer longingly to "the Dean's comeback." So far had Howells' reputation declined by the time Sinclair Lewis made his disdainful Nobel acceptance-speech reference to "Victorian and Howellsian timidity" in 1930, ten years after Howells' death, that its restoration to a level even approaching that he had held during his lifetime was perceived as an uphill struggle, with the struggling done by underdogs. But the general process of restoration now seems to have reached its conclusion. Given Howells' own modesty and the consciously moderate limitations he imposed on his own art, the intensity of passion for esthetic ideals or the moral outrage against injustice large and small which make Henry James and Mark Twain — the more spectacular contemporaries between whom he stood as literary friend and critical supporter in the development of American realism — so exciting are not present. Indeed, much of the enthusiasm which does exist around Howells is the enthusiasm of critics eager to make Howells more provocative by deemphasizing his critical and personal sanity and touting instead his inconsistency, his doubt, his moments of anguish over suffering and loss that plagued him no more than they plague anyone. Even so, such acts of unfortunate distortion have succeeded in drawing more attention to Howells, and every year brings deeper and wider study of the incredible variety and quantity of his achievements as novelist, poet, literary and social critic, editor, public personality, influential and active friend. The culminating point in the Howells revival was the initiation in the early 1960s of the still-ongoing "A Selected Edition of W. D.

From Earl N. Harbert and Robert A. Rees, editors, *Fifteen American Authors before 1900: Bibliographic Essays on Research & Criticism* (Madison: The University of Wisconsin Press; © 1984 by the Board of Regents of the University of Wisconsin System); may be reproduced only by permission of the publisher.

Howells," with the aim of making the texts of the major works available in reliable form for use in both classroom and study. Both the research drawn upon in the work of the "Howells Edition" and the scholarship being generated simultaneous with it — sometimes under its influence — are indications that Howells is now fully a topic of serious interest, and no longer the mere figurehead of an age.

BIBLIOGRAPHY

As sources of basic information about items written by Howells, the listings in the various editions of Merle Johnson's (later Jacob Blanck's) *American First Editions*, in the *Cambridge History of American Literature*, in the "Bibliography" volume of *The Literary History of the United States*, and, for drama, in the Howells "Bibliography and Play-List" in Volume One of Arthur Hobson Quinn's *A History of the American Drama from the Civil War to the Present Day* (New York, 1936) are convenient and generally accurate even if incomplete. The major comprehensive bibliographies remain the Howells section in Volume Four of Jacob Blanck, *Bibliography of American Literature* (New Haven, Conn., 1963), and William M. Gibson and George Arms, *A Bibliography of William Dean Howells* (*BNYPL*, Sept. 1946–Aug. 1947; New York, 1948; reprinted, New York, 1971). *BAL*, for all its importance, has significant limitations, particularly in its treatment of Howells. It is essentially a collector's and librarian's bibliography of first editions, and so excludes any reference to periodical publication — and one of Howells' strengths was his knowledgeable use of the magazine medium and his constant and skillful placement of his novels in monthly installments. *BAL* details pagination, signatures, binding variants, and locations of copies examined, even for the books in a section of secondary works which follows the primary listing, but it fails to offer any information about content, especially crucial, for instance, in the case of collections of essays like *Literature and Life* (1902) or *Impressions and Experiences* (1896). It is unsatisfactory, as every Howells bibliography has been, in identifying important first editions of the major novels of the 1880s published by David Douglas of Edinburgh. (On these editions, see Scott Bennett, "David Douglas and the British Publication of W. D. Howells' Works" [*SB*, 1972].) Finally, *BAL* supplies no index or brief introductory listing to guide the user through the welter of chronological entries.

Gibson & Arms, on the other hand, remains despite its date the indispensable Howells bibliography. It identifies both book and magazine and newspaper publications, in separate chronological sections fully cross-referenced to each other so that the relation of periodical items to assem-

bled volumes is immediately clear. The listings also specify the items reviewed and/or general topics discussed in periodical essays whose titles
don't convey that information — a valuable component of the bibliography given the unspecific nature of the continuing titles of columns to which
Howells contributed, for example "The Editor's Study" and "The Editor's
Easy Chair." Gibson & Arms also provides a full index to persons and
subjects in Howells' writings, both periodical materials and books; a selected list of secondary materials published through the early 1940s; an
introductory guide to Howells' book publications year by year; and a record of the dates of his association with individual newspapers and journals. Given the date of its publication and the difficulty of searching out
all of Howells' far-flung productions over a writing career covering almost seventy years, Gibson & Arms is incomplete. But nothing has yet
replaced it. (A Scarecrow Press bibliography of Howells edited by Vito J.
Brenni [Metuchen, N.J., 1973] does little more than rearrange the information in Gibson & Arms — inaccurately, at that.) A new bibliography
is promised as the final volume of the Howells Edition — whenever the
editing work is completed. In the meantime, the individual volumes of
the edition supply comprehensive bibliographical information relevant
to their contents.

Other scholars have made piecemeal additions to the canon of primary
works. The most productive is George Monteiro: "William Dean Howells:
Two Mistaken Attributions" (PBSA, 1962), "William Dean Howells and
The Breadwinners" (SB, 1962), "William Dean Howells: A Bibliographical Amendment" (PBSA, 1964), "A Speech by W. D. Howells" (SB, 1967),
and "Thomas Sergeant Perry: Four Attributions" (PBSA, 1965) — identifying one Perry item written in collaboration with Howells. Other scholars
have described bibliographical discoveries made in the course of their
larger research: Rudolf and Clara Kirk, "Howells' Guidebook to Venice"
(AL, May 1961), and "Niagara Revisited, by William Dean Howells: The
Story of Its Publication and Suppression," in Essays in Literary History,
edited Rudolf Kirk and C. F. Main (New Brunswick, N.J., 1960); Edwin H.
Cady, "William Dean Howells in Italy: Some Bibliographical Notes" (Sym,
May 1953) and "Howells Bibliography: A 'Find' and a Clarification" (SB,
1959), on Howells' translation of an Italian guidebook and his studies of
Italian poetry, and on a "lost" poem; and Ulrich Halfmann, "Addenda
to Gibson and Arms: Twenty-three New Howells Items" (PBSA, 1972).
The segment of his long and prolific writing career least satisfactorily
represented by bibliographical research remains the mostly unsigned journalism Howells did for his family's newspaper, the Ashtabula Sentinel,
and for other Ohio newspapers before 1861.

If Howells' longevity and productivity make a primary bibliography difficult, his prominence in a period when writers were the popular celebrities make an inclusive secondary bibliography almost inconceivable; the New York and Boston daily newspapers of the 1880s and 1890s, for example, are littered with news items and gossip about his latest trip, his next book, his views on today's crucial subject. Selected bibliographies of major scholarship appear in many of the volumes of selections by or about Howells identified below, as well as in the major critical studies and in the crucial American literature reference works mentioned in the preface to this volume. Only one attempt at a comprehensive secondary bibliography has been made—and it introduces itself with caveats about its provisional nature: "A Bibliography of Writings about William Dean Howells" (*ALR*, Special Number 1969), in two parts, 1860–1919 by James Woodress and 1920–present by Stanley P. Anderson. Both parts identify in separate alphabetical groups books, articles, and reviews; the second section adds bibliographical items and dissertations in two additional groups, and includes summaries of contents, though these are so vague and sophomoric as to not deserve the space. The work is not only incomplete but unjustifiably inaccurate. Corrections to Part One alone take up yet another bibliographical essay: Ulrich Halfmann and Don R. Smith, "William Dean Howells: A Revised and Annotated Bibliography of Secondary Comment in Periodicals and Newspapers, 1868–1919" (*ALR*, Spring 1972).

In the matter of contemporary reviews of Howells' fiction, Clayton L. Eichelberger, *A Guide to Critical Reviews of United States Fiction, 1870–1910* (Metuchen, N.J., 1971) is essential, though it leaves to the user the equally difficult task of identifying the authors of the items. Two selected bibliographies of secondary material, one devoted to contemporary and one to modern works, are more sensible still in their selection and arrangement. Eichelberger's *Published Comment on William Dean Howells Through 1920: A Research Bibliography* (Boston, 1976) provides an informative chronological survey of newspaper and magazine items together with summaries suggesting the shape of Howells' reputation and the terms of the ongoing debate about his achievement. And Maurice Beebe caps an excellent special Howells number of *Modern Fiction Studies* (Autumn 1970) with "Criticism of William Dean Howells: A Selected Checklist," whose special feature is a section listing discussions of individual works by Howells.

EDITIONS

Whether Howells' reputation has been affected by the absence for so long of a collected or other edition of his works is a modest "what if" for literary history. Howells participated in arrangements for what could have become a comprehensive edition early in the 1900s, and even began preparing prefaces for individual titles (frustratingly conscious of the awesome example recently set by Henry James in the New York Edition issued by Scribner). The project was beset by difficulties, however, most of them centering on disagreements over the rights and republication terms between the two major publishers involved—Houghton, Mifflin, which controlled the titles first issued before 1887, including *A Modern Instance* and *The Rise of Silas Lapham*, and Harper & Brothers, holders of the rights to virtually everything after that date. The end of their dispute— and of the edition—was the release by Harper & Brothers in 1911 of a six-volume "Library Edition" of Howells consisting entirely of Harper titles: *My Literary Passions/Criticism & Fiction, The Landlord at Lion's Head, Literature and Life, London Films/Certain Delightful English Towns, A Hazard of New Fortunes,* and *Literary Friends and Acquaintance.* Except for the introductory "Bibliographical" prefaces, which mostly identify Howells' original intentions and his problems with writing, and which seem to consciously avoid any larger Jamesian analysis, there is little that is special about these texts. Howells did revise *Criticism & Fiction* in stylistic rather than argumentative ways, and he added two essays —"A Belated Guest," on Bret Harte, and "My Mark Twain"— to *Literary Friends.* Harpers prepared new typesettings of other titles, and even advertised more volumes as forthcoming, but nothing further was published in the edition. An additional group of prefaces written by Howells and set in type but not used because the volumes for which they were intended were not released is printed in George Arms, "Howells's Unpublished Prefaces" (*NEQ,* Dec. 1944). A thorough history of the fate of the edition is provided in Robert W. Walts, "William Dean Howells and His 'Library Edition'" (*PBSA,* 1958).

The need for a large-scale edition of Howells became a matter of serious discussion among scholars as early as the late 1940s, and the topic eventually merged with a more comprehensive concern among Americanists for soundly researched texts of major American writers. Finally, in 1965, "A Selected Edition of W. D. Howells," centered at Indiana University, Bloomington, and published by the Indiana University Press, was formally launched as one of the projects associated with the Modern Language Association's Center for Editions of American Authors and one of the first recipients of a grant from the then newly established National Endowment for the Humanities. The general editors of the Howells Edition, working with an executive committee of Howells and American literature specialists and a central staff of Indiana faculty and graduate research assistants, have been, successively, Edwin H. Cady, who outlined the general content of the edition and supplied much of the initiating energy, Ronald Gottesman, who had begun as the textual editor and developed the specific textual theory and practice, Don L. Cook, and David J. Nordloh. The original plan for the edition called for a total of thirty-five volumes, but that number was revised first upward to accommodate additional significant titles and then downward to acknowledge the realities of scholarly energy and government and press support. Through the end of 1981, twenty of the now thirty-two volumes in the final plan had been published; the first volume, *Their Wedding Journey*, was released in 1968.

Of the published titles, thirteen are novels: *Their Wedding Journey, A Chance Acquaintance, A Modern Instance, Indian Summer, The Rise of Silas Lapham, The Minister's Charge, April Hopes, A Hazard of New Fortunes, The Shadow of a Dream/An Imperative Duty* (two novels in one volume), *The Quality of Mercy, The Kentons, The Son of Royal Langbrith*, and *The Leatherwood God*. Of the remainder, one is a collection of Howells' Utopian fiction under the collective title *The Altrurian Romances*; two contain works of autobiography and literary reminiscence, *Years of My Youth* and *Literary Friends and Acquaintance*; and four are *Selected Letters* (volume 1: 1852–1872, volume 2: 1873–1881, volume 3: 1882–1891, volume 4: 1892–1901). Yet to be published—the original plans called for the completion of the entire series in 1975!—are three more volumes of novels (*A Foregone Conclusion/The Vacation of the Kelwyns, The Undiscovered Country*, and *The Landlord at Lion's Head*), a volume of selected novelle, the complete poetry, Howells' first and most significant travel book, *Venetian Life*, three volumes of selected literary criticism, two additional volumes of letters (volume 5: 1902–1911, volume 6: 1912–1920), and a complete primary bibliography. Indiana University Press continues as the publisher of the major portion of work, but G. K. Hall & Co., Boston, has taken on the six volumes of letters; the fact of two publishers for the same edition, employing two separate sets of volume numbers, has created some confusion among scholars, librarians, and order departments.

The emphasis in "A Selected Edition" is on the authenticity and accuracy of the text, and not on its critical context. As the result of this policy, the introductions to the volumes, each prepared by a different Howells scholar, emphasize genesis, biographical background, and history of publication and reception rather than innovative critical perception. Even so, several of them—most notably those of Kermit Vanderbilt for *April Hopes*, Martha Banta for *The Shadow of a Dream/An Imperative Duty*, and George C. Carrington, Jr., for *The Kentons*—overcome that presumed limitation with rounded and relevant commentary. The textual work is done by a continuing editorial team, and the texts are edited in accordance with principles first enunciated in W. W. Greg's "The Rationale of Copy-text" and elaborated upon by Fredson Bowers in both theoretical essays and a variety of editions. Thus the Howells volumes incorporate Howells' identifiable intentions in both major and minor details, based on a full analysis of all the extant forms of the texts, on the relevant correspondence, publishers' and printers' records, and associated documents, and on a cumulative knowledge of Howells' stylistic preferences and working methods; simultaneously the editorial process aims at eliminating the errors and non-authorial alterations made in the earlier versions of the texts. The textual situation and editorial treatment are fully described in a "textual commentary" in each volume, and supported by technical apparatus which identifies changes made in the text and alternate readings in the other extant forms. Besides this technical documentation, the volumes also contain explanatory annotation; in many of them, particularly the novels, this supplementary material is often too sparing and too cryptic, but in the *Selected Letters* it is succinct and thorough, and especially helpful in setting out the context of the correspondence within which the printed letters were originally written. The extremes of the hostile and favorable reaction to the plan and content of the edition are voiced by Edmund Wilson, "The Fruits of the MLA: I. *Their Wedding Journey*" (*NY Review of Books*, 26 September 1968), and Hershel Parker, "The First Nine Volumes of A Selected Edition of W. D. Howells: A Review Article" (*Proof* 2, 1972).

Important selections of Howells' work have also appeared in various other forms over the years, often with useful critical introductions. Almost simultaneous in their publication were Henry Steele Commager's sizable *The Selected Writings of William Dean Howells* (New York, 1950), which reprints in their entirety *The Rise of Silas Lapham, A Modern Instance, My Mark Twain,* and *A Boy's Town,* and the somewhat slimmer *William Dean Howells: Representative Selections,* edited by Clara M. and Rudolf Kirk (New York, 1950), sampling portions of longer works and individual literary and social essays. The Kirks have also contributed *Criticism and Fiction and Other Essays* (New York, 1959) and *European and American Masters* (New York, 1963), both concentrating on Howells' reviews and critical essays. George Arms, William M. Gibson, and Frederic Marston collected Howells' contributions to the published work of other authors in the facsimile reprint *Prefaces to Contemporaries (1882–1920)* (Gainesville, Fla., 1957). Albert Mordell brought together all of Howells' reviews of and essays on Henry James in *Discovery of a Genius: William Dean Howells and Henry James,* with an introduction by Sylvia E. Bowman (New York, 1961). More important, because they are more thorough and more soundly informed, are Walter Meserve's *The Complete Plays of W. D. Howells* (New York, 1960), the title of which doesn't hint how complete the historical research and critical analysis supporting the texts manage to be, and Edwin H. Cady's contribution to "The Routledge Critics Series," *W. D. Howells as Critic* (London and Boston, 1973), reprinting chronologically fifty-four of Howells' best essays on literary subjects, with introductions and headnotes setting the context and defining the terms of Howells' ongoing critical arguments.

Relatively inaccessible Howells items are made available in other editions. William M. Gibson has edited Howells' manuscript lecture, "Novel-Writing and Novel-Reading," for *Howells and James: A Double Billing* (New York, 1958). *The Life of Abraham Lincoln*, the 1860 campaign biography that proved influential in Howells' career, has been reprinted twice, first by the Abraham Lincoln Association (Springfield, Ill., 1938), and then by the Indiana University Press (Bloomington, 1960).

There have been more than twenty simple reprint editions of various Howells titles since 1920. Given their ephemeral nature and the disinclination of most libraries to bind paperbacks, most are now difficult to find. Even so, the search is made worthwhile by the quality of the critical introductions attached. The best of the lot are Booth Tarkington's for *The Rise of Silas Lapham* (Boston, 1937), and those of Howard Mumford Jones (London and New York, 1948), George Arms (New York, 1949), Harry Hayden Clark (New York, 1951), and Edwin H. Cady (Boston, 1957) for the same title; William M. Gibson for *A Modern Instance* (Boston, 1957); Benjamin DeMott (New York, 1965) and Tony Tanner (London, 1965) for *A Hazard of New Fortunes*; Gibson (New York, 1951) for *Indian Summer*; and Eleanor Tilton (New York, 1964) for *The Landlord at Lion's Head*. Marilyn Austin Baldwin provides fine introduction, full explanatory notes, and carefully prepared text for *My Mark Twain* (Baton Rouge, La., 1967). And Ulrich Halfmann has compiled "Interviews with William Dean Howells" (*ALR*, Fall 1973; also available as a book), expanding substantially the group of "Five Interviews with William Dean Howells" gathered thirty years earlier by George Arms and William M. Gibson (*Americana*, Apr. 1943).

Survey lists of the editions of individual titles are included in the Kirks' *Representative Selections* and in Beebe's *Modern Fiction Studies* checklist.

MANUSCRIPTS AND LETTERS

References in his correspondence — especially that in later years with friends and institutions inquiring about donations of significant items — suggest that Howells had in his possession many of the manuscripts of already published work. Some things he proceeded to donate into security, for example the manuscript of *A Foregone Conclusion* to the Buffalo and Erie County Public Library and the manuscript of *The Leatherwood God* to the American Academy of Arts and Letters for its collection of founding members, but others were apparently lost in one or another of his constant changes of address. The present whereabouts of the manuscripts of such novels as *Indian Summer, April Hopes, The Rise of Silas Lapham*, and *A Hazard of New Fortunes* are unknown, and only little more than the first third of *A Modern Instance* has been located. The major part of what he retained went to Howells' children and grandchildren. Some important things remain in the family, but the bulk is now institutionally held — and the major portion of that is in the Houghton Library, Harvard University, to which items and groups of items have been either donated or sold over the years. The New York Public Library and the Huntington, Princeton, Virginia, Yale, and University of Texas libraries have smaller collections.

The best source of information about the present location of manuscripts, as well as of diary and journal materials and of letters, is *American Literary Manuscripts*, second edition, edited by J. Albert Robbins *et al.* (Athens, Ga., 1977). The crucial disadvantage of this guide, however, is that in its compact system of reference it does not identify by name the items in a given institution. Much fuller information about Howells' manuscripts, providing not only locations but physical descriptions and notes on contents, appears in John K. Reeves, "The Literary Manuscripts of W. D. Howells: A Descriptive Finding List" and "The Literary Manuscripts of W. D. Howells: A Supplement to the Descriptive Finding List" (*BNYPL*, June, July 1958; Sept. 1961). In the twenty years since the publication of Reeves' second list, other manuscripts have been found or made public, and some already known have changed hands; the bulk of the Charles Feinberg Howells collection, for example, is now in the Barrett Collection in the Alderman Library, University of Virginia. Up-to-date information about the manuscripts of individual works can be found in the volumes of "A Selected Edition," whose textual commentaries survey all pre-publication material relevant to the editorial work, including library accessions since Reeves' work was published and often supplemented with detailed physical descriptions. In addition, the Howells Center in Bloomington maintains a working manuscript union list, and can answer inquiries. But a new, more detailed manuscript listing would be a contribution to Howells studies.

For diaries, journals, and letters, *American Literary Manuscripts* is basic. But it doesn't list private holdings — scores of individual letters are in private collections — and it appeared before the acquisition by Alfred

University, Alfred, New York, of the Howells/Fréchette Papers, including letters to and from Howells, and missed the Howells, Mead, Noyes, and Dock Family Papers in the Massachusetts Historical Society, Boston; on both of these collections, see Ginette de B. Merrill, "Two Howells Collections" (*RALS*, Spring 1981). The extant letters especially are concentrated in the same libraries holding manuscripts, with the Houghton Collection by far the most extensive. Harvard also has the only known Howells diaries and journals. The Harvard Howells letters are enumerated and abstracted by Richard H. Ballinger, "A Calendar of the William Dean Howells Collection in the Library of Harvard University" (Harvard dissertation, 1953). The enumerative portion of that list has now been superseded by the unpublished typescript catalogue prepared by the Houghton. Only one library catalogue focused exclusively on Howells holdings has been published: Fannie Mae Elliott and Lucy Clark, *The Barrett Library W. D. Howells* (Charlottesville, Va., 1959).

Because of the sheer bulk of the letters (an estimated 21,000 extant letters *by* Howells, and perhaps an equal number to him) and the wide variation in their importance, from perfunctory social notes to business correspondence to intimate personal exchanges with family and friends to public statements concerning political, social, and literary events, a complete edition is probably not crucial or likely. The two-volume *Life in Letters of William Dean Howells* prepared by his daughter Mildred Howells (Garden City, N.Y., 1928) remains valuable both by the representativeness of its selection and the intimately informed source of the headnote information about Howells' attitudes and friendships. That edition has not been entirely superseded by the *Selected Letters* in "A Selected Edition," since the latter does not include all the items printed earlier. *Selected Letters* does have several advantages, however: the texts of the letters it does print are complete (Mildred Howells omitted what she considered personal or trivial detail) and more accurate, the locations of the original manuscripts are identified, and the published letters (only letters *by* Howells appear in full in the body of the text) are annotated in the context of the larger correspondences of which they are a part, often with extensive quotation and reference to manuscript and printed sources of other relevant letters. But neither edition indicates which letters may be printed elsewhere or supplies a calendar listing *all* extant correspondence; the scholar who wishes to move beyond the limits of the editions, therefore, still has much basic research to do — though the working letters files at Indiana, with their fairly complete background information and records of collections, can be drawn upon in the majority of cases.

Despite the importance of many of Howells' literary friendships, only two attempts have been made to collect complete single correspondences.

Mark Twain–Howells Letters, an edition in two volumes by Henry Nash Smith and William M. Gibson (Cambridge, Mass., 1960), is a fascinating record of the peaks and troughs of the thirty-five-year relationship of two energetic thinkers and writers, delightfully readable in the letters and in its wide-ranging explanatory annotation. But not complete: the later one-volume *Selected Mark Twain–Howells Letters*, prepared by Frederick Anderson, Smith, and Gibson (Cambridge, Mass., 1967) adds two new Mark Twain letters to the record. On a more modest scale, and with less potential for real excitement, George Monteiro and Brenda Murphy have collected the *John Hay–Howells Letters* (Boston, 1980), to which are appended Howells' reviews and essays on Hay. The volume highlights Howells' early political acquaintance with Hay, through whom his Venetian consular appointment of the 1860s became possible, and their social and literary sympathies, reflected especially in Howells' outspoken critical support for Hay's controversial and anonymous *The Breadwinners* (1884).

Letters by and to Howells also appear, of course, in editions of other authors. The most important of these are Doris Arthur Jones, *The Life and Letters of Henry Arthur Jones* (London, 1930), Robert W. Stallman and Lillian Gilkes, *Stephen Crane: Letters* (New York, 1960), and James C. Austin, *Fields of the Atlantic Monthly* (San Marino, Ca., 1953). Letters to Howells, but not by him, have appeared more widely. The major collections are Percy Lubbock, *Letters of Henry James* (two volumes, New York, 1920), and more recently Leon Edel's ongoing Belknap Press edition of *Selected Henry James Letters*, the latter rife with misreadings and superficially annotated; Evan E. Charteris, *Life and Letters of Sir Edmund Gosse* (New York and London, 1931); Charles R. Williams, *Diary and Letters of Rutherford Birchard Hayes* (five volumes, Columbus, Ohio, 1922–1926); M. A. De Wolfe Howe, *New Letters of James Russell Lowell* (New York and London, 1932); and Allan Nevins, *The Letters and Journal of Brand Whitlock* (two volumes, New York and London, 1936).

Several periodical items which identify and print letters move beyond the opportunistic "recently discovered" to attempting fuller coverage. Most notable among these efforts are the early "The Letters of Howells to Higginson," by George Hellman (*Twenty-Seventh Annual Report of the Bibliophile Society, 1901–1929*, Boston, 1929); George Arms, " 'Ever Devotedly Yours'—the Whitlock-Howells Correspondence" (*JRUL*, Dec. 1946); Kjell Ekström, "The Cable-Howells Correspondence" (*SN*, no. 1, 1950); James L. Woodress, "The Lowell-Howells Friendship: Some Unpublished Letters" (*NEQ*, Dec. 1953); Robert W. Ayers, "W. D. Howells and Stephen Crane: Some Unpublished Letters" (*AL*, Jan. 1957); Joseph Schiffman, "Mutual Indebtedness: Unpublished Letters of Edward Bellamy to

William Dean Howells" (*HLB*, Autumn 1958); Clara and Rudolf Kirk, "Letters to an 'Enchanted Guest': W. D. Howells to Edmund Gosse" (*JRUL*, June 1959); Jean Downey, "Three Unpublished Letters: Howells-[Rose Terry] Cooke" (*AL*, Jan. 1961) and "*Atlantic* Friends: Howells and Cooke" (*AN&Q*, May 1963); Howard Wilson, "William Dean Howells's Unpublished Letters about the Haymarket Affair" (*Journal of the Illinois State Historical Society*, Spring 1963); and Richard Cary, "William Dean Howells to Thomas Sergeant Perry" (*CLQ*, Dec. 1968).

BIOGRAPHY

Still the best—and, curiously, the only attempt at a complete—biography is that of Edwin H. Cady, whose pioneering critical-biographical triumph fills two separately titled volumes: *The Road to Realism: The Early Years, 1837–1885, of William Dean Howells*, and *The Realist at War: The Mature Years, 1885–1920, of William Dean Howells* (Syracuse, N.Y., 1956, 1958). Howells is fully placed within and growing away from family and Midwestern influences, solidly attuned to and sometimes caught in the social and intellectual dilemmas of the age, increasingly anguished but always productive and sane. Cady is perhaps too insistent on Howells' prophetic liberalism, but the first biography of a major author, particularly one ending thirty-five years of disdain and then disregard, can play advocate with perhaps more justice than its successors. The discussion in these volumes is sometimes more allusive than precise, and the references to source materials too general to be used easily, but the essential outlines of the life and the place of the major writing in it haven't been surpassed. Kenneth Lynn's more recent *William Dean Howells: An American Life* (New York, 1971) sets the works aside and concentrates on biography alone, annotates its sources (it draws most heavily on the correspondence) more thoroughly—and only carries its subject fully into the 1890s, arguing that the last twenty-five years of Howells' life aren't worth the same serious attention as the rest. Lynn labors even harder than Cady to demonstrate Howells' importance, emphasizing the tensions in the man, familial and social, emotional and intellectual, that make him modern, ignoring the centrality of his place and his ideas to his time rather than to ours. The perspective tends to isolate Howells from his world and attribute to him a fastidiously tortured mind. The notion is not quite convincing, partly because Lynn gives the impression of not seriously believing it himself, partly because Howells so obviously betrayed the thesis by remaining consistently level-headed enough to not let his concerns debilitate him. Still, the underlying factual scholarship is sound.

Other book-length studies, not clearly or exclusively biographies, are

also important in providing biographical information. Van Wyck Brooks'
final statement on Howells, *Howells: His Life and World* (New York, 1959)
is understandably better in placing Howells in his literary context than
in making him live, but the appreciative tone of the book and Brooks'
fuller acceptance of Howells' importance and the vitality of his literary
imagination compensate for the nagging insistence about Howells' shal-
lowness which had filled the earlier *New England: Indian Summer, 1865–
1915* (New York, 1940). Edward Wagenknecht's *William Dean Howells:
The Friendly Eye* (New York, 1969) is "psychograph"—study of character
and personality—rather than biography, and eschews chronological sequence for sometimes artificial topical divisions emphasizing Howells as
family man, social thinker, artist ("Mr. Papa," "Mr. American," "Mr.
Twelvemough," and such). The Humpty-Dumpty method, though, has
its compensations in the wealth of detailed information from both life
and writing. Clara M. Kirk and Rudolf Kirk's *William Dean Howells*
for "Twayne's United States Authors Series" (New York, 1962) — to be replaced shortly by a completely new volume in the same series by Kenneth Eble — supplies a comprehensive overview weighted toward Howells as social thinker. The Kirks' favorite Howells is the Howells of social
complicity, the economic novels, and Altruria, the Howells of the late
1880s and early 1890s. And William M. Gibson, *William D. Howells*
(UMPAW, no. 63, 1967), offers a brief but sensibly balanced introduction; the essay is also reprinted in *Six American Novelists of the Nineteenth Century: An Introduction* edited by Richard Foster (Minneapolis,
Minn., 1968).

A number of critical studies present essential biographical information. Among the best for their focus on specific periods of Howells' life
are James Woodress, *Howells & Italy* (Durham, N.C., 1952), which concentrates on life and literary work during the Venetian consulship of
1861–1864, and Kermit Vanderbilt, *The Achievement of William Dean
Howells: A Reinterpretation* (Princeton, N.J., 1968), which describes biographical issues relevant to four novels of Howells' major period, *The Undiscovered Country, A Modern Instance, The Rise of Silas Lapham,* and
A Hazard of New Fortunes. Also quite useful within their even more
limited perspectives are the contemporary appreciations by Thomas Sergeant Perry, "William Dean Howells" (*Century,* Mar. 1882), and William Henry Bishop, "Mr. Howells in Beacon Street, Boston" (*Critic,* 27
November 1886), the latter reprinted in Joseph B. and Jeannette L. Gilder,
eds., *Authors at Home* (New York, 1888) as "Mr. Howells in Beacon Street."
Essential modern studies are F. C. Marston, Jr., "The Early Life of William Dean Howells, A Chronicle, 1837–1871" (unpublished dissertation,
Brown University, 1944); Edd W. Parks, "A Realist Avoids Reality: William

Dean Howells and the Civil War Years" (*SAQ*, Jan. 1953); two essays by Clara M. Kirk and Rudolf Kirk, "Abraham Cahan and William Dean Howells: The Story of a Friendship" (*American Jewish Historical Quarterly*, Sept. 1962) and "William Dean Howells, George William Curtis, and the 'Haymarket Affair'" (*AL*, Jan. 1969); Ginette de B. Merrill, "Redtop and the Belmont Years of W. D. Howells and His Family" (*HLB*, Jan. 1980); and David J. Nordloh, "W. D. Howells at Kittery Point" (*HLB*, Oct. 1980). Howells' one serious effort at a lecture tour, through the Midwest in 1899, is perhaps the most fully studied single event of his life: Harrison T. Meserole, "The Dean in Person: Howells' Lecture Tour" (*WHR*, Autumn 1956), and Robert Rowlette, "In 'The Silken Arms of the Aristocracy': William Dean Howells' Lecture in Indianapolis, 1899" (*Indiana Magazine of History*, Dec. 1973) and "William D. Howells' 1899 Midwest Lecture Tour" (*ALR*, Spring 1977) — the factual errors in the last corrected by Thomas Wortham, "W. D. Howells' 1899 Midwest Lecture Tour: What the Letters Tell" (*ALR*, Autumn 1978).

CRITICISM

The swings in Howells' critical reputation have been so wide — from the low point of H. L. Mencken's essay "The Dean" (*Prejudices, First Series*, New York, 1919) and Sinclair Lewis's Nobel speech to the current concern for finding the right perspective from which to make him the most interesting and exciting — that no brief survey of materials can quite do it justice. Edwin H. Cady set the essential tone of the newer Howells in identifying "The Howells Nobody Knows" (*Mad River Review*, Winter 1964–65), the Howells whose novels contain more psychological depth than usually acknowledged, and in defining "The Neuroticism of William Dean Howells" (*PMLA*, Mar. 1946). Cady's "neurotic" Howells was anything but. The more recent tendency, however, particularly in Lynn's biography and Vanderbilt's *The Achievement of William Dean Howells*, already mentioned, and in the essays of John Crowley referred to below, is to claim importance or relevance for Howells with the notion of him as unusually distressed, distracted, or self-deluded. But there are also more modest claims made for Howells the craftsman, Howells the steadily developing artist and social thinker, and Howells the archivist of the immediate and the transitory in American life.

Two survey collections of critical essays provide a useful introduction to the material in the field, and help to clarify the terms of the ongoing debate. Edwin H. Cady and David L. Frazier, eds., *The War of the Critics over William Dean Howells* (Evanston, Ill., 1962) reprints sixty-eight essays or parts of essays, from the hostile commentaries of Lewis and Gertrude Atherton ("Why is American Literature Bourgeois?") to the deeper appreciations of Carl Van Doren and Henry Steele Commager, and including as well three essays by Henry James, Newton Arvin's "The Useableness of Howells" (*NR*, 30 June 1937) and Lionel Trilling's "W. D. Howells and the Roots of Modern Taste" (*Partisan Review*, Sept.–Oct. 1951). Kenneth Eble's *Howells: A Century of Criticism* (Dallas, Tex., 1962) covers much the same territory, but is more heavily weighted to items published during Howells' lifetime. The time is right for a similar volume surveying work done in the twenty years since the almost simultaneous appearance of these collections. In its absence, Kermit Vanderbilt, "Howells Studies: Past, or Passing, or to Come" (*ALR*, Spring 1974), and John Crowley's two-part "Howells in the Seventies: A Review of Criticism" (*ESQ*, Third and Fourth Quarters 1979) are good overviews, though the latter is strongly biased toward psychological criticism. The seven essays which appear in the "William Dean Howells Special Number" of *Modern Fiction Studies* (Autumn 1970) are a good sampling of the range and quality of more recent work; especially good both in themselves and for their reference to the varieties of perspective on Howells are Joseph H. Gardner, "Howells: The 'Realist' as Dickensian," and Sanford E. Marovitz, "Howells and the Ghetto: 'The Mystery of Misery'." And another excellent starting-point, not for criticism but for comprehension of the primary materials, is the non-critical but critically essential guide by George C. Carrington, Jr., and Ildikó de Papp Carrington, *Plots and Characters in the Fiction of William Dean Howells* (Hamden, Conn., 1976).

Overviews, Theories, and Definitions

The number of comprehensive critical studies of Howells isn't great, but the excellence of some of them is compensation. Van Wyck Brooks' *Howells*, Cady's two-volume biography, and Woodress's *Howells & Italy*, discussed earlier, must be cited as essential. Three very early volumes — Alexander Harvey, *William Dean Howells: A Study of the Achievement of a Literary Artist* (New York, 1917; reprinted, New York, 1972), Delmar Gross Cooke, *William Dean Howells, A Critical Study* (New York, 1922), and Oscar W. Firkins, *William Dean Howells, A Study* (Cambridge, Mass., 1924; reprinted, New York, 1973) — are now dated in their judgments but nicely unstrident in their perspectives on the limits of Howells' social vision and admiring of the breadth of his accomplishment in fiction and criticism. Most important of the modern studies — and striking by their contrast of approach — are Everett Carter, *Howells and the Age of Realism* (Philadelphia, 1954), which sets Howells solidly within the intellectual ferment of his age, and George C. Carrington, Jr., *The Immense Complex Drama: The World and Art of the Howells Novel* (Columbus, Ohio, 1966), an attempt at New Criticism which concentrates on structure and concludes that Howells' fiction constitutes a romantically flawed effort at the exploration of individual perception. The soundest critical reading of the major novels as a group is the two-book sequence by George N. Bennett, *William Dean Howells: The Development of a Novelist* (Norman, Okla., 1959) and *The Realism of William Dean Howells, 1889–1920* (Nashville, Tenn., 1973); in both Bennett takes as his starting-point Howells' own expressed intention as realist for his works as studies of individuals in their social context, and judges Howells, most often favorably, against those intentions. Other volumes with valuable special perspectives are Robert L. Hough, *The Quiet Rebel: William Dean Howells as Social Commentator* (Lincoln, Neb., 1959), Clara M. Kirk, *W. D. Howells and Art in His Time* (New Brunswick, N.J., 1965) and *W. D. Howells: Traveler from Altruria, 1889–1894* (New Brunswick, N.J., 1962), and — concentrating on Howells' fiction to 1882 — Olov W. Fryckstedt, *In Quest of America: A Study of Howells' Early Development as a Novelist* (Cambridge, Mass., 1958).

Howells is well — but not necessarily favorably — represented in major historical and critical overviews. Vernon L. Parrington, after first setting out his thesis in an essay on "The Development of Realism" in Norman Foerster's *The Reinterpretation of American Literature* (New York, 1928), sharpened his language and broadened his evidence about Howells' Victorian limitations and lack of imaginative power in "William Dean Howells and the Realism of the Commonplace," in *Main Currents in American Thought*, volume 3 (New York, 1930). Carl Van Doren is appreciative but cautious in "Howells and Realism," *The American Novel* (New York, 1921). V. F. Calverton, still grudging of Howells' achievement, includes his discussion in "From Sectionalism to Nationalism," in *The Liberation of American Literature* (New York, 1932). Walter Fuller Taylor needs only a few pages in *The Economic Novel in America* (Chapel Hill, N.C., 1942) to dispense with Howells' "perception without force." Richard Chase, in *The American Novel and Its Tradition* (Garden City, N.Y., 1957), complains of a Howells who didn't try hard enough. Daniel Aaron treats of Howells in two major studies, *Men of Good Hope* (New York, 1951), in which "William Dean Howells: The Gentleman from Altruria" examines Howells' notion of the reform of the individual by the community, and *The Unwritten War: American Writers and the Civil War* (New York and London, 1975), which draws upon *A Hazard of New Fortunes* in evaluating Howells' attitude toward the struggle whose ideals he supported but for which he did not go into uniform. Morton G. White and Lucia White elucidate, provocatively but with insufficient depth, "The Ambivalent Urbanite: William Dean Howells" in *The Intellectual Ver-*

sus the City (Cambridge, Mass., 1962). Michael Millgate places Howells firmly into the mainstream of a specific literary tradition in *American Social Fiction: James to Cozzens* (New York, 1964). Howells becomes a central figure for both theory and example in Robert Falk's *The Victorian Mode in American Fiction, 1865–1885* (East Lansing, Mich., 1965) and in Warner Berthoff's contribution to intellectual history, *The Ferment of Realism* (New York, 1965). For both Berthoff and Larzer Ziff, in "Literary Hospitality: William Dean Howells," *The American 1890's* (New York, 1966), Howells is, despite his influence, too kind, too shallow, too inclined in his art to explore human dimensions that are only possible rather than morally and esthetically appropriate. (Implicit support for the charge, from a more laudatory perspective, is offered by William C. Fischer, Jr., "William Dean Howells: Reverie and the Nonsymbolic Aesthetic" [*NCF*, June 1970]; Fischer identifies Howells' use of the reverie convention as a stylistic and intellectual device necessarily limiting the possibility of expressing moral truth.) H. Wayne Morgan places "William Dean Howells: The Realist as Reformer" among his *American Writers in Rebellion* (New York, 1965). Jay Martin's *Harvests of Change: American Literature, 1865–1914* (Englewood Cliffs, N.J., 1967), though perhaps too sweeping and allusive, locates him within the major lines of significant development of the period. And Jay B. Hubbell offers a succinct eight pages on Howells in *Who Are the Major American Writers?* (Durham, N.C., 1972), following him from his triumphant first visit to Boston in 1860 through the critical revival of the 1950s.

Howells the Realist, both theorist and practitioner, is naturally a focal figure in attempts at a definition of the term. Several essays by Donald Pizer first published separately and then revised and collected into *Realism and Naturalism in Nineteenth-Century American Literature* (Carbondale, Ill., 1966) emphasize the sources of Howells' ideas, particularly in relation to evolutionary science, and examine in his fiction the unique characteristics of his version of realism. Edwin H. Cady's *The Light of Common Day: Realism in American Fiction* (Bloomington, Ind., 1971) sets Howells' ideas against the bugaboos of romanticism and sentimentality Howells himself attacked in both criticism and fiction. And Harold H. Kolb, Jr., *The Illusion of Life: American Realism as a Literary Form* (Charlottesville, Va., 1969), though rejecting elements of the definitions supplied by Pizer, Cady, and others, relies just as heavily as they on Howells for essential evidence. More narrowly argued essays explore these and similar questions. Roger B. Salomon, "Realism as Disinheritance: Twain, Howells and James" (*AQ*, Winter 1964), postulates that crucial to the sense of realism as a contemporary ethic is the discontinuity of present and past. Gary Stephens, "Haunted Americana: The Endurance of American Realism" (*Partisan Review* 44, 1977), seeks to determine the sources

of the continuing popularity of this now apparently old-fashioned literature. William L. Stull, "The Battle of the *Century:* W. D. Howells, 'Henry
James, Jr.,' and the English" (*ALR*, Autumn 1978) explores the impact
of Howells' famous essay on the contemporary who was his principal evidence that "the art of fiction has, in fact, become a finer art in our day
than it was with Dickens and Thackeray." Louis J. Budd makes a very
convincing study of Howells' toleration of more than realism in "W. D.
Howells' Defense of the Romance" (*PMLA*, Mar. 1952).

Howells the social critic and social thinker has attracted a still wider
variety of analysis. The opening of the modern discussion is Walter Fuller
Taylor, "On the Origins of Howells' Interest in Economic Reform" (*AL*,
Mar. 1930) and "William Dean Howells and the Economic Novel" (*AL*,
May 1932), the latter included in Eble's *Howells: A Century of Criticism*, mentioned above. Taylor's Howells is no vague aesthetician or closet
radical but an engaged thinker, active in defense of the anarchists, committed to Tolstoy, eager to learn — and sadly limited by his ties to an overly
moderate past. George Arms, "The Literary Background of Howells's Social Criticism" (*AL*, Nov. 1942) describes Howells' debt to the thought
of Laurence Gronlund. Louis J. Budd contributes several strenuously
argued and deeply reasoned studies: "William Dean Howells' Debt to
Tolstoy" (*American Slavic and East European Review*, Dec. 1950), "Howells, the *Atlantic Monthly*, and Republicanism" (*AL*, May 1952), "Altru-
ism Arrives in America" (*AQ*, Spring 1956), and "Twain, Howells, and
the Boston Nihilists" (*NEQ*, Sept. 1959). Arnold B. Fox explicates a dominant theme of the Howells novels of the major period in "Howells' Doctrine of Complicity" (*MLQ*, Mar. 1952). Clara Kirk and Rudolf Kirk in
"Howells and the Church of the Carpenter" (*NEQ*, June 1959) provide
the record of Howells' association with a socialistic religious movement
during his almost frantic search for a solution to contemporary social dilemmas. Richard Foster, "The Contemporaneity of Howells" (*NEQ*, Mar.
1959), praises Howells' identification of the modern themes of discontinuity and intellectual loss. Frank Turaj, "The Social Gospel in Howells'
Novels" (*SAQ*, Summer 1967) reviews Howells' interest in Christian Socialism as social practice and not simply theory. Everett Carter, "The Haymarket Affair in Literature" (*AQ*, Fall 1950) describes Howells' commitment to a cause for which so few others had the courage — or sense — to
speak. Arthur Boardman, "Social Point of View in the Novels of William
Dean Howells" (*AL*, Mar. 1967), faults Howells for showing in his fiction a strong preference for the highest society, in contradiction to his
professed egalitarianism. Howells' relation to racial matters is studied by
Clare R. Goldfarb, "The Question of William Dean Howells' Racism"
(*BSUF*, Summer 1971), which explicates *An Imperative Duty*, and by
William L. Andrews, "William Dean Howells and Charles W. Chesnutt:

Criticism and Race Fiction in the Age of Booker T. Washington" (AL, Nov. 1976), which equates the shifts in Howells' critical posture toward Chesnutt's work with the prevalent tendency to forego literary comment for sociological in dealing with Afro-American writing. Sam B. Girgus, "Howells: The Rebel in the One-Dimensional Age," in The Law of the Heart: Individualism and the Modern Self in American Literature (Austin, Tex., 1979), touts Howells as precursor of Herbert Marcuse in lamenting the impact of modern life on personal freedom. Joseph A. Dowling examines the whole range of Howells' pronouncements on the trans-Atlantic topic in "Howells and the English: A Democrat Looks at English Civilization" (BNYPL, 1972), matching his earlier look at Howells as the English saw him in his "W. D. Howells' Literary Reputation in England, 1882–1897" (DR, Autumn 1965). And William M. Gibson's chapter on Howells in Theodore Roosevelt Among the Humorists (Knoxville, Tenn., 1980) demonstrates how canny a political analyst Howells could be.

Howells' conception of types and the importance of perceived and accepted behavior are examined in several strong studies of the American social environment. Edwin H. Cady's The Gentleman in America (Syracuse, N.Y., 1949) argues that Howells' gentleman was Christian and unconcerned with class. James W. Tuttleton, The Novel of Manners in America (Chapel Hill, N.C., 1972) praises Howells' perceptive dissections of the middle class. Stow Persons, The Decline of American Gentility (New York, 1973) defines a Howells typical of his age in blaming the decline of old values on such generalized villains as money and the Jews.

Howells was regarded even among his contemporaries as a novelist for and about women. In "William Dean Howells: The Indelible Stain" (NEQ, Dec. 1959), William Wasserstrom explores Howells' attitude toward female imperfection and his treatment of sex. John Roland Dove's "Howells' Irrational Heroines" (Univ. of Texas Studies in English, 1956) speculates on the consistency of Howells' treatment of female psychology. Alfred Habegger adds "life-denying discipline" to irrationality as elements of Howells' definition of the modern feminine mind in "W. D. Howells and the 'American Girl'" (Texas Quarterly, Winter 1976), and Sidney H. Bremer elaborates on another view of the incomplete but wholly human woman in "Invalids and Actresses: Howells's Duplex Imagery for American Women" (AL, Jan. 1976). In his broader study of several authors, Paul John Eakin in The New England Girl (Athens, Ga., 1976) traces the shaping of the Howells vision of woman away from the abstract and ideal.

Individual Works

That more recent studies of individual Howells works move beyond the most commonly read major novels to lesser-known titles is a refreshing sign of increasing interest. Many of the full-length studies already mentioned explore several titles. In addition, two essays — Clara M. Kirk's "Reality and Actuality in the March Family Narratives of W. D. Howells" (*PMLA*, Mar. 1959) and Robert Gillespie's "The Fictions of Basil March" (*CLQ*, Mar. 1976) — analyze the works in which the fictional characters most closely patterned after the Howellses themselves play a prominent part. Kirk stresses Howells' use of himself and his own experiences and attitudes as a means of achieving realistic effects. Gillespie finds Basil March unsatisfactorily shallow, and his weaknesses symptomatic of Howells' narrowness as social thinker. Treating two major novels, Seymour Gross and Rosalie Murphy in "Commonplace Reality and the Romantic Phantoms: Howells' *A Modern Instance* and *The Rise of Silas Lapham*" (*SAF*, Spring 1976) note the uncertainty and ambiguity of Howells' supposedly "smiling" vision.

A *Modern Instance* alone is examined in several strong essays. James W. Gargano, "*A Modern Instance*: The Twin Evils of Society" (*TSLL*, Autumn 1962), describes the opposition of the principal male characters, Bartley Hubbard and Ben Halleck, as polarities of social corruption. Sam B. Girgus, "Bartley Hubbard: The Rebel in Howells' *A Modern Instance*" (*RS*, 1971), argues that, despite Hubbard's many and obvious values, he is at least self-made and challenges typical middle-class values. In "The Significance of the Legal Profession in *A Modern Instance*," published in *From Irving to Steinbeck: Studies of American Literature in Honor of Harry R. Warfel*, edited by Motley Deakin and Peter Lisca (Gainesville, Fla., 1972), Nathalia Wright perceives the law as crucial to both structure and theme. And George Perkins, "*A Modern Instance*: Howells' Transition to Artistic Maturity" (*NEQ*, Sept. 1974), argues that it is not divorce but the conflict of country and city values which demonstrates the crucial failures of individual and society.

The Rise of Silas Lapham remains the mostly widely discussed of the novels. George Arms and William M. Gibson in "'Silas Lapham,' 'Daisy Miller,' and the Jews" (*NEQ*, Mar. 1943) provide background on Howells' use of striking contemporary topics — in the case of "Daisy Miller" an anachronistic one — to establish the social context of the events in the novel. W. R. Macnaughton's "The 'Englishmen' in *The Rise of Silas Lapham*" (*Mark Twain Journal*, Summer 1976) explicates a meaningful minor detail. In two essays —"The Architecture of *The Rise of Silas Lapham*" (*AL*, Jan. 1966) and "The Boston Seasons of Silas Lapham" (*SNNTS*, Spring 1969) — G. Thomas Tanselle defines the underlying structures of the narrative. Eric Solomon emphasizes a metaphorical pattern which creates a similar effect in "Howells, Houses, and Realism" (*ALR*, Fall 1968). By contrast, Edwin T. Bowden in "The Commonplace and the Grotesque,"

printed in his *The Dungeon of the Heart* (New York, 1961), urges that
the seemingly unformed and literal quality of the novel and of its characters, particularly Lapham himself, constitutes a means of establishing
the real sources and practical applications of the fiction. Paul A. Eschholz in "The Moral World of Silas Lapham: Howells' Romantic Vision
of America in the 1880s" (*RS*, June 1972) interprets the novel as Howells'
way of asserting the continuing value of "Jeffersonian morality" in the
face of dubious economic and industrial progress and rapid alteration
of social classes. Herbert Edwards describes Howells' attempt — typically
unsuccessful in his experience with works which began as fiction — to trans-
form novel into play in "The Dramatization of *The Rise of Silas Lapham*" (*NEQ*, June 1957). Donald Pizer's "The Ethical Unity of *The Rise
of Silas Lapham*" (*AL*, Nov. 1960) is reprinted in his *Realism and Naturalism*, already mentioned.

A Hazard of New Fortunes, the subject of significant discussion in the
second volume of Cady's critical biography, in the chapter on Howells
in the Whites' *The Intellectual Versus the City*, and in Vanderbilt, has
generated surprisingly few good articles. Paul A. Eschholz provides another fine reading of a Howells novel in the self-explanatory "William
Dean Howells' Recurrent Character Types: The Realism of *A Hazard of
New Fortunes* (*English Record*, Spring 1973). George Arms lays out the
basic materials of the novel and defines the ambivalent authorial attitudes underlying it in "Howells' New York Novel: Comedy and Belief"
(*NEQ*, Sept. 1948).

Several other novels of Howells' major period, usually defined as framed
by *The Undiscovered Country* (1880) and *The Landlord at Lion's Head*
(1897), have received critical attention. *The Undiscovered Country* provides a prominent example of the literary mistrust of popular spiritualis-
tic cults explored by Howard Kerr in *Mediums, and Spirit-Rappers, and
Roaring Radicals: Spiritualism in American Literature, 1850–1900* (Urbana, Ill., 1972). Robert Emmet Long contrasts the reconciling impulse
of the novel with the satirical intent of Henry James's *The Bostonians*
in exploring the debt of both works to Hawthorne in "Transformations:
The Blithedale Romance to Howells and James" (*AL*, Jan. 1976). *Indian
Summer* (1886) receives a good introductory explication, with emphasis
on the protagonist's eventual acknowledgment of his own coming to true
middle age, in David L. Frazier's "Time and the Theme of *Indian Summer*" (*ArQ*, Autumn 1960). Jack H. Wilson compares characters in *April
Hopes* (1888) to those in the George Eliot novel Howells knew best and
referred to most frequently in "Howells' Use of George Eliot's *Romola*
in *April Hopes*" (*PMLA*, Oct. 1969). Kermit Vanderbilt demonstrates how
Howells used the novel to dramatize his esthetic ideas in "The Conscious

Realism of Howells' *April Hopes*" (*ALR*, Winter 1970). Louis J. Budd attempts a definition of realism using Howells' 1889 novel as his model in "*Annie Kilburn*" (*ALR*, Fall 1968). *The Shadow of a Dream* (1890) gets three intriguingly different treatments: Elaine Hedges, "Howells on a Hawthornesque Theme" (*TSLL*, Spring 1961), contrasts Howells' realistic treatment to Hawthorne's romantic use of the same material; George Spangler, "*The Shadow of a Dream*: Howells' Homosexual Tragedy" (*AQ*, Mar. 1971), dissects the book with a Freudian scalpel; and Barbara L. Parker, "Howells's *Oresteia*: The Union of Theme and Structure in *The Shadow of a Dream*" (*AL*, Mar. 1977), demonstrates Howells' illumination of the theme of complicity by analyzing parallels with Greek tragedy. Another Howells novel is also compared to Hawthorne in Scott A. Dennis, "*The World of Chance*: Howells' Hawthornian Self-Parody" (*AL*, May 1980). And the final novel of the major period is studied by Paul A. Eschholz in "*The Landlord at Lion's Head*: William Dean Howells' Use of the Vermont Scene" (*Vermont History*, Winter 1974); in Susan Allen Toth's "Character and Focus in *The Landlord at Lion's Head*" (*CLQ*, June 1975), which concentrates on Howells' shaping his novel around the personal and esthetic limitations of the artist, Westover; and in Gary P. Storhoff's "Ironic Technique in *The Landlord at Lion's Head*" (*NDQ*, Spring 1978), offering a comparison of Westover to Howells' interestingly modern and amoral "hero," Jeff Durgin.

Howells' earliest novels, *Their Wedding Journey* (1872), *A Chance Acquaintance* (1873), and *A Foregone Conclusion* (1875), form the basis for William M. Gibson's analysis of Howells' development of his craft in "Materials and Form in Howells's First Novels" (*AL*, May 1947). John K. Reeves evaluates Howells' transformation of the materials of his earlier unpublished story "Geoffrey Winter" into *Their Wedding Journey* in "The Limited Realism of Howells' *Their Wedding Journey*" (*PMLA*, Dec. 1962). The same novel has received more attention since its publication as the first volume of "A Selected Edition" in 1968. Marion W. Cumpiano, "The Dark Side of *Their Wedding Journey*" (*AL*, Jan. 1969), points out the disturbing qualities of modern life which gnaw at the Marches during their middle-age honeymoon. Kenneth Seib sees the roots of Howells' later despair in these same elements of the novel in "Uneasiness at Niagara: Howells' *Their Wedding Journey*" (*SAF*, Spring 1976). David L. Frazier, "*Their Wedding Journey*: Howells' Fictional Craft" (*NEQ*, Sept. 1969), illustrates the processes and effects of journey as both structure and meaning. D. B. Graham comments on Howells' use of American folklore in "A Note on Howells, Williams, and the Matter of Sam Patch" (*NConL*, Mar. 1974). The most skillful study of the metaphorical and psychological dimensions of this apparently simple travel-book-made-fiction is

Gary A. Hunt, "'A Reality That Can't Be Quite Definitely Spoken': Sexuality in *Their Wedding Journey*" (*SNNTS*, Spring 1977).

The ending of a Howells novel is defended by John Crowley in "'A Completer Verity': The Ending of W. D. Howells' *A Foregone Conclusion*" (*ELN*, Mar. 1977). Another novel of the early period, *The Lady of the Aroostook*, is compared with Henry James's vision of American innocence in Annette Kar, "Archetypes of American Innocence: Lydia Blood and Daisy Miller" (*AQ*, Spring 1953). John Crowley analyzes the same novel and its rejection of European and Eastern ideals — as well as its failure to make Howells' Western alternative convincing — in "An Interoceanic Episode: *The Lady of the Aroostook*" (*AL*, May 1977). *The Leatherwood God*, the fictionalization at the other end of Howells' career of an actual episode of religious imposture on the Ohio frontier, has drawn some attention. Arnold B. Fox, "Howells as a Religious Critic" (*NEQ*, June 1952), uses the novel to demonstrate Howells' distinction between social and dogmatic Christianity. Haskell Springer details Howells' reshaping of the historical account that served as his source in "*The Leatherwood God:* From Narrative to Novel" (*Ohio History*, Summer 1965). Charles Feigenoff explores the psychological disruption underlying the religious veneer in "Sexuality in *The Leatherwood God*" (*SNNTS*, Fall 1980).

Howells' shorter fiction is considered less effective than his novels, since its confines seem less amenable to his broader, more leisurely story-telling pace. Even so, some shorter works have their critical admirers. "Editha" (1905), the most widely anthologized, is treated by William J. Free, "Howells' 'Editha' and Pragmatic Belief" (*SSF*, Spring 1966) as a capsule example of Howells' practical, contextual ethic, and by Michael O. Bellamy, in "Eros and Thanatos in William Dean Howells's 'Editha'" (*ALR*, Autumn 1979), as a study in feminine psychological aberration. Charles Feigenoff argues for hidden dimensions in Howells' thought in "'His Apparition': The Howells No One Believes In" (*ALR*, Spring 1980). The longer story "A Fearful Responsibility" (1881) is offered as Howells' "first predominantly bleak work" and the first step in his rejection of his early idea of pragmatism in Allen F. Stein's "A New Look at Howells's *A Fearful Responsibility*" (*MLQ*, June 1978). John Crowley defines the same work as Howells' exorcism of his guilt about failing to participate in the Civil War in "Howells's Obscure Hurt" (*JAmS* 9, 1975). Crowley also studies Howells' exploration of directions beyond realism for the experience of psychic and psychological issues in "Howells' *Questionable Shapes:* From Psychologism to Psychic Romance" (*ESQ*, Third Quarter 1975). And with Charles L. Crow, Crowley explicates a single story in that same collection in "Psychic and Psychological Themes in Howells' 'A Sleep and a Forgetting'" (*ESQ*, First Quarter 1977). George C. Carrington, Jr., turns

Howells' light and affectionate seasonal stories into projections of anxiety and guilt in "Howells' Christmas Sketches: The Uses of Allegory" (*ALR*, Summer 1977).

Disappointingly little has been done with Howells' many works of non-fiction. In "Howells' English Travel Books: Problems in Technique" (*PMLA*, Mar. 1967), George Arms studies Howells' solution to the special difficulties of the genre. James L. Dean, building on Arms' basic conception, provides the only book-length analysis of the travel books, all nine of them, in *Howells' Travels Toward Art* (Albuquerque, N.M., 1970). The major volume of literary reminiscence, *Literary Friends and Acquaintance* (1900) is seen as Howells' understated suspicion of his own betrayal of an ideal of the literary life in Lewis P. Simpson, "The Treason of William Dean Howells," collected in *The Man of Letters in New England and the South* (Baton Rouge, La., 1973). Kermit Vanderbilt, emphasizing reconciliation rather than destruction, takes the same work as an effort to unify the discrete sensibilities of Howells the naive young Midwesterner and Howells the mature Eastern artist in "The Perception and Art of *Literary Friends and Acquaintance*" (*ALR*, Summer 1977). *A Boy's Town* (1890), Howells' fictionalized and distanced reminiscence of his boyhood, is explored in its contrasting romantic and realistic perspectives and its revelation of the subconscious in Thomas Cooley, "The Wilderness Within: Howells's *A Boy's Town*" (*AL*, Jan. 1976), expanded in Cooley's *Educated Lives: The Rise of Modern Autobiography in America* (Columbus, Ohio, 1976). Tom H. Towers studies the same work as Howells' definition of meaningful social growth in "Savagery and Civilization: The Moral Dimensions of Howells's *A Boy's Town*" (*AL*, Jan. 1969).

Washington Irving

JAMES W. TUTTLETON

How GREAT A WRITER is Washington Irving, how durable, permanently pleasurable, influential? Such questions go to the heart of a writer's stature in the field of American letters. Several ways of answering the question are suggested in this review of criticism and scholarship, which brings to light what others have thought and felt about the man and his work.

There can be no doubt that Irving was immensely popular during his lifetime. "The Father of American Literature" is the understandable, if inaccurate, sobriquet by which he was long known. Before his death his works sold extensively, he was wined and dined by the eminent on both sides of the Atlantic and, afterwards, there were banks, schools, towns, saloons, cigars, and athletic teams named in his memory. No wonder that George P. Putnam brought out Irving's collected writings in fifteen volumes between 1848–50; Irving was the first American author to be so acknowledged. And shortly after his death he was memorialized in a four-volume biography (1862–1864) by Pierre M. Irving that defined the "Life and Letters" as a genre of literary biography in the nineteenth century.

If he was an "American" writer, he belonged in his lifetime to the nations, as Lincoln in death belonged to the ages. For one notes that in *Stories of American Life* (London, 1830) — recently reprinted by Clarence Gohdes (3 vols., New York, 1972) — Mary Russell Mitford excluded Irving from her list of American short story writers because "his writings are essentially European and must be content to take their station amongst the Spectators and Tatlers of the mother country." This puts Irving on a par with Addison and Steele, while Europeanizing him. The judgment

From Earl N. Harbert and Robert A. Rees, editors, *Fifteen American Authors Before 1900: Bibliographic Essays on Research & Criticism* (Madison: The University of Wisconsin Press; © 1984 by the Board of Regents of the University of Wisconsin System); may be reproduced only by permission of the publisher.

of London was of course crucial in 1830, for as Jay B. Hubbell remarks in *Who Are the Major American Writers?* (Durham, N.C., 1972), England imposed great pressure on American writers to prove their worth. As "'the father of American literature,' Irving was perhaps the first great American writer to secure an enthusiastic British audience."

Yet Irving has experienced an odd critical neglect that makes it appropriate, at the point of the bicentennial of his birth, to review the significant criticism and scholarship devoted to his life and work. As is made clear in the following account, which brings up to date Henry Pochmann's excellent survey in the first edition of *Fifteen American Authors Before 1900* (1971), Irving continues to enjoy a great deal of popular affection and esteem as befitting the versatile man of letters who produced clever epistolary journalism in *Oldstyle* and *Salmagundi*; excellent short stories in *The Sketch Book, Bracebridge Hall,* and *Tales of a Traveller*; highly readable biographies in *Oliver Goldsmith, Mahomet,* and *Life of George Washington*; scholarly and romantic histories in *Columbus, Companions of Columbus, Granada* and *The Alhambra*; and pioneering Western treatments in *Astoria, Captain Bonneville,* and *A Tour of the Prairies.*

Even so, there still exists a tendency to treat Irving as the genial humorist of trifling whim-whams, to pedestal him as a benign satirist of light follies, to accord his romantic histories a smile of tolerant benevolence, while locating our "best literature" in the dark consciousness of overtly symbolic writers like Poe, Melville, Faulkner, and Pynchon. In consequence, Irving has not been closely studied by our major literary critics, like Edmund Wilson, nor our critical theorists, like Northrop Frye or Kenneth Burke. Irving continues to be most frequently and successfully studied by editors and literary historians.

Yet Irving's importance cannot be measured by the forms of critical neglect evident in the following review. He is a significant innovator in nearly every genre of his time. And his range of materials — English town and country life, moorish Spain, Dutch colonial history, the discovery of the Americas, Revolutionary era politics, the American West — is voluminous, yet on the whole composed with an agreeableness of temper, a charm of personality, and a winsomeness of style that make for continued pleasure, a style that Eudora Welty in *The Eye of the Story* (New York, 1970) has described as elegant, direct, spontaneous, and meticulously observed in its details.

BIBLIOGRAPHY

Generations of dedicated bibliographical scholars have simplified the task of the modern student and researcher. Amongst the early compilers of information about the manuscripts and printed texts of Irving were Henry Pochmann in his "Selected Bibliography" in the American Writers Series edition of *Washington Irving: Representative Selections* (New York, 1934); Thomas H. Johnson in his bibliographical essay in Volume Three of the *Literary History of the United States* (New York, 1959); the collector's bibliography compiled by William R. Langfeld and Philip C. Blackburn, originally published in the *BNYPL* (June–Dec. 1932) and in book form the following year. Stanley T. Williams and Mary Allen Edge also produced a *Bibliography* (New York, 1936), based on the data developed during Williams's research for the *Life of Washington Irving* (discussed below). In large measure, all of these early accounts have been superseded by the coverage accorded to Irving in the fifth volume of Jacob N. Blanck's *Bibliography of American Literature*, which provides essential information about issues, states, and impressions of first editions and significant later editions. Yet even though Blanck's good work appears to have proved indisputable the Williams-Edge contention that Irving had attained "the most complete bibliographical record of any American literary figure," Blanck is not always accurate. As Edwin T. Bowden discovered and as John H. McElroy has shown in his "Textual Commentary" of *The Life and Voyages of Christopher Columbus* (Boston, 1981), readers — including Irving — have always thought that John Murray, Irving's London publisher, refused to publish a second edition of *Columbus*. In fact, Murray did publish, but he never told Irving about it; and Blanck misinterpreted the printing data.

Herbert L. Kleinfield's "A Census of Washington Irving Manuscripts" (*BNYPL*, Jan. 1964) has laid the groundwork for a thorough scholarly account of the description and location of Irving papers and manuscripts. But so much new material has been discovered in the past two decades that a new census is in order. Most of the new discoveries have been made in connection with the preparation of a new thirty-volume edition of *The Complete Writings of Washington Irving* (1970–   ), discussed below. Thus, for the most complete and accurate information about manuscripts and printed editions of individual Irving titles, the reader should consult the "Textual Commentary" of the relevant volume, if it has appeared. On the basis of such gathering bibliographical data, Edwin T. Bowden, the Textual Editor of the Irving Edition, will prepare a new and comprehensive bibliography of the author's works.

One of the most valuable bibliographical works in recent years has been Haskell Springer's *Washington Irving: A Research Guide* (Boston, 1976), which offers a year-by-year account of the developing "scholarship, criticism, reviews, and miscellaneous commentary" appearing between 1807 and 1974. Springer's annotations, particularly of old and inaccessible items, are especially valuable. Readers ought also to consult the quarterly listings of bibliographical information in *American Literature* and the annual lists and surveys in *PMLA* and *American Literary Scholarship*.

MANUSCRIPTS AND LETTERS

As remarked above, H. L. Kleinfield's "A Census of Washington Irving Manuscripts" (*BNYPL*, Jan. 1964) offers the most comprehensive list of the contents and whereabouts of Irving holographs. Readers may also consult Andrew B. Myers's "Washington Irving and the Astor Library" (*BNYPL*, June 1968) and other accounts of Irving exhibits and collections in *BNYPL* for Nov. 1914; May 1920; Feb. 1926; Apr. 1929; Feb. 1943; and Mar. 1964. Lesser collections are described in the *Library of Congress Quarterly* (Feb. 1948) and *YULG* (Apr. 1966; Oct. 1966; Jan. 1967). The New York Public Library contains the largest repository of Irving manuscripts; these are described in part in *The Seligman Collection of Irvingiana* (New York, 1926) and *Catalogue of the Hellman Collection of Irvingiana* (New York, 1929). Other valuable collections are housed at the Yale, Huntington, and Harvard University libraries. Clifton Waller Barrett has given his important Irving collection to the University of Virginia Library; and other notable collections are housed in the Carl H. Pforzheimer Library in New York City and at Sleepy Hollow Restorations in Tarrytown, New York. Irving's diplomatic papers are available in the Library of Congress and in the files of the National Archives in Washington.

Some of Irving's letters began to be published shortly after his death, notably in Evert A. Duyckinck's *Irvingiana: A Memorial to Washington Irving* (New York, 1860) and in Charles R. Leslie's *Autobiographical Recollections* (Boston, 1860). A fuller collection subsequently appeared in Pierre M. Irving's *The Life and Letters of Washington Irving* (discussed below). These letters are sometimes fully reproduced but are most often extracted and in any case are highly selective, as befitting perhaps a family biography done by the writer's nephew. An exceptional instance of Pierre's method is suggested by Ben Harris McClary in "Irving's Literary Pimpery" (*AN&Q*, June 1972), which reprints in full a letter of Irving's, which had been merely excerpted by Pierre, illustrating Irving's help to John Howard Payne in procuring a manuscript Payne intended to plagiarize.

George S. Hellman's *Washington Irving, Esquire: Ambassador at Large from the New World to the Old* (New York, 1925), prints some of Irving's diplomatic correspondence from the 1840s. And other more specialized collections are the correspondence of Irving and John Howard Payne in

Scribner's Magazine (Oct., Nov. 1910); Irving and the Renwicks (New York, 1910); Irving and Henry Brevoort, edited by G. S. Hellman (2 vols., New York, 1918); Stanley T. Williams' editions of *Letters from Sunnyside and Spain* (New Haven, 1928) and *Washington Irving and the Storrows* (Cambridge, Mass., 1933); S. T. Williams and Leonard B. Beach, "Washington Irving's Letters to Mary Kennedy" (*AL*, Mar. 1934); Barbara D. Simison, "Letters to Sarah Storrow from Spain . . . ," in *Papers in Honor of Andrew Keogh* . . . (New Haven, Conn., 1938); Clara and Rudolf Kirk, "Seven Letters of Washington Irving [1804–1805]," *JRUL* (Dec. 1945 and June 1946); Clara L. Penney, "Washington Irving in Spain: Unpublished Letters Chiefly to Mrs. Henry O'Shea, 1845–1854," *BNYPL* (Dec. 1958); and Everett H. and Katherine T. Emerson, "Some Letters of Washington Irving, 1833–1843," *AL* (May 1963). Lesser collections are itemized in *LHUS* and *Supplement* and in more recent bibliographies.

One extremely valuable collection of Irving's correspondence is contained in *Washington Irving and the House of Murray: Geoffrey Crayon Charms the British, 1817–1856*, edited by Ben Harris McClary (Knoxville, Tenn., 1969), which prints Irving's correspondence with his first British publisher.

But by far the most comprehensive and scholarly edition of Irving's correspondence is that contained in *The Complete Writings of Washington Irving*, which aspires to completeness. *Letters: Volume I, 1802–1823; Volume II, 1823–1838; Volume III, 1839–1846;* and *Volume IV, 1847–1859* (Boston, 1979–1982) have been edited by Ralph M. Aderman, Herbert L. Kleinfield, and Jenifer S. Banks. Each volume, meticulously edited and sealed by the CEAA/CSE, presents the correspondence in chronological order and usefully identifies the recipients.

EDITIONS

Irving's popularity from almost the very beginning guaranteed that very nearly every one of his books stayed in print, in one edition or another. Amongst his early publishers were Murray, Carvill, Carey and Lea, Galignani, and George P. Putnam. As Henry Pochmann remarked in his review of scholarship mentioned in my introduction, "the quantity and variety of selected works and of single titles appearing at home and abroad throughout the years are simply staggering. A mere listing of them occupies some 150 pages in the Williams-Edge checklist." Such a massive number of editions precludes specificity here, but some remarks about significant editions and collections are warranted.

Aside from the always important first editions, English and American, often published in concert to protect copyright, the first significant collection was the "Author's Revised Edition" of the works of Irving, published in fifteen volumes by George P. Putnam in New York between 1848–1851. To these were later added *Salmagundi* and the five-volume *Life of George Washington* in 1860, to make twenty-one volumes for the "New Author's Revised Edition." The merit of this collected, but not complete, edition is that Irving himself revised the texts of the "ARE" and saw them through the press. Thus the edition generally incorporates his final intention.

All subsequent Putnam editions, including the Riverside (21 vols., 1850–1860), Kinderhook (28 vols. in 14, 1850–1880), Sunnyside (28 vols., 1860), National (21 vols., 1860), Knickerbocker (27 vols., 1869), Geoffrey Crayon (27 vols., 1880–1883), Spuyten Duyvil (12 vols., 1881), Hudson (27 vols., 1882), another Knickerbocker (40 vols., 1891), Autograph (40 vols., 1895), People's (23 vols., 1901), and such other twentieth-century reissues as the Hudson, Nepperhan, Stuyvesant, Knickerbocker, Sunnyside, Pocantico, and Popular are all based on the original Author's Revised Edition, as are most of the unauthorized editions issued in great numbers by stray publishers in America, England, Spain, France, and Germany, sometimes pirated, sometimes in translation.

Other editions include Pierre M. Irving's two-volume *Spanish Papers and Other Miscellanies* (1860), which was incorporated into later Putnam collected editions; George S. Hellman's *Abu Hassan* and *The Wild Huntsman* (New York, 1924); William R. Langfeld's edition of *The Poems of Washington Irving* for the *BNYPL* (Nov. 1930); and Martin Roth's *Washington Irving's Contributions to "The Corrector"* (Minneapolis, 1968), presenting forty-five anonymous essays, in defense of Aaron Burr, originally appearing in 1804 in a New York political newspaper. Irving never republished them either because they were too ephemeral, too controversial, or too scurrilous. Stanley T. Williams and E. E. Leisy edited " 'Polly Holman's Wedding': Notes by Washington Irving" in the *Southwest Review* (July 1934). And William J. Scheick, in " 'The Seven Sons of Lara': A Washington Irving Manuscript" (*RALS*, Autumn 1972), edits an eighteen-page manuscript translation from Ambrosio de Morales's *La Crónicas General de España* (1586) that Irving used in writing "The Seven Sons of Lara."

Wayne R. Kime has recently culled newspapers and magazines with good effect, as reported in "Washington Irving and 'The Extension of the Empire of Freedom': An Unrecorded Contribution to the *Evening Post*, May 14, 1804" (*BNYPL* 76, 1972); in "The First Locomotive to Cross the Rocky Mountains: An Unidentified Sketch in the *Knickerbocker Magazine*, May 1839, by Washington Irving" (*BNYPL* 76, 1972); in Washington Irving and *The Empire of the West* " (*WAL*, Winter 1971), an Irving review dealing with the westering movement and America's national destiny; and in "An Actor Among the Albanians: Two Rediscovered Sketches of Albany by Washington Irving" (*NYH* 56: 4, 1975). And finally Joanne F. Diderich takes note of "The Moorish Drum," a popular song attributed to Irving, in "Washington Irving as Lyricist" (*PBSA*, First Quarter 1975).

Irving's home at Sunnyside is maintained by Sleepy Hollow Restorations, which also operates the Van Cortlandt Manor and Phillipsburg Manor. SHR has published, over the years, a number of beautiful gift books that may, at the same time, be valuable to the student and scholar. Amongst these are facsimile editions of Irving's illustrated "Author's Revised Edition" of *The Sketch Book*, *A History of New York*, *The Alhambra*, and *Bracebridge Hall*, as well as composites like *Old Christmas*, *The Wit and Whimsey of Washington Irving*, the *Life of George Washington* (a useful abridgement by Jess Stein), and the F. O. C. Darley illustrated *Rip Van Winkle & The Legend of Sleepy Hollow*, introduced by Haskell Springer and prefaced by Andrew B. Myers. Future SHR publications include *The Artists and Illustrators of Washington Irving*, *Astorian Adventure: The Journal of Alfred Seton*, *The Irving Family Genealogy*, and *Washington Irving and the Performing Arts: A Bibliography*.

By far the most important edition of Irving in the past 150 years is *The Complete Writings of Washington Irving*, to which I have already alluded. This edition, proposed by Henry L. Pochmann, was begun in the 1960s with the support of the Center for Editions of American Authors (now the Center for Scholarly Editions) and the Modern Language Association. With a team of Irving experts and editors from all over the country, Pochmann and his Editorial Board (which, over the years, has included Lewis Leary, Edwin T. Bowden, Richard Beale Davis, Andrew B. Myers, C. Hugh Holman, Walter A. Reichart, and H. L. Kleinfield), set in motion a project to publish Irving's complete works in thirty meticulously edited volumes, to be published by the University of Wisconsin Press. Each volume was to be based on a full analysis and collation of all existing manuscripts and significant printed texts.

The first fruits of that project was *Journals and Notebooks: Volume I, 1803–1806*, edited by Nathalia Wright (Madison, 1969). And at irregular intervals the following have since appeared: *Mahomet and His Successors*, edited by Henry A. Pochmann and E. N. Feltskog (Madison, 1970); *Journals and Notebooks: Volume III, 1819–1827*, edited by Walter A. Reichart (Madison, 1970). After the University of Wisconsin found itself unable to continue with the edition, it was taken over by the Boston publisher Twayne-G. K. Hall and, with the deaths of Professors Pochmann and Kleinfield, Richard Dilworth Rust became the General Editor. Since then the following titles have appeared under the Twayne imprint: *As-*

toria, or Anecdotes of an Enterprize beyond the Rocky Mountains, edited by Richard Dilworth Rust (Boston, 1976); *The Adventures of Captain Bonneville*, edited by Robert A. Rees and Alan Sandy (Boston, 1977); *Bracebridge Hall or the Humorists: A Medley by Geoffrey Crayon, Gent.*, edited by Herbert F. Smith (Boston, 1977); *Letters of Jonathan Oldstyle, Gent. & Salmagundi; or the Whim-whams and Opinions of Launcelot Langstaff, Esq. & Others*, edited by Bruce I. Granger and Martha Hartzog (Boston, 1977); *The Sketch Book of Geoffrey Crayon, Gent.*, edited by Haskell Springer (Boston, 1978); *The Crayon Miscellany*, edited by Dahlia Kirby Terrell (Boston, 1979); *Wolfert's Roost*, edited by Roberta Rosenberg (Boston, 1979); *The Life and Voyages of Christopher Columbus*, edited by John Harmon McElroy (Boston, 1981); and the *Life of George Washington*, edited by Allen Guttmann and James A. Sappenfield (3 vols., Boston, 1982).

The remaining volumes, soon to be published or already in print at the time of the publication of this essay, include *Journals and Notebooks, Volume II: 1807–1822*, edited by Walter A. Reichart and Lillian Schlissel; *Volume IV: 1827–1829*, edited by Andrew B. Myers and W. R. Kime; and *Volume V: 1832–1842*, edited by Sue Fields Ross and C. Hugh Holman. To these may be added *Oliver Goldsmith: A Biography and Poetical Remains of the Late Margaret Miller Davidson*, edited by Elsie Lee West; *A History of New York*, edited by Michael L. Black; *Tales of a Traveller*, edited by Brom Weber and David Wilson; *Voyages and Discoveries of the Companions of Columbus*, edited by James W. Tuttleton; *A Chronicle of the Conquest of Granada by Fray Antonio Agapida*, edited by Earl Harbert and Miriam Shillingsburg; *The Alhambra: A Series of Tales and Sketches of the Moors and Spaniards*, edited by William Lenehan and Andrew B. Myers; *Washington Irving: Miscellaneous Writings, 1803–1859*, edited by Wayne R. Kime; and *Irving Bibliography*, edited by Edwin T. Bowden. Very likely a *Nineteenth-Century Fiction* reviewer was right in observing that "By its [Twayne's Irving series] completion we will have one of the finest scholarly editions of an American author ever to be produced."

For the present, then, this edition of Irving would appear to be definitive. Each text is based on minute and extensive collations of all relevant forms of the work; each presents a clear rationale for copy-text; and each contains a full apparatus of emendations, rejected substantives, discussions of adopted readings and the like. It is to be hoped that subsequent reprints, by whatever publisher, will be based on these rather than older, corrupt texts.

Even so, the rationale of the Irving Board of Editors, in presenting the journals, was the occasion for a review by William H. Gilman in "How

Should Journals Be Edited?" (*EAL*, Spring 1971). In that article, Gilman, the chief editor of the Emerson edition sponsored by the CEAA/CSE and published by the Harvard University Press, argues that there are three kinds of editions that might be produced from private manuscripts: the facsimile text, the clear text with full report of changes, and the inclusive text. Gilman believes that the Irving journal editors were right to choose the inclusive text (as the Emerson edition does), but by declining the kind of editorial intervention evident in the Emerson journals, the Irving journals do not satisfy the need for "a quotable text at the minimal level." Those who have tried merely to read, let alone quote, the cluttered pages of the Emerson journals in the Harvard edition, will find much to wonder at in this remark.

With respect to accuracy of reprinted editions, Irving will be well represented in the new Library of America series. This publishing venture is intended to keep the classic American writers continuously in print in the best available texts. The first of two volumes of Irving's work, edited by James W. Tuttleton, will include *Oldstyle, Salmagundi, A History of New York*, and *The Sketch Book*. Each work is based on a CSE text, with the exception of *A History of New York*, which is not yet available in a CSE text; here the 1809 text is presented. The publication of this inexpensive one-volume selection is scheduled to coincide with the bicentennial of Irving's birth. A second volume will include the Western writings as well as other works.

BIOGRAPHY

If Irving has been fortunate in respect to the availability of his texts (though often in corrupt or pirated editions), he has also, on the whole, been lucky in his biographers. Pierre M. Irving's *The Life and Letters of Washington Irving* (New York, 1862–1864) gave immediate, direct, and full access to Irving's life. This work of Irving's nephew was based on the writer's private papers and was written with the cooperation of the subject, toward the end of his life. Wayne R. Kime has now analyzed the ways in which the nephew's biography served to shape Irving's "posthumous fame" in *Pierre M. Irving and Washington Irving: A Collaboration in Life and Letters* (Waterloo, Ont., 1977).

Owing to their astute collaboration, Irving's reputation in the nineteenth century crystalized as that of the genial and revered man of letters. Succeeding biographies by Charles Adams (New York, 1870), Adolf Laun (Berlin, 1870), David J. Hill (New York, 1879), Charles Dudley Warner (Boston, 1881 — inexplicably reprinted in New York by Chelsea in 1981, with a new introduction by Philip McFarland), Daniel Wise (New York,

1893), Richard Henry Stoddard (New York, 1886), Francis H. Underwood (Philadelphia, 1890), George W. Curtis (New York, 1891), and Henry W. Boynton (Boston, 1901) add little to the portrait, though they do reflect the changing literary climate as the ideologies of realism and naturalism emerged.

Serious twentieth-century biographical work on Irving commenced with George S. Hellman's *Washington Irving, Esquire: Ambassador at Large from the New World to the Old* (New York, 1925). Hellman presented Irving as the first major American writer to have had an impact on Europe and emphasized Irving's diplomatic experience in England and Spain. According to Pierre M. Irving, the writer never married because of grief at the early death of his beloved Matilda Hoffman. Hellman argued that in fact Irving proposed marriage to Emily Foster in March 1823 but was rejected. Hellman's claim, which appeared to refute Pierre's sentimental image of Irving as the faithful mourner of his first love, sparked a controversy that is argued back and forth in the Introduction to Stanley T. Williams's edition of Irving's Dresden journal; in Hellman's reply in *MLN* (May 1932); in Williams's "Washington Irving, Matilda Hoffman, and Emily Foster" (*MLN*, Mar. 1933); in Walter A. Reichart's "Washington Irving, the Fosters, and the Forsters" (*MLN*, Jan. 1935); in Francis P. Smith's "Washington Irving, the Fosters, and Some Poetry" (*AL*, May 1937); and in Walter A. Reichart's "Baron Von Gumppenberg, Emily Foster, and Washington Irving" (*MLN*, May 1945). Whatever the case, it is clear that Irving was attracted to a number of women over his lifetime, while maintaining confirmed bachelorhood. Perhaps to Matilda Hoffman and Emily Foster we may now add Serena Livingston, whom Irving thought of marrying, according to M. A. Witherspoon in "1815–1819: Prelude to Irving's *Sketch Book* (*AL*, Jan. 1970).

But for many years now, the standard biography has been Stanley T. Williams's *The Life of Washington Irving* (2 vols., New York, 1935), a work of massive research and scholarship that, in the words of one reviewer, "marks the arrival at maturity of American biography." It was based on all the known or available printed records concerning Irving as well as upon collections of Irving's manuscripts, both in America and abroad. Even so, it is a troubling biography to read, largely because Irving's life and work are not so much intrinsically studied as they are presented as a mirror of the age — the pre-Civil War era of elegant gentility. "Indeed, as I continued my study of the age in which Irving lived," Williams observed, "the question became not at all the measuring of his literary work by the immemorial touchstones of the past, tested by which he is often trivial, or by the standards of to-day, by which he has been outmoded, but a study of his career and writings in fusion with the liter-

ary criteria of his own time. For through such an approach he becomes
a clarifying mirror of some aspects of culture in America during the first
half of the nineteenth century. To understand Irving's hold upon his generation is to understand a dominating tendency of American literature
prior to the Civil War, which, beginning only two years after Irving's
death, helped to destroy the cult of elegance and made comprehensible
the voices of a Whitman or a Clemens."

Trivial, outmoded, the cult of elegance: these terms suggest the point
of view, the tone, which dominates the Williams biography. To bring
American literature (and American biography) to full maturity in the
1930s seemed to require students like Williams virtually to dismiss our
elegant cosmopolitan writers (Europeanized palefaces) and to praise authentic (i.e., crude or raw) American writers like Twain and Whitman
(who were not so easily measured against their English brethren). In fact,
Williams's biography is one of a number of more or less "debunking" biographies to be written in the wake of Strachey's *Eminent Victorians*,
of which, in America, Van Wyck Brooks's *The Pilgrimage of Henry James*
is exemplary. While students of Irving for the past half century have therefore been indebted to Williams for his establishment of the facts of Irving's life and work, they have sometimes asked the question often posed
of Mark Schorer's biography of Sinclair Lewis: if he felt that way about
his subject, why did he spend all of those years writing the life?

More moderate, as befitting the subject, is Edward Wagenknecht's
Washington Irving: Moderation Displayed (New York, 1962), which takes
Williams gently to task for his tone, corrects a few details, and paints
a more sympathetic portrait of the man. In this connection, useful corrective biographical notes are also provided by David E. Sloane in "Washington Irving's 'Insufferable Diffidence'" (*AL*, Mar. 1971), on Irving's
aversion to speaking in public; and Albert Burton, Jr., in "Alexander Robertson: Irving's Drawing Teacher" (*AN&Q*, June 1971), which claims that
young Irving's art teacher was not Archibald but rather his brother
Alexander Robertson. More sympathetic portraits of Irving are also to
be found in Harold Dean Cater's *Washington Irving at Sunnyside* (Tarrytown, N.Y., 1957) and George Sanderlin's *Washington Irving: As Others
Saw Him* (New York, 1975).

Scholars, however, will find little use of Johanna Johnston's *The Heart
That Would Not Hold* (New York, 1971), an altogether too fanciful treat-
ment of Irving's life without documentation. A more interesting treat-
ment of Irving, counterpointed against contemporaries like John Brown,
Mary Shelley, John Jacob Astor, Walter Scott and others, is offered in Philip
McFarland's *Sojourners* (New York, 1979), which undertakes to establish
Irving's historical and cultural context by diverging from his life to ex-
plain what others were doing elsewhere in the world.

It has long been recognized, then, that a more objective, if not sympathetic scholarly treatment of Irving's life is in order—one tending toward a balance between the somewhat hagiographical nineteenth-century studies and the manifestly irritated treatment evident in Williams, yet without the blandness of Wagenknecht's study. Such a biography is at present in progress. The author, Andrew B. Myers, has been involved with Irving studies for several decades—as an editor, compiler of criticism, critic, and President of the Washington Irving Society. Myers's biography, the appearance of which is scheduled to coincide with the bicentennial of Irving's birth, promises to bring to bear on the life a great deal of the new information developed by individual text editors and to refocus the image of Irving both as man and writer in relation to his time and to the modern era.

LITERARY HISTORY AND CRITICISM

The character of Irving scholarship has not appreciably changed since 1970, when Henry Pochmann observed that, "For Irving more than for most American writers, . . . literary history is inseparable from literary criticism, and until recently there was very little of the latter *per se.*" Literary history, biography, and textual and bibliographical discussion provide the most significant forms of publication.

One of the best general introductions is still one of the earliest, Pochmann's long introduction to *Washington Irving: Representative Selections* (New York, 1934), which Stanley T. Williams described at the time as "the most informative volume in existence concerning Washington Irving" (*AL*, Jan. 1935). It is a model of concise, judicious criticism by one deeply steeped in Irving's life and work. Perhaps more up to date is Pochmann's "Washington Irving: Amateur or Professional," in *Essays on American Literature in Honor of J. B. Hubbell*, ed. Clarence Gohdes (Durham, N.C., 1967), which ascribes Irving's literary success to an acute grasp of his own strengths, so that he appears less the divine amateur "toying with esoteric aspirations beyond his reach than the canny professional gauging his grasp by his reach." Comparable assessments are to be found in the summary judgments of George Snell in "Washington Irving: a Revaluation" (*MLQ*, Sept. 1956), Ernest E. Leisy's "Irving and the Genteel Tradition" (*SR*, Sept. 1947); Leonard Beach's "Washington Irving: The Artist in a Changing World" (*UKCR*, Summer 1948). And of particular high quality is Lewis Leary's Minnesota Pamphlet (no. 25), *Washington Irving* (Minneapolis, 1963), which offers an acute and concise summary of the writer's career.

Turning now to book-length critical studies, of primary importance is William L. Hedges's *Washington Irving: An American Study, 1802–*

1832 (Baltimore, 1965), which accents Irving's roots in the national culture, the influences on him of Swift and Addison, his American predecessors, and his effect on Cooper, Poe, Hawthorne, Emerson, Thoreau, Melville, Twain, and Howells. Of particular interest is Hedges's dissection of those less than genial moods in Irving, his persistent self-deprecation, insecurity, depression, and negativism. Hedges's account of Irving's role in the development of the American short story form is also adroitly handled. Although Hedges' work stops at the point of Irving's return to America, it is an indispensable account of Irving's formative and productive early career.

Also dealing principally with the early career is Martin Roth's *Comedy and America: The Lost World of Washington Irving* (Port Washington, N.Y., 1976), which culminates in a full-scale treatment of *A History of New York*. In Roth's view this is a burlesque comedy lacking, like satire and humor, "all moral reference." Roth believes that Irving succeeded in creating an authentic American voice, in Diedrich Knickerbocker, but the voice was that of a "childish neurotic and solipsist" which served only those early materials and was useless to the later sketches, where the Crayon persona served better the morally referential prose.

As remarked above, Ben H. McClary's *Washington Irving and the House of Murray: . . .* (Knoxville, Tenn., 1969) brings together the letters between Irving and his British publisher John Murray II and his son. Through careful introductions and annotations, McClary traces Irving's earliest dealings with his publisher and the growing estrangement between them, illustrating at the same time some fascinating features of British and American literary relationships during the period (1817–1856). Of equally high caliber is Walter A. Reichart's *Washington Irving in Germany* (Ann Arbor, Mich., 1957), which offers an exhaustive account of all of Irving's relations with Germany. In this connection one may also consult Henry A. Pochmann's "Irving's German Sources in *The Sketch Book*" (*SP*, July 1930), "Irving's German Tour and Its Influence on His Tales" (*PMLA*, Dec. 1930), and *German Culture in America* (Madison, Wis., 1957).

Students in particular will find a useful introduction to the writer in Mary Weatherspoon Bowden's *Washington Irving* (Boston, 1981), a volume in the Twayne United States Authors Series that provides a concise account of the author's life and work, a brief chronology of important dates, and a short annotated bibliography.

Amongst collections of essays devoted to Irving, the most valuable is clearly *A Century of Commentary on the Works of Washington Irving, 1860-1974*, edited by Andrew B. Myers (Tarrytown, N.Y., 1976), which brings together some forty-five essays, in whole or in part, representing the most essential criticism of Irving between William Cullen Bryant's

1860 eulogy on Irving to 1974. Myers has also edited *Washington Irving: A Tribute* (Tarrytown, N.Y., 1972), which contains valuable essays by Haskell S. Springer on *The Sketch Book*; Carl H. Woodring on literary England in the 1820s; Lorman A. Ratner on American nationalism; Myers on Irving in Spain; H. L. Kleinfield on Irving in his letters; Joseph T. Butler on Sunnyside; and William M. Gibson on the American literary scene, 1815–1860. Myers has also edited valuable collections in *The Worlds of Washington Irving, 1783–1859: An Anthology Exhibition from the Collections of the New York Public Library* (Tarrytown, 1974), which usefully collects and annotates a valuable collection of manuscripts, letters, prints, and drawings; and in *The Knickerbocker Tradition; Washington Irving's New York* (Tarrytown, 1974), which brings together six scholarly essays on various aspects of the subject. Particularly valuable is Myers's essay "Sunnyside: From Saltbox to Snuggery to Shrine," which recounts the changing condition of Irving's house as the man himself became an institution. It should be read alongside Joseph T. Butler's *Washington Irving's Sunnyside* (Tarrytown, 1968).

As should be evident from the previous paragraph, Myers and his colleagues at Sleepy Hollow Restorations in Tarrytown have been very active in the past decade in publishing highly valuable compendia and symposia of Irving's scholarship. Tarrytown is also the headquarters of the newly formed Washington Irving Society, an organization now allied with the Modern Language Association. The aim of the society, of which Myers is the first and current president, is to promote more extensive knowledge and understanding of the life and works of Irving and of his time. A very valuable new semi-annual newsletter of the Washington Irving Society, *Postscript*, offers a forum of information about meetings of the Society and stimulating commentary on the life and work of Irving. The address of the WI Society is 150 White Plains Road, Tarrytown, N.Y. 10591.

A great deal of useful criticism of Irving's work is to be found in books not exclusively devoted to Irving. Amongst these should be mentioned Daniel G. Hoffman's *Form and Fable in American Fiction* (New York, 1961); William L. Hedges's "Washington Irving: Nonsense, the Fat of the Land and the Dream of Innocence," in *The Chief Glory of Every People: Essays on Classic American Writers*, ed. Matthew Bruccoli (Carbondale, Ill., 1973); Henry Seidel Canby's *Classic Americans* (New York, 1931); Leo Marx's *The Machine and the Garden* (New York, 1964); and Lewis Leary's excellent *Soundings: Some Early American Writers* (Athens, Ga., 1975). Other essay treatments in books will be mentioned below, as appropriate, as this review proceeds from a consideration of Irving's art to criticism of his books in the order in which they were published.

Those interested in Irving's idea of the craft of writing will find him usefully excerpted and discussed in Stanley Banks's *American Romanticism: A Shape for Fiction* (New York, 1969), which discusses his art in the context of other writers. Irving in relation to other early practitioners of fiction is admirably treated in Henri Petter's *The Early American Novel* (Columbus, Ohio, 1971), which marks an advance on the work of Lillie D. Loshe. These matters are also usefully outlined in William C. Spengemann's *The Adventurous Muse: The Poetics of American Fiction, 1789–1900* (New Haven, Conn., 1977), which is particularly acute on theoretical considerations.

In "Irving's Use of the Gothic Mode" (*SLitI*, Spring, 1974), Donald A. Ringe claims for Irving a commitment to the philosophy of the Scottish school of common sense, with the effect that, however fascinated Irving might have been with the world of gothic fantasies, he is finally anchored in "the world of common sense and prosaic daylight. . . ." Readers should also consult John Clendenning's "Irving and the Gothic Tradition" (*BuR*, May 1964). On Irving's art of the short story, so ably analyzed in Hedges's book, Eugene Current-Garcia — in "Irving Sets the Pattern: Notes on Professionalism and the Art of the Short Story" (*SSF*, Fall 1973) — takes a fresh look at the claim that Irving inaugurated the American short story and comes to the conclusion that he did "indeed set the pattern for the artistic re-creation of common experience in short fictional form. . . ." In a subsequent essay—"'Soundings and Alarums': The Beginning of Short Fiction in America" (*MQ*, Summer 1976) — Current-Garcia remarks that prior to 1800, short fiction pointed its moral rather overtly. Irving is praised for extending the development of the short tale by his gift for nascent realism, "a feeling of life-likeness and immediacy."

These discussions of realism, gothicism, and romantic fantasy have a significant bearing on matters of style and point of view. Of those who have dealt significantly with such issues are Lewis Leary, in "The Two Voices of Washington Irving" in *From Irving to Steinbeck: Studies of American Literature in Honor of Harry R. Warfel*, eds. Motley Deakin and Peter Lisca (Gainesville, Fla., 1972), which points out the differences between the comic voices of Geoffrey Crayon and Diedrich Knickerbocker so as to discriminate the styles of Irving's comedy. How the point-of-view character shapes style is also the subject of Guido Fink's "Il 'Corsivo Vivente' di Washington Irving" (*SA* 16, 1970). Fink's *I testimoni dell'-immaginario* (Roma, 1978) brings up to date his analysis of Irving's use of the mask or persona as narrator. Finally, John C. Kemp, in "Historians Manqués: Irving's Apologetic Personae" (*ATQ*, 1974), claims that the whimsical personae Knickerbocker and Crayon foreshadow the wayward failures of Hawthorne, Twain, Fitzgerald and J. D. Salinger. Kemp argues that after Irving abandoned his whimsical sketches for serious history, he abandoned as well the ineffectual persona type, and that later, when Irving returned to fiction, the revival of this persona was unsuccessful.

Let us turn now to the criticism of specific Irving titles, in the order of their appearance, with allowances for some overlapping.

Oldstyle and *Salmagundi* have sparked little criticism. But amongst the items worth noting are Bruce I. Granger's "From Silence Dogood to Launcelot Langstaff" (*EAL*, Spring 1968), which surveys the American periodical essay from Franklin through Irving. Expanding on his treatment of Irving's place in the serials tradition, Granger published *American Essay Serials from Franklin to Irving* (Knoxville, Tenn., 1978), comparing Irving to Joseph Dennie, Freneau, Trumbull, and others. Granger sees only a tenuous connection between the early serials in *Oldstyle* and *Salmagundi* and Irving's mature work. An offshoot of Bruce Granger and Martha Hartzog Stocker's edition of these serials is Granger's charming essay "The Whim-Whamsical Bachelors in *Salmagundi*" (*Costerus* 2, 1972), as well as Stocker's "*Salmagundi:* Problems in Editing the So-called First Edition (1807–08)" in *PBSA* (First Quarter, 1973). On the sources of the latter, readers may consult Mary Weatherspoon Bowden's "Cocklofts and Slang-Whangers: The Historical Sources of Washington Irving's *Salmagundi*" (*NYH* 61:2, 1980). Irving's sources are central to Martin Roth's "Irving and the Old Style" (*EAL*, Winter 1977), which argues Irving's dependency on Goldsmith, Addison, and Steele rather than the perhaps more valuable American examples like Franklin's "Do-good Papers." However that may be, Roth finds little to commend in *Oldstyle* because Irving's models were alien to his comic intent: "It was characteristic of Irving in his first period to choose to write in traditional genres that carried with them a heavy burden of moralizing; yet, because of his temperament and talents, the world he projected in his writings was a comic one in which moral and physical evil left no traces." These views are more fully elaborated in Roth's *Comedy and America.*

Irving's *A History of New York* has fared somewhat better, so far as volume of criticism is concerned. Readers may consult Stanley T. Williams and Tremaine McDowell's introduction to their edition of the 1809 text (New York, 1917). Edwin T. Bowden also has enlightening things to say about the work in the Introduction to his edition of the 1812 text (New Haven, 1964). On the sources of the work the following are of especial value: James E. Evans's "The English Lineage of Diedrich Knickerbocker" (*EAL*, Spring 1975), which cites sources in Swift, Fielding, and Sterne; Robert C. Wess's "The Use of Hudson-Valley Folk Tradition in Washington Irving's *Knickerbocker's History of New York*" (*NYFQ* 30, 1974), which locates sources in the traditions of the old Dutch settlers; W. L. Hedges's

"Knickerbocker, Bolingbroke, and the Fiction of History" (*JHI*, June–Sept. 1959); Charles W. Jones's "Knickerbocker Santa Claus" (*New York Historical Society Quarterly*, Oct. 1954); and Henry M. Lydenberg's "Irving's *Knickerbocker* and Some of Its Sources" (*BNYPL*, Nov.–Dec. 1952).

Edwin A. Greenlaw was first to elaborate on Irving's satire on Jeffersonian Republicanism in the work, in "Washington Irving's Comedy of Politics" (*Texas Review*, Apr. 1916). Mary Weatherspoon Bowden extends the analysis in "Knickerbocker's *History* and the 'Enlightened' Men of New York City" (*AL*, May 1975), identifying the sources of Irving's wit in easily identifiable contemporary figures and institutions, like Mayor DeWitt Clinton, who, like many other New Yorkers, found Irving's *History* to be "perfectly disgusting to good taste." Finally, Michael L. Black's "Political Satire in Knickerbocker's *History*" (in Myers's collection, *The Knickerbocker Tradition: Washington Irving's New York* [Tarrytown, N.Y., 1974]) claims for Irving the status of "one of the best writers of American political satire, a genre that has not flourished in this country."

On the matter of the tone of *A History*, Charlton G. Laird finds "Tragedy and Irony in *Knickerbocker's History*" (*AL*, May 1940), but most readers have found it satirical and comic. Another adjective, however, is suggested by Marvin E. Mengeling in "The Crass Humor of Irving's Diedrich Knickerbocker" (*SAH*, Oct. 1974). In David Durant's "Aeolism in Knickerbocker's *A History of New York*" (*AL*, Jan. 1970), a claim is made for the unity of the work in Irving's satiric treatment of Aeolism — "the inflation of empty subjects into false importance through idle words." Durant argues that "the Aeolistic narrator is a historian whose work involves, as an allegory, a satiric attack on political Aeolism and includes, as a casebook of bombast, a similar attack on Aeolistic historians." Wayne R. Kime has analyzed "The Satiric Use of Names in Irving's *History of New York*" (*Names*, Dec. 1968), finding satirical as well as serious onomastic discussion. Kime remarks that by using "burlesque etymologies, insulting sobriquets, and fanciful interpretations of topographical, generic, and family names, Irving utilized his own interest in name study." Donald R. Nobel notes an obscenity relevant to Stuyvesant's name in Irving's *History* in "Washington Irving's 'Peter' Pun" (*AN&Q*, Mar. 1970), though frankly I think that Irving has more fun with Anthony's nose. In any event, the 1809 text did have its embarrassments for the older genteel Irving, who revised the text in the late 1840s. Some of his changes are taken up in Clarence Webster's "Irving's Expurgation of the 1809 *History of New York*" (*AL*, Nov. 1932). While we await Michael L. Black's CSE-Twayne edition of the work, his dissertation, "Washington Irving's *A History of New York* With Emphasis on the 1848 Revision" (Columbia, 1967) offers a comparatively full study of Irving's changes and expurgations. Finally, in "The Compulsive Design," Irving Mailin finds Testy a prototype of the American hero who tries to master his environment by constructing an inflexible design that eventually destroys him (*American Dreams, American Nightmares*, ed. David Madden [Carbondale, Ill., 1970]).

The Sketch Book is perhaps Irving's most popular work, but virtually all the accumulated criticism deals with "Rip Van Winkle" and "The Legend of Sleepy Hollow." George Monteiro in "Washington Irving: A Grace Note on 'The Pride of the Village'" (*Research Studies* [Wash. St. U.], Dec. 1968) tries to absolve a minor tale of the charge of "sickly pathos." But most critics have limited themselves to the former two stories. Martin Roth links "Rip Van Winkle" to *A History* in "The Final Chapter of Knickerbocker's New York" (*MP*, Feb. 1969) by noting that both works explore the same mythic contest between the Yankees and the Dutch as symbols of opposing views of history and culture. On this issue the reader may also profitably consult Donald A. Ringe's "New York and New England: Irving's Criticism of American Society" (*AL*, Jan. 1967).

On the sources of "Rip" readers may consult the following: Louis Le Fevre (*YR*, Sept. 1946), Elmer Brooks (*AL*, Jan. 1954), John T. Krumpelmann (*Archiv*, 1956), Walter A. Reichart (*Monatshefte*, Jan. 1956 and *Archiv*, 1957), and Henry A. Pochmann (*SP*, July 1930).

The origin of the story in folklore has offered critics an exceptional opportunity to engage in symbolic or allegorical readings. Amongst those who have written instructively on the possible larger meanings of the tale are Terence Martin in "Rip, Ichabod, and the American Imagination" (*AL*, May 1959), which argues a split in Irving's heroes between the visionary and imaginative, in their almost timeless situations, and the practical and pragmatic (Columbus, Washington); Philip Young, whose "Fallen from Time: The Mythic Rip Van Winkle" (*KR*, Autumn 1960) superbly dissects the latent implications of Rip's flight; Marcel Heiman, whose "Rip Van Winkle: A Psychoanalytic Note on the Story and Its Author" (*AI*, Spring 1959) finds Rip's flight an objectification, not of American concerns, but of a deeply personal anxiety about marriage; David J. Kann, whose "'Rip Van Winkle': Wheels within Wheels" (*AI* no. 2, 1979) finds the "mechanism of the dream" as the closest analogue to the process of Irving's tale. Extending Young's analysis, Kann notes both the infantile fantasy of the bulk of the tale, yet registers Irving's own satirical distance at the end.

These analytic, or psychoanalytic, interpretations of Rip's relationship to his wife and society have not been lost on the developing feminist critics. In *The Resisting Reader: A Feminist Approach to American Fiction* (Bloomington, Ind., 1978), Judith Fetterley argues that "American literature is male" and that "Our literature neither leaves women alone nor allows them to participate" in the American dream. She believes that the woman reader is "co-opted into participation in an experience from which she is explicitly excluded; she is asked to identify with a selfhood that defines itself in opposition to her; she is required to identify herself against herself." How is the modern woman to read "our first and most famous" tale, she asks, if the subject is "the avoidance of woman, which means the avoidance of one's wife? What is the impact of this American dream on her?" Needless to say, Irving is roughly handled, with some justice, although the subtlety of his wit and irony is sacrificed in the service of ideology; and the human poignance of sexual anxiety, of either sex, is not felt. Irving's attitude toward women is also discussed by Kenneth T. Reed in "'Oh These Women!' Irving's Shrews and Coquettes" (AN&Q, June 1970) and in William L. Hedges's "Irving, Hawthorne, and the Image of the Wife" (ATQ, First Quarter 1970), where it is argued that the principal archetype of the wife in Irving's fiction is a conventional "womanly woman" marked by fortitude in adversity and sustaining love, in contrast to Hawthorne's more carnal "post-lapsarian Eve." Hedges's Washington Irving (Baltimore, 1965) also offers some valuable observations about women in Irving's early works. As a follow-up to these matters the reader may consult Richard Ellmann's "Love in the Catskills" (NY Review of Books, 5 Feb. 1976) and the rejoinders by Nina Baym, Thomas H. Pauley, and Ellman on 13 May 1976.

It seems somewhat prosaic to turn from these charged issues to "On the Plot Structure of 'Rip Van Winkle' and 'Rip Rip'" (Romance Notes, Winter 1980), but Henry J. Richards's account of how the story is put together is useful. On the "Americanness" of Rip, readers may consult "Buckskin West: Leatherstocking at High Noon" (NYFQ, 1968), where Warren S. Walker finds Rip to be a typical folklore hero, solitary, individualistic, and avoiding the responsibilities of domesticity and social life. And Daniel L. Plung finds "Rip" different from its intriguing models in European folklore, since it is an Americanized version of the "quest for individualism and self-reliance" in "'Rip Van Winkle': Metempsychosis and the Quest for Self-Reliance" (Rocky Mountain Review of Language and Literature, 1977).

If Philip Young pointed to Rip as "fallen from time," in some mythic sense, John F. Lynen's The Design of the Present: Essays on Time and Form in American Literature (New Haven, 1969) argues that Irving conceived of momentary experience against a background of "eternal time," a dialectic of simultaneous involvement and transcendence that Lynen traces to the puritan consciousness. See also Walter Shear's useful "Time in 'Rip Van Winkle' and 'The Legend of Sleepy Hollow'" (MQ, Winter 1976). The timeliness of "Rip" is also suggested in Tom Scanlan's "The

Domestication of Rip Van Winkle: Joe Jefferson's Play as Prologue to a Modern American Drama" (*VQR*, Winter 1974), where Jefferson's greater stress on the *importance* of the family, in his nineteenth-century play adaptation, leads directly to the conflicted family situations in O'Neill, Williams, and Miller. In "Dreiser's Hurstwood and Jefferson's Rip Van Winkle" (*PMLA* 87, 1972), John R. Byers, Jr., argues that Jefferson's adaptation, which Carrie, Hurstwood and Drouet see one evening, suggested to Dreiser "the tragic possibilities in the usually comic Rip for the development of Hurstwood," who likewise comes to be "a once prosperous man locked out of his home."

Finally, readers may also wish to consult Robert H. Woodward's "Dating the Action of 'Rip Van Winkle'" (*NYFQ*, Spring 1959); Marvin E. Mengeling's "Characterization in 'Rip Van Winkle'" (*EJ*, Dec. 1964) and "Structure and Tone in 'Rip Van Winkle': The Irony of Silence" (*Discourse*, Autumn 1966); Helen Lee's "Clue Patterns in 'Rip Van Winkle'" (*EJ*, Feb. 1966); and K. W. Cameron's "The Long-Sleep-and-Changed-World Motif in 'Rip Van Winkle'" (*ESQ*, Second Quarter 1960). Lastly, "Rip" has finally come of age (the Age of Barthes, Lacan, and Todorov) in Jean Béranger's "Analyses structurales de 'Rip Van Winkle'" (*Revue Française d'Études Américaines*, Apr. 1978).

"The Legend of Sleepy Hollow" has not been so extensively analyzed, although, as the previous paragraphs suggest, it is often paired with "Rip Van Winkle" in critical discussions. Among the best treatments are those by Daniel Hoffman in "Irving's Use of American Folklore in 'The Legend of Sleepy Hollow'" (*PMLA*, June 1953) and in *Form and Fable in American Fiction* (New York, 1961), where the conflict between Brom Bones and Ichabod is related to the tension between frontier and seaboard values; in Walter Shear's *MQ* article (cited above), which finds Ichabod and Rip to be "betrayed by history" and thus illustrative of the theme that American notions "of fame, happiness, and contentment" are "distributed capriciously by a random Eternal Justice"; in Marjorie Bruner's "The Legend of Sleepy Hollow': A Mythological Parody" (*CE*, Jan. 1964); and James W. Clark's "Washington Irving and New England Witchlore" (*NYFQ*, Dec. 1973), which invokes Cotton Mather's *Magnalia* to illustrate his definition of witchlore. Several articles, finally, have tried to identify the prototype for Ichabod: Herbert Reed in *The Staten Island Historian* (Apr.–June 1963); Truman Strobridge and Edwin Turnblath in *PNJHS* (July 1966); Patrick Conley in *AL* (Mar. 1968); and Ben Harris McClary in *N&Q* (Jan. 1968).

The Sketch Book was Irving's first book to be published in England. It may therefore be appropriate to pause here in the chronological survey to comment on the literature of Irving's relation to the mother country.

Ferdinand Künzig was first to treat the topic in *Washington Irving und seine Beziehungen zur englishen Literatur des 18. Jahrhunderts* (Heidelberg, 1911). Robert E. Spiller's *The American in England during the First Half Century of Independence* (New York, 1926) and Ernest Earnest's *Expatriates and Patriots: American Artists, Scholars and Writers in Europe* (Durham, N.C., 1968) also treat Irving in England, the latter relating Irving to more recent expatriates and expressing admiration for those who remained patriots. Irving's complicated relationship with Dickens is treated in Ernest Boll's "Charles Dickens and Washington Irving" (*MLQ*, Dec. 1944); Christof Wegelin's "Dickens and Irving: The Problem of Influence" (*MLQ*, Mar. 1946); W. C. Desmond Pacey's "Washington Irving and Charles Dickens" (*AL*, Jan. 1945); and Maunsell F. Field's *Memories of Many Men and Some Women* (New York, 1874). In "Walter Scott and Washington Irving: 'Editors of the Land of Utopia'" (*JAmS*, Apr. 1976), Kathryn Sutherland points out the mutual influence these friends had on one another, particularly Irving's contribution to Scott's narrative personae. Wayne R. Kime offers evidence of a literary relationship in "Washington Irving and 'To a Mountain Daisy': An Anecdote of Robert Burns in America" (*Studies in Scottish Literature*, Jan. 1973). And evidence of Irving's immense popularity in England is suggested by William S. Ward's "American Authors and British Reviewers, 1798–1826: A Bibliography" (*AL* 49, 1977), which finds Irving and Cooper more extensively reviewed than any other American writers.

Bracebridge Hall has evoked little scholarly interest. Aside from Herbert F. Smith's remarks in his CSE Twayne edition, Ben H. McClary argues, through an analysis of a letter of Irving's to the Reverend Cornelius H. Reaston Rodes, that Rodes's home, Chesterfield, was the model for Bracebridge Hall in "A Bracebridge-Hall Christmas for Van Buren" (*ELN*, Sept. 1970) And "Dolph Heyliger" is thematically analyzed in Horst Kruse's *Schlüsselmotive der amerikanischen Literatur* (Düsseldorf, 1979). *Tales of a Traveller* fares somewhat better. Nathalia Wright's "Irving's Use of His Italian Experiences in *Tales of a Traveller:* The Beginning of an American Tradition" (*AL*, May 1959) is a useful source study, as is Michael Clark's "A Source for Irving's 'The Young Italian'" (*AL*, Mar. 1980), which cites Allston's *Monaldi*. G. Thomas Couser traces the transformation of the garden image in "The Ruined Garden of Wolfert Webber" (*SSF*, Winter, 1975). James E. Devlin's "Irving's 'Adventure of the German Student'" (*SAF*, Spring 1979) finds in Gottfried Wolfgang's fantasies about "female beauty" a preoccupation with masturbation, such self-abuse "naturally" leading to insanity and institutionalization in a madhouse. Readers may also consult Kelley Griffith, Jr., "Ambiguity and Gloom in Irving's 'The Adventures of the German Student'" (*CEA*, 1975) and Elizabeth Teichmann's "Deux adaptations inconnues du conte de

W. Irving: 'The Adventures of the German Student'" (*MP*, Aug. 1955). Roger Asselineau, incidentally, has some interesting things to say about this tale in his bilingual French-English edition, *Washington Irving — Contes Fantastique: Rip Van Winkle, L'Etudiant Allemand, Le Gouverneur des Sept Cités*, translated by Henri Parisot with an Introduction and Notes by Roger Asselineau (Paris, 1979). Finally, Charles D. Zug in "The Construction of 'The Devil and Tom Walker'" (*NYFQ*, Dec. 1968) has argued that Irving's tale constitutes a virtual handbook of folklore motifs: the sale of a man's soul to the devil, the existence of buried treasure, the notion of a tree of life, an oath, and the figure of the devil as a huntsman or a strong black man. Zug argues that, in addition, Irving added the American legend of Captain Kidd, a domestic wrangle, and colonial usury in Boston.

Irving's Spanish travels and writing have generated considerably more interest than other works of the 1820s. Readers should consult John DeLancey Ferguson's *American Literature in Spain* (New York, 1916), Claude G. Bowers's *The Spanish Adventures of Washington Irving* (Boston, 1940), and Stanley T. Williams's *The Spanish Background of American Literature* (2 vols., New Haven, Conn., 1955). Irving as a hispanist is studied by C. A. Baiocco in "Washington Irving's Hispanic Literature" (*Américas*, Apr. 1972), her essay illustrating the importance of Irving's residence in Spain in the 1820s and afterwards, in the 1840s, while he served in the diplomatic corps in Madrid.

William L. Hedges's "Irving's *Columbus:* The Problem of Romantic Biography" (*Américas*, Oct. 1956) deals with the relationship between biographical and historical writing in the age of Emerson, Prescott, and Bancroft. And John Harmon McElroy's "The Integrity of Irving's *Columbus*" (*AL*, Mar. 1978) refutes Stanley T. Williams's insinuation that "anyone who praises the scholarship of Irving's *Columbus* can have made 'no genuine investigation' into the matter." McElroy, whose investigation has been more probing than that of any other researcher, shows that Irving's research was extensive, thoroughgoing, original, and responsible to the Spanish texts which he tracked down in several libraries in Spain, digested, synthesized, and reshaped into a great early biography. The only modern treatment of Irving's *Voyages and Discoveries of the Companions of Columbus* is James W. Tuttleton's "The Romance of History: Irving's *Companions of Columbus*" (*ATQ*, 1974), which analyzes this series of lives of the minor navigators who sailed with Columbus as romantic history, focusing on New World navigations and explorations as an extension of the spirit of the Crusades and containing Irving's analysis of "the conflict between national and racial attributes" brought "under the moral scrutiny of the author."

The best work in the past decade on *Granada* has been done by Earl N.

Harbert in several essays. His "The Manuscripts of A *Chronicle of the Conquest of Granada:* A Revised Census with Commentary" (*BRH* 82:1, 1979) expands Kleinfield's earlier census, documents the author's slipshod compositional methods, yet at the same time stresses Irving's "unwavering commitment through the years to historical accuracy and improved narrative economy." In his "Fray Antonio Agapida and Washington Irving's Romance with History" (*TSE* 17, 1969) and "Washington Irving's *Conquest of Granada:* A Spanish Experiment that Failed" (*CLIO,* June 1974) Harbert argues that Irving sought to counterbalance his Romantic tendencies in storytelling by "employing the weight of documentation," arguing in the latter essay that the experiment failed with the public, Irving concluding that the balance between fact and fantasy "should be reworked to become a more conservative exposition of verifiable history." Finally, Harbert's "Irving's *A Chronicle of the Conquest of Granada:* An Essay in the History of Publication, Revision, and Critical Reception" (*BNYPL,* Summer 1976) offers helpful information about differences between the early British and American editions and Irving's revisions for the ARE in the late 1840s. Readers should also consult Louise Hoffman's "Irving's Use of Spanish Sources in *The Conquest of Granada*" (*Hispania,* Nov. 1945). On the other Spanish books not much is available. Barton L. St. Armand finds Irving a possible source for the raven and for the term "arabesque" in "Some Poe Debts to Irving's *Alhambra*" (*Poe Studies,* Dec. 1977); and *Mahomet* elicits Montgomery Watt's "Muhammad in the Eyes of the West" (*Boston University Journal,* 1974).

Irving's Western writings have also generated a considerable amount of commentary. Readers may consult the criticisms and annotations provided in older editions of some of the Western works: Henry Leavitt Ellsworth's *Washington Irving on the Prairie or A Narrative of a Tour of the Southwest in the Year 1832,* edited by Stanley T. Williams and Barbara D. Simison (New York, 1937); [Charles Joseph] *Latrobe's Tour with Washington Irving. From Letters in The Rambler in North America* (London, 1835), edited and annotated by Muriel H. Wright and George H. Stirk (Oklahoma City, Okla., 1955); George E. Spaulding's *On the Western Tour with Washington Irving: The Journal and Letters of Count de Pourtales,* translated by Seymour Feiler (Norman, Okla., 1968); *A Tour on the Prairies,* edited by John F. McDermott (Norman, Okla., 1956); and *Astoria* (Norman, Okla., 1964) and *Bonneville* (Norman, Okla., 1961), both edited by Edgeley W. Todd.

Edgeley W. Todd has commented on the genesis of these Western works in "Washington Irving Discovers the Frontier" in *WHR* (Winter 1957), a topic enlarged upon by the Twayne edition editor of *Astoria,* Richard D. Rust, in "Irving Rediscovers the Frontier" (*ATQ,* 1973). In *Washington*

Irving: The Western Works (Western Writers Series 14, 1974), Richard H. Cracroft studies the Western tales, concluding that Irving is "the first American writer to discover a literary bonanza in the trans-Mississippi West." Arguing that Irving included "too much foreground and too little background" to really exploit his Western materials, Cracroft suggests that Irving wavered "between hymning the ideal, the primitive, and the romantic, and hymning the economic exploits of hard-headed realistic businessmen and their often uncouth and uncivilized employees." Irving's treatment of the landscape of the West is taken up in Donald Ringe's *The Pictorial Mode: Space and Time in the Art of Bryant, Irving and Cooper* (Lexington, Ky., 1971), where the landscapes of Thomas Cole suggesting the despoliation of nature are the model for Irving's treatment of what will happen to the prairie landscape.

On *A Tour on the Prairies*, Wayne R. Kime finds a satisfying fulness in "The Completeness of Washington Irving's *A Tour on the Prairies*" (*WAL*, Spring–Summer 1973). In "How the West Won: Irving's Comic Inversion of the Westering Myth in *A Tour on the Prairies*" (*AL*, Nov. 1978), William Bedford Clark argues that this work subverts the notion that civilization must inevitably overtake the West: "Civilized man's assault upon the virgin West, a theme rich with heroic possibilities, is portrayed as an exercise in comic futility, a lesson in human limitations." A comparable subject is treated in William J. Scheick's "Frontier Robin Hood: Wilderness, Civilization and the Half-Breed in Irving's *A Tour on the Prairies*" (*Southwestern American Literature*, 1978), which analyzes the half-breed Pierre Beatte as representative of "a hybrid race epitomizing the radical tension between civilization and the wilderness which permeates the narrative." Scheick sees in Beatte a suspended ambivalence about the relative values of the East and West, an ambivalence that gives way, later, to a greater appreciation of the East. On Irving's representation of minorities, readers may also wish to consult "The Indian in Knickerbocker's New Amsterdam" (*Indian Historian*, Summer 1974), where Per Seyersted finds Irving's treatment of the Indians in *A History* (book 1, chapter 4) quite sympathetic, in contrast to Irving's "later treatments of the original Americans," which mark "a sad anticlimax for a writer who started out as one of America's strongest critics of his countrymen's merciless robbing and killing of the Indians." Not irrelevant to this subject is Kenneth T. Reed's "Washington Irving and the Negro" (*Negro American Literature Forum*, July 1970), where Reed notes the evident fact that Irving shows little concern for slavery and deals with the black in stereotypical ways, raising a question about Irving's humanity in a time of abolitionist agitation. Finally, to return to *A Tour*, William C. Spengemann's *The Adventurous Muse: The Poetics of American Fiction, 1789–*

1900 (New Haven, Conn., 1977) is particularly interesting, as is Martha Dula's "Audience Response to *A Tour . . .* in 1835" (*WAL*, Spring–Summer 1973).

On *Bonneville*, readers may consult J. F. McDermott's "Washington Irving and the Journal of Captain Bonneville," (*Mississippi Valley Historical Review*, Dec. 1956) and Thomas J. Lyon's "Washington Irving's Wilderness" (*WAL*, Fall 1966). In "The Misadventures of Irving's Bonneville: Trapping and Being Trapped in the Rocky Mountains," in *The Westering Experience in American Literature: Bicentennial Essays*, edited by Merrill Lewis and L. L. Lee (Bellingham, Wash., 1977), Wayne Franklin rescues *Astoria* and *Bonneville* from the charge of being paid hackwork by arguing that they are important histories that defined for later authors how the Western prairie experience was to be rendered and what, in the largest sense, "the West" meant in relation to the East.

On the language and form of *Astoria*, Kenneth S. Rothwell notes, in "In Search of a Western Epic: Neihardt, Sandburg, and Jaffe as Regionalists and 'Astoriadists'" (*Kansas Quarterly* 2, 1970), that Irving's work offers a useful term, *Astoriad*, for defining a work that transforms history, saga, and tale into an epic dealing with "themes of settlement and conquest." Wayne R. Kime analyzes Irving's language in "Washington Irving and Frontier Speech" (*American Speech*, Feb. 1967), by cataloguing, in three of these Western works, Irving's interest in American language and his glossary of new frontier expressions. Kime also notes, in "Washington Irving's Revision of the *Tonquin* Episode in *Astoria*" (*WAL*, Spring 1969), that Irving's revisions of this episode reveal, through his heightening of the drama, Irving's increasing narrative art. The journal of Alfred Seton is also cited by Kime in "Alfred Seton's Journal: A Source for Irving's *Tonquin* Disaster Account" (*Oregon Historical Quarterly*, Dec. 1970). *Astoria* as an influence is explored in Kime's "Poe's Use of Irving's *Astoria* in 'The Journal of Julius Rodman'" (*AL*, May 1968).

On Irving's biography of George Washington, little has been published. George S. Hellman's "Irving's *Washington* and an Episode in Courtesy" (*Col*, 1930) may be consulted, as well as Elsie Lee West's "Washington Irving, Biographer," in *Washington Irving Reconsidered: A Symposium*, ed. Ralph M. Aderman (Hartford, Conn., 1969). Andrew B. Myers commends the life, in "The New York Years in Irving's *The Life of George Washington*" (*EAL*, Spring 1976), for consciously making the complicated narrative a story of rugged individuals and for making Washington "a flesh-and-blood general, and president, not any Olympian demi-god."

In conclusion, let me mention some recent studies of Irving in foreign countries. On Irving's works in Rumania, see Lucia Pavel's "Opera lui Washington Irving în România" (*Transilvania*, 1977). Irving's status in

Italy is admirably accounted for in three chapters of Rolando Anzilotti's *Studie ricerche di letteratura americana* (Florence, 1968). Maria Colombo supplies the text of a minor essay on "French Romance" in "Un Inedito di Washington Irving" (*SA* 12, 1966). And in *Il re nascosto: Saggio su Washington Irving* (Roma, 1979), Alessandro Portelli approaches Irving from the standpoint of a mixed Freudianism and Marxism, finding in Irving an awareness of the tensions of American society, yet restlessly searching for rhetorical stratagems to prevent the conflict from erupting into his pages. Irving's complicated feelings about "rabble power," Jacksonianism, progress, free enterprise, and the treatment of the Indian are suggestively analyzed in this study. Irving appears to retain more interest amongst Germanists than any other early nineteenth-century American writer, notable examples being Helmbrecht Breinig's *Irvings Kurzprosa: Kunst Und Kunstproblematik im erzählerischen und essayistischen Werk*, Angelsächsisch Sprache Und Literature, no. 6 (Frankfurt, 1973) and "'The Sober Page of History': Irvings kürzere historisch — biographische Schriften zwischen Faktographie und Dichtung" (*Amerikastudien*, 1975), on the blending of fact and fiction. Irving as a travel writer is explored in Waldemar Zacharasiewics's "Skizzen eines Reisenden: Bemerkungen zu einem bestimmenden Thema im Werk Washington Irvings" (*Salzburg Studies in English Literature*, 1977). Finally, in Morton Nirenberg's *The Reception of American Literature in German Periodicals, 1820–1850* (Heidelberg, 1970), it is suggested that while the Transcendentalists received short shrift during the period indicated, German periodicals were hospitable to the work of Irving.

This review has not undertaken to list all doctoral dissertations on Irving and his works, which may be discovered in *Dissertation Abstracts International*, or to cite all of the scores of minor notes, source studies, and stray articles on Irving's influence on subsequent writers. Readers may find them listed in the two-volume *Articles on American Literature*, edited by Lewis Leary (Durham, N.C., 1954, 1970), the Springer reference guide cited earlier, annual bibliographies of *PMLA* and the annual volumes of *American Literary Scholarship*.

To have cited all of the published scholarship and criticism would require a book very nearly of the size of *Fifteen American Authors before 1900*. Even so, a review of merely the items selected here for attention suggests certain conclusions about his art. First, it is apparent that Irving continues to enjoy the attention of serious literary critics, textual editors, biographers, and historians. In part this attention is a reflection of his preeminence, not merely as the first major American writer to have made his living from his literary productions but also as the first exceptional, all-round practitioner of several important literary genres: the travel sketch, epistolary journalism, the short story, comic and serious history, and biography. While Irving has not been accorded the significance of those American writers who, in Harry Levin's words, cultivated "the power of blackness," he remains an unusually popular writer whose esteem with the general public lies perhaps in the extent to which his personality, as reflected in his congenial prose, expresses the deeply grounded optimism of the American people. In any case, the pleasures of his style—as expressed in his wit and whimsy, his gift for satire, his urbane moral sense and his social conscience—suggest that he will continue to enjoy an appreciative audience, whatever the coming fluctuations of literary taste, however much the reputations of other writers may rise and fall.

Henry Wadsworth Longfellow

RICHARD DILWORTH RUST

As THE CHIEF American poet of his time, Henry Wadsworth Longfellow has been included in practically every discussion of American literature of the nineteenth century. Furthermore, many of the literary elite of Longfellow's era who were also his friends or acquaintances left their reminiscences and evaluations of him. Despite the hundreds of books, articles, and reviews from the 1830s through the 1910s, it was not until approximately fifty years after Longfellow's death that there was serious consultation of manuscripts and letters at the Craigie-Longfellow House, and approximately seventy-five years until the first impartial full-length biography appeared.

Longfellow criticism is especially interesting as an index to changing aesthetic tastes. The man whom Hawthorne considered "the head of our list of native poets" was disparaged by some in the 1920s and '30s as the epitome of Victorianism, didacticism, Brahminism, and the genteel tradition. Critical interest in Longfellow has increased since that time, yet not in any widespread manner. In the last twenty years (as represented in the *PMLA* bibliographies for 1961 through 1980) there were ninety-nine articles, five books, six scholarly editions, and three doctoral dissertations — hardly a tenth of the output on Longfellow's friend Hawthorne. While several of the most significant books on Longfellow were published in the 1960s, the decade of the 1970s saw relatively little in the way of major reexaminations of Longfellow.

From Earl N. Harbert and Robert A. Rees, editors, *Fifteen American Authors Before 1900: Bibliographic Essays on Research & Criticism* (Madison: The University of Wisconsin Press; © 1984 by the Board of Regents of the University of Wisconsin System); may be reproduced only by permission of the publisher.

BIBLIOGRAPHY

In Volume Five of Jacob Blanck's *BAL* we have the first full Longfellow bibliography of primary books and reprints and the first listing of Longfellow material in books by authors other than Longfellow, sheet music with lyrics derived from Longfellow, and some secondary criticism and biographies. Blanck's material supersedes Luther S. Livingston's *A Bibliography of the First Editions in Book Form of the Writings of Henry Wadsworth Longfellow* (New York, 1908; reprinted, 1968), which still has value for its notes accompanying some entries.

The earliest Longfellow bibliography appeared in the *Literary World*, 26 February 1882, and was revised and enlarged to form an appendix to Samuel Longfellow's *Final Memorials of Henry Wadsworth Longfellow* (Boston, 1887). (In 1891, *Final Memorials* was in turn integrated into the earlier *Life of Henry Wadsworth Longfellow* to form a three-volume biography; rpt. 1969.) To this bibliography of books, translations, and reviews, Samuel Longfellow added a list of Longfellow's poems and dates of composition. The original *Literary World* bibliography is further expanded by a lengthy list of contemporary reviews at the end of Eric S. Robertson's *Life of Henry Wadsworth Longfellow* (London, 1887; rpt. 1972) and by Thomas Wentworth Higginson's additions to the list of translations, in an appendix to his *Henry Wadsworth Longfellow* (Boston, 1902).

The most complete bibliography of books on Longfellow in foreign languages is Paul Morin's *Les Sources de l'Oeuvre de Henry Wadsworth Longfellow* (Paris, 1913), in which Morin lists 145 biographies and critical writings and 320 reviews and appreciations. A more accessible list of foreign and English language biographies and criticism is found at the end of Volume Two of *CHAL*. This bibliography on Longfellow, prepared by H. W. L. Dana, also includes periodical contributions not contained in the *Complete Works*.

An annotated bibliography is found in Harry H. Clark's *Major American Poets* (New York, 1936), an excellent anthology which also has extensive notes on selected poems. This is complemented by the annotated bibliography in Odell Shepard's *Henry Wadsworth Longfellow: Representative Selections, with Introduction, Bibliography, and Notes* (New York, 1934). More exhaustive and up-to-date bibliographies are in Edward Wagenknecht's *Longfellow: A Full-Length Portrait* (New York, 1955); the *LHUS* and Supplements (New York and London, 1974); and Lewis Leary's *Articles on American Literature, 1900–1950, 1950–1967, and 1968–1975.*

EDITIONS

Editions of Longfellow's complete works, single works, selections, and translations are legion. Blanck has 173 pages on Longfellow, the most extensive amount on any author treated thus far in *BAL*. As Henry Pochmann and Gay Wilson Allen note in their *Introduction to Masters of American Literature* (Carbondale, Ill., 1969), Longfellow's writings have been translated into Russian, Hebrew, Dutch, French, German, Italian, Spanish, Portuguese, Swedish, Norwegian, Danish, Pennsylvania-Dutch, Yiddish, and Icelandic (and, they might have added, Latin, Polish, and Persian).

Many separate and collected Longfellow works appeared during his lifetime, the most significant of which are listed in the *LHUS* bibliography. Four years after his death, the Houghton Mifflin Company published an authorized Riverside Edition of Longfellow's works (11 vols., Boston, 1886). Five years later, Samuel Longfellow's three-volume *Life* was added to form the Standard Library Edition of *The Works of Henry Wadsworth Longfellow* (Boston, 1891; available in reprint from AMS Press). This edition is divided into two volumes of prose works, six of poetical works, three of the *Divine Comedy*, and the biography. Two years later, and in many reprintings thereafter, appeared a one-volume edition of *The Complete Poetical Works of Henry W. Longfellow*, edited by Horace E. Scudder (Boston, 1893). It currently is in print (Boston, 1975) under the title, *The Poetical Works of Longfellow*.

Judicious selections of both poetry and prose are in Odell Shepard's *Longfellow: Representative Selections*. A current edition of a Longfellow novel is *Kavanagh, A Tale*, edited, with an introduction surveying critical reception of the book, by Jean Downey (New Haven, Conn., 1965). Useful collections of poetry are: *The Poems of Henry Wadsworth Longfellow*, edited by Louis Untermeyer (New York, 1943); the Modern Library edition of *The Poems of Longfellow* (New York, 1945), which includes the four major narrative poems but excludes the best sonnets; *Longfellow: Selected Poetry*, edited by Howard Nemerov (New York, 1959); *The Essential Longfellow*, edited by Lewis Leary (New York, 1963); *Favorite Poems*, edited by H. S. Canby (Garden City, N.Y., 1967); *Poems*, edited by Edmund Fuller (New York, 1967); and several reprintings of *The Poetical Works of Longfellow* (New York, 1973, 1975, 1981). In addition to these, perusal of current book lists showing multiple editions of individual poems such as *Evangeline, Hiawatha*, and "Paul Revere's Ride" would suggest that Longfellow's poetry continues to be a staple of elementary and junior high school reading.

MANUSCRIPTS AND LETTERS

The majority of Longfellow manuscripts and letters belong to the Henry Wadsworth Longfellow Trust and are on deposit in the Houghton Library at Harvard University. Located there are 242 volumes of papers by or pertaining to Longfellow, including manuscripts of his works, lectures, and journals. Also on deposit are 3,913 letters from Longfellow to various persons and letters from 6,507 identified persons to Longfellow. Harvard has many volumes from Longfellow's personal library, some of which were donated by Alice Longfellow about 1905, and the remainder of which were deposited by the Longfellow Trust.

The Bowdoin College Library has 17 Longfellow manuscripts and 61 letters by Longfellow and 80 to him. In addition, the library has over a thousand volumes of Longfellow's works and more than seven hundred musical scores of Longfellow poems. Parts of this collection are described very attractively in Richard Harwell's *Hawthorne and Longfellow: A Guide to an Exhibit* (Brunswick, Maine, 1966), with commentary on Longfellow's college years and some letters and documents pertaining to Longfellow at Bowdoin.

Although Longfellow letters and manuscripts are scattered throughout the country, the following libraries account for the remaining bulk of them. The Massachusetts Historical Society has about 160 letters written by Longfellow to various correspondents. The Boston Public Library has 10 manuscripts and 87 letters. There are 7 manuscripts and 52 letters at Yale University. Longfellow materials at the Pierpont Morgan Library include 13 manuscripts and 76 letters. The Berg Collection at the New York Public Library has 25 manuscripts and 145 letters. The Library of Congress has 7 manuscripts and 45 letters. The Clifton Waller Barrett Library at the University of Virginia has 7 manuscripts of Longfellow's prose, 45 of verse, and 318 letters. At the Henry E. Huntington Library are 15 Longfellow manuscripts, 203 letters by Longfellow, and 173 letters to him. And at the University of Washington there are 2 manuscripts and 121 letters.

The 5,000 or so extant letters presented a formidable mass, yet Andrew Hilen successfully completed the task of editing a selection from them in an accurate and readable format. The first two volumes of *The Letters of Henry Wadsworth Longfellow* were published by Harvard Press (Cambridge, 1966) and cover the period from 1814 to 1843. Volumes Three and Four cover from 1844 to 1865 (Cambridge, 1972). The last two volumes, covering 1866 to 1882, appeared in 1983. In each of the volumes published, Hilen provides an informative biographical introduction and thorough notes. His purpose, as he states in "The Longfellow Letters"

(*Manuscripts*, Summer 1955), is "to rescue Longfellow through the publication of authentic texts of his best letters, from the morass of Victorian misinterpretation and modern misunderstanding into which he has fallen." Along with the accurate printing of the letters, the publication of Longfellow's journals in their original form is essential for a more thorough understanding of his character and conflicts. To date we have to rely almost solely on Samuel Longfellow's extensive but altered versions of the journals in his *Life*. The late Robert S. Ward began editing the journals, a project now being carried forth by J. Chesley Mathews. Segments of journals pertaining to Longfellow's visits in Spain, Scandinavia, and France are in Andrew Hilen's *Longfellow and Scandinavia: A Study of the Poet's Relationship with the Northern Languages and Literature* (New Haven, Conn., 1947); Iris Lilian Whitman's *Longfellow and Spain* (New York, 1927); and C. L. Johnson's "Longfellow's Journey along the Loire, 1826" (*FR*, Oct. 1966).

BIOGRAPHY

Longfellow's letters and journals, reminiscences of his family and friends, autobiographical novels, and standard biographies provide an abundance of material on Longfellow's life. Three books of the last sort appeared shortly after his death: William Sloane Kennedy's *Henry W. Longfellow* (Cambridge, Mass., 1882; rpt. 1973); Francis H. Underwood's *Henry Wadsworth Longfellow: A Biographical Sketch* (Boston, 1882; rpt. 1973); and George Lowell Austin's *Henry Wadsworth Longfellow: His Life, His Works, His Friendships* (Boston, 1883; rpt. 1977). Although Kennedy sought out reminiscences from Longfellow's friends, he turned mostly to printed reviews in newspapers and journals to produce his disjointed and second-hand work. Underwood's biography likewise is derivative, although he pays more attention than other biographers of the 1880s to Longfellow as poet. In 1876, Austin started gathering memoranda from Longfellow himself, but postponed this work until Longfellow's death terminated the project. Regretting his failure to complete what would have been the closest thing to an authorized biography, Austin later enlisted the help of John Owen, Longfellow's cousin, to finish his partial biography and collection of anecdotes.

Andrew Hilen in the *Letters* warns us that "equipped with scissors and paste and a divinity-school training," Samuel Longfellow tampered with the manuscripts at his disposal and "created a portrait in soft tones of a saint without force, a man without troubles or anger or sex." Despite its weaknesses, Samuel Longfellow's *Life of Henry Wadsworth Longfellow* remains the standard biography. The body of the *Life* consists of selections from Longfellow's journals and letters which allow Longfellow to "tell his own story as far as possible" and thus show "how a man of letters spends his time, and what occupies his thoughts." Filling in his portrait with segments of letters and favorable reviews as well as his own reminiscences, Samuel Longfellow delineates his brother as "the good son, devoted husband, affectionate father; the generous, faithful friend; the urbane and cultivated host; the lover of children; the lover of his country; the lover of liberty and of peace."

Samuel Longfellow's opinion of Longfellow the man is echoed in Annie Fields's *Authors and Friends* (Boston, 1893). She writes from the vantage point of the daughter of Longfellow's publisher, James T. Fields, and embellishes her highly anecdotal and slightly naive account with information from correspondence between Fields and Longfellow. Holding a similarly high opinion of Longfellow but tempering his enthusiasm with critical acuity, Thomas Wentworth Higginson gives us fresh and readable accounts of Longfellow in *Old Cambridge* (New York, 1899) and *Henry Wadsworth Longfellow*. The latter biography contrasts markedly with the biographies of the eighties and nineties in its smooth-flowing narrative; moreover, it introduces new material from unpublished letters, Harvard records, and uncollected early writings.

The most notorious Longfellow biography is Herbert S. Gorman's *A Victorian American, Henry Wadsworth Longfellow* (New York, 1926; rpt. 1967). Lacking in original information, slightly condescending in tone, and burdened by a thesis, Gorman's book presents Longfellow as "a sort of American Queen Victoria" who had "a total lack of moralistic analysis and an eminently 'safe' observation of life." Gorman's subthesis is that the greater part of Longfellow's mental and intellectual sustenance was drawn from the Old World; yet he undercuts the positive aspect of this thesis by saying that the "facile and kindly" sage used European culture only as a prop.

In contrast with Gorman's derivative work, the biographies of the thirties and forties contain new insights by scholars who returned to the original sources, especially the letters and journals at the Longfellow-Craigie House. Entitling his book *New Light on Longfellow* (Boston, 1933; rpt. 1970), James Taft Hatfield concerns himself more with Longfellow's temperament than with his poetic achievement. Hatfield does provide some "new light," particularly regarding Longfellow's relations to Europe and his mastery of European languages and poetic forms; yet his insights are limited by his uncritical rating of Longfellow's position as "worthy of Apollo."

Lawrance Thompson's *Young Longfellow (1807–1843)* (New York, 1938; rpt. 1969) is an important milestone in Longfellow biography. Reacting

against the Samuel Longfellow stereotype of Henry Wadsworth Longfellow, Thompson emphasizes the human elements in Longfellow's life
and concentrates on "the conflicting problems which confronted Longfellow as a young man," particularly a strain of Yankee opportunism in
him which was at odds with his dominantly romantic attitude toward
life. Thompson's narrative is coherently written and well documented;
moreover, by its close attention to original documents and dispassionate
scrutiny of Longfellow's early life it provides a significant reinterpretation of him.

Any biographical study of Longfellow the poet must of necessity be
accompanied by an examination of Longfellow the professor who devoted
twenty-four years of his life to teaching languages and literature. Thompson is thorough in his treatment of the Bowdoin years and early Harvard
years. Carl L. Johnson's *Professor Longfellow of Harvard* (Eugene, Oreg.,
1944) focuses somewhat narrowly on Longfellow's professional responsibilities as Smith Professor of Modern Languages and on his dealings with
the Harvard administration. Rounding out the portrait of Longfellow
as teacher are the Bowdoin and Harvard lectures printed at the end of
Robert Stafford Ward's dissertation, "Longfellow's Lehrjahre" (Boston
Univ., 1951), and E. C. Dunn's "Longfellow the Teacher" (*NAR*, Feb. 1920)
in which Longfellow is considered as a fighter against Philistinism in
America and as a bold innovator in the teaching of French.

Edward Wagenknecht combines the explorative spirit of Hatfield and
Thompson and the narrative sense of Higginson in his major critical biography, *Longfellow: A Full-Length Portrait*, which he rewrote in modified and shortened form as *Henry Wadsworth Longfellow: Portrait of
an American Humanist* (New York, 1966). Based on painstaking and exhaustive study of manuscript materials as well as published sources,
Wagenknecht's biography presents Longfellow in an illuminating historical perspective. Instead of simply following a strict chronology, Wagenknecht explores diverse aspects of Longfellow's life such as his reading,
friendships, family relationships, and artistic theory and practice. The
result is a finely balanced view of Longfellow, the man and the artist,
which resolves many of the misconceptions concerning him. As just one
example, Wagenknecht finds that Longfellow's conventionalism is over-
stressed and that Longfellow achieved in his poetry a "combination of
spontaneity and careful craftsmanship."

Two ancillary contributions to Longfellow biography are Wagenknecht's
edition of *Mrs. Longfellow: Selected Letters and Journals of Fanny Appleton Longfellow (1817–1861)* (New York, 1956)) and *Clara Crownin-
shield's Diary: A European Tour with Longfellow, 1835–1836*, edited by
Andrew Hilen (Seattle, 1956). The latter is an "artless and unpretentious"

journal which provides a glimpse into the private life of the Longfellows before Henry achieved his popularity as a poet. Three Longfellow critical biographies of the 1960s which I intend to discuss in detail later are Newton Arvin's *Longfellow: His Life and Work* (Boston, 1963; rpt. 1977), Edward L. Hirsh's *Henry Wadsworth Longfellow* (Minneapolis, 1964), and Cecil Brown Williams's *Henry Wadsworth Longfellow* (New York, 1964).

A number of shorter pieces in the 1970s are of biographical value. In the Longfellow symposium published in *ESQ* (First Quarter 1970) we find "Voices of Longfellow: *Kavanagh* as Autobiography" in which Steven Allaback argues that *Kavanagh* is a rich source for personal and essentially private information about Longfellow; "Longfellow and Music" by Robert L. Volz; "Librarian Longfellow" by Richard Harwell; Ernest J. Moyne's "Longfellow and Kah-ge-ga-gah-bowh," discussing Longfellow's Chippewa acquaintance, George Copway, who lectured in the United States and Europe; and "Longfellow's Studies in France" in which Carl L. Johnson recounts Longfellow's language and literature studies during his first trip abroad. Robert A. Ferguson makes insightful use of the first four volumes of Longfellow *Letters* in his essay, "Longfellow's Political Fears: Civic Authority and the Role of the Artist in *Hiawatha* and *Miles Standish*" (*AL*, May 1978). Ferguson argues convincingly that rather than being an escapist poet running in distaste from his times, Longfellow took an intense interest in the world around him, especially in the turbulent 1850s, and consciously or unconsciously reflected his anxieties and tensions in *Hiawatha* and *The Courtship of Miles Standish*.

CRITICISM

Three dominant modes of evaluating Longfellow are found in the early criticisms by Nathaniel Hawthorne, Edgar Allan Poe, and Margaret Fuller, and have continued to the present. Hawthorne represents those who admire Longfellow the man and comment, sometimes extravagantly, on the virtues they find in his writings. Thus, in his letter of 26 December 1839 (quoted by Samuel Longfellow), Hawthorne says concerning Longfellow's poems, "Nothing equal to some of them was ever written in this world, this western world, I mean; and it would not hurt my conscience much to include the other hemisphere." Again, in his review of *Evangeline*, reprinted by Randall Stewart in "Hawthorne's Contributions to *The Salem Advertiser*" (*AL*, Jan. 1934) and discussed by H. H. Hoeltje in "Hawthorne's Review of *Evangeline*" (*NEQ*, June 1950), Hawthorne praises the poem for the "simplicity of high and exquisite art" with which it is told.

Poe's criticisms of Longfellow are often brilliant and incisive, yet they demonstrate what Longfellow called "the irritation of a sensitive nature chafed by some indefinite sense of wrong." Poe represents critics whose evaluations are negatively biased by their seeing Longfellow as a representative of imitative poetry, superficiality, sentimentality, and the like. Poe's reviews, collected in *The Complete Works of Edgar Allan Poe* (New York, 1902), contain guarded praise for several poems but are in the main disparaging. Reviewing *Hyperion* in 1839, Poe considers Longfellow "singularly deficient in all those important faculties which give artistical power, and without which never was immortality effected. He has no combining or binding force." Reviewing *Ballads and Other Poems*, Poe criticizes the theory of poetry which regards the inculcation of a moral as essential. Then, in reviewing *The Waif* in 1845, Poe started "the Longfellow war" by charging Longfellow with plagiarism — a charge he repeated later that year. (For a summary of Poe's criticisms, see Wagenknecht, *Longfellow: A Full-Length Portrait*, and Perry Miller, *The Raven and the Whale* [New York, 1956].)

Margaret Fuller, like Poe, resented the excessive praise given Longfellow, but nevertheless demonstrated a kind of balancing of strengths and weaknesses which is found in the most penetrating Longfellow criticism. In *Papers on Literature and Art* (London, 1846) and in *The Writings of Margaret Fuller*, edited by Mason Wade (New York, 1941), she says: "Longfellow is artificial and imitative. He borrows incessantly, and . . . is very faulty in using broken or mixed metaphors. The ethical part of his writing has a hollow, secondhand sound. He has, however, elegance, a love of the beautiful, and a fancy for what is large and manly, if not a full sympathy with it. His verse breathes at times much sweetness; and if not allowed to supersede what is better, may promote a taste for good poetry. Though imitative, he is not mechanical." Again, his work is "of little original poetic power, but of much poetic taste and sensibility."

Reputation

Longfellow's readership and popularity during his lifetime was immense in the United States (as indicated by Wagenknecht and by L. E. Hart, "The Beginnings of Longfellow's Fame" [*NEQ*, Mar. 1963]) and was unequalled by any other writer of the period throughout the world (as noted by Clarence Gohdes in *American Literature in Nineteenth Century England* [New York, 1944]). Gohdes says that in England Longfellow was better known than Tennyson or Browning; critical reviews there mixed harsh criticism with extravagant praise. Extensive quotations showing the response of Victorians to Longfellow are found in Kenneth Walter Cameron's *Longfellow Among His Contemporaries: A Harvest of Estimates*,

Insights, and Anecdotes from the Victorian Literary World (Hartford, Conn., 1978). Speaking of this period, James Woodress in his article, "The Fortunes of Longfellow in Italy" (*SA*, 1970), says: "To study Longfellow's reputation is to inquire into the tastes and preoccupations of the Victorian era." Woodress goes on to reveal that there are more translations of Longfellow into Italian than into any other language; nevertheless, "the dying embers have just about burned out for Longfellow in Italy." In Russia, according to David Hecht, "Longfellow in Russia" (*NEQ*, Dec. 1946), Longfellow was one of the first American poets who was widely read. Hecht cites ten Russian translators of Longfellow before 1900, and notes that from 1918 to 1935 the appearance of seven editions of his poems indicated Longfellow's popularity under the Soviet regime. And in South America, Longfellow has had the largest number of poems translated by the greatest number of South American translators, although he lost ground in the twentieth century to Poe and Whitman, as J. E. Englekirk tells us in "Notes on Longfellow in South America" (*Hispania* [Stanford], Oct. 1942). (For an overview of Longfellow's reputation in Latin America, see Robert S. Ward's introductory note to Ernest J. Moyne's "The Origin and Development of Longfellow's *Song of Hiawatha*" [*Journal of Inter-American Studies*, Jan. 1966].)

Longfellow's position and popularity reached a peak in the 1880s and remained high through the Longfellow centennial in 1907. Expressing a widely held opinion, Charles Eliot Norton in *Tributes to Longfellow and Emerson by The Massachusetts Historical Society* (Boston, 1882) states: "It was not by depth of thought or by original views of nature that he won his place in the world's regard; but it was by sympathy with the feelings common to good men and women everywhere, and by the simple, direct, sincere, and delicate expression of them, that he gained the affection of mankind." Longfellow's appeal to Eric S. Robertson, as shown in his *Life of Henry Wadsworth Longfellow* (London, 1887; rpt. 1972), was his ability to embellish the common and to produce "a wealth of tender and beautiful sayings that in every civilized land . . . became household favorites." And William Dean Howells, in *Literary Friends and Acquaintance* (New York, 1900) and in "The Art of Longfellow" (*NAR*, Mar. 1907), praises Longfellow as a poet who saw beyond his native New England to express the universal in the sense that "the poet has nothing to tell, except from what is acually or potentially common to the race."

A sampling of criticism during or near the Longfellow centennial finds Longfellow lauded for his moral purpose (R. B. Steele, "The Poetry of Longfellow" [*SR*, Apr. 1905]), his "trustworthy and graceful" translations (Leon H. Vincent, *American Literary Masters* [Boston, 1906]), his popularizing "our scant store of American traditions" (M. C. Crawford, "Longfellow: Poet of Places" [*Putnam's Monthly Magazine*, Feb. 1907]), his simplicity, reverence, and grace which appeal to the "intellectual middle class" (Bliss Perry, "The Centenary of Longfellow" [*AtM*, Mar. 1907]), his interpreting to his generation "the hitherto alien treasures of European culture" (Bliss Perry, *Park-Street Papers* [Boston, 1908]), and his mastery of the sonnet (Paul Elmer More in *Shelburne Essays, Fifth Series* [New York, 1908], and H. W. Mabie, "Sonnets from the *Divine Comedy*" [*Outlook*, Jan. 1909]). Summing up Longfellow's reputation at the turn of the century, Thomas Wentworth Higginson in *Henry Wadsworth Longfellow* affirms that "he is a classic" who "will never be read for the profoundest stirring, or for the unlocking of the deepest mysteries" but "will always be read for invigoration, for comfort, for content."

Paradoxically, it was often the elements praised by Norton, Higginson, Perry, Stedman, and others that were deprecated by later critics. Thus Longfellow's ability to reach all levels of society is dismissed by Gamaliel Bradford as mere commonplace ("Portraits of American Authors" [*Bookman*, Nov. 1915]) or is considered by John Macy to be an appeal to "simple minds" (*The Spirit of American Literature* [New York, 1913]). Instead of Longfellow's being an adaptor of "the beauty and sentiment of other lands to the convictions of his people" (E. C. Stedman, *Poets of America* [Boston, 1913]), he is considered a grizzled old man to whom "the world was a German picture-book, never detaching itself from the softly colored pages" (Van Wyck Brooks in *America's Coming-of-Age* [New York, 1915], reprinted in Philip Rahv, *Literature in America* [Cleveland, 1957]). And rather than a "story-teller in verse" with "power to transplant to American literature some of the colour and melody and romantic charm of the complex European literature he had studied" (William P. Trent, "Longfellow" [*CHAL*]), Longfellow is considered "bounded by his books and he cannot see beyond them" (Gorman, *A Victorian American*).

That Longfellow ceased to appeal to certain moderns of the twenties and thirties is illustrated by I. A. Richards's experiment, described in *Practical Criticism* (New York, 1929), in which 92 percent of his students judged Longfellow's "In the Churchyard at Cambridge" unfavorably — "by far the most disliked" of the thirteen poems they criticized. And Ludwig Lewisohn in *Expression in America* (New York, 1932) says: "Who, except wretched schoolchildren, now reads Longfellow? . . . He never touches poetry. He borrows form and accepts content from without. . . . To minds concerned with the imaginative interpretation of man, of nature and of human life, Longfellow has nothing left to say."

Responding to the type of disparagement found in Lewisohn and others (such as V. L. Parrington) who found "little intellect" and "little creative originality" in Longfellow, G. R. Elliot in "Gentle Shades of Longfellow," in *The Cycle of Modern Poetry* (Princeton, N.J., 1929), argues persuasively that the modern taste is too caught up in aesthetic dogmas to recognize Longfellow's vital place in the mainstream of American poetry. Saying that the academics have "a fatal aversion for American näiveté," Elliott proposes a literary-historical study of American literature which views its past growth "more largely and more organically." Commenting on Longfellow's simplicity, George Saintsbury in *Prefaces and Essays* (London, 1933) asserts that while one never has to question Longfellow's meaning, his meaning is never contemptible and is sometimes very admirable. Saintsbury advocates selectivity in evaluating Longfellow's poetry—which already had been a practice of Longfellow's most discerning critics but which allowed a hasty discounting, in Saintsbury's case, of *Evangeline*, "The Arsenal at Springfield," and the sonnets.

An important contribution to the revaluation of Longfellow during the thirties was Odell Shepard's introduction to *Representative Selections* of Longfellow's writings. Discussing Longfellow's environment, opinions, limitations, and popularity, Shepard notes weaknesses such as Longfellow's uncritical temper, incomprehensive grasp of contemporary fact, self-indulgent romanticism, escape to the past, and flinching "from all violence, satire, and stern denunciation"; yet he balances these by praising Longfellow's success in "saying what all have thought and in singing what all have felt," his "harmony and unity of the whole composition," and his deepening "our sense of the American past," thereby providing a link with what we have been. In the same vein as Shepard, Howard Mumford Jones called for a revaluation of Longfellow, first in "The Longfellow Nobody Knows" (*Outlook*, 8 August 1928) and later in *American Writers on American Literature*, edited by John A. Macy (New York, 1934). While recognizing that Longfellow lacks depth and sharpness of philosophy, Jones esteems his narrative talent, sense of humor, and command of the sonnet, and considers "lucidity, gentleness, musicality" his essential qualities. It was also in the midthirties that Van Wyck Brooks in *The Flowering of New England* (New York, 1936) revised his earlier opinion and asserted that while "Longfellow's flaccidity debarred him from the front rank," his work possessed "a quality, a unity of feeling and tone, that gave him a place apart among popular poets."

Three of the most disinterested views of Longfellow's place in literature appeared approximately a century after the publication of *Evangeline* and *The Song of Hiawatha*. Norman Holmes Pearson writes about Longfellow's function as "laureate of the common man" and as poet "of the castle and the court" in "Both Longfellows" (*University Review*, Summer 1950). In justifying Longfellow's fame, Pearson emphasizes his powers in myth-making by which he helps restore to a nation a "past function of poetry." George Arms in *The Fields Were Green: A New View of Bryant, Whittier, Holmes, Lowell, and Longfellow* (Stanford, Calif., 1953) says the "schoolroom poets" are unpopular with twentieth-century moderns because of differences in conceptions of poetry or aesthetic taste. "Longfellow's age took comfort in extensive moral explanation and was uneasy when wit was forced to its attention; our age is hot for wit and boggles at direct moral intent." Arms sums up his succinct and fair-minded evaluation by asserting that "though Longfellow does not go deeply into human experience, he sees with a good deal of clarity and poise that life which comes to his view." Howard Nemerov in his introduction to *Longfellow: Selected Poetry* (New York, 1959) affirms that Longfellow is a genuine, though minor poet who employs allegory, personification, and anecdote rather than symbol, metaphor, and myth. Recognizing that Longfellow stretched his modest gifts too far, Nemerov nevertheless defends Longfellow's didacticism and clarity against the now-current fashion for obscurity and implication. Longfellow's moralizing is often "poetically just"; that is, it grows organically from the body of the poem and has "the force of a formal close" which brings the measure and the meaning to a resolution together. Arms is not so generous with the didactic element, and he suggests the improvement of several poems by excluding certain lines and stanzas — particularly the moral at the end. It is interesting that William Dean Howells similarly suggested in "The Art of Longfellow" that "The Village Blacksmith" would be improved by omitting the last two stanzas "which make it a homily."

Critical views in the sixties and seventies which diminish Longfellow's reputation are found in Roy Harvey Pearce's *The Continuity of American Poetry* (Princeton, N.J., 1961); Marcus Cunliffe's *The Literature of the United States* (Baltimore, Md., 1964); Richard Ruland's "Longfellow and the Modern Reader" (*EJ*, Sept. 1966); Hyatt H. Waggoner's *American Poets: From the Puritans to the Present* (Boston, 1968); and the introduction to Longfellow selections in Cleanth Brooks's, R. W. B. Lewis's, and Robert Penn Warren's anthology, *American Literature: The Makers and the Making* (New York, 1973). Pearce says that Longfellow "glosses over hard fact and harder motivation," and that "desiring the universal, he failed to see that it could be achieved only through a meticulous attention to the particular." Indicating his dislike of priggishness in Longfellow's novels and unreality in *Hiawatha*, Cunliffe is of the opinion that Longfellow's reputation has declined not because of his Brahminism, but because of "an inability to transcend the requirements of his generation which he so admirably met." Ruland attributes Longfellow's decline to the limited conception held by the nineteenth-century writer and audience alike that the poet's role is to state the values of his culture in language and forms which are both acceptable and beautiful. Contrary to his stated desire to rehabilitate the "schoolroom poets," Waggoner comes down hard on Longfellow. He severely criticizes "The Psalm of Life" and "Excelsior"— horses which already had been beaten to death — and by selecting a few lines expressing Longfellow's "true" inner doubts and feeling, concludes that Longfellow "was a very sad poet who became not simply banal but incoherent and confused when he tried to cheer himself or others." Brooks, Lewis, and Warren call Longfellow "the nearly perfect embodiment of the various impulses of the time," but then see those impulses as sentimental, restricted by taboos, and superficial. Authentically a poet when he "looks out from a safe corner on action long past, long distant, or irrelevant," Longfellow could not or would not look into his heart to acknowledge "the buried self whose struggles were made manifest only in a pervasive and unaimed melancholy."

There is an element of truth in these criticisms — Longfellow did have inner doubts and troubles and was not simply a facile optimist as Waggoner says; further, as Brooks, Lewis, and Warren point out, we find little in Longfellow's poetry that shows him breaking "through the crust of the conventional self that concealed the real and unacknowledged self." Yet to take these views exclusively means to discount much of Longfellow's poetry as vapid and hypocritical from a somewhat condescending twentieth-century perspective. A more historically balanced view is found in William Charvat's essay, "Longfellow," in *The Profession of Authorship in America, 1800–1870* (Columbus, Ohio, 1968). Separating Longfellow the "public poet" from "private poets" such as Emily Dickinson and "mass poets" such as James Whitcomb Riley, Charvat declares that Longfellow recognized the unpleasant realities of frustration, failure, weariness, deprival, and death in the life of the average citizen, and taught in his poetry the acceptance of life's labors and sorrows. Also affirming the viability of Longfellow as "public poet" is George Monteiro in his introduction to *The Poetical Works of Longfellow* (Boston, 1975). Monteiro argues that Longfellow was "actually at his best writing for a large public whose interests and tastes he uncannily understood and served through a long professional life" and that he deliberately sought to write the more public forms of poetry until after the death of Fanny Longfellow.

The most recent book-length studies of Longfellow are Edward L. Hirsh's *Henry Wadsworth Longfellow*, Cecil Brown Williams's *Henry Wadsworth Longfellow*, and Newton Arvin's *Longfellow: His Life and Work*. Hirsh's brief but compact UMPAW study presents a generally sympathetic yet objective analysis of Longfellow's prose and poetry. Longfellow's chief faults, according to Hirsh, are an "inability to probe life's dark or sordid aspects," fondness for literary diction, and "explication of the already-evident"; yet Longfellow has an "impressive tonal range," and "within the age's literary conventions, Longfellow used language skillfully and sensitively." Williams divides his TUSAS book into biography and criticism, the latter being mainly appreciative. Considering Longfellow not a major poet but not a minor one either, Williams calls for a reappraisal of Longfellow — produced by objectively seeing him in terms of biography and literary history.

Arvin's critical biography is by far the most thorough critical study of Longfellow. Written in his usual well-modulated style, Arvin's study provides in-depth analyses of Longfellow's major works and of numerous minor poems. Following the method of balancing strengths and weaknesses (sometimes too apologetically), Arvin finds Longfellow was at times "facile and flaccid" and "could fall a victim to the bad sentimental taste of his age"; yet "at his best he is an accomplished, sometimes an exquisite, craftsman" who had the strain of the folk poet in his make-up. In his epilogue, Arvin sums up the various critical attitudes held regarding Longfellow. His conclusion is that Longfellow was a minor writer who suffered in the twentieth century from a shift in taste, yet as a demotic poet, he should have an enduring place in our esteem. Certainly critics of stature such as Arvin, Wagenknecht, Thompson, and Charvat have through their perceptive and thorough studies helped ensure that esteem.

Sources and Influences

Given Longfellow's eclectic reading and his methods of composition, it is obvious there is an important place in Longfellow criticism for examination of his sources and influences. An extremely narrow way to look at the subject is to see Longfellow as being mainly a plagiarist. Since Poe's time, however, few have faulted Longfellow for plagiarism. Nor have they generally criticized him for being simply derivative, as did Margaret Fuller in her left-handed defense of Longfellow (*Writings*): "We have been surprised that anyone should have been anxious to fasten special charges [of plagiarism] upon him, when we had supposed it so obvious that the greater part of his mental stores were derived from the works of others." Rather, the large number of persons who have written about Longfellow sources, parallels, echoes, and influences have usually taken Margaret Fuller's premise without her caustic tone and have recognized Longfellow's indebtedness to writings from many countries which he transmuted artistically into his own work.

The most complete study in this last category is Paul Morin's *Les Sources de l'Oeuvre de Henry Wadsworth Longfellow*. Morin begins his 637-page work by asserting it was natural for Longfellow to assimilate — sometimes unconsciously — writings of European authors into his own poetry or prose.

In defense of Longfellow, Morin affirms that literary borrowing was no more a sin for Longfellow than it was for Chaucer or Shakespeare. Morin's method for the most part is to rely greatly on parallel texts, although for major works he lists definite sources and possible sources — finding for *Evangeline*, for example, fifteen books of the former type and twenty-eight of the latter. Another general treatment of Longfellow's sources is Francesco Viglione's *La Critica Literaria di Henry Wadsworth Longfellow* (2 vols., Florence, 1934) which examines extensively Longfellow's relationships with various people and places in America and Europe — with the information being digested mainly from Viglione's wide reading in secondary works. Edward Wagenknecht surveys "Longfellow's Reading" both in an article by that title (*Boston Public Library Quarterly*, Apr. 1955) and in his biography; a more detailed list is given by Kenneth Walter Cameron in "Longfellow's Reading in Libraries; the Charging Records of a Learned Poet Interpreted" (*ATQ*, Fall 1976).

Robert S. Ward argues in "Longfellow's Roots in Yankee Soil" (*NEQ*, June 1968) that Yankee folklore, especially oral tradition, was important in Longfellow's works — a position amplified by Donald A. Sears in "Folk Poetry in Longfellow's Boyhood" (*NEQ*, Mar. 1972) who discusses the nature of the ballads to which Longfellow would have been exposed as a boy in Portland and holds that the poet unconsciously learned from the ballads. The mass of studies of this sort, though, deal almost exclusively with European sources and influences. A succinct and comprehensive survey of these commentaries is made by Arvin in his critical biography. For a discussion of French influences, Edmond Estève in his Bowdoin lecture, *Longfellow et la France* (Brunswick, N.J., 1925), gives a limited but interesting overview; Carl L. Johnson treats the subject much more extensively in his dissertation, "Longfellow and France" (Harvard, 1933). In regard to Italy, Emilio Goggio in "Italian Influences on Longfellow's Works" (*RR*, July 1925) shows that Longfellow's Italian scholarship was both intensive (in the case of Dante) and extensive (in the case of the more minor figures). And as for Spain, Iris Lilian Whitman's *Longfellow and Spain* contains many extracts from Longfellow's writings which show his practical and academic grasp of Spanish materials, leading her to conclude that Spain broadened his appreciation of life and helped him as much as other European countries to form his literary career. Taking a more scholarly and objective approach than Whitman, Stanley T. Williams adds to her examination in *The Spanish Background of American Literature* (2 vols., New Haven, Conn., 1955), in which he points to Longfellow's comprehension of the Spanish spirit and his "long service of introducing to America the literature of Spain"— most remarkably through his translations or adaptations.

A great deal has been written about the influence of Germany and German literature on Longfellow, beginning with a series of doctoral dissertations emerging from German universities. Two examples of this sort which cite Longfellow's references to Germany and German subjects and which suggest his work is infused with the German spirit are J. Perry Worden's *Über Longfellows Beziehungen zur Deutschen Litteratur* (Halle, 1900) and Friedrich Kratz's *Das Deutsche Element in den Werken H. W. Longfellow* (Wasserburg, 1920). J. T. Hatfield's subtitle to *New Light on Longfellow — With Special Reference to His Relations to Germany —* indicates his special focus. Hatfield discounts some of the German borrowings and influences earlier ascribed to Longfellow, yet still finds the German influence to be large. Hatfield's study is especially valuable in its account of Longfellow's friendship with Bernard Rolker, Ferdinand Freiligrath, and others, and in its lists of Longfellow's German friends and correspondents and German studies and reading. Orie W. Long's *Literary Pioneers: Early American Explorers of European Culture* (Cambridge, Mass., 1935) has a chapter on Longfellow derived in part from examination of letters and journals at the Craigie-Longfellow House. Long considers Longfellow the most important of the early "ambassadors of learning" who "made Goethe a living figure in academic halls." In a balanced article on "Longfellow and Germany" (*DN*, 1952), Anna J. De-Armond concludes that while the German influence broadened Longfellow, it also encouraged his tendency to formlessness and softness. Henry A. Pochmann in *German Culture in America: Philosophical and Literary Influences, 1600–1900* (Madison, Wis., 1957) believes that Longfellow was most influenced by the German spirit because of his natural sympathy for German literature, his stays in Germany, and his work with German literature after his returns to America. More recently, Frederick Burwick in "Longfellow and German Romanticism" (*CLS*, Mar. 1970) analyzes Longfellow's description of the course of German romanticism and shows how his interest waned after his enthusiastic response to Freiligrath, whom he met in 1842. According to John Griffith in "Longfellow and Herder and the Sense of History" (*TSLL*, Summer 1971), Longfellow's historiography was congruous with — if not influenced by — Herder's democratic notion that history should focus on national character, on the spirit of the *Volk*.

Longfellow's relationship with Scandinavia is examined by Andrew R. Hilen in *Longfellow and Scandinavia: A Study of the Poet's Relationship with the Northern Languages and Literature* (New Haven, Conn., 1947; rpt. 1970). Hilen is especially good in tracing the influence of Tegnér and concludes that Longfellow's relationship with Scandinavia "was essentially the product not of scholarly inquisitiveness but of his interest as

a romanticist in remote and unfamiliar scenes." Of ancillary interest is
Gerald R. Griffin's thesis in "'Tegnér's Dream': A Reappraisal" (*ATQ*, Fall
1978) that Longfellow imitates the two kinds of major verse for which
Tegnér was renowned in order to praise through imitation.

Much of what has been written about the long narratives deals with
influences and sources. In regard to *Evangeline*, Edward Thostenberg
in "Is Longfellow's *Evangeline* a Product of Swedish Influence?" (*Poet-
Lore*, Autumn 1908) first pointed out the parallels between Longfellow's
Nova Scotia and the Swedish landscape described in his article on Tegnér's *Frithiof's Saga*. Similarities or a "rapprochement" between *Jocelyn*
and *Evangeline* are illustrated by Mario Mormile in *L'idylle épique de
Lamartine et Longfellow: Étude de Joselyn et d'Evangeline* (Rome, 1967).
M. G. Hill in "Some of Longfellow's Sources for the Second Part of *Evangeline*" (*PMLA*, Nov. 1916) examines as source material Fremont's *Expedition to the Rocky Mountains*, Sealsfield's *Life in the New World*, and
Kip's *Early Jesuit Missions*. And Manning Hawthorne and H. W. L. Dana
in *The Origin and Development of Longfellow's "Evangeline"* (Portland,
Maine, 1947) consider anew the historical background, genesis, and in-
ception of Longfellow's work. They also suggest that *Evangeline* undoubtedly has stimulated the production of more than 250 books and
articles on the subject of the Acadians since the poem was published.

The Song of Hiawatha has been the subject of intense source studies
ever since Thomas C. Porter in the *Washington National Intelligencer*
(26 November 1855) charged that Longfellow borrowed "the entire form,
spirit, and many of the most striking incidents" of *Kalevala*. This began
a series of attacks and responses, discussed thoroughly by Ernest J. Moyne
in *Hiawatha and Kalevala: A Study of the Relationship between Longfellow's "Indian Edda" and the Finnish Epic* (Helsinki, 1963). Moyne ex-
onerates Longfellow of plagiarism, but shows how Longfellow used An-
ton Schiefner's translation of the *Kalevala* as a model for the meter and
form of *Hiawatha*. Although proven wrong in his thesis that Longfellow
did not borrow from the *Kalevala*, Waino Nyland in "*Kalevala* as a Re-
puted Source of Longfellow's *Song of Hiawatha*" (*AL*, Mar. 1950) does
point, in his attention to Indian songs, to an interesting area of related
study. The subject of Indian folklore elements in *Hiawatha* has in fact
been discussed perceptively by Christabel F. Fiske, "Mercerized Folklore
in *Hiawatha*" (*Poet-Lore*, Dec. 1920); Stith Thompson, "The Indian Legend of Hiawatha" (*PMLA*, Mar. 1922); Albert Keiser, *The Indian in American Literature* (New York, 1933); and R. M. Davis, "How Indian is *Hiawatha*?" (*MF*, Spring 1957). Fiske shows how in *Hiawatha* the fabric of
primitive myths was "mercerized"; that is, "its fibers were shrunken, its
surface more lustrous, its colors more vivid or pastel-like than of old."

Thompson notes Longfellow's erroneous identification of Hiawatha with Manabozho (which was Schoolcraft's error as well) and then says that Longfellow humanizes Manabozho and emphasizes romantic and poetic elements, thereby departing greatly from the spirit of the myth. Keiser also observes these discrepancies but partially justifies them as stemming from the poet's "kind and delicate nature" and to his tailoring the poem for his contemporaries. Davis, with Fiske and Thompson, says that Longfellow does not grasp the animistic modes of thought behind Indian myths. Despite the validity of these criticisms, we should remind ourselves that Longfellow did not have access to twentieth-century information about Indian anthropology, but rather derived most of his material from George Catlin, J. G. E. Heckewelder, and particularly from Henry Rowe Schoolcraft. These sources, especially the last, are discussed at great length but disjointedly by Chase S. and Stellanova Osborn in *Schoolcraft-Longfellow-Hiawatha* (Lancaster, Pa., 1942).

Sources for *Tales of a Wayside Inn* and *The Golden Legend* are fairly obvious and have not been subjects of controversy. Besides Arvin, W. E. A. Axon, "On the Sources of Longfellow's *Tales of a Wayside Inn*" (*Royal Society Literary Transactions*, 1911), and John Van Schaick, *The Characters in "Tales of a Wayside Inn"* (Boston, 1939; rpt. 1974), have discussed sources of the *Tales*; the latter book is devoted mainly to biographical sketches of Longfellow's real-life models. Hartmann von Aue's *Der arme Heinrich* as the main source for *The Golden Legend* is discussed superficially in Friedrich Münzner's *Die Quellen zu Longfellows Golden Legend* (Dresden, 1898). By contrast, Carl Hammer, Jr.'s *"Golden Legend" and Goethe's "Faust"* (Baton Rouge, La., 1952) is a carefully documented examination of the many echoes of *Faust*. More important than single correspondences, though, "is the impression that Longfellow's poem derives much of its afflatus" from *Faust*.

Poetic Forms and Methods

Longfellow's poetics have always interested critics, with the best and most expansive discussions being those by Gay Wilson Allen, *American Prosody* (New York, 1935), George Arms, and Newton Arvin. Earlier critics often focused on narrow aspects of Longfellow's poetry, with a disproportionate amount of energy in the nineteenth century and the first decade of this century spent in debating the appropriateness of his hexameters. A learned article which stands above the others of the time is Cornelius C. Felton's review of *Ballads and Other Poems* (*NAR*, July 1842) which places Longfellow's hexameters in the context of the history of the hexameter from the early Greek poetry to the modern-day English and American poetry. In such a context, Felton concludes, Longfellow's is not

a true hexameter. Modern criticism, though, is considerably more pragmatic. Allen, for example, analyzes varieties of Longfellow's forms and
meters in terms of their effectiveness, and concludes, "On the whole, Longfellow's hexameters are appropriate for his purposes." Likewise, Arvin
in discussing *Evangeline* says, "At its most successful, the verse has a kind
of grave, slow-paced, mellifluous quality, like a slightly monotonous but
not unmusical chant, which is genuinely expressive of its mournful and
minor theme." Regarding *Hiawatha*, Celia Millward and Cecelia Tichi
in "Whatever Happened to *Hiawatha*?" (*Genre*, Sept. 1973) demonstrate
how Longfellow followed epic-heroic conventions in the poem and assert
that the intrusion of mid-nineteenth-century American cultural values
makes it impossible for the work to succeed in its epic form.

Poetic matters more closely related to Longfellow's current and future
reputation as a poet are his handling of diverse forms of poetry, the technical and lyrical qualities of his nondidactic poems — particularly the sonnets, and his translations. Allen exemplifies a current critical viewpoint
when he says Longfellow's translations and imitations of foreign forms
directed attention to systems of versification unfamiliar to America and
gave us "a wide acquaintance with the chief poetic techniques of the
world." Possibilities still exist for close readings of his poems, two admirable examples being G. Thomas Tanselle's "Longfellow's 'Serenade' (*The
Spanish Student*)" (*Expl*, Feb. 1965) and Michael Zimmerman's "War
and Peace: Longfellow's 'The Occultation of Orion'" (*AL*, Jan. 1967).
Tanselle's method is to show the poem's movement from the remote to
the near and from the concrete to the abstract, reflecting the lover's state
of mind. Zimmerman pays close attention to allusions and ambiguities
in the poem and to the milieu in which the poem was written to demonstrate Longfellow's "ability to impress upon us a significant, more or less
complex feeling by means of metaphor and image, tone, and dramatic
situation." In regard to the sonnets, one reason for their success and continuing interest for modern readers, according to Arms, is that they limit
the poet to a two-stage movement (scene and analogy) and thus omit a
third stage — frequently found in Longfellow's poems — of statement or
homily.

As for Longfellow's translations, they continue to receive generally high
praise. Whitman (*Longfellow and Spain*) finds that Longfellow's translations from the Spanish hold fairly true to his ideal of "rendering literally
the words of a foreign author while at the same time [preserving] the
spirit of the original" (Longfellow's "Preface" to the *Coplas*, 1833). Stanley T. Williams (*Spanish Background*) agrees with this thesis and proposes that Longfellow is a good translator because of his gift with words,
his facility in verse, and his respect for the original. Longfellow's transla-

tions of Dante were held in esteem by his contemporaries; John Fiske in *The Unseen World and Other Essays* (Boston, 1876) declares that Longfellow's translation rises to "something like the grandeur of the original." A more temperate view is held by Angelina La Piana (*Dante's American Pilgrimage*, New Haven, Conn., 1948) who says that general response to Longfellow's translation was favorable, although adverse criticism focused on his literalness, Latinate diction, excessive inversions, and rhythmical irregularities. Finally, Arvin somewhat equivocally illustrates that Longfellow's translation of the *Divine Comedy* compares favorably with those by Henry F. Cary and Laurence Binyon. Yet he concludes by esteeming Longfellow as a translator who could preserve the meaning and form of the original lines because "he was a poet himself, because his feeling for languages was so intuitive, and because, for some sorts of poetry, his resources in his own language were so adequate."

Samuel Johnson points out in "Preface to Shakespeare" that a century after an author's death, when advantages from personal allusions and local customs have been lost, we can determine lasting literary merit. Measured in this perspective, Longfellow retains established, if minor, fame. The maintenance of his works in print points to a continuing popular audience — as do treatments such as Harry Hansen's attractively illustrated guide to Longfellow sites, *Longfellow's New England* (New York, 1972), and current anthologizing of some three dozen of Longfellow's sonnets and other short lyrics suggests a degree of ongoing attention on the part of college professors and their students. As Steven Allaback says in the *Dictionary of Literary Biography*, vol. 1 (Detroit, 1978), Longfellow has left "at least thirty to fifty short, unpretentious lyrics, in addition to a few longer pieces, that are likely to have readers far into the future." William R. Harmon in *Poetry Pilot* (May 1976) indicates some favor among poets as well by selecting six favorite Longfellow lyrics for "American Retrospectives" and by commenting not only on what was bad about some of Longfellow's poems but also on "what was good—very good indeed—about some others."

Future studies of Longfellow probably will continue along lines pursued in the 1960s and 1970s. These will include further examination of Longfellow in his milieu of the sort suggested by several of the papers presented at a commemorative conference held at the Longfellow National Historic Site in Cambridge on April 2 and 3, 1982: Andrew Hilen, "Longfellow and Scandinavia Revisited"; Edward Wagenknecht, "Longfellow in His Family Relations"; Rena Coen, "Longfellow, Hiawatha, and American Nineteenth Century Painters"; and Frederick Wagner, "Longfellow and the Concord Authors." There is still room for additional source and influence studies, as evidenced by Hans-Joachim Lang's and Fritz

Fleischmann's thoughtful essay on MacKenzie's *Encyclopedia Americana* article as a source: "'All This Beauty, All This Grace': Longfellow's 'The Building of the Ship' and Alexander Slidell MacKenzie's 'Ship'" (*NEQ*, Mar. 1981). We can expect to see Edward L. Tucker's scholarly edition entitled *Longfellow's "John Endicott": Its History, Including Two Early Versions*; in addition, he is working on a similar treatment of *The Courtship of Miles Standish*. One could hope for more biographical essays revealing the "inner" Longfellow along the lines pursued by Steven Allaback in "*Kavanagh* as Autobiography" and by Robert A. Ferguson in "Longfellow's Political Fears." These will be strengthened by the availability of Andrew Hilen's six volumes of *Letters* and eventually by the publication of Longfellow's journals. We might well see more examinations of Longfellow's themes of the sort probed by Phyllis Franklin in "The Importance of Time in Longfellow's Works" (*ESQ*, First Quarter 1970). Ironically, it may be that the most stimulating criticism will be by persons such as Tanselle and Zimmerman who use some of the methods of the "new critics" who so readily dismissed Longfellow. Finally, there surely will continue to be a steady appearance of critical and biographical notes of various sorts — testifying that while Longfellow does not absorb our attention, he still remains of interest.

James Russell Lowell

ROBERT A. REES

HOLMES SAID of Lowell, "He was alive, alive all over." Not an isolated poet nor an inward-oriented artist patiently growing toward perfection, Lowell blossomed early in direct relationship to his individual background and the general atmosphere and issues of his time—and he blossomed perennially, but in many varieties of bloom. In studying Lowell, one must keep in mind his versatility, his interaction with his milieu, and his vitality.

Some writers can be studied in their texts alone; others are understood far better by referring also to biographical background and historical context. Lowell, an enormously talented man of letters who never had a real mentor and who was not divinely endowed with patience or self-criticism, is one of the latter. Although his talent was not efficiently channeled, it may have been greater than that of contemporaries who have—deservedly—fared better with the critics.

BIBLIOGRAPHY

The most current as well as the most comprehensive and reliable bibliography of Lowell is Jacob Blanck's *Bibliography of American Literature*, vol. 6 (1973). It includes listings under the headings of "Primary Books," "Reprints of Lowell's Own Books," "Books by Others than Lowell, Containing Material by Him," and "Official Publications," which contains a sampling of Lowell's writings when he was ambassador.

Another recent bibliography is that contained in the WPA Project, *Literary Writings in America: A Bibliography*, vol. 5 (Millwood, N.Y., 1977),

From Earl N. Harbert and Robert A. Rees, editors, *Fifteen American Authors Before 1900: Bibliographic Essays on Research & Criticism* (Madison: The University of Wisconsin Press; © 1984 by the Board of Regents of the University of Wisconsin System); may be reproduced only by permission of the publisher.

379

which includes 45 pages of listings under "Bibliography," "Collected Works," "Edited Editions," "Periodical Publications," "Biography," "Criticism," and "Reviews," the later two sections containing entries not found in other bibliographies.

The earliest bibliography of value is the one at the end of Volume Two of Horace E. Scudder's biography, *James Russell Lowell* (2 vols., Boston, 1901). The works are arranged chronologically in order of appearance and the listings include the place of first publication. The first Lowell bibliography in book form was George W. Cooke's *A Bibliography of James Russell Lowell* (Boston, 1906). It contains primary and secondary bibliography, each separated into useful categories, and it is still the only bibliography dealing extensively with nineteenth-century critical literature. Although some entries are inaccurate and the volume is now badly out of date, it is unique and valuable. It provides relatively few references to periodical literature before 1870.

Careful scholarship within a limited area is available in Luther S. Livingston's *A Bibliography of the First Editions in Book Form of the Writings of James Russell Lowell* (New York, 1914; reprinted, 1968), which is based to a large extent on a collection of Jacob C. Chamberlain (and is therefore sometimes called the "Chamberlain Bibliography"). In spite of the title, it includes a few of the Lowell biographies written after his death and describes items of the broadside or souvenir type. Fewer than fifty primary items are in book form. Although more limited in its coverage than Cooke's, Livingston's collection contains more information on certain entries and is generally more reliable.

The selective bibliography of the 1917–1921 edition of *CHAL* lists 35 primary works, 19 works which Lowell edited or to which he contributed, and about 120 biographical and critical items.

Since the publication of Cooke's and Livingston's bibliographies, a number of articles, notes, dissertations, and books have added new items which have helped to clarify and refine certain aspects of the Lowell canon.

Although nominally devoted to history, Grace Griffin's *Writings on American History* (Washington, D.C., 1936) cites "representative" works in many areas and provides leads which do not appear in other bibliographies and guides. The annotated bibliography in Harry Hayden Clark and Norman Foerster's *James Russell Lowell: Representative Selections* (New York, 1947) is a valuable guide to the most significant Lowell scholarship before 1946. It supersedes an earlier and slightly shorter version in Clark's *Major American Poets* (New York, 1936).

The chapter notes to Leon Howard's *Victorian Knight-Errant: The Early Literary Career of James Russell Lowell* (Berkeley, Calif., 1952) provide some useful bibliographic information on material covering Lowell's career up to the Civil War.

Martin Duberman's *James Russell Lowell* (Boston, 1966) was written chiefly from manuscript sources and its bibliography is not intended to include all previous scholarship. However, the explanatory remarks on pp. 373–80 and the categorically arranged bibliographies evaluate certain titles and provide an excellent orientation to a number of earlier works.

TEXTS AND EDITIONS

The standard edition is *Writings of James Russell Lowell*, published by Houghton, Mifflin & Co., in 1890 (Boston and New York). This edition, known as the Riverside edition, is preferred by most scholars because the selections for the ten volumes (six of prose and four of poetry) were made by Lowell himself. An eleventh volume, published after Lowell's death, includes essays selected by Charles Eliot Norton, Lowell's literary executor. The Elmwood edition of 1904 is almost identical to the Riverside, but includes three volumes of letters edited by Norton, which had been published separately ten years earlier. In this edition, Norton added new letters, corrected errors, and identified additional addressees in the earlier letters.

Many Lowell writings excluded in these editions appeared in collections published subsequently. The most important of these are: *The Function of the Poet and Other Essays*, early essays and reviews edited by Albert Mordell (Boston, 1920); *Lectures on the English Poets*, Lowell's 1855 lectures at the Lowell Institute (Cleveland, Ohio, 1897); and *The Anti-Slavery Papers of James Russell Lowell* (Boston, 1902), two volumes of essays from the *Pennsylvania Freeman* (1844) and the *National Anti-Slavery Standard* (1845–1850).

The Cambridge edition of *The Complete Poetical Works of James Russell Lowell* (Boston, 1897; "sixth printing," 1968) is the only comprehensive anthology of Lowell's poetry. It includes the poetry from the Riverside edition plus a small group of poems published in C. E. Norton's edition of *Last Poems of James Russell Lowell* (Boston, 1895). This volume contains a biographical sketch, headnotes, and a chronological list of Lowells' poems — all by Horace Scudder.

The only new volumes of poetry to appear in the twentieth century are the *Uncollected Poems of James Russell Lowell* (Philadelphia, 1950), edited by Thelma Smith and based on her 1945 University of Pennsylvania dissertation, and *The Poetical Works of James Russell Lowell* (Boston, 1978), edited and with an introduction by Marjorie R. Kaufman. Smith's volume includes 135 poems printed originally in newspapers and magazines, which were omitted from the Elmwood edition but not specifically rejected by Lowell. While admitting that Lowell's best poems "are still to be found among those selected by the poet for his collected works," Smith nevertheless feels that these additional poems, which span Lowell's lifetime, are necessary for a full view of the poet. She thinks Lowell would have included some of these in the Riverside edition had he remembered them. Smith's annotated edition identifies available manuscript sources and provides bibliographic information about the publication of each poem. She mistakenly attributes a poem by Arthur Hugh Clough to Lowell.

Kaufman's edition, an update of Scudder's Cambridge Edition, includes "three previously uncollected poems . . . within the text of the introduction," all of which were identified and published by Smith.

Clark and Foerster's *James Russell Lowell: Representative Selections* includes a carefully balanced collection of poems, letters, and prose. *Lowell: Essays, Poems and Letters*, edited by William Smith Clark II (New York, 1948), is the only other modern anthology devoted exclusively to Lowell.

Of special interest is Scully Bradley's facsimile edition of the *Pioneer* (New York, 1947), the journal edited by Lowell and Robert Carter in 1843. Bradley's introduction is excellent and his footnotes are extensive.

The only modern edition of Lowell's criticism is Herbert F. Smith's *Literary Criticism of James Russell Lowell* (Lincoln, Neb., 1969). Smith arranges selected criticism under "Defense of Poetry," "Principles of Criticism," "American Provincial," and "American Contemporaries." Smith's general introduction as well as his headnotes to the various essays provide an excellent introduction to Lowell's criticism and the best assessment yet that we have of Lowell as critic.

The most important single edition of Lowell's work to appear in recent years is Thomas Wortham's *The Biglow Papers (First Series): A Critical Edition* (De Kalb, Ill., 1977). Approved by the CEAA, Wortham's edition includes an historical introduction, annotation, and a complete textual apparatus. It is in almost every respect the epitome of the sound scholarly edition.

The work of Lowell's which has been reprinted most often is *The Vision of Sir Launfal*, probably because it lent itself to moralistic interpretations, which were popular in schools until recent decades. With the advent of the reprint houses, most of Lowell's works, as well as many works about him, are now available, including the Elmwood edition and Norton's edition of the *Letters*.

MANUSCRIPTS AND LETTERS

Lowell's early recognition and a long, creative life suggest that his manuscripts would be found in quantity and in diverse places. *American Lit-*

erary Manuscripts (Austin, Tex., 1960) lists sixty-two depositories of Lowell manuscripts and letters.

As Lowell was a Harvard alumnus (by the skin of his teeth) and a Harvard professor, it is not surprising that many collections of his manuscripts and letters are to be found at Harvard; the Houghton Library contains the largest collections of Lowell material. Other significant collections are in the following public and private libraries: Boston Public, Colby College, Harvard University Archives, Hispanic Society (New York), Huntington, Library of Congress, Massachusetts Historical Society, Morgan Library, New York Public, University of Pennsylvania, University of Texas, University of Virginia, and Yale University.

The best guide to manuscript sources is Duberman, who provides a detailed list of the holdings in public and private libraries as well as in eleven privately owned collections. Duberman also includes a list of auction house catalogues, some of which describe manuscripts now lost.

The first collection of Lowell's letters was edited by Charles Eliot Norton, who brought out his two-volume *Letters of James Russell Lowell* in 1894. Like many nineteenth-century letter collections, Norton's has limited value. While acknowledging that "few writers have given in their letters a more faithful representation of themselves, and of few men is the epistolary record more complete from youth to age," Norton gives a bowdlerized version of the letters with the justification that "portions of every man's life are essentially private, and knowledge of them belongs by right only to those intimates whom he himself may see fit to trust with his entire confidence" (that is, Norton). After stating that "there was nothing in Mr. Lowell's life to be concealed and excused," Norton makes considerable use of ellipses, saying, "Nothing will, I hope, be found in these volumes which [Lowell] himself might have regretted to see in print." A literary executor has many difficult choices, but to the modern reader it seems unnecessary for the private Lowell to have been mutilated to preserve the formal public image. Norton's excising and clipping seem especially unfortunate because many of the letters to which he had access have since been lost or destroyed. As an early critic remarked, "The result is like a photograph from which the retoucher has taken all lines that give strength and character to the face. . . . For the greater part of the thousand pages we ponder over the asterisks of omission, and wonder, in no spirit of idle curiosity, what Lowell really wrote" (William B. Cairns, "James Russell Lowell: A Centenary View" [*Nation*, 22 February 1919]).

The only other published volume of Lowell letters is M. A. de Wolfe Howe's *New Letters of James Russell Lowell* (New York, 1932)). These letters, most of them to Lowell's daughter, are edited more honestly than those presented by Norton, and from them a clearer picture of Lowell emerges.

In addition to small groups of letters published in scholarly journals (such as those from Lowell to Nathan Hale, Jr., edited by Philip Graham for *TSLL*, Winter 1962), Lowell letters have appeared in volumes of published correspondence of his friends: *Letters of John Holmes to James Russell Lowell and Others* (Boston, 1917); *The Scholar Friends: Letters of Francis James Child and James Russell Lowell*, edited by M. A. de Wolfe Howe and G. W. Cottrell, Jr. (Cambridge, Mass., 1952); and *Browning to His American Friends: Letters Between the Brownings, the Storys and James Russell Lowell*, edited by Gertrude Reese Hudson (London, 1965). Also of interest is Ada Nisbet's dissertation, "Some Letters of Thomas Hughes to James Russell Lowell: A Chapter in Anglo-Americana" (U.C.L.A., 1947), and Quentin G. Johnston's M.A. thesis, "The Letters of James Russell Lowell to Robert Carter, 1842–1876" (Oregon, 1956). Miss Nisbet's notes documenting the Hughes letters quote extensively from unpublished Lowell letters. The forty-seven letters from Lowell to Carter are now in the Berg Collection of the New York Public Library.

Some of Lowell's diplomatic correspondence as Minister to Spain is published in *Impressions of Spain* [by] *James Russell Lowell*, compiled by J. B. Gilder and with an introduction by A. A. Adee (Boston, 1899).

Since Lowell was one of the greatest letter writers in American literature and since his letters have been so inadequately edited, a new scholarly edition of his correspondence is long overdue.

BIOGRAPHY

Though Lowell is extensively discussed in literary histories and critical works and though he is mentioned in biographies of other great men of his time, there are relatively few biographies of Lowell. Of these only three qualify as full-scale historical biographies: Horace Scudder's *James Russell Lowell: A Biography* (Cambridge, 1901), Martin Duberman's *James Russell Lowell* (Boston, 1966), and Edward Wagenknecht's *James Russell Lowell: Portrait of a Many-Sided Man* (New York, 1971).

Scudder's book was preceded by such works as Francis H. Underwood's *The Poet and the Man: Recollections and Appreciations of James Russell Lowell* (Boston, 1892) and Edward Everett Hale, Jr.'s *James Russell Lowell and His Friends* (Boston, 1899). Written shortly after his death by those who saw him as the dominant literary figure of America, these books have little to recommend them to the modern scholar. Both authors are more interested in praising than in portraying and evaluating Lowell. An anonymous reviewer lamented particularly the superficiality of Hale's biography since Hale was "perhaps the one surviving man best acquainted with Lowell and his career from the brilliant start to the honored close."

He saw Hale's book as "a series of gossipy reminiscences" which were "interesting . . . but also disappointing" ("Littérateur, Ambassador, Patriot, Cosmopolite," *Academy*, 29 July 1899).

Two noteworthy views by Lowell's later contemporaries are those of Henry James and William Dean Howells, both of whom had long and intimate associations with Lowell. In his "Studies of Lowell" (a reprint of an essay in the September 1900 issue of *Scribner's*) in *Literary Friends and Acquaintance* (New York, 1900), Howells warmly recalls many visits with Lowell, especially at Elmwood. He concludes, "I believe neither in heroes nor in saints; but I believe in great and good men, and among such men Lowell was the richest nature I have known. His nature was not always serene and pellucid; it was sometimes roiled by the currents that counter and cross in all of us; but it was without the least alloy of insincerity, and it was never darkened by the shadow of a selfish fear. His genius was an instrument that responded in affluent harmony to the power that made him a humorist and that made him a poet, and appointed him rarely to be quite either alone."

Henry James recalled his long friendship with Lowell in two *Atlantic Monthly* essays (Jan. 1892 and Jan. 1897; the first was reprinted in *Essays in London and Elsewhere*, New York, 1893). James, who certainly was not blind to Lowell's shortcomings, considered him "completely representative." After rereading Lowell, James says, "He looms, in such a renewed impression, very large and ripe and sane, and if he was an admirable man of letters there should be no want of emphasis on the first term of the title." He concludes, "He was strong without narrowness; he was wise without bitterness and bright without folly. That appears for the most part the clearest ideal of those who handle the English form, and he was altogether in the straight tradition. This tradition will surely not forfeit its great part in the world so long as we continue occasionally to know it by what is so solid in performance and so stainless in character."

Scudder's two-volume study is a surprisingly competent work for its time. Scudder was the first scholar to use letters and manuscripts in telling the story of Lowell's life, and he is the first to suggest the complexities of the man. While Scudder, like Norton, is cautious and conservative when it comes to the proprieties of biography, one must credit him at least with an attempt at objectivity. It is a tribute to Scudder that subsequent biographers have been indebted to him and that his work was the standard biography for over sixty years.

Ferris Greenslet, *James Russell Lowell: His Life and Work* (Boston, 1905), proposed to write "a biography of the mind," but Greenslet, like others before him in the nineteenth century, set limitations which precluded any presentation of a viable image of the mind or the man. In his introduction Greenslet says, "In this narrative . . . there will be little occasion to adduce any piece of 'bare truth' that the man himself in his essays, his poems, and his letters has not made a part of the record." In spite of these limitations, and in spite of the fact that his work is derivative, Greenslet is at times accurate and perceptive about some aspects of Lowell's life. His chapter on Lowell's poetry is especially penetrating. Greenslet's later study, *The Lowells and Their Seven Worlds* (Boston, 1946), which is devoted to the Lowell family, adds little to his picture of Lowell. Perhaps the best brief biography of Lowell was that written for the *DAB* (1933) by M. A. de Wolfe Howe, who makes a masterful summary of Lowell's life and an estimate of his place in American literature.

Only two major biographical studies of Lowell appeared between Greenslet's work and Duberman's: Richmond Croom Beatty's *James Russell Lowell* (Nashville, Tenn., 1942) and Leon Howard's *Victorian Knight-Errant: A Study of the Early Literary Career of James Russell Lowell.* Both studies are limited. In his preface Beatty admits to a bias ("almost everybody appears to have one") and then proceeds to manifest that bias on almost every page. As a southerner, Beatty seems incapable of forgiving Lowell for being a northerner and an abolitionist. He says Lowell "never understood history, . . . never comprehended politics. . . . Moreover, Harvard scholar though he was, he never made any effort worth mentioning to understand the civilization of the South. He proved himself, from his undergraduate days, a dupe of the most irresponsible propaganda his age afforded." Nor does Beatty give Lowell much credit as a thinker and a critic: "For the central facts about [Lowell's] mind were its discursiveness, its self-conscious irrelevance, and inner certainty, the compulsion of which was always present to disperse his meditations. . . . The evidence is unmistakable that any basic coherence in his thinking about literature appears to have come to him only at intervals, and by happy though sadly infrequent accidents." At times Beatty shows enough insight into Lowell to suggest he might have written a far better book.

Beatty's view on Lowell and the South does not jibe with that of Howells, who said of Lowell, in his reminiscence mentioned above (*Scribner's,* Sept. 1900): "He had a great tenderness for the broken and ruined South, whose sins he felt that he had had his share in visiting upon her, and he was willing to do what he could to ease her sorrows in the case of any particular Southerner." Howells's view is supported by Max L. Griffin's "Lowell and the South" (*TSE,* 1950). Griffin feels that Lowell's abolitionism was moral and philosophical rather than political and sectional, and that it did not affect his personal friendships with southerners.

Leon Howard's study is limited by design. Howard did not intend to write a full or a conventional biography; instead he wanted "to discover the extent to which a meticulous examination of an individual's entire literary output, within the human context of its origin, could improve one's understanding of the individual himself and of the age in which he lived." Howard's book is an interesting study in literary research; it is also the most comprehensive view we have of Lowell's life and times through his literature. Howard may give more information than some readers would wish, but he draws extensively and intelligently upon the canon of Lowell's creative work to provide us with many new biographical insights. One should not quibble with the limits stipulated by Howard, but one cannot help but wish he had carried his study past the year 1857 when, for him, Lowell reached a state of arrested development; the success of Howard's approach to the early Lowell makes us want to see all of Lowell in such a context.

Although written earlier than Howard's book, H. H. Clark's biographical introduction to *James Russell Lowell: Representative Selections* presents an interesting view that differs from Howard's premise. For Clark, Lowell's life underwent progressive change from beginning to end. Clark traces the development of Lowell's life and career through three major stages — the Humanitarian (to 1850), the Nationalist (1850 to 1867), and the Natural Aristocrat (1867 to 1891) — and makes a convincing argument that the evolution from one to the other was organic. This argument is based on Clark's earlier study, "Lowell — Humanitarian, Nationalist, or Humanist?" (*SP*, July 1930), in which he argued that Lowell's life was "an essentially progressive and symmetrical expansion from a center, a steady widening of circles."

Duberman's intended scope was all-inclusive, and he had access to practically every manuscript relevant to Lowell's life. He made good use of those materials in filling in the gaps and fleshing out the details of Lowell's life and in correcting errors that have accumulated over the years. Duberman states that his purpose in writing the book was not "to restore Lowell's stature as a Renaissance figure or a literary giant" (he feels Lowell was neither), but "to restore him as a man." Duberman is interested more in Lowell as a virtuous man, as a man of character, than as a man of letters. One has the feeling that part of the real Lowell is still missing and that Duberman's easy dismissal of Lowell as an artist ("There are many moments in his poetry, long sections in his essays, which deserve respect, . . . but they remain incidental; rather than high-lighting a consolidated achievement, they call attention to its absence.") suggests that he does not fully understand Lowell. But Duberman's study is likely to be the best that we will have for some time. Perhaps it need disappoint only those who still consider Lowell primarily as a litterateur, as a man

who gave American letters a dignity that it has seldom had in our history.
Claire McGlinchee's TUSAS *James Russell Lowell* (New York, 1967),
is hardly worthy of mention. A glib and superficial study, it contributes
nothing to our understanding of Lowell.

Wagenknecht's study of Lowell, like his biographies of other American writers, is "a psychograph or character portrait." As such, it attempts
to explore the "Lowell Problem" by focusing on various aspects of Lowell's character and accomplishment, by examining Lowell's complexities
and contrarities, by showing the ways in which seemingly contradictory
elements in Lowell's life are balanced. While Wagenknecht's study is general and interpretive and gives us a rounded rather than a detailed portrait, several of his chapters, especially those dealing with Lowell's creativity and his religion, provide fresh insight if not new information.

C. David Heymann's *American Aristocracy: The Lives and Times of
James Russell, Amy and Robert Lowell* (New York, 1980), highly derivative of Duberman and other sources, adds nothing to our understanding
of Lowell as man or writer or to his influence on the two later Lowell
poets. Besides factual errors and questionable interpretation of biographical facts and poetry, Heymann, who acknowledges "informed conspira-
tors" among his sources, reports gossip, anecdote, and family stories without documentation as if they were fact.

One of the difficulties that have faced his biographers and one of the
reasons why the essential Lowell has in one way or another eluded all
of his biographers, is that he was so diverse and so versatile. If comparison often places him second in some category of literary or other endeavors, rarely has one man demonstrated excellence in so many facets. He
was: poet, essayist, humorist, letter-writer, linguist, critic. He was also:
abolitionist, journalist, crusader for political and other reform, diplomat,
teacher of modern foreign languages and literatures, public lecturer, after-
dinner speaker, and editor (*The Pioneer, The Atlantic Monthly*, and *The
North American Review*). As Frank R. Stockton said in a "Personal Tribute to Lowell" written at the time of Lowell's death, "Without occupying the highest rank in any of his vocations, he stood in front of his fellow
citizens because he held so high a rank in so many of them" (*The Writer*,
Sept. 1891).

There are areas of Lowell's life which need further attention. Though
a great deal is known of Lowell and Lowell's thinking from the time of
his youth, his letters are revelatory on some matters and carefully silent
on others. These areas of reverberating silence involve his relationships
with his family and his feeling about his mother's insanity. The silence
is entirely in keeping with nineteenth-century reticence; it indicates no
scandal, but it cuts off a means of insight into Lowell as a creative artist.

That he had a morbid streak far deeper than his contemporaries realized or reported can be deduced from many passim remarks. And no one has satisfactorily come to terms with Lowell's mysticism, an aspect of his life on which there is a good deal of divided opinion. Psychoanalysis, applied through the veil of over a century and based on fragmentary evidence, would be foolish and dangerous, but some new attempt to evaluate and to interpret all of Lowell's character and personality is needed.

Another area that needs further exploration is the influence of Lowell's wives upon his moral and intellectual patterns. There is speculation that Maria was more devoted to abolition than he was and that she was more creative. There are also indications that Frances did not like Lowell's dialect poetry; since moderns consider this one of his strongest areas, did she inhibit him from developing further along this line?

Perhaps there are parts of the Lowell puzzle which we will never find, but until we understand more about the complexities of his personality we will never completely understand him as a creative artist. Perhaps the key to the puzzle lies in the works themselves. And until a biographer comes along who has a greater interest in Lowell's total creative output — bad as well as good — we are not likely to get the story of Lowell's life which we need and which he deserves.

CRITICISM

James Russell Lowell's critical reputation has never been very secure. In almost every decade since he started writing, he has been praised by some critics and damned by others — sometimes for the same thing. One could generalize, however, that before his death Lowell was praised for things that were not true of him and after his death damned for things that were.

Lowell's critics seem always to lament that he was not something other than he was: a more disciplined poet, less a dilettante, more patriotic, less a Puritan, more a scholar, less an Anglophile, more an abolitionist, and so on. Critics wishing that Lowell were not himself seem to reflect Poe's sentiment on first meeting Lowell: "He is not half the noble looking person I expected to see."

While a good deal of nineteenth-century criticism is essentially effusive and of little critical worth to modern readers, there have been from the beginning a few critics who have tried to be objective about Lowell. Of Lowell's early contemporaries, perhaps the views of Edgar Allan Poe and Margaret Fuller are most significant. Poe felt that Lowell was the best poet in America with the exception of Longfellow and "perhaps one other" (presumably Poe himself), essentially because of the vigor of Lowell's imagination. Poe, however, felt that Lowell's ear for rhythm was imperfect and his artistic ability of second rank. Poe was less than enthusiastic about *A Fable for Critics*, which he found "essentially 'loose'— ill conceived and feebly executed as well in detail as in general" and lacking polish (*Southern Literary Messenger*, Mar. 1849). Poe's estimate may have been colored by Lowell's finding him "two-fifths sheer fudge" in the *Fable*.

Margaret Fuller was more sharply critical of Lowell and, in her estimate of his reputation, almost prophetic. Speaking of Longfellow, she says, "Though imitative, his [poetry] is not mechanical. We cannot say as much for Lowell, who, we must declare it, though to the grief of some friends, and the disgust of more, is absolutely wanting in the true spirit and tone of poesy. His interest in the moral questions of the day has supplied the want of vitality in himself; his great facility at versification has enabled him to fill the ear with a copious stream of pleasant sound. But his verse is stereotyped; his thought sounds no depth, and posterity will not remember him." In retaliation, Lowell painted a most unflattering portrait of Miss Fuller in the *Fable* and refused to remove or soften it in later editions.

Lowell's death in 1891 stimulated some of the most vigorous criticism of him in the nineteenth century. Thomas Wentworth Higginson is perhaps representative of those who were extravagant in their evaluations of Lowell. Higginson (*Nation*, 13 August 1891) called the "Commemoration Ode" "the finest single poem yet produced in this country"; and Lowell himself "our foremost critic." If Higginson is close to the mark in these estimates, he was clearly off the mark in stating that "no American author, unless it be Emerson, has achieved a securer hold upon a lasting fame."

An opposite, almost violent reaction to Lowell is found in an anonymous review of his *Last Poems* (1895) in the *Athenaeum* (4 January 1896). The reviewer considers Lowell a third-rate poet primarily because of his inability to use metaphor properly: "The figure of speech was to him speech at its finest elevation; and he laid violent and indiscriminate hands on everything that could be compared to anything else." He adds, "But after all it is not the prevalence of bad lines, of false metaphors, of any other external blemish, that forbids us to assign Lowell any place among the conspicuous poets of his time; it is his radically prosaic attitude of mind and his radically prosaic construction of verse. . . . He gets the right number of syllables in his lines, but he seems to get them by counting on his fingers." He concludes, "That he should ever have seemed to the American critic or the American public a poet of national importance is, perhaps, the severest criticism on itself that the American nation has ever made."

A more rational and perceptive English view is that in "An English Estimate of Lowell" (*ForumNY*, Oct. 1891) by Frederic William Farrar. Farrar points out that Lowell "might have been greater, had he in some respects been less. He might have done more, had he not known so much." Farrar felt that *A Fable for Critics* had been underestimated, that it had "a very unusual power of seeing the real men through the glamour of temporary popularity and the cloud of passing dislike." Farrar is just as perceptive when it comes to Lowell's poetry: "The chief element of his strength, and not of his weakness, was the intensity of that moral sympathy which makes his best poetry distinctly didactic. The best chords of his lyre are exactly those in which he means to preach." Farrar sees Lowell's poetry as being too imitative; "sometimes defective in distinctness, and sometimes in symmetry, as well as sometimes in melody"; and lacking "a clear, definite impression."

A final nineteenth-century estimate worthy of mention is that of Henry James in Charles Dudley Warner's edition of *A Library of the World's Best Literature, Ancient and Modern* (New York, 1897). James was impressed with Lowell's learning and his versatility, which gave him "among Americans of his time, the supreme right to wear the title of a man of letters." James praises *The Biglow Papers* as "an extraordinary performance and a rare work of art" which established Lowell as "the master and the real authority" of dialect and colloquial writing. Of Lowell's poetry, James remarks, "The chords of his lyre were of the precious metal, but not perhaps always of the last lyric tenuity. He struck them with a hand not idle enough for mere moods, and yet not impulsive enough for the great reverberations. He was sometimes too ingenious, as well as too reasonable and responsible."

While others criticized Lowell for his Puritanism, James praised him for it: "It is the recognition of the eternal difference between right and wrong that gives the ring to his earliest melodies, the point to his satire, the standard to his critical judgments, the sublimity to his Commemoration Ode" (*AtM*, Jan. 1897).

Ferris Greenslet's biography of Lowell did not add much to Scudder's in terms of biographical fact, but he far surpassed Scudder in his critical evaluation of Lowell as a writer. In speaking of Lowell's weakness as a poet, Greenslet observes, "The expression of his views and opinions meant more to him — in all save his most ecstatic poetic moods — than the production of a perfect poem; and he was never steadily able to distinguish between the stress of opinions seeking utterance and the pure poetic impulse." In spite of these shortcomings, Greenslet feels that much of Lowell's poetry succeeds because of "the utter and fervent sincerity of the moods expressed in it"; "the amount of mind that lay back of it"; and "the constant ideality, which was both root and branch of his sincerity and of his abounding intellectual life."

Like others before and after him, Greenslet found the best and the worst of Lowell's prose related to Lowell's conversational style. It is loosely structured and lacking in intellectual unity, but full of learning and emotionally convincing.

An important early twentieth-century essay on Lowell was that by William C. Brownell in his *American Prose Masters* (New York, 1909).[1] For Brownell, Lowell had a "representative rather than individual turn of mind" and "was not an original but an independent thinker" whose chief qualities were his poise; his passion for patriotism, books, and nature; his "ingrained cleverness" and "his extraordinary personal charm." Brownell feels that, although Lowell's prose "has the piquancy of Pegasus in harness, . . . at least it is never prose poetry. It is masculine, direct, flexible, and energetic prose." While he feels that Lowell wrote "a good deal too much verse," Brownell believes that "a great deal of it is very fine, very noble and at times very beautiful, and it discloses the distinctly poetic faculty of which rhythmic and figurative is native expression." Brownell is of the opinion that Lowell's "patriotic poetry is altogether unmatched — even unrivalled."

Bliss Perry took the occasion of the commemoration of the centenary of Lowell's birth to answer some of Brownell's charges against Lowell. In "James Russell Lowell" (*Harvard Graduate Magazine*, June 1919), Perry felt that Brownell failed to answer the question as to why, in spite of his defects, Lowell's essays were read "with such pleasure by so many intelligent" people. Perry felt that Lowell's greatness was due to the fact that he wrote in a great tradition of literary essays and that he was so much a man of learning and culture. If Lowell was not a great poet, Perry feels, it was because "his was a divided nature, so variously endowed that complete integration was difficult."

In *The Spirit of American Literature* (Garden City, N.Y., 1913), John Albert Macy states that, with the exception of *The Biglow Papers*, Lowell's poetry is not successful, "the music simply does not happen." *The Biglow Papers*, however, "have no rivals. . . . Occasional poems, they have wings that lift them above occasion to immortality. In them Lowell is possessed by his genius, by a genius that never visited anyone else in the same shape." Macy is one of the few who considers the second series of *The Biglow Papers* superior to the first.

---

1. A new edition of Brownell's study was edited by Howard Mumford Jones in 1963 (Cambridge, Mass.). Jones's introduction to the text is valuable for the information it provides on Brownell as a literary critic.

Further praise of *The Biglow Papers* is found in Edward M. Chapman's "*The Biglow Papers* Fifty Years After" (*YR*, Oct. 1916). Chapman sees *The Biglow Papers* as Lowell's chief contribution to literature because they are written "in a field [humorous wit] where his learning was most profound and his heart most enlisted."

The most extravagant praise of *The Biglow Papers* is found in Lewis H. Chrisman's "Permanent Values in *The Biglow Papers*" in his *John Ruskin, Preacher, and Other Essays* (New York, 1921). Chrisman feels that "in American literature in the field of satire we have nothing better to show than Lowell's Biglow Papers." He adds, "No other writer has written in dialect lines so pathetically beautiful and enchantingly melodious." *The Biglow Papers* contain "some of the ripest, richest, and most virile thoughts in American literature." Less hyperbolic but as appreciative is Jennette Reid Tandy's estimate in her *Crackerbox Philosophers in American Humor and Satire* (New York, 1925): "Lowell's range and penetration in satirical portraiture are unsurpassed in America. As a piece of sustained irony *The Biglow Papers* has escaped the careful study of present-day critics. We have no other satirist at once so witty and so racy."

An opposite view of *The Biglow Papers* is seen in V. L. Parrington's *The Romantic Revolution in America* (New York, 1927). Parrington says, "The native clutter of Lowell's mind is there laid bare — the grotesque mixture of homely satire, moral aphorisms, Yankee linguistics, literary criticism — an unwieldy mass that he could neither simplify nor reduce to order. The machinery spoils the propaganda and weighs down the satire." This is characteristic of Parrington's entire estimate of Lowell. He sees Lowell as limited by his Brahmin and Puritan background and to the last "extraordinarily parochial." For Parrington, Lowell "never speculated widely or analyzed critically. Ideas, systems of thought, intellectual and social movements, he had no interest in; he was content to remain a bookish amateur in letters, loitering over old volumes for the pleasure of finding apt phrases and verbal curiosities. With all his reading, history remained a blank to him; and science he would have none of."

The most comprehensive and most responsible evaluation of *The Biglow Papers* is Thomas Wortham's introduction to the new critical edition cited above. Wortham establishes the clearest biographical and social context we have for the spirit that inspired Lowell's satirical personae. As Wortham notes, and as his careful scholarship confirms, "What holds *The Biglow Papers* together, what makes it a book, are irony and its form, unique both in conception and execution. From its beginning in deft parodies of contemporary literary notices to its outrageous 'Index,' *The Biglow Papers* is a masterpiece of sustained irony, the irony of an earnest young man who sees the good sense of truth and justice, but realizes the blindness of those around him." A more succinct assessment of the *Biglow Papers* by Wortham can be found in his essay on Lowell in the *Dictionary of Literary Biography*, vol. 2, *American Humorists, 1800–1950*, pt. 1 (Detroit, 1982).

In his essay on Lowell in *Nature in American Literature* (New York, 1923), Norman Foerster says that "although nature is the theme or background of most of the poems, [Lowell] never writes of her with sustained spontaneity." Foerster ponders why Lowell's poetry of nature is not better than it is and concludes that it is due to Lowell's failure as an artist to revise and polish his verse and to "the paralyzing effect of the spirit of the times" which confused Lowell's heart and mind.

In the thirties and forties there was a general critical reaction against Lowell. Writing with a definite Marxist bias, Granville Hicks, in *The Great Tradition* (New York, 1933), sees Lowell as inexorably locked into his Brahminism to the extent that he always looked backwards. For Hicks, Lowell belonged to a class of writers who were "kindly men, well-informed, well-intentioned, full of eloquent professions of patriotic and literary zeal, but they were nevertheless parasites — parasites upon the past, upon foreign culture, upon an industrial order that they did not try to understand, did not think of reforming, and did not even venture to defend and advance."

Hicks's point of view is echoed in Percy Boynton's *Literature and American Life* (Boston, 1936) and, to a lesser extent, in Van Wyck Brooks's *The Flowering of New England* (New York, 1936).

In his *American Prosody* (New York, 1935), Gay Wilson Allen found no system or theory of prosody in Lowell's poetry. He concludes, "We must decide that Lowell made no direct contribution to American prosodic thought, but his versification introduced into American poetry the freedom which we find in the first two or three decades of nineteenth-century English poetry."

The anti-Lowell sentiment of the thirties and forties can perhaps best be summarized by quoting the conclusion of Arthur W. M. Voss's 1949 essay on "James Russell Lowell" (*UKCR*, Spring 1949): "He was a significant force in furthering our cultural development and is therefore a worthy subject of study for the literary scholar and historian. But he wrote no books which have true literary power. A volume of considerable literary merit might be culled from his writings, but it would be made up of passages and parts, not wholes. Lowell served the cause of humane letters well, but whoever holds that only the best of intellects, the greatest of literary artists, are worthy of the reader's serious attention may ignore him."

Although Leon Howard's interest in Lowell's writings is essentially biographical, his study nevertheless contains a good deal of astute critical commentary. For Howard, the main value of the poems and essays is not in the literary merit they possess, but in the insight they give into Lowell's life and the age he lived in: "Lowell never achieved the quality of excellence which makes some literature so great that it possesses a life of its own, independent of time and place. He was intimately a part of nineteenth-century America, and his importance is determined by that intimacy rather than by the inherent quality of his writings."

Howard sees Lowell's early poetry as his best because Lowell was "fighting wholeheartedly for a poet's place in a difficult world." For Howard, Lowell became less a true poet in middle and later life, because he confused the role of the poet with that of the preacher or moralist and because he "accepted the wisdom of the market place instead of pursuing something less tangible. . . . As a poet, he applied his craftsmanship to writing up to the occasion which called forth his verses, instead of trying to compete with the best that had been thought and said in the world before him."

In spite of such sentiments, Lowell has continued to have his defenders. In his *The Conservative Mind from Burke to Santayana* (Chicago, 1953), Russell Kirk notes that it had become fashionable to belittle Lowell. Kirk answers such critics as Parrington and Harold Laski (*The American Democracy*, New York, 1948) in saying of Lowell:"But how civilized a man, and how versatile! Whoever reads Lowell's letters is not likely to dismiss him summarily. . . . Lowell founded the major American school of literary criticism; he was a poet of high, if limited talent; and he represented the best in Brahmin culture."

George Arms believes that part of the decline in Lowell's reputation is related to the fact that he has been so poorly represented in anthologies, something Arms attempts to correct in the selections of Lowell's poetry he includes in *The Fields Were Green* (Stanford, Calif., 1953). Though Arms feels that Lowell is essentially a failure as a poet ("These closing pages are not written with the hope of making the reader forget the enormously disheartening effect that Lowell's verses as a whole produce."), he feels his best poetry has been wrongly judged by association with his worst. For Arms, Lowell "had a real genius for a certain kind of poem" and Lowell's reputation as a poet must rest on a handful of poems (in addition to *The Biglow Papers* and *A Fable for Critics*): "Agassiz," "Fitz Adam's Story," "To the Dandelion," "Auspex," "The Cathedral," and "Ode Recited at the Harvard Commemoration."

In *The Continuity of American Poetry* (Princeton, N.J., 1961), Roy Harvey Pearce sees Lowell as the poet of the ideal, who wrote poetry "to give direction and coherence to men living in the real world and save them from their temptation to take seriously the natural world." As such, Lowell is the "poet as patriarch" and preacher, who writes good public but not good private poems, who sings Songs of Ourselves, but no Song of Myself.

In "The Craftsmanship of Lowell: Revisions in *The Cathedral*" (*BNYPL*, Jan. 1966), G. Thomas Tanselle demonstrates that Lowell was a better craftsman that he is usually accounted.

A revisionist assessment of Lowell's place in the history of American poetry is that of Marjorie R. Kaufman in her introduction to *The Poetical Works of James Russell Lowell* (Boston, 1978). Kaufman uses three previously uncollected poems as well as examples from the Lowell canon in her "search for the unfaded Lowell." In speaking of Lowell's use of vernacular speech in *The Biglow Papers*, Kaufman confirms Walter Blair's 1937 assessment (*Native American Humor*) when she says: "A quarter of a century before Twain's achievement, the poet was displaying the same invention on surprisingly similar materials with much the same effect: the artistic freedom gained by the use of vernacular rather than literary speech to attack official but morally decayed institutions and attitudes, a freedom created when the artist chooses a hero and an idiom not from his own world but from the bottom of the social and cultural heap." Kaufman also praises *A Fable for Critics* ("The first extended statement of its kind and quality in American letters, undertaken as something other than pure puffery of native writers over British"), *The Vision of Sir Launfal* ("for the reader curious about the history of American sensibility, the poem remains a major document"), as well as other poems. In concluding, Kaufman expresses hope for a new look at Lowell as poet: "Now, with Whitman's reputation safe, with the recovery of the fragile and eccentric but genuine poetry of artists like Henry Tuckerman and Jones Very, we may at least be able to afford a place for the *successes* of Lowell. . . . In addition to its importance to literary history, much of the poetry remains its own excuse for being."

The matter of Lowell's reputation as a critic deserves special mention if for no other reason that that it has been given special attention by critics and literary historians. Lowell was considered by his contemporaries to be the foremost critic in American letters. This was undoubtedly due in part to his astute appraisal of his contemporaries (and himself) in *A Fable for Critics* and to the fact that he expressed his critical views on a variety of subjects over a long period of time.

Although Lowell's reputation as a critic was relatively more secure in the nineteenth century, there were those who belittled that reputation. Two early essays point to the weaknesses that twentieth-century critics were to emphasize. In "Professor Lowell as Critic" (*Lippincott's Monthly*

Magazine, June 1871), John Foster Kirk feels that Lowell is "narrow, shallow, and hard, destitute of the insight, the comprehension, the sympathy, by which the true critic, the true poet, searches the domain of thought and the recesses of the mind, illumines the emotions and kindles them." In a long article on "Mr. Lowell's Prose" (*Scribner's*, May, June, July 1872), William Cleaver Wilkinson grants Lowell the wide literary background, the ability to empathize with other writers, and the artistry requisite to the good critic, but feels that Lowell fails as a critic because he has no basic and systematic critical position.

While admiring Lowell as a scholar and man of culture, William C. Brownell, in *American Prose Masters*, feels that Lowell was deficient as a critic because "he occupied himself mainly with genius. As a subject . . . the best was good enough for him." This, according to Brownell, led to Lowell's proclivity to rank poets rather than to evaluate and describe them. Lowell's failure as critic was related to three characteristics, according to Brownell: his criticism grew out of his reading and not out of his thought; he was insensitive to the plastic arts; and he had "no philosophic view to advocate or express."

In the first comprehensive treatment of Lowell as critic (*James Russell Lowell as A Critic* [New York, 1915]), Joseph J. Reilly expands on Brownell's view. He considers Lowell a failure because he was limited in his critical interest; he was deficient in his knowledge of art and history; he lacked sympathy for science and classical art; and he had little interest in drama and fiction. According to Reilly, "If Lowell is to survive, it must be frankly as an impressionist, for so far as criticism approaches a science, so far as it depends to any serious extent on ultimate principles, so far, in a word, as it is something more fundamental and abiding than the *ipse dixit* of an appreciator, Lowell is not a critic."

George E. De Mille in "The Critic from Cambridge" (*SR*, Oct. 1924) does not try to determine how good a critic Lowell is, but what kind of critic. If Lowell is measured by the standards of the scientific critic "we can hardly say that Lowell is a critic at all. If, on the other hand, we accept Professor Brewster's definition . . . that criticism is simply 'talk about books,' . . . Lowell takes a very high rank indeed."

In *The Romantic Revolution in America* V. L. Parrington takes Reilly's first definition and finds Lowell sorely wanting: "He had no standards other than ethical, only likes and dislikes; no interest in ideas, only a pottering concern for the text; no historical backgrounds, only isolated figures dwelling in a vacuum. He was puzzled over new schools and unfamiliar technic, and was at ease only in praising established reputations and confirming approved judgments."

In "Lowell's Criticism of Romantic Literature" (*PMLA*, Mar. 1925),

H. H. Clark says that Lowell did not like romantic literature "because it failed to fulfill the requirements of his poetic creed." C. M. Lombard argues that Clark and others were incorrect in their judgment of Lowell's attitude toward the Romantics and that Lowell gave the Romantics reasonable praise ("Lowell and French Romanticism" [*Revue de Littérature Comparée*, Oct.–Dec. 1964]). In "Lowell on Thoreau" (*Sp*, July 1930), Austin Warren feels that in his infamous essay Lowell as humanist reacts more to romanticism than to Thoreau.

A convincing defense of Lowell as critic has been made by Norman Foerster. In "The Creed of Lowell as Literary Critic" (*SP*, July 1927), Foerster counters Brownell's contention that Lowell's criticism "lacks the unity of a body of doctrine." In a fuller treatment published the following year in his *American Criticism: A Study in Literary Theory from Poe to the Present* (Boston and New York, 1928), Foerster calls Lowell "our most distinguished literary critic," and defends him against the charge of being merely an impressionist. Foerster feels that Lowell had a "comprehensive vision of the task of the critic. It involves sensitiveness to impressions, historical understanding, and an aesthetic-ethical judgment." If Foerster's views seem at times too much influenced by New Humanism, his defense of Lowell helped to pave the way for a more balanced view of Lowell as critic.

Although generally appreciative of Lowell's critical ability, Bernard Smith (*Forces in American Criticism* [New York, 1939]) points out that Lowell did not understand or sympathize with contemporary literary movements after the Civil War. He had nothing to say about Twain and little about James, Howells, or Whitman. Nevertheless, Smith feels Lowell is the "*beau idéal* of gentlemanly critics."

Richard D. Altick defends Lowell against earlier critics (Reilly, Clark, Parrington, and others) who charged that Lowell was unaware of the importance of historical perspective in formulating his critical judgment. In fact, Altick accuses these critics with the same charges they had raised against Lowell, for they failed to evaluate correctly the resources available to Lowell and thus judged him by modern standards. According to Altick, Lowell "was by no means ignorant of the value or the nature of historical criticism, and . . . his critical essays abound with evidences of his awareness of the power exerted by contemporary circumstance upon the literature of a given era" ("Was Lowell an Historical Critic?" [*AL*, Nov. 1942]).

The culmination of the discussion of Lowell as critic is seen in three well-balanced views. Although John Paul Pritchard (*Criticism in America* [Norman, Okla., 1965]) is realistic about Lowell's shortcomings as critic—"His ignorance of America south of Philadelphia and west of the

Alleghenies narrowed considerably his capacity to speak for and of the whole country; his aristocratic point of view . . . made him unable to *feel* the nobility of toil; his inability to adapt himself to the age of science restricted his understanding of later writers; and he was too much Man Reading"—he still sees him at times as surprisingly modern, as in his theory of the lyric: "Here eighty years before the relation of poetic texture and structure were discussed by John Crowe Ransom and Allen Tate, Lowell adumbrated the approach to lyric poetry which these well-known New Critics have amplified."

Richard H. Fogle in "Organic Form in American Criticism: 1840–1870" (in *The Development of American Literary Criticism*, edited by Floyd Stovall [Chapel Hill, N.C., 1955]) sees Lowell's conservatism and his inhospitality to new writers as having two causes: "He comes at the end of a *great tradition* [the organic tradition of Herder, Goethe, and Coleridge], which at the last failed in energy to revitalize itself; and there really was much in the new generations which Lowell did well to reject." Fogle feels that "Lowell's criticism is eclectic, but organicist in its very eclecticism. . . . He shows the organicist willingness to sympathize, to assimilate, to absorb before he passes judgment. And his judgments generally stand up well. His essay on Keats, for example, written in 1854, contains in the germ all that modern scholarship has fathomed of Keats's identity, his unique fusion of experience and thought, his sensuous power and his idealism."

The most recent and perhaps the soundest appraisal of Lowell's critical abilities is Herbert F. Smith's introduction to his collection of Lowell's critical writings, *Literary Criticism of James Russell Lowell* (Lincoln, Neb., 1969). Noting that during the 20th century "Lowell's reputation as a critic has been an esthetic battlefield," in which "the stridence of his debunkers . . . is marked by the idolatry of his supporters," Smith attempts realistically to assess Lowell's strengths and weaknesses and to establish his true place in American literary criticism once and for all. Summarizing Lowell's weaknesses, Smith says, "He wrote too much; he is repetitive; few principles of criticism seem, at first sight, to make his work cohere; he was traditional and conservative—indeed, he was inconsistent and even self-contradictory in many of his judgments." In spite of such faults, Smith contends that "the critical writings of a man with such taste, such erudition, and such esthetic sympathies may not be written off either as outdated or as evidence of the immaturity of the man and his epoch." Noting that most of Lowell's criticism avoids extremes, Smith astutely comments, "Therein, probably, lies the reason for the wild swings of Lowell's critical reputation. Firmly located in the center as he is, humble and undemonstrative as he is, he is either looked up to or looked down on, as the case demands, by modern factionalist critics, as though he were a satellite and they the mother earth. Lowell professes as guide and principle for his criticism only humility and catholicity, taste and erudition." In summary, Smith contends that Lowell "was the only American critic for some fifty years who consistently defended art on the Philistine's home ground — that is, that it had value in a raw democracy." Smith says: "If we persist in our examination of him, if we break through the formality of his presentation, . . . he comes to seem remarkably contemporary. We discover that what seemed to have only an antiquarian interest was really written under conditions which still prevail, and his voice, which seems at first merely quaint, is one to which the modern reader ought to listen."

Influence on Lowell's thinking and writing have been traced by a number of scholars. In his chapter on Lowell in *Return to the Fountains* (Durham, N.C., 1942), John Paul Pritchard finds a significant indebtedness to classical literature, an indebtedness he explored in two earlier essays, "Lowell's Debt to Horace's *Ars Poetica*" (*AL*, Nov. 1931) and "James Russell Lowell and Aristotle's Poetics" (*Classical Weekly*, 15 January 1934). Of Aristotle's influence on Lowell, Pritchard says, "It is not too much to say that Lowell's important position in American letters and criticism is based largely upon his knowledge of the principles advocated by Aristotle in the Poetics and his adherence to them." In two later studies, "Lowell and Longinus" (*Transactions of the American Philological Association*, 1945) and "A Glance at Lowell's Classical Reading" (*AL*, Jan. 1950), Pritchard adds Longinus, Plato, and Plutarch to the list of Lowell's classical mentors.

Related to Pritchard's work is George P. Clark's Ph.D. dissertation on "Classical Influences and Background in the Writings of James Russell Lowell" (Yale, 1948), and his "James Russell Lowell's Study of the Classics Before Entering Harvard" (*JA*, 1963).

In "James Russell Lowell's Interest in Dante," J. Chesley Mathews documents Lowell's lifelong preoccupation with Dante but concludes that Dante's influence on Lowell's poetry was slight (*Italica*, June 1959). According to Lawrence H. Klibbe, the Spanish influence on Lowell was not great except for Cervantes and Calderón, both of whom "are vital to the analysis of Lowell's literary theories" (*James Russell Lowell's Residence in Spain, 1877–1880* [New York, 1964]). The Spanish influence on Lowell is further explored by Stanley T. Williams in *The Spanish Background of American Literature* (2 vols., New Haven, Conn., 1955).

Charles Oran Stewart's *Lowell and France* (Nashville, Tenn., 1951) examines the influence of French culture and literature in a number of

Lowell's works, showing that they provided him with both subject matter and inspiration.

Like many of his contemporaries, Lowell rejected the Bible as a religious text early, but used it extensively in his writing throughout his life. William J. De Saegher concludes his study of "James Russell Lowell and the Bible" (Ph.D. dissertation, U.C.L.A., 1964) by remarking that Lowell understood the Bible well and used it often and variously in his writing, so that "biblical material pervades every facet of his work."

If this review of scholarly work on Lowell reveals anything it is that Lowell continues to be a figure to be reckoned with in the American literary landscape. Although he has been disparaged, devalued, and damned by numerous critics for over a hundred and fifty years, Lowell's versatility and vitality have kept his position as a pre-eminent man of letters at least a matter of continuing controversy. While he is no longer regarded with the same esteem that he held in his own century, his influence on so many aspects of American literary and critical expression guarantee that he will continue to be seen as a central figure of that first flowering from which all American Literature has sprung. As W. C. Brownell said in 1909, "He will doubtless cease to be one of our superstitions, but he will always remain one of our chief glories."

Frank Norris

WILLIAM B. DILLINGHAM

BIBLIOGRAPHY

No AREA OF STUDY on Frank Norris has flourished more in recent years than that of bibliography. Until 1959 the student of Norris was greatly hampered by the absence of bibliographical information. An early mimeographed bibliography by Joseph Gaer (California Literary Research Project, 1934) was brief and unreliable. With the publication of *Frank Norris: A Bibliography* (Los Gatos, Calif., 1959) by Kenneth A. Lohf and Eugene P. Sheehy, a major step was taken toward greatly improving the situation. Lohf and Sheehy's bibliography includes sections on Norris's collected works, individual works, dramatizations, film adaptations, translations, and Norris's contributions to periodicals. Another section is devoted to writings about Norris, including reviews. William White's "Frank Norris: Bibliographical Addenda" (*BB*, Sept.–Dec. 1959) lists forty-six additional items not found in Lohf and Sheehy; and Richard Leekley adds information concerning editions of *Moran of the Lady Letty* in "Addendum to Lohf and Sheehy: Frank Norris" (*PBSA*, no. 1, 1976). John S. Hill's *Checklist of Frank Norris* (Columbus, Ohio, 1970) lists books and major separate publications, editions, letters, bibliographies, checklists, biographies, and scholarship and criticism. Ernest Marchand's *Frank Norris: A Study* (Stanford, Calif., 1942) contains a bibliographical essay (Chapter Six) which is particularly valuable for a survey of contemporary reviews. An excellent bibliographical essay is also to be found in Warren French, *Frank Norris* (New York, 1962). French published in ad-

From Earl N. Harbert and Robert A. Rees, editors, *Fifteen American Authors Before 1900: Bibliographic Essays on Research & Criticism* (Madison: The University of Wisconsin Press; © 1984 by the Board of Regents of the University of Wisconsin System); may be reproduced only by permission of the publisher.

dition an abbreviated bibliography on Norris in *ALR* (Fall 1967). For a checklist of Norris's literary criticism, the bibliography in Donald Pizer's edition of *The Literary Criticism of Frank Norris* (Austin, Tex., 1964) is useful. Joseph Katz adds important bibliographical information about several articles that Norris published in the Brooklyn *Daily Eagle* in "The Elusive Criticisms Syndicated by Frank Norris" (*Proof* 3, 1973). To date the most nearly complete bibliography of Norris's contributions to periodicals is Katz's "The Shorter Publications of Frank Norris" (*Proof* 3, 1973). Katz's valuable introduction details the history of past checklists, especially errors in and shortcomings of the one that was published in the 1903 edition of *The Responsibilities of the Novelist*. Sensibly disclaiming definitiveness for their work (or, indeed, for any future bibliography on Norris), Jesse S. Crisler and Joseph R. McElrath, Jr., in *Frank Norris: A Reference Guide* (Boston, 1974), have compiled a highly useful annotated bibliography of published writings in English about Norris beginning in 1891. The volume also contains a brief but excellent bibliographical overview in the introduction and sections on doctoral dissertations and works published in foreign languages. McElrath has listed, divided into appropriate categories, and discussed forty-four doctoral dissertations on Norris in *ALR* (Autumn 1975). James B. Stronks added twelve items to Crisler and McElrath (*PBSA*, no. 1, 1977, and *ALR*, Spring 1978). Selected bibliographies of Norris's works and of principal works about him are included in Pizer's *The Novels of Frank Norris* (Bloomington, Ind., 1966; reprinted, New York, 1973) and Don Graham's *The Fiction of Frank Norris: The Aesthetic Context* (Columbia, Mo., 1978). An annotated bibliography of works about Norris is to be found in William B. Dillingham's *Frank Norris: Instinct and Art* (Lincoln, Neb., 1969). Don Graham's introduction to *Critical Essays on Frank Norris* (Boston, 1980) is a well informed bibliographical essay with suggestive observations about recent trends in writings about Norris.

EDITIONS

Both Collier and Son's *The Complete Works of Frank Norris* (4 vols., 1898–1903) and Doubleday, Page and Company's *The Complete Works of Frank Norris* (7 vols., 1903) omit *Vandover and the Brute*, which was not published until 1914. The standard edition is *The Complete Edition of Frank Norris* (Garden City, N.Y., 1928) in ten volumes. Actually released in the early part of 1929, this edition is dated 1928. Although it is better than the early editions of many writers, the *Complete Edition* is not complete. Notable is the omission of some of Norris's critical essays. Norris scholars would welcome a new edition incorporating the many items by Norris discovered in recent years and utilizing the careful methods of modern textual scholarship.

Frank Norris of "The Wave": Stories and Sketches from the San Francisco Weekly, 1893 to 1897, has a foreword by Norris's writer brother, Charles, and an introduction by Oscar Lewis. Published in 1931 (San Francisco), this was long a rare item, but it was reprinted in 1970. Donald Pizer's edition of *The Literary Criticism of Frank Norris* supersedes *The Responsibilities of the Novelist* (New York, 1903), the first collection of Norris's essays. In 1970, James D. Hart published his long awaited edition of Norris's Harvard themes along with *Blix* and *Vandover and the Brute. A Novelist in the Making: A Collection of Student Themes and the Novels Blix and Vandover and the Brute* (Cambridge, Mass.) is indispensable to anyone studying Norris's development as a novelist.

The availability of Norris's works has vastly improved over the past few years. Currently all of his seven novels are in print, *McTeague* in no less than seven editions, *The Pit* six editions, *The Octopus* four. *Vandover and the Brute*, out of print when the original version of this essay was published, is now available in both hard and paper covers. Even the lesser novels, *Moran of the Lady Letty, Blix*, and *A Man's Woman*, have been reprinted. In addition, two reprintings of Norris's 1903 volume *A Deal in Wheat and Other Stories of the New and Old West* have appeared in relatively inexpensive editions and *The Responsibilities of the Novelist* (1903) has been reprinted by the Greenwood Press.

MANUSCRIPTS AND LETTERS

Norris's manuscripts and letters are scarce. The most important single collection is in the Bancroft Library of the University of California at Berkeley. Many of the manuscripts for the novels have been lost, but through persistent effort, James D. Hart managed to collect much of the manuscript of *McTeague*. He recorded his experiences in reassembling this manuscript and in obtaining several other valuable papers for the Bancroft Library in a fascinating article, "Search and Research: The Librarian and the Scholar" (*College and Research Libraries*, Sept. 1958). Joseph Katz recounts the history of the *McTeague* manuscript, lists all known pieces of it — ninety-four, about one-third of the total — and indicates where they are to be found in "The Manuscript of Frank Norris's *McTeague*: A Preliminary Census of Pages" (*RALS*, Spring 1972). The Norris collection at the Bancroft Library includes Franklin Walker's interview notes for his biography on Norris, several books owned by Norris, various clippings, notes by Norris, letters, and scrapbooks.

A slim volume of Norris's letters edited by Franklin Walker (*The Letters of Frank Norris*, San Francisco) was published in 1956, and "Ten Letters by Frank Norris" which Walker did not include were edited and published by Donald Pizer in 1962 (*Quarterly News-Letter* of the Book Club of California). In 1973, James B. Stronks published an additional letter (*Quarterly News-Letter* of the Book Club of California).

BIOGRAPHY

As little is known about Frank Norris the man as about any novelist of importance in American literature. He lived only thirty-two years, and his whereabouts can easily be accounted for in each one of those years — Chicago, San Francisco, Paris, Berkeley, Harvard, South Africa, New York, Cuba, and trips between New York and San Francisco. We know who his parents were, where he went to school, what he studied, what grades he made, where he worked, whom he married, what he wrote, and where and how he died. We can read reports of what he was like from his friends and acquaintances: Harry M. Wright's reminiscence, "In Memoriam — Frank Norris, 1870–1902" (University of California *Chronicle*, Oct. 1902); Isaac Marcosson's account of his friendship with Norris in *Adventures in Interviewing* (London, 1920); Wallace W. Everett's anecdotal treatment of Norris the fraternity man in "Frank Norris in His Chapter" (*The Phi Gamma Delta*, Apr. 1930); Grant Richards's sparkling account of how Norris defended Dreiser's *Sister Carrie* in *Author Hunting By an Old Literary Sportsman* (New York, 1934); and comments about Norris by his lifelong close friend Ernest Peixotto in "Romanticist Under the Skin" (*SatR*, 27 May 1933). Despite all these articles by those who apparently knew him best, Frank Norris remains elusive. One strongly suspects that he could not have been as uncomplicated, boyish, and superficial as these reminiscences depict him and still have written books like *Vandover and the Brute*, *McTeague*, and *The Octopus*.

Probably the most influential article yet published about Norris's life is Charles C. Dobie's "Frank Norris, or Up From Culture" (*AM*, Apr. 1928, reprinted as the introduction to vol. 7 of the *Complete Edition*). It is the source of several ideas about Norris, some of them doubtful or erroneous, that have been expressed through the years. Written for a wide audience, this article is more popular than scholarly. Sensational aspects of Norris's life are dramatized throughout: the difference between Mr. Norris, the down-to-earth businessman, and Frank, the sensitive son; the avid desire of Mrs. Norris, an ex-actress and a socialite, for a career in the arts for her sensitive son against the wishes of her husband; Norris's "lead soldier stage," when he made up stories to please his younger brother; Dwight L.

Moody's choirmaster talking Mr. Norris into letting Frank study art in London at the "Kensington School of Art," and then in Paris; Frank's indifference to his art studies; Mr. Norris's discovering some installments of a romantic novel Frank was writing and sending home to his brother Charles and his subsequent cabling to Frank to return home at once. Many of these stories cannot stand close scrutiny. Norris's father, for example, was a far more complicated person than Dobie suggested. No one had to persuade him to escort Norris to Europe, and probably it was more Frank's decision than his father's to return home. Norris was not nearly so cavalier about painting as Dobie claimed, and incidentally, if one sets out seriously to retrace Norris in London and to find "the Kensington School of Art," failure awaits. The school in London which Norris probably attended was the National Art Training School, but biographers and critics continued for a generation to repeat Dobie's error in this as well as in most of his other oversimplifications or inaccuracies.

Norris's younger brother, Charles G. Norris, himself a minor novelist, was responsible to a large extent for the smoke screen one must get through to get at the real Frank Norris. Most of what has been written about Norris's life either came directly from Charles Norris or had his stamp of approval. He was understandably concerned about protecting his brother from too intimate a probing. His memory sometimes made honest errors; a few times he simply gave misinformation. In his foreword to the *Complete Edition* volume of *Vandover and the Brute*, for example, he concocted the story which has been repeated countless times by biographers and critics that the manuscript of *Vandover* had been temporarily packed away in a crate and stored in a warehouse in San Francisco after Norris's death. When the fire and earthquake occurred, the warehouse burned, and it was assumed *Vandover* was lost forever. Then years later a letter was received from the storage company stating that the crate had been moved just before the fire and was safe. Since the manuscript did not have the author's name on it, however, more years went by before someone recognized Norris's style. Then the novel was at last published. When Franklin Walker questioned Charles Norris about this matter in 1930, Charles admitted that he had made up the entire story, that the manuscript had actually been in the hands of Norris's widow all along, and that he did it to explain the long delay before the novel was published.

Walker had a great deal more information about Norris than he used in his *Frank Norris: A Biography* (Garden City, N.Y., 1932), the only full-length biography yet published. His interview notes are extremely important to anyone seriously interested in Norris's life. Considering the fact that Walker worked very closely with Charles and Jeannette Norris

(Frank's widow), the biography is amazingly good. In fact, it is so judiciously balanced that it has had, ironically, an adverse effect. Few new facts about Norris's life have come to light since it was written, and its competence discourages would-be biographers. Consequently, no new biography has appeared in fifty years, an extraordinary situation for a writer of Norris's importance, especially when one counts the biographies of Crane (whose life was even shorter) and Dreiser, Norris's fellow naturalists.

As sound as Walker's biography is, it is clear that he exercised a certain restraint in dealing with the more intimate questions of Norris's life such as his marriage, which may not have been quite the made-in-heaven match usually pictured, and with his general psychological make-up. Charles Norris was greatly pleased with the Walker biography, and wrote the foreword to it, stating that "in other hands the personality of my brother might have suffered." Walker was also unquestionably influenced by Dobie's article, from which he sometimes quoted. That a generally accurate and useful biography emerged is much to Walker's credit, but the fact is that biographical work on Norris is now lagging far behind criticism of his fiction. What is urgently needed is a new appraisal of Norris, a look at the inner man. While provocative new ideas are being expressed about his work, all biographical discussion, to paraphrase Hemingway, comes from one book by Franklin Walker. There was nothing before. There has been nothing as good since.

William B. Dillingham's two biographical chapters in his *Frank Norris: Instinct and Art* make a start in the right direction. Dillingham explores to some extent Norris's fear of failure, corrects some previous biographical mistakes, and deals with the much neglected area of French painting as an influence on his life and writings. Still, a fuller portrait of Norris is needed. Since new facts are difficult to come by and since his life has been so long shrouded in a cloak of "boyishness," the task will be a most difficult undertaking.

Biographical details and especially useful information about Norris's experiences at Harvard are provided in James D. Hart's lengthy introduction to *A Novelist in the Making*, but like previous biographers Hart perpetuates the image of Norris as the child that never quite grew up: "Norris remained boyish until he died in his early thirties. He retained always a kind of youthful playfulness."

Though not a full-scale corrective to the conventional portrait of a "boy Zola," "Frank Norris: A Biographical Essay" (*ALR*, Autumn 1978) by Joseph R. McElrath, Jr., is a fresh and thoughtful beginning. McElrath's point of departure is the body of eulogies and memoirs published immediately after Norris's death (McElrath has collected many of these in

"Frank Norris: Early Posthumous Responses," *ALR*, Spring 1979). The
Frank Norris represented in these accounts does not appear to be the im-
mature fraternity brother depicted by biographers and critics or a literary iconoclast preoccupied with human aberrations: "The psychological
irregularities manifested in the works are contradicted in testimony after
testimony" of those who knew Norris best. McElrath's conclusion is that
Norris had matured rapidly so that by the time of his death he had become not only an admirer of American middle-class values but also "a
conventional believer, with friends in the ministry," a "practicing Episcopalian." In this dramatic journey from a kind of split personality in his
early years, a "temperamental paradox," to a settled and integrated being, his marriage was the turning point. McElrath finds the change sig-
naled by Norris's "attempts at high art" in his final novels, *The Octopus*
and *The Pit:* "It was perhaps no accident that Curtis Jadwin . . . was
Norris's final full-scale hero. Jadwin's middle-class solidity and his beginning of a new life with his wife at the conclusion of *The Pit* may be of
some real biographical relevance."

CRITICISM

From the death of Norris in 1902 until 1930, he received little critical
attention.[1] The situation is illustrated in a 1911 statement by Frederic
Taber Cooper: "The work of Norris, taken as a whole, has been thrown
into an unjust and misleading remoteness. We are apt to think of him
as belonging to a bygone generation, as an influence which after showing a brief potentiality suddenly withered once and for all." During Norris's lifetime and shortly thereafter, William Dean Howells was one of
his strongest supporters. He paid high tribute to Norris in his reviews of
McTeague (Literature, 24 March, 1899) and *The Pit (Harper's Weekly,*
14 March 1903) and in an essay which was occasioned by Norris's sudden
death (*NAR,* Dec. 1902). After this, however, even Howells seemed all
but to forget the young author who has been called by one critic "the
last and most powerful of Howells's protégés."

Cooper's essay in *Some American Story Tellers* (New York, 1911) was
the first serious and sustained scholarly estimate of Norris's work. In pointing out Norris's literary split personality — the realist and the romantic —
Cooper struck a note still heard today in Norris criticism. "It is impossible to read Norris's works," Cooper wrote, "without perceiving that from

---

1. For surveys of contemporary reviews of Norris's works, see Paul H. Bixler, "Frank
Norris's Literary Reputation" (*AL,* May 1934) and Ernest Marchand's concluding chapter
in *Frank Norris: A Study.*

first to last there was within him an instinct continually at war with his chosen realistic methods; an unconquerable and exasperating vein of romanticism that led him frequently into palpable absurdities — not because romanticism in itself is a literary crime, but because it has its own proper place in literature, and that place is assuredly not in a realistic novel." Through the years this question has been the single most controversial issue in writings about Norris. The inability to see Norris's work for what it is, whole, coherent, and cohesive, has been perhaps the greatest failure of numerous critics from Cooper onward. Cooper's commentary also launched another perennial question: how good is *The Pit?* Like a few recent critics, Cooper preferred it to most of Norris's other novels, including *The Octopus*, but for the unusual and tenuous reason that "the symbolism is kept further in the background."

If Cooper felt that Norris's romantic tendency was his greatest shortcoming, John Curtis Underwood saw it as a typical American trait and Norris as the very best America had to offer. In *Literature and Insurgency* (New York, 1914), Underwood set Norris up as "unrivaled, unassailed and unassailable" for the reason that Norris loved and wrote for "the Plain People" and dealt with "the material of our common national life." Full of lengthy, tedious plot summaries and indiscriminate praise, Underwood's essay is valuable today chiefly as a dramatic means of seeing how far criticism on Norris has come.

A much briefer but far more illuminating early commentary is that by Theodore Dreiser, which he wrote as an introduction to *McTeague* in the *Complete Edition*. It is illuminating both for what it says about Norris and for what it suggests about Dreiser. The strongest link between these two giants of American literary naturalism was their uncanny talent for capturing a moment in American culture. Dreiser admired Norris most of all for his ability to depict scenes like Polk Street, a phenomenon wholly "indigenous to America, and California, and San Francisco — a brilliant and accurate picture of a certain phase of life in this most amazing of new lands." Norris had that same awareness of the historical moment which Robert Penn Warren has praised Dreiser for possessing.

The decade of the thirties was the Dark Age of criticism. Ideological critics found truths where they did not exist, and dogmatic literary historians were too prudish or too opinionated (or both) to offer objective evaluations. Considering the perils of the time, Norris fared very well. Vernon Louis Parrington did not live to complete his third volume of *Main Currents in American Thought* (New York, 1930), but his notes indicate that he found Norris "the most stimulating and militant of our early naturalists." Even that guardian of literary good taste, Fred Lewis Pattee, had warmed to Norris somewhat by 1930. In an earlier volume, *A*

History of American Literature Since 1870 (New York, 1915), he gave Norris only summary treatment. But in Pattee's *The New American Literature, 1890–1930* (New York, 1930), Norris is awarded an entire chapter, and *The Octopus* heralded as being almost "the great American novel." Paul H. Bixler assessed Norris's position in American literature in "Frank Norris's Literary Reputation" (*AL*, May 1934). Reviewing the new *Complete Edition* of Norris's work, Edward Wagenknecht in "Frank Norris in Retrospect" (*VQR*, Apr. 1930) was probably the only critic who has aimed his praise and admiration particularly at Norris's "fundamental decency and sanity," a position eminently justified.

One of the most wrongheaded but persistent theories about Norris's work is that it was moving steadily in the direction of social protest when his death occurred. *The Octopus*, of course, is the book such theorists have in mind. A recent college desk dictionary, thoroughly reliable in most respects, labels Norris "Author of novels of social protest." This label became indelibly stamped upon him in the 1930s. By misreading *The Octopus* and then making the further mistake of ignoring most of Norris's other work, a critic like Russell Blankenship in *American Literature as an Expression of the National Mind* (New York, 1931) could conclude that "from *The Octopus* to the soap-box and the indignant, perfervid eloquence of Upton Sinclair is only a step" and could make the astounding statement that *The Pit* "must stand as an example of what a naturalist can produce when he becomes too much interested in sociology." Arthur Hobson Quinn in *American Fiction* (New York, 1936) voiced a similar but quieter objection to *The Octopus* when he complained that Norris "made the railroad so completely black" that the book is not convincing. In *The Foreground of American Fiction* (New York, 1934), Harry Hartwick wrote accurate plot summaries but dubious generalizations, one of which was that Norris was on his way to socialism.

Norris did not go far enough for Granville Hicks, who was in those days a card-carrying Communist. Instead of ending with a clear-cut Marxist position, Norris, in Hicks's view, sadly went into philosophical fibrillation. The year before Hicks's *The Great Tradition* (New York, 1933) appeared, John Chamberlain in *Farewell to Reform* (New York, 1932) laid the groundwork for the controversy on philosophical inconsistency in *The Octopus*, a problem over which Norris's tireless critics are still butting their heads. Chamberlain questioned whether the "good" which Norris wrote of at the end of *The Octopus* is supported by the facts of the plot. Hicks picked up the argument and made it popular. He charged that Norris never really understood the philosophical implications of determinism. What bothered him most, however, was that Norris admired the giants of industry at the same time that he expressed sympathy for the common people. Hicks's co-Marxist, V. F. Calverton, emphasized what he considered Norris's inherent and justified pessimism in *The Liberation of American Literature* (New York, 1932); and in *Expression in America* (New York, 1932), Ludwig Lewisohn offered the highly original but profoundly tenuous notion that Norris was influenced deeply by Octave Mirbeau. In Lewisohn's opinion, only *McTeague* was worth preserving of all Norris's work.

The 1930s also ushered in the first serious studies of Norris's sources and of influences upon his writing. The earliest extended treatment of Zola's influence upon Norris was Marius Biencourt's *Une Influence du Naturalisme Française en Amérique: Frank Norris* (Paris, 1933). In "Frank Norris's Reading at Harvard College" (*AL*, May 1935), Willard E. Martin, Jr., used the borrower's record of the Harvard College Library to reveal books Norris checked out while he was a student there in 1894–95 and writing both *Vandover and the Brute* and *McTeague*.

Only two other commentaries on Norris from the thirties deserve mention. In *Companions on the Trail* (New York, 1931), Hamlin Garland reminisced about Norris and his reaction to Norris's death. ("Nothing of late has so stirred me and grieved me.") This essay also included the text of an earlier critical estimate of Norris's work which Garland had published in *The Critic* (Mar. 1930). Alfred Kazin in "Three Pioneer Realists" (*SatR*, 8 July 1939) stressed the point that Norris "was the product of many diverse influences, and to the end betrayed them all often simultaneously." What seemed to impress Kazin most about Norris was his "unquenchable joy in life that one finds only in the younger Elizabethan poets, a joy that is like the first discovery of the world, splendid in its freshness and eager to absorb every flicker of life." Kazin corrected factual errors in this essay (such as his statement that Norris was once a student at the University of Southern California), revised it slightly, and included it three years later in his book *On Native Grounds*.

Criticism of the 1940s focused largely upon *The Octopus*. The controversy over philosophical inconsistency which Chamberlain and Hicks had inaugurated some years before now raged with stalwarts on both sides of the issue. The beginning of the decade found H. Willard Reninger attempting to answer the charges of Hicks and others. In "Norris Explains *The Octopus*: A Correlation of His Theory and Practice" (*AL*, May 1940), Reninger took the position that Norris was following his own literary theory as set out in *The Responsibilities of the Novelist*, a set of philosophical and aesthetic values which Reninger considered coherent. Unfortunately, the article was not a convincing answer to Chamberlain, Hicks, and others because it overrated Norris as a literary critic. *The Responsibilities of the Novelist*, Reninger wrote, "is a far more penetrating volume than any student of American criticism has yet revealed." And, further, "*The Responsibilities* stands as the climax of American critical theory of the novel in the nineteenth century."

In a brief note, "Frank Norris on Realism and Naturalism" (*AL*, Mar. 1941), Charles Child Walcutt, who was a few years later to become one of the most important critics of Norris and American literary naturalism, answered Reninger by revealing an obvious error in one of his key quotations and by pointing out a glaring flaw in the logic of his position: "The relation of theory and practice in his [Norris's] work is to be determined not by a study of his own critical *dicta*—for authors have been notoriously prone to rationalize their works into a theoretical consistency —but by careful analysis of his novels in relation to the ideas which they pretend to express and to which they attempt to give significant form."

In his long intellectual history, *Intellectual America: Ideas on the March* (New York, 1941), Oscar Cargill surveyed Norris's career and his writings and found *The Octopus* to be "Frank Norris at his best." Cargill quarreled with Norris's characterization of Presley, Behrman, and Shelgrim, but seemed to detect no inconsistency in the theme.

Walter Fuller Taylor generally agreed with Walcutt. In *The Economic Novel in America* (Chapel Hill, N.C., 1942), he credited Norris with having lifted the "romance of economic conflict," which was being depicted by inferior authors, to a new "literary level." Furthermore, Norris showed that the philosophy of naturalistic determinism was "peculiarly appropriate" to stories which have as "the principal human value the thrill of successful struggle for survival." Nevertheless, "the survival in his work of moral themes and attitudes, the mingling of deterministic and undeterministic strains of thought, shows to what extent the contradictory leadings of two widely divergent views of life left him confused." Taylor felt that "in any discriminating judgment of Norris's worth, this confusion of mind must necessarily be remembered to his detriment." Perhaps an even severer charge, however, was that Norris did not possess "a certain 'fusing' quality of imagination," which would make the elements of his stories seem organic "as if they had grown together naturally and of themselves." After spending a great deal of time in supporting these arguments of philosophical inconsistency, especially as revealed in *The Octopus*, and of structural and stylistic defects, Taylor concludes his consideration of Norris with the astounding thought that the objections he raised were not very important after all "when weighed against the solid worth" of Norris's writing. The failure in philosophical consistency and in style are merely "failures in certain useful accessories of fiction, not in its absolute essentials." Critics as well as novelists can indulge in philosophical confusion.

The first really effective defense of *The Octopus* was George W. Meyer's "A New Interpretation of *The Octopus*" (*CE*, Mar. 1943). In showing the thematic unity of *The Octopus*, Meyer was the first critic to make it plain that the wheat ranchers of the San Joaquin Valley were themselves partly responsible for their defeat, that they were in the business of making money, and that they were scarcely less selfish than the railroad. Meyer further pointed out that Shelgrim's speech did not necessarily reflect Norris's beliefs, nor did Presley always represent Norris. Meyer's chief contribution, however, was his suggestion that nature in *The Octopus* was neither malevolent nor benevolent, but a great force which could seem benevolent if man aligned himself with it instead of against it. Only when Meyer attempted to discuss the subject of moral blame and to establish a subtle distinction between determinism and fatalism did he falter, for Norris then looks too much like a didactic moralist, and more questions about the nature of human responsibility are raised than could possibly be answered.

Meyer's case for *The Octopus* seemed to go unheard by three other critics who echoed earlier objections to the novel. Malcolm Cowley in "Naturalism's Terrible McTeague" (*New Republic*, 5 May 1947) expressed his preference for *McTeague*, and of *The Octopus* he wrote: "At the end it declined into muzzy sentiments and fine writing." Describing and evaluating Norris's writing in *The Shapers of American Fiction, 1798–1947* (New York, 1947), George Snell accepted what had become the majority opinion of *The Octopus*—that it contained too many antithetical elements and that thematically it was disorderly, diverse, and distracting. By this time, critical analysis of *The Octopus* began to sound strangely like the early reviews of *Moby-Dick*. Robert E. Spiller called *The Octopus* "the most ambitious novel of its generation," but he echoed the old charge of inconsistency: "The book finally fails as tragic drama because Norris has no consistent position on the vast economic and metaphysical problems he raises" (*LHUS*). One commentary on *The Octopus* which did not confront this long-standing controversy was Irving McKee's "Notable Memorials to Mussel Slough" (*PHR*, Feb. 1948), which recounted the details of the Mussel Slough incident of 1880 and indicated how Norris utilized the event in his novel.

With the exception of Lars Åhnebrink's *The Influence of Émile Zola on Frank Norris* (Cambridge, Mass., 1947), which was superseded by his later book (discussed below), the only book to be published on Norris during the decade of the 1940s was Ernest Marchand's *Frank Norris: A Study* (Stanford, Calif., 1942). Marchand read Norris with a level head and with much more care than many previous critics. He thoroughly digested Norris's critical writings, and furthermore he read and evaluated carefully most of the reviews and articles on Norris. In his treatment of Norris's fiction, Marchand is eminently sound in his evaluations and accurately descriptive. What is missing is a probing of depth into the methods and motives of Norris, the literary artist. Marchand does not take us very deep; he does not tell us *why* Norris felt it essential, for example, to use detail so extensively, or what fundamentally he was trying to achieve as a symbolist. Nevertheless, as a pioneering critical study, it is admirable, especially in comparison with initial books on many authors.

A critic is always impressive when he takes upon himself the enormous task of describing and analyzing an entire group of writers, whether they be the classicists, the neoclassicists, the romantics, the realists, the naturalists, the lost generation, the beats, or any others who have been grouped and labeled chiefly for convenience by literary historians. When such an attempt fails, as it does more often than not, the failure seems abysmal. Such, precisely, is the case with Malcolm Cowley's ambitious attempt to characterize the naturalistic movement in America, "'Not Men': A Natural History of American Naturalism" (*KR*, Summer 1947). Using outmoded generalizations about literary naturalism, Cowley treated Norris, Dreiser, and Crane, three very different kinds of writers, as if they all believed the same things and wrote the same way.[2] Of greater significance are two articles on Norris by Charles C. Walcutt, "Frank Norris and the Search for Form" (*UKCR*, Winter 1947) and "The Naturalism of *Vandover and the Brute*" (in *Forms of Modern Fiction*, Minneapolis, Minn., 1948). Revised versions of both articles were incorporated later into Walcutt's book, which will be discussed below.

The next ten years saw nearly as many critical commentaries published on Norris as had been produced in the forty-eight years from his death to 1950. Many of these are significant enough to constitute both a substantial upsurge of interest in Norris and a thoughtful reconsideration of his place in American literature. By this period Norris's stature had been determined: he would not be regarded as a minor writer like his contemporaries Robert Herrick, David Graham Phillips, or even Harold Frederic. He had risen far above Jack London and had taken his place beside Crane, Dreiser, Howells, and others just below the highest rank of such American novelists as Hawthorne, Melville, and James. The most unfortunate aspect of this particular rank is that it leaves a critic somewhat uncertain about how much he can take for granted in dealing with

2. A revised and expanded version of Cowley's essay (which was originally delivered as a lecture at Princeton) was published as "Naturalism in American Literature" in *Evolutionary Thought in America*, edited by Stow Persons (New Haven, Conn., 1950).

such a writer's works. He cannot, that is, assume that the reader had read the works of Norris or Howells with the same confidence that he could assume a reader's knowledge of the novels of Hawthorne or Melville. As a result, readers who wish to acquaint themselves adequately with the criticism must wade through plot summary after plot summary.

A book which illustrates this point well is Lars Åhnebrink's celebrated work, *The Beginnings of Naturalism in American Fiction* (Cambridge, Mass., 1950). A substantial portion of Åhnebrink's discussion of Norris is taken up with plot summaries and with biographical information which contributes nothing at all new. Insofar as criticism on Norris is concerned, the most important part of the book is the third section of Chapter Ten, which deals with the influence of Zola. It establishes once and for all the extent of Zola's influence with more than enough evidence and example. When Åhnebrink leaves Zola for other possible influences, he is frequently unconvincing. His case for Huysman's influence, for example, is shaky at best, and when he gets to Turgenev and Ibsen, he seems to be clutching at straws. In Chapter Twelve, he indicates that no scholar has suggested that Turgenev might have had a direct influence on Norris, admits that "there is no reference whatever to Turgenev in Norris's works," and then proceeds to show parallels. It becomes clear that in this part of his book, Åhnebrink is discussing *resemblance*, not direct influence, and the results are not fruitful. Of *The Octopus* he writes: "The atmosphere of anarchism, conspiracy, and revolt which pervades the latter part of *The Octopus* is *somewhat reminiscent* [italics mine] of that of *Virgin Soil*." In the inevitable "summing up" that concludes each chapter, Åhnebrink sometimes sums up more than he has proved, as in the case of Turgenev: "Norris's debt to Turgenev can be traced in at least two novels: *The Octopus* and *The Pit*." In trying to show Ibsen's influence, Åhnebrink makes the following statement: "In the autobiographical *Blix*, the heroine is a young, independent, modern woman, reminiscent of Nora in *A Doll's House*." Such tenuous comparisons are all too frequent in this book.

The interest in Norris's sources continued with Charles Kaplan's "Norris's Use of Sources in *The Pit*" (*AL*, Mar. 1953), in which he discusses Curtis Jadwin's similarity to Joseph Leiter, who tried to corner the wheat market in 1897, and "Fact into Fiction in *McTeague*" (*HLB*, Autumn, 1954), an enlightening treatment of Norris's extensive reliance on Thomas Fillebrown's *A Text-book of Operative Dentistry* for technical details in *McTeague*. Even minor novels were examined for their possible sources, as in John C. Sherwood's "Norris and the *Jeannette*" (*PQ*, Apr. 1958), which shows how the early scenes of *A Man's Woman* follow the published records of an actual expedition, Commander De Long's *The Voyage of the Jeannette* (1884) and Chief Engineer Melville's *In the Lena Delta* (1884).

A different kind of influence was pointed out by Joseph J. Kwiat in "The Newspaper Experience: Crane, Norris, and Dreiser" (*NCF*, Sept. 1953). Kwait suggests that several of the typical aspects of these three naturalistic writers can be traced to their experience as newspaper men: "All three . . . discovered that their value to a newspaper depended upon the cultivation of technical facility and an awareness of the human interest angle. All three attempted to be 'detached' observers who accepted life as it was for its facts and drama."

One of the most significant contributions to the study of Norris in the fifties was a doctoral dissertation, Robert D. Lundy's "The Making of *McTeague* and *The Octopus*" (University of California, 1956), which should have been published but has not been. Lundy convincingly established the chronology of composition of these two novels and discussed the important themes which Norris wrote for Gates at Harvard. He was the first to show in some detail how much *The Octopus* owed in its philosophy to Norris's science professor at the University of California, Joseph Le Conte. Lundy's brief introduction to *The Octopus* (New York: American Century Series, 1957) argues that Norris borrowed techniques from Zola but not materialistic determinism. Norris's own position Lundy calls "evolutionary transcendentalism."

The influence Norris might have had on later writers was greatly neglected during this period. Perhaps because Norris was so heavily indebted to Zola, critics did not have much inclination to explore the mark he might have made on others. Henry Dan Piper's "Frank Norris and Scott Fitzgerald" (*HLQ*, Aug. 1956) should have set critics off on a new kind of search, but it did not. Piper pointed out the influence of Norris's work, especially *Vandover*, on Fitzgerald.

If the 1950s began with Åhnebrink's attempt to fit Norris into the European stream of literary naturalism, much of the remainder of the decade was spent trying to denaturalize him. He began to be treated more as an individual and less as an example of a literary trend. One way of doing this was through utilizing the tools of Freudian psychology. Norris's psychoanalyst of the fifties was Maxwell Geismar. His *Rebels and Ancestors: The American Novel, 1890–1915* (Boston, 1953) opened with a lengthy chapter on Norris. In his preface, Geismar explained: "Because Frank Norris illustrates the impact of the new age upon the old so clearly in the meeting of the Angel and the Brute in our fiction at the turn of the century, I have used him to open this volume and to serve as a figurehead for the period." Geismar's penetratingly interesting essay probes be-

NORRIS • *Criticism* 417

neath the boyish surface of Frank Norris and discovers a man afraid of drives within himself that he did not understand — the "obsessive preoccupation of a spirit in the grip of what is considered to be a destructive physical or psychological process." Geismar finds, however, that Norris's "wound was also a source of his power; the animal instincts were the origin of his most human insights; and even the tormented rites of reversionary emotions became a path of liberation in the works of art." Geismar's persistent use of the jargon of psychology is annoying, but his essay is one of the most original and incisive discussions yet to be published on Norris.

Not so incisive is Kenneth S. Lynn's attempt to examine Norris's work in terms of a mother-father conflict (*The Dream of Success* [Boston, 1955]). Lynn's argument involves him in a tremendous amount of guessing, some of it wide of the mark. "There is no doubt," he writes of young Norris's broken arm, "that Norris's failure to prove himself to his father on the playing field was a crucial event in his life." Or, referring to Norris's fascination with Froissart's *Chronicles:* it was "another way his [the father's] son took to hide his naked hero worship of his father." Norris's heroines, Lynn claims, are all tall and strong because they represent his mother: "It is not so much that they are of abnormal size, but that the viewpoint from which they are described is that of a small boy looking at his mother." In the end, Lynn asserts, Norris finally cast off the mother influence. Whereas Geismar, despite all his talk of morbidity, oedipal relationships, and castration complexes, has contributed significantly to an understanding of Norris and his work, Lynn seems to have performed an exercise in futile conjecture. More perceptive is Lynn's introduction to *The Octopus* (Boston: Riverside Editions, 1958), although his analysis of Presley as "Norris's intellectual" does not take enough into account the important role of instinct in the novel.

Two articles in 1955 were of particular interest in the new attempt to understand Norris's work not merely as naturalistic fiction but for what it is. Charles G. Hoffmann in "Norris and the Responsibility of the Novelist" (*SAQ*, Oct. 1955) argued that "by the time Norris came to write *The Octopus* and *The Pit*, he explored the power of love as man's saving element in a world of impersonal forces. Thus the regenerative power of love seems to be Norris's solution to the dilemma presented by the interaction of deterministic forces and social responsibilites on his characters. The solution is fundamentally a moral one." Therefore, Hoffmann rightly concluded, "the key to Norris's literary practice lies not in his adherence to any one theory of the novel such as 'naturalism.'" Donald Pizer, in the first of several important articles on Norris, reconsidered the charge of philosophical inconsistency so often leveled against Norris. In "Another

Look at *The Octopus*" (*NCF*, Dec. 1955), Pizer made clear what had for some reason remained fuzzy in the minds of many previous critics, that much of the ostensible inconsistency in *The Octopus* was not Norris's wavering between positions of free will and determinism but the character Presley's, through whom much of the story is told. If Presley's role is understood, the problem of thematic fragmentation is largely solved. Pizer also pointed out that *The Octopus* owed as much to the transcendentalists as to naturalism.

For students of American naturalistic writing, the most important book to be published in the fifties was Charles Child Walcutt's *American Literary Naturalism, A Divided Stream* (Minneapolis, Minn., 1956). Walcutt thoughtfully surveyed the work not only of Norris, Crane, London, and Dreiser but also that of certain important realists such as Harold Frederic, Hamlin Garland, and Winston Churchill. In addition, he related the naturalism of the older authors to more recent writers like Anderson, Farrell, Steinbeck, Hemingway, and Dos Passos. Walcutt's chapter on Norris is uneven; it includes most of the ideas expressed in his previously published articles and thus in some ways reflects an earlier critical position. At a time when critics were beginning to move away from the idea that Norris was a muddled thinker in *The Octopus*, for example, Walcutt stuck to the position taken by Chamberlain and Hicks twenty years before, that "the wheat books, magnificently conceived, fail structurally because they contain conflicting and contradictory sets of ideas." Walcutt's most thoughtful contribution is in his discussion of *Vandover and the Brute*, which he says narrowly misses being a modern tragedy. In reexamining the characteristics of literary naturalism, Walcutt made the long overdue point that naturalism was not a world-view which was new and terrible but a new pronouncement of old truths: "In short, so long as it is essentially transcendental, naturalism will give full recognition to the power and immensity of the physical world but will also assume a meaning in it that is akin to and ideally accessible to the mind of man; so that man achieves tragic dignity as he strives to penetrate and master his own nature and the physical universe. . . . Seen in this light, naturalism is no revolutionary departure from the world-view of Shakespearian tragedy. It is rather a mode of presenting in realistic 'modern' terms the forces, microcosmic and macrocosmic, against which man has always tragically contended. Naturalism is the modern approach to Fate." The oversimplifications of literary historians about naturalism as an ogre-offspring of Darwin should have been answered once and for all by this clarification.

If all of the old and tired generalizations about Norris and naturalism were not completely silenced, at least they were not heard so frequently as in the past. Norris was being examined in new ways and by discriminating and thoughtful critics. Richard Chase, for example, gave Norris a chapter in *The American Novel and its Tradition* (Garden City, N.Y., 1957) among the exclusive company of Hawthorne, Melville, James, Twain, and Faulkner. Although Chase's treatment of Norris is provocative, some of his ideas are questionable. Seeing Norris as being in deep sympathy "with the doctrines of American Populism, the movement of agrarian protest and revolt which was in its heyday when Norris was forming his ideas in the 1880's and 1890's," Chase is led to conclude that Norris hated the city. "The City (even San Francisco) is the abode of evil and decay, like the East, in Norris's Populist mythology." What Chase overlooks is that Norris's attitude toward big centers of population was ambivalent — there was, to be sure, evil and decay there, but there was also vitality, force, in a word, Life. San Francisco never failed to fascinate Norris because he considered it a cross section of all that was vigorous and exciting in American life. Chase is undoubtedly correct, however, in his observation that "there is all through his work a tension between Norris the liberal humanist and ardent democrat and Norris the protofascist, complete with a racist view of Anglo-Saxon supremacy . . . and a portentous nihilism. . . ." This was a restatement in fresh terms of an old idea, the split between Norris the romantic and Norris the naturalist. Chase was the first to call Norris what he no doubt was, "a classic case of the modern lowbrow novelist, something of an intellectual himself to be sure, and yet a lowbrow because of his native temperament and conviction — but also because . . . lowbrowism is one of the most successful literary poses in modern America," and to fit him into a tradition of "anti- or nonintellectualism shown by most of the important modern novelists except those who belong to the school of James and Howells."

Three other essays of this period took another look at Norris's world view. Arnold L. Goldsmith in "The Development of Frank Norris's Philosophy" (*Studies in Honor of John Wilcox* [Detroit, Mich., 1958]) traced Norris's vacillation between positions of determinism and free will, concluding that he was neither romantic nor naturalist: "It is this optimistic world view which places his complete works on the literary bridge between romanticism and naturalism." In "Romantic Individualism in Garland, Norris and Crane" (*AQ*, Winter 1958), Donald Pizer defined Norris's final position as "an imaginative and emotional reliance upon self in the presence of nature." And in "Frank Norris and the Werewolf of Guilt" (*MLQ*, Sept. 1959), Stanley Cooperman argued that "Frank Norris, in *McTeague* and *Vandover*, was motivated far more directly by Calvinist-Christian guilt than by scientific naturalism." By now, it was becoming extremely difficult to consider Frank Norris in the simplistic terms of "naturalist" or "determinist" which at one time had been so freely used to sum him up.

The several literary histories of the fifties reflected this growing trend to view Norris in a more complex light. In his crisply written essay, "Facts of Life *versus* Pleasant Reading" (*The Literature of the American People* [New York, 1951]), Clarence Gohdes commented that "*The Octopus* shows how the author had learned to mix Zola and Hugo, Tolstoi and Dickens, with perhaps a dash of Stevenson, into a palatable literary cocktail all his own." Grant C. Knight surveyed most of Norris's work in his two volumes, *The Critical Period in American Literature* (Chapel Hill, N.C., 1951) and *The Strenuous Age in American Literature* (Chapel Hill, N.C., 1954). He pointed out the extent to which Norris brought American life vividly to the reading public. Only Van Wyck Brooks, who deplored Norris's "confused" naturalism, reverted atavistically to the stale arguments of yesteryear in his *The Confident Years: 1885–1915* (New York, 1952). Norris also received brief attention in more specialized literary histories such as Everett Carter's *Howells and the Age of Realism* (Philadelphia, 1954) and Frederick J. Hoffman's *The Modern Novel in America, 1900–1950* (Chicago, 1951). Edward Wagenknecht, who had written a sensitive estimate of Norris's work over twenty years earlier, reexamined it in *Cavalcade of the American Novel* (New York, 1952). Taking note of the long-standing argument over philosophical inconsistency in *The Octopus*, Wagenknecht raised a new point: "Whether it is artistically unified would seem to be a more important consideration."

By 1960 very few critical assumptions about Norris's work had gone unchallenged. Above all, it was no longer meaningful (or even intelligent) to categorize Norris as a "naturalist" without important qualifications or, indeed, to talk about naturalism in the old simplistic terms. In "Frank Norris and the Genteel Tradition" (*TSL*, 1960), William B. Dillingham cautioned against overemphasizing Norris's break with the fiction of polite society, for in retrospect his differences with the genteel tradition can be seen as far less pronounced than they appeared to readers of his time and a few decades thereafter.

One critical viewpoint which had been expressed repeatedly throughout previous years by numerous critics without serious dissent was that *McTeague* was flawed by the "romantic" subplot involving the old people, Grannis and Miss Baker. In "The Old Folks of *McTeague*" (*NCF*, Sept. 1961), William B. Dillingham pointed out that there are no fundamental differences between the forces that bring Old Grannis and Miss Baker together and those that destroy McTeague and Trina. The issue is a broad one, for the tendency to see everything in Norris's work which is pleasant and ends happily as "romantic" and everything which is unpleasant and destructive as "naturalistic" constitutes a failure to understand Norris's most basic belief — that the forces to which man is subjected, especially his deepest instinctive drives, may lead to fulfillment and happiness as well as to destruction.

George W. Johnson's article on "Frank Norris and Romance" (*AL*, Mar. 1961) places Norris, as did Stanley Cooperman a few years earlier, in the Calvinist tradition "of spiritual antinomies in a cosmos whose causation was ordered yet inscrutable." According to Johnson, Norris was attempting "to reconstitute romance in American letters" on the basis of "a precarious balance between the centrifugal pull of large abstractions [romance] and a centripetal interest in careful observation [realism]." Johnson's otherwise provocative article is blemished by his insistence that McTeague is a sort of agrarian hero: "Gullible, mute, and unmalicious, McTeague is an Anglo-Saxon country boy, a figure of archetypal innocence destroyed by an evil objectified in the city." Johnson presented fundamentally the same argument in "The Frontier Behind Frank Norris' *McTeague*" (*HLQ*, Nov. 1962), where he described McTeague as something of a frontiersman out of place in civilization, "a debased version of the folkloristic mountain man, like a muted Mike Fink." In stressing Norris's Populist bent, Johnson was following the lead of Richard Chase, and in doing so he made fundamentally the same error in overemphasizing the purity of McTeague and the evil of the city. In formulations like the following, however, he goes much further than Chase: "*McTeague* does reflect the agrarian distrust of urban life as parasitic, corrupting, and degenerate. In Trina's unexplained pallor, we find the Populist conception of the city girl's vitiation; in McTeague's perversion we find the Populist conviction that trade was a harlot and the metropolis a Babylon. The overwrought emphasis on gold in the novel mirrors the agrarian preoccupation with the money power, and in McTeague's victimization by the law, one might argue, there is worked out the Populist melodrama of the struggle between the only two urban classes, the robbers and the robbed."

That McTeague is not simply a good-natured country boy driven to crime by urban evil was pointed out concurrently by William B. Dillingham in "Themes and Literary Techniques in the Fiction of Frank Norris" (University of Pennsylvania doctoral dissertation, 1961) and by Donald Pizer in "Evolutionary Ethical Dualism in Frank Norris' *Vandover and the Brute* and *McTeague*" (*PMLA*, Dec. 1961). Dillingham and Pizer argued that in his characterization of McTeague, Norris was following to a large extent the theories of the popular Italian criminologist Cesare Lombroso and that McTeague is a clear representative of a type Lombroso termed the born criminal. Even though McTeague was not meant to represent a typical Anglo-Saxon with healthy heritage, it is still possible for the reader to feel sympathy for him as a human being. Indeed,

Pizer further pointed out in "Nineteenth-Century American Naturalism: An Essay in Definition" (*BuR*, Dec. 1965) that the essence of American literary naturalism is partly the tension between the forces that determine a character's life and his own individual suffering and striving. Another tension completed Pizer's definition of naturalism: that between the common and ordinary on the one hand and the sensational and extraordinary on the other hand. Pizer convincingly examined *McTeague*, *Sister Carrie*, and *The Red Badge of Courage* with these two sets of contrasts in mind. His contention was that traditional definitions of naturalism have "handicapped thinking both about the movement as a whole and about individual works within the movement. It has resulted in much condescension toward those writers who are supposed to be naturalists yet whose fictional sensationalism (an aspect of romanticism) and moral ambiguity (a quality inconsistent with the absolutes of determinism) appear to make their work flawed specimens of the mode."

Pizer's thoughtful work on the theory of American naturalism has added immensely to our understanding of that complicated literary movement. Several of his previously published articles were collected and reprinted as *Realism and Naturalism in Nineteenth-Century American Literature* (Carbondale, Ill., 1966), an indispensable volume to the student of this period. Not only is Pizer's analysis of what constitutes a naturalistic novel original and penetrating, but his argument about the relevance of naturalistic fiction lifts it from the barrenness of the cold Darwinian winter to the realm of human values: "It involves a belief that life on its lowest levels is not so simple as it seems to be from higher levels. It suggests that even the least significant human being can feel and strive powerfully and can suffer the extraordinary consequences of his emotions, and that no range of human experience is free of the moral complexities and ambiguities which Milton set his fallen angels to debating. Naturalism reflects an affirmative ethical conception of life, for it asserts the value of all life by endowing the lowest character with emotion and defeat and with moral ambiguity, no matter how poor or ignoble he may seem."

An important assumption underlying most of Pizer's work on Norris is that "the naturalistic novel is . . . not so superficial or reductive as it implicitly appears to be in its conventional definition." In "Synthetic Criticism and Frank Norris; Or, Mr. Marx, Mr. Taylor, and *The Octopus*" (*AL*, Jan. 1963), reprinted as Chapter Thirteen of *Realism and Naturalism*), Pizer objected to oversimplification and distortion by critics who try to make a literary work fit a pre-established pattern. He particularly objected to Leo Marx's analysis of *The Octopus*, which, he charged, does not take into account the intrinsic pattern of the novel but attempts to superimpose an extrinsic pattern upon it. Pizer's own approach to *The*

Octopus can be seen in "The Concept of Nature in Frank Norris' *The Octopus*" (*AQ*, Spring 1962). In his continuing effort to show the artistic integrity of Norris's work, Pizer examined *The Octopus* from the standpoint of evolutionary theism, that eclectic view of the late nineteenth century which attempted to reconcile religion with the new theories about evolution. Norris's teacher in this area was Joseph Le Conte at Berkeley, who combined in the manner of John Fiske "Spencerianism, transcendentalism and utilitarianism" into a philosophical brew that could take care of almost any conflicting problems. Evolution could be viewed as both scientific and theistic; evil could be seen as real but temporary; God and Force could be identified. It is this view, Pizer argued, which accounts for the optimistic ending of *The Octopus*, and to this coherent system of ideas the novel is true from beginning to end. Those who complain of philosophical inconsistency are actually quarreling "with such basic Christian paradoxes as the coexistence of free will and determinism, the eternity of life despite death and the emergence of good out of evil."

A much different and less convincing interpretation of *The Octopus* was offered by James K. Folsom. In "Social Darwinism or Social Protest? The 'Philosophy' of *The Octopus*" (*MFS*, Winter 1962–63), Folsom found the novel's optimistic ending ironic and reverted to the muckraking interpretation of the book which had not been offered in several years. *The Octopus*, Folsom concluded, was clearly a novel of social protest and not otherwise philosophical in its content. Most serious readers of Norris's work will find this interpretation untenable.

Oscar Cargill agreed that Norris began his novel as an out and out protest against the Southern Pacific Railroad but contended that the writer's plans were drastically altered when he interviewed Collis P. Huntington. This essay is one of the few where one may find an accurate and concise summary of the Mussel Slough incident, the model for the pitched battle at the irrigation ditch in *The Octopus*. Although Cargill's essay, which appeared as the afterword to the Signet Classics edition of *The Octopus* (1964) and as a chapter in his volume *Toward a Pluralistic Criticism* (Carbondale, Ill., 1965), is admittedly based upon speculation, it is fascinating reading. According to Cargill, Norris was greatly impressed by Huntington, who told Norris something he had not heard before, namely that the wheat farmers had tried to "pack" the state rate-fixing commission. The surprised Norris then found it difficult to see the conflict in the same terms as before, with the railroad as the villain and the farmers as victims. He then set to work and shifted the emphasis of the book. The interview, argued Cargill, "took the heart out of Norris and . . . this explains the flatulence of *The Pit*."

It has been fashionable since Norris's death to speculate as to what kind of fiction he might have written had he lived beyond his short thirty-two years. Michael Millgate, unlike most recent critics, feels that the two volumes of Norris's proposed wheat trilogy seem so unalike and rife with inconsistencies because they represent a partial job. In *American Social Fiction: James to Cozzens* (London, 1964), Millgate writes: "Had Norris lived, it is conceivable that he might have been able, in *The Wolf*, to round off the trilogy into a satisfactory whole, making the apparent inconsistencies within individual works fully comprehensible as parts of an overall pattern." As is, Millgate does not rate Norris very high, but shows how his work, especially *The Pit*, fulfills what James had stated the American novel of business might be: "The epic heroism, the 'wounds of the market,' the 'ferocity of battle,' the imagery of war and the aura of romance, the central importance of the relationship between the businessman and his 'immitigable womankind.'"

Various kinds of literary histories in the sixties surveyed Norris's work. H. Wayne Morgan in *American Writers in Rebellion from Mark Twain to Dreiser* (New York, 1965) praised Norris highly but added little that was new to a critical interpretation of his work. Robert W. Schneider's *Five Novelists of the Progressive Era* (New York, 1965) likewise covered ground that had already been well covered. In *The American 1890s: Life and Times of a Lost Generation* (New York, 1966), Larzer Ziff argued that though Le Conte's influence on Norris may have been in some ways beneficial, *The Octopus* would have been better without it: "In short, the realism of the scene works powerfully to make *The Octopus* a first-rate novel, while the LeContian theory, used as a Zolaesque organizing principle, drags it back into the confusing and the second-rate." Nevertheless, Ziff concluded, "the genius which was released, once this handle to the world [popular Darwinism] was grasped, brought into American literature not only a new cast of characters but a closer observation and shrewder delineation of the problems they shared with their fellows— not the least of which was sexuality."

This thesis was developed further by Gordon O. Taylor in *The Passages of Thought: Psychological Representation in the American Novel 1870–1900* (New York, 1969). Taylor indicated that in *McTeague* sex "is more clearly acknowledged as psychological fact" than in earlier American novels. Norris treated sex, argued Taylor, as a "process which is physiologically determined, unconsciously experienced by the character, and detachedly observed by the author." Yet the influence of Le Conte is apparent, for the force behind the process "is an abstract conception removed from the action and from the passage of time, and positing a moral consciousness or a moral instinct to struggle with purely physical urges."

One of the most provocative comments from a literary history of this period came from Jay Martin's *Harvests of Change: American Litera-ture, 1865–1914* (Englewood Cliffs, N.J., 1967). Martin saw the real sub-ject of *The Octopus* as the writing of an American epic: "Presley is a writer preparing, at the conclusion of the novel, to write the epic he has lived; the novel is in a sense hung upon his growing insight into the nature of an American epic, as he has lived through it. During the book, he rejects most of the genteel notions of the epic." Presley, then, has undergone the basic training of heart and mind and has at the end been brought through several steps to the point of being able to begin the epic he wanted to write in the beginning, and "the quest for the epic becomes the subject of the epic."

Three commentaries on Norris from this period were largely unsym-pathetic. Warner Berthoff, in *The Ferment of Realism: American Litera-ture, 1884–1919* (New York, 1965), admitted that "Frank Norris may be the writer this history will be most unjust to." Berthoff found it difficult to account for Norris's "continuing reputation as a serious figure in Ameri-can literature"; dismissed *The Octopus* as "preposterous"; and described Norris's style "as if Cole Porter had written novels." Philip Walker com-plained in "*The Octopus* and Zola: A New Look" (*Sym*, Summer 1967) that Norris's "most Zolaesque" novel, *The Octopus*, falls far short of Zola's work because of heavy-handedness in the use of metaphor, obtrusive "ro-mantic wishfulfillment," and "metaphysical anxiety," which becomes in the concluding pages "shrill, dominant, infinitely disturbing." A like ob-jection is expressed by W. M. Frohock (*Frank Norris*, UMPAW [Minne-apolis, 1968]), who argues that *The Octopus* is greatly indebted to Zola but much inferior to the master's work. The thesis of Frohock's essay is that Norris "emerges as an instinctive melodramatist working with natu-ralist materials." Frohock's discussion of Norris's life and work is unfor-tunately pervaded by a tone of somewhat amused condescension. Fro-hock writing about Norris reminds one of Norris writing about McTeague. In Frohock's appraisal, Norris suffers greatly from not having written like Henry James, who "has reformed our notion of the novel."

At no other time in the history of criticism on Norris has there been so much interest in his essays as in the 1960s. The posthumously pub-lished collection *The Responsibilities of the Novelist* (1903) was for many years the only source of Norris's literary criticism. Willard E. Martin pub-lished "Two Uncollected Essays by Frank Norris" (*AL*, May 1936), but it was not until 1964 that a new collection of Norris's essays on literature appeared. Much more comprehensive than the earlier *Responsibilities* (which Norris had no hand in putting together), Donald Pizer's edition of *The Literary Criticism of Frank Norris* includes articles which Norris wrote for the San Francisco *Wave*, as well as several of the "Weekly Letters" from the *Chicago American Literary and Art Review*, all of which were omitted from the earlier volume. In contrast to *Responsibilities*, Pizer's edition is arranged carefully, with Norris's essays on literary theory coming first, followed by numerous articles that reveal Norris applying these theories to specific works or problems. Pizer is one of few critics who have considered Norris seriously as a literary critic. The result is a thoughtful, comprehensive, and logically presented body of editorial comment in this volume. In every respect, Pizer's work supersedes *Responsibilities* as the standard edition of Norris's literary criticism. The remaining seven letters which Norris had written for the *Chicago American* and which Pizer did not include in his edition were edited and published by Richard Allan Davison (*ALR*, Summer 1968).

Both the editorial commentary in *The Literary Criticism of Frank Norris* and Pizer's earlier "Frank Norris' Definition of Naturalism" (*MFS*, Winter 1962–63) admit that the critical essays are "poorly written, repetitious, and occasionally plain silly," but Pizer is able to see that despite their crudity they "contain a coherent critical attitude of some importance." As Pizer sees it, Norris "conceived of naturalism as a fictional mode which illustrated some fundamental truth of life within a detailed presentation of the sensational and low." Such a concept resolved the differences between romanticism and realism by taking from the one the idea of "philosophical depth," from the other the technique of "detailed accuracy," and adding a third ingredient which both romanticism and realism neglect, the use of the "sensational and low" as subject matter.

After examining Norris's criticism on literature and his opinions about social responsibility, Joseph J. Kwiat concluded that the two strains were separate and conflicting. In "Frank Norris: The Novelist as Social Critic and Literary Theorist" (*ArQ*, Winter 1962), Kwiat stated that "any attempt to reconcile completely Norris' aesthetic theories with his social theories is an ill-fated venture." Nevertheless, Kwiat argued that in his essays Norris reflected the same intellectual struggle experienced by several other important American writers, including Melville, Twain, Stephen Crane, Dreiser, Hemingway, Steinbeck, Dos Passos, and Farrell.

After Ernest Marchand's critical study appeared in 1942, another book-length work on Norris was not published until the 1960s, when three appeared. Warren French's lively *Frank Norris* (TUSAS, New York, 1962) summarizes Norris's life in a chapter and then surveys his work chronologically. French's contention is that Norris was not so much a naturalist in the European tradition as he was "a scion of the transcendentalists." Although this thesis is certainly tenable, French tends to carry it too far. As a transcendentalist, Norris must hate urban civilization, find nature benevolent, and be optimistic in all of his works. To make him so, French has to perform a number of critical contortions. To get around Norris's comment in *The Octopus* that nature is indifferent, for example, French argues that Norris did not really mean indifferent but "unconscious": "Nature, he [Norris] feels, does good without thinking about it — but it does do good in the long run." French rates *The Octopus* and *McTeague* somewhat lower than usual and considers *The Pit* "the only work in which Norris shows promise of achieving intellectual maturity."

Donald Pizer's *The Novels of Frank Norris* (Bloomington, Ind., 1966) uses the foundation that he had established in several previously published articles to show that "Norris' novels are philosophical novels in the sense that they contain coherent systems of belief and value." Although some readers will feel that Pizer somewhat overemphasizes the influence of Joseph Le Conte on Norris and attributes too much in Norris's work to his belief in "evolutionary theism," this book represents an enormous contribution to criticism on Frank Norris. Its greatest strength is that it considers Norris in a new context, in fresh terms, and avoids entrapment in the tired generalizations that had been piling up for years.

William B. Dillingham's *Frank Norris: Instinct and Art* deals with both Norris's life (see *Biography*, above) and writings. Dillingham views Norris as being similar to D. H. Lawrence, who insisted on the gods within "that come and go." The gods for Norris were man's instinctive drives, sometimes creative, sometimes destructive, but always the primary force of life. No external influence upon Norris was as important as his own instincts (and the source of those will remain an eternal mystery). Dillingham argues that although much of what Norris wrote was not successful, his attempt was extremely ambitious, especially in the area of literary symbolism.

The keynote for studies of Norris in the 1970s was struck by Crisler and McElrath in their introduction to *Frank Norris: A Reference Guide* (Boston, 1974): "Virtually all critics of the 1950s and 1960s pause to point out Norris's clumsiness and inability to control his excesses. Ultimately, one comes to wonder why, exactly, so many people . . . spend so much time writing about a novelist who seems to give them so little pleasure." The defensive tone of this remark resounds through much written about Norris in the last decade. Previously Norris had had serious and perceptive critics of his work, but in the 1970's *champions* emerged who were determined to set the record straight and to elevate Norris to his true position in American literary history. The results have been mixed.

One aspect of this new determination to lift Norris from the ranks of the minors can be seen in the many articles that take as their basic premise that he was an artist of the highest order who knew exactly what he was about in virtually all of his writings. In "*McTeague:* The Imagistic

Network" (*WAL*, Summer 1972), Suzy Bernstein Goldman states: "Norris was a far more conscious artist than we have yet realized," and convincingly demonstrates in a method strikingly reminiscent of the New Critics how image patterns in *McTeague* develop character and theme. She argues, as did Dillingham earlier, that the novel's ending is not melodramatic but skillfully prepared for through recurrent imagery.

No one in the 1970s was a more faithful champion of Frank Norris than Joseph R. McElrath, Jr. In several articles he assumed the role of corrector of past blunders about Norris's work and of guide into the golden realm of a much more subtle and artistically sophisticated Norris than, he felt, had been dreamed of earlier. Attempting to reveal still another dimension to Norris's multiple abilities, McElrath published "The Comedy of Frank Norris's *McTeague*" (*SAH*, Oct. 1975). In the early part of the novel, McElrath argues, Norris proves himself a talented humorist, employing especially "ironic inflation" as "the major comic device." McElrath attempted more and gained less with his effort to redeem Norris's pot boilers and to establish them as serious works of art. In "The Erratic Design of Frank Norris's *Moran of the Lady Letty*" (*ALR*, Spring 1977), McElrath argues that "Moran and Wilbur are parodic exaggerations of stark adventure-romance characters." Norris is perceived as intentionally writing a bad novel in order to create satire on bad novels. If we can bring ourselves to think of the book this way, Norris can be seen as a sophisticated and accomplished artist even in what has been mistakenly considered a terrible novel. "When the satire and parodic dimensions of *Moran* are recognized, many of the major *faults* disappear." Though ingenious, the argument probably will not convince many, even among those who would like to believe it. McElrath also finds *Blix* a more consciously wrought novel than have past critics. In "Allegory in Frank Norris's *Blix:* Its Relevance to *Vandover*" (*MR*, Winter 1979), he points to certain "allegorical instances" and concludes that they add to the depth of characterization in that novel. In a sense Debra D. Munn supported McElrath's contention that Norris wrote *Blix* with a high degree of conscious artistry in her examination of the novel's revisions. In "The Revision of Frank Norris's *Blix*" (*RALS*, Spring 1980), she shows that Norris carefully revised the serialized version of *Blix* that appeared in the *Puritan* magazine (Mar.–Aug. 1899).

When novelists achieve a reputation for greatness, their works tend to be examined in a manner different from that in which lesser writers are discussed. The obvious is not what it seems; characters have hidden depths; clues are deftly scattered about so that unsuspected but justified meanings may be uncovered. To analyze Norris's works in this way is thus to suggest that he is among those few American novelists whose writings can support the assumption of the rich hidden stratum. Stuart L. Burns, in "The Rapist in Frank Norris's *The Octopus*" (*AL*, Jan. 1971), takes us on such a clue-hunting expedition in order to conclude that Norris has placed Angèle's mysterious rapist right before our very eyes if we would but open them to see. The priest, Father Sarria, he argues, is the culprit. In "Eroticism in American Literary Realism" (*SAF*, Spring 1977), Joseph Katz similarly goes deep into the dark realm of suggestiveness to find what is certainly not obvious in *The Pit*, namely that Laura has sexual intercourse with the artist Corthell. Norris, states Katz, was always keenly aware not only of his own complex artistry but also of his audience, and he arranged to have the eroticism of *The Pit* available only to the most sophisticated of readers.

Evidence of this new respect for Norris can be seen even in treatments of his short stories and sketches. Several such articles appeared during the 1970s, including Lee Ann Johnson's "Western Literary Realism: The California Tales of Norris and Austin" (*ALR*, Summer 1974) and Christian Messenger's "Frank Norris and the College Sportsman" (*ALR*, Autumn 1979). John K. Swensson published a previously unpublished short story called "The Great Corner in Hannibal and St. Jo" (*ALR*, Summer 1971), which Norris apparently wrote about the same time as *The Pit*; and Wayne W. Westbrook (*ALR*, Spring 1977) further annotated references and allusions in the story.

Two books published during the 1970s have as their *raison d'être* the furthering of the new image of Norris as sophisticate rather than as boy Zola, as aesthetic strategist rather than as inspired amateur. In *The Fiction of Frank Norris: The Aesthetic Context* (Columbia, Mo., 1978), Don Graham early informs his readers: "It is my opinion that Norris deserves more credit as an artist than he has received." Graham's excellent book builds on articles that he published separately, notably "Art in *McTeague*" (*SAF*, Autumn 1975) and "Frank Norris and Les Jeunes: Architectural Criticism and Aesthetic Values" (*ALR*, Autumn 1978). The word *art* in Graham's book and in his article on *McTeague* refers both to Norris's artistry as a conscious author and to "the extensive references to all manner of art in Norris's fiction, including paintings, interior decor, drama, literature, sculpture, music, landscapes." In chapters devoted to *Vandover*, *McTeague*, *The Octopus*, and *The Pit*, an introduction that touches on Norris's three lesser novels, and an afterword, Graham demonstrates how "aesthetic objects function as an index of character value and as keys to the evaluation of interior and exterior landscapes." Graham's book and his article on Les Jeunes are important not only in upgrading Norris as a conscious artist but also in filling in the background of his interests and associations in the other areas of art.

Coming at the end of the decade, *Critical Essays on Frank Norris* (Boston, 1980), which Graham edited, is unmistakable evidence of the increased stature that Norris enjoys in the eyes of many. The collection was painstakingly put together, edited with professional skill, and carefully balanced between early reviews and the best of recent biography and criticism. It is an indispensable volume for the serious student of Norris.

Though not so loud, a less positive note was being sounded during the decade of the 1970s that was reminiscent of the past. Some critics insisted upon reminding us that Norris was no Henry James after all and that he really *did* detest fine style and attention to revision. In 1972 Mukhtar Ali Isani published (*AN&Q*, Apr.) a statement that Norris made in the Philadelphia *Book News* a short time after *McTeague* appeared, a statement that "appears to have escaped the attention of scholars." What Norris said highlights that side of him that should not be obscured through gallant efforts to make him a sophisticated conscious artist. "My chief object in writing 'McTeague,'" he wrote, "was to produce an interesting story—nothing more. It has always seemed to me that this should be the final test in any work of fiction independent of style, 'school,' or theory of art. If I had any secondary motive in its production it was in the nature of a protest against and a revolt from the 'decadent,' artificial and morbid 'prose fancies' of latter-day fiction. I believe that the future of American fiction lies in the direction of a return to the primitive elemental life, and an abandonment of 'elegant prose' and 'fine writing.'" Nothing ever became more important to Norris than that "primitive elemental life."

A few other critics during this period found Norris failing in some of his major novels and attempted to explain why. In this vein is William L. Vance's "Romance in *The Octopus*" (*Genre*, Jun. 1970), a highly intelligent article that does not elevate Norris to the position of a great writer but finds him deserving of close attention and intense interest because of the nature of his failure. *The Octopus*, Vance concludes, is a confused book because of Norris's "preoccupation with literary types—with the epic, the romantic, the tragic, the realistic, the naturalistic, and the melodramatic," genres that are in some measure incompatible. Norris not only indulged in all of them in *The Octopus* but "introduced at the center of his book a character similarly obsessed." Less original in explaining the failure of the novel is Robert Micklus, "Ambivalent Warriors in *The Octopus*" (*WAL*, Summer 1981), who argues that Vanamee has been too much out of the action to be the spokesman, as Norris meant him to be, for the novel's final philosophical stance. Thomas C. Ware, "'Gold to Airy Thinness Beat': The Midas Touch in Frank Norris's *McTeague*" (*Interpre-*

tations, Fall 1981), charges Norris with writing from real life without creating characters that are actually lifelike.

Generally, however, Norris has been treated generously of late. Critics' desire to cast off the boy Zola tag has been manifested not only in the tendency to treat Norris seriously as a skillful conscious artist but also in a growing conviction that his writings were not of a single piece but marked by a steady growth toward greater complexity and a mature understanding of life. Richard Allan Davison argues that "*The Octopus* (along with *The Pit*) is the culmination of Norris's growing belief in a morally ordered universe" and sees Norris accepting the "far-reaching implications of St. Paul's optimistic philosophy" ("Frank Norris's *The Octopus:* Some Observations on Vanamee, Shelgrim and St. Paul," in *Literature and Ideas in America*, edited by Robert Falk [Columbus, Ohio, 1976]). Davison feels that Norris the writer got better and better as his career progressed. In another essay, Davison states that *The Pit* is a highly complex novel with "Norris's most mature observations" that establish him finally not as a naturalist but as a deep and wise author of Christian convictions ("A Reading of Frank Norris's *The Pit*," in *The Stoic Strain in American Literature: Essays in Honour of Marston LaFrance*, edited by Duane J. MacMillan [Toronto, 1979]). Joseph R. McElrath, Jr., follows suit in "Frank Norris's *The Octopus:* The Christian Ethic as Pragmatic Response" (in *Critical Essays on Frank Norris*, edited by Don Graham [Boston, 1980]), arguing that the conclusion of *The Octopus* is mere irony and that "Norris's own view, final view, is that the best of all possible ethics is that expressed in the Sermon on the Mount." McElrath's position here parallels that of his earlier biographical essay (*ALR*, Autumn 1978) in which he sees Norris moving more and more in his life and art toward middle-class and conventional religious values, a movement which McElrath considers maturation.

That the modern drive to raise Norris's literary reputation has met with at least some success is indicated by the large number of articles published in the last few years that deal both with the sources of his writings and with the influence his work has had on other authors. In "Frank Norris's *McTeague:* A Possible Source in H. C. Bunner" (*NCF*, Mar. 1971), James B. Stronks suggests that Norris got the idea for his Old Grannis-Miss Baker subplot from Bunner's story "The Love Letters of Smith." Charles S. Watson claims that Norris used Dante's *Inferno* ("A Source for the Ending of *McTeague*," *ALR*, Spring 1972), and Joseph H. Gardner sets out to prove that there is much in Norris's works that derives from Charles Dickens ("Dickens, Romance, and *McTeague:* A Study in Mutual Interpretation," *EL*, Spring 1974). The most enlightening of these studies dealing with where Norris got his materials for *McTeague*, however, is Keith S. Sheppard's modest "A New Note for McTeague's Canary" (*WAL*, Fall 1974). Critics have long dwelt on McTeague's canary, but Sheppard appears to be the first to point out that it is grounded in actual fact, for "song birds were used in deep shaft mining to detect lethal gases. As long as the bird sang the miners knew that all was well. When the singing stopped, death was near." Thus it was natural for McTeague to have such a bird while he was a miner and brought it with him from the mines. The canary as a "danger-detector" opens up interesting new possibilities for the symbolism of the novel.

Surprisingly, even Norris's least successful novels have come in for their share of source studies. In "John Kendrick Bangs Criticizes Norris's Borrowings in *Blix*" (*AL*, Nov. 1970), James B. Stronks raises the question as to whether Norris may have come close to plagiarism in *Blix* by "his near duplication of striking details used recently by the best-selling Conan Doyal." Though it still seems of little importance what sources Norris may have used for *A Man's Woman* since the novel turned out so poorly, Fritz H. Oehlschlaeger in "An Additional Source for Frank Norris's *A Man's Woman*" (*ALR*, Spring 1980) has added Nansen's *Farthest North* to the list.

In two articles on *The Octopus*, Don Graham argues first that Norris probably was influenced by the French writer Stéphane Mallarmé, though "one can only speculate about whether Norris knew Mallarmé's poem ["The Afternoon of a Faun"] directly" (*PLL*, Summer 1974), and in "Studio Art in *The Octopus*" (*AL*, Jan. 1973), Graham identifies "the Japanese youth" who comes to Mrs. Cedarquist's salon to read his poetry as Yone Noguchi, a figure much a part of the San Francisco art scene of the 1890s and a contributor to the little magazine *The Lark*. Charles L. Crow sought to identify the real Vanamee of *The Octopus* as a "San Francisco painter, stained-glass craftsman, writer and art patron named Bruce Porter." "The Real Vanamee and His Influence on Frank Norris' *The Octopus*" (*WAL*, Summer 1974) is an intelligent and convincing article, one of the most provocative to appear during the 1970s, for it proves that the optimistic philosophy that Presley espouses at the end, the "compromise between evolution and humanism," which Norris himself accepted, may well have come from Porter, who wrote along the same lines and who had been strongly influenced by Bergson. Much has been made of the influence of Joseph Le Conte, one of Norris's teachers at Berkeley, on Norris's philosophy, but Crow may have uncovered an even more immediate influence in Bruce Porter, one of Norris's closest friends. The possibility deserves further exploration. In "The Other *Octopus*" (*ALR*, Spring 1981), Glen A. Love and David A. Carpenter argue that *The Octopus* may have been based in part on John R. Robinson's exposé of the railroads, also called *The Octopus* and published in 1894. Robinson's work was not a novel, but one of many pieces of reform journalism of the time pointing out the corruption of the railroads. There is no direct evidence that Norris read it. John S. Hill traced, as did Pizer and Dillingham before him, Norris's use of Cesare Lombroso's theories ("The Influence of Cesare Lombroso on Frank Norris's Early Fiction" [*AL*, Mar. 1970]). Stephen Tatum finds that Joseph Le Conte's ideas on evolution are not so important in "Lauth" as has been theorized and that Lemattre's article "On the transfusion of Blood" (1873) is a more likely source, though more "diffused" than direct ("Norris's Debt in 'Lauth' to Lemattre's 'On the Transfusion of Blood,'" *ALR*, Autumn 1978). In "A Source for Norris's 'A Deal in Wheat'" (*ALR*, Spring 1978), Joseph R. McElrath, Jr., points to an anecdote in Richard Harding Davis's *The West Through a Car-Window* (1892) as the possible source for a plot detail in Norris's story. With the exception of those by Sheppard, Crow, and possibly Tatum, these articles and notes on influences are for the most part insignificant and in some instances even farfetched, but collectively they suggest the seriousness with which Norris's works are currently being taken. In addition, the articles of Crow and Tatum may well signal the beginning of a new era in Norris studies when Le Conte will no longer be seen as the dominant influence in Norris's evolutionary philosophy.

If many critics of the 1970s concerned themselves with the sources that Norris utilized, some were eager to study Norris's own influence on other writers. As Mukhtar A. Isani pointed out in "Jack London on Norris' *The Octopus*" (*ALR*, Winter 1973), London expressed his admiration of Norris in a review of *The Octopus* that appeared in *Impressions;* and Charles N. Watson, Jr., documented the influence of Norris's *Moran of the Lady Letty* on London's *The Sea-Wolf:* "Sexual Conflict in *The Sea Wolf:* Farther Notes on London's Reading of Kipling and Norris" (*WAL*, Fall 1976). Don Graham found the description of the valley of ashes in Fitzgerald's *The Great Gatsby* remarkably similar to a passage in *Vandover* dealing with a "blighted urban landscape of San Francisco" as seen from the Lick Hotel ("Fitzgerald's Valley of Ashes and Frank Norris' 'Sordid and Grimy Wilderness,'" *Fitzgerald-Hemingway Annual*, 1972). In "Eliot's 'Red Rock' and Norris's *McTeague*" (*N&Q*, Sept. 1973), George M. Spangler argues that a line in *McTeague* is a source for a line in *The Waste Land* (though "there is no record of Eliot's having read *McTeague*"). It may be that learned journals are overly eager to publish articles and notes that deal with sources and influences, for many such essays seem to be inadequately supported by fact. At any rate, another kind of influence discussion, George Wead's "Frank Norris: His Share of Greed" (in *The*

Classic American Novel and the Movies, edited by Gerald Peary and Roger Shatzkin [New York, 1977]), is convincing in showing that Erich von Stroheim misunderstood *McTeague* and that the resulting film, *Greed*, is a misinterpretation of Norris's novel. Long held to be a reasonably faithful rendition of the novel, *Greed* is not really true to the theme or the art of *McTeague*.

The formative influence of Norris's early journalistic experiences continues to be the subject of critical commentary. In "Stephen Crane and Frank Norris: The Magazine and the 'Revolt' in American Literature in the 1890's" (*WHR*, Autumn 1976), Joseph J. Kwiat concludes that for both writers the "little magazine" and the "popular magazine" served "as artistic vehicles for expressing the truth about the nature of nature, the nature of man, and the nature of society." Kwiat alludes to Norris's "earlier newspaper training" as he did in his earlier article on "The Newspaper Experience: Crane, Norris, and Dreiser" (*NCF*, Sept. 1953), an article which prompted Joseph Katz to write a rebuttal, "Frank Norris and 'The Newspaper Experience'" (*ALR*, Winter 1971), in which he points out that the newspaper world of Crane and Dreiser "simply was not the school Frank Norris attended. The situation in which he learned his craft was fundamentally different from theirs" since the San Francisco *Wave* was not a newspaper at all but a weekly magazine. Robert A. Morace also corrected Kwiat's misconception about Norris as a newspaper man in "Frank Norris and the Magazine Experience" (*MR*, Summer 1980) and further took issue with Kwiat's linking of Norris with Crane relevant to their experiences with little magazines. *The Wave*, Morace correctly states, was "very much unlike the cheap popular magazines to which Crane contributed." In another essay, "The Writer and His Middle Class Audience: Frank Norris: A Case in Point" (in *Seasoned Authors for a New Season: The Search for Standards in Popular Writing*, edited by Louis Filler [Bowling Green, 1980]), Morace concludes that "among the several benefits Norris received as a result of his tenure on the San Francisco *Wave* was the opportunity to write for a clearly defined audience and to learn to adapt his writing so as to accommodate his own artistic purposes as well as the values of his readers."

The several other recent critical treatments of Norris's work can be broadly divided into three categories: the philosophical — those that deal with Norris's philosophy of life and art; the psychological — those that seek to apply the methods of modern psychological analysis to Norris and his characters; and the sociological — those that see him as mainly interested in those forces which were sweeping across the American scene of his time. In probing Norris's world view, S. S. Moorty finds it to be highly moralistic: "Norris was not a thoroughgoing naturalist and any attempt to relate him narrowly to a consistent deterministic pessimistic philosophy is bound to be misleading." Norris felt, according to Moorty, that it was only through self-discipline and fundamental virtues that man can achieve his highest potential ("Norris and Fitzgerald as Moralists," in *Studies in American Literature*, edited by Jagdish Chander and Narindar S. Pradhan [Delhi, 1976]). Other critics of the 1970s disagreed, seeing Norris very much as a determinist. Leonard Lutwack, in *Heroic Fiction: The Epic Tradition and American Novels of the Twentieth Century* (Carbondale, Ill., 1971), argues that *The Octopus* is by genre an epic and that "Norris is in this tradition, his naturalistic philosophy casting the same shadow over the exploits of men as the fate of the earlier epic poets." In "Naturalism as Expediency in the Novels of Frank Norris" (*MR*, Feb. 1971), Bryant N. Wyatt agrees that Norris "utilizes the deterministic concept — to make predictable the actions of his characters." But in doing so, Wyatt concludes, Norris made determinism his "crutch" and made no attempt to shape his characters "into convincing and consistent personages who are vital and believable in their own right." William B. Stone tries, with special attention to *The Pit*, to demonstrate in "Idiolect and Ideology: Some Stylistic Aspects of Norris, James, and DuBois" (*Style*, Fall 1976) that Norris's determinism dictated his sentence structure. For example, "periodic sentences, with initial modifiers which may be said to 'predetermine' the main clauses, are prevalent in Norris's writing." Stone's argument is flawed because it is based upon a major premise about Norris's outlook that is somewhat distorted and simplistic. James K. Folsom's "The Wheat and the Locomotive: Norris and Naturalistic Esthetics" (in *American Literary Naturalism: A Reassessment*, edited by Yoshinobu Hakutani and Lewis Fried [Heidelberg, 1975]) is an attempt to reassess the way Naturalism manifests itself in Norris's fiction, not so much in the theme of determinism as opposed to free will but as "internal character traits" which are "projected outward in the signs and symbols of the novel."

Norris's insistence that Zola was a romanticist has for years puzzled critics and literary historians. A good explanation of that long troublesome statement is John E. McClusky's "Frank Norris' Literary Terminology: A Note on Historical Context" (*WAL*, Summer 1972), which anchors Norris's terminology of "realist" to describe Howells and "romanticist" to describe Zola in the time. Others — including H. Rider Haggard, Albion Tourgée, and Hamlin Garland — were referring to Zola in precisely the same way, as a romanticist, defined as one who deals not with the commonplace and "prosaic activities of ordinary people" but with "variations from the type of normal life."

The psychological approach to Norris and to his characters has not yielded much in the past several years that is truly illuminating perhaps because many of the enticements he holds out to Freudians do not reflect as much of his real and deepest self as they seem to. He is elusive; he *appears* to be a more ready subject for psychological analysis than he actually is. Consequently, his psychoanalysts are sometimes reduced to conjectures that add no new dimensions to him or his work. For example, Doris Grieser Marquit guesses from what she can derive about sex from Norris's works that he was repelled even by normal sex and found it dirty and destructive ("Nature and Human Nature in Frank Norris" [*GyS*, Winter 1977]). George M. Spangler appears to agree, though his argument is more cogent and substantive. In "The Structure of *McTeague*" (*ES*, Feb. 1978), he suggests that Norris had "a repressed fear of castration," which is reflected in his treatment of Trina as the "villain" of *Mc-Teague* and in his characterization of the dentist as "the victim of Norris's version of the fatal woman, who . . . 'makes small of him.'" Running through *McTeague*, Spangler feels, is an undercurrent of "terror at female sexuality." William Freedman supplies Freudian labels in "Oral Passivity and Oral Sadism in Norris's *McTeague*" (*Language and Speech*, no. 2, 1980). "The behavior of McTeague and a number of other figures in the novel, notably Trina and Marcus," he states, "is characteristically — and often neurotically — oral-erotic."

The fundamental aim of Edwin Haviland Miller in two articles on Norris is not so much to supply Freudian labels to what we already know about characters (though he does do that) as it is to use the psychological approach, as other critics have used other approaches, to convince readers that Frank Norris should enjoy a much higher place in American literary history than he has been accorded. In "The Art of Frank Norris in *Mc-Teague*" (*MR*, Summer 1979), Miller compares Norris to Proust and Hawthorne for his "sensitivity" and argues that if he does not create the "subtleties" of Henry James or the "baroque accretiveness" of Thomas Mann, it is because "there is no room" for them in *McTeague*. He tells us, as have other Freudian critics, that McTeague has "castration anxiety" (as witnessed in his remark, "Don't make small of me") and that the brute dentist does not mature beyond the oral stage. Marcus and Mc-Teague, Miller feels, have a "latently homosexual relationship." This article, like its companion, piece, "The Art of Frank Norris in *Vandover and the Brute*" (*MR*, Summer 1981), is largely a recapitulation of plot details in Freudian perspective. Miller finds Vandover's trouble all brought on by his reaction to his mother's death when he was eight (he feels rejected). In summary, Miller finds that "the psychology of the novel is profound and the art, as to be expected, matches the psychology: they are one."

In many ways, the America in which Norris spent his brief life was as fraught with change and electric excitement as in any other time in its history. Unquestionably, the forces in Norris's environment were powerful stimuli to this powerful young Lochinvar. Recognizing this, several recent critics have approached his work from the standpoint of his reaction to his environment. Joseph J. Kwait has described Norris's sense of mission to reflect real life around him, his "confidence in the Plain People," and his conviction that literature is "the most democratic of all the arts" ("The Social Responsibilities of the American Painter and Writer: Robert Henri and John Sloan; Frank Norris and Theodore Dreiser," *CR*, Winter 1977). In "The American Painter and Writer's Credo of 'Art for Truth's Sake': Robert Henri and John Sloan; Frank Norris and Theodore Dreiser" (*JAC*, Summer 1978), Kwiat argues that Norris rejected the "desiccated conception of the role of the creative artist and thinker as an isolate" and accepted "the idea of the creator as a forceful instrument for social and cultural change within a 'new' American community." According to Robert E. Morsberger ("The Inconsistent *Octopus*," *WAL*, Summer 1981), *The Octopus* is inconsistent philosophically, but it possesses great vitality that reflects "the mixed mind of America at the turn of the century."

Some critics see Norris looking negatively at his world and depicting, as Lewis Fried claims, "the alienation of man — not from his sensual capacities — but from his self-created modes of labor and exchange, so that the world he inhabits not only furthers his dehumanizations, but becomes a dead world, one of junk, feces, and waste" ("The Golden Brotherhood of *McTeague*," *Zeitschrift für Anglistik und Amerikanistik*, Jan. 1975). Similarly in "Frank Norris's *Vandover and the Brute*: Narrative Technique and the Socio-Critical Viewpoint" (*SAF*, Spring 1976), Joseph R. McElrath, Jr., sees *Vandover* as "a critical attack upon nineteenth-century popular morality and the archaic life-vision of a world of fixed certainties which informed it." Warren French agrees in his introduction to *Vandover* (Lincoln, 1978), denying that the novel is part of some "naturalistic" movement in favor of its being a "contribution to the brief but intense outburst of a preoccupation with decadence in late nineteenth-century American literature." The novel, he feels, is a "protest against an inert and constricting society that, like a vampire, destroys individuals in order to give its already dead form a semblance of life." Glen A. Love's "Frank Norris's Western Metropolitans" (*WAL*, Spring 1976) focuses on the necessity in Norris's novels for a "return to — rather than escape from — the city." In surveying the novels, Love sees a shift "from characters who are either somehow unfitted for modern urban life, or who turn their backs upon it in favor of escapist adventuring in wild nature, to those who can function successfully on both levels but who are primarily committed to an urban existence and who discover in industrialized contemporary life the opportunities for high enterprise."

Love's thoughtful article along with several others published in the last dozen years goes a long way toward filling two needs mentioned in the original version of this essay. One is attention to Norris as a mine of Americana, as an ideal subject to study for an understanding of the culture and thought of late nineteenth-century America. As critics are now seeing, in Norris the principal American myths and national contradictions of his time are reflected with rare clarity. He was both roughrider and velvet-jacketed gentleman, racist and liberal, traditionalist and progressive, artist and lowbrow. Like F. Scott Fitzgerald, who read and admired him, Norris was of that unusual breed of writers who seem totally fused with the dominant spirit of their times and yet manage to see life from a larger perspective as well with a clear, honest vision. The other pressing need was for greater consideration of Norris as an ambitious literary artist. After the publication of the first edition of this volume, critics turned their considerable talents more toward the examination of Norris as a conscious artist than they had ever done before, and this has been the single most conspicuous aspect of the criticism in recent years. It may be that a few of Norris's new champions have gone too far in attributing to him a degree of conscious artistry that he did not in reality possess. One does not have to assume that Norris always succeeded in his works to find them, even the failures, interesting in their unique way and instructive.

Edward Taylor

NORMAN S. GRABO and JANA WAINWRIGHT

DESPITE THE vigorous attention lavished in the 1970s on other colonial poets—Anne Bradstreet, Phyllys Wheatley, Benjamin Tompson, Ebenezer Cooke, and others—Edward Taylor remains our most significant poet, certainly before Freneau and Bryant, and possibly before Poe. He is a genuine, if sometimes ragged, poet, whose voice realized the beauty of an otherwise often dismal religion, and whose presence has necessitated a deep rethinking of the character of American culture in the seventeenth and eighteenth centuries. Before 1937 he was essentially unknown; by 1970 he could not be avoided; since then the availability of his thought and writing has doubled, work the implications of which can be absorbed only very slowly, but work which has already established Taylor's permanence among the furniture of American Literature.

BIBLIOGRAPHY

Useful information on early bibliographical work on Taylor may still be found in the earlier version of this essay. The most complete and comprehensive bibliography, however, is Constance J. Gefvert's *Edward Taylor: An Annotated Bibliography, 1668–1970*, The Serif Series 19 (Kent, Ohio, 1971). This lists 306 primary and secondary items and is the necessary beginning for any investigation of the poet. Broader in some respects, narrower in others, is the section on Taylor in William J. Scheick and JoElla Doggett, *Seventeenth-Century American Poetry: A Reference Guide* (Boston, 1977). Items are arranged chronologically from 1937

From Earl N. Harbert and Robert A. Rees, editors, *Fifteen American Authors before 1900: Bibliographic Essays on Research & Criticism* (Madison: The University of Wisconsin Press; © 1984 by the Board of Regents of the University of Wisconsin System); may be reproduced only by permission of the publisher.

through 1975, and include all doctoral dissertations (which Gefvert reports only selectively). Gefvert is more useful in locating social and biographical materials; Scheick and Doggett place Taylor in a context of seventeenth-century poetics and aesthetics, alongside other poets of the period. For more selective but also more evaluative comments on published work since 1975, readers should consult the "Literature to 1800" essays by Robert D. Arner and later by William J. Scheick in the annual *American Literary Scholarship*, ed. James Woodress and J. Albert Robbins (Durham, N.C.). One special bibliography deserves attention. From an inventory made shortly after Taylor's death, Thomas H. Johnson compiled a list of 192 titles in Taylor's library for his edition of *The Poetical Works*. The list has some minor errors, but considering the meager evidence provided in the inventory and the lack at that time of many of Taylor's manuscripts, Johnson's identifications are remarkably astute. As Harrison T. Meserole proposes in one of the very few attempts to deal with the sources of Taylor's thought, "Edward Taylor's Sources" in *Directions in Literary Criticism: Contemporary Approaches to Literature* (University Park, Penn., 1973), much more investigation of the critical implications of Taylor's sources is warranted, towards which Johnson's list provides relatively untapped information.

EDITIONS

There is no collected edition of Taylor's works and no complete edition of his poems, all of which, but for two stanzas from "Upon Wedlock and Death of Children" included in Cotton Mather's *Right Thoughts in Sad Hours* (London, 1689), remained in manuscript until the 1930s. After announcing the significance of the manuscript "Poetical Works" (at a meeting of the Modern Language Association in 1936), Thomas H. Johnson, in "Edward Taylor: A Puritan 'Sacred Poet'" (*NEQ*, June 1937), published "Huswifery," "Upon Wedlock and Death of Children," "The Ebb and Flow," four poems and some shorter excerpts from *Gods Determinations*, nine meditations, and a short excerpt from "My Last Declamation in the Colledg Hall."

Response to the poems was swift and favorable. Norman Holmes Pearson and William Rose Benét printed eight selections in the very successful *Oxford Anthology of American Literature* (New York, 1938), Perry Miller incorporated references to Taylor's manuscript poems in the now classic *The New England Mind: The Seventeenth Century* (Cambridge, Mass., 1939), and Miller and Johnson made room for several poems in *The Puritans: A Sourcebook of Their Writing* (New York, 1938).

Johnson then published a very ample selection of the poems in a limited edition of 925 copies under the title, *The Poetical Works of Edward Taylor* (New York: Rockland Editions, 1939). This volume was reissued in 1943 by the Princeton University Press, and released yet again in paperback by Princeton in 1966. The standard edition for twenty years, it includes a brief biography and descriptive evaluation of the poetry, a glossary, notes, a list of Taylor's library, a description of the manuscript, a bibliography, and the following poems: all of *Gods Determinations*, "An Address to the Soul Occasioned by a Rain," "Upon a Spider Catching a Fly," "Huswifery," "Upon Wedlock and Death of Children," "The Ebb and Flow," and thirty-one meditations. The quality of Johnson's selections may be indicated by the fact that no subsequent anthology of the period ignores Taylor, and there is hardly an anthologized poem that did not first appear here. Johnson's texts, however, are not reliable.

In 1942 Johnson also published "The Topical Verses of Edward Taylor" (*Publications of the Colonial Society of Massachusetts*, Feb. 1942), including the following poems: "Elegy on Mr. Sims," "Elegy on Francis Willoughby," "Declamation in the Colledg Hall," "Elegy on Mr. John Allen," "Elegy on Mr. Charles Chauncey," "Acrostic Love Poem to Elizabeth Fitch," "Elegy on Mrs. Elizabeth Taylor," "Elegy on Mr. Sam Hooker," "Elegy on Mrs. Mehetabel Woodbridge," "Elegy on Dr. Increase Mather," and "Verses made upon Pope Joan." The following year, in "Some Edward Taylor Gleanings" (*NEQ*, June 1943), Johnson edited "Upon a Wasp Child with Cold," "Huswifery II," "Upon the Sweeping Flood," and eight previously unpublished meditations. Several additional poems from the "Poetical Works" were published between then and 1960 (all listed in Stanford, *Poems*).

In 1953, Donald E. Stanford transcribed all the poems from the Yale manuscript in his dissertation, "An Edition of the Complete Poetical Works of Edward Taylor." Done before the discovery of the Redwood Library manuscripts, this is the closest approach to date to a complete edition of the poems. Although its texts are not as exact as those of the printed *Poems* (1960), they are still an improvement over Johnson's, and are the basis for the Yale edition. Stanford's 189-page introduction is the fullest discussion thus far of Taylor's biography, theology, and poetry, and Stanford also transcribes Taylor's diary and his letter to Increase Mather.

In 1960, Stanford's texts, refined from their dissertation state but not representing all the poems in the manuscript "Poetical Works," were published as *The Poems of Edward Taylor*, with a foreword by Louis L. Martz; a twenty-four page introduction by Stanford on Taylor's biography, theology, previous editions, and the texts of the poems; a bibliographical appendix on previous editions; another detailed appendix on the Taylor manuscripts (see *Manuscripts and Letters*, below); a glossary of technical, theological, and dialectal terms (essentially the same as the glossary of the 1953 dissertation); and the following poems: all 217 *Preparatory Meditations*, all of *God's Determinations*, "When Let by Rain," "Upon a Spider Catching a Fly," "Upon a Wasp Child with Cold," "Huswifery" "Another upon the Same," "Upon Wedlock and Death of Children," "The Ebb and Flow," "Upon the Sweeping Flood," "A Funeral Poem [upon his wife Elizabeth]," "An Elegy upon the Death of . . . Mr. Samuel Hooker," "A Fig for Thee Oh! Death," and extracts from the *Metrical History of Christianity*. This edition was reissued, abridged, in 1963, as a Yale paperback. It deletes both the foreword and introduction, replacing them with a new introduction by Donald Stanford, and deletes the excerpt from the *Metrical History*, both elegies, "A Fig for Thee Oh! Death," both bibliographical appendices, and sixty-six meditations.

Stanford published his typescript of the whole 21,500-line *Edward Taylor's Metrical History of Christianity* (Cleveland, Ohio: Micro Photo, Inc.) in 1962, from the Redwood Library collection, and from that same collection, "The Earliest Poems of Edward Taylor" (*AL*, May 1960), selecting "A Letter sent to his Brother Joseph Taylor and his wife after a visit," "The Lay-Mans Lamentation," "an epigram on the Archbishop of Canterbury," "A dialogue in verse between the writer and a Maypole dresser," "this in a letter I sent to my schoolfellow, W. M.," and "Another Answer [to a Popish Pamphlet]," as verses originally by Taylor, presumably before his emigration to America.

Until the discovery of the Redwood Library cache, it was assumed that Taylor's diary, first published in *PMHS* (1880), had been lost. Since then, the diary, which covers Taylor's expedition from England, his college years at Harvard, and his final settlement in Westfield, has been reedited with an introduction by Francis Murphy as *The Diary of Edward Taylor* (Springfield, Mass., 1964).

Norman S. Grabo edited a diplomatic text of *Edward Taylor's Christographia* (New Haven, Conn., 1962), with an introduction arguing that these fourteen sacrament-day sermons preached between 1701 and 1703 constitute a kind of poetic workbook for the *Preparatory Meditations* (Second Series, 42–56), since the poems were "Chiefly upon the Doctrin preached," and therefore presumably followed the sacramental sermons in order of composition, in structure, and in controlling logic and imagery. The full title of the Yale manuscript is "CHRISTOGRAPHIA, or A Discourse touching Christs Person, Natures, the Personall Union of the Natures, Qualifications, and Operations Opened, Confirmed, and Practically improoved in Severall Sermons delivered upon Certain Sacrament Dayes unto the Church and people of God in *Westfield*."

Eight more sermons — these from the Prince Collection of the Boston

Public Library, and untitled by Taylor—were edited by Norman S. Grabo as *Edward Taylor's Treatise Concerning the Lord's Supper* (East Lansing, Mich., 1965). The editor's introduction argues that these sermons belong to the ecclesiastical and theological Stoddardean controversy over qualifications for admission to the sacrament of the Lord's Supper, and moreover, to the developing theories of "signs" or knowable marks of God's grace as they were expounded by Thomas Shepard and Jonathan Edwards. A practical rather than a definitive text, modernizing and regularizing some usage, this edition lacks adequate textual notes regarding substantive emendations and readings, but the "Explanatory Notes" are exceptionally full, making considerable use of the sources Taylor used in composing the sermons.

Two editions are too recent to permit judicious assessment, although both promise to be enormously valuable in expanding and deepening our understanding of Taylor. Most auspicious is the three-volume *Unpublished Writings of Edward Taylor* (Boston, 1981), edited admirably by Thomas M. and Virginia L. Davis. Volume One, *Edward Taylor's "Church Records" and Related Sermons*, includes Westfield's "Profession of Faith," the "Public Relations" of the church's foundation members, Taylor's "Foundation Day Sermon," his record of disciplinary cases, the revised Foundation Day sermon, and two disciplinary sermons. Volume Two, *Edward Taylor vs. Solomon Stoddard: The Nature of the Lord's Supper*, makes available for the first time the documents by which to understand Taylor's long and important role in the Stoddardean Controversy. Volume Three, *Edward Taylor's Minor Poetry*, collects for the first time Taylor's English poems before his arrival in America, the elegies, the baroque marriage proposal to Elizabeth Fitch, the "occasional" poems, and numbers of Biblical paraphrases and translations from Latin—in short, work that was previously available only in Stanford's dissertation or in fugitive essays. This is an extraordinary range and volume of material. No substantial amount of Taylor has been edited flawlessly, and no doubt the flaws will appear in these three volumes in time, despite their ample textual apparatus, but no one with the slightest exposure to Taylor's faded, torn, blotted, and scrawled manuscripts will be able to withhold admiration for the subtlety and sophistication of the Davises' editing. Volumes One and Two have especially good and long introductions, and all three are carefully and fully annotated.

The other edition is still in progress: in 1977 Charles W. Mignon identified a collection of thirty-six sermons entitled "Upon the Types of the Old Testament" discovered in Lincoln, Nebraska. When published, these will constitute a unique opportunity to study Taylor's system of typological symbolism in both his poems and his theology.

MANUSCRIPTS AND LETTERS

In the sketch of Edward Taylor supplied for William Sprague's *Annals of the American Pulpit* (1866), the Hon. Henry W. Taylor wrote that most of the books Taylor used were manuscript copies transcribed by Taylor: "His manuscripts were all handsomely bound in parchment by himself, of which tradition says he left, at his death, more than a hundred volumes." Detailed description of fourteen of these may be found in Stanford's *Poems*. The manuscripts described by Stanford, with their location, are:

1. "Poetical Works" (Yale University Library). Several brief or incomplete or simply very bad poems are transcribed in Stanford's dissertation, "An Edition of the Complete Poetical Works of Edward Taylor," and are now printed in Davis and Davis, *Unpublished Writings*, 3 (1981).

2. "Poems found in the Binding of 'Poetical Works'" (Yale University Library); these are described in some detail and evaluated in Donald Junkins, "Edward Taylor's Revisions" (*AL*, May 1965).

3. "Manuscript Book" (Yale University Library).

4. "China's Description and Commonplace Book" (Yale University Library).

5. "Metallographia" (Yale University Library).

6. "Dispensatory" (Yale University Library).

7. "Christographia" (Yale University Library). These are fully published and described in Norman S. Grabo, ed., *Edward Taylor's Christographia*.

8. "The Public Records of the Church at Westfield" (Westfield Athenaeum). John Hoyt Lockwood relied heavily upon this material, quoting portions of it in passing, in *Westfield and Its Historical Influences, 1669–1919: The Life of an Early Town* (Springfield, Mass., 1922). Part of the manuscript is printed in Donald Stanford, "Edward Taylor's 'Spiritual Relation'" (*AL*, Jan. 1964); this document is discussed in the context of "Traditional Patterns in Puritan Autobiography" by Daniel B. Shea in *Spiritual Autobiography in Early America* (Princeton, N.J., 1968). A microfilm of the entire manuscript was prepared by the Genealogical Society, Salt Lake City, Utah.

9. "Copy Book of the Council of Trent" (Westfield Athenaeum).

10. "Origen's *Contra Celsus* and *De Principiis*" (Westfield Athenaeum); described in Francis E. X. Murphy, "An Edward Taylor Manuscript Book" (*AL*, May 1959).

11. "Commonplace Book" (The Massachusetts Historical Society); two

of the forty-two items — an exchange of letters — are published in Norman S. Grabo, "The Poet to the Pope: Edward Taylor to Solomon Stoddard" (*AL*, May 1960), and Davis and Davis, *Unpublished Writings*, 2 (1981).

12. "Diary, Theological Notes, and Poems" (Redwood Library and Athenaeum). The diary has been twice published, and the poems appeared in Donald Stanford, "The Earliest Poems of Edward Taylor" (see *Editions*, above).

13. "A Metrical History of Christianity" (Redwood Library and Athenaeum); described fully in Donald E. Stanford, "Edward Taylor's Metrical History of Christianity" (*AL*, Nov. 1961).

14. "Harmony of the Gospels" (Redwood Library and Athenaeum). Charles W. Mignon discusses several of these manuscripts in "Some Notes on the History of the Edward Taylor Manuscripts" (*YULG*, Apr. 1965), also mentioning an additional manuscript:

15. "Notes on Divinity" (Yale University Library).

16. "Extracts, by Rev. Edward Taylor, Westfield" (Boston Public Library); see *The Prince Library: A Catalogue* for a description of the contents. Of this material, Taylor's expanded foundation sermon, "A Particular Church Is God's House" (1679), the original of which is in Item 8 above, is described in Norman S. Grabo, "Edward Taylor on the Lord's Supper" (*Boston Public Library Quarterly*, Jan. 1960). Eight sermons delivered at Westfield in 1693–94 are published as *Edward Taylor's Treatise Concerning the Lord's Supper*, ed. Norman S. Grabo (East Lansing, Mich. 1965). Related items pertaining to the Stoddardean controversy are published in Davis and Davis, *Unpublished Writings*, 2 (1981).

17. "Commonplace Book" (Yale University Library); Charles W. Mignon describes this book in "Another Taylor Manuscript at Yale" (*YULG*, Oct. 1966).

18. "Upon the Types of the Old Testament" (University of Nebraska). Thirty-six sermons on typology, many of them sacrament-day sermons with corresponding poetic meditations, dated 1693–98 and 1703–6. These are described in Charles W. Mignon, "The Nebraska Edward Taylor Manuscript: 'Upon the Types of the Old Testament'" (*EAL*, 1977/78), and illustrated by Mignon in "Christ the Glory of All Types: The Initial Sermon from Edward Taylor's 'Upon the Types of the Old Testament'" (*WMQ*, 1980).

The manuscript letters of Taylor are all listed in Stanford, *Poems* (1960); it also lists all the letters previously printed, with the exception of the letter to Stoddard, cited above, Item 11. For manuscripts pertaining to Taylor, see Thomas H. Johnson, "Secondary Works," in *The Poetical Works*, and Alexander Medlicott, "Notes on Edward Taylor from the Diaries of Stephen Williams" (*AL*, May 1962).

BIOGRAPHY

Despite the fact that Taylor's relative obscurity has led to numerous biographical comments since his poetry first came to light, there is so far nothing approaching a full, authoritative, and reliable, not to say definitive, biography. While a good number of facts have by now been accumulated, they have mostly been put to the service of explaining episodes in Taylor's long poetic career. The central biographical problems have been these: When was he born? Was he by training and faith theologically orthodox by his contemporary standards? If he was, how could he have composed such sensuous poetry in an Anglo-Catholic and "Metaphysical" manner? And why did he suppress the publication of his poetry?

Prior to 1975 the fullest printed outline of Taylor's life was Norman S. Grabo's *Edward Taylor*, based primarily upon previously published information. Grabo argues for Taylor's complete orthodoxy, and tries to record Taylor's inward biography as revealed in his prose and poetry and by the social occasions that provided the context for Taylor's writing.

Briefer, less interpretative (and in tone more temperate) are Donald E. Stanford's several biographical sketches. The first appeared in his introduction to the 1960 edition of the *Poems*, a much reduced, lightly documented version of the life that appeared in his dissertation. For the second edition of the *Poems* (1963), Stanford prepared a new introductory essay. It incorporates new evidence regarding Taylor's parentage and birth, and his earliest poetry, concluding that

Taylor, then, seems to have been endowed with most of those qualities usually connoted by the word *puritan*. He was learned, grave, severe, stubborn, and stiff-necked. He was very, very pious. But his piety was sincere. It was fed by a long continuous spiritual experience arising, so he felt, from a mystical communion with Christ. The reality and depth of this experience is amply witnessed by his poetry.

Another and expanded essay covering essentially the same factual material, but now interlarded with comments and judgments upon the documents, designed to emphasize that "Taylor is an anomaly," was published by Stanford in *Edward Taylor* (Minneapolis, 1965). This 46-page pamphlet makes evident the fact that the question of Taylor's birth date cannot be established with certainty because no official record of his birth has been discovered and because "the baptismal entries of the Taylor family in the parish church of Burbage, England, are incomplete." But Stanford decides that it must have been 1642, ignoring other hypothetical dates as late as 1646 on the grounds of circumstantial evidence and the long-held family tradition supporting the early date.

The most up-to-date biographical information on Edward Taylor is in Karl Keller's *The Example of Edward Taylor* (Amherst, 1975). Keller rehearses the known biographical information on Taylor in his 67-page biographical chapter, which provides the most personal and detailed view of Taylor to date. Keller also devotes one chapter to describing Taylor in one of the senses in which he is exemplary — in his Americanness, and in his repeated poetic defense of the New England Way of theology, since that way required him to link his piety with community polity and his introspectiveness with citizenship in the New Israel in America.

When Thomas H. Johnson announced Taylor's poetry in 1937, he inadvertently raised a question that has plagued Taylor scholar-critics ever since. In "Edward Taylor: A Puritan 'Sacred Poet,'" Johnson clearly indicated "Taylor's artistry in stating orthodox covenant theology in terms of sensuous imagery," but in his emphatic conclusion he suggested that Taylor belonged to the tradition of Anglo-Catholic conceitists and that he "turned to Anglican and, perhaps, to Catholic poets for example." Two years later, and much more circumspect in his introduction to the *Poetical Works*, Johnson insisted that the "reader need not search afield for analogues among the verses of the seventeenth-century conceitists to explain Taylor's choice of subject," and again that "the *Meditations* need no analogues among Anglo-Catholic sacramentalists to explain their adoration of Christ." He then went on to discriminate very carefully and accurately the points at which Congregational, Calvinist, Anglican, and Roman Catholic sacramental theology coincided, in order to explain the "orthodoxy" of Taylor's poetic expression. But the damage had already been done; the issue of Taylor's orthodoxy has only recently abated.

The importance of Taylor's personal religious orthodoxy to American literary history can only be appreciated if one compares him to the other known poets of the period — Wigglesworth, Bradstreet, Tompson — upon whose work had been elaborately constructed a seemingly satisfactory explanation for the dreariness of colonial poetry. As Puritans, it was argued, they saw mainly mnemonic and utilitarian value in verse, they admired plainness and were suspicious of figurative language, and if not religiously averse to all forms of earthly beauty, they nonetheless detested all sensuality, all imagery (especially in a religious context), all eroticism, and certainly such objects as altars, censers, crosses, and vestments. And yet Taylor, a "stiff-necked" New England minister, seemed to violate every assumption about American Puritans, presenting a highly artificial, mannered, sensual, even erotic poetry abounding in imagery drawn from ancient Christian, and therefore Catholic, rituals. He so obviously did not fit the picture that the easiest explanation must be that he was not, truly, a Puritan.

This explanation proved attractive to a number of influential writers: Kenneth B. Murdock, in *Literature & Theology in Colonial New England* (Cambridge, Mass., 1949), suggested that although Taylor "was an orthodox Puritan, he felt as a poet a sense of constraint within the bounds of the ordinary plainness and sobriety of Puritan literary style," adding that his contemporaries would probably have found his "erotically suggestive imagery" offensive, a suggestion he repeats again in *The Literature of the American People*, edited by A. H. Quinn (New York, 1951). In two essays Willie T. Weathers implied that Taylor's theology was a fundamentally pagan and Platonic conception flimsily covered with Calvinistic trappings—"Edward Taylor: Hellenistic Puritan" (*AL*, Mar. 1946) and "Edward Taylor and the Cambridge Platonists" (*AL*, Mar. 1954). Perry Miller shifted the argument somewhat by suggesting that Taylor's verse technique itself was one that "Puritans considered suitable only to the sensualities of the Church of England" (*The New England Mind: From Colony to Province* [Cambridge, Mass., 1953]). And Samuel Eliot Morison posited, albeit rhetorically, that "Such intensity of devotion, such richness in color and imagery, one looks for in the Anglo-Catholic poets rather than among puritans," *The Intellectual Life of Colonial New England* (New York, 1956). Morison goes on to deny the implication, but the suggestion is stronger than his rebuttal of it.

An obvious alternative explanation for Taylor's unusualness is simply that prevailing theories of Puritan aesthetics were wrong. Such an alternative is suggested by Keller's *Example*, but is more clearly and forcefully argued for in Robert Daly's *God's Altar: The World and the Flesh in Puritan Poetry* (Berkeley, 1978). Daly claims that the traditional view of Puritanism derived primarily from "Perry Miller's 'monolithic' New England mind" and did not take into account the "'pluralistic' reality." His main argument centers on the idea that the sheer amount of imagery and symbolism in Puritan poetry belies the theory that Puritans were averse to those things. Daly's primary explanation for the symbolic fact, contra the figureless theory, is that Puritans had a great deal of faith in the sensible world as a comprehensible metaphor for their incomprehensible God. The world was, therefore, itself symbolic and its beauties were symbolic of the beauties of God.

Daly's point is convincingly taken and works well when applied to two of the three poets he discusses in detail—Bradstreet and Wigglesworth. When he discusses Taylor, however, he is less than persuasive. In keeping with two earlier essays, "Edward Taylor: A Note on Visual Imagery" (*EAL*, 1973) by Jeff Hammond and Thomas M. Davis, and "The Imagination of Death in the Poetry of Philip Pain, Edward Taylor, and George Herbert" (*SLitI*, 1976) by Donald E. Stanford, Daly focuses on Taylor's view of death as positive, in that it serves as an "intersection of this life and the next and, for the saint, of earth and heaven." His examples from Taylor's poetry, however, are too often atypical and even so, strain the point that death, since it symbolically bridges the gap between this world and the next, is a comforting or positive aspect of the sensible world. It cannot be disputed that Taylor's poetry is resplendent with symbolism and sensuous imagery, but Taylor so overwhelmingly denied the adequacy of his lush metaphors that he seems to be stressing everywhere the antithetical qualities of the visible human world and the invisible divine one. Daly's observations about Taylor's view of death may be accurate, but those views alone are not sufficient to claim that Taylor's perception of the sensible world in general was positive. Notwithstanding, Daly's ideas about Puritan aesthetics are refreshing and most provocative.

The final explanation for Taylor's seemingly anomalous poems has been primarily biographical. Donald E. Stanford, not persuaded by these hints of unorthodoxy, and maintaining that orthodoxy is not an aesthetic or poetic question, but strictly a doctrinal one, argued vigorously in his dissertation that Taylor was a thoroughly orthodox Calvinist and not a deviant New England covenant theologian. But that has never been argued in print. More to the point was his description of Taylor's "orthodoxy" in the long-lasting argument with Solomon Stoddard, especially as the issues are encountered in Taylor's *Meditations* 2: 102–11. Stanford mentions the disagreement with the Johnson-Miller Covenant/Calvinist distinction, but does not press it, in "Edward Taylor and the Lord's Supper" (*AL*, May 1955). Taylor's orthodoxy, both theological and ecclesiastical, in this running battle with Stoddard, is discussed in much greater detail in Grabo's *Edward Taylor*, "Edward Taylor on the Lord's Supper," and the introduction and notes to *Edward Taylor's Treatise Concerning the Lord's Supper*. But Thomas M. Davis defines Taylor's doctrinal history more solidly and accurately than others in his fine "Introduction" to Volume Two of Davis and Davis, *The Unpublished Writings* (1981), *Edward Taylor vs. Solomon Stoddard*.

In "Catholic Tradition, Puritan Literature, and Edward Taylor" (*PMASAL*, 1960), Grabo also makes a case for the Puritan acceptance of originally Catholic devotional practices, suggesting that Taylor's contemporaries would not have been as surprised or shocked by his performance as earlier critics supposed. But the weakest point in this argument, and the strongest for the proponents of Taylor's heterodoxy, whether doctrinal or poetic, was Taylor's prohibition of the publication of his poems. This prohibition was reported in a letter written in 1851 by Taylor's great grandson Henry Wyllys Taylor, a New York judge, to William B. Sprague who was then collecting information for his *Annals of the American*

Pulpit, which appeared in 1857. Edward Taylor, reported the judge, previous to his death "enjoined it upon his heirs never to publish any of his writings." The remark was repeated in Sprague's entry for Edward Taylor, and echoed again in John L. Sibley's *Biographical Sketches of Graduates of Harvard College*, vol. 2 (Cambridge, Mass., 1881). When Johnson announced and published his selections of Taylor's poetry in 1937 and 1939, he carefully repeated Sibley's phrasing, that Taylor "gave orders that his heirs should never publish any of his writings." And when S. Foster Damon reviewed Johnson's *Poetical Works* in *NEQ* (Dec. 1939), he remarked that Taylor's "large library contained a manuscript volume of his poems, the publication of which he forbade."

Thus began to form a kind of mystery—why did Taylor forbid the publication of his poems? While the "fact" of his injunction (now particularized to cover only the poetry) received constant reinforcement in anthologies, in critical essays, and in historical reviews, its significance took a new turn after Richard D. Altick popularized the story of the recovery of Taylor's poetry in *The Scholar Adventurers* (New York, 1950), and Perry Miller insinuated that Taylor must have had something to hide by keeping his lyrics "secretive" (*The New England Mind: From Colony to Province*). He asserts this interpretation most strongly in the introduction to Taylor in his anthology, *The American Puritans: Their Prose and Poetry* (New York, 1956). Quietly contesting this interpretation, Stanford nonetheless recorded in his 1960 edition of the *Poems* that "Taylor did not publish his poems and he forbade his heirs to publish them," and Grabo, returning to the language reported in Sprague and Johnson, reminded readers of *Edward Taylor* (1961) that "actually Taylor forbade the publication of any of his writing, though this fact tends to be overlooked by critics wishing to further the myth that Taylor's poetry would have been considered evil by his contemporaries."

But not everyone was fooled. Shortly after Emmy Shepard in "Edward Taylor's Injunction Against Publication" (*AL*, Jan. 1962) suggested that perhaps Taylor's motive in forbidding publication "was simple, genuine humility, touched by self-respect and pride in his work and perhaps—lightly—by the perversity of the aged," Francis Murphy pointed out that curiously "no questions have ever been raised concerning the basis of authority for this controversy." Murphy declares flatly and convincingly, in "Edward Taylor's Attitude Toward Publication: A Question Concerning Authority" (*AL*, Nov. 1962), that "there is no documentary evidence whatsoever regarding Edward Taylor's final intention toward his work. Henry Taylor's remark can only be based on some family tradition, and whether it grew up early or late, we shall never know. The major point to be made is that in the absence of any documentary evidence all serious consideration of this question is impossible." So ended a regrettable, but not entirely useless controversy.

CRITICISM

The pattern Taylor criticism has assumed in its four decades since the publication of Johnson's *Poetical Works* is almost suspiciously pat. Each decade seems dominated by a different kind of interest or method, partly perhaps a reflection of critical interests and fads in literary criticism, but more probably a reflection of the primary problem of characterizing, describing, indeed identifying this rare poet in a poetic desert. What primarily distinguished criticism of the forties from that of the fifties and sixties was the critical context that then seemed most relevant to and instructive regarding Taylor's poetry. In the forties the most relevant context seemed to be poetic history, and critics pointed to Taylor's dependence upon or similarities with various poetic traditions — Metaphysical, Baroque, the medieval morality plays, or a variety of Greek and Roman classics. The fifties saw a definite shift in emphasis. It began with Sidney Lind's protest that Taylor did not deserve the dignity the comparisons of the forties implied because of his religious culture, and was reinforced by Roy Harvey Pearce's insistence that Taylor's poetic accomplishment must be understood and measured by his own Puritan culture. Criticism in this decade addressed the questions of Taylor's theological and intellectual background with increased emphasis, without entirely ignoring contextual questions raised by the first decade of Taylor critics. At the end of this decade, Donald E. Stanford's ample edition of the *Poems* (1960) provided a basis for renewed and deeper consideration of both the poetic and intellectual traditions to which Taylor's poetry belongs, but more important, turned attention to the poetic qualities of the poems themselves. The sixties therefore saw an increasing interest in the explication of single poems, in the details of Taylor's poetic technique, and in the quality of his poetic accomplishment. And in the seventies and early eighties, Taylor has come into his own and been accepted as an important figure in American literary history. The past decade has seen two book-length critical studies, a three-volume edition of the unpublished writings and inclusion in larger thematic studies of both American and British writers for Edward Taylor. The movement since 1939 has been, then — and not surprisingly — from understanding to evaluation to acceptance.

Poetic Traditions

All Taylor criticism has deepened, without changing the essential contours of Thomas H. Johnson's earliest appraisals. Johnson, in "Edward

Taylor: A Puritan 'Sacred Poet,'" maintained from the beginning that Taylor was a completely orthodox New England Puritan who was also "a poet of real, not merely historic, importance"; that he was "not indifferent to poetry as an art"; and that if one must seek "parallels or analogues for Taylor's verse," one will find them naturally in the seventeenth-century conceitists, especially Herbert, Quarles, and Crashaw. With the kind of overstatement that has marked Taylor criticism until very recently, the publishers of *Poetical Works* predicted in 1939 that "a re-evaluation of early American letters will be made in the light of this publication." In 1966, when the *Poetical Works* was reissued, Johnson could quite rightly say, "Indeed it is no exaggeration to say that the twentieth-century reassessment of Puritanism, especially in those aspects which reveal the Puritan's feeling for beauty in his hungry search for Heaven, has been given impetus by the appearance of Taylor's poetry."

Austin Warren, with deft analysis and informed perceptions, began the history of modifications that Johnson's judgments would undergo for forty years. In "Edward Taylor's Poetry: Colonial Baroque" (*KR*, Summer 1941), Warren argued that Taylor's verse belongs to the seventeenth-century tradition that would have been described as "false wit" by late seventeenth-century critics such as Addison. Metaphysical in neither the cosmic sense of Du Bartas nor the psychological sense of Donne, it nonetheless performed the "humble baroque ingenuities" that other New England poetasters found so attractive. A poet of wit whose chief instrument was "the homely conceit," Taylor was largely unaware of the intellectual implications of his method, associating his devices, "in baroque fashion, about surprises." The effects, illustrated in Taylor's "Meditation Eight" and "The Reflexion"— both analyzed very sensitively — may be amateurish, but still powerful, though Warren's final judgment is that "Taylor is sometimes a neat little artisan but more often an unsteady enthusiast, a naïve original, an intermittently inspired Primitive." Slightly altered, this essay was reprinted as "Edward Taylor" in Warren's *Rage for Order* (Ann Arbor, Mich., 1948).

Wallace Cable Brown disagreed sharply with Warren, arguing that at his best Taylor went beyond baroque devices "and became a full-fledged, if minor, metaphysical poet" in "Edward Taylor: An American 'Metaphysical'" (*AL*, Nov. 1944). He supported this argument by tracing a variety of characteristics Taylor's poetry shared with Donne's and Herbert's: kinds of metrical roughness, syntactic complexity, wit, heterogeneous ideas, "the peculiar effect on the imagination of the great distances between focal points of the imagery," the "sensuous apprehension of thought," and the tight logical structure or "intellectuality in the presence of strong personal emotion." Brown concludes that with "the exception of tight logical structure, which he does not always manage to achieve, Taylor's work exhibits all the 'earmarks' (as he himself would say) of the metaphysical esthetic."

In *The First Century of New England Verse*, printed originally in *PAAS* (Oct. 1943) and issued the following year under separate cover (Worcester, Mass., 1944), Harold S. Jantz rejected Brown's characterization in favor of Warren's: "Taylor employs his treasure of images in a typically late Baroque manner: lavishly but purposefully and consequentially, in an ordered, well-disposed intricacy." But Jantz's remarks are general rather than analytical, proceeding in part from the larger purpose of his study and in part from his unwillingness to grant so much to Taylor's poetic quality or significance as was at least implied by earlier critics.

Undaunted by Jantz's cautious approach, two writers discovered somewhat more remote literary alliances in the same issue of *American Literature* (Mar. 1946). Nathalia Wright, beginning by observing the "flair for drama" that runs through all of Taylor's verse, developed one set of parallels in "The Morality Tradition in the Poetry of Edward Taylor." She focuses on *Gods Determinations* to demonstrate points in common with four well-known morality plays: the *Coventry XI* pageant, the *Castle of Perseverance*, *Mary Magdalen*, and *Wisdom*. Plot, stock themes, hints of costuming, the use of various verse forms, allegorical devices, and tricks of characterization all contribute to the medieval character of Taylor's poem. Professor Wright concludes: "Taylor may thus have been led to the morality tradition, not by one, but by a combination of influences; a keen dramatic sense, a congeniality with the thought of the Middle Ages, and long habits of theological speculation." Early in her essay, however, distinguishing Taylor from other Renaissance poets who used morality elements, she remarks that Taylor "lacks the classical background upon which they constantly drew." But Willie T. Weathers maintains that "Miss Wright is clearly mistaken" about this, in "Edward Taylor, Hellenistic Puritan." Pointing to the six volumes of classical poetry in Taylor's library, Professor Weathers compiles a series of "cursory findings" revealing Taylor's debt to Theocritan song-contests and bits and passages that seem to owe their inspiration to Greek and Latin sources. The analogies become very tenuous, however, as the crippled man of *Gods Determinations* suggests "the hero of Oedipus," or Taylor's line, "As Spot barks back the sheep again," prompts the interpretation that "Spot is obviously the 'flock-dog' often mentioned in Theocritan pastorals, and by one shepherd given the name 'White-Tail.'"

Intellectual and Theological Traditions

Sidney E. Lind, obviously irked by the amount of critical attention paid Taylor, "as though he were a poet of high merit whose resurrection has added significantly to the cultural hoard of America," argued to the contrary, in "Edward Taylor: A Revaluation" (*AL*, Dec. 1948), that "he is at best a mediocre poet, as he was doomed to be, whatever his inherent poetic gifts, by reason of his station in life." Lind's point is that New England Puritan culture — a "highly codified theologico-cultural system" fully and accurately described by Perry Miller's *New England Mind* — provided too narrow a basis for the production of "sustained passages of real beauty" or for "the flawless blending of communication and art." Taylor only occasionally lapsed from the Puritan standards of doctrinal primacy, utility, and intelligibility, into poetry, and the criticism that ignores the Puritan limits of Taylor's culture is an exercise in empty rhetoric.

Despite Lind's questionable assumptions regarding the nature of Puritan culture, his insistence that Taylor must be related to it did not go unattended. Without sharing Lind's evaluation of Taylor's poetic worth, Roy Harvey Pearce in "Edward Taylor: The Poet as Puritan" (*NEQ*, Mar. 1950) agreed that critics had been reluctant to read Taylor simply as a colonial poet. For Pearce this meant that Taylor's culture limited his achievement to "one of discovery, most often the discovery of God-informed unity in man's experience in and of his world. Whatever struggle is involved in making such a discovery, however, is not in the poem; it is external, anterior to the poem." Taylor's method and purpose are therefore characterized as essentially Ramistic. This Pearce demonstrates in comments upon "Huswifery," "Meditation Six," *Gods Determinations*, and "Meditation Eight." All show that "for Taylor technique is little or nothing," and that the poetry of discovery is essentially undramatic. The Puritan culture that made his poetry what it is "indeed, cut Taylor down (or should one say, built Taylor up?) to its size. However adequate that culture might have been for major religious experience, it was yet inadequate for major poetry; for it allowed for little play of the individual will — in the last analysis for little real human drama." But however much Pearce and Lind agreed, one senses none of Lind's superficial assumptions about New England Puritanism and its desiderata in Pearce's remarks, which were essentially reprinted in Pearce's *The Continuity of American Poetry* (Princeton, 1961).

Kenneth Murdock's treatment of Taylor in "A Little Recreation of Poetry," in *Literature & Theology in Colonial New England*, was sympathetic, but like Jantz's, cautious in its claims, and did not much advance critical discriminations already made, although it also treated Taylor primarily in terms of his colonial culture. But Herbert Blau's "Heaven's Sugar Cake: Theology and Imagery in the Poetry of Edward Taylor" (*NEQ*, Sept. 1953) brought a new sensibility to bear upon Taylor's poems, and one that focused upon his theology. Blau believed that at his best Taylor was the equal of Donne and Crashaw, but when locked (as Pearce had pointed out) in the game of "discovery," his search for signs of grace often led him poetically astray. Blau shows that Taylor profoundly accepted a Calvinist paradox that allowed him to argue as if repentance were possible despite the doctrine of absolute predestination. Rejecting *Gods Determinations* as "fairly tedious, inconsistent theologically, and neither a good narrative nor a good *débat*," Blau concentrates upon the *Meditations* and analyzes their diction, prosody, and syntax in greater depth and with a finer eye for detail than any previous critic. His comparisons range from Gascoigne and Greville through Donne, Herbert, and the other metaphysicals to Blake, Dickinson, T. S. Eliot, and Ezra Pound — both unexpectedly and justly. Blau is especially sharp-sighted in defining and illustrating Taylor's most persistent fault-lapses in taste and decorum.

The following year, Willie T. Weathers again argued for Taylor's Classicism, but this time centered on Taylor's relationships with seventeenth-century Platonists who were also eminent theologians, in "Edward Taylor and the Cambridge Platonists." Weathers points to the exceptional lapses from colonial Puritanism that Lind had acknowledged, but sees them as manifestations of Taylor's "personal Platonism," which opened for him mystical, erotic, aesthetic, and imaginative possibilities that the public doctrines of Puritanism seemed to deny. Weathers distinguishes at length this liberal, Platonic temperament from the dominant authoritarian and scholastic one, defining seven precise areas in which Neoplatonism differed from orthodox Puritanism — in each of which Taylor sides with the Neoplatonists. But Weathers misreads *Gods Determinations* — from which the bulk of her evidence comes — rather badly. Evidence not fully available when she wrote disproves every major point, indicating that what she calls Taylor's "ingenuity" is rather her own. But to the extent that Platonic thought and imagery permeated Renaissance religious writing and were thus available to Taylor, these speculations are very suggestive and deserve reexamination in the light of subsequent findings.

Donald E. Stanford pulled both Blau and Weathers back to earth by explaining that Taylor's mystical response to the Lord's Supper was perfectly orthodox in Puritan terms, in "Edward Taylor and the Lord's Supper." Regrettably, Mindele Black seems not to have availed herself of Stanford's work; if she had, her otherwise excellent "Edward Taylor: Heaven's Sugar Cake" (*NEQ*, June 1956) would have been even better. Black begins by pointing out Taylor's affinity with pre-Restoration English poets — particularly Herbert — as somewhat inconsistent, but reasons that "the seeming inconsistency lies not so much in Taylor himself as in the devotional tradition to which he belongs." That tradition Black identifies primarily with the sacramental writings of Increase Mather, Thomas Doolittle, and Samuel Willard, agreeing with E. I. Watkin that "this side of Puritan devotion, as opposed to the theological, was not a genuine Protestant development but an influx of direct or indirect borrowings from

Catholic spirituality." This view permits her acceptance of Taylor's proximity to Herbert and Crashaw, despite their differences theologically, and she bolsters her argument with quotations from Taylor's *Christographia* sermons. But again this is a case of intuition exceeding careful reading: Black assumes, for example, that *Gods Determinations* is, like Wigglesworth's *Day of Doom*, about Judgment Day. Nonetheless, Mindele Black distinctly narrowed the circle of relevant traditions, and brought the decade's search for intellectual contexts within appropriate limits.

Notes and articles of a historical or explicatory nature were published before the decade ended, but few were of any critical significance. In the year 1960 an even dozen articles and reviews appeared, mostly occasioned by the publication of Stanford's edition of the *Poems*, opening a new era of Taylor criticism.

The Poetry Itself

The most important critical essay of 1960 was Louis L. Martz's foreword to the *Poems*. In *The Poetry of Meditation* (New Haven, Conn., 1954), Professor Martz had provided the rationale behind Mindele Black's argument for a specific devotional tradition. Martz argued that the devotional methods of Ignatius of Loyola, modified by later Jesuits, provided models first for Anglican adaptation in the work of Joseph Hall and then for adaptation by Presbyterian and Independent churchmen through Richard Baxter's *Saints Everlasting Rest*. Moreover, he demonstrated most persuasively that Donne, Herbert, and Crashaw, among others, showed the effects of formal Ignatian meditation in their poems, and mentioned Taylor in passing. In the foreword, therefore, it is no accident that Taylor is closely related to the "metaphysical" poets, particularly Herbert, and that the meditative tradition is peculiarly appropriate for Taylor: "In Baxter's arguments for the use of sensory images in meditation we have, I believe, the grounds of justification for Taylor's bold and often unseemly use of common imagery." Often with very particular and acute examples and analytical comments, Martz accentuates the metaphysical-meditational qualities of Taylor's verse.

Norman S. Grabo was the most enthusiastic follower of Martz's suggestions in "Catholic Tradition, Puritan Literature, and Edward Taylor," arguing like Mindele Black that Taylor's contemporaries were not at all averse to Catholic devotional practices and, like Martz, that the method of Ignatian meditation was known to them and favored by some of them. In 1961 Grabo expanded the implications of this principle into his book-length survey of Taylor's work, *Edward Taylor*. There Grabo surveys Taylor's active life and characterizes his inward or contemplative life as recorded in his writings to conclude that Taylor was essentially a mystic, that his meditative procedures reflect the various stages of Western Christian mysticism while remaining thoroughly within the orthodox teaching of New England Calvinism, and that his poetry was the natural result of his mysticism. This is demonstrated by showing the extent to which Taylor's sacramental preaching — especially in the *Christographia* sermons for which there are corresponding meditations — determined the structure, themes, images, and general development of his poems. Two final chapters consider the early poems as Taylor's apprenticeship to poetry, and the *Preparatory Meditations* and *Gods Determinations* as his major accomplishments. The questions raised about Taylor's art are not particularly new, but the scope of the book allows for more particular analyses of Taylor's techniques and significance than had been afforded earlier. Grabo's emphasis upon Taylor's personal mysticism has proved the most objectionable and least tenable part of the study.

Following Grabo's book, several good general definitions of Taylor's accomplishment were published, the best being Donald E. Stanford's introduction to the second edition of the *Poems* and his pamphlet, *Edward Taylor*, both of which penetrate deeper into the area of Taylor's own reading. Grabo's introduction and explanatory notes to *Edward Taylor's Christographia* contribute to this general intellectual history and explicate in detail the thesis that Taylor's *Preparatory Meditations* are determined by his sacrament-day sermons. Likewise, his introduction and notes to *Edward Taylor's Treatise Concerning the Lord's Supper* explore Taylor's use of theological and ecclesiastical polemics as they relate to the poems, locating Taylor's sacramentalism in a literary-theological tradition that runs from Shepard to Edwards and seeks to determine the extent to which a man's spiritual condition may be judged from his observable behavior. Several essays in the sixties explore these implications.

But the major change in Taylor criticism since 1960 has been an intensified examination of particular poems or devices, by asking questions narrower in scope and pursuing them more deeply, while at the same time attending to the poetic surface more exactly than before. William R. Manierre II discusses the presence and significance of "polyptotonic play," in "Verbal Patterns in the Poetry of Edward Taylor" (*CE*, Jan. 1962), focusing on the effectiveness of *ploce* and *polyptoton* in the "Preface" to *Gods Determinations*. John Clendenning, arguing that "We now need a deepened understanding of particular poems, a task which few of Taylor's critics have adequately attempted," provides a close reading of "The Reflexion," tracing the four basic images that control the poem — food, light, flowers, and sex — in "Piety and Imagery in Edward Taylor's 'The Reflexion'" (*AQ*, Summer 1964). And Norman S. Grabo explores the meaning of Taylor's "Huswifery" by examining the use of spinning, weaving, and clothing imagery throughout his poetry and prose in "Edward Taylor's Spiritual Huswifery" (*PMLA*, Dec. 1964).

With a wholly different approach, Donald Junkins tests previous critical generalizations by a careful look at Taylor's manuscript for indications of his artistry. In "Edward Taylor's Revisions," he concludes that "all the evidence shows that he wrote, re-wrote, crossed out, and incorporated, that he revised painstakingly, and that his process was artistically sound." This sense of Taylor's artistic self-consciousness is also supported by Charles W. Mignon's "Diction in Edward Taylor's 'Preparatory Meditations'" (AS, Dec. 1966) which analyzes Taylor's "difficult words"— obsolete, dialect, Americanisms, and special terms. Mignon shows that Taylor's "Meditations have a higher incidence of difficult words per page than any random sampling selected from the published verse of Taylor's contemporaries of New England," suggesting that this relative obscurity substantiates Taylor's privateness and "reflects Taylor's desire to write for no one but himself."

Somewhat more conventional is the series of articles on Taylor's images that appeared around mid-decade. Cecilia Halbert discussed "Tree of Life Imagery in the Poetry of Edward Taylor" (AL, Mar. 1966). Although it is misinformed, the main value of this discussion is that it provoked Ursula Brumm to establish the theological tradition of that image as Taylor would most probably have known and used it, in "The 'Tree of Life' in Edward Taylor's Meditations" (EAL, Fall 1968), a translation of her earlier article cited below, and one of the more sophisticated contributions to Taylor scholarship in recent years. Thomas Werge emphasizes the Puritan use of this image in "The Tree of Life in Edward Taylor's Poetry: The Sources of a Puritan Image" (EAL, Winter 1968–69), but though he usefully associates Thomas Shepard and Jonathan Edwards with the image, he does not avail himself of Brumm's more thoroughgoing and suggestive discussion. Werge does underline Taylor's own reading, however, and that is likewise the emphasis of Jean L. Thomas's "Drama and Doctrine in Gods Determinations" (AL, Jan. 1965), particularly his reading in homiletic and devotional literature. Thomas E. Johnston, Jr., dwells on yet another line of devotional imagery in "Edward Taylor: An American Emblematist" (EAL, Winter 1968–69).

Inevitably, emphasis upon Taylor's own reading as a source for ideas and images leads away from the poetry and towards intellectual history. Stephen Fender, a British scholar, in "Edward Taylor and 'The Application of Redemption'" (MLR, July 1964), emphasizes the parallel aspects of Taylor's poetic-meditative method and that developed by Thomas Hooker. Robert M. Benton challenges Grabo's interpretation that the poems followed the sermons in composition and therefore developed the "doctrine" of the sermons rather than the scriptural texts by showing how Meditations II:47 and II:43 use images from the scriptural contexts rather than from the sermons, in "Edward Taylor's Use of His Text" (AL, Mar.

1967). And Allen Richard Penner argues that, understood in terms of Taylor's theology and method, "Meditation One" escapes the facile critical descriptions of early Taylor critics. We must, Penner says in "Edward Taylor's Meditation One" (*AL*, May 1967), "re-create as well as we are able the intensity and significance of the theology which inspired those meditations," in order to appreciate them fully. But this line of inquiry is essentially a continuation of the criticism of the fifties, though in many respects more particular.

Another continuation is evident in the foreign attention paid to Taylor. General introductions to Taylor have appeared in Italy, Germany, and Japan. Biancamaria Tedeschini-Lalli's introduction to what was then known of Taylor appeared in *Studi Americani*, 1956. Very like it, but better informed, is Ken Akiyama's in *Studies in Humanities* (Doshisha University, 1963). And there are signs of appreciation of Taylor's mysticism by Indian scholars. But it is so far only in Germany that Taylor has received serious critical examination. The general and derivative comments in Henry Lüdeke's *Geschichte der amerikanischen Literatur* (Bern, 1954) and Alfred Weber's review of Stanford's edition of the *Poems* (*JA*, 1962) only prepared the way for the intensive studies of Ursula Brumm and Peter Nicolaisen. Brumm devotes a chapter to Taylor in her very well received *Die religiöse Typologie im amerikanischen Denken* (Leiden, 1963), entitled "Edward Taylor's Meditationen über das Abendmahl" (that is, on the Lord's Supper), in which she analyzes Taylor's use of types, emblems, signs, and metaphors to place him in a tradition that reaches through Jonathan Edwards to Emerson and thus into the main tradition of American writing through Faulkner. In "Der 'Baum des Lebens' in den Meditationen Edward Taylors" (*JA*, 1967) Brumm presents the background to Taylor's Tree of Life imagery as developed in English a year later. Both studies emphasize Taylor's reliance on the Bible and on traditional ways of explicating and applying biblical material.

Somewhat different is Peter Nicolaisen's excellent monograph on Taylor's imagery, *Die Bildlichkeit in der Dichtung Edward Taylors* (Neumünster, 1966). Nicolaisen's is the first printed examination of this most irresistible aspect of Taylor's art. American dissertations by Thomas Wack, Elizabeth Wiley, and Emma L. Shepard at the beginning of the decade elaborately categorized and analyzed Taylor's images, but Nicolaisen goes beyond such studies by fitting his analysis to a controlling thesis—that Taylor uses images, especially images of amplification, to support his sense that the attempt of the human understanding and imagination to comprehend God is doomed to failure. Thus the poems do not express achieved union of man and God but only testify to its desirable impossibility. Nicolaisen emphasizes the biblical sources of Taylor's imagery and minimizes origins in Taylor's personal experience, expecially in the *Pre-*

paratory Meditations, using the Anglican Herbert as a foil to help define the peculiar nature of Taylor's art. A good five-page English abstract declares the general thesis at the end of the book.

Since mid-decade, commentary has been increasingly general. Acknowledging that Taylor's poems do indeed work, critics seek to explain more exactly just how they do so. Clark Griffith, in "Edward Taylor and the Momentum of Metaphor" (*ELH*, Dec. 1966), maintains in comments on "Meditation Eight," "Huswifery," and the "Preface," that Taylor's poems move from allegorical, rational images and tropes to increasingly idiosyncratic conceits, thereby generating the energy that is so striking in the poems. Peter Force, on the other hand, in "Edward Taylor as a Poet" (*NEQ*, Sept. 1966), contends that it is exactly at those points of potential hindrance to appreciation of Taylor's poetry that the elevating force of poems frequently originates. He illustrates with examples of troubling diction, punctuation, syntax, sound-sense relationships, imagery, and structure.

A good number of quite competent studies appeared between 1967 and 1970, especially in the pages of *EAL*, but three essays of very recent vintage seem to epitomize the direction of Taylor studies in the sixties, and perhaps to suggest the direction of studies to come. With an uncommonly rich knowledge of all of Taylor's work and previous Taylor criticism, E. F. Carlisle writes very elegantly of "The Puritan Structure of Edward Taylor's Poetry" (*AQ*, Summer 1968). Carlisle reasons that behind, or beneath the evident form of Taylor's sermons and poems there is a personalized and intense "deep form" determined by Taylor's personal response to his Puritan faith. Like several previous critics, he sees the crucial root of Taylor's work in a "fundamental sense of vast difference" between the world of human experience and the transcendent realm of godly ideals. But Carlisle sees four "formal"— in a sense structural — principles inherent in this sense and basic to the movement of several poems, including the "Prologue," Meditation I: 6, Meditation II: 46, and "Huswifery." These principles of contrast, ascension, question-and-answer, and metaphor or symbol both clarify the difference between the public and private qualities of Edward Taylor's verse, and bring "the Puritan minister, man and poet together in the underlying structure of the poetry." Charles Mignon's similar interest in Taylor's privateness also finds support in the "Prologue," "The Reflexion," and Meditation II:77, in "Edward Taylor's *Preparatory Meditations*: A Decorum of Imperfection" (*PMLA*, Oct. 1968). Like Carlisle, Mignon sees the vast disparity between man's fallen condition and his high poetic purpose at the root of Taylor's aesthetic, which first diminishes man by meiosis and then amplifies God by hyperbole drawn from the scriptures. Mignon concludes that "Taylor has a decorum peculiar to himself with subjects recognizable in their general outlines as Puritan: the ineffectiveness of fallen rhetoric itself, and the impossibility of successfully praising God with this rhetoric." Coincidentally, the same subject occupies Donald Junkins in "'Should Stars Wooe Lobster Claws?': A Study of Edward Taylor's Poetic Practice and Theory" (*EAL*, Fall 1968). Junkins argues that Taylor's anguished sense of his own spiritual imperfections is embodied in his numerous images of writing. Poetry is thus a metaphor of his spiritual condition, especially clear in images of self-abasement cast as criticism of his own poetic incompetence: "The poem, then, is the medium through which he experiences both art and religion." Faith and poetic intention are indistinguishably intertwined in what Junkins calls a "religio-Aesthetic process," delineating an original sense of the relationship of religion and art in Taylor's work. The focus of examination in these three essays, one notes, is very similar to Nicolaisen's thesis, and all four address with varying degrees of consciousness the challenge issued by Sidney Lind in 1948 to put Taylor into the context of his Puritanism — not, however, by going to secondhand intellectual history, but by examining the dynamics of the poems themselves.

By the early seventies, Taylor studies had reached a fairly complicated and postadolescent, if not entirely mature, state. The Taylor issue of *EAL* (Winter, 1969) testified to the growing interest and intensity of Taylor criticism; publication of Gene Russell's concordance to the poems promised new directions for critical energies; and the appearance of two extensive bibliographic studies provided scholars with maps to the territory. Of course some of the earlier interests continued. Though considerably fewer in number, discussions of individual poems, for example, were offered throughout the seventies, including several commentaries on frequently anthologized "Miscellaneous" poems as well as individual meditations.

Notable among more general criticism was Karen Rowe's "Sacred or Profane? Edward Taylor's Meditations on the Canticles" (*MP*, 1974), which points out that many problematic images in Taylor's poems come directly from the Canticles, and furthermore that the meditations change during Taylor's life from being derivative of Biblical and exegetical sources to more personal statements of his hope for redemption. A similar point about the derivation of Taylor's imagery is made in Michael Schuldiner's "Edward Taylor's 'Problematic' Imagery" (*EAL*, 1978).

In addition to discussions of miscellaneous poems and meditations, other issues resurfaced in the seventies. The altercation between Taylor and Stoddard is addressed in James Barbour's "The Prose Context of Edward Taylor's Anti-Stoddard Meditations" (*EAL*, 1975), which provides a very useful survey of Taylor's prose over a thirty-year period, and points out that the poet's thought during that time could consistently predict his later position against Stoddard. David L. Parker, "Edward Taylor's Preparationism: A New Perspective on the Taylor-Stoddard Controversy" (*EAL*,

1976/77), defines "preparationism" as the process by which man readies himself to receive grace or be admitted to the Lord's Supper. He uses various poetic, epistolary, doctrinaire, and sermonic sources to compare Stoddard and Taylor on what is involved in "proper" preparation. The surprising upshot is that Taylor proves the more liberal cleric, in that for him all actions, not just the sacrament, were preparation; if pious, they would eventually lead to a decision for election. Stoddard, on the other hand, would not be pinned down on the relationship between preparation and any ultimate moment of conversion, so Taylor's view, which allowed for good works to play some part in conversion, gave more hope to the sinful than Stoddard's.

Another essay germane to past issues is Kathleen Blake's "Edward Taylor's Protestant Poetic: Nontransubstantiating Metaphor" (*AL*, 1971), which indirectly addresses the Catholic vs. Protestant controversy surrounding Taylor. Although Blake does not specifically mention the traditional dispute, her theory—that for Protestants the metaphoric nature of the Sacrament justifies the use of metaphor in general, while the literal Catholic teaching offers no such aesthetic implications—provides good evidence for those arguing for Taylor's orthodoxy. Norman Grabo attempts to extend the intellectual bases of Taylor's lyricism in "Puritan Devotion and American Literary History" in *Themes and Directions in American Literature*, ed. Ray B. Browne and Donald Pizer (Lafayette, Ind., 1969), and the question is deepened immeasurably in the very fine *Moral Philosophy at Seventeenth-Century Harvard* by Norman Fiering (Chapel Hill, N.C., 1981). Fiering provides an indispensable guide to Taylor's mind without once mentioning Taylor.

One last essay contributing to earlier issues deserves acknowledgment: Alan B. Howard's "The World as Emblem: Language and Vision in the Poetry of Edward Taylor" (*AL*, 1972) argues that Taylor's poetry is more emblematic than metaphysical, as many previous scholars had contended, and that its emblematic nature limits its success as poetry.

Also during the seventies, essays on Taylor continued to appear in collections of offerings on early American literature. Besides Robert Daly's *God's Altar*, discussed previously, Donald Stanford's essay, "Edward Taylor," appeared in *Major Writers of Early American Literature*, edited by Everett H. Emerson (Madison, Wis., 1971). This is a general discussion of Taylor's work that includes information on the *Preparatory Meditations, Gods Determinations*, and several critical and biographical issues. Two essays appeared in the collection, *Discoveries and Considerations: Essays on Early American Literature and Aesthetics Presented to Harold Jantz* (Albany, N.Y., 1976), edited by Calvin Israel. The first article, "American Baroque: Three Representative Poets" is by Jantz himself, and traces baroque elements in Fiske, Johnson, and Taylor. The second article, "Edward Taylor's 'A Fig for Thee Oh! Death!'" by Arthur Forstater, explores several issues related to Taylor's imagery in the poem, but most notably discusses the interaction between death and sex images.

Three essays on Taylor appeared in the most significant collection of the seventies, *Typology and Early American Literature*, edited by Sacvan Bercovitch (Amherst, 1972), inspired by the growing awareness of the importance of typology in seventeenth-century literary symbolism, and abetted by the translation of Ursula Brumm's seminal study of 1963, now available as *American Thought and Religious Typology* (New Brunswick, N.J., 1970). The first, Robert Reiter's "Poetry and Doctrine in Edward Taylor's *Preparatory Meditations*, Series 2, 1–30," discusses the problems Taylor faced in writing successful poetry on so rigid a subject as what Reiter concludes is a series of typological topics. The second essay, Karl Keller's "'The World Slickt up in Types': Edward Taylor as a Version of Emerson," argues that Taylor's use of wit "is not mere play with types, but serious delight in the relationships that language gives to reality . . . Taylor seems, like Emerson, to have apprehended words as signs of spiritual facts." The last article on Taylor in this collection is Ursula Brumm's "Edward Taylor and the Poetic Use of Religious Imagery." Here Brumm uses an extended analysis of "Meditation I, 10" to demonstrate that for Taylor "typological parallels link the best in all creation to the Godhead." This use of typology goes beyond merely employing traditional Biblical types and anti-types and, according to Brumm, provides an essential element of Taylor's thought and poetic craft. These essays appeared before Mignon's discovery of Taylor's sermons "Upon the Types." One can expect their speculations to be clinched and modified by Mignon's edition.

One of the most prevalent critical issues of the seventies centered on Taylor's use of language and metaphor as subject matter in his poetry — Taylor's writing about writing and his inclination to use figurative language declaratively. Other image studies take a different approach. Cheryl Oreovicz's "Edward Taylor and the Alchemy of Grace" (*SCN*, 1976), for example, is an image study, but merely points out the occurrence of alchemical images. Gene Russell's "Dialectical and Phonetic Features of Edward Taylor's Rhyme" (*AL*, 1971), while most informative, is concerned entirely with linguistic features of Taylor's work. But another image study, Sibyl Jacobson's "Image Patterns in Edward Taylor: Prayer and Proof" (*CP*, 1973), points out that the seemingly inconsistent images, if seen as reflecting the persona's relationship to Christ, are not inconsistent at all. Such an emphasis on the interrelationship between the poet, persona, poem, and imagery is characteristic of this recent critical direction in Taylor studies.

A clearer example is Michael D. Reed's "Edward Taylor's Poetry: Puritan Structure and Form" (*AL*, 1974), in which Reed points out that both the disparate images of Taylor's conceits and the hypothetical mode of most of the *Meditations* are used purposefully to make the declarative point that the chasm between man and God cannot be bridged. But the most sophisticated essay concerned with Taylor's self-referential use of metaphor and language is Michael North's "Edward Taylor's Metaphors of Promise" (*AL*, 1979). Here North claims that Taylor's recognition of the metaphoric nature of the Lord's Supper, as symbolic of God's promise of salvation and as a physical manifestation of spiritual grace, leads him to use the notion of metaphor as a paradigm for his poetry. The discovery and use of metaphoric significance in common things is, for Taylor, a Godcraft. Such a reading of Taylor explains many of the earthy metaphors in the *Meditations* and would further inform his fascination with systems of metaphor like typology.

This critical emphasis may be a subtle response to recent trends in literary criticism, reflecting the dissemination of the ideas of Roland Barthes, Jacques Derrida, Paul de Man, and others. Indeed, Karl Keller in "'Stamp Thy Holy Print on My Unholy Heart': The Regeneration of Early American Literature via French Structuralism" (*Actes du Congrès de Grenoble de 1973*, 1976) clearly advocates such ideas. But whatever the reason for the emergence of this language and self-referential centered criticism, one interesting fact about it is that it is wholly preoccupied with the poetry itself; it no longer makes apologies for Taylor and is one of the indications that the poet is now accepted without reservation as a major American literary figure.

The same critical trend is evident in both the book-length critical studies of the last decade. And their appearance is another clear indication of a wider acceptance of Taylor, since between 1937 and 1974, Grabo's *Taylor* and Peter Nicolaisen's *Bildlichkeit* were the only book-length studies published. But in 1974, William J. Scheick's *The Will and the Word: The Poetry of Edward Taylor* (Athens, Ga.) filled the need for more extensive critical treatment than had been previously offered.

In his study Scheick attempts to find a single idea or theme that unifies, explains, and justifies Taylor's *Meditations*. Scheick finds such a key in the idea of the will, which in a human relationship to God occupies a mediate position between the human and the divine. Scheick further asserts that metaphor in Taylor's poetry occupies a similar position in that "it yokes the sublime to the ordinary" and imitates Christ's or "the Word's mediation" between humankind and Godhead. According to Scheick, then, Taylor's reason for writing his poems is to express love, the necessary condition for conversion, and his mode of writing them, that is his use of startling metaphors and his insistence on their inadequacy, imitates the Word's divine mediation.

The first three chapters of *The Will and the Word* comprise Part One and discuss the Calvinistic and Augustinian backgrounds for Taylor's theological understanding of human reason. These chapters further explain the relationship between reason, the will, and the writing of the *Meditations*. Part Two, the last three chapters, demonstrates Taylor's use of metaphor and language in the poems themselves and elaborates on the idea that there is a corrolary relationship between Christ's position relative to God and man and a metaphor's relationship to its tenor and vehicle.

The other book is Karl Keller's *The Example of Edward Taylor* (Amherst, Mass., 1975). Besides the first two biographical chapters, which were discussed earlier, there are nine others, which discuss specific poetic works, speculate on Taylor's position in a New England literary tradition, examine Taylor's prosody, and place him among the humanists of Western civilization. Keller discusses both Taylor's poetic and prose styles, outlining an idea central to the rest of his discussion of the poet's work—that Taylor used style and language to reflect and resolve the problems of his metaphoric religious beliefs and world view. The idea is treated at length in chapters on *Gods Determinations, The Metrical History of Christianity,* and especially the *Preparatory Meditations*. A chapter on Taylor as myth-maker presents the poet's mythic dimensions in three respects. First he is part of the New England Puritan theology and mythology; second, he contributed to a New England tradition in which other American writers, most notably Jonathan Edwards and Emily Dickinson lived and worked; and third, he was the first to establish a mythically significant place for the writing of poetry as a vehicle to free himself from and define himself within his culture. The chapter discussing prosody in Keller's book makes an extended comparison between Taylor's rough metrics and American primitive painters, in that for both it is the flaws and failures which give vitality, interest, and personality to the works. And in the final chapter Keller presents Taylor as a "Puritan Humanist" who glorified mankind as a participant in the theanthropic nature of Christ and in his position between the anti-humanistic medieval world and the liberated romantic one.

Perhaps the most obvious bench-mark of Taylor's integration into the canonical community of literary artists is his inclusion in critical studies of literature not limited to the colonial period. One such is Albert Gelpi's *The Tenth Muse: The Psyche of the American Poet* (Cambridge, Mass., 1975), which contends that there are two sorts of poetry: typological and tropological. By this distinction Gelpi means that the tropological poet renders experience in concrete images; the typological poet uses tropes as symbols to express some absolute identity between language and experience. According to Gelpi, even though Taylor's poetry has abundant tropes, it is essentially typological in that it uses "radical experiments in language" to express what for Taylor were the theological truths of the mystery of the incarnation and the schism between God and man. Gelpi speculates about Taylor's indebtedness to and departures from the work of George Herbert and Isaac Watts, and fits him into a typological American poetic tradition including Emerson, Whitman, Pound, Williams, Olson, Levertov, Ginsburg, and Everson. In a much too brief and narrowly focused commentary in *American Poets from the Puritans to the Present* (Boston, 1968), Hyatt H. Waggoner questions the extent to which Taylor might profitably be placed in the poetic tradition that yielded Emerson, Whitman, and Dickinson—"a question everyone will want to answer for himself." More successful is Karl Keller's use of Taylor to help define Emily Dickinson's Puritan myth as well as her poetic endeavors within it. In "My Puritan Spirit: Emily Dickinson and Edward Taylor," Chapter Two of *The Only Kangaroo among the Beauty: Emily Dickinson and America* (Baltimore, 1979), Taylor is aligned with Bradstreet, Edwards, Stowe, Hawthorne, Emerson, Whitman, Frost, and others, all related to each other subtly through their relationship to Emily Dickinson.

Broader and deeper than these general studies is Barbara Kiefer Lewalski's *Protestant Poetics and the Seventeenth-Century Religious Lyric* (Princeton, 1980), which returned the treatment of Taylor to the discussion of his place among the English "Metaphysicals" that so occupied criticism of the Forties. But Lewalski places him now without apology or question among "the major religious lyric poets of the century—Donne, Herbert, Vaughan, and Traherne." According to Lewalski, "far from eschewing aesthetics for a rhetoric of silence or a deliberate anti-aesthetic strategy, the poets committed themselves to forging and employing a Protestant poetics, grounded upon scripture, for the making of Protestant devotional lyrics." Besides a common dependence on Biblical subjects, she also finds a concentration on the "classic Protestant paradigm of sin and salvation" as a characteristic thematic and structural influence on these poets.

In her chapter, "Edward Taylor: Lisps of Praise and Strategies for Self-Dispraise," Lewalski discusses these two Protestant aspects of Taylor's work. In the first part of her study she considers Biblical sources for Taylor's metaphors, pointing out that the Protestant understanding of the metaphoric nature of the scriptures was especially important to Taylor in that he saw words and figures as having an analogous power to God's metaphoric manifestations to humankind. She focuses on Taylor's use of analysis or association, meiosis, and antithesis to express man's metaphoric relationships to Christ. In the second half of her essay she explores Taylor's concentration on the other Protestant preoccupation—the drama of sin and salvation. She argues that this theme is dominant in the second series of *Meditations*, and she demonstrates how Taylor used types, emblems, and poems based on the Canticles to elucidate questions of redemption.

In one of the most mature and learned recent books on colonial thought and writing, Mason I. Lowance, Jr.'s *The Language of Canaan: Metaphor and Symbol in New England from the Puritans to the Transcendentalists* (Cambridge, Mass., 1980), there is a brilliant and exact discourse on Taylor's language of Canaan derived from his sermons "Upon the Types" and his use of Canticles in the *Meditations*. Lowance extends this tradition to include Samuel and Cotton Mather, Edwards, Barlow, and (briefly) Emerson and Thoreau. With a broader brush Taylor is also given passing but telling attention in general studies such as Allan I. Ludwig's *Graven Images: New England Stonecarving and Its Symbols, 1650–1815* (Middletown, Conn., 1966), John F. Lynen's *The Design of the Present: Essays on Time and Form in American Literature* (New Haven, 1969), and David Leverenz's *The Language of Puritan Feeling: An Exploration in Literature, Psychology, and Social History* (New Brunswick, N.J., 1980).

Scholarship such as Keller's, Lewalski's, and Lowance's does indeed indicate Taylor's integration into broad literary communities, but some crucial needs for specific Taylor studies still exist. For example, *Gods Determinations* was the subject of several good essays during the sixties and seventies. Michael J. Colacurcio's "God's Determinations Touching Half-Way Membership: Occasion and Audience in Edward Taylor" (*AL*, 1967) shrewdly reconstructs the immediate context for the writing of the poem, and two other essays — John Gatta, Jr.'s "The Comic Design of God's Determinations Touching His Elect" (*EAL*, 1976), which identifies the comic character of the poem, and Karl Keller's chapter in *The Example of Edward Taylor*, which argues that *Gods Determinations* is Taylor's strongest statement of covenant theology — both add significant, broad, contextual information about the poem. More specific studies have been done by Robert D. Arner in "Proverbs in Edward Taylor's *Gods Determinations*" (*SFQ*, 1973), which identifies Taylor's proverbs and comments upon their artistic and affective impact, and by William J. Scheick in "The Jawbones Schema of Edward Taylor's *Gods Determinations*," in *Puritan Influences in American Literature*, edited by Emory Elliott (Urbana, Ill., 1979), which discusses the unifying effect of the "jawbones" structure of the poem. But an exhaustive reading and interpretation of *Gods Determinations* remains to be done and there is still a crucial need for a full biography of Taylor. Beyond these needs, Taylor's own reading and his use of centuries of theological and Biblical commentary have only barely been tapped, and studies of the implications of his accomplishment for our understanding of the Puritan mind and its influence on later literary traditions have just begun.

John Greenleaf Whittier

KARL KELLER

JOHN GREENLEAF WHITTIER has been more important as a personality
and as a historical force than he has been to literary criticism. Affection
has at most points taken the place of analysis and documentation the
place of discussion. Whittier has been a writer to love, not to belabor.
More attention has been shown him than most other schoolroom poets;
he has been most fortunate in the hands of his biographers and critics
and, as I hope this essay shows, deserves considerably more study.

BIBLIOGRAPHY

Students of Whittier have a superb bibliography in the work of
Thomas F. Currier, *A Bibliography of John Greenleaf Whittier* (Cambridge, Mass., 1937). Currier has accurately identified and described most
of Whittier's works — the poetry, the essays and tales, letters to the press,
and contributions to the newspapers, anthologies, and tracts which Whittier edited. Included in Currier's volume is Pauline F. Pulsifer's bibliography of the biographical and critical writings on Whittier up to 1936.

In 1976 Albert J. von Frank published his *Whittier: A Comprehensive
Annotated Bibliography* (New York, 1976). It is indeed comprehensive
and the annotations are immensely helpful in understanding and balancing all of the writings by and about Whittier. This amazing work,
with its several thousand items, all described fairly fully, makes Whittier live again in the criticism. Only book reviews of Whittier's works
and of works about Whittier have been excluded. Frank's bibliography

From Earl N. Harbert and Robert A. Rees, editors, *Fifteen American Authors before 1900:
Bibliographic Essays on Research & Criticism* (Madison: The University of Wisconsin Press;
© 1984 by the Board of Regents of the University of Wisconsin System); may be reproduced
only by permission of the publisher.

goes well beyond the brief ones in Lewis Leary's *Articles on American Literature, 1900–1950 and 1950–1967* (Durham, N.C., 1954 and 1970) and in Edward Wagenknecht's *John Greenleaf Whittier: A Portrait in Paradox* (New York, 1967), and well beyond the 1971 version of this bibliographical essay.

Although subsumed in large part by the Currier and Frank works, of bibliographical interest are the *Stephen H. Wakeman Collection of Books of Nineteenth-Century American Writers* issued by the American Art Association (New York, 1924) and *Thirteen Author Collections of the Nineteenth-Century*, vol. 2, compiled by Jean C. Wilson and David A. Randall (New York, 1950). Less significant but accessible bibliographies are by Harry H. Clark in *Major American Poets* (New York, 1936) and by Harry Hartwick in Walter F. Taylor's *History of American Letters* (Boston, 1936). There is a brief bibliography in Robert E. Spiller et al., eds., *The Literary History of the United States* (New York, 1948), which was brought up to date to 1959 by Richard M. Ludwig with the third edition. A *Whittier Newsletter* has been published since 1966 by John B. Pickard for bibliographical and review purposes.

EDITIONS

Fortunately, Whittier is one of America's most accessible poets. The first collection of Whittier's poems was the Boston edition of 1837 and the first collection of his prose was the Boston edition of 1866. Since 1857 Houghton Mifflin has held the copyrights to all editions of Whittier's works, the most comprehensive of which is *The Writings of John Greenleaf Whittier*, the Riverside Edition of 1888 (7 volumes), edited by Horace E. Scudder with Whittier's assistance. All editions — including such admirable reprintings as the Artists' Edition of 1892, the Cambridge Edition of 1895, and the Household Edition of 1873 — derive from the Riverside Edition. Of these the Cambridge Edition, *Complete Poetical Works of John Greenleaf Whittier* (New York, 1895), is the most convenient. In "Making Whittier Definitive" (*NEQ*, June 1939), Eleanor M. Tilton describes the exchange between Scudder and Whittier that made the Riverside Edition accurate and full. There were as many as 17 maverick editions of Whittier's poems between 1880 and 1900; these are valuable because they have poems in them excluded from the authorized editions.

In fact, many items were lost before the Riverside Edition or were rejected by Whittier in the course of the work with Scudder, and as unearthed since have been published in scattered places, often in inaccurate form. *Whittier on Writers and Writing*, edited by Harry H. Clark and Edwin H. Cady (Syracuse, N.Y., 1950), is a gathering of literary reviews and criticism by Whittier from various periodicals of his day; other fugitive prose is reprinted in the *Boston Evening Transcript*, 7 February 1925 (*NEQ*, Dec. 1933), and in a collection of Whittier columns by John M. Moran, Jr., "Editor Whittier and the *New England Weekly Review* (*ESQ*, First Quarter 1968). The complete *Legends of New England*, as edited by J. B. Pickard, has been reissued (Gainesville, Fla., 1965), as has *The Supernaturalism of New England*, edited by Edward Wagenknecht (Norman, Okla., 1969). Yet unfortunately only a small portion of Whittier's prose has been reprinted.

On the other hand, the search for Whittier's unpublished poems—particularly the earliest ones—has been productive. These are published in *The Independent* (Nov. 1893), *NEM* (Nov. 1903; Feb. 1904), *Whittier-Land* by Samuel T. Pickard (Boston, 1904), *Congregationalist and Christian World* (Dec. 1907), *AL* (May 1932), *BFHA* (Spring 1936), *American Collector* (Dec. 1926), *JRUL* (June 1944), *NEQ* (Dec. 1937; March 1961), *EIHC* (Apr. 1955), and *ESQ* (Third Quarter 1965). Two collections of previously uncollected Whittier verse, with commentaries on sources and secrets of the search, are Frances M. Pray's *A Study of Whittier's Apprenticeship as a Poet, 1825–1835* (Bristol, N.H., 1930) and a thesis by Edward F. Grier, "The Uncollected Periodical Poems of John Greenleaf Whittier" (Columbia, 1938). Thomas F. Currier discusses peculiar problems of editing Whittier's early verse in "The Whittier Leaflet 'Pericles'" (*Library Quarterly*, Apr. 1934). The Frank bibliography lists 28 additional sources for uncollected poetry and prose. But no definitive edition of the poetry has been attempted since 1888. As a result, a large body of Whittier's writings remains inaccessible and a new edition of Whittier is needed.

The Household Edition is still the most usable one-volume selection of Whittier's poems; it, the Cambridge Edition, and the seven-volume Riverside Edition are currently in print. Louis Untermeyer's edition of poems (New York, 1945) is generally available but does not have an adequate introduction or notes and lacks full representation of Whittier's thinking and activity. The most recent editions of poems are by Donald Hall for Dell (New York, 1960) and Robert Penn Warren's edition for the University of Minnesota Press, *John Greenleaf Whittier's Poetry: An Appraisal and a Selection* (Minneapolis, 1971). Both are excellent if frugal editions.

It may be valuable to note the books of Whittier's which have stayed in print or have been reprinted in the 1980s. The Anti-Slavery Crusade of America has kept a collection of Whittier in print, *Anti-Slavery Poems: Songs of Labor and Reform*, an 1888 reprint. The Black Heritage Library has honored Whittier with a facsimile edition from 1865, *National Lyrics*.

The renewed interest in Whittier as folklorist and regionalist has brought three of his works back into print: *Leaves from Margaret Smith's Journal, Legends of New England,* and *The Supernaturalism of New England.*

MANUSCRIPTS AND LETTERS

The Whittier manuscripts are at the Haverhill Public Library; at the Whittier homestead at Oak Knoll, Haverhill, Mass.; at the Morgan Library; and at the Essex Institute in Salem — all of which are described by Harriet S. Tapley in *EIHC* (Apr. 1931) and in *A Descriptive Exhibition of Rare Whittieriana,* edited by D. K. Campbell and Pauline F. Pulsifer (Haverhill, Mass., 1938). Albert H. Whittaker and Shang-chao Liu have prepared *The Holdings of the Haverhill Public Library: The John Greenleaf Whittier Collection* (Haverhill, Mass., 1976). There are important manuscripts in the Quaker Collection at Haverford College, which are described by Edward D. Snyder in two articles: "Whittier Returns to Philadelphia after a Hundred Years" (*PMHB,* Apr. 1938) and "Notes on Whittier and Haverford College" (*BFHA,* Spring 1936). Still other manuscripts are in the Friends Historical Library at Swarthmore College, at the Harvard Library, the Boston Public Library, the Berg Collection at the New York Public Library, the Longfellow House in Cambridge, and at the Thomas B. Aldrich Library in Portsmouth, New Hampshire.

Superior collections of works by and about Whittier can be found at Haverhill Public Library, at the Library of Haverford College, at the Essex Institute, and at Yale University.

Much of Whittier's life was lived in his correspondence. At times of literary value in themselves because of their wit and charm and concern for style, his letters give us as much of Whittier's mind as he ever revealed at any time. More important, though, like the letters of William Lloyd Garrison and Wendell Phillips, they are primary documents in the history of the pre-Civil War period; indeed, they made the history of the times.

In 1976 J. B. Pickard published with Harvard University Press *The Letters of John Greenleaf Whittier* in three volumes. In his introduction Pickard makes an attractive case for Whittier as an important letter-writer. Pickard's notes give a running history of Whittier and his times from 1828 until his death in 1892. Entirely new kinds of study of Whittier could now come from this collection of letters. By and large, however, collectors have used his correspondence to document a particular relationship or an individual idea but have had little interest in giving us the whole man. Pickard's edition now corrects this. An attempt was made by Samuel T. Pickard in his *Life and Letters of John Greenleaf Whittier* (Boston, 1894) to form a life around some of Whittier's letters, though some of them had to be altered for Pickard's purposes. Most of them were selected to show Whittier's problems of publishing or part of his abolition work, and few reveal personal matters or the full range of his social conscience. Several other small collections have helped to fill such gaps: John Albree's edition of *Whittier Correspondence from the Oak Knoll Collections* (Salem, Mass., 1911), made up of letters showing the life of the Whittier family and their Quaker friends; M. V. Denervaud's edition of the letters to Whittier's first sweetheart; Elizabeth Lloyd, in *Whittier's Unknown Romance* (Boston, 1922), expanded by Thomas F. Currier in *Elizabeth Lloyd and the Whittiers* (Cambridge, Mass., 1939); "Letters of John Greenleaf Whittier in the Roberts Collection at Haverford College," edited by Edward D. Snyder and Anna B. Hewitt for *BFHA* (Spring 1936), which has thirteen letters on Whittier's family life and abolitionist worries; and Martha H. Shackford's picture of family relationships in the Quaker world of the Whittiers, *Whittier and the Cartlands: Letters and Comments* (Wakefield, Mass., 1950). Before Pickard's edition, these collections, along with the biographies of Whittier, were the main purveyors of Whittier's correspondence.

For more than sixty years Whittier waged a difficult but successful war against slavery and discrimination — with his verse, his newspapers, and his profuse correspondence. Most of his correspondence in the service of abolition is lost but what remains shows his force of mind and great influence. In 1900 Samuel T. Pickard collected Whittier's letters to a fellow Quaker abolitionist, Elizur Wright, Jr., in *Whittier as a Politician* (Boston, 1900), and he has published letters showing Whittier's influence on the British abolitionist John Bright (*Independent*, January 1899; *NEQ*, Dec. 1935). Other abolitionists with whom Whittier had a significant exchange of letters are William Francis Channing, the son of William Ellery Channing (*AL*, Nov. 1930); Thomas Clarkson, the British abolitionist (*AL*, Jan. 1936); Henry B. Stanton (*JRUL*, Dec. 1945), and Gerrit Smith (*AL*, May 1950) — the last of these having importance because they document Whittier's shift from Garrisonian abolitionism to the abolitionism of the Liberty Party in 1840. Another letter on this schism is in *NEQ* (June 1964). Of special significance is the correspondence between Whittier and Henry Clay in 1837 on the relation between slavery and the annexation of Texas, discussed in the *Kentucky Historical Society Register* (1953). But no doubt the single abolitionist letter most important to the history of American literature is Whittier's 1845 letter to Emerson attempting to enlist him in the cause of abolition and the Liberty Party, edited and discussed by Roland H. Woodwell in *EIHC* (Oct. 1957). An important debate on the subject of abolition — to partisans of the slavery question, North and South, pro and con — is constructed from the letters exchanged during and after the Civil War between Whittier and Paul Hamilton Hayne edited by Max L. Griffin in *AL* (Mar. 1947).

A number of Whittier letters document his relations with other writers of the period. They show not only the wide range of Whittier's reputation and influence but also some of his esthetic principles and literary judgments. Whittier's most important literary relationship was with James T. Fields of the *Atlantic* between 1861 and 1881; this relationship is documented by letters in James C. Austin's *Fields of the Atlantic Monthly* (San Marino, Calif., 1953). Whittier's relation with the editors Willis G. Clark and Lewis G. Clark is documented by new letters edited by John C. Hepler in *BNYPL* (Nov. 1966). Other letters of literary-historical import are the ones to George Washington Cable (*NEQ*, March 1949), to Oliver Wendell Holmes about the poetry of Walt Whitman (*Walt Whitman Review*, Mar. 1958), and to Paul Hamilton Hayne about the poetry of Henry Timrod (in *The Last Years of Henry Timrod*, edited by Jay B. Hubbell [Durham, N.C., 1941]). There are also letters that show that Whittier was important to the emerging careers of a series of minor writers of the period: the poet Lydia Maria Child (in her *Letters* [Boston, 1883]); Rose Terry Cooke, a local-colorist of Connecticut (*QH*, Spring 1963); Harriet Prescott Spofford and Sarah Orne Jewett (*Dial*, Dec. 1907); the novelist Richard Henry Stoddard (in his *Recollections Personal and Literary* [New York, 1903]); William J. Allinson, a young Quaker writer (*BFHA*, Spring 1948); Harriet McEwen Kimball, an aspiring young poet (*EIHC*, Jan. 1959); and the popular short-story writer S. R. Crockett (*Independent*, Oct. 1899). Richard Cary has edited further letters to Sarah Orne Jewett for *ESQ* (First Quarter 1968). Joseph M. Ernest's dissertation "Whittier and the American Writers" (Tennessee, 1952) lists hundreds of letters written by Whittier to writers of the time who sought both to learn from and do honor to him as a poet.

Additional published letters show Whittier's literary, political and religious influence among Quakers in the Midwest. These were edited by Charles A. Hawley (*EIHC*, Oct. 1931; *IJHP*, Apr. 1937; *Palimpsest*, Sept. 1937; *BFHA*, Autumn 1939; and Spring 1941). Still others record personal and family matters (*BFHA*, Autumn 1940, Autumn 1960; *EIHC*, Jan. 1933, Oct. 1939, Oct. 1940; and *LHJ*, Dec. 1899, Jan. 1900). Whittier's letters to Mary Emerson Smith, an early sweetheart, edited by J. B. Pickard (*AL*, Jan. 1967), suggest a more passionate Whittier than has been suspected by most of his biographers.

The corrupting of Whittier's letters to make him fit a particular religious or political bias is discussed by Richard Cary, "Whittier Regained" (*NEQ*, June 1941). Cary has in mind in particular the letters on Whittier's faith doctored by Charlotte F. Bates for McClure's *Magazine* (Jan. 1894). Edward D. Snyder is also concerned with the recovery of Whittier's original intent in his letters in "Whittier MS. Discovered 'to Order'" (*The Friend*, 12 December 1936).

There are five main manuscript collections of Whittier letters. Swarthmore has over six hundred in manuscript, mainly from the early years. The Houghton Library has a useful collection of four hundred from the early period and has well over a thousand in its Pickard-Whittier collection. The Essex Institute houses the famous Oak Knoll Collection of over five hundred letters, plus hundreds written to Whittier, most of these from the period after 1860. The Huntington Library has about three hundred fifty from Whittier's correspondence with James T. Fields and Thomas Wentworth Higginson. And Central Michigan University has over five hundred by and to Whittier from the Oak Knoll period; John Hepler of Central Michigan has an unpublished manuscript which includes the best of these.

J. B. Pickard's 1976 edition of the letters includes all the extant letters from the important years 1828 to 1860 and all the letters after 1860 of biographical, literary, social, or political significance. This edition is a major contribution to the understanding of Whittier for a number of reasons: it recovers the newspaper correspondence that made up Whittier's historically significant personal warfare on behalf of abolition; it documents the almost daily progress of Whittier from farm boy to national reformer as an example of The American Dream; and it assists in reconciling the paradox of lyric poet and didactic reformer that has troubled Whittier's biographers.

BIOGRAPHY

Whittier is unusual in American literary history in that he is important as a writer mainly because of his life, rather than the other way around. That fact puts him in a class with, say, Winthrop, Jefferson, and Lincoln. As with these others, the writing of Whittier's life has evolved from the fondling of his memory to a kind of hagiography and then to critical reaction against legend. By and large, the Whittier Lives succeed in being a justification of part of the history of the nation (as microcosm, as myth, as example), more than a contribution to the life of the mind in America.

Edward D. Snyder attempted an overview, "Seventy Years of Whittier Biographies, 1882–1952" (*BFHA*, Spring 1954), but its sectarian prejudice makes it a disappointing account of the regard paid Whittier over the years. Another, closer look is needed.

The first biography of Whittier was William Sloane Kennedy's *John Greenleaf Whittier: His Life, Genius, and Writings* (Boston, 1882). Whittier had not authorized it and disliked it intensely. Published at the height of the veneration of Whittier, the view of his life and work is remarkable for its objectivity. Kennedy clearly loved the man and saw an intimacy between his personality and his work. But what he finds to praise in Whittier — his piety, his passion, and his politics — to him only degraded his art: "He has three crazes that have nearly ruined the mass of his poetry. They are the reform craze, the religious craze, and the rhyme craze." In this, Kennedy identified the key problem for biographers of Whittier: the disparity between the passionate man and the pale poet. Heroic as Kennedy finds Whittier's life, he finds the reasons for the pale poet in the qualities of the passionate man: he was for Kennedy too much the Quaker, too much the militant for the good of his art. Kennedy finds Whittier's life so much dominated by the Puritan strain of his Quaker faith that he could not love beauty for its own sake. Whittier's triteness, lack of originality in form or idea, and ultimately his tameness are to Kennedy due to "the subdued and art-chilling atmosphere of his Quaker religion." This view of his life, a view that Kennedy expanded in his 1892 biography, *John Greenleaf Whittier: The Poet of Freedom* (New York, 1892), no doubt cut Whittier to the quick.

On the other hand, Francis H. Underwood's *John Greenleaf Whitter: A Biography* (Boston, 1884) was undertaken with the approval though not with the cooperation of Whittier and was "not intended as a critical study, but as a friendly guide and interpreter." The portrait of Whittier therefore glows: the background is fortunate, the motives are just right, the actions heroic, the poetry pure, the interest in reform and the interest in literature perfectly united. Everything is magnified so as to be incomparable, and the process of mythologizing Whittier was begun. "Some imperfection clings to all souls." Underwood writes, "but few have been observed in our time so well poised, so pure, and so stainless as his." This formed the pattern for the inflated level of most discussions of Whittier's life since.

The biography that Whittier authorized as the picture he wanted painted of himself was Samuel T. Pickard's *Life and Letters of John Greenleaf Whittier* (Boston, 1894). Because of Pickard's personal affection for Whittier, his study is often sentimental in championing the purity of Whittier's homelife, the intimacy of his poetry with his life, the sincerity of his journalism, the devotion of Whittier to the various causes of reform, and the genuineness of Whittier's literary and political success in his own time. Pickard's central argument in the biography is that Whittier's political ambition gradually overwhelmed his literary ambition, both strengthening and temporizing his art. Pickard's *Life* was based on the broadest survey of Whittier letters ever attempted and done with thousands of personal interviews and contacts, but it is an idealization of Whittier that we get, even an attempt at mythologizing him. For most purposes, it remains the standard biography, however, and the basis for most biographies that followed.

Those that followed almost kill Whittier with indiscriminate sentimentality. Such is the case in B. O. Flower's *Whittier: Prophet, Seer and Man* (Boston, 1896). Though an attempt is made to show him as barefoot boy, prophet of freedom, and modern spiritual apostle, Whittier loses his toughness in the process. This is true too in the Lives of Whittier published in England, all of them derivative and all of them sentimentalizations— Wilfred Whitten, *John G. Whittier* (London, 1892), and W. J. Linton, *Life of John Greenleaf Whittier* (London, 1893), both deriving from Kennedy and Underwood; G. K. Lewis, *John Greenleaf Whittier: His Life and Work* (London, 1913), a Christian Life; Henry Hudson, *Whittier and His Poetry* (London, 1918), the best of the British Lives; Arthur Rowntree, *Whittier: Crusader and Prophet* (London, 1944), in which Whittier is pictured as one of the pilgrims sustaining Christianity through the whole of a godless century. The worst of this kind is Fredrika S. Smith's *John Greenleaf Whittier: Friend and Defender of Freedom* (Boston, 1948), a Horatio Alger success story in fiction form in which Whittier is a simple country boy who conquers the century with his verse.

The long tradition of loving and laudatory reminiscences of Whittier is best represented by Mary B. Claflin's *Personal Recollections of John G. Whittier* (New York, 1893) and Annie Field's *Whittier: Notes of His Life and of His Friendships* (New York, 1893). It is easy to forget that in the nineteenth century the reminiscence was a widely accepted form of literary criticism. Used on Whittier, the form is standard: the general sketch of a background of hardship, the randomly selected anecdotes that make a list of virtues, the few quoted lines of verse to imply a life of the mind, the attention to the uniqueness of wit, and the deep feeling for the poet that is intended to suggest his own deep feeling for life.

Many such personal reminiscences found their way into print, most of them recalling visits to Whittier in his later years that upon reflection take on the stature of pilgrimages, with anecdotes that teach his example. They were for the most part sensational fodder for the press. Caroline Cadbury makes "A Visit to Whittier in 1881." (*BFHA*, Autumn 1957). Ellen E. Dickinson recalls "A Morning with the Poet Whittier" (*Churchman*, June 1882). Walter M. Merrill makes a delightful summary discussion of many who claimed, "We Talked with Whittier" (*EIHC*, April 1958). Samuel J. Cappen reports "A Visit to John Greenleaf Whittier"

(*Leisure Hour*, Sept. 1888). Charles H. Battey remembers finding "Whittier at Home" (*Friend's Intelligence and Journal*, Nov. 1891). Sarah E. Palmer, in "A Memory of Whittier" (*Century*, Nov. 1893), tells the events of an evening visit with Whittier shortly before his death. In her "Personal Recollections of Whittier" (*NEM*, June 1893), Charlotte Grimke tells of several visits to Whittier to express the gratitude of the Negro race for Whittier's abolition work. Isaac Wilson tells of his "Visit to John Greenleaf Whittier" (*Friend's Intelligence and Journal*, June 1894) and Helen Burt of a summer spent with Whittier in 1880 in West Ossippee, in "Reminiscences of the Poet Whittier" (*Bookman*, June 1895). Robert S. Rantoul tells about Whittier's simplicity, practicality, and self-assurance in "Some Reminiscenses of the Poet Whittier" (*EIHC*, Apr. 1901). Wyatt Eaton tells in his "Recollections of American Poets" of Whittier's homey personality during the painting of a portrait (*Century*, Oct. 1902). Among his "Reminiscences of a Long Life," Carl Schurz recalls a visit to the "kindly" Whittier (*McClure's*, Jan. 1907). J. Warren Thyng's *Reminiscences of the Poet Whittier* (Manchester, N.H., 1908) is a collection of memories of Whittier in his home setting. In his "Reminiscense of the Poet Whittier," W. H. Beckford retells a conversation (*Book News Monthly*, Sept. 1914). Caroline Ticknor, in *Glimpses of Authors* (New York, 1922), recalls memories of problems in publishing Whittier's works. Others remember Whittier for his humor — Josiah L. Pickard, "The Humor of Whittier" (*Midland Monthly*, May 1897); Elizabeth Stuart Phelps, "Whittier's Sense of Humor" (McClure's Magazine, July 1896); Samuel T. Pickard, "Whittier's Sense of Humor," in his *Whittier-Land*. The last in this long line of personal reminiscences was Emily B. Smith's *Whittier* (Amesbury, Mass. 1935). Many of these memory pieces were no doubt written out of genuine affection for the man; others were mere obsequiousness or attempts at promoting Quakerism.

The collections of anecdotes about Whittier are only a little less annoying. George Stewart tells "Bits of Gossip" about Whittier in *Belford's Monthly Magazine* (Oct. 1877). In her *Chapters from a Life* (Boston, 1897), Elizabeth Stuart Phelps tells stories showing Whittier's sense of humor. The anecdotes that Charlotte F. Bates remembers about Whittier make up her "Whittier Desultoria" (*Cosmopolitan*, Jan. 1894). G. F. Carter reprints "Some Little-known Whittierana" in *Literary Collector* (July 1904). Anecdotes from his life, selected to make Whittier a hero and saint, make up F. C. Sparhawk's *Whittier at Close-Range* (Boston, 1925).

Kennedy's more serious view of Whittier as a man larger than his work was revived by Richard Burton in his *John Greenleaf Whittier* (Boston, 1901). "What we are," he quotes Whittier as saying, "will then be more important than what we have done or said in prose or rhyme." But Bur-

ton finds an irony in this, for it was because of his work as reformer, though
he was for so much of his life rejected in that role, that Whittier became
known as a representative American poet. The religiosity of his life turned
him quite naturally into a reformer and his obsession with reform turned
him quite naturally into a didactic poet. So his life and his work became one.

Pickard had challenged that position befoিc the turn of the century
by arguing that the strong qualities of Whittier's character had made his
verse strong. T. W. Higginson took up that same challenge against Kennedy and Burton in his *John Greenleaf Whittier* (New York, 1902), written for the English Men of Letters series. To Higginson, Whittier was
more man than reformer or writer. Whittier's strong personal qualities
—his simplicity, his intimacy, his life lived "near the people," and above
all his Quaker quietism—were important creative forces. It was because
of these qualities that as a reformer he preferred legislative change and
nonresistance to violence, and because of these that as a writer he preferred to work on the public conscience rather than confronting the enemy
more directly as in politics or debate. It was these qualities, more than
the events around him, that transformed a young man of little promise
into "the leading bard of the greatest moral movement of the age." To
Higginson, an ardent literary nationalist, Whittier was the epitome of
those ethical values fundamental to a democracy.

George R. Carpenter was selected to write the biography of Whittier
for the American Men of Letters series, *John Greenleaf Whittier* (Boston, 1903), even though he had little sympathy for the moral idealism
and social reform of Whittier and the period. To Carpenter the main
interest in Whittier's life was politics rather than poetry. But because of
his poor health, poverty, and quietism, Whittier was disappointed in his
political ambitions, and so came to write a kind of poetry of politics—
that is, a poetry of public occasions, local history, and humanitarian interests. Carpenter feels that Whittier was essentially an inner rather than
an outer man and so was ineffective in public affairs. Indeed, according
to Carpenter, from Whittier's abolitionism and involvement in other public matters came his poetry's narrow range, its lack of wide human sympathy, its esthetic poverty. Occasions gave his writings an importance
wholly out of proportion to their artistic merits. Yet though the reformer
in him killed the poet in him, he was more effective as journalist, pam-
phleteer, and poet than he could have been as a politician; reform poetry
and tracts made it possible for him to be the man of action he could not
otherwise have been.

Bliss Perry, in his *John Greenleaf Whittier: A Sketch of His life* (Boston, 1907), argues further against Kennedy's thesis about the poet made

bad by his piety, passion, and politics. To Perry, Whittier's passion for justice, especially in the dangerous business of abolitionism, purged his verse of melancholy, provincialism, and triteness, or at least made these characteristics negligible. The saintliness of Whittier's life came from his strong social conscience, and without a storm to strengthen his lines, his writings were merely occasional, though effectively so. It was issues, after all, that made Whittier a poet and so his attention to "the great interests of humanity" saved him from literary oblivion.

A repudiation of the Whittier legend built by all the biographers from Kennedy to Perry, Albert Mordell's *Quaker Militant: John Greenleaf Whittier* (Boston, 1933) was the first psychoanalytic study of Whittier. In it the modest, mild, and sexless saint gives way to a militant and radical but sexually repressed agitator. The young man that Mordell found was one devoured by desire for worldly success but frustrated in his political ambition by his idealism. Similarly, the "natural man" that Mordell felt he found under Whittier's skin was one obsessed with a love of women but frustrated by a puritan conscience. In all cases his idealism controlled everything he did, leaving his life with a psychic impotence, his personal poetry without warmth, and his reform work centering more around propaganda than active involvement. His prolonged virginity was to Mordell the source of the nervous condition that limited his political ambitions; it had a ruinous effect artistically upon his poems; and it left Whittier a frustrated celibate in his less radical years.

Fascinating as Whittier's sexual repression is to Mordell as an explanation for Whittier's limitations, he is much more interested in Whittier as a radical, He finds Whittier unique in poeticizing the cause of social justice (this makes his reform poetry superior to his domestic and pious poetry), and finds him effective in manipulating men and agitating masses in the cause of abolition. Though his Quaker idealism dampened much of his fire, it also made him militant against worldliness. A number of Mordell's arguments are suspect, yet they succeed in moving Whittier criticism to a different plane — away from mythology and toward analysis.

Whitman Bennett was infuriated by Mordell's Freudianized Whittier and so wrote his *Whittier, Bard of Freedom* (Chapel Hill, N.C., 1941) in reply. What Mordell called a wound of passion in Whittier, Bennett found to be little more than a dramatized series of casual platonic crushes. What Mordell called sublimation of sexuality into the channels of reform work, Bennett found to be simply a soul on fire. Bennett's interest in Whittier is much simpler and more reasonable: Whittier exerted a dynamic influence throughout the nation, not because he was a man of genius, but because he was enormously devoted to a significant cause. A weak body kept Whittier's strong soul from involvement in the reform work, journalism, and political activity that he loved, but produced a mind sensitive to nature and spirit. Bennett's is a good sketch of the nation-shaking political and reformist events into which Whittier fit and which Bennett finds him affecting mightily with his pen.

Though John A. Pollard's intent in *John Greenleaf Whittier, Friend of Man* (New York, 1949) was to show Whittier as a well-balanced man with a broad range of interests, experiences, and abilities, it is like most of the biographical studies since the 1930s, mainly a political life — one in which the politician is a prophet of the people and the prophet is a poet. To Pollard, Whittier's importance was his concern with the whole life of man in the world rather than merely with literary art. He wanted to be known in a more socially relevant capacity than as a maker of rhymes; so his poetry was written mainly in the service of his various social roles — as politician, as propagandist, as reformer, as moralist. Great movements exalted him and with his pen he became a kind of prophet of an age. Like Amos he lived within a small radius but with his voice he remade the age in his own image. Pollard documents Whittier's important place in American history better than anyone else, showing his influence on humanitarian reforms, his creation of a national conscience over slavery, his construction of a new national morality. Whittier's home life, love life, and religion all seem incidental over against Pollard's magnification of Whittier's public life.

Lewis Leary's *John Greenleaf Whittier* (New York, 1961) is the antithesis of the political lives. Forced to fit the format of the TUSAS, the biography is but an overview of Whittier's life and work, yet the emphasis is clear: Leary's Whittier is a man of peaceful nature, a gentle man, a man of simple faith and compassionate humility. He is a man of sense among violently emotional issues; a man of passive resistance in the face of militance; a man who drew quietly into himself when war threatened; a man of holiness in materialistic times. Yet to Leary, Whittier was not primarily a personality but a poet, or rather a personality turned into an important poet by popularity, by the course of events, and by his holy regard for the world around him.

The best critical biography of Whittier (and it is a temptation to say the only sensitively analytical biography) is Edward Wagenknecht's *John Greenleaf Whittier: A Portrait in Paradox* (New York, 1967). By identifying the paradoxes of Whittier's life, Wagenknecht is able to destroy most of the stereotypes. The result is the fullest and most humane view of Whittier's temperament and mind. The paradoxes that Wagenknecht finds in Whittier make him a complex man: the fact that he lived celibate and yet was strongly attracted to women; his desire for fame as opposed to his moral obligation to the work of reform; his desire for power amid his love of man; his interest in reform as opposed to his interest in poetry; the fact that he was a pacifist and yet militant; his view of beauty as grace though also as a snare; his Quaker cosmology vs. his nature worship.

With the exception of Wagenknecht's study, the Whittier biographies appear to have been written either to create the hero-saint or to explain Whittier's severe limitations as a writer. Roland H. Woodwell is currently at work on a definitive life.

The hero-worship of Whittier led to an inordinate interest in the stock he came from. The Whittier genealogy is discussed in D. B. Whittier's *Genealogy of Two Branches of the Whittier Family from 1620 to 1873* (Boston, 1873) and Charles C. Whittier's *Genealogy of the Whittier Family, 1622–1882* (Boston, 1882). Two other branches of Whittier's genealogy are discussed in James E. Greenleaf's *Genealogy of the Greenleaf Family* (Boston, 1896); in Alonzo H. Quint, "The Hussey Ancestry of the Poet Whittier" (*NEHGR*, 1896); and in Roland H. Woodwell and Martha H. Dureen, "The Hussey Ancestry of the Poet Whittier" (*EIHC*, Jan. 1934). A tribute to Whittier's sister and her services in furthering his literary efforts is Annie R. Marble, "Elizabeth Whittier and the Amesbury Home" (*Outlook*, Sept. 1907). Lloyd W. Griffin has pointed out the importance to literary history of Whittier's brother, Matthew Franklin Whittier, known in the humorist circles of Artemus Ward and Mark Twain as "Ethan Spike" (*NEQ*, Dec. 1941).

Whittier lived most of his life in one place and out of devotion to the area became one of our literature's first regionalists. The fascination with Whittier's locale led Samuel T. Pickard to compile his handbook of North Essex, *Whittier-Land* (Boston, 1904), an illustrated guide. George M. White attempts to identify "The Local Associations of Whittier's Poems" (*HM*, Feb. 1883). A great deal of fuss has been made about Whittier's moves between Amesbury and Oak Knoll in Danvers, Mass. Abby J. Woodman attempts to describe his daily life in her *Reminiscences of John Greenleaf Whittier at Oak Knoll* (Salem, Mass., 1908). Other fuss is made by S. W. Phillips, "Further Light on the Question of the Residence of John Greenleaf Whittier" (*EIHC*, Jan. 1933), and by Roland H. Woodwell, "Whittier's Place of Residence from 1876 to 1892" (*EIHC*, Oct. 1932), and by C. B. Rice, "Mr. Whittier at Home" (*LW*, 1877). Harriet Prescott Spofford tried to sum up the debate in her "John Greenleaf Whittier at Amesbury" (*The Critic*, 1884). In Katharine Abbott's *Old Paths of New England* (New York, 1903) and Edwin Bacon's *Literary Pilgrimages in New England* (New York, 1902) we have two pleasantly antiquarian views of Whittier country. In her *Gleanings from Merrimack Valley* (Portland, Maine, 1881) Rebecca Davis explains the Essex County associations of a number of Whittier's poems, as does S. T. Frost in an article, "Geography in Whittier" (*Common School Education*, Jan. 1891). "Whittier's New Hampshire" is the subject of essays by D. L. Maulsby (*NEM*, Aug. 1900) and Eugene R. Musgrove (*GM*, July 1903). The efforts to preserve Whittier's birthplace are told by Edmund C. Stedman, "The Whittier Home Association" (*Independent*, May 1902). Donald P. Wright has made a photographic documentary of Whittier's life in his *John Greenleaf Whittier: A Profile in Pictures* (Haverhill, Mass., 1967). Another collection of pictures is in J. B. Pickard, *Memorabilia of John Greenleaf Whittier* (Hartford, Conn., 1968, reprinted from *ESQ*, First Quarter, 1968). A more recent collection of Whittier visuals, really a pictorial biography of the poet, is *Whittier and Whittierland: Portrait of a Poet and His World*, edited by Donald C. Freeman, John B. Pickard, and Roland H. Woodwell (North Andover, Mass., 1976).

One of the special problems in Whittier's biography is his influence as a young newspaperman in Philadelphia. Thomas F. Currier writes on the events and people in his life at this time, in "Whittier's Philadelphia Friends in 1838" (*BFHA*, Autumn 1938), and Arthur H. Reede documents the political influence of Whittier in Pennsylvania in "Whittier's Pennsylvania Years, 1837–1840" (*Pennsylvania History*, Oct. 1958).

The special problem raised by Mordell's biography — the facts of Whittier's various romances — is discussed effectively by Norman Foerster in "Whittier as Lover" (*Freeman*, Feb. 1923). Foerster's concern is especially with Whittier's ill-fated romance with Elizabeth Lloyd. Whittier's romance with Evelina Bray is discussed by M. M. Barrows, "The Love Story of Whittier's Life" (*NEM*, Apr. 1905). Albert Mordell has two additional notes to support his argument on Whittier's romance with Lucy Hooper, both in *NEQ* (June 1934). Other possible romances of Whittier's were Cornelia Russ, discussed by Thomas C. Richards in the Boston *Evening Transcript*, 28 Feb., 1931, and Mary Emerson Smith, discussed by J. B. Pickard in *AL* (1967). There is fairly good substantiation for all of these romances.

Perhaps the single most contradictory event in Whittier's later life was the occasion of his seventieth birthday celebration, when tributes were mixed with satire of the old poet. The great praise that came to Whittier can be seen in *The Literary World*, 1 December 1877, and George H. Brownell documents the differing reactions to "Mark Twain's Speech at the Whittier Banquet" (*American Book Collector*, Aug. 1933). Bernard De Voto's account in *Mark Twain's America* (Boston, 1932) is a justification of Twain's attack on Whittier on esthetic grounds. Henry Nash Smith, in "That Hideous Mistake of Poor Clemens's" (*HLB*, Spring 1955) and in "The Backwoods Bull in the Boston China Shop" (*AH*, Aug. 1961), tells why Twain turned the dinner into a public scandal; Twain was daring to suggest that the cult of the writers taking Whittier as a model was an elaborate fraud.

Whittier's life as an unceasing struggle to overcome his pride and to achieve a life that was modest, meek, selfless, and serene is argued by J. J. McAleer, "Whittier's Quest for Humility" (*QH*, Spring 1961). This is one of the most attractive views of Whittier proposed, for it resolves what other biographers have abandoned as paradoxes of his life and mind.

As should be evident, the Whittier Lives have been a gradual recognition of what H. E. Hurd calls "The Paradoxes in the Life and Poetry of John Greenleaf Whittier" (*Poetry Review* [London], Aug. 1926). Hurd, in summary, lists the main paradoxes as these: (1) Whittier was a man of limited culture and opportunity, yet he captured the affections of educated men; (2) violating the conventions of verse, he became a poet; (3) he was an ardent lover who never married; (4) Whittier spiritualized the hard life that crushed him; (5) he was a dreamer who could scheme; (6) Whittier, a prophet of peace, sharpened the swords of the North for the Civil War; (7) even without a pulpit, he was a powerful preacher.

CRITICISM

The shape of Whittier criticism from the middle of the nineteenth century to the middle of this century has been discussed by Lewis E. Weeks, "Whittier Criticism Over the Years" (*EIHC*, July 1964). Weeks has found two phases in the critical fortunes of Whittier. The first phase (up to Whittier's death in 1892) is characterized by a double attitude: he is the kindly, honest Quaker and the dreaded, vigorous abolitionist; he is violently loved (because he is loyally American, domestic, public, and a simple, earnest, sincere writer) and violently hated (because he is an anarchist, an overpassionate libertarian, overweeningly didactic, and a poet without adequate technique or range). Beginning in mistrust, the criticism becomes increasingly elegiac toward the end of the century. But because Whittier was such a personal force, there was difficulty in assessing his work esthetically. The second phase (the twentieth century) is concerned mainly with placing Whittier in perspective. The result by and large is a minor rank for him, yet not obscurity. His morality is worth rescuing but not his moralizing, his courage but not his voice, his passion for writing but not the poems he wrote passionately. Our concern has therefore turned in this century from his substance to his reputation.

Although Whittier was noticed almost everywhere during his lifetime, only a few of the notices now seem very important. One of the earliest serious assessments of Whittier was Rufus Griswold's *Poets and Poetry of America* (Philadelphia, 1842). Whittier's *Supernaturalism in New England* appeared in 1847 and it was one of literary history's "shocks of recognition" when Hawthorne reviewed it in *The Literary World* (reprinted in *NEQ*, Sept. 1936); Hawthorne saw Whittier as too practical-minded to "believe his ghost story while he is telling it," too pedantic and fussy, too far removed from the folk life from which New England legends spring; Whittier, Hawthorne said, "did not care much for literature." Orestes Brownson, in a review of Whittier's *Songs of Labor* in *Brownson's Quarterly Review* (Oct. 1850), went further and saw Whittier as the devil incarnate; to Brownson, Whittier sought to undermine faith, eradicate loyalty, break down authority, and establish the reign of anarchy: "He is a Quaker, an infidel, an abolitionist, a philanthropist, a peace man, a Red Republican, a nonresistant, a revolutionist, all characters we hold in horror and detestation, and his poems are the echo of himself." In contrast, David Wasson, representative of the period's Transcendentalists, thought of Whittier as a kind of Biblical poet-prophet (*AM*, Mar. 1864); like a prophet, Whittier spoke plainly to plain men, had a firm "moral sentiment," and was a reformer of the world around him.

Near the end of his life and immediately following his death, as Currier and Pulsifer have noted in their Whittier bibliography and Frank in his, discussions of Whittier, most of them by Friends and friends, ran into the hundreds. Harriet Prescott Spofford's is typical of these (*HM*, Jan. 1884); because he is democratic, simple, rustic, moral, a man of broad interests and natural esthetic sense, Whittier is promoted as the ideal American poet, the nation's poet laureate. Edmund Gosse's *Portraits and Sketches* (London, 1912) is also typical; like Gosse, many found his personality "sweet" and "Quakerly" but his verse "primitive" and "redundant." Yet interestingly enough, the first assessment of Whittier from a nearly esthetic point of view was not made until 1881 when Richard Henry Stoddard wrote *The Homes and Haunts of Our Elder Poets* (New York) and until 1885 when Edmund C. Stedman wrote *Poets of America* (Boston). Both found that the power of Whittier's poetry comes not from the man so much as from his background (the Colonial past, the injustices in the society around him) and yet both also attempt to account for his failings as a poet: he is too naive, too moralistic, too simplistic. Unfortunately, most of the critical comments on Whittier at his death serve better as nostalgia than as literary criticism.

Whittier's reputation in America during his lifetime has been discussed by T. W. Higginson, "The Place of Whittier among the Poets" (*Reader*, Feb. 1905), and his reputation abroad by John A. Pollard, "Whittier's Esteem in Great Britain" (*BFHA*, Spring 1949). A brief note on Whittier's reputation is C. Marshall Taylor, "The 1849 Best Seller" (*BFHA*, Autumn

1950). The problem of keeping Whittier's reputation alive is discussed by C. Waller Barrett, "John Greenleaf Whittier: The 100th Anniversary of His Birth" (*American Antiquarian Society Proceedings*, 1957) and by Donald C. Freeman, "The History of the Haverhill Whittier Club" (*ESQ*, First Quarter 1968).

As Weeks has mentioned, almost all of the Whittier criticism since the turn of the century is concerned essentially with Whittier's reputation, rather than with his thought or art. Three attempts to account for Whittier's universal appeal in the nineteenth century but neglect in the twentieth are Rica Brenner, *Twelve American Poets before 1900* (New York, 1932); Desmond Powell, "Whittier" (*AL*, Nov. 1937); and W. Harvey-Jellie, "A Forgotten Poet" (*Dalhousie Review*, Apr. 1939).

There are almost formidable problems in reading Whittier in the twentieth century. Stanley Kunitz has articulated best, in *American Authors, 1600–1900* (New York, 1938), how invalid Whittier's assumptions about life and art and how irrelevant his writings now seem. He was "the middle nineteenth-century New England farmer and small town dweller," but ours is a different world. In *The Fields Were Green* (Stanford, Calif., 1953), George Arms, while defending him as a poet, sees Whittier's single-mindedness as the central problem in reading him today. To Arms, Whittier was a personal poet, a poet of personal experience, who tended to have only one interest, the Quaker view of man, even going so far as to identify English Romanticism with Quaker cosmology. As a result Whittier was uneasy as a poet; he could not accept art as an essential expression of life. Like Arms, Howard Mumford Jones, in "Whittier Reconsidered," in his *History and the Contemporary* (Madison, Wis., 1964), bemoans the inattention given Whittier's values and Christian gentlemanliness in our own time, but sees that the central problems for us are the superficiality of Whittier's indignation and his monotony and sentimentality.

Yet for all the problems in reading Whittier, much of the Whittier criticism has attempted to find what is redeemable in the man and his art. One of the most balanced early views is that by John Vance Cheney, *That Dome in Air* (Chicago, 1895); Cheney feels that though Whittier is stiff and provincial, what he has left to generations after him is the idea of the poet as lover of man. Like this view is Paul Elmer More's, in *Shelburne Essays, Third Series* (Boston, 1906): for all Whittier's faults of taste, he had an indisputable, simple grace. To More, Whittier is the poet who brought the quiet affections of the home into our literature; his poetry is unmatched in the genre of "poetry of the hearth." Bliss Perry, in "Whittier for Today" (*AtM*, Dec. 1907), explains Whittier's relevance on other grounds—his courage and humanity, his involvement in social affairs. To Perry, there are two issues on which Whittier is always right: his insistence that there must not be any race issue and his demand for international peace. An extension of Perry's claim for Whittier is Ernest D. Lee's argument, in "John Greenleaf Whittier" (*The Westminster Review*, Jan. 1908), that Whittier should be preserved as an example of the phenomenon of a national poet.

Winfield Townley Scott, in his excellent essay "A New Consideration of Whittier's Verse" (*NEQ*, June 1934) and in his poem "Mr. Whittier," deplores the schoolroom use to which Whittier has been put and argues that Whittier can be restored to eminence if emphasis is placed on the poetry written after the Civil War, especially the religious verse. Hyatt H. Waggoner, in his *American Poets from the Puritans to the Present* (Boston, 1967) and in "What I Had I Gave: Another Look at Whittier" (*EIHC*, Jan. 1959), also finds Whittier's religious verse that which should recommend him to our own time. Waggoner shows how Whittier moved from moralizing and propagandizing to symbolizing and spiritualizing the world as he knew it, making him one of our literature's few Christian poets. To Waggoner there is value in relearning how to read Whittier; his contemporaries read him as a religious poet, as a poet of universal and humane causes, as a poet documenting God's part in the progress of The American Dream, and we must do so too.

Yet to read Whittier today, as Donald Hall has argued in "Whittier" (*Texas Quarterly*, Autumn 1960), requires an effort of the historical imagination. To Hall it is the nineteenth-century themes of goodness and optimism that give Whittier a firm place in our literary history. George E. Woodberry, in his essay on Whittier in *Makers of Literature* (New York, 1901), was one of the first to see how representative Whittier was of his time. John Macy, in *The Spirit of American Literature* (New York, 1913), saw Whittier as the poet who best represents the crudeness, banality, and prejudices, but also the idealism and exaltation, of the nineteenth century. To William M. Payne, writing in *CHAL*, Whittier was the representative man of "the epic days" preceding the war. Yet as Daniel W. Smythe has pointed out in "Whittier and the New Critics" (*ESQ*, First Quarter 1968), Whittier continues to suffer disparagement under contemporary critical methods.

Whittier's development as an artist has been discussed best by H. H. Clark, J. B. Pickard, and Edward Wagenknecht. Clark, in an essay, "The Growth of Whittier's Mind" (*ESQ*, First Quarter 1968), assigns Whittier's work to the three conventional phases of his life: up to 1833, Whittier was interested mainly in sensational local legend; from 1833 to 1857 his mind was preoccupied with outward reformism; and from 1857 until his death he turned to the inward life. Pickard, in the critical essays in *John Greenleaf Whittier: An Introduction and Interpretation* (New York,

1961), sees his growth not so much in subject matter as in movement between genres, that is, from folk forms to protest forms and finally to nature poems and religious lyrics. Wagenknecht, on the other hand, sees, in *John Greenleaf Whittier: A Portrait in Paradox,* the growth of Whittier's mind in terms of coming to grips with the contradictions in his thinking; that is, the resolution of his fears, his pride, his senses (all of which conflicted with his otherworldly interests) into a sense of grace.

The earliest work on Whittier's esthetics and literary theory was done by Samuel T. Pickard, "Whittier's Literary Methods" (*Independent,* Sept. 1897) and by Harry H. Clark, in his notes on Whittier in *Major American Poets.* J. B. Pickard's work on the artistry of Whittier (especially in an essay, "Poetic Creed and Practice," in his *John Greenleaf Whittier*) shows that Whittier's views on art and beauty are dominated by a conflict between the lure of external natural beauty and the strict plainness of the Quaker lifestyle. Confusing religion with esthetics, Whittier's view of the purpose of art remained obscured throughout his life. Edward Wagenknecht's Life, like Pickard's, is mainly a concern for Whittier's esthetics, and like Pickard he finds Whittier torn between regarding beauty as grace and beauty as a snare. Wagenknecht's discussion of Whittier's worship of nature, "The Light That Is Light Indeed," is excellent in reconciling Whittier's regard for art with his regard for religion. Lewis Leary, in his *John Greenleaf Whittier,* finds Whittier's literary principles centered around the idea of "the beauty of holiness, of purity, of that inward grace which passeth show," as opposed to the idea of the holiness of beauty of his Romantic contemporaries. Like Emerson, Whittier felt that a high seriousness made language poetic, and though he lacked that esthetic education which might have provided the literary counterbalance to the moralist in him, he compensated for it with sincerity, devotion, humor, and stinging words. Though Leary is often more interested in Whittier's performance than in his poetics, he does demonstrate how a sense of the past, a consciousness of life being lived, and the meditating on one's own worth and humility were to Whittier more important parts of the poet's esthetics than his prosody or imagery. Roy Harvey Pearce, in discussing the esthetics of the Fireside Poets in *The Continuity of American Poetry* (Princeton, N.J., 1961), distorts Whittier in arguing that his literary principles were dominated by a fantasy principle, that is, by the belief that the poet has special access to the common man's dreams and fantasies. Whittier's poems, Pearce maintains, are therefore dominated by visions, dreams, nostalgia, idealistic indulgence, romanticizing of the past, and blind faith in the future.

With regard to Whittier's literary theory, what is largely lacking in the criticism is an extended discussion of Whittier's concern for form.

We have Gay Wilson Allen's discussion of rhythm and stanza form in his *American Prosody* (New York, 1935) and two notes on "Whittier's Rhymes" by Kathryn A. McEuen and S. T. Byington (*AS*, Feb. 1945 and Feb. 1946), but Whittier's use of conventions and his many innovations have gone largely unexplored.

Whittier himself promoted the popular legend that he was not a well-read man, but scholars have gone to great pains to prove otherwise. The closest we have to a list of Whittier's reading is "The Library of John G. Whittier" (*ESQ*, First Quarter 1964). Alwin Thaler, in "Whittier and the English Poets" (*NEQ*, Mar. 1951; *ESQ*, First Quarter 1968), lists all of the British writers that Whittier knew. Thaler persuasively argues Whittier's wide reading and frequent use of his reading in his poems, especially Elizabethan and Romantic writings.

Whittier's legend also excluded the problem of literary influence, but the writers who influenced Whittier the most are revealed in an unpublished dissertation, Joseph M. Ernest's "Whittier and the American Writers" (Tennessee, 1952). As with other New England writers of the period, some of the strongest influences on Whittier were Elizabethan, German, and Oriental — all of which Whittier in his strict Quaker orthodoxy was largely able to resist. Iola K. Eastburn shows Whittier's catholic interests and wide reading in *Whittier's Relation to German Life and Thought* (Philadelphia, 1915); though Whittier was interested in German legends and reform movements, the German influence on him was not strong. Whittier was not a mystic, either, not a promoter of faith in the transcendent, and yet his Oriental interests were strong. Arthur E. Christy, "The Orientalism in Whittier" (*AL*, Jan. 1930 and Nov. 1933), found that what appealed to the orthodox Quaker was mainly the moral tone and the general ethical principles of Eastern thought; Whittier's was not a spiritual and philosophical affinity with the Orient like Emerson's, for he was blind to distinctions between Christian and Oriental principles.

The influences on Whittier have been explored with vigor. J. C. Mathews found "Whittier's Knowledge of Dante" (*Italica*, Dec. 1957). When it comes to the influence of English writers on Whittier, Whittier and Campbell have been discussed by Jack Stillinger (*PQ*, Oct. 1959), and Whittier and Tennyson, probably the most significant influence, have been discussed by W. J. Fowler (*Arena*, Dec. 1892) and by Alwin Thaler (*PQ*, Oct. 1949). More study of the influence of British poetry on Whittier's is needed, but the best summary essay is Alwin Thaler, "Whittier and the English Poets" (*NEQ*, Mar. 1951).

As a critic, as Edwin H. Cady and H. H. Clark show in their collection *Whittier on Writers and Writing*, Whittier was much more interested in the moral, the sublime, the antiquarian, and that which would reform society than he was in technical skill. The best discussions of Whittier's critical principles are two unpublished dissertations: C. P. Marcy, "The Literary Criticism of John Greenleaf Whittier" (Boston University, 1945) and J. M. Ernest, "Whittier and the American Writers." Marcy outlines the formative influences on Whittier's critical thought — his home-life, his education, his religion and politics — and finds Whittier most concerned with a writer's morality, the sensitivity of his response to nature, and the functionality of his imagination. Marcy's conclusion is that Whittier was not a discriminating critic of literature, and what limited him most severely was his idea that literature should conform to the conventions of a society controlled by Quaker tenets of morality and simplicity. Ernest, on the other hand, is interested mainly in showing how Whittier was one of the great promoters of American literature. He had a deep interest in seventeenth-century American writings and he kept abreast of the literary movements of his time by meeting and corresponding with, reading and reviewing, most of the authors of his day. But as a critic, because his interests were primarily ethical rather than esthetic, he did not usually consider the work as distinct from the author. Not until he was older did his esthetic sense outgrow his crusading zeal.

Whittier's relationships with writers who were his contemporaries have been taken up separately to show what John J. McAleer calls "Whittier's Selective Tolerance" (*ESQ*, First Quarter 1968). McAleer finds Whittier both consoling and severe in his work with other writers. While the relationship between Whittier and Tennyson, as William J. Fowler (*Arena*, Dec. 1892) and Alwin Thaler (*PQ*, Oct. 1949) have both found, was one of mutual admiration, Whittier's regard for Carlyle, discussed by Roland H. Woodwell in *ESQ* (First Quarter 1968), was one of growing disgust because of Carlyle's refusal to support humanitarian causes important to Whittier.

The best discussion of Whittier's relations with American writers contemporary with him is still in unpublished form, Joseph M. Ernest's dissertation "Whittier and the American Writers" (Tennessee, 1952). Whittier's contacts with these writers were considerable.

The regard that Whittier and Bryant had for one another is discussed by Charles D. Deshler, *Afternoon with the Poets* (New York, 1879), and by Charles I. Glicksberg, "Bryant and Whittier" (*EIHC*, Apr. 1936); what they had in common was the cause of human freedom and an ardent patriotism. Longfellow's indebtedness to Whittier is discussed by Frank B. Sanborn, "Whittier and Longfellow Compared as Poets of New England" (*Boston Evening Transcript*, 24 July 1902), and by O. S. Coad, "The Bride of the Sea" (*AL*, Mar. 1937). Whittier's indebtedness to Bayard Taylor is discussed by Joseph M. Ernest in *Friend's Intelligencer* (Sept. 1952).

Ernest has also documented Whittier's influence on American women writers in the latter half of the century in "Whittier and the 'Feminine Fifties'" (AL, May 1956). Ernest gives credit to Whittier for the phenomenon of so many women writers in the period; more than anyone else, Whittier gave them practical help and encouragement in their liberal causes.

J. G. Pulsifer discusses Whittier and Alice and Phoebe Cary (EIHC, Jan. 1973); Jean Downey discusses Whittier and Rose Terry Cooke (BFHA, Spring 1963); Richard Cary discusses Whittier and Sarah Orne Jewett (ESQ, First Quarter 1968 and EIHC, Oct. 1971), as does Carl J. Weber (NEM, Sept. 1945); Grace F. Shepard discusses Whittier and Lucy Larcom (NEQ, July 1930). There are other important relations with American writers. Arlin Turner discusses the association with Cable in "Whittier Calls on George W. Cable" (NEQ, Mar. 1949). Max L. Griffin discusses the association with Paul Hamilton Hayne in "Whittier and Hayne: A Record of Friendship" (AL, Mar. 1947).

Whittier's thorniest relationship was with Whitman. Joseph M. Ernest, in "Whittier and Whitman: Uncongenial Personalities" (BFHA, Autumn 1953), blames Whittier for this. Whittier threw his copy of Leaves of Grass into the fire, would not mention Whitman's name, and then publicly denounced him in 1885. Lewis E. Weeks's documentation of the relationship, "Whittier and Whitman" (ESQ, First Quarter 1968), finds great similarity between them but also inevitable incompatibility. Weeks continues his discussion in "Did Whittier Really Burn Whitman's Leaves of Grass?" (WWR, Mar. 1976).

Whittier is one of the pioneer regionalists in our literature. The attention to nation, region, land, and folk called for by Emerson was already appearing, though from a different, less self-conscious, less programmatic perspective than Emerson's, in the writings of Whittier. Mamoru Ohmori has written of this in "J. G. Whittier and American National Literature" in his Essays in English and American Literature (New York, 1961). The causes that led Whittier to use folk materials in his poems are discussed by George C. Carey, "Whittier's Place in New England Folklore" (ESQ, First Quarter 1968) and "Whittier's Roots in a Folk Culture" (EIHC, Jan. 1968). Carey shows that Whittier was the product of a folk milieu, born and raised in the context of rural New England story-telling. So where most of the writers of the time were patricians, Whittier was a new phenomenon to our literature, the peasant poet. Henry W. Wells, in "Cambridge Culture and Folk Poetry," in his The American Way of Poetry (New York, 1943), sees Whittier as a type—"the New England Quaker," a role Whittier played so well that he gave us a form of folk poetry. In "Whittier's Ballads: The Making of an Artist" (EIHC, Jan. 1960), J. B. Pickard discusses Whittier's ballads as the best re-creation of native folklore and legend written in the nineteenth century. A special study of a folktale type is Harry Oster, "Whittier's Use of the *Sage* in His Ballads," in *Studies in American Literature*, edited by Waldo McNeir and Leo B. Levy (Baton Rouge, La., 1960).

The attention to New England folk ways and history resulted in an early if sometimes awkward and sentimental form of regional writing, as has been shown by Albert Mordell in his biography *Quaker Militant* and by Theodore R. Garrison in a dissertation, "John Greenleaf Whittier: Pioneer Regionalist and Folklorist" (Wisconsin, 1960). The use to which Whittier put New England history is given general treatment by Thomas F. Waters, "Whittier, the Poet, as Historian" (*Massachusetts Magazine*, Jan. 1908) and M. Jane Griswold, "American Quaker History in the Works of Whittier, Hawthorne, and Longfellow" (*Americana*, 1940). How willing a contributor to the Puritan legend Whittier was — and in this regard as a forerunner of Hawthorne and Melville — is discussed by Louis C. Schaedler, "Whittier's Attitude toward Colonial Puritanism" (*NEQ*, Sept. 1948). Though Whittier's attitude turned initially from impartiality to hostility, the more he dealt with Puritan materials the more appreciative he became. Cecil B. Williams, in a work devoted entirely to Whittier's regionalism, *Whittier's Use of Historical Material in "Margaret Smith's Journal"* (Chicago, 1936), shows the care with which Whittier used colonial records and New England historians in the construction of his prose legend. An excellent example of the possibilities of studying the art in Whittier's regionalist works is Donald Ringe, "The Artistry in Whittier's *Margaret Smith's Journal*" (*EIHC*, July 1972). Whittier's fine use of New England folklore may yet prove the most fertile field of Whittier study, as seen in George Casey's "John Greenleaf Whittier and Folklore: The Search for a Traditional American Past" (*NYFQ*, Mar. 1971). An informal survey of Whittier's interest in folk superstitions, ghosts, witches, and the like is David V. Craig's "John Greenleaf Whittier: The Devil's Chronicler" (*New England Galaxy*, Spring 1976). The quality of Whittier's imagination is seen in his use of the legend genre to turn historical material into protest literature. This approach inspired much of the local color writing toward the end of the century. The skillful construction of this work is discussed further by Lewis Leary, "A Note on Whittier's Margaret Smith" (*ESQ*, First Quarter 1968).

Discussions of individual works by Whittier are for the most part attempts either at checking Whittier's facts and sources or making one aware of Whittier's values. Whittier's poem "Barbara Frietchie" and his poems on John Brown ("Brown of Ossawatomie") and Daniel Webster ("Ichabod") are cases in point. As early as 1875, historians began questioning Whittier's use of the Revolutionary War story of Barbara Frietchie; see especially Jubal Early, "Barbara Frietchie: The Poet's Base of Facts" (*Boston Daily Advertiser*, 8 May 1875) and "Letter on the Barbara Frietchie Myth" (*Southern Historical Society Papers*, 1879) and Henry M. Nixdorff, *Life of Whittier's Heroine, Barbara Frietchie* (Frederick, Md., 1887). Others, however, have rushed to Whittier's defense with information from Maryland history: Caroline H. Dall, *Barbara Frietchie, a Study* (Boston, 1892); R. M. Cheshire, "More About Barbara Frietchie" (*Book of the Royal Blue*, July 1903); D. M. Quynn and W. R. Quynn, "Barbara Frietchie" (*Maryland Historical Magazine*, Sept. 1942 and Dec. 1942).

In the case of the John Brown poem, Cecil D. Eby has tried to prove the accuracy of Whittier's information, first in "Whittier's 'Brown of Ossawatomie'" (*NEQ*, Dec, 1960) and then in "John Brown's Kiss" (*Virginia Cavalcade*, May 1961). In the case of the Webster poem, two brief notes have tried to show the features of Webster's life and personality that Whittier uses in his poem: Margaret H. Gangewer, "Whittier's Poem 'Ichabod'" (*AN&Q*, Mar. 1889) and Motley S. Maddox, "Whittier's 'Ichabod'" (*Expl*, Apr. 1960).

Even with more explicable poems like "Skipper Ireson's Ride" and "Snow-Bound," the critical comments have had more to do with historical and biographical background than with art. There are a number of discussions of the biographical and historical associations of "Skipper Ireson's Ride" and these show how accurate Whittier tried to be: J. W. Chadwick, "Marblehead," (*Harper's*, July 1874); Margaret B. Wright, "A Poet's Town" (*The Chautauquan*, Sept. 1891); S. T. Pickard, "The Original Version of the Skipper Ireson Ballad" (Boston *Evening Transcript*, Oct. 13, 1900); E. E. Ericson, "'John Hort' and 'Skipper Ireson'" (*NEQ*, Sept. 1937); and Jules Zanger, "A Note on Skipper Ireson's Ride" (*NEQ*, June 1956). Likewise, there are a number of notes identifying the characters in "Snow-Bound" and these show how personal the poem was: Nathaniel L. Sayles, "A Note on Whittier's 'Snow-Bound'" (*AL*, Nov. 1934); Helen L. Drew, "The Schoolmaster in 'Snow-Bound'" (*AL*, May 1937); Elizabeth F. Hoxie, "Harriet Livermore: 'Vixen and Devotee'" (*NEQ*, June 1945); W. Gary Groat, "Harriet Livermore: A Whittier Recollection" (*AN&Q*, May 1966); Harry Fenn, "The Story of Whittier's 'Snow-Bound'" (*St. Nicholas*, Apr. 1893); Garland Greever, *Three American Poems* (Chicago, 1910); Lucy A. Sloan, *Whittier's "Snow-Bound": A Study and Interpretation* (Chicago, 1913). But there are four long discussions of the poem (the only two real explications among all of the comments on Whittier's individual poems) which are excellent: J. B. Pickard, "Imagistic and Structural Unity in 'Snow-Bound'" (*CE*, Mar. 1960); Elizabeth V. Pickett, "'Snow-Bound' and the New Critics" (*ESQ*, First Quarter 1968); Sidney Poger, "'Snow-Bound' and Social Responsibility" (*ATQ*, First Quarter

1969); and Leonard B. Trawick, "Whittier's 'Snow-Bound': A Poem about the Imagination" (*Essays in Literature*, Western Illinois University, Spring 1974). These four essays show that the greatest need in Whittier criticism is for full discussions of individual poems.

There are two collections of essays about Whittier, John B. Pickard's *Memorabilia of John Greenleaf Whittier* for the Emerson Society (Hartford, Conn., 1968), and Jayne K. Kribbs's *Critical Essays on John Greenleaf Whittier* (G. K. Hall, Boston, 1980). Both gather previously published works. The two finest critical essays on Whittier's poetry, however, are the introductions which Donald Hall and Robert Penn Warren wrote for their paperback editions of Whittier poems, mentioned above.

Most Whittier criticism has had to deal in one way or another with Whittier's faith, which was important personally and culturally. "In Whittier," wrote Whitman, "lives the zeal, the moral energy that founded New England." Whittier's place in American religious literature in the nineteenth century is explored by Augustus H. Strong, *American Poets and Their Theology* (Philadelphia, 1916), and Elmer J. Bailey, *Religious Thought in the Greater American Poets* (Boston, 1922). Whittier's Quaker contribution to our literature is examined by Howard H. Hintz, *The Quaker Influence in American Literature* (New York, 1940). Three essays in Howard H. Brinton's *Byways in Quaker History* (Wallinford, Pa., 1944) are a good introduction to the three major concerns about Whittier's faith. Rufus M. Jones, in "Whittier's Fundamental Religious Faith," agrees that Whittier's faith leaned neither to the orthodox nor to the unitarian side of nineteenth-century American Quakerism, but as the result of the influence of Coleridge and Emerson, it was unique in its strong Platonism, and as such is the finest expression of Quaker beliefs in American life. Henry J. Cadbury, in "Whittier as Historian of Quakerism," shows how Whittier found in historic Quakerism the full expression of his social philosophy and therefore tried to protect it from misrepresentation or abuse. C. Marshall Taylor, in "Whittier, the Quaker Politician," shows Whittier's faith as the main force behind his interest in social reform.

The broad religious interests of Whittier — Biblical, Quaker, Oriental — are discussed in a dissertation by Charles R. Tegen, "The Religious Poetry of John Greenleaf Whittier" (Central Wesleyan, 1968). Whittier's specific principles are discussed by Luella Wright, "Whittier on the Dignity of Man" (*The Friend*, Dec. 1945) and by Elfriede Fecalek in an unpublished work, "Die Wertwelt John Greenleaf Whittiers" (Vienna, 1946). His general morality is commented on by C. M. Severance, F. M. Larkin, and J. C. Carr in a Whittier symposium in *Pacific Monthly* (Spring 1891).

Whittier was seen, by Friends and others, as an important religious force in his time. Early comments like Henry Blanchard's "The Theology of Whittier" (*The Friend*, May 1866) and G. R. Baker's "John Greenleaf Whittier" (*Friends Quarterly Examiner*, Oct. 1871), show how important he was to Quakers on both sides of the Atlantic as a purveyor of the faith. Estimates like those of Annie Fields, "The Inner Life of John Greenleaf Whittier (*The Chautauquan*, Nov. 1899), and Oliver Wendell Holmes, "Whittier's Religion" (*Unity*, Dec. 1892), show how important he was to writers of the time as a sustainer of Christian thought. Other brief comments emphasizing how much Whittier's Quaker ancestry, environment, and faith meant to him are John W. Chadwick, "Whittier's Spiritual Career" (*New World*, Mar. 1893); William H. Savage, "Whittier's Religion (*Arena*, July 1894); and Will D. Howe, "Whittier," in *American Writers on American Literature*, edited by John Macy (New York, 1931).

A number of the separate titles on Whittier are merely Quaker tracts, in which the Quaker life is celebrated as much as Whittier's orthodoxy: Julius W. Atwood, *The Spiritual Influence of John Greenleaf Whittier* (Providence, R.I., 1894); Ernest E. Taylor, *John Greenleaf Whittier, the Quaker* (New York, 1954); and Benjamin F. Trueblood, *The Faith of John Greenleaf Whittier* (Amesbury, Mass., 1957). The significance of Whittier's poetry in transmitting Quaker ideas to the common man is emphasized by T. T. Munger, "The Religious Influence of Whittier" (*Christian Union*, 24 September 1892), and by Frederick M. Meek, "Whittier the Religious Man" (*ESQ*, First Quarter 1968). Most promotional was simply *A Selection from the Religious Poems of John Greenleaf Whittier* (Philadelphia, 1934) for Friends' use.

Yet for all of the faith in Whittier's faith, a battle has raged over whether he was really orthodox. His leanings toward New England Puritanism are discussed by James Mudge in "The Quaker Laureate of Puritanism" (*Methodist Review*, Jan. 1908), by M. E. Kingsley in "A Quaker Poet in Puritan New England" (*Poet-Lore*, Oct. 1910), and by Louise C. Schaedler, "Whittier's Attitude toward Colonial Puritanism" (*NEQ*, Sept. 1948). On the other side of the nineteenth-century Quaker spectrum, it is argued that Whittier inclined toward Unitarianism, an accusation Whittier fought all his life. Richard H. Thomas, "Was Whittier Unitarian?" (*Friend's Review*, 17 November 1892), and Edward D. Snyder, "Whittier and the Unitarians" (*BFHA*, Autumn 1960), attempt to show that though he was not Unitarian, Whittier had mild pro-Unitarian feelings that made him a man of interdenominational good will. Lewis H. Chrisman argues, in "The Spiritual Message of Whittier" (in his *John Ruskin, Preacher and Other Essays* [Cincinnati, Ohio, 1921]), that Whittier's fundamentalism was a reaction against the popularity of a nebulous Unitarianism, as does J. C. Fletcher, "Whittier's Christian Belief" (*New York Evangelist*, Dec. 19, 1892).

Other defenses of Whittier's orthodoxy have been made on the basis of the principle of the Inner Light. Chauncey J. Hawkins, in *The Mind of Whittier: A Study of Whittier's Fundamental Religious Ideas* (New York, 1904), shows how Whittier's faith depended on the concept of the immanence of God; hope and humanitarianism were to Whittier man's main courses of action, but both spring from the conviction of immanence in self and others. Catherine Albright, in "Whittier's Religious Message" (*FI*, Dec. 2 and 9, 1911), makes Whittier's Inner Light very Transcendental. Edward Wagenknecht, in "Whittier and the Supernatural — a Test Case" (*ESQ*, First Quarter 1968), is also able to defend Whittier's orthodoxy on the basis of his belief in immanence; Whittier survived nineteenth-century religious currents because he took the Inner Light rather than the Bible, tradition, or superstition, as the supreme authority in his life.

This does not mean, however, that Whittier was a mystic, as some have carelessly labeled him: S. M. Crothers, "Whittier the Mystic" (*Unity*, Dec. 1892); Rufus M. Jones, "Whittier the Mystic," (*American Friend*, Dec. 1907); and Lyman Abbott, "John G. Whittier, Mystic" (*Outlook*, Jan. 1921). W. Harvey-Jellie, in "A Forgotten Poet" (*DR*, Apr. 1939), argues, however, that the element of mysticism in his best poetry is the best way to rehabilitate Whittier. The role of nature in Whittier's religious outlook is discussed by Norman Foerster, *Nature in American Literature* (New York, 1923), a role disputed by Percy H. Boynton, *American Poetry* (New York, 1921). As Arthur E. Christy has shown in his discussions of Whittier's Oriental interests in "The Orientalism in Whittier" (*AL*, Jan. 1930; Nov. 1933), Whittier was not so much resistant to other religious systems as he was selective of those values from them which coincided with his own.

Still, Whittier has been looked at from a wide variety of sectarian positions, perhaps indicating the universality of his values. For a Roman Catholic view, see John L. Spalding, "John Greenleaf Whittier" (*Catholic World*, Jan. 1877); for a Universalist view, W. T. Stowe, "Whittier" (*University Quarterly*, July 1867); for a Presbyterian view, A. MacLeod, "The Great Poets of America: Whittier" (*Catholic Presbyterian*, July 1882); for a Unitarian view, Edward Everett Hale, "Curtis, Whittier, and Longfellow" (in his *Five Prophets of Today*, Boston, 1892) and George W. Cutter, "Whittier" (*The Unitarian*, Nov. 1891); for a Methodist view, Camden M. Cobern, "The Religious Beliefs of John Greenleaf Whittier" (*Methodist Review*, Mar. 1895); for a Congregational view, J. W. Buckham, "Whittier Face to Face" (*Congregational Quarterly*, Sept. 1935); and for a Disciples of Christ view, Henry J. Cadbury, "Whittier's Religion" (*Christian Century*, 5 February 1958). The best discussion of Whittier as a writer of primarily religious poetry is Charles R. Tegen, "The Religious Poetry of John Greenleaf Whittier" (unpub. diss., Georgia, 1968).

There are three studies of Whittier and the Bible: S. Trevena Jackson, "Whittier's Use of the Bible" (*Christian Advocate*, Dec. 1907), James S. Stevens, *Whittier's Use of the Bible* (Orono, Maine, 1930), and Alice N. Townsend, "The Scope of Whittier's Bible References" (*FI*, Jan. 28, 1899), all showing Whittier to be a literalist. This literal use resulted in a large body of religious verse, as Edward D. Snyder had pointed out in "Whittier's Religious Poetry" (*Friends Quarterly Examiner*, April 1934). Whittier as a writer of religious verse for hymns has been discussed by William C. Gannett, "Whittier in Our Hymn Books" (*Unity*, Dec. 1892), and by C. Marshall Taylor, "Whittier Set to Music" (*EIHC*, Jan. 1952).

Whittier's connection with the founding of a Quaker township in California, Whittier, near Los Angeles, is discussed in Errol T. Elliott, *Quakers on the American Frontier* (Richmond, Ind., 1969) and in Charles W. Cooper, *Whittier Independent College in California* (Los Angeles, 1967).

Unfortunately, most of the commentary on Whittier's faith deals with the phenomenon of Quaker theology and says little about Whittier himself in this regard. Two studies that are enlightening on the religious Whittier are by Philip C. Moon and Perry Miller. Moon, in "Observations on the Religious Philosophy and Method of Whittier" in *Voices of Freedom* (*EIHC*, Oct. 1957), demonstrates that it was the influence of Garrison, not Quakerism, that gave Whittier his messianic humanitarianism, his conscientious devotion, and his religious-reformist zeal. But Miller, in "John Greenleaf Whittier: The Conscience in Poetry" (*Harvard Review*, Spring 1964), identifies Whittier's Quaker role as a method of self-defense, a convenience, a life-long act; beneath his quietism was a ferocity that characterized the real Whittier. The regard for Whittier as abolitionist could not have been higher in his lifetime. As Samuel J. May put it, in *Some Recollections of our Anti-Slavery Conflict* (Boston, 1869), "Of all our American poets, John G. Whittier has from first to last done most for the abolition of slavery. All my anti-slavery bretheren, I doubt not, will unite with me to crown him our laureate." The anti-slavery movement and Whittier's place in it are discussed effectively in Gilbert H. Barnes, *The Anti-Slavery Impulse* (New York, 1933), and in *The Anti-Slavery Vanguard*, edited by Martin Duberman (Princeton, N.J., 1965). Whittier's part in the reconciliation of North and South after the war is discussed in Paul H. Beck, *The Road to Reunion* (Boston, 1937).

Many other contemporaries celebrated Whittier as a poetic prophet of the movement — David V. Barlett, *Modern Agitators* (New York, 1855); William Lloyd Garrison II, *John Greenleaf Whittier* (Brooklyn, N.Y.,

1892); T. W. Higginson,"Whittier as a Combatant" (*Book News Monthly*, Dec. 1907); Frank B. Sanborn, "Whittier as Man, Poet and Reformer" (*Biblia Sacra*, Apr. 1908). Seldom did anyone take issue, as William Dean Howells did in his *Literary Friends and Acquaintance* (New York, 1900), with those who considered him a great reformer. The most extensive treatment of Whittier's antislavery ideas and activities is an unpublished work, Siegfried Krugmann's "John Greenleaf Whittiers Kampf gegen die Sklaverei" (Erlangen, 1953).

However, Whittier's abolition poetry, roughly one-third of the canon, has seldom been discussed critically. Most comments are like John V. Cheney's "Whittier" (*Chautauquan*, Dec. 1892), arguing that Whittier is the ideal poet for democracy and that his antislavery poems are central to that position, or like Alfred Kreymborg's "A Rustic Quaker Goes to War" in his *Our Singing Strength* (New York, 1928), arguing that Whittier's poetry is autobiographical and that his best poetry resulted from his abolition work. The only discussion of artistic qualities of the poetry is in J. B. Pickard's "Whittier's Abolitionist Poetry" (*ESQ*, First Quarter 1968). "At best," Pickard concludes, "their earnest simplicity and religious intensity redeemed their topical nature, simplified their digressive tendency, and toughened their derivative phrasing."

The wide range of Whittier's social conscience has been celebrated best by V. L. Parrington, *Main Currents in American Thought* (New York, 1927), but many others have cited his historical significance for liberalism. J. Wilfred Holmes shows this wide range in his collection, *Whittier's Prose on Reforms Other than Abolition* (Pittsburgh, Pa., 1945). Whittier's work against capital punishment is discussed in David Brion Davis, "The Movement to Abolish Capital Punishment in America, 1787–1861" (*AHR*, Oct, 1957). His concern for laborers and labor conditions is discussed in Thomas F. Currier, "Whittier and the Amesbury-Salisbury Strike" (*NEQ*, Mar. 1935), and John A. Pollard, "Whittier on Labor Unions" (*NEQ*, Mar. 1939). That Whittier belongs to the tradition of Hawthorne and Melville in reacting against the advance of technology is argued by Richard Olson, "Whittier and the Machine Age" (*ESQ*, First Quarter 1968); in the conflict, Whittier preferred the garden, that is, the idyllic and humane, to the machine.

Whittier's relationships with other reformers, political or abolitionist, reveal the uniqueness and limitations of his thinking. His political idealism resulted in an intimate friendship like that with Charles Sumner, as J. Wilfred Holmes claims in "Whittier and Sumner: A Political Friendship" (*NEQ*, Mar. 1957), though a number of differences were dictated by Whittier's Quakerism. The same is true of his relation with Thomas Clarkson, as C. Marshall Taylor notes (*BFHA*, Autumn 1954). The relation with William Lloyd Garrison was more of a test, however. The main source of information on the Whittier-Garrison quarrel is Wendell Phillips Garrison and Francis Jackson Garrison, *William Lloyd Garrison* (Boston, 1885). Philip C. Moon, in "Observations on the Religious Philosophy and Method of Whittier in *Voices of Freedom,*" argues that Garrison was the main creative influence in Whittier's life, and Cecil B. Williams, in "Whittier's Relation to Garrison and ᵤᵢe *Liberator*" (*NEQ,* June 1952), shows how Garrison helped Whittier's career as poet and journalist. T. W. Higginson's was perhaps the earliest serious comparison of the two, "Garrison and Whittier" (*Independent,* Dec. 1905); to him the men complemented each other. C. Marshall Taylor's comparison, "Whittier vs. Garrison" (*EIHC,* July 1946), though heavily biased in favor of Whittier's pacifism, patience, idealism, and faith, identifies the cause of their differences in Whittier's heavy sense of sin. Whittier's growing detachment from active reform participation is discussed by John B. Pickard, "John Greenleaf Whittier and the Abolitionist Schism of 1840" (*NEQ,* June 1964) and by Samuel T. Pickard, *Whittier as a Politician* (Boston, 1900). John Brown put Whittier to an even more severe abolitionist test, as Cecil D. Eby argues in "Whittier's 'Brown of Ossawatomie'" (*NEQ,* Dec. 1960). Other discussions of Whittier as an editor of abolitionist periodicals are Bertha-Monica Stearns, "John Greenleaf Whittier, Editor" (*NEQ,* June 1940), and Thomas F. Currier, "Whittier and the *New England Weekly Review*" (*NEQ,* Sept. 1933). The greatest twentieth-century put-down of Whittier as politician and abolitionist is Edmund Wilson, *Patriotic Gore* (New York, 1962).

The black view of Whittier as an abolitionist is shown by Beatrice J. Fleming, "John G. Whittier, Abolition Poet" (*Negro History Bulletin,* Dec. 1942). J. Wilfred Holmes, in "Whittier's Friends among the Lowly" (*ESQ,* First Quarter 1968), discusses Whittier's association with and attitude toward blacks. Even though he finds Whittier's poems to have been evoked more by specific events than by humanitarian values, Osborn T. Smallwood, in "The Historical Significance of Whittier's Anti-Slavery Poems as Reflected in Their Political and Social Background" (*Journal of Negro History,* Apr. 1950), recognizes that Whittier's poems are an important part of the protest literature that molded public opinion and finally elected Lincoln. J. Wilfrid Holmes discusses "Whittier's Concerns for Negro Education" (*Phylon,* Second Quarter 1946). That Whittier may have been the author of a slave narrative is argued by P. K. Foley, "Whittier and the 'Narrative of James Williams'" (*Nation,* Apr. 29, 1897).

Whittier's abolitionist influence extended to the Midwest, where through his correspondence he worked to keep new states free; these were among his most successful political moves. Whittier's influence on affairs in Iowa and Nebraska is discussed by Charles A. Hawley in *IJHP* (Apr. 1936) and in *BFHA* (Autumn 1939 and Spring 1941). His influence in Kansas is discussed by Wayne Delavan, "Whittier Promoted Free Kansas" (*Arena*, Spring 1941), and by Cora Dolbee, "Kansas and 'The Prairied West' of John G. Whittier" (*EIHC*, Oct. 1945, Jan. 1946, and Apr. 1946). Whittier's concern over freedom abroad is discussed by Livio Jannattoni, "Whittier e la Beecher Stowe d'accordo su Garibaldi" (*La Fiera Letteraria*, Oct. 1951), and by Francis B. Dedmond, "A Note on Whittier and Italian Freedom" (*BFHA*, Autumn 1951).

In conclusion it must be said that, in depth, the Whittier criticism leaves much to be desired. Though Whittier does not fit easily into any mode of criticism, he has been dealt with honestly if not fully. In the criticism, we have much of Whittier's life, mind, soul, and times, but not yet all of the life and liveliness that may be hidden in the poetry itself.

Notes on Contributors

JAMES FRANKLIN BEARD, born in Memphis, Tennessee, in 1919, is Professor of English and Chairman of the English Department at Clark University. Educated at Columbia College (A.B.), Columbia University (M.A.), and Princeton University (Ph.D.), he has taught at Princeton, at Dartmouth, and since 1955 at Clark. Among other awards, he has held Guggenheim Fellowships, 1952–53, 1958–59, and a Senior Fellowship of the National Endowment for the Humanities, 1967–68. Author of numerous articles, reviews, and introductions, he collected and edited the six-volume *Letters and Journals of James Fenimore Cooper* (1960–68) and is presently Editor-in-Chief of the collaborative edition of *The Writings of James Fenimore Cooper*, ten volumes of which have been published by the State University of New York Press. He is also preparing a critical biography of Cooper.

WILLIAM B. DILLINGHAM is Professor of English at Emory University. Born in Atlanta in 1930, he holds degrees from Emory (B.A. and M.A.) and the University of Pennsylvania (Ph.D.). He was a Fulbright-Hays lecturer in American literature at the American Institute, University of Oslo, Norway, 1964–65 and has been a National Endowment for the Humanities Fellow (1978–79) and a Guggenheim Fellow (1982–83). His books include *Frank Norris: Instinct and Art* (1969), *Humor of the Old Southwest* (edited with Hennig Cohen, 1964; 2nd ed., 1974), *An Artist in the Rigging: The Early Work of Herman Melville* (1972), and *Melville's Short Fiction, 1853–1856* (1977). His essays on American literature have appeared in *College English, Nineteenth-Century Fiction, Philological Quarterly, American Literature, English Studies*, and other journals.

EVERETT EMERSON is Professor of English at the University of North Carolina at Chapel Hill and editor of the journal *Early American Lit-*

erature. He has taught in Virginia, Louisiana, Pennsylvania, Florida, Massachusetts, New York, and California, as well as in North Carolina. He is author or editor of eight books including *Major Writers of Early American Literature* and *American Literature, 1764–1789: The Revolutionary Years*, both published by the University of Wisconsin Press, and most recently *The Authentic Mark Twain: A Literary Biography of Samuel L. Clemens.*

NORMAN S. GRABO was born in Chicago in 1930, educated at Elmhurst College (B.A.) and UCLA (M.A. and Ph.D.). He has taught at Michigan State University, University of California at Berkeley, Texas A&M University, and St. John's College (Santa Fe), and is presently University Professor in English at the University of Tulsa. A Fellow of the Folger Shakespeare Library (1959), the Society for Religion in Higher Education (1966–67), the Guggenheim Memorial Foundation (1970–71), and the National Endowment for the Humanities (1980), he is the author of *Edward Taylor* (1961) and *The Coincidental Art of Charles Brockden Brown* (1981), and editor of *Edward Taylor's Christographia* (1963), *Edward Taylor's Treatise Concerning the Lord's Supper* (1965), *American Thought and Writing* (1965), and *American Poetry and Prose* (1970). He is presently preparing a history of early American literature called "American Literary Design, 1520–1820."

BRUCE GRANGER, Professor Emeritus of English at the University of Oklahoma, was born in Philadelphia in 1920 and educated at Cornell (A.B., M.A., Ph.D.). He has taught at the University of Wisconsin, the University of Denver, and the University of Oklahoma as well as at the University of Vienna as a Fulbright Lecturer. He is the author of *Political Satire in the American Revolution* (1960), *Benjamin Franklin: An American Man of Letters* (1964), and *American Essay Serials from Franklin to Irving* (1978), and co-editor (with Martha Hartzog) of *Oldstyle-Salmagundi* (1977), which is the first volume of *The Complete Works of Washington Irving.*

EARL N. HARBERT is Professor of English at Northeastern University, Boston, Massachusetts. He received an A.B. from Hamilton College, an M.A. from the Johns Hopkins University, and a Ph.D. from the University of Wisconsin-Madison. He has taught at George Washington University, Tulane University, and Harvard University, and held a Fulbright appointment to Spain. He is author and editor of numerous publications, including *The Force So Much Closer Home: Henry Adams and the Adams Family.*

KARL KELLER has published extensively in American literary studies, especially in the early period (Taylor, Stoddard, and Edwards) and in the nineteenth century (Emerson, Thoreau, Whittier, Dickinson, and Whitman). The University of Massachusetts Press published his book *The Example of Edward Taylor* in 1975 and The Johns Hopkins University Press published his book *The Only Kangaroo Among the Beauty: Emily Dickinson and America* in 1979. The University of Illinois Press will soon publish Keller's manuscript on Whitman, *Be Not Afraid of My Body: The Whitman Difference*. Keller's most recent work is a book on American religious fundamentalism and social change, *The Mormons Are Coming, the Mormons Are Coming*. Keller is professor of American literature at San Diego State University and is on the Board of Editors of *American Quarterly*.

BARRY MENIKOFF, Professor of English at the University of Hawaii, was born in Brooklyn, New York, in 1939. He received his B.A. from Brooklyn College and his M.A. and Ph.D. from the University of Wisconsin-Madison. He has served as a Fulbright Lecturer at the University of Santiago, Santiago de Compostela, Spain, as a Visiting Associate Professor at the University of Southern California, and as a Huntington Library–NEH Fellow. His *Robert Louis Stevenson and 'The Beach of Falesa': A Study in Victorian Publishing* was recently published by Stanford University Press.

DAVID J. NORDLOH, born in 1942, in Cincinnati, Ohio, received his A.B. at Holy Cross College, Worcester, Massachusetts, and his Ph.D. at Indiana University. He is Professor of English at Indiana, where he has taught since 1968, and general editor and a textual editor of the ongoing "A Selected Edition of W. D. Howells." He was chairman of the MLA's Committee on Scholarly Editions, which reviews and supervises the work of a variety of editorial projects, from 1979 to 1982, and serves as consultant to several editions. He is also an editor for "Twayne's United States Authors Series." He has held a visiting appointment at the University of Virginia, and in 1982–83 was Fulbright Senior Professor at the University of Heidelberg, West Germany.

DONALD PIZER, who was born in New York City, received his Ph.D. from the University of California, Los Angeles, in 1955. After service in the Army, he joined the faculty of Newcomb College, Tulane University, where he is now Pierce Butler Professor of English. He has received fellowships from the Guggenheim Foundation, the American Council of Learned Societies, and the National Endowment for the Humanities. During 1967–68 he was a Fulbright Lecturer at the Hamburg University. He is the author of *Hamlin Garland's Early Work and Career* (1960), *The Novels of Frank Norris* (1966), *Realism and Naturalism in Nineteenth-Century American Literature* (1966), *The Novels of Theodore Dreiser: A Critical Study* (1976), and *Twentieth-Century American Literary Naturalism: An Interpretation* (1982). He has also prepared editions of works by Hamlin Garland, Frank Norris, Stephen Crane, Theodore Dreiser, and Jack London.

ROBERT A. REES is Assistant Dean of the College of Fine Arts and Director of Arts Extension at UCLA, where he also served on the Faculty of English for a number of years. Educated at Brigham Young University (B.A.) and the University of Wisconsin (M.A., Ph.D.), he has published articles and essays on American literature and various aspects of the humanities. He is co-editor of *15 American Authors before 1900* and Washington Irving's *The Adventures of Captain Bonneville*. A published poet, Rees is currently making a documentary film on Simon Rodia's Towers in Watts.

JAMES E. ROCKS is Associate Professor and Director of Graduate Programs in English at Loyola University of Chicago, where he has also served as Assistant Chairman. He received his A.B. from Western Reserve University and his M.A. and Ph.D. from Duke University, where he was a James B. Duke Fellow for two years; he taught previously at Tulane University. His articles on nineteenth- and twentieth-century American literature have appeared in *Mississippi Quarterly*, *Poe Studies*, *South Atlantic Quarterly*, *Southern Humanities Review*, *Southern Review*, *Tulane Studies in English* and *University of Mississippi Studies in English*.

RICHARD DILWORTH RUST is Professor of English and Adjunct Professor of American Studies at the University of North Carolina at Chapel Hill. He was born in Provo, Utah, in 1937, and was educated at Brigham Young University and the University of Wisconsin, where he received his Ph.D. in 1966. He has published articles on Irving, Longfellow, Hawthorne, Melville, Mark Twain, and Eugene O'Neill, and has edited *Glory and Pathos: Responses of Nineteenth-Century American Authors to the Civil War* (1970), Washington Irving's *Astoria* (1976), and James Fenimore Cooper's *The Pathfinder* (1981). During 1971–72 and 1977–78 he was a Fulbright Lecturer at the University of Heidelberg. Currently he is General Editor of *The Complete Works of Washington Irving*.

JAMES W. TUTTLETON is Professor of English at New York University. He was born in St. Louis, Missouri, in 1934, and was educated at Harding College and the University of North Carolina, where he received the Ph.D. in 1962. He is the author of *The Novel of Manners in America* and *Thomas Wentworth Higginson*, and the editor of Irving's *Voyages and Discoveries of the Companions of Columbus* in *The Complete Works of Washington Irving* (Twayne) and *The Works of Washington Irving* in the Library of America series.

JANA D. WAINWRIGHT, born in Baton Rouge, Louisiana, in 1948, holds a B.A. from Colorado State University and an M.A. from Austin Peay State University in Clarksville, Tennessee. She is currently a Ph.D. student at Texas A&M University and is working on a dissertation on American narratives of the period between 1789 and 1820.

JAMES WOODRESS, Professor of English at the University of California at Davis, was born in Webster Groves, Missouri, in 1916. He was educated at Amherst (A.B.), N.Y.U. (M.A.), and Duke (Ph.D.). He is the author of biographies of Booth Tarkington, Joel Barlow, and Willa Cather and a study of Howells in Italy. He has been a Guggenheim Fellow and Fulbright Lecturer in France and Italy. He was the founder and editor of *American Literary Scholarship*. He has recently edited *Critical Essays on Walt Whitman* and Willa Cather's *The Troll Garden*.

Index

507

COMPOSED BY METRICOMP
GRUNDY CENTER, IOWA
MANUFACTURED BY INTER-COLLEGIATE PRESS, INC.
SHAWNEE MISSION, KANSAS
TEXT AND DISPLAY LINES ARE SET IN CALEDONIA

Library of Congress Cataloging in Publication Data
Main entry under title:
Fifteen American authors before 1900.
Includes bibliographies and index.
1. American literature—History and criticism—
Abstracts. 2. American literature—Bio-bibliography.
I. Harbert, Earl N., 1934–
II. Rees, Robert A., 1935–
PS55.F53 1984   016.81'09   83-40263
ISBN 0-299-09590-8